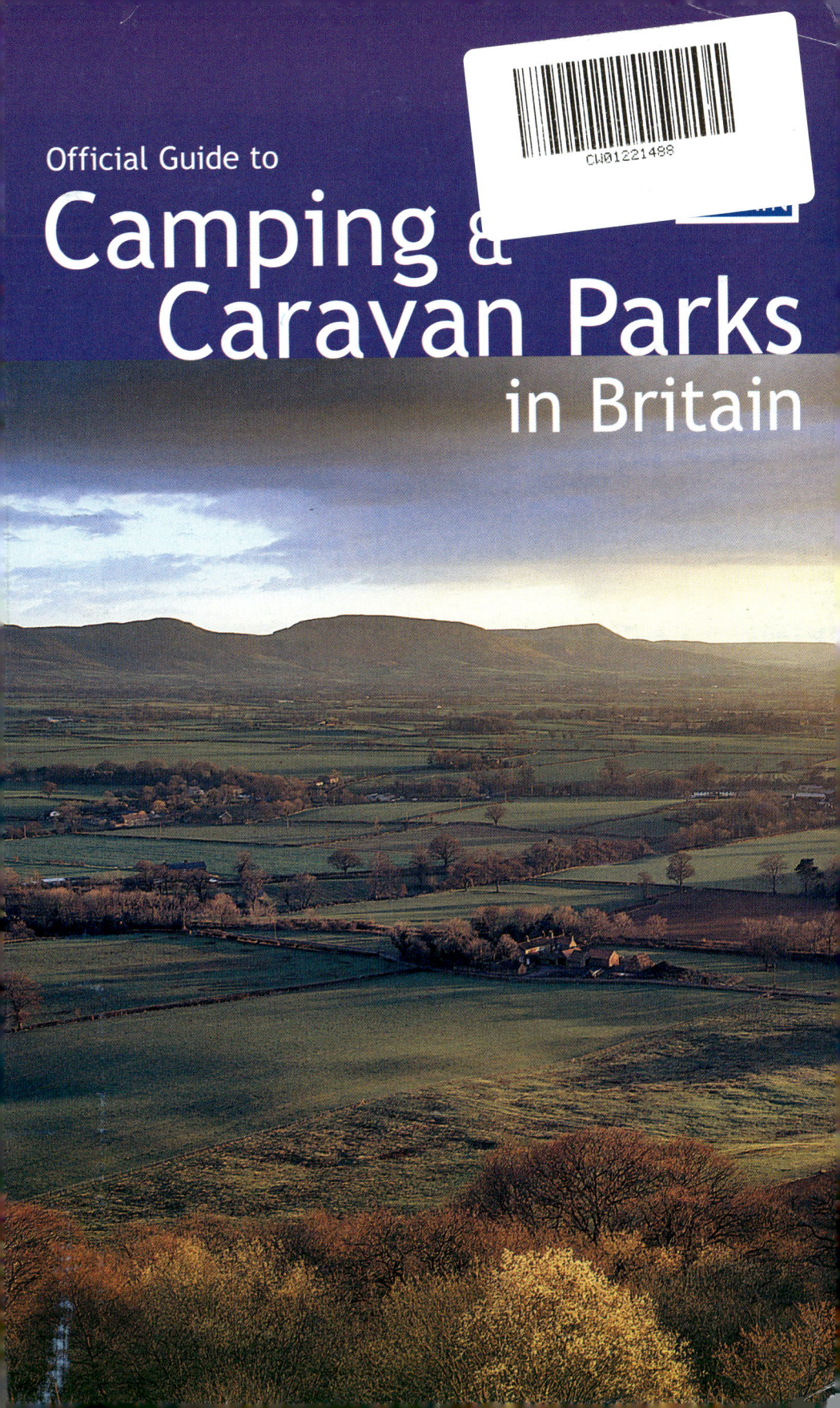

Official Guide to
Camping & Caravan Parks
in Britain

Contents

Welcome to Where to Stay

TOURING BRITAIN	**4**
Le tourisme en Grande-Bretagne	6
Unterwegs in Großbritannien	7
Rondtrekken in Groot-Brittannië	9
Alla scoperta della Gran Bretagna	11
HOLIDAY COMPETITION	**14**
ACCOMMODATION LOCATION MAPS	**15-29**
HOW TO USE THIS GUIDE	**31**
Mode d'emploi du guide	34
Benutzung dieses Reiseführers	38
Hoe u deze gids moet gebruiken	42
Come usare questa Guida	46
CARAVAN HOLIDAY HOME AWARD SCHEME	**45**

Places to stay and things to do

CAMPING AND CARAVAN PARKS, PLACES TO VISIT, REGIONAL TOURIST BOARD CONTACT DETAILS AND TRAVEL TO THE AREA

England	
London	51
Cumbria	59
Northumbria	71
North West	81
Yorkshire	89
Heart of England	101
East of England	113
South West	125
South of England	153
South East England	171
Scotland	**183**
Wales	**201**

Events for 2001

Manifestations en 2002/Veranstaltung in 2002/
evenementen in 2002/calendario degli avvenimenti nel 2002

England	222-227
Scotland	228-229
Wales	230-231

Where to Stay in Britain 2002
England · Scotland · Wales

Further Information

USEFUL ADDRESSES — 218
Adresses utiles/nützliche Anschriften/nuttige adressen/indirizzi utili

STANDARDS FOR CARAVAN AND CAMPING PARKS — 219
Normes requises pour les terrains de camping et pour caravanes/
Regeln für Camping- und Caravanplätze/aan caravan en camping parken
gestelde eisen/norme imposte ai campeggi per tende e roulottes

TOURIST INFORMATION IN BRITAIN — 232
Information pour les touristes/Touristen-Information/ toeristische
informatie/informazioni per turisti

NATIONAL ACCESSIBLE SCHEME — 233

BTA OVERSEAS OFFICES — 234

INDEX TO PARKS — 241
RÉPERTOIRE DES TERRAINS/PLÄTZVERZEICHNIS/REGISTER VAN CAMPINGS/
INDICE DEI CAMPEGGI

INDEX TO TOWNS — 245
Annuaire par villes/Städteverzeichnis/index van steden/indice delle città

COMPETITION — 14
Win a week's family holiday park break.

CONCOURS — 14
Gagnez un séjour d'une semaine pour toute la famille dans un parc de vacances.

PREISAUSSCHREIBEN — 14
Gewinnen Sie einen einwöchigen Familienurlaub in einem Feirenpark.

PRIJSVRAAG — 14
Win een vakantie van een week voor het hele gezin op een vakantiepark.

CONCORSO — 14
Vincete una vacanza di una settimana per tutta la famiglia in un parco vacanze.

KEY TO SYMBOLS
Inside back cover flap

Signes Conventionnels — 34
Zeichenerklärung — 38
Verklaring van de tekens — 42
Spiegazione dei simboli — 46

Britain is a country of beautiful landscapes and historic interest where the traveller can enjoy a great variety of scenery within short distances. Camping or caravanning is a good way to see Britain. You can go as you please without sticking to a set programme, enjoy the country air and have a lot of fun. Wherever you stay, you can use your park as a base for sightseeing and touring the surrounding area.

Le tourisme en Grande-Bretagne	(Voir page 6)
Unterwegs in Großbritannien	(Lesen Sie Seite 7)
Rondtrekken in Groot-Brittannië	(Zie pag 9)
Alla scoperta della Gran Bretagna	(Vedi 11)

Touring Britain

As the birthplace of camping, Britain has a large number of places to stay of every kind – from small, quite spots to big lively parks offering a wide range of facilities and entertainment. Many have a restaurant, bar, nightclub, regular barbeques and evening entertainment (eg dinner dance, cabaret).

An increasing number of parks now make ideal centres for an activity holiday. Fishing, sailing and golfing and are just three of the more popular activities offered by more and more parks. Many also have indoor swimming pools, tennis courts, games room and provide a wide range of facilities and activities to keep the children amused.

Most parks admit tents, touring and motor caravans and provide a wide range of central facilities for the tourer. Many have caravan holiday homes for hire. These are often very spacious, luxurious and well equipped with two to three good sized bedrooms, a lounge with comfortable furnishings and a separate dining area. Many have modern conveniences such as colour televisions, fridges, hot showers, en-suite bathrooms and microwaves. In addition to caravan holiday homes, many parks also have chalets and lodges for hire, designed and equipped to the same standard as the caravans. All are truly a home from home, giving you the facilities and freedom you need to enjoy your holiday.

To help you select the type of park to suit you, with the facilities and standards you require, the British Graded Holiday Parks Rating Scheme will be of great assistance. Each park involved in this scheme has been visited by an independent assessor and given a rating based on cleanliness, environment and the quality of facilities and services provided.

Many parks are open all year and can be an excellent way to have a short break in the spring, autumn and even in the winter months. Prices will be cheaper than during the main season and many facilities will still be available (although it might be wise to check).

If you intend to stay in a popular holiday area during the main season (June to September), you are advised to book in advance. It is essential either to send written confirmation of any reservations made or to arrive very early at your chosen park.

Le tourisme en Grande-Bretagne

La Grande-Bretagne est un pays qui abonde en panoramas superbes et en sites d'intérêt historique, où les touristes n'ont pas besoin de parcourir des kilomètres pour pouvoir admirer des paysages très variés. Le camping et le caravaning sont d'excellents moyens d'explorer la Grande-Bretagne. On peut aller où on le désire sans adhérer à un plan fixe, profiter du bon air de la campagne et se divertir. Quelle que soit la région où se trouve le terrain dans lequel on séjourne, on peut s'en servir comme point de chute pour faire du tourisme et rayonner dans la région.

C'est en Grande-Bretagne qu'est né le camping, on y trouve donc un grand nombre de terrains de toutes sortes, allant de petits terrains tranquilles à de grands parcs pleins d'animation proposant une vaste gamme d'équipements et de distractions. Un grand nombre de terrains possèdent des restaurants, bars, night-clubs, et organisent régulièrement des barbecues et des distractions nocturnes (par ex. dîners dansants, spectacles de cabaret).

Les terrains de camping sont des endroits merveilleux pour passer des vacances à thème, et un nombre de plus en plus important de terrains proposent cette formule. La pêche, la navigation de plaisance et le golf, entre autres, font partie des activités les plus populaires qu'on peut pratiquer dans des terrains de plus en plus nombreux. Un grand nombre de terrains mettent également à la disposition des vacanciers des piscines couvertes chauffées, des courts de tennis, des salles de jeux, et proposent une large gamme d'installations et d'activités destinées aux enfants.

La plupart de terrains acceptent les tentes, les caravanes de tourisme et les camping-cars, et mettent un vaste éventail d'équipements à la disposition des vacanciers. Un grand nombre de terrains louent des caravanes fixes, qui sont souvent très spacieuses, luxueuses et bien aménagées, comportant deux ou trois belles chambres à coucher, un salon confortable et un coin salle à manger séparé.

Un grand nombre de ces logements de vacances ont tout le confort moderne: télévision couleur, réfrigérateur, douche avec eau chaude, salle de bains et four à micro-ondes. En plus des caravanes de vacances, de nombreux terrains louent également des chalets et des pavillons, conçus et équipés avec le même soin et dotés du même confort. Vous vous sentirez comme chez vous dans tous ces terrains et vous y trouverez les aménagements et la liberté dont vous avez besoin pour profiter au mieux de vos vacances.

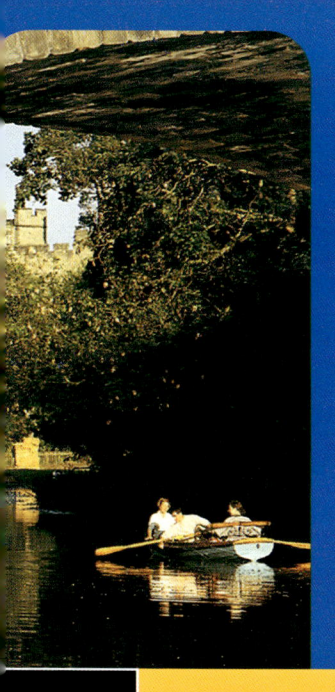

Pour sélectionner le meilleur terrain/centre offrant les services et normes dont vous avez besoin, le British Graded Holiday Parks Rating Scheme (système d'évaluation des centres de vacances/terrains de camping britanniques) vous sera très utile. Des inspecteurs indépendants ont visité chaque terrain participant à ce projet et les ont classés selon la propreté, l'environnement et la qualité de leurs services.

De nombreux terrains sont ouverts toute l'année, et permettent ainsi de prendre quelques jours de vacances agréables au printemps, en automne et même en hiver. Les tarifs sont moins élevés que pendant la haute saison, et de nombreux équipements sont encore à la disposition des vacanciers (il est toutefois prudent de vérifier).

Si vous avez l'intention de séjourner, en haute saison (de juin à septembre), dans une région de villégiature très fréquentée, nous vous conseillons de réserver à l'avance. Il est indispensable soit de confirmer toute réservation par écrit, soit d'arriver très tôt au terrain de votre choix.

Mit Zelt und Wohnwagen unterwegs in Großbritannien

Großbritannien ist reich an schönen Landschaften und historischen Stätten und die Natur zeigt sich dem Besucher innerhalb weniger Kilometer von ihrer abwechslungsreichsten Seite. Die Übernachtung auf dem Campingplatz oder im Wohnwagen eignet sich gut, um Großbritannien kennen zu lernen. Sie können nach Lust und Laune ins Blaue fahren, die würzige Landluft genießen und viel Interessantes erleben. Wo Sie sich auch aufhalten mögen, Ihr Platz ist stets ein idealer Ausgangsort für Besichtigungstouren und Ausflüge in die Umgebung.

Großbritannien ist der Geburtsort des Zeltens und bietet eine große Anzahl an Plätzen jeder Art - von kleinen, ruhigen bis zu großen, lebhaften Plätzen mit einer großen Auswahl an Einrichtungen und einem reichen Unterhaltungsprogramm. Zahlreiche Plätze verfügen über ein Restaurant, eine Bar, einen Nachtklub und veranstalten regelmäßige Grillpartys und Abendunterhaltung (z.B. Abendessen mit Tanz, Kabarett).

Immer mehr Plätze sind ideale Ferienorte für Aktivferien. Angeln, Segeln und Golf, nur drei der beliebtesten Aktivitäten, werden von einer wachsenden Zahl von Plätzen angeboten. Viele verfügen auch über ein Hallenbad, Tennisplätze, Spielzimmer und bieten eine große Auswahl an Einrichtungen und Aktivitäten für Kinder.

Die meisten Plätze sind für Zelte, Wohnwagen und Wohnmobile eingerichtet und bieten dem Besucher eine Reihe von Einrichtungen. Zahlreiche Plätze vermieten Wohnwagen. Diese sind oft äußerst geräumig, luxuriös und gut ausgestattet und verfügen über zwei oder drei Schlafzimmer, ein Wohnzimmer mit komfortablen Möbeln und einen getrennten Essbereich. Viele bieten auch Farbfernseher, Kühlschrank, Dusche mit warmem Wasser, Bad und Mikrowellenherd. Zusätzlich zu den Wohnwagen gibt es auf zahlreichen Plätzen auch Chalets und Hütten mit demselben Komfort. Alle sind in der Tat ein zweites Zuhause und bieten die Einrichtungen und die Unabhängigkeit, die für erfolgreiche Ferien unerlässlich sind.

Um Ihnen bei der Auswahl des Parktyps zu helfen, dessen Standards und Leistungsumfang Ihren Anforderungen und Wünschen am besten entspricht, wird Ihnen das British Graded Holiday Parks Rating Scheme (Beurteilungssystem für britische Ferienparks) von großem Nutzen sein. Alle an diesem System beteiligten Parks sind von unabhängigen Gutachtern besucht und im Hinblick auf Sauberkeit, Umwelt und Qualität von Angebot und Service beurteilt worden.

Zahlreiche Plätze sind ganzjährig geöffnet und ideal für Kurzurlaube im Frühling, Herbst oder auch Winter. Die Preise sind während der Nebensaison billiger als während der Hochsaison und zahlreiche Einrichtungen sind immer in Betrieb (es ist jedoch ratsam, sich zuerst zu erkundigen).

Falls Sie während der Hochsaison (Juni bis September) eine beliebte Feriendestination wählen, ist es ratsam, im Voraus zu buchen. Sie müssen die Buchung entweder schriftlich bestätigen oder sehr früh auf dem Platz Ihrer Wahl eintreffen.

Rondtrekken in Groot-Brittannië

In Groot-Brittannië vindt u prachtige landschappen en een interessante geschiedenis. De reiziger treft op korte afstand van elkaar allerlei verschillende gebieden aan, en kamperen met de tent of de caravan is de ideale manier om echt van Groot-Brittannië te genieten. Ga en sta waar u wilt, zonder aan een programma vast te zitten, geniet van de frisse lucht en maak plezier! Waar u ook bent, u kunt uw kampeerplaats uw basis maken en in het omliggende gebied rondtrekken.

Groot-Brittannië is het geboorteland van het kamperen, en wij hebben dan ook een groot aantal terreinen in allerlei soorten en maten: vanaf kleine rustige terreintjes tot en met grote gezellige parken met allerlei faciliteiten en amusement. Vele hebben een restaurant, bar, nachtclub, en organiseren regelmatig barbecues en amusement 's avonds (zoals diner dansant, cabaret).

Steeds meer parken vormen tegenwoordig een ideaal centrum voor een actieve vakantie. Vissen, zeilen en golfen zijn slechts drie mogelijkheden die steeds meer terreinen organiseren. Vaak vindt u ook overdekte zwembaden, tennisbanen, spellenkamers en allerlei faciliteiten en activiteiten om de kinderen bezig te houden.

Op de meeste terreinen worden tenten, trekcaravans en kampeerauto's toegelaten en vindt u een groot aantal centrale faciliteiten voor de trekker. Ook zijn er vaak stacaravans te huur: deze zijn vaak zeer ruim, luxueus en goed uitgerust, met twee of drie ruime slaapkamers, een zitkamer met gerieflijk meubilair en een aparte eetkamer. Vaak vindt u er ook moderne gemakken zoals kleuren t.v., ijskast, warme douches, en-suite badkamers en magnetronovens.

Vele parken bieden niet alleen stacaravans maar ook huisjes te huur, die al net zo goed zijn ingericht en uitgerust. Geniet van de faciliteiten en de vrijheid om echt vakantie te vieren.

Om u te helpen met het selecteren van een bepaald type park met voorzieningen en op het niveau dat u zoekt, zal het British Graded Holiday Parks Rating Scheme u zeker van pas komen. Elk park dat aan dit systeem meedoet is bezocht door een onafhankelijke controleur en heeft een classificatie gekregen op basis van hygiëne, omgeving en de kwaliteit van de voorzieningen en diensten die er aanwezig zijn.

Vele parken zijn het hele jaar open en bieden de ideale manier om er even tussenuit te gaan in de lente, herfst of zelfs in de winter. De prijzen zijn dan lager dan in het hoogseizoen, terwijl toch vele faciliteiten beschikbaar zijn (het is wel raadzaam dit van te voren na te gaan).

Als u in een populair vakantiegebied denkt te verblijven in het hoogseizoen (juni tot september), raden wij u aan van te voren te reserveren. Bevestig de reservering schriftelijk of kom zeer vroeg aan op het terrein.

South Coast
and New Forest

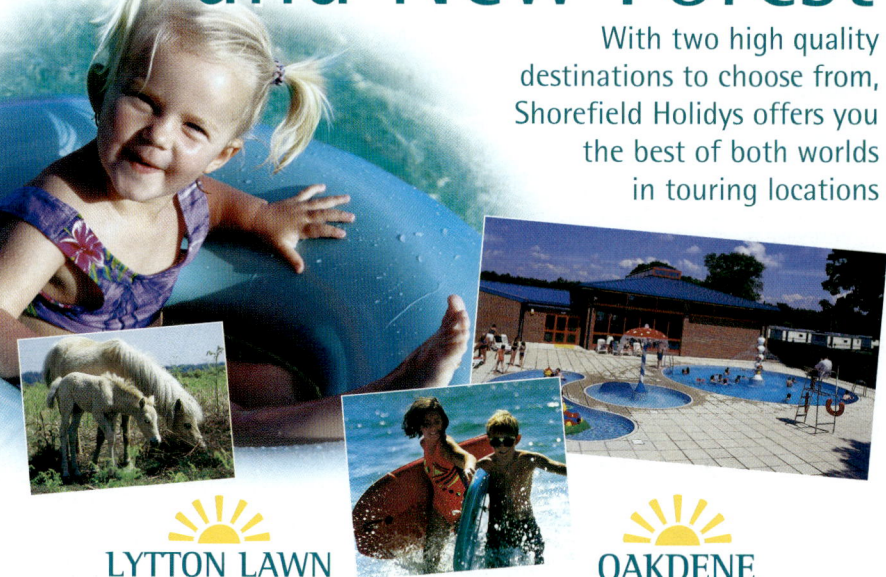

With two high quality destinations to choose from, Shorefield Holidys offers you the best of both worlds in touring locations

LYTTON LAWN
TOURING PARK

Set in beautiful natural parkland close to Milford beach and the historic New Forest with views to the Isle of Wight. Peaceful, unspoilt and relaxing. Electricity hook-up, showers, laundrette, shop, 'Premier Pitches' and a children's area. Optional Leisure Club facilities $2^{1}/_{2}$ miles away, at Shorefield

OAKDENE
FOREST PARK

Over 55 acres of beautiful parkland giving direct access to the Avon Forest, and only 9 miles from Bournemouth's sandy beaches. New 'Premier Pitches', indoor and outdoor pools, sauna, steam room, spa bath, flume, gym, adventure playground, club with entertainment, cafeteria, takeaway, general store and launderette.

SHOREFIELD
HOLIDAYS LIMITED

For further details telephone
01590 648331 Ref. WTST

RALLIES WELCOME AT BOTH SITES

Oakdene Forest Park, St. Leonards, Ringwood, Hants BH24 2RZ
Lytton Lawn, Lymore Lane, Milford on Sea, Hants SO41 0TX
e-mail: holidays@shorefield.co.uk   www.shorefield.co.uk

2000 DAVID BELLAMY CONSERVATION AWARD GOLD

ENGLAND FOR EXCELLENCE
THE ENGLISH TOURIST BOARD
AWARDS FOR TOURISM

Alla scoperta della Gran Bretagna

La Gran Bretagna è uno stupendo paese di grande interesse storico che offre un'ampia varietà di paesaggi. Il campeggio in tenda o roulotte è uno dei modi più efficaci di visitare la Gran Bretagna, dato che consente di viaggiare quando e dove si vuole, senza dover rispettare un itinerario prestabilito, divertendosi e respirando l'aria fresca della campagna. Ovunque si decida di andare, il campeggio può servire da base dalla quale il turista può visitare la zona circostante.

Il campeggio è un'invenzione britannica, ne consegue che in Gran Bretagna vi sono numerosissimi campeggi di tutti i tipi: da quelli piccoli e tranquilli a quelli grandi e animatissimi che offrono un'ampia gamma di strutture e intrattenimenti. Molti campeggi offrono anche ristoranti, bar, locali notturni, banchetti all'aperto con barbecue e spettacoli serali (p.es. serate di ballo, cabaret).

Molti campeggi sono ideali per trascorrere periodi di vacanza di tipo più dinamico, dato che un numero sempre maggiore di essi offre la possibilità, ad esempio, di pescare, praticare la vela o giocare al golf.

Molti dispongono di piscine, campi da tennis e palestre al coperto e di numerose strutture e attività per il divertimento dei bambini.

La maggior parte dei campeggi accetta tende, campers e roulottes e offre un'ampia gamma di strutture centralizzate per il campeggiatore. Molti offrono anche roulottes a noleggio Queste roulottes sono spesso spaziosissime, lussuose e ben attrezzate con due o tre camere doppie, un salotto comodamente ammobiliato e una sala da pranzo separata. Molte offrono anche altre moderne comodità come televisioni a colori, frigoriferi, docce calde, camere con bagno e forni a microonde. Oltre alle roulottes a noleggio, molti campeggi offrono anche chalet e casette a noleggio progettate e attrezzate con gli stessi criteri. Sono tutte abitazioni dove ci si sente come a casa propria, e che offrono libertà e tutte le attrezzature necessarie a godersi la propria vacanza.

Caravan & Camping
Haven
BRITISH HOLIDAYS

We've come together to offer you more
Where great family holidays are made!

Prices start from
***£4 Per night**

*Based on nights in Spring or Autumn and includes the 2 for 1 offer.

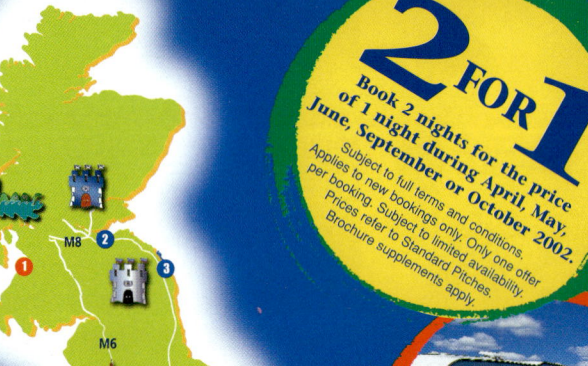

SCOTLAND, THE NORTH WEST AND NORTHUMBERLAND
1. Craig Tara
2. Seton Sands
3. Haggerston Castle
4. Blue Dolphin
5. Primrose Valley
6. Reighton Sands
7. Lakeland
8. Marton Mere

THE EAST OF ENGLAND
9. Thorpe Park
10. Golden Sands
11. Cherry Tree
12. Wild Duck
13. Orchards

DORSET
14. Rockley Park
15. Seaview
16. Weymouth Bay
17. Littlesea

DEVON, SOMERSET AND CORNWALL
18. Devon Cliffs
19. Perran Sands
20. Doniford Bay
21. Burnham on Sea

WALES
22. Kiln Park
23. Greenacres
24. Presthaven Sands

We Welcome...
✓ Touring Caravans, Motorhomes
✓ Trailer Tents and Tents

For Haven or British Holidays call now on:
08705 13 44 02
or see your local travel agent quoting BTA01

Haven Holidays/British Holidays, 1 Park Lane, Hemel Hempstead, Herts. HP2 4YL.

2 FOR 1
Book 2 nights for the price of 1 night during April, May, June, September or October 2002. Applies to new bookings only. Only one offer per booking. Subject to limited availability. Prices refer to Standard Pitches. Brochure supplements apply. Subject to full terms and conditions.

What A Perfect Mix...
- Freedom to choose from even more coastal locations throughout the UK
- Freedom to enjoy on-Park life
- Freedom to relax with the familiarity of your own touring caravan, motorhome, tent or trailer tent

Per aiutare a scegliere il tipo di parco più adatto, che offra i requisiti e gli standard richiesti, sarà molto utile il British Graded Holiday Parks Rating Scheme (progetto di assegnazione di punteggio ai parchi vacanze del Regno Unito). Ogni parco iscritto viene ispezionato da ispettori indipendenti, con assegnazione di punteggio sulla base dei criteri di pulizia, qualità dell'ambiente e delle risorse e dei servizi offerti.

Molti dei campeggi sono aperti tutto l'anno e sono dunque ideali per trascorrere una breve vacanza anche in primavera, in autunno o in inverno, stagioni in cui i prezzi sono più bassi che durante i mesi di alta stagione, anche se restano disponibili molte delle strutture (consigliamo comunque di controllare prima dell'arrivo).

Si consiglia a chi intenda trascorrere una vacanza in una delle località turistiche più frequentate durante i mesi di alta stagione (da giugno a settembre) di prenotare in anticipo. È essenziale confermare la prenotazione per iscritto o arrivare molto presto al campeggio prescelto.

Want To Win A Holiday?

Bring your own Touring Caravan, Tent, Motorhome or Trailer Tent

JUST SOME OF OUR AWARDS

Just answer the question below!

Haven and British Holidays & Where to Stay: Camping and Caravan Parks are delighted to offer you the chance to win a wonderful seven night Touring family holiday, with three runners-up prizes of Touring family breaks at a Haven or British Holidays Park.

With a choice of 24 coastal locations throughout England, Scotland and Wales, all Parks offer an extensive range of facilities such as Indoor and Outdoor Heated Swimming Pools, meet Rory the Tiger or Bradley Bear at the Kids Club, Excellent Sports, Family Entertainment, Great Bars and Restaurants and much more.

The lucky first prize winner will be staying on an electric pitch for 7 nights including full use of all the Amenities.
Normal Terms & Conditions apply.

Q **What is the name of the British Holidays Park in Somerset?**

Fill in your answer and details on the coupon below and send to: Julie Freedman, Bta Competition, Haven Holidays/British Holidays, 1 Park Lane, Hemel Hempstead, Herts. HP2 4YL.
Closing date 30th November 2002.
Please see page 240 for competition rules.

Answer:
Name:
Address:
                                    Postcode:
Telephone Number: E-Mail Address:

Haven
www.havenholidays.com

BRITISH HOLIDAYS
www.british-holidays.co.uk

For Haven or British Holidays call now on:

08705 13 44 02

or see your local travel agent quoting BTA01

MAP 1

Location Maps

SEE MAP 2 FOR KEY TO MAPS

Key to numbered Unitary Authorities
1: NEATH PORT TALBOT
2: BRIDGEND
3: RHONDDA CYNON TAFF
4: MERTHYR TYDFIL
5: CAERPHILLY
6: CARDIFF
7: TORFAEN
8: NEWPORT

SEE MAP 3 & 4

0 — 25 Miles
0 — 40 Km

Key to regions: Wales

All place names in black offer parks in this guide.

15

MAP 2

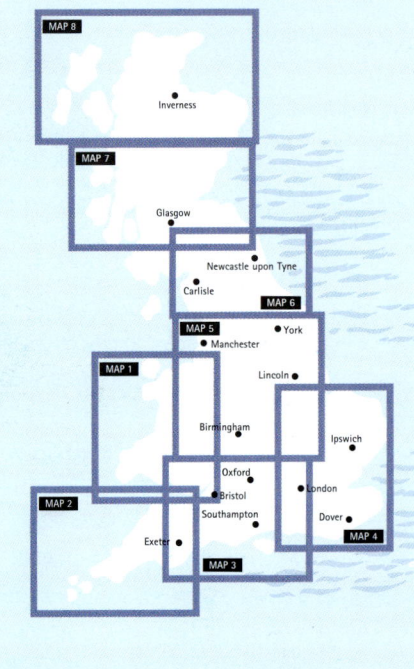

Every place name featured in the regional accommodation sections of this Where to Stay guide has a map reference to help you locate it on the maps which follow. For example, to find Colchester, Essex, which has 'Map ref 3B2', turn to Map 3 and refer to grid square B2.

All place names appearing in the regional sections are shown in black type on the maps. This enables you to find other places in your chosen area which may have suitable accommodation - the Town Index (at the back of this guide) gives page numbers.

Key to regions: South West

MAP 2

All place names in black offer parks in this guide.

MAP 3

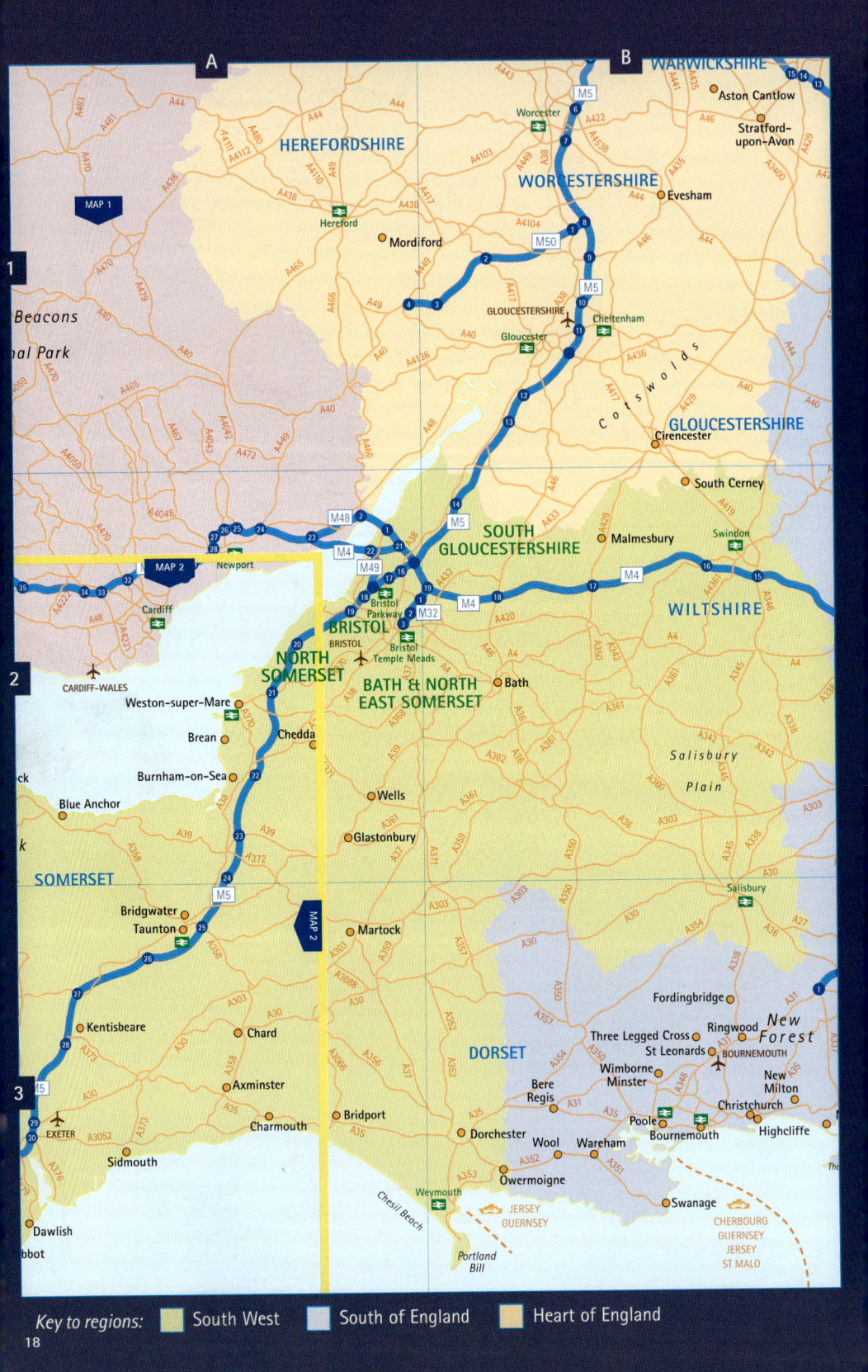

MAP 3

MAP 4

MAP 4

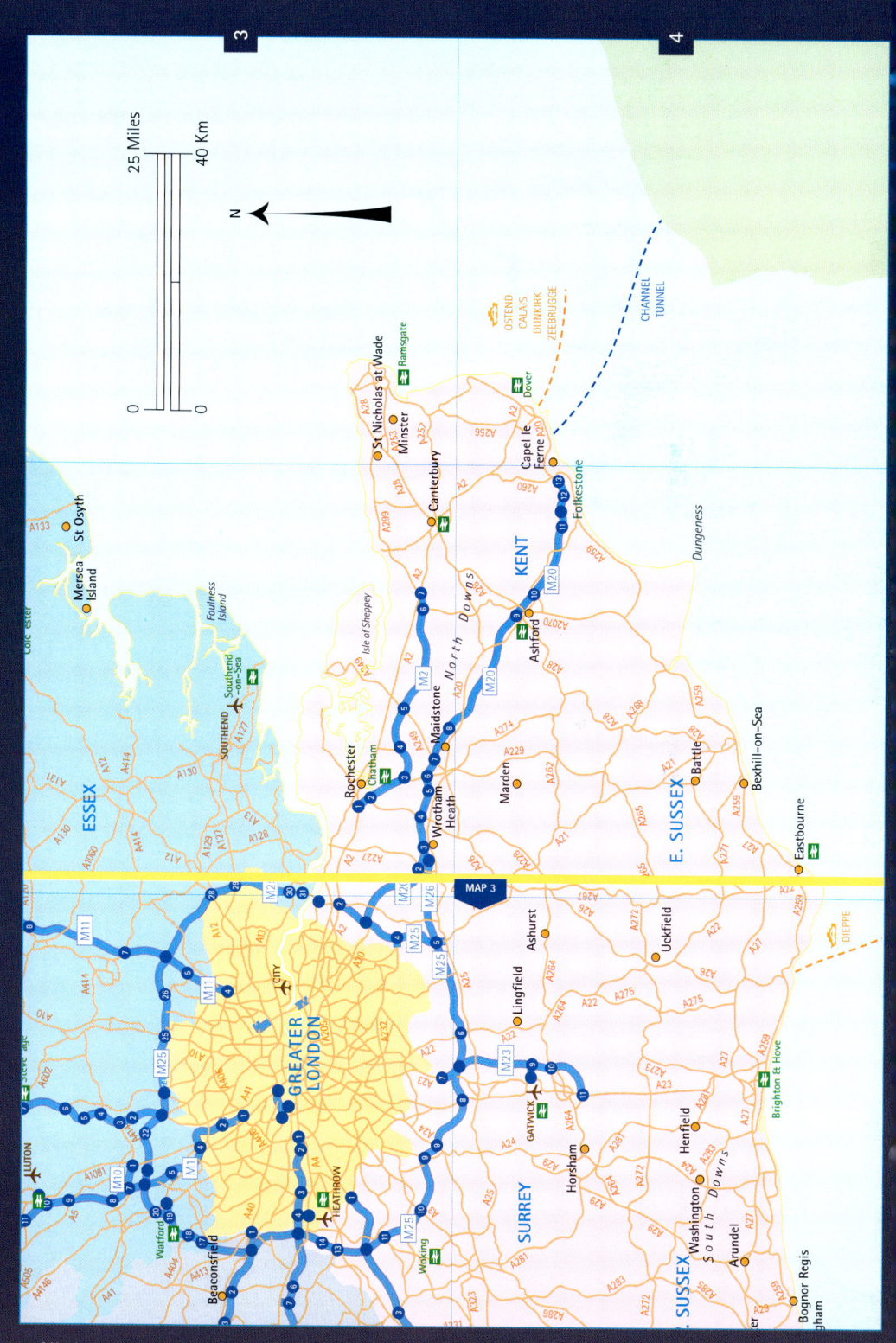

All place names in black offer parks in this guide.

MAP 5

Key to regions: North West · Yorkshire · Heart of England · East of England

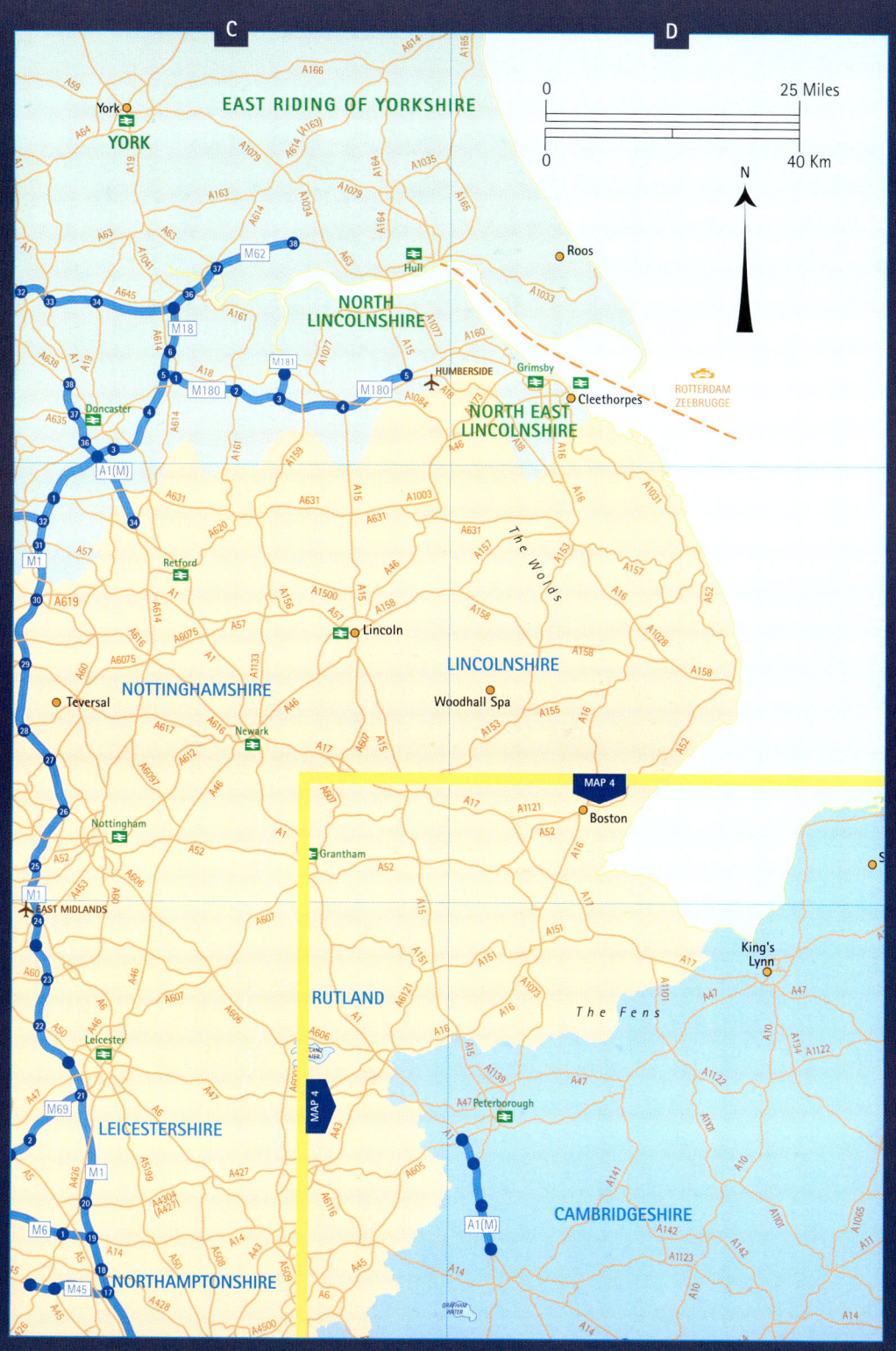

MAP 5

All place names in black offer parks in this guide.

MAP 6

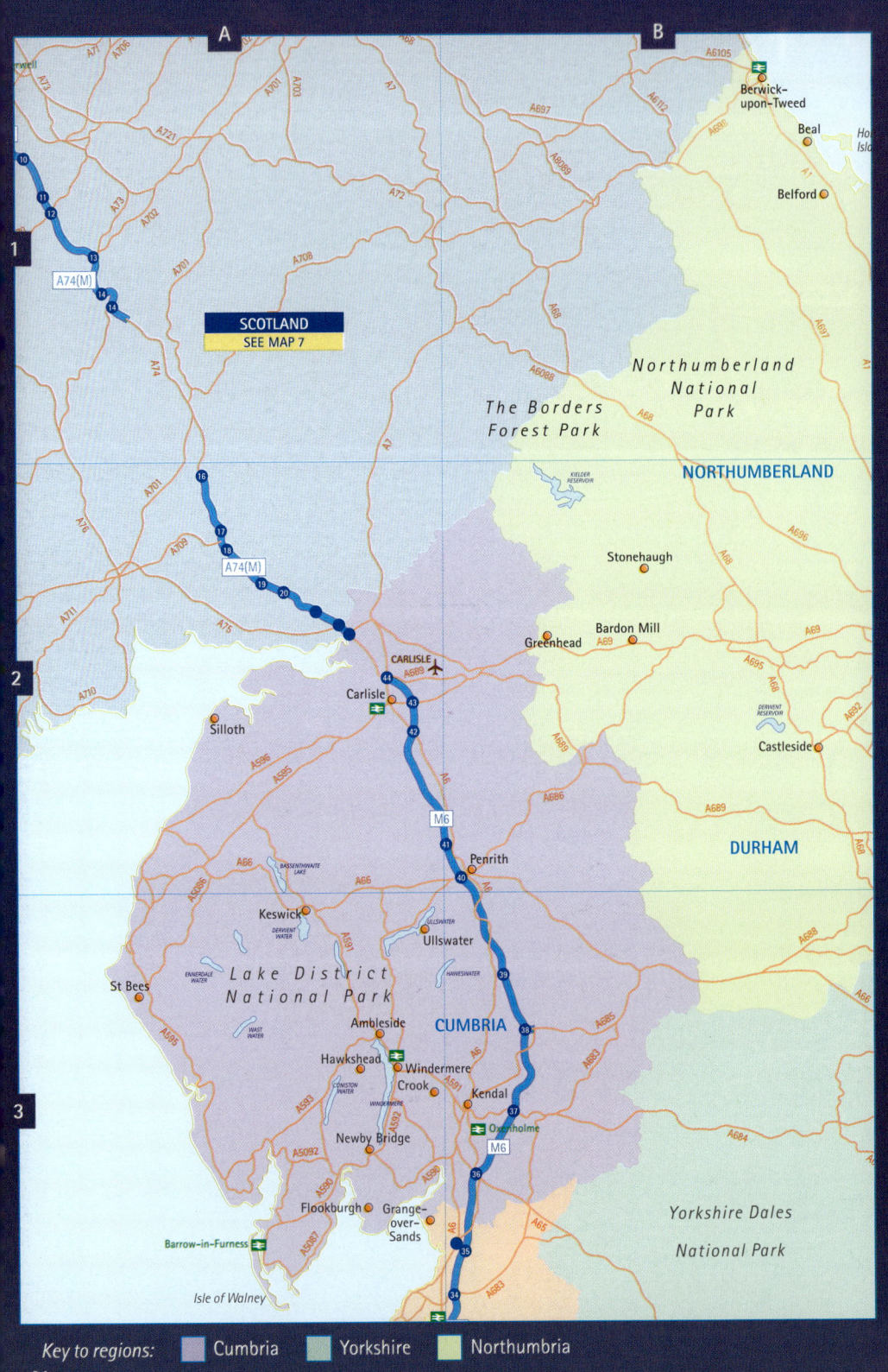

SCOTLAND SEE MAP 7

Key to regions: Cumbria | Yorkshire | Northumbria

MAP 6

All place names in black offer parks in this guide.

MAP 7

A **B**

1

Coll
Tiree
Island of Mull
Fort William
Glencoe
Oban
Ardlui
Inveruglas
Aberfoyle

ARGYLL AND BUTE

2

Colonsay
Lochgilphead
Jura
Islay
Lochranza
Isle of Arran
Balloch
Greenock
Wemyss Bay
Skelmorlie
Lochwinnoch
GLASGOW
Glasgow

NORTH AYRSHIRE
Ardrossan

EAST AYRSHIRE

PRESTWICK
Ayr

Key to numbered Unitary Authorities
1: WEST DUNBARTONSHIRE
2: EAST DUNBARTONSHIRE
3: CITY OF GLASGOW
4: EAST RENFREWSHIRE
5: THE CLACKMANNANSHIRE
6: CITY OF EDINBURGH

SOUTH AYRSHIRE

Galloway Forest Park

3

LARNE
BELFAST
Cairnryan
Stranraer
Glenluce
Sandhead

NORTHERN IRELAND

Key to regions: Scotland

MAP 7

All place names in black offer parks in this guide.

MAP 8

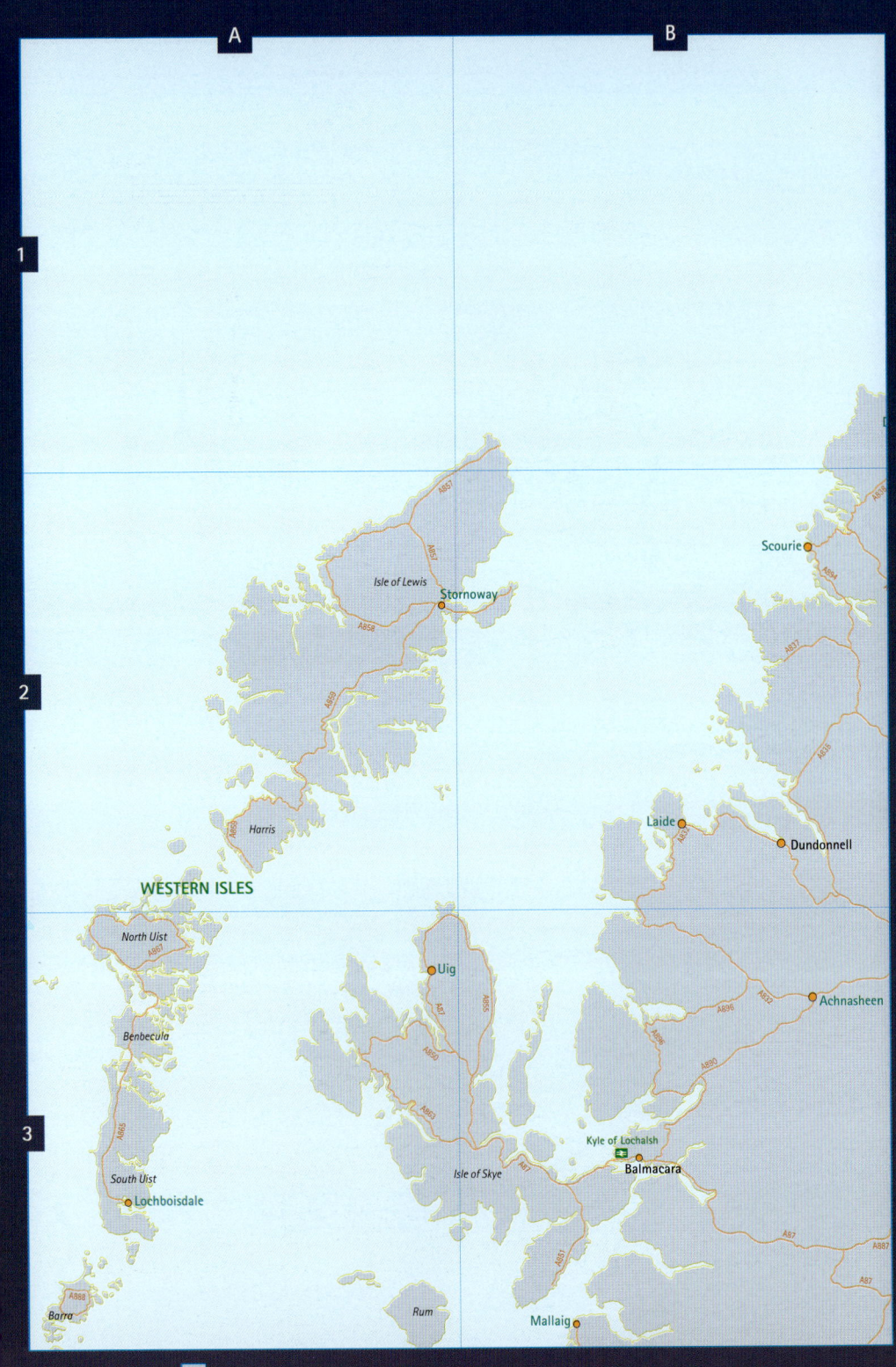

A B

1

2

Isle of Lewis
Stornoway
Scourie
Harris
WESTERN ISLES
Laide
Dundonnell

3

North Uist
Uig
Achnasheen
Benbecula
South Uist
Lochboisdale
Isle of Skye
Kyle of Lochalsh
Balmacara
Barra
Rum
Mallaig

Key to regions: Scotland
28

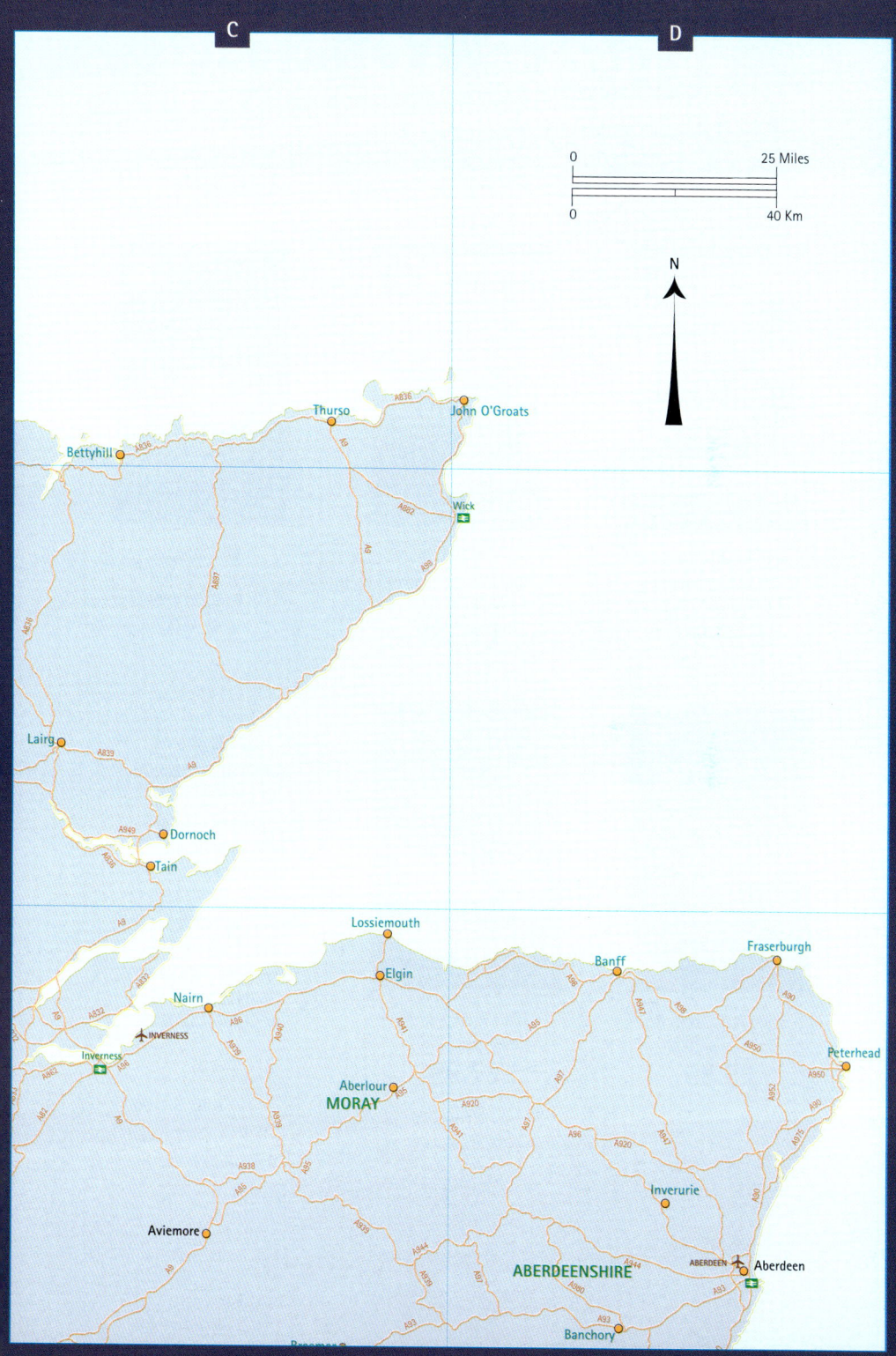

MAP 8

All place names in black offer parks in this guide.

Where to Stay 2002

The official and best selling guides, offering the reassurance of quality assured accommodation

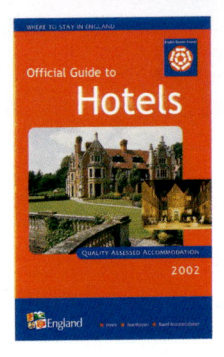

Hotels, Townhouses and Travel Accommodation in England 2002
£10.99

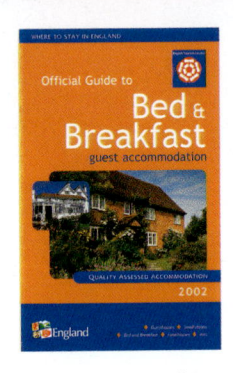

Guesthouses, Bed & Breakfast, Farmhouses and Inns in England 2002
£11.99

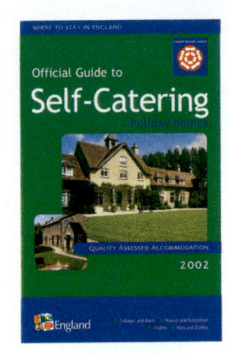

Self Catering Holiday Homes in England 2002
£9.99

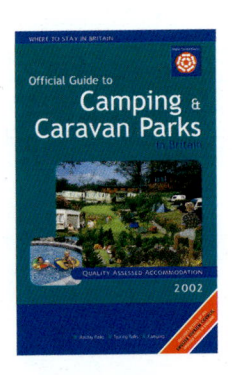

Camping & Caravan Parks in Britain 2002
£5.99

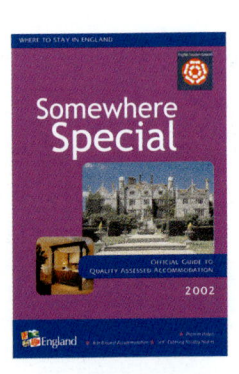

Somewhere Special in England 2002
£7.99

Look out also for:
SOMEWHERE SPECIAL IN ENGLAND 2002

Accommodation achieving the highest standards in facilities and quality of service –

the perfect guide for the discerning traveller.

NOW ALSO FEATURING SELF CATERING ACCOMMODATION

The guides include
- Accommodation entries packed with information • Full colour maps
- Places to visit • Tourist Information Centres

INFORMATIVE • EASY TO USE • GREAT VALUE FOR MONEY

From all good bookshops or by mail order from the ETC Fulfilment Centre,
PO Box 22489, London W6 9FR
Tel: 0870 606 7204 Fax: 020 8563 3048
Email: fulfilment@englishtourism.org.uk Web: www.englishtourism.org.uk

How to use this guide

Most parks listed here have accommodation for touring caravans or tents or both and most welcome motor caravans. Many parks also have caravan holiday homes to let.

The Quality Assurance Standard

When you're looking for a place to stay, you need a rating system you can trust. The British Graded Holiday Parks Scheme, relaunched in 2000, gives you a clear guide of what you can expect, in an easy-to-understand form. The scheme has quality at its heart and reflects consumer expectation.

The English Tourism Council uses Stars to show the quality rating of parks participating in the scheme. Parks are visited annually by trained, impartial assessors who award a rating from One to Five Stars. These are based on cleanliness, environment and the quality of facilities and services provided.

Parks are also given a 'designator' so you can identify the type of site at-a-glance - a Holiday Park, a Touring Park or a Camping Park, for example. (If no rating or designator is shown, the park was awaiting assessment at the time of going to press.)

The British Graded Holiday Parks Scheme was devised jointly by the national tourist boards for England, Northern Ireland, Scotland and Wales in association with the British Holiday & Home Parks Association (see page 45) and the National Caravan Council (see page 49).

Facilities

Facilities are indicated by means of the at-a-glance symbols explained on the fold-out back cover flap.

Prices

Prices given for touring pitches are based on the minimum and maximum charges for one night for two persons, car and either caravan or tent. It is more usual in Britain to charge simply for the use of the pitch, but a number of parks charge separately for car, caravan or tent, and for each person. Some parks may charge extra for caravan awnings. Minimum and maximum prices for caravan holiday homes are given per week. Prices quoted are those supplied to us by the park operators concerned, and are intended to give an indication of the prices which will be charged during the currency of this publication. Prices are shown in pounds (£) and pence (p). VAT (Value Added Tax) at 17.50% is included in the prices shown. In order to avoid misunderstandings, it is particularly advisable to check prices with the park concerned when making reservations.

Making a Booking

When enquiring about accommodation, as well as checking prices and other details, you will need to state your requirements clearly and precisely - for example:

- arrival and departure dates with acceptable alternatives if appropriate.
- the accommodation you need.
- tell the management about any particular requirements.

Misunderstandings can occur very easily over the telephone so we recommend that all bookings be confirmed in writing if time permits. Remember to include your name and address and please enclose a stamped addressed envelope or an international reply coupon (if writing from outside Britain) for each reply.

Deposits and Advance Payments

In the case of caravan, camping and chalet parks and holiday centres the full charge often has to be paid in advance. This may be in two instalments - a deposit at the time of booking and the balance by, say, two weeks before the start of the booked period.

Cancellations

When you accept offered accommodation, in writing or on the telephone, you are entering into a legally binding contract with the proprietor of the establishment. This means that if you cancel a reservation, fail to take up the accommodation or leave prematurely (regardless of the reasons) the proprietor may be entitled to compensation if it cannot be relet for all or a good part of the booked period. If a deposit has been paid it is likely to be forfeited and an additional payment may be demanded.

It is therefore in your interest to advise the management immediately if you have to change your travel plans, cancel a booking or leave prematurely.

Electric hook-up points

Most parks now have electric hook-up points for caravans and tents. Voltage is generally 240v AC, 50 cycles, although variations between 200v and 250v may still be found. An adaptor for use with hook-ups may be necessary. Parks will usually charge extra for this facility, and it is advisable to check rates when making a booking.

Finding your Park

Parks in this guide are listed in England by region followed by Scotland and Wales. They are listed alphabetically under the name of the town in or near which they are situated. The Town Index on page 245 and colour location maps at the front of the guide show all cities, towns and villages with park listings in this guide.

Use these as a quick and easy way to find suitable accommodation. If you know which park you wish to stay at, check under the Index to Parks on page 241.

If the place you wish to stay is included in the Town Index, turn to the page number given to find the parks available there. The town names appear in black on the maps at the front of the guide as indicated by the map reference in the entry. Also check on the colour maps to find other places nearby which also have parks listed in this guide.

If the place you want is not in the town index - or you only have a general idea of the area in which you wish to stay - use the colour location maps.

The maps show all place names under which a park is listed in this guide. For a precise location read the directions in each entry. If you have any difficulties finding a particular park, we suggest that you ask for final directions within the neighbourhood.

The International Direction Signs shown here are in use in Britain and are designed to help visitors find their park. They have not yet been erected for all parks and do not display the name of any particular one. They do show, however, whether the park is for tents or caravans or both.

The International Camping Carnet is rarely recognised in Britain except at parks organised by the major clubs.

London sites
London is a great attraction to many visitors, so the camping and caravan parks in the Greater London area tend to become full very quickly, and early booking is required. Parks are also available at most ports of entry to the country and many of these are listed in this guide and marked on the maps at the front.

Park finding services
Tourist Information Centres throughout Britain (see end pages) are able to give campers and caravanners information about parks in their areas.

Some Tourist Information Centres have camping and caravanning advisory services which provide details of park availability and often assist with park booking. At present, in England, these advisory Tourist Information Centres cover areas in the New Forest, (0131) 314 6505; and Cornwall, (01872) 274057. In Wales, many Tourist Information Centres can supply information on pitch availability in their area from the end of May to the end of August.

Avoiding Peak Season Problems
In the summer months of June to September, parks in popular areas such as North Wales, Cumbria, the West Country or the New Forest in Hampshire may become full. Campers should aim to arrive at parks early in the day or, where possible, should book in advance. Some parks have overnight holding areas for visitors who arrive late. This helps to prevent disturbing other campers and caravanners late at night and means that fewer visitors are turned away. Caravans or tents are directed to a pitch the following morning.

Other Caravan and Camping Places
If you enjoy making your own route through Britain's countryside, it may interest you to know that the Forestry Commission operates forest camp parks in Britain's seven Forest Parks as well as in the New Forest. Some offer reduced charges for youth organisations on organised camping trips, and all enquiries about them should be made, well in advance of your intended stay, to the Forestry Commission.

Camping Barns
These are usually redundant farm buildings which have been converted to provide simple accommodation, for up to 15 visitors, at a reasonable cost. Facilities are basic with somewhere to sleep, eat and prepare food, a supply of cold running water and flush toilet.

The Youth Hostels Association has a network of camping barns stretching from the Forest of Bowland in Lancashire, through Durham and into North Yorkshire. Further information and bookings details can be obtained from the YHA, Trevelyan House, Dimple Road, Matlock, Derbyshire DE4 2YH
Tel: (017687) 72645 (for camping barns in Lake District)
Tel: (01200) 420102 (for barns in all areas except Lake District)
Internet: www.yha.org.uk

Camping barns are also available in the Peak National Park. Further information and details can be obtained from Peak District National Park Authority, Aldern House, Baslow Road, Bakewell, Derbyshire DE45 1AE.
Tel: (01629) 816200
Note that bookings are handled by the YHA (see above).

Pets
Many places accept guests with dogs, but we do advise that you check this when you book, and ask if there are any extra charges or rules about exactly where your pet is allowed. The acceptance of dogs is not always extended to cats and it is strongly advised that cat owners contact the establishment well in advance. Some establishments do not accept pets at all. Dogs are welcome where you see this symbol 🐕.

Bringing Pets to Britain
The quarantine laws have recently changed in England and a Pet Travel Scheme (PETS) is currently in operation. Under this scheme pet dogs are able to come into Britain from over 35 countries via certain sea, air and rail routes into England.

Dogs that have been resident in these countries for more than 6 months may enter the UK under the Scheme, providing they are accompanied by the appropriate documentation.

For dogs to be able to enter the UK without quarantine under the PETS Scheme they will have to meet certain conditions and travel with the following documents: the Official PETS Certificate, a certificate of treatment against tapeworm and ticks and a declaration of residence.

For details of participating countries, routes, operators and further information about the PETS Scheme please contact the PETS Helpline, DEFRA (Department for Environment, Food and Rural Affairs),
1a Page Street, London SW1P 4PQ
Tel: +44 (0) 870 241 1710 Fax: +44 (0) 20 7904 6834
Email: pets.helpline@defra.gsi.gov.uk, or visit their web site at www.defra.gov.uk/animalh/quarantine

Drugs Warnings for Incoming Tourists

The United Kingdom has severe penalties against drug smuggling. Drug traffickers may try to trick travellers. If you are travelling to the United Kingdom avoid any involvement with drugs. Never carry luggage or parcels through customs for someone else.

Legal Points

The best source of legal advice for motorists in Britain will be your motoring organisation. What the caravanner or camper needs to know in addition is relatively simple.

If you are towing a caravan or camping trailer you must not exceed 96 kph (60 mph) on dual carriageways and motorways, 80 kph (50 mph) on single carriageways, and on a motorway with three lanes each side you must not enter the third (fastest) lane. Do not light cooking stoves in motorway service areas.

In most towns parking is restricted both by regulations and practical difficulties. Cars with trailers may not use meter-controlled parking spaces, and many town car parks are designed with spaces for single vehicles only. However, a number can accommodate long vehicles as well as cars.

At night a trailer or a car attached to a trailer, if parked on the roadway, must show two front and two rear lights even where a car by itself would be exempt.

The brakes, lights, weight etc. of foreign vehicles do not have to comply with British technical requirements. However, a trailer must not exceed the British size limits - 7 metres (23 feet) long and 2.3 metres (7 feet 6 inches) wide. They must carry your national identification plates. Do not stop overnight on roadside grass verges or lay-bys, because these are considered by law to be part of the road.

Finally, it is important to find out the time you are expected to vacate your pitch on your departure day. You should then leave in good time in the morning, or you may be asked to pay an extra day's charge.

Advice for Visitors

The British Tourist Authority welcomes your comments on any aspects of your stay in Britain, whether favourable or otherwise. We hope that you will have no cause to complain, but if you do, the best advice is to take up the complaint immediately with the management of the enterprise concerned: for example the park, shop or transport company. If you cannot obtain satisfaction in this way, please let us know and we ourselves may investigate the matter or suggest what action you might take.

You may bring currency in any denomination and up to any amount into Britain and there is no restriction on the number of travellers' cheques you can change. If you need to change money when the banks are closed you can do so at some large hotels, travel agents and stores or at independent bureaux de change. Be sure to check in advance the rate of exchange and the commission charges. All large shops, department stores and most hotels and restaurants will accept the usual internationally recognised credit cards. If you go shopping in local street markets, patronise only the large, recognised ones, and examine goods carefully.

Always ask the price of goods and services before committing yourself. Beware of pick-pockets in crowded places.

If your possessions are stolen or if you are involved in an accident or fire, telephone 999 (no charge will be made) and ask for the police, the ambulance service or the fire brigade.

Every effort has been made by the British Tourist Authority/English Tourism Council (BTA/ETC) to ensure accuracy in this publication at the time of going to press. The information is given in good faith on the basis of information submitted to the BTA/ETC by the promoters of the caravan parks listed. However, BTA/ETC cannot guarantee the accuracy of this information and accepts no responsibility for any error or misrepresentation. All liability for loss, disappointment, negligence or other damage caused by reliance on the information contained in this guide or in the event of the bankruptcy or liquidation of any company, individual or firm mentioned, or in the event of any company, individual or firm ceasing to trade, is hereby excluded. It is advisable to confirm the information given with the establishments concerned at the time of booking.

All parks in this guide conform to Tourism Council Standards. A list of these Standards for Camping and Caravan Parks may be found on page 219.

All the establishments included in the full colour section of this guide have paid for inclusion.

Mode d'emploi du guide

La plupart des terrains répertoriés ici possèdent des emplacements pour les caravanes de tourisme ou les tentes, ou les deux, et la plupart accueillent volontiers les camping-cars De nombreux terrains ont aussi des caravanes fixes à louer.

La Norme d'Assurance-Qualité

Lorsque vous cherchez un endroit où faire étape, vous voulez un système d'évaluation de confiance. Le British Holiday Parks Scheme, relancé en l'an 2000, vous indique clairement et en toute simplicité à quoi vous attendre. La qualité reste la préoccupation principale de ce système, en réponse aux exigences des consommateurs.

L'English Tourism Council (office de tourisme anglais) utilise des Etoiles pour indiquer la qualité des terrains et centres de vacances participant à ce système. Des inspecteurs agréés et impartiaux visitent ces terrains chaque année et les récompensent de une à cinq Etoiles. Celles-ci indiquent la propreté, l'environnement et la qualité des services fournis.

Les terrains reçoivent également un symbole pour vous permettre d'identifier le type de terrain en un clin d'œil - centre de vacances familial, terrain de camping ou de caravanes, par exemple (si aucun symbole/aucune étoile n'est indiqué pour un terrain/centre particulier, celui-ci n'a pas encore reçu son évaluation à l'heure de mise sous presse).

Le British Graded Holiday Parks Scheme (système d'évaluation des centres de vacances/terrains de camping britanniques) a été conçu par les agences de tourisme d'Angleterre, d'Irlande du Nord, d'Ecosse et du Pays de Galles en collaboration avec The British Holiday & Home Parks Association (l'Association britannique des centres familiaux de vacances et de terrains de camping) (voir page 45) et le National Caravan Council (le bureau national des caravaniers) (voir page 49).

Equipements

Les installations sont indiquées au moyen de symboles illustratifs, dont la légende est donnée ici.

SIGNES CONVENTIONNELS

- **M** Membre d'un Office de tourisme régional
- **BH&** British Holiday &
- **HPA** Home Parks Association (voir page 45)
- **NCC** National Caravan Council (voir page 49)
- Caravanes admises (suivi du nombre d'emplacements et des tarifs)
- Camping-cars admis (suivi du nombre d'emplacements et des tarifs). Dans certains cas, les emplacements pour camping-cars sont compris dans le total des emplacements pour caravanes
- Tentes admises (suivi du nombre d'emplacements et des tarifs)
- Nombre de caravanes disponibles pour la location (voir la rubrique 'emplacements' ci-dessous)
- Location de bungalows et logements similaires
- Place de parking à côté de l'unité
- **P** Parking dans le terrain
- Aire de séjour d'une nuit
- Branchements électriques pour caravanes (voir la rubrique 'alimentation électrique pour caravanes' ci-dessous)
- Douches
- Eau chaude à tous les lavabos
- Eclairage dans les compartiments WC, etc.
- Décharge pour WC chimiques
- Service de remplacement des bouteilles de gaz butane ou propane
- Magasin d'alimentation fixe/itinérant
- Café/restaurant
- Club/bar/magasin avec vente de boissons alcoolisées
- Salle de télévision couleur
- Cabine(s) teléphonique(s)
- Laverie
- Dispositifs de séchage du linge
- Matériel de repassage
- Prises électriques pour rasoirs
- Salle de jeux
- Aire de jeux pour les enfants
- Location de vélos
- Piscine couverte chauffée sur le terrain
- Piscine de plein air sur le terrain
- Installations de plongée sous-marine (avec compresseur)
- Ski nautique depuis le terrain
- Canotage/canoë sur le terrain
- Voile depuis le terrain
- Equitation/randonnée à dos de poney depuis le terrain
- Tennis sur le terrain
- Pêche sur le terrain
- Golf sur le terrain ou à proximité
- Chasse privée
- Les chiens sont acceptés
- Distractions nocturnes
- Réservations recommandées l'été
- **T** Les réservations peuvent s'effectuer par l'intermédiaire d'une agence de voyages

Tarifs

Les tarifs indiqués pour les emplacements sont établis sur la base du tarif minimum et du tarif maximum pour une nuitée et pour 2 personnes accompagnées d'une voiture et d'une tente ou d'une caravane La pratique générale veut qu'en Grande-Bretagne on ne fasse payer que l'emplacement, mais certains terrains de camping pratiquent des tarifs séparés pour la voiture, la tente ou la caravane ainsi que pour chaque personne. Certains terrains appliquent parfois des suppléments pour les auvents des caravanes. Les tarifs minimum et maximum de location des caravanes sont donnés par semaine. Les prix indiqués nous ont été fournis par les responsables des terrains concernés, et ont pour but de donner une idée des prix en vigueur au moment de la publication de ce guide. Les prix sont libellés en livres (£) et pence (p). La T.V.A. (Taxe à la Valeur Ajoutée) de 17,5% est comprise dans les tarifs indiqués Afin d'éviter tout malentendu, il est fortement conseillé de vérifier les prix auprès du terrain de camping concerné au moment d'effectuer les réservations.

Modalités de réservation

Lorsque vous vous renseignerez sur l'hebergement offert ainsi que sur les tarifs et autres détails, vous devrez énoncer avec clarté et précision quels sont vos besoins, notamment;

- dates d'arrivée et de départ, avec dates de remplacement acceptables le cas échéant.
- type d'hebergement requis.
- autres besoins particuliers à signaler à la direction.

Les malentendus sont très courants par téléphone, aussi vous est-il recommandé de confirmer par écrit toutes vos réservations si les délais vous le permettent. N'oubliez pas de mentionner votre nom et votre adresse et prenez soin de joindre une enveloppe timbrée à votre adresse ou un coupon-réponse international (si vous écrivez depuis l'étranger) pour la réponse.

Arrhes et paiements anticipés

Les terrains de camping, de caravaning, ou avec bungalows, ainsi que les centres de vacances exigent souvent le versement intégral du paiement à l'avance. Celui-ci peut s'effectuer en deux fois: vous devez payer des arrhes lors de la réservation et vous acquitter du solde deux semaines avant le début de la période de location, par exemple.

Annulations

Lorsque vous acceptez l'hébergement qui vous est offert par écrit ou par téléphone, bous êtes lié par contrat avec le propriétaire de l'établissement. Cela signifie que si vous annulez une réservation, si vous ne venez pas prendre possession du logement ou si vous partez plus tôt que prévu (quelle qu'en soit la raison), le propriétaire est en droit d'exiger un dédommagement s'il ne peut pas relouer pour la durée totale ou une grande partie de la location. Si vous avez versé des arrhes, vous ne serez probablement pas remboursé, et l'on peut vous demander de payer une somme supplémentaire.

Vous avez donc intérêt à aviser immédiatement la direction si vous devez changer vos projets de voyage, annuler une réservation ou partir plus tôt que prévu.

Point de branchement électrique:

La plupart des terrains ont à présent des points de branchement électrique pour les caravanes et les tentes. Le voltage est en général de 240v 50Hz en courant alternatif, bien qu'on puisse encore trouver des courants variant entre 200v et 250v. Il se peut qu'un adaptateur soit nécessaire pour le branchement. En général, les terrains font payer un supplément pour ce service, et il est conseillé de se renseigner sur les tarifs en vigueur au moment de la réservation.

Comment choisir un terrain

Les terrains sont répertoriés dans ce guide en plusieurs sections : Angleterre (par région), Écosse et Pays de Galles. Dans chaque section, ils sont répertoriés par ordre alphabétique selon le nom de la ville la plus proche. L'Index des Villes en page 245 ainsi que les cartes en couleur au début du guide vous indiquent toues les villes et villages pour lesquels un terrain apparaît dans ce guide. Utilisez-les pour trouver un terrain rapidement et très facilement. Si vous savez quel est le terrain où vous voulez séjourner, vous le trouverez immédiatement en consultant l'index des terrains en page 241.

Si le lieu où vous désirez séjourner figure dans l'index des villes, reportez-vous au numéro de page indiqué pour voir quels terrains y sont disponibles. Le nom de la ville est indiqué en noir sur les cartes au début du guide à l'endroit indiqué par la référence carte donnée dans chaque entrée. Consultez également les cartes en couleur pour trouver des lieux proches pour lesquels des terrains sont également répertoriés dans ce guide.

Si le lieu où vous désirez séjourner ne figure pas dans l'index des villes (ou bien si vous avez seulement une idée générale du lieu dans lequel vous désirez séjourner), utilisez les cartes en couleur. Certaines régions apparaissent sur plus d'une carte mais les noms de villes (imprimés en noir sur les cartes) sont indiqués une fois seulement.

Toutes les localités dans lesquelles un terrain est répertorié dans le guide figurent sur la carte. Pour avoir la position précise du terrain, veuillez consultez la rubrique qui lui est consacrée. Si vous avez des difficultés pour trouver un terrain donné, nous vous suggérons de demander votre chemin dans le voisinage.

Pour aider les visiteurs à trouver leur terrain de camping, la Grande-Bretagne emploie les panneaux de signalisation internationaux ci-contre. Tous les terrains ne sont pas encore signalés de cette manière et les panneaux n'affichent pas le nom de terrains particuliers. Ces panneaux indiquent en revanche si le terrain peut accueillir des tentes, des caravanes ou les deux.

L'International Camping Carnet est rarement reconnu en Grande-Bretagne sauf dans les terrains gérés par les grands clubs.

Sites à Londres
Londres attire de nombreux visiteurs, aussi les terrains de Camping-caravaning du Grand Londres ont-ils tendance à se remplir tres rapidement. Des terrains sont également disponibles dans la plupart des ports d'entrée du pays: bon nombre d'entre eux sont répertoriés dans ce guide et indiqués sur les cartes au début du guide.

Services-conseils disponibles
Les Centres d'Information Touristique de toute la Grande-Bretagne (voir dernières pages) sont en mesure de donner aux campeurs et au caravaniers des renseignements sur les terrains de leur région.

Certains Centres d'Information Touristique possèdent des services-conseils pour le camping-caravaning qui vous donneront des détails sur les terrains disponibles et pourront souvent vous aider à effectuer votre réservation. A l'heure actuelle, en Angleterre, ces Centres d'Information Touristique couvrent les régions suivantes: New Forest, (0131) 314 6505; et Cornouailles, (01872) 274057. Au Pays de Galles, de nombreux Centres d'Information touristique peuvent fournir des renseignements sur les emplacements disponibiles dans leur région depuis la fin du mois de mai jusqu'à la fin du mois d'août.

Précautions à prendre en haute saison
Lors des mois d'été, de juin à septembre, les terrains situés dans des régions très fréquentées comme le Nord Gallois, le Cumbria, le Sud-Ouest de l'Angleterre ou la New Forest, dans le Hampshire, risquent d'être complets. Les campeurs doivent s'efforcer d'arriver sur les terrains de bonne heure dans la journée ou, si c'est possible, de réserver à l'avance. Certains terrains ont des aires de séjour temporaire ou les visiteurs arrivant tard le soir peuvent passer la nuit. Cela permet de ne pas déranger les autres campeurs et caravaniers pendant la nuit et d'accepter un plus grand nombre de vacanciers. Les caravanes et les tentes se voient attribuer un emplacement le lendemain matin.

Autres terrains de camping-caravaning
Si vous souhaitez suivre votre propre itinéraire dans la campagne britannique, il peut vous être utile de savoir que la Forestry Commission gère des terrains de camping en forêt dans les sept Parcs forestiers de Grande-Bretagne ainsi que dans la New Forest. Certains terrains offrent des tarifs réduits pour les organisations de jeunesse effectuant des séjours de groupes: il vous est conseillé de vous renseigner à ce sujet auprès de la Forestry Commission très à l'avance.

Granges aménagées pour le camping
Ce sont en général des bâtiments de ferme aujourd'hui superflus qui ont été aménagés pour permettre d'héberger - en toute simplicité - jusqu'à 15 personnes, à un prix raisonnable. Les installations sont ce qu'il y a de plus simple: un endroit pour dormir, manger et préparer les repas, l'eau froide et les WC avec chasse d'eau.

La Youth Hostels Association exploite un réseau de granges aménagées pour le camping qui va de la région de Forest Bowland dans le Lancashire au North Yorkshire, en passant par Durham. Pour obtenir de plus amples renseignements et des détails sur la façon de réserver, veuillez vous adresser à: YHA, Trevelyan House, Dimple Road, Matlock, Derbyshire DE4 2YH
Tel: (017687) 72645
(pour les granges aménagées dans le Pays des Lacs)
Tel: (01200) 420102
(pour les granges aménagées dans toute les régions sauf le Pays des Lacs)
Internet: www.yha.org.uk

On peut également séjourner dans des granges aménagées pour le camping dans le Peak National Park. Pour obtenir de plus amples renseignements et des détails, veuillez vous adresser auprès du Peak District National Park Authority, Aldern House, Baslow Road, Bakewell, Derbyshire DE45 1AE.
Tel: (01629) 816200
Notez que les réservations sont prisées en charge par la YHA.

Les animaux
De nombreux terrains acceptent les chiens, mais nous vous conseillons de vérifier si c'est bien le cas lorsque vous réservez. Demandez également s'il y a des frais supplémentaires et si votre chien sera exclu de certaines zones. Lorsque les chiens sont acceptés, les chats ne le sont pas automatiquement et nous conseillons vivement aux propriétaires de chats de contacter l'établissement longtemps à l'avance. Certains terrains n'acceptent aucun animal familier. Les chiens sont acceptés lorsque vous voyez ce symbole 🐕.

Amener votre animal en Grande-Bretagne
Les lois sur la quarantaine ont récemment changé en Angleterre. Un système, appelé Pet Travel Scheme (PETS) est actuellement à l'essai. Ce système autorise les chiens venus de 35 autres pays d'entrer en Angleterre à certains points (par avion, bateau et train).

Les chiens qui résident dans ces pays depuis plus de 6 mois peuvent entrer au Royaume-Uni grâce au système PETS, pourvu qu'ils possèdent la documentation nécessaire.

Pour que les chiens puissent entrer au Royaume-Uni sans quarantaine grâce au système PETS, ils doivent répondre à certaines conditions et avoir les documents suivants: certificat officiel PETS, certificat de traitement contre le ténia et les tiques et déclaration de résidence.

Pour avoir la liste des pays participant à ce programme, ainsi que la liste des points d'entrée et des opérateurs, ou pour tout complément d'information sur le projet pilote PETS veuillez contacter le téléphone rouge PETS, DEFRA (Department for Environment, Food and Rural Affairs), 1a Page Street, London SW1P 4PQ
Tel: +44 (0) 870 241 1710 Fax: +44 (0) 20 7904 6834

Email: pets.helpline@defra.gsi.gov.uk, ou consultez le site web www.defra.gov.uk/animalh/quarantine

Réglementation contre la drogue

Le Royaume-Uni applique des sanctions sévères contre la contrebande de la drogue. Les trafiquants de drogue peuvent essayer de duper les voyageurs. Si vous voyagez à destination du Royaume-Uni, ne soyez pas mêlé au trafic de drogue. Ne passez jamais de bagages ou de colis pour autrui par les douanes.

Aspects juridiques

La meilleure source de renseignements juridiques pour les automobilistes voyageant en Grande-Bretagne reste l'association des automobilistes de leur pays d'origine. Les détails supplémentaires que doivent connaître le campeur ou le caravanier sont relativement simples.

Si vous tractez une caravane ou une remorque de camping, vous ne devez pas dépasser 96 km/h sur les voies express ou sur les autoroutes, 80 km/h sur les routes à deux voies; en outre, sur les autoroutes ayant trois voies dans chaque direction, vous ne devez pas rouler sur la troisième voie (la plus rapide). N'allumez pas de réchauds à gaz sur les aires de service des autoroutes.

Dans la plupart des villes, le stationnement est limité à la fois par la réglementation et par le manque de place. Les voitures dotées de remorques ne peuvent pas occuper les espaces de stationnement limité à parcmètres et de nombreux parcs de stationnement de ville ne sont conçus que pour accueillir des véhicules indépendants. Toutefois, certains parcs peuvent accueillir des véhicules plus longs en plus des voitures.

La nuit, les remorques ou les voitures dotées de remorques, lorsqu'elles sont en stationnement au bord de la route, doivent avoir les deux feux avant et les deux feux arrière allumés même dans le cas où cela n'est pas jugé nécessaire pour une voiture seule.

Les freins, l'éclairage, le poids, etc. des véhicules étrangers n'ont pas à respecter les prescriptions techniques britanniques. Toutefois, une remorque ne doit pas dépasser les limites dimensionnelles britanniques: 7m de long et 2,3m de large. Elle doit être munie de votre plaque d'immatriculation nationale. Vous ne devez pas vous arrêter pour la nuit sur les accotements ou sur les petites aires de stationnement des bas-côtés car la loi stipule que ces emplacements font partie de la route.

Enfin, il est important de vous renseigner sur l'heure à laquelle il vous est demandé de libérer votre emplacement le jour du départ. Vous devrez prévoir de partir assez tôt, sans quoi vous risquez d'avoir à payer une journée de location supplémentaire.

Conseils aux visiteurs

L'Office de Tourisme de Grande-Bretagne vous invite à formuler vos observations sur tout aspect de votre séjour en Grande-Bretagne, qu'elles soient favorables ou non. Nous espérons que vous n'aurez pas lieu de vous plaindre, mais dans l'affirmative, il vous est conseillé de faire part de votre mécontentement immédiatement auprès de la direction de l'établissement concerné comme par exemple:
camping, magasin ou société de transport. Si vous ne pouvez pas obtenir satisfaction de cette manière, veuillez nous le faire savoir et nous examinerons la question nous-mêmes ou nous vous suggèrerons une procédure éventuelle à suivre.

Vous pouvez emporter en Grande-Bretagne les devises de votre choix en quantité illimitée et aucune restriction ne s'applique a la quantité de chèques de voyage changés. Si vous avez besoin de devises britanniques pendant les heures de fermeture des banques, vous pouvez vous les procurer dans certains grands hôtels, agences de voyages, grands magasins ou dans les bureaux de change indépendants. Ne manquez pas de vérifier à l'avance le taux de change et la commission appliqués.

Tous les grands magasins et boutiques et la plupart des hôtels et restaurants accepteront les cartes de crédit usuelles reconnues dans le monde entier. Si vous aimez faire vos achats au marché, limitez-vous aux grands marchés de rue officiels et examinez toujours les articles soigneusement.

Demandez toujours le prix des marchandises avant de vous engager. Prenez garde aux pickpockets en cas d'affluence. Si l'on vous vole des objets personnels ou si vous vous trouvez sur le lieu d'un incendie ou d'un accident, composez le 999 (numéro gratuit) et demandez la police, les services d'ambulance ou les pompiers.

La British Tourist Authority (BTA) et l'English Tourism Council (ETC) ont pris toutes les dispositions nécessaires pour assurer l'exactitude des Informations contenues dans la présente publication au moment de mettre sous presse. Ces Informations sont fournies en toute bonne foi sur la base des renseignements donnés à la BTA/ETC par les exploitants des terrains de camping répertoriés. Toutefois, la BTA/ETC ne peut pas garantir l'exactitude de ces renseignements et décline toute responsabllité en cas d'erreur ou de déformation des faits. Toute responsabilité est également déclinée pour toutes pertes, déceptions, négligences ou autres dommages que pourrait subir quiconque se fie aux renseignements contenus dans le présent guide, pour les cas de faillite ou de liquidation de toute personne morale ou physique mentionnée, et pour les cas de cessation d'activités de toute personne morale ou physique. Il est conseillé de se faire confirmer les renseignements fournis par les établissements concernés lors de la réservation.

Tous les terrains inclus dans ce guide respectent les normes du Tourism Council (bureau national de tourisme). On trouvera à la page 219 une liste de ces normes relatives aux terrains de camping-caravaning.

Tous les établissements répertoriés dans la section eu couleurs figurent dans le présent guide à titre payant.

Unterwegs in Großbritannien

Die meisten der hier aufgeführten Parks verfügen über Stellplätze für Wohnwagen bzw. Zelte oder beides und die meisten nehmen auch Wohnmobile auf. Des Weiteren vermieten viele Parks auch Ferienwohnwagen.

Qualitätsgewährleistungsstandard

Bei der Suche nach einer geeigneten Unterkunft braucht man ein verlässliches Einstufungssystem. Das 'British Graded Holiday Parks Scheme' (britisches Beurteilungssystem für Ferienparks), das im Jahr 2000 neu lanciert wurde, vermittelt Ihnen in leicht verständlicher Form einen klaren Eindruck von dem, was Sie erwarten können. Das System spiegelt die Kundenerwartungen wider und beurteilt in erster Linie die Qualität.

Das English Tourism Council (englischer Fremdenverkehrsrat) kennzeichnet die Qualitätsstufe der an diesem Programm teilnehmenden Parks durch die Vergabe von Sternen. Die betreffenden Parks werden jährlich von sachlich geschulten, unparteiischen Prüfern inspiziert und dann mittels einer Skala von einem bis fünf Sterne eingestuft. Die Anzahl der vergebenen Sterne hängt von der Sauberkeit, dem Ambiente sowie der Qualität der vorhandenen Einrichtungen und gebotenen Dienstleistungen ab.

Außerdem werden die einzelnen Parks nach Typ gekennzeichnet, so dass man auf einen Blick erkennt, um was für eine Art von Gelände es sich handelt - z.B. Ferienpark, Touringpark oder Campingpark. (Weist der Park keine Einstufung oder Kennzeichnung auf, so bedeutet das, dass die Beurteilung zum Zeitpunkt der Drucklegung noch nicht stattgefunden hat.)

Das 'British Graded Holiday Parks Scheme' entstand in partnerschaftlicher Zusammenarbeit der nationalen Fremdenverkehrsstellen für England, Nordirland, Schottland und Wales, in Verbindung mit der British Holiday & Home Parks Association (siehe Seite 45) und dem National Caravan Council (siehe Seite 49).

Einrichtungen

Die jeweiligen Einrichtungen sind durch Symbole bezeichnet, deren Bedeutung Sie der Zeichenerklärung auf einen Blick entnehmen können.

ZEICHENERKLÄRUNG

- **M** Mitglied eines regionalen Tourist Board
- **BH&** British Holiday &
- **HPA** Home Parks Association (siehe Seite 45)
- **NCC** National Caravan Council (siehe Seite 49)
- Wohnwagen zugelassen (mit Anzahl der Stellplätze und Preisen)
- Wohnmobile zugelassen (mit Anzahl der Stellplätze und Preisen)
- Zelte zugelassen (mit Anzahl der Stellplätze und Preisen)
- Anzahl der vermietbaren Ferienwohnwagen (mit Anzahl und Preisen)
- Bungalows, Chalets, Wohnkabinen zum Vermieten
- Parkmöglichkeit neben der Wohneinheit
- **P** Parkplatz auf dem Gelände
- Auffangstelle für spät im Park eintreffende Gäste
- Stromanschluß für Wohnwagen und Zelte
- Duschen
- Heißes Wasser für alle Waschbecken
- Beleuchtung im Toilettenbau
- Chemische Toiletten
- Umtauschstelle für Butan- /oder Propangaszylinger
- Lebensmittelgeschäft/Wagen für Lebensmittelverkauf
- Restaurant
- Klub mit Alkoholausschank/Bar
- Aufenthaltsraum mit Farbfernseher
- Öffentliche Fernsprecher
- Wäscherei
- Wäschetrockner
- Bügelmöglichkeiten
- Anschlüsse für Elektrorasierer
- Hallenspiele
- Kinderspielplatz
- Fahrradverleih
- Hallenbad
- Freibad
- Tauchen
- Wasserski vom Park aus
- Bootsfahrten/Kanufahrten
- Segeln
- Reiten/Ponyreiten in der Nähe
- Tennis
- Angeln
- Golf im Park oder in der Nähe
- Private Jagdrechte
- Haustiere willkommen
- Abendunterhaltung
- Im Sommer Reservierung empfohlen
- Buchung durch Reisebüros möglich

Preise

Die angegebenen Preise für Stellplätze beruhen auf den Mindest- bzw. Höchstgebühren pro Nacht für zwei Personen, ein Auto und einen Wohnwagen bzw. ein Zelt. In Großbritannien ist es im Allgemeinen üblich, einfach eine Gebühr für die Nutzung des Stellplatzes zu berechnen, allerdings erheben einige Parks separate Gebühren für das Auto, den Wohnwagen bzw. das Zelt und pro Person. Manche Parks verlangen unter Umständen eine Zusatzgebühr für am Wohnwagen angebrachte Sonnenzelte. Die Mindest- und Höchstpreise für Ferienwohnwagen sind pro Woche angegeben. Die Preise wurden jeweils von der betreffenden Parkleitung zur Verfügung gestellt und bilden lediglich eine Richtschnur für die tatsächlich berechneten Preise während der Gültigkeit der vorliegenden Veröffentlichung. Die Preise sind in Pfund Sterling (£) und Pence (p) angegeben. Die Mehrwertsteuer (VAT) zum Satz von 17,5% ist im Preis enthalten. Um etwaigen Missverständnissen vorzubeugen, ist es ratsam, sich bei der Reservierung nach den genauen Preisen zu erkundigen.

Reservierungen

Bei Anfragen über mögliche Unterkünfte, Preise und weitere Angaben sollten Sie Ihre Wünsche klar und genau angeben - zum Beispiel:

- Ankunfts- und Abreisetermin, falls möglich mit akzeptablen Ausweichterminen
- gewünschte Unterkunft
- Teilen Sie der Parkleitung mit, falls Sie besondere Anforderungen haben.

Bei Telefongesprächen kommt es leicht zu Missverständnissen. Deshalb empfehlen wir Ihnen, Ihre Reservierung schriftlich zu bestätigen, falls dies zeitlich möglich ist. Denken Sie bitte daran, Ihren Namen und Ihre Anschrift anzugeben und einen adressierten Freiumschlag, bei Anfragen aus dem Ausland einen internationalen Antwortschein, beizulegen

Anzahlungen und Vorauszahlungen

Bei Wohnwagen-, Camping-, Chaletparks und Ferienzentren ist der gesamte Betrag häufig im Voraus zu entrichten. Die Zahlung kann in zwei Raten erfolgen: bei der Reservierung wird eine Anzahlung fällig und der Restbetrag ist zwei Wochen vor Beginn des Aufenthalts zu leisten.

Stornierungen

Wenn Sie ein Unterkunftsangebot schriftlich oder telefonisch akzeptieren, gehen Sie mit dem Besitzer der betreffenden Unterkunft einen rechtlich bindenden Vertrag ein. Das hat zur Folge, dass der Besitzer, wenn Sie eine Reservierung stornieren, nicht wahrnehmen oder die Unterkunft (gleichgültig aus welchen Gründen) vorzeitig räumen, unter Umständen berechtigt ist, Schadensersatz zu verlangen, sofern er nicht in der Lage ist, die Unterkunft für den ganzen bzw. einen Teil des gebuchten Zeitraums weiterzuvermieten. Falls eine Anzahlung geleistet wurde, wird sie wahrscheinlich hierfür angerechnet und unter Umständen erfolgt eine weitere Zahlungsforderung.

Es ist daher in Ihrem Interesse, die Geschäftsleitung umgehend zu benachrichtigen, wenn Sie Ihre Reisepläne ändern, eine Reservierung stornieren oder die Unterkunft vorzeitig verlassen möchten.

Anschluss ans Stromnetz

Die meisten Parks verfügen inzwischen über Stromanschlussstellen für Wohnwagen und Zelte. Es handelt sich dabei im Allgemeinen um Wechselstrom mit einer Spannung von 240 Volt, 50 Schwingungen, allerdings können Spannungsschwankungen zwischen 200 V und 250 V auftreten. Unter Umständen benötigen Sie einen Adapter. Die Parks erheben normalerweise eine Zusatzgebühr für diesen Service und es ist ratsam, sich bei der Reservierung nach deren Höhe zu erkundigen.

So finden Sie Ihren Park

In der vorliegenden Broschüre sind die Parks in England nach Region, danach die Parks in Schottland und Wales aufgeführt. Sie sind in alphabetischer Reihenfolge unter dem Namen der Ortschaft, in der oder in deren Nähe sie liegen, verzeichnet. Im Ortsverzeichnis auf Seite 245 und auf den farbigen Lagekarten am Anfang dieser Veröffentlichung sind alle Städte, Ortschaften und Dörfer aufgeführt, die in dieser Broschüre mit einem Park vertreten sind. Anhand des Verzeichnisses und der Karten finden Sie schnell und mühelos eine geeignete Unterkunft. Wenn Sie bereits wissen, in welchem Park Sie übernachten möchten, schlagen Sie im Verzeichnis der Parks auf Seite 241 nach.

Wenn die Ortschaft, in der Sie übernachten möchten, im Ortsverzeichnis aufgeführt ist, schlagen Sie auf der angegebenen Seite nach, wo die dort vorhandenen Parks verzeichnet sind. Die Namen der Ortschaften sind gemäß des beim betreffenden Eintrag genannten Planquadrats auf den Karten am Anfang dieses Reiseführers schwarz gedruckt. Sehen Sie auch auf den farbigen Karten nach, um Ortschaften in der Nähe zu finden, wo sich ebenfalls Parks befinden, die in dieser Veröffentlichung aufgeführt sind.

Falls die Ortschaft, in der Sie übernachten möchten, nicht im Ortsverzeichnis aufgeführt ist oder Sie nur eine ungefähre Vorstellung von der Gegend haben, in der Sie übernachten möchten, so benutzen Sie die farbigen Lagekarten.

Auf den Karten sind alle Orte verzeichnet, die in der vorliegenden Veröffentlichung mit einem Park vertreten sind. Die genaue Lage ist jeweils in den betreffenden Einträgen beschrieben. Sollten Sie Schwierigkeiten haben, einen bestimmten Park zu finden, so schlagen wir vor, dass Sie sich vor Ort eine genaue Wegbeschreibung geben lassen.

Die hier abgebildeten internationalen Hinweisschilder, die in Großbritannien vielfach zu finden sind, erleichtern Ihnen das Auffinden eines Parks. Allerdings sind sie noch nicht für alle Camping-, Wohnwagen- bzw. Ferienparks vorhanden und geben nicht den Namen des Parks an, doch zeigen sie, ob es sich um einen Park für Wohnwagen, Zelte oder beides handelt. Der internationale Campingausweis ist in Großbritannien nur in Parks gültig, die von größeren Klubs verwaltet werden.

Plätze in London
Da London ein großer Anziehungspunkt für Besucher ist, sind die Camping- und Wohnwagenparks im Umkreis der britischen Hauptstadt schnell ausgebucht, daher ist eine frühzeitige Reservierung ratsam. Auch in den meisten Einreisehäfen gibt es entsprechende Parks, von denen viele in dieser Veröffentlichung aufgeführt und auf den Karten am Anfang verzeichnet sind.

Informationsdienste
Die Touristeninformationszentren in allen Teilen Großbritanniens (auf den letzten Seiten aufgeführt) geben Ihnen gerne Auskunft über die Camping- und Wohnwagenparks in ihrem Gebiet.

Einige Touristeninformationszentren haben einen Wohnwagen- und Camping-Beratungsdienst, der über freie Plätze Auskunft geben und häufig auch Reservierungen vornehmen kann. Zur Zeit sind in England folgende Beratungsdienste vorhanden: New Forest, (0131) 314 6505 und Cornwall (01872) 274057. Viele Touristeninformationszentren in Wales können Ihnen Auskunft über von Ende Mai bis Ende August verfügbare Stellplätze in ihrem Gebiet geben.

Vermeiden von Problemen in der Hochsaison
In den Sommermonaten Juni bis September sind die Camping- und Wohnwagenparks in den beliebten Urlaubsgebieten wie etwa Nordwales, Cumbria, im West Country oder im New Forest in Hampshire schnell ausgebucht. Treffen Sie daher frühzeitig am Tag am Park ein oder buchen Sie nach Möglichkeit im Voraus. Manche Parks verfügen über Auffangstellen für spät eintreffende Gäste. Auf diese Weise werden die anderen Gäste zu fortgeschrittener Stunde nicht gestört und es werden weniger Besucher abgewiesen. Es wird dann am nächsten Morgen ein Stellplatz zugewiesen.

Sonstige Wohnwagen- und Campingplätze
Wenn Sie Ihre Reiseroute durch die britische Landschaft lieber auf eigene Faust planen, dürften Sie an den Campingplätzen in Waldgebieten interessiert sein, die von der Forestry Commission verwaltet werden. Hierzu gehören sieben Forest Parks und der New Forest. In einigen erhalten Jugendorganisationen beim Campingurlaub Preisermäßigungen. Alle diesbezüglichen Anfragen sind frühzeitig im Voraus an die Forest Commission zu richten.

Camping in der Scheune
Bei dieser Campingalternative handelt es sich um ehemalige Scheunen, die zu einfachen, günstigen Unterkünften für bis zu 15 Personen umgebaut wurden. Die Einrichtungen sind anspruchslos. Es gibt eine Schlaf-, Koch- und Essstelle, kaltes Wasser und ein WC.

Die Youth Hostels Association (der Jugendherbergsverband) verfügt über ein Netz von Camping-Scheunen, das sich vom Forest of Bowland in Lancashire über Durham bis nach North Yorkshire erstreckt. Für weitere Informationen und Reservierungen wenden Sie sich bitte an die YHA, Trevelyan House, Dimple Road, Matlock, Derbyshire DE4 2YH

Tel: (017687) 72645
(für Camping-Scheunen im Lake District)
Tel: (01200) 420102 (für Scheunen in allen Gebieten, außer im Lake District)
Internet: www.yha.org.uk

Camping-Scheunen sind auch im Peak Nationalpark zu finden. Für weitere Auskünfte wenden Sie sich bitte an die Peak District National Park Authority, Aldern House, Baslow Road, Bakewell, Derbyshire DE45 1AE.
Tel: (01629) 816200
Wir weisen darauf hin, dass die Reservierungen von der YHA (siehe oben) bearbeitet werden.

Haustiere
In vielen Unterkünften werden Gäste mit Hunden aufgenommen, allerdings raten wir Ihnen, sich bei der Reservierung danach zu erkundigen. Außerdem sollten Sie fragen, ob für den Hund eine zusätzliche Gebühr berechnet wird, und ob es Regeln gibt, wo genau Ihr Haustier sich aufhalten darf. Der Umstand, dass Hunde aufgenommen werden, bedeutet nicht unbedingt, dass das Gleiche auch für Katzen gilt und wir raten Katzenbesitzern dringend, sich diesbezüglich frühzeitig mit der betreffenden Unterkunft zu verständigen. Manche Unterkünfte lassen überhaupt keine Haustiere zu. Wo Sie das Zeichen 🐕 sehen, sind Haustiere willkommen.

Das Mitbringen von Haustieren nach Großbritannien
In England wurden kürzlich die Quarantänevorschriften novelliert und momentan läuft das 'Pet Travel Scheme (PETS)'. Im Rahmen dieser Aktion können als Haustier gehaltene Hunde auf bestimmten Schiffs-, Flug- und Bahnstrecken aus über 35 Ländern nach England mitgebracht werden.

Hunde, die länger als 6 Monate in den betreffenden Ländern gehalten wurden, können im Rahmen der Aktion nach Großbritannien eingeführt werden, vorausgesetzt, dass die entsprechenden Dokumente vorhanden sind.

Um im Rahmen der Aktion PETS ohne Quarantäne nach Großbritannien einreisen zu können, müssen Hunde bestimmte Kriterien erfüllen und es müssen folgende Unterlagen vorgelegt werden: das offizielle PETS-Zertifikat, eine Behandlungsbescheinigung gegen Bandwurm, Zecken sowie eine Bestätigung des Haltungsorts.

Für weitere Auskünfte über die an dieser Aktion teilnehmenden Länder, die Strecken, Reiseunternehmer sowie ausführlichere Informationen über die Aktion PETS wenden Sie sich bitte an die PETS Helpline, DEFRA (Department for Environment, Food and Rural Affairs), 1a Page Street, London SW1P 4PQ,
Tel: +44 (0) 870 241 1710, Fax: +44 (0) 20 7904 6834,

E-Mail: pets.helpline@defra.gsi.gov.uk oder schauen Sie auf der Website vorbei:
www.defra.gov.uk/aimalh/quarantine

Drogenwarnung für einreisende Touristen

Großbritannien geht gegen Rauschgiftschmuggel sehr scharf vor. Drogenhändler versuchen häufig, unschuldige Reisende in ihre Geschäfte zu verwickeln. Seien Sie daher bei der Reise nach Großbritannien sehr auf der Hut und tragen Sie niemals Gepäckstücke für andere Personen durch die Zollkontrolle.

Rechtliches

Wenden Sie sich vor dem Antritt Ihrer Reise am besten an Ihren Automobilverband, der Ihnen gerne Auskunft über alle rechtlichen Fragen in Bezug auf Reisen in Großbritannien gibt. Wenn Sie mit dem Wohnwagen oder Zelt unterwegs sind, sollten Sie zusätzlich ein paar einfache Regeln beachten.

Wenn Sie mit einem Wohnwagen oder einem Camping-Anhänger unterwegs sind, dürfen Sie auf vierspurigen Fernstraßen und Autobahnen höchstens 96 km/h fahren. Auf zweispurigen Fernstraßen gilt das Tempolimit 80 km/h. Auf sechsspurigen Autobahnen dürfen Sie niemals - auch nicht zum Überholen - in der dritten (schnellsten) Spur fahren. Auf den Raststätten an der Autobahn dürfen keine Kochöfen angezündet werden.

In den meisten Städten ist das Parken durch gesetzliche Bestimmungen oder praktische Probleme stark eingeschränkt. Autos mit Anhängern dürfen nicht an Parkuhren parken. Ferner nehmen die meisten Parkplätze nur Wagen ohne Anhänger auf. Allerdings sind einige Parkplätze vorhanden, die überlange Fahrzeuge und Fahrzeuge mit Anhängern zulassen.

Nachts müssen auf der Straße geparkte Anhänger bzw. Autos mit Anhänger vorn und hinten jeweils zwei Lampen aufweisen. Dies gilt auch an Stellen, wo ein Auto ohne Anhänger davon ausgenommen wäre.

Die britischen Vorschriften über Bremsen, Beleuchtung, zulässiges Gewicht und sonstige technische Punkte gelten nicht für ausländische Fahrzeuge. Ein Anhänger muss jedoch die britischen Vorschriften erfüllen und darf nicht länger als 7 m und nicht breiter als 2,30 m sein. Anhänger müssen mit den amtlichen Zulassungsschildern Ihres Heimatlandes versehen sein. Übernachten Sie nicht auf dem Grasrand einer Straße oder in einer Ausweichbucht, weil diese Stellen als zur Straße gehörig angesehen werden.

Abschließend sei betont, wie wichtig es ist, dass Sie sich erkundigen, wann Sie den Stellplatz in einem Camping- oder Wohnwagenpark am Abreisetag räumen müssen. Reisen Sie morgens rechtzeitig ab, sonst müssen Sie vielleicht die Gebühr für einen weiteren Tag bezahlen.

Ratschläge für Besucher

Die British Tourist Authority würde sich über Ihren Kommentar hinsichtlich aller Gesichtspunkte Ihres Aufenthalts in Großbritannien freuen, ganz gleich, ob er positiv oder negativ ausfällt. Wir hoffen, dass Sie keinen Grund zur Beanstandung haben, falls Sie aber doch Anlass zu Beschwerden haben sollten, ist es am besten, sich sofort an die Leitung des entsprechenden Unternehmens zu wenden, z. B. des Parks, des Geschäfts oder der Verkehrsgesellschaft. Wenn Sie mit der Behandlung, die Sie dort erfahren, nicht zufrieden sind, so geben Sie uns bitte Bescheid. Wir werden dann der Angelegenheit entweder selbst nachgehen oder Sie darüber beraten, welche Maßnahmen Sie ergreifen können.

Sie können Währungen jeder Art in beliebiger Höhe nach Großbritannien mitbringen. Reiseschecks werden in beliebiger Anzahl eingelöst. Wenn Ihnen das Bargeld ausgeht, wenn die Banken geschlossen sind, so können Sie Geld in einigen großen Hotels, Reisebüros, Kaufhäusern und in unabhängigen Wechselstuben umtauschen. Prüfen Sie vor dem Geldumtausch, welcher Wechselkurs Anwendung findet und wie hoch die Bearbeitungsgebühr ist. Alle größeren Geschäfte, Kaufhäuser und die meisten Hotels und Restaurants akzeptieren international gängige Kreditkarten als Zahlungsmittel. Wenn Sie auf örtlichen Straßenmärkten einkaufen, so halten Sie sich an die großen, bekannten Märkte und prüfen Sie die Waren sorgfältig.

Erkundigen Sie sich vor dem Kauf stets nach dem Preis der Waren oder Dienstleistungen. Nehmen Sie sich in Menschenmengen vor Taschendieben in Acht.

Wenn Sie Opfer eines Diebstahls oder Zeuge eines Unfalls oder Brands werden, wählen Sie den Notruf unter der Nummer 999 (der Anruf ist kostenlos) und verlangen Sie die Polizei (police), einen Krankenwagen (ambulance) oder die Feuerwehr (fire brigade).

Die British Tourist Authority und das English Tourism Council (BTA/ETC) haben sich alle erdenkliche Mühe gegeben, die Richtigkeit der in der vorliegenden Veröffentlichung gemachten Angaben zum Zeitpunkt der Drucklegung zu gewährleisten. Die Informationen werden in gutem Glauben erteilt und beruhen auf den Angaben, die der BTA/dem ETC von den aufgeführten Wohnwagenparks erteilt wurden. Die BTA/das ETC geben jedoch keine Garantie für die Genauigkeit der Angaben und übernehmen keinerlei Verantwortung für Fehler oder fälschliche Darstellungen. Hiermit ausgeschlossen wird die Haftung für Verluste, nicht erfüllte Erwartungen, Fahrlässigkeit oder andere Schäden, die sich daraus ergeben, dass sich Leser auf die Informationen in der vorliegenden Veröffentlichung verlassen, oder die sich daraus ergeben, dass in der Veröffentlichung genannte Unternehmen, Firmen oder Einzelpersonen Konkurs anmelden, in Liquidation gehen oder ihre Geschäftstätigkeit einstellen. Es wird empfohlen, sich die in der vorliegenden Veröffentlichung gemachten Angaben bei der Reservierung von den betreffenden Stellen bestätigen zu lassen.

Alle in diesem Reiseführer genannten Parks entsprechen den Standards des Tourism Council (Fremdenverkehrsrat). Eine Liste der Standardbedingungen für Camping- und Wohnwagenparks befindet sich auf Seite 219.

Sämtliche im farbigen Teil dieser Veröffentlichung genannten Stellen haben für die Aufnahme eine Gebühr entrichtet.

Hoe u deze gids moet gebruiken

Op de meeste vermelde terreinen zijn trekcaravans, tenten of kampeerauto's of alledrie welkom. Bij de meeste zijn vakantiecaravans te huur.

De Kwaliteits Garantie Standaard

Als u een verblijfsplaats zoekt, dan heeft u een classificatiesysteem nodig dat u kunt vertrouwen. De British Graded Holiday Parks Scheme, in 2000 opnieuw gepubliceerd, geeft u een duidelijk overzicht van wat u kunt verwachten in een gemakkelijk te begrijpen vorm. Het systeem houdt kwaliteit hoog in het vaandel en weerspiegelt de verwachtingen van de consument.

De English Tourism Council gebruikt sterren om de kwaliteitsclassificatie van de deelnemende parken weer te geven. De parken worden jaarlijks door getrainde, onafhankelijke controleurs bezocht, die 1 tot 5 sterren toekennen. Deze zijn gebaseerd op hygiëne, omgeving en kwaliteit van de voorzieningen en diensten, die er aanwezig zijn.

De parken hebben ook een 'aanwijzer' zodat u het type standplaats in één oogopslag kunt herkennen b.v. een vakantie park, een tourcaravan park en een camping. (Als er geen gradatie of aanwijzer is gegeven dan is men in afwachting van een classifcatie ten tijde van het drukken van deze brochure.)

The British Graded Holiday Parks Scheme is gezamenlijk ontworpen door de nationale toeristencentra van Engeland, Noord-Ierland, Schotland en Wales en de British Holiday & Home Parks Association (zie pagina 45) en de National Caravan Council (zie pagina 49).

Faciliteiten

De faciliteiten worden aangeduid d.m.v. de hieronder in het kort verklaarde tekens.

Prijzen

De vermelde tarieven zijn de minimale en maximale prijzen voor een overnachting voor 2 personen, auto plus caravan of tent. Over het algemeen berekent men in Groot-Brittannië voor de staanplaats, maar een aantal terreinen belast u apart voor de auto, caravan of tent, en elke persoon. Bij sommige parken moet u eventueel extra

VERKLARING VAN DE TEKENS

- **M** lid van een regionale toeristenraad
- **BH&** British Holiday &
- **HPA** Home Parks Association (zie blz 45)
- **NCC** National Caravan Council (zie blz 49)
- caravans toegestaan (met aantal staanplaatsen en tarieven)
- kampeerauto's toegestaan (met aantal staanplaatsen en tarieven) In sommige gevallen is het aantal plekjes voor kampeerauto's opgenomen in het totaal voor toercaravans
- tenten toegestaan (met aantal plekjes en tarieven)
- aantal vakantiecaravans te huur (Zie 'Vakantiecaravans')
- bungalows/chalets/huisjes te huur
- parkeerplaats naast staanplaats
- **P** parkeerruimte op terrein
- terrein voor late aankomers op het park
- elektrische aansluiting voor caravans (zie 'Elektriciteit. Elektrische aansluiting voor caravans)
- douches
- alle wastafels hebben warm water
- verlichting in toiletten, etc.
- lozing van chemische toiletten mogelijk
- omwisseling van butaan- en propaangasflessen
- levensmiddelenwinkel/rijdende winkel
- **X** café/restaurant
- klub/barwinkel met vergunning
- Zitkamer met kleurentelevisie
- openbare telefoons
- wasserette op terrein aanwezig
- drogen van wasgoed mogelijk
- strijken van wasgoed mogelijk
- stopcontacten voor scheerapparaten
- recreatiekamer
- speeltuin
- fietsenverhuur
- verwarmd binnenbad op park
- openluchtbad op park
- onderwaterzwemmen op terrein (zuurstofflessen verkrijgbaar)
- waterskiën op terrein
- boten/kano's op terrein aanwezig
- zeilen op terrein
- manège (paard/pony) op terrein
- tennis op terrein
- vissen op terrein
- golf op of bij park
- particuliere jachtvergunning
- huisdieren welkom
- amusement 's avonds
- raadzaam voor de zomermaanden te boeken
- kan geboekt worden bij reisbureaus

betalen voor een tent of voortent die aan een caravan vastgebouwd is. Minimale en maximale tarieven voor vakantiecaravans zijn per week. Vermelde prijzen werden verstrekt door de terreinbeheerders en dienen als richtlijn voor de prijzen die tijdens de geldendheid van dit boekje gerekend zullen worden. Vermelde prijzen zijn in ponden (£) en pence (p). VAT (BTW) à 17,5% is bij de prijzen inbegrepen. Om misverstanden te vermijden, raden wij u dringend aan de prijzen te controleren als u een reservering maakt.

Reserveren

Bij het maken van een reservering, of het inwinnen van inlichtingen, moet u vooral duidelijk en precies aangeven wat u wilt - bij voorbeeld:

- aankomst- en vertrekdata met mogelijke alternatieven.
- gewenste accommodatie.
- vertel de beheerder vooral wat voor speciale wensen of eisen u heeft.

Misverstanden kunnen heel gemakkelijk voorkomen over de telefoon en wij raden u daarom aan alle reserveringen, als de tijd dat toelaat, schriftelijk te bevestigen. Vergeet vooral niet uw naam en adres te vermelden en een aan uzelf geadresseerde envelop met postzegel of internationale antwoordcoupon (als u uit het buitenland schrijft) in te sluiten voor elk antwoord.

Aan- en vooruitbetalingen

Campings, caravanterreinen, bungalow- en vakantieparken moeten meestal van tevoren geheel betaald worden. Dit kan gedaan worden in tweeën - een aanbetaling bij de reservering en betaling van het saldo bijvoorbeeld twee weken voor de aanvang van de geboekte periode.

Annuleren

De aanvaarding van geboden accommodatie, hetzij schriftelijk of telefonisch, wordt over het algemeen beschouwd als een wettelijk bindend contract. Dit betekent dat als u annuleert, niet verschijnt op het park, of vroegtijdig het park verlaat (het geeft niet om welke reden), de eigenaar compensatie van u kan verlangen als de staanplaats voor het overgrote deel van de geboekte periode niet opnieuw verhuurd kan worden. Als u een aanbetaling gedaan heeft, kan deze vervallen worden verklaard en een aanvullend bedrag van u verlangd worden.

Het is daarom in uw eigen belang de bedrijfsleiding onmiddellijk in kennis te stellen, als u uw reisplannen moet wijzigen, een boeking moet annuleren, of voortijdig moet vertrekken.

Elektrische aansluiting:

De meeste parken hebben elektrische aansluitpunten voor caravans en tenten. De voltage is meestal 240v AC, 50Hz, hoewel nog steeds voltages tussen 200v en 250v kunnen worden aangetroffen. Het kan zijn dat u een adaptor nodig heeft voor de aansluiting. Meestal moet u extra betalen voor deze faciliteit. Het is raadzaam de tarieven na te vragen voor u reserveert.

Het vinden van een park of terrein

De parken in dit gidsje zijn ingedeeld in Engeland per regio, gevolgd door Schotland en Wales. Zij staan in alfabetische volgorde onder de naam van de meest nabijgelegen plaats. De index van plaatsen op blz 245 en de gekleurde lokatiekaarten voorin de gids vertonen alle steden, plaatsen en dorpen met parken die in deze gids voorkomen. Zo kunt u snel en gemakkelijk ergens een park vinden. Als u al weet op welk park u wilt staan, kunt u de index van parken raadplegen op blz 241.

Als uw bestemming in de index van plaatsen voorkomt, raadpleeg dan de gegeven bladzij, waar de aldaar gevestigde parken worden vermeld. De plaatsnamen staan in zwart op de kaarten voorin het gidsje, aangeduid met coördinaten bij de vermelding. Ook kunt u de kleurenkaarten raadplegen om nabijgelegen plaatsen te vinden die ook in de gids voorkomende parken hebben.

Als uw bestemming niet in de index van plaatsen voorkomt, of als u alleen een vaag idee heeft van het gebied dat u wilt bezoeken, kunt u eveneens de kleurenkaarten raadplegen. De kaarten bevatten alle plaatsnamen waaronder een park in het gidsje wordt vermeld. Voor de precieze locatie dient u de routebeschrijvingen bij iedere vermelding te raadplegen. Heeft u moeite met het vinden van een bepaald park, dan raden wij u aan in de buurt om verdere aanwijzingen te vragen.

De hiernaast vertoonde internationale verkeersborden worden in Groot-Brittannië gebruikt en zijn speciaal ontworpen voor het gebruik van de parkbezoekers en kampeerders. Ze zijn nog niet bij alle parken opgesteld en vermelden niet de naam van een park of camping. Ze duiden echter wel aan of het park geschikt is voor caravans, tenten of beide.

Het Internationale Kampeerkarnet wordt maar weinig in Groot-Brittannië erkend, behalve op terreinen die beheerd worden door de grote clubs.

Campings bij Londen

Londen is een grote trekpleister voor toeristen en daarom raken de campings en caravanterreinen in de streek van Greater London erg snel vol en boeking ver van tevoren is daarom noodzakelijk. Bij de meeste aankomsthavens zijn ook campings te vinden en de meeste worden vermeld in deze gids en aangeduid op de kaarten voorin.

Hulp bij het vinden van een park

De Toeristische Informatiecentra over heel Groot-Brittannië (zie aan het einde van deze gids) kunnen kampeerders en caravaneigenaars informatie verschaffen over lokale parken en terreinen. Een aantal Toeristische Informatiecentra biedt ook een adviesdienst, die inlichtingen kan geven over mogelijke plaats op campings en vaak kan helpen met het maken van een reservering. Momenteel beslaan de volgende TIC's in Engeland de streken: New Forest, 0131-314-6505; en Cornwall, 01872-274057.

In Wales kan tussen mei en eind augustus een groot aantal Tourist Information Centres inlichtingen verstrekken over beschikbare staanplaatsen in hun streek.

Vermijding van problemen in het hoogseizoen

In de zomermaanden juni t/m september kunnen parken in populaire gebieden, zoals Noord-Wales, Cumbria, de West Country en het New Forest in Hampshire bijzonder vol raken. Bezoekers moeten proberen zo vroeg mogelijk op de dag bij het park aan te komen, of nog beter, van tevoren boeken. Een aantal parken heeft een speciaal terrein voor bezoekers die laat in de avond arriveren. Dit is om te voorkomen dat andere bezoekers in hun slaap gestoord worden en minder kampeerders weggestuurd worden. De volgende morgen worden de caravans en tenten dan een juiste plek gegeven.

Andere mogelijkheden voor caravans en tenten

Als u ervan houdt om door landelijke streken in Groot-Brittannië te trekken, vindt u het misschien interessant te weten, dat de Forestry Commission (staatsbosbeheer) bos-kampeerterreinen in zeven van Groot-Brittannië's Forest Parks en het New Forest beheert. Sommige bieden gereduceerde tarieven voor jeugdorganisaties op georganiseerde kampeertochten, en alle inlichtingen hierover moeten ver van tevoren ingewonnen worden bij de Forestry Commission.

Kampeerschuren

Dit zijn meestal niet meer in gebruik zijnde boerengebouwen die zijn verbouwd tot simpele logies voor een groep tot 15 personen, tegen redelijke prijs. De faciliteiten zijn eenvoudig: u kunt er slapen, eten, en eten bereiden, er is koud stromend water en een doortrek w.c. De Jeugdherberg Vereniging heeft een heel netwerk van kampeerschuren, van de Forest of Bowland in Lancashire tot en met Durham en Noord-Yorkshire. Meer informatie bij de YHA, Dimple Road, Matlock, Derbyshire DE4 2YH Tel: (017687) 72645
(voor kampeerschuren in het Lake District)
Tel: (01200) 420102
(voor kampeerschuren in alle andere regio's)
Internet: www.yha.org.uk

Kampeerschuren zijn ook in het Peak National Park beschikbaar. Meer informatie verkrijgbaar bij Peak District National Park Authority, Aldern House, Baslow Road, Bakewell, Derbyshire DE45 1AE.
Tel: (01 629) 816200 Let op: reserveringen worden afgehandeld door de YHA.

Huisdieren

Op veel parken zijn honden toegestaan, maar we raden u aan voor het reserveren na te vragen of dit het geval is, of er een extra tarief wordt geheven, en waar uw hond precies is toegestaan. Als er honden worden toegelaten, wil dit niet altijd zeggen dat ook katten toegestaan zijn, en we raden u ten sterkste aan van te voren contact op te nemen met het establissement als u uw kat mee wilt nemen. Op sommige parken zijn huisdieren in het geheel niet toegestaan. Honden zijn toegestaan als u dit symbool ziet 🐕.

Uw huisdier meenemen op vakantie in Groot-Brittannië

De quarantainewetten zijn onlangs gewijzigd in Engeland, en er is op dit moment een zgn. Pet Travel Scheme van toepassing. Onder dit systeem kunnen honden uit meer dan 35 landen Engeland binnen via bepaalde zee-, lucht- en treinroutes.

Honden die langer dan zes maanden in die landen hebben vertoefd mogen Groot-Brittannië binnen mits de eigenaar de juiste documentatie bij zich heeft voor de dieren.

Als u zonder quarantaine een hond mee wilt nemen naar Groot-Brittannië, onder het PETS-systeem, dan moet het dier aan bepaalde voorwaarden voldoen en u over de volgende documentatie beschikken: het officiële PETS-certificaat, een certificaat van behandeling tegen lintworm en teken, en een verklaring van verblijf.

Neem voor meer informatie over deelnemende landen, toegestane routes, reisoperators en andere details van het PETS-systeem, contact op met de PETS-lijn, DEFRA (Department for Environment, Food and Rural Affairs), 1a Page Street, Londen, SW1P 4PQ, Engeland.
Tel: +44 (0) 870 241 1710, fax: +44 (0) 20 7904 6834.
E-mail: pets.helpline@defra.gsi.gov.uk, of bezoek hun website op www.defra.gov.uk/animalh/quarantine

Drugswaarschuwing voor inkomende toeristen

In het Vereningd Koninkrijk staan er zware straffen op het illegaal invoeren van drugs. Drugshandelaars proberen onschuldige reizigers te misleiden en wij raden u daarom aan alle betrokkenheid met drugs te vermijden. Draag nooit pakjes of bagage door de douane die niet van uzelf zijn.

Wettelijke bepalingen

De allerbeste bron van wettelijk advies voor automobilisten is een Club voor Automobilisten (b.v. ANWB). Wat de kampeerder of caravaneigenaar nog meer moet weten is betrekkelijk eenvoudig. Als u een caravan of kampeerwagentje achter de auto heeft, mag u niet meer dan 96 km (60 mijl) per uur rijden op tweebaanswegen of snelwegen, 80 km (50 mijl) per uur op eenbaanswegen, en op snelwegen met drie banen aan elke kant mag u niet in de derde (snelste) baan. Kooktoestellen mogen niet bij een wegrestaurant met benzinestation aangestoken worden.

In de meeste steden is parkeren beperkt, zowel door wettelijke bepalingen als uit praktische overwegingen. Auto's met aanhangende caravans mogen niet parkeren bij een parkeermeter en vele stadsparkeerterreinen zijn alleen geschikt voor auto's zonder aanhangende caravans of kampeerwagentjes.

's Nachts moet een kampeerwagen, of een auto verbonden met een aanhangwagen, die aan de weg geparkeerd staat, zowel z'n twee voorlichten als z'n achterlichten aanhebben, terwijl een auto alleen dit niet hoeft.

De remmen, lampen, het gewicht, etc. van buitenlandse voertuigen hoeven niet te voldoen aan de Britse technische voorschriften. Hoe dan ook, een aanhangwagen mag de Britse wettelijke afmetingsbepalingen - 7m lang en 2,3m breed - niet overschrijden. Ze moeten het internationale kenteken (NL of B) voeren en niet overnachten in de berm of op de parkeerhavens, daar deze wettelijk onderdeel uitmaken van de weg.

Tenslotte is het ook heel belangrijk van tevoren uit te vinden hoe laat u op de dag van vertrek moet opbreken. U moet zich daar aan houden, anders kan men u een extra dag in rekening brengen.

Advies aan bezoekers

De BTA stelt er prijs op uw op- of aanmerkingen op uw verblijf in Groot-Brittannië te vernemen. wij hopen dat u geen reden tot klagen heeft, maar mocht dit toch het geval zijn, raden wij u dringend aan om uw klacht onmiddellijk kenbaar te maken aan de leiding van het desbetreffende park, de winkel of vervoersmaatschappij. Indien u hieruit geen genoegdoening verkrijgt, laat u ons dit dan weten, zodat wij zelf een onderzoek kunnen instellen, of u kunnen adviseren over eventuele verder te nemen stappen.

U mag het geeft niet hoeveel geld, en in welke munteenheid dan ook, meenemen en er bestaan geen beperkingen op het aantal inwisselbare reischeques. Als u geld wilt wisselen als de banken gesloten zijn, kunt u dit doen bij de grotere hotels, reisbureaus en warenhuizen of bij onafhankelijke wisselkantoren. Controleer vooral van tevoren de berekende wisselkoers en commissietarieven.

Alle grote winkels, warenhuizen, en de meeste hotels en restaurants accepteren de gebruikelijke, internationaal erkende credit cards. Als u ook graag op markten winkelt, koop dan alleen op grote, erkende markten, en bekijk de artikelen eerst zorgvuldig.

Vraag altijd wat de prijs is voor u tot de aankoop overgaat. Pas op voor zakkenrollers in drukke menigten.

Indien u bestolen bent, of betrokken bent bij een ongeval of brand, bel dan 999 (waarvoor geen geld nodig is) en vraag om de 'police' (politie), 'ambulance service' (ambulance) of de 'fire brigade' (brandweer).

De British Tourist Authority/English Tourism Council (BTA/ETC) heeft alle pogingen in het werk gesteld om deze publicatie bij het ter perse gaan van nauwkeurigheid te verzekeren. De informatie werd in goed vertrouwen verstrekt, gebaseerd op inlichtingen gegeven aan de BTA/ETC door de organisatoren van de vermelde caravanparken en campings. De BTA/ETC kan echter niet garanderen dat deze informatie correct is en kan geen verantwoording aanvaarden voor foute of onjuiste voorstellingen. De BTA/ETC kan beslist niet verantwoordelijk worden gesteld voor verlies, teleurstelling, nalatigheid of enige andere schade die voortvloeit uit het vertrouwen in de informatie in deze gids, of problemen voortkomend uit het faillisement of liquidatie van enige vermelde maatschappij, individu of bedrijf, of indien een maatschappij, individu of bedrijf ophoudt handel te drijven. Het is daarom raadzaam de gegeven informatie bij het maken van een reservering goed te controleren.

Alle parken in deze gids houden zich aan de richtlijnen van de Tourism Council. Een lijst van de aan de campings en caravanparken gestelde eisen kunt u vinden op pagina 219.

All genoemde instellingen in het gedeelte in kleur hebben betaald voor hun vermelding in deze gids.

BRITISH HOLIDAY AND HOME PARKS ASSOCIATION

The Association represents commercial operators of all kinds throughout Britain. Its aim is to ensure a high standard of excellence in members' parks for the satisfaction of the visitor.

Parks listed in this Guide all conform to the standards set by the British Tourist Authority but BH&HPA Members' Parks, which are identified in the Guide by (BH&HPA), must also abide by the BH&HPA Code of Conduct. This gives the visitor an assurance of a high standard of facilities and reliability.

The BH&HPA works with the British Tourist Authority, English Tourism Council, and the national and regional tourist boards to safeguard tourist interests. It also works with Government and local government authorities to ensure that all aspects of legislation and control are applied and that proper safety measures are carried out for the comfort and protection of the visitor.

The BH&HPA will investigate problems encountered by visitors and can provide details of self-catering holidays and residential parks. Contact:

British Holiday and Home Parks Association Ltd, Chichester House, 6 Pullman Court, Great Western Road, Gloucester GL1 3ND.
Telephone: (01452) 526911
Fax: (01452) 508508.

Come usare questa Guida

I campeggi elencati in questa guida sono per la maggior parte aperti sia alle roulottes che alle tende e molti di essi accolgono anche i camper e le motorhome. Molti campeggi dispongono anche di roulottes a noleggio.

Standard di garanzia di qualità

Per chi va in cerca di un posto dove soggiornare, è necessario un sistema di classificazione affidabile. Il programma britannico di classificazione dei parchi vacanze (British Graded Holiday Parks Scheme) del 2000 offre una guida chiara e comprensibile su ciò che ci si può aspettare. Il programma è sempre imperniato sulla qualità e rispecchia le aspettative del cliente.

L'organo per il turismo inglese (English Tourism Council) utilizza ora delle stelle per illustrare le categorie dei parchi partecipanti al programma. I parchi vengono ispezionati annualmente da funzionari competenti e imparziali, che assegnano una classificazione da una a cinque stelle, basandosi sulla pulizia, sull'ambiente e sulla qualità delle strutture e dei servizi offerti.

Inoltre, i parchi vengono ora contrassegnati da un simbolo, in modo che se ne possa identificare immediatamente il tipo - ad esempio Parco Vacanze, Parco Turistico o Campeggio. (L'assenza di classifica o contrassegno significa che il parco in oggetto non è stato ancora valutato al momento di andare in stampa).

Il programma di classificazione è stato ideato congiuntamente dagli enti nazionali per il turismo dell'Inghilterra, dell'Irlanda del Nord, della Scozia e del Galles in collaborazione con l'associazione britannica dei parchi per roulotte e vacanze (British Holiday & Home Parks Association) (vedere a pagina 45) e con l'organo nazionale per le roulotte (National Caravan Council) (vedere a pagina 49).

Strutture

Le strutture vengono indicate per mezzo di simboli, comprensibili a prima vista, spiegati qui di seguito.

SPIEGAZIONE DEI SIMBOLI

- **M** Socio del Regional Tourist Board
- **BH& HPA** British Holiday & Home Parks Association (v. pagina 45)
- **NCC** National Caravan Council (v. pagina 49)
- Roulottes ammesse (con numero di posteggi e prezzi)
- Camper/motorhome ammessi (con numero di posteggi e prezzi) In alcuni casi il numero di posteggi per camper/motorhome è compreso nel numero di posteggi per roulottes
- Tende ammesse
- Numero di roulottes a noleggio (v. posteggi per roulottes a noleggio a seguito)
- Bungalow/chalet/casette a noleggio
- Parcheggio vicino all'alloggio
- **P** Parcheggio sul post
- Zona di pernottamento temporaneo
- Allacciamento elettrico per roulottes (v. Alimentazione elettrica: prese di allacciamento per roulottes)
- Docce
- Aqua calda per tutti i lavandini
- Illuminazione dei WC ecc.
- WC a trattamento chimico
- Cambio di bombole di gas butano o propano
- Negozio/negozio ambulante di alimentari
- Bar/ristorante
- Club/bar/negozio autorizzato alla vendita di bevande alcoliche
- **TV** Salone con televisione a colori
- Telefono pubblico
- Lavanderia sul posto
- Attrezzature per asciugare la biancheria
- Attrezzature per stirare i vestiti
- Prese per rasoi elettrici
- Sala giochi
- Zona giochi per i bambini
- Locazione biciclette
- Piscina riscaldata al coperto sul posto
- Piscina all'aperto sul posto
- Strutture per gli sport subacquei sul posto (comprese le bombole di ossigeno)
- Sci d'acqua sul posto
- Imbarcazioni/canottaggio sul posto
- Vela sul posto
- Equitazione/escursioni a dorso di pony partendo dal campeggio
- Tennis sul posto
- Pesca sul posto o nelle vicinanze
- Golf sul posto o nelle vicinanze
- Galleria per armi da fuoco privata
- **p** Si accettano animali domestici
- Spettacoli/intrattenimenti serali
- Si consiglia di prenotare in estate
- **T** Prenotazione possible tramite agenzie di viaggio

Prezzi

I prezzi indicati per i posteggi sono il prezzo minimo e il prezzo massimo di un pernottamento per 2 persone, un'automobile e una tenda o una roulotte. I campeggi britannici preferiscono in genere includere tutto in un solo prezzo, benché in alcuni vi siano prezzi separati per automobili, roulottes o tende e per ogni persona. In alcuni campeggi possono essere richiesti supplementi per i tendoni delle roulottes. I prezzi minimi e massimi delle roulottes a noleggio sono i prezzi per settimana. I prezzi indicati sono quelli forniti dagli esercenti dei campeggi in questione e sono un'indicazione dei prezzi che verranno praticati per il periodo di validità di questa pubblicazione. I prezzi indicati sono in sterline (£) e pence (p). L'IVA (Imposta sul Valore Aggiunto) al 17,5% è compresa nei prezzi indicati. Per evitare qualsiasi equivoco, si consiglia vivamente di controllare i prezzi al momento di effettuare la prenotazione.

Prenotazione

Nel richiedere informazioni sulle possibilità di sistemazione, è necessario, oltre a controllare il prezzo, illustrare chiaramente le proprie esigenze, per esempio:

- date di arrivo e partenza, e se possibile date alternative;
- tipo di sistemazione richiesto;
- qualsiasi particolare esigenza.

Quando si prenota per telefono c'è sempre il rischio di errori. Tempo permettendo, si consiglia dunque di confermare sempre le prenotazioni per iscritto. Ricordarsi di indicare il proprio nome e indirizzo e di accludere, per ogni risposta, una busta preindirizzata e preaffrancata o un buono internazionale per riposta pagata.

Anticipi

Per la prenotazione di posti nei campeggi per tende, roulottes e chalets, il prezzo intero va normalmente versato in anticipo. Il versamento può normalmente essere effettuato in due rate: un anticipo al momento della prenotazione e il saldo circa due settimane prima dell'inizio del periodo prenotato.

Annullamenti

Nel Regno Unito, l'accettazione di un alloggio offerto, sia per iscritto che per telefono, equivale per legge alla firma di un contratto vincolante tra l'inquilino e il proprietario dell'alloggio. Ciò significa che se l'inquilino annulla la propria prenotazione, non prende domicilio o parte prima del previsto (per qualsiasi ragione), il proprietario potrebbe avere diritto a un risarcimento qualora non riuscisse a riaffittare l'alloggio per tutto o parte del periodo prenotato. Se è stato versato un anticipo, è probabile che venga ritenuto dal proprietario, il quale potrebbe anche esigere un ulteriore addebito.

È consigliabile dunque avvisare immediatamente il proprietario sia di qualsiasi cambiamento di itinerario, sia dell'intenzione di annullare una prenotazione o di partire prima del previsto.

Prese di allacciamento elettrico:

I campeggi dispongono per la maggior parte di prese di allacciamento alla rete di distribuzione dell'energia elettrica adoperabili sia per la roulottes che per le tende. La tensione è di 240V circa e 50Hz, benché in alcuni casi possa ancora variare tra 200V e 250V. In alcuni campeggi potrebbe essere necessario un adattatore per l'allacciamento. La fornitura di energia elettrica è normalmente soggetta ad un addebito supplementare e si consiglia di controllare le tariffe al momento della prenotazione.

Come trovare il campeggio prescelto

I campeggi in questa guida sono raggruppati per regione in Inghilterra, seguiti dalle liste relative a Scozia e Galles, e sono stati elencati in ordine alfabetico sotto il nome della città in cui si trovano, o vicino a cui si trovano. L'Indice delle Città a pagina 245 e le Mappe a colori all'inizio della guida riportano tutte le città, i centri e i villaggi che hanno un campeggio elencato in questa guida. Usate questi riferimenti per trovare in un modo facile e veloce un alloggio adatto. Se sapete in quale campeggio volete stare, controllate l'Indice dei Campeggi a pagina 241.

Se il luogo dove volete stare è compreso nell'indice delle città, andate alla pagina indicata per trovarvi i campeggi disponibili. I nomi delle città appaiono in nero sulla mappa all'inizio della guida nel modo in cui sono stati indicati dal riferimento alla mappa nella voce relativa. Controllate anche le mappe a colori per trovarvi altri luoghi vicini che hanno anche dei campeggi elencati in questa guida.

Se il luogo dove volete stare non si trova nell'indice delle città – o avete solo un'idea generale della zona in cui volete stare – usate le cartine a colori.

Le cartine illustrano tutti i nomi delle località in cui viene elencato un campeggio nella guida. Per trovare la località precisa leggete le indicazioni di ogni voce. In caso di difficoltà è consigliabile chiedere indicazioni a qualcuno nelle vicinanze del campeggio.

I segnali internazionali indicati qui vengono usati in Gran Bretagna per aiutare i visitatori a trovare i campeggi. Non sono ancora stati installati per tutti i campeggi e non indicano il nome di nessun campeggio. Indicano però se il campeggio è per tende, roulottes o ambedue.

Il carnet internazionale del campeggiatore è raramente riconosciuto in Gran Bretagna, salvo nei campeggi organizzati dai principali club.

Campeggi di Londra

Londra rappresenta una grande attrazione per molti visitatori, per cui i campeggi per tende e roulotte nell'area della Greater London tendono a riempirsi molto rapidamente, e bisogna prenotare molto in anticipo.

Sono anche disponibili campeggi presso la maggior parte dei porti d'entrata nel paese, e molti di questi sono elencati in questa guida e indicati sulla mappa all'inizio.

Servizi di ricerca campeggi

I Tourist Information Centre di tutta la Gran Bretagna (v. pagine finali) possono fornire ai campeggiatori informazioni sui campeggi nelle loro zone di responsabilità.

Alcuni Tourist Information Centre offrono servizi di ricerca campeggi che forniscono informazioni sulla disponibilità di posteggi e spesso aiutano a effettuare le prenotazioni. I Tourist Information Centre che attualmente offrono questo servizio coprono le seguenti zone del paese: New Forest, (0131) 314 6505; Cornovaglia, (01872) 274057. Nel Galles, molti Tourist Information Centres possono fornire informazioni sulla disponibilità di posti dalla fine di maggio alla fine di agosto.

Come evitare i problemi dell'alta stagione

Nei mesi estivi, da giugno a settembre, i campeggi nelle zone più frequentate del paese: Galles settentrionale, Cumbria, Inghilterra sud-occidentale e la New Forest nel Hampshire, registrano molto presto il tutto esaurito. Si consiglia ai campeggiatori di arrivare presto o, se possibile, di prenotare in anticipo. Alcuni campeggi dispongono di zone di pernottamento temporaneo per i campeggiatori che arrivano tardi. Queste zone di pernottamento consentono di non disturbare gli altri campeggiatori durante la notte e di accogliere un maggior numero di nuovi arrivati, i quali vengono condotti a uno dei posti liberi la mattina seguente.

Altri luoghi di campeggio

A chi preferisce seguire il proprio itinerario attraverso la campagna britannica potrebbe interessare sapere che la Forestry Commission gestisce dei campeggi forestali nei sette parchi forestali del paese e nella New Forest. Alcuni offrono tariffe ridotte a gruppi organizzati di giovani in campeggio. Tutte le richieste d'informazioni vanno indirizzate direttamente alla Forestry Commission con qualche mese di anticipo sulla data di arrivo.

Granai da campeggio

Sono spesso degli edifici agricoli inutilizzati e trasformati in semplici alloggi per un massimo di 15 visitatori a prezzi ragionevoli. Le strutture sono le minime indispensabili: un posto per dormire, mangiare e cucinare, acqua corrente fredda e WC.

La Youth Hostel Association dispone di una rete di granai da campeggio che copre la zona tra Forest Bowland nel Lancashire, Durham e lo Yorkshire settentrionale. Per ulteriori informazioni, anche sulle modalità di prenotazione, rivolgersi a: YHA, Dimple Road, Matlock, Derbyshire DE4 2YH Tel: (017687) 72645 (granai del Lake District) Tel: (01200) 420102 (granai di utte le altre zone).

I granai da campeggio esistono anche nel Peak National Park. Per ulteriori informazioni, scrivere al seguente indirizzo: Peak District National Park Authority, Aldern House, Baslow Road, Bakewell, Derbyshire DE45 1AE

Tel: (01629) 816200 Le prenotazioni sono gestite dalla YHA.

Animali domestici

Molti campeggi accettano ospiti con cani, ma si consiglia di controllare al momento della prenotazione e di chiedere se è necessario versare un supplemento o se esistono delle regole particolari per l'ammissione degli animali domestici. Spesso anche se sono ammessi i cani, non è consentito portare gatti; è consigliabile per i proprietari di gatti contattare l'esercizio in anticipo. Gli esercizi che accettano animali domestici sono contrassegnati dal simbolo 🐕.

Ingresso degli animali domestici in Gran Bretagna

Ultimamente in Inghilterra la normativa sulla quarantena è stata modificata; attualmente è in vigore PETS, un programma per l'ingresso degli animali domestici, che consente l'ingresso in Gran Bretagna dei cani provenienti da oltre 35 paesi diversi attraverso determinati itinerari in nave, aereo e treno.

L'ingresso nel Regno Unito dei cani residenti da oltre 6 mesi in questi paesi è consentito ai sensi del Programma, a condizione che gli animali siano accompagnati dalla relativa documentazione.

Per entrare nel Regno Unito senza quarantena ai sensi del programma PETS, i cani devono rispondere a determinate condizioni e viaggiare con i seguenti documenti: Certificato ufficiale PETS, un certificato di cura contro tenia e zecche e dichiarazione di residenza.

Per particolari sui paesi partecipanti, gli itinerari, gli operatori e altre informazioni sul programma PETS, rivolgersi a: PETS Helpline, DEFRA (Department for Environment, Food and Rural Affaris), 1a Page Street, London SW1P 4PQ Tel: +44 (0) 870 241 1710 Fax: +44 (0) 20 7904 6834 Email: pets.helpline@defra.gsi.gov.uk www.defra.gov.uk./animalh/quarantine

Avvertimento sugli stupefacenti per i turisti in arrivo

Le leggi britanniche sul contrabbando di stupefacenti prevedono delle sanzioni estremamente severe per i trasgressori. I trafficanti di droga tentano a volte di ingannare i viaggiatori. Si consiglia a chiunque abbia deciso di visitare il Regno Unito di evitare qualsiasi coinvolgimento con lo spaccio di stupefacenti e di non attraversare mai la dogana portando le valige o i pacchi di altri viaggiatori.

Aspetti giuridici

La migliore fonte d'informazioni per gli automobilisti che intendono visitare la Gran Bretagna è l'organizzazione automobilistica del paese di origine. Le regole che deve conoscere l'automobilista campeggiatore sono relativamente semplici.

Le automobili con roulotte o rimorchi al traino non

devono superare i 96 chilometri orari (60 miglia all'ora) sulle strade a doppia carreggiata e sulle autostrade, e gli 80 chilometri orari (50 miglia all'ora) sulle strade normali. Sulle autostrade a tre carreggiate in ogni direzione, le roulotte ed i rimorchi non sono ammessi nella terza carreggiata (la più veloce). È vietato accendere fornellini nelle aree di servizio autostradali.

Nella maggior parte delle città, parcheggiare è reso difficile sia dai regolamenti che da difficoltà pratiche. Alle automobili con rimorchio è vietato l'uso di spazi con parchimetri e i posteggi di molti parcheggi cittadini sono intesi per automobili senza rimorchio, sebbene in alcuni di essi vi siano spazi anche per veicoli più lunghi.

Se parcheggiati sulla strada di notte, i rimorchi, o le automobili attaccate ai rimorchi, devono avere due luci anteriori e due luci posteriori accese, anche dove l'automobile senza il rimorchio sarebbe esonerata da quest'obbligo.

I freni, le luci, il peso ecc. dei veicoli provenienti dall'estero non devono soddisfare i criteri tecnici delle norme britanniche. I rimorchi tuttavia non devono superare i limiti britannici, che sono: 7 metri di lunghezza e 2,3 metri di larghezza. I rimorchi devono recare il numero di targa del paese di provenienza. È vietato sostare di notte sui lati erbosi o nelle piazzole di sosta delle strade, dato che queste zone sono per legge considerate parti della strada.

Per concludere, è importante sapere l'ora entro la quale si è obbligati a liberare il posteggio nel giorno previsto per la partenza. Si consiglia di partire presto la mattina per evitare di dover pagare il prezzo di una giornata in più.

Consigli per i visitatori

La British Tourist Authority è sempre lieta di ricevere i commenti e le osservazioni dei turisti su qualsiasi aspetto del loro soggiorno in Gran Bretagna, che siano o meno favorevoli. Ci auguriamo che chiunque visiti il nostro paese non abbia mai occasione di lamentarsi. Se vi fosse ragione di lamentarsi, il consiglio è di rivolgersi in primo luogo alla gestione del campeggio, negozio o società di trasporti. Qualora la risposta non sia soddisfacente, consigliamo ai turisti di rivolgersi alla BTA che prenderà in esame la questione o suggerirà le misure da prendere.

Si possono portare in Gran Bretagna valute di qualsiasi denominazione senza limiti di quantità. Si può cambiare anche qualsiasi numero di traveller's cheque. Per cambiare le valute straniere durante le ore di chiusura delle banche ci si può rivolgere alle recezioni di alcuni grandi alberghi, alle agenzie di viaggio, alle agenzie di cambiavalute indipendenti. Raccomandiamo di controllare il tasso e la commissione di cambio prima di cambiare i soldi.

Tutti i grandi negozi, i grandi magazzini la maggior parte degli alberghi e dei ristoranti accettano le carte di credito normalmente riconosciute nel mondo. A chi decida di fare spese nei mercati consigliamo di comprare solo in quelli grandi e riconosciuti e di esaminare accuratamente gli articoli prima di acquistarli.

Consigliamo di chiedere sempre il prezzo dei beni e dei servizi prima di impegnarsi all'acquisto e di fare attenzione ai borsaioli nei luoghi affollati.

Chiunque sia vittima di un furto, o coinvolto in un incidente o un incendio può telefonare al 999 (chiamata gratuita) e chiedere la polizia, il servizio ambulanze o i vigili del fuoco.

La British Tourist Authority e l'English Tourism Council (BTA/ETC) hanno fatto di tutto per garantire l'esattezza delle informazioni contenute in questa pubblicazione al momento di andare in stampa. Le informazioni vengono date in buona fede in base ai dati forniti A BTA/ETC dai promotori del campeggi elencati. La BTA e l' ETC tuttavia non possono né garantire l'esattezza delle informazioni né assumersi la responsabilltà di qualsiasi errore o falsità. È esclusa tutta la responsabilità di perdite, delusioni, negligenza o di altri danni che risultino dall'aver fatto affidamento sulle informazioni contenute in questa guida o dal fallimento o dalla liquidazione di qualsiasi società, individuo o ditta, o dalla cessazione delle attività di qualsiasi società, individuo o ditta. Si consiglia di verificare l'esattezza delle informazioni al momento di effettuare la prenotazione.

Tutti i parchi elencati in questa guida sono conformi agli Standard del Tourism Council. A pagina 219 riportiamo un elenco di queste norme applicabili ai campeggi per tende e roulottes.

Tutti i campeggi elencati nella seqione a colori hanno pagato per la loro inserzione nella guida.

THE NATIONAL CARAVAN COUNCIL

The National Caravan Council is the representative body of the British caravan industry.

The Council operates an approval system for caravans, certifying that they are manufactured in accordance with the European Standard. All Dealer members and Park Operator members, which are identified in the Guide by (NCC), agree to comply with Conditions of Membership which require them to provide their customers with a high standard of service.

The Council works closely with the British Tourist Authority, English Tourism Council, and the national and regional tourist boards to promote tourism and particularly to promote the important role which all kinds of caravans play in providing tourists with the facilities they require.

Full information on its members and its activities together with assistance on any difficulties encountered can be obtained from:

The National Caravan Council,
Catherine House, Victoria Road, Aldershot,
Hampshire GU11 1SS.
Telephone: (01252) 318251
Fax: (01252) 322596
E-mail: info@nationalcaravan.co.uk
Internet: www.nationalcaravan.co.uk

Caravan Holiday Home
Award Scheme

Rose Award,
English Tourism Council,
Thames Tower, Black's Road,
Hammersmith, London W6 9EL.

Thistle Award,
Scottish Tourist Board,
Thistle House, Beechwood Park North,
Inverness IV2 3ED.

Dragon Award,
Wales Tourist Board, Brunel House,
2 Fitzalan Road, Cardiff CF24 0UY.

The English Tourism Council and the national tourist boards for Scotland and Wales run similar Award schemes for holiday caravan homes on highly graded caravan parks. They recognise high standards of caravan accommodation and enable you to step into a comfortable, fully furnished holiday home set amongst landscaped surroundings with all amenities you could wish for.

All the caravan parks included in the Award scheme have been inspected and meet the criteria demanded by the scheme. In addition to complying with joint tourist board standards for 'Holiday Caravan Parks and in Caravan Holiday Homes' all Award caravans must have a shower or bath, toilet, mains electricity and water heating (at no extra charge) and a refrigerator (many also have a colour television).

A complete list of the parks in each country, plus further information about them, can be obtained free from the national tourist boards (see page 232). Look out for these plaques displayed by all Award winning parks, and by each caravan which meets the required standards. Many parks listed in this guide are participating in these schemes and are indicated accordingly.

CAMPING AND CARAVAN PARKS IN BRITAIN
Published by:
British Tourist Authority and English Tourism Council, Thames Tower, Black's Road, Hammersmith, London W6 9EL.
ISBN 0 7095 7407 X
Distribution code M2CACEN
Publishing Manager: Michael Dewing
Production Manager: Iris Buckley
Technical Manager: Marita Sen
Compilation, Design & Production: www.jacksonlowe.com
Typesetting: Tradespools Ltd, Somerset and Jackson Lowe Marketing, Lewes
Maps: © Maps In Minutes™ (1999)
Printing and Binding: Mozzon Giuntina S.p.A., Florence and Officine Grafiche De Agostini S.p.A., Novara.
Advertisement Sales: Jackson Lowe Marketing, 173 High Street, Lewes, East Sussex BN7 1EH. (01273) 487487
© British Tourist Authority (except where stated)

Cover Pictures:
Front Cover Inset: Carlyon Bay Caravan & Camping Park, Carlyon Bay, Cornwall
Photo Credits:
Cumbria - Cumbria Tourist Board; Northumbria - Northumbria Tourist Board, Graeme Peacock, Mike Kipling;
Colin Cuthbert and Michael Busselle; North West - North West Tourist Board, Cheshire County Council,
Lancashire County Council, Marketing Manchester; Yorkshire - Yorkshire Tourist Board;
Heart of England - Heart of England Tourist Board; East of England - East of England Tourist Board Collection;
South West - South West Tourism; South of England - Southern Tourist Board, Peter Titmuss, Chris Cove-Smith and Iris Buckley;
South East England - South East England Tourist Board, Chris Parker and Iris Buckley; Scotland - Scottish Tourist Board; Wales - Wales Tourist Board

Important:
The information contained in this guide has been published in good faith on the basis of information submitted to the British Tourist Authority/English Tourism Council (BTA/ETC) by the proprietors of the premises listed, who have paid for their entries to appear. The BTA/ETC cannot guarantee the accuracy of the information in this guide and accepts no responsibility for any error or misrepresentation. All liability for loss, disappointment, negligence or other damage caused by reliance on the information contained in this guide, or in the event of bankruptcy, or liquidation, or cessation of trade of any company, individual or firm mentioned, is hereby excluded. Please check carefully all prices and other details before confirming a reservation.

LONDON

A dynamic mix of history and heritage, cool and contemporary. Great museums, stunning art collections, royal palaces, hip nightlife and stylish shopping, from ritzy Bond Street to cutting-edge Hoxton.

classic sights
St Paul's Cathedral – Wren's famous church
Tower of London – 900 years of British history
London Eye – spectacular views from the world's highest 'big wheel'

arts for all
National Gallery – Botticelli, Rembrandt, Turner and more
Tate Modern – 20th century art in a former power station
Victoria & Albert Museum – decorative arts

city lights
Theatre: musicals – West End; drama – Royal Court and National Theatre;
Music: classical – Wigmore Hall and Royal Festival Hall;
jazz – Ronnie Scott's; ballet & opera – Royal Opera House

insider london
Dennis Severs's House, E1 – candlelit tours of this authentically 18th century house

Greater London, comprising the 32 London Boroughs

FOR MORE INFORMATION CONTACT:
London Tourist Board
6th Floor, Glen House, Stag Place,
London SW1E 5LT
Telephone enquiries - see London Line on page 56
Internet: www.LondonTouristBoard.com

The Pictures:
1 Tower Bridge
2 Hampton Court
3 Piccadilly Circus

Places to Visit - see pages 52-56
Where to Stay - see pages 57-58

PLACES to visit

You will find hundreds of interesting places to visit during your stay, just some of which are listed in these pages. Contact any Tourist Information Centre in and around London for more ideas on days out.

Bank of England Museum
Bartholomew Lane, London, EC2R 8AH
Tel: (020) 7601 5545 www.bankofengland.co.uk
The museum is housed within the Bank of England. It traces the history of the Bank from its foundation by Royal Charter in 1694 to its role today as the nation's central bank.

British Airways London Eye
Jubilee Gardens, South Bank, London, SE1
Tel: (0870) 5000 600 www.ba-londoneye.com
At 443 ft (135 m) high, this is the world's highest observation wheel. It provides a 30-minute slow-moving flight over London

British Library
96 Euston Road, London, NW1 2DB
Tel: (020) 7412 7332 www.bl.uk
Exhibition galleries, bookshop, piazza displaying Magna Carta, Gutenberg Bible, Shakespeare's First Folio and illuminated manuscripts, temporary exhibitions.

British Museum
Great Russell Street, London, WC1B 3DG
Tel: (020) 7323 8000 www.thebritishmuseum.ac.uk
One of the great museums of the world, showing the works of man from prehistoric to modern times with collections drawn from the whole world.

Cabinet War Rooms
Clive Steps, King Charles Street, London, SW1A 2AQ
Tel: (020) 7930 6961 www.iwm.org.uk
The underground headquarters used by Winston Churchill and the British Government during World War II. Includes Cabinet Room, Transatlantic Telephone Room and Map Room.

Chessington World of Adventures
Leatherhead Road, Chessington, KT9 2NE
Tel: (01372) 729560 www.chessington.com
Visitors will be in for a big adventure as they explore the theme park's amazing new attractions.

Design Museum
28 Shad Thames, London, SE1 2YD
Tel: (020) 7403 6933 www.designmuseum.org
The Design Museum is one of London's most inspiring attractions, concerned solely with the products, technologies and buildings of the 20thC and 21stC.

Hampton Court Palace
Hampton Court, East Molesey, KT8 9AU
Tel: (020) 8781 9500 www.hrp.org.uk
The oldest Tudor palace in England with many attractions including the Tudor kitchens, tennis courts, maze, State Apartments and King's Apartments.

HMS Belfast
Morgan's Lane, Tooley Street, London, SE1 2JH
Tel: (020) 7940 6300 www.iwm.org.uk
World War II cruiser weighing 11,500 tonnes, now a floating naval museum, with 9 decks to explore.

LONDON

Imperial War Museum
Lambeth Road, London, SE1 6HZ
Tel: (020) 7416 5320 www.iwm.org.uk
Museum tells the story of 20thC war from Flanders to Bosnia. Special features include the Blitz Experience, the Trench Experience and the World of Espionage.

Kensington Palace State Apartments
Kensington Gardens, London, W8 4PX
Tel: (020) 7937 7079 www.hrp.org.uk
Furniture and ceiling paintings from Stuart-Hanoverian periods, rooms from Victorian era and works of art from the Royal Collection. Also Royal Ceremonial Dress Collection.

Kew Gardens (Royal Botanic Gardens)
Kew Richmond TW9 3AB
Tel: (020) 8940 1171 Rec.
300 acres (121 ha) containing living collections of over 40,000 varieties of plants. Seven spectacular glasshouses, 2 art galleries, Japanese and rock garden.

London Dungeon
28-34 Tooley Street, London, SE1 2SZ
Tel: (020) 7403 7221 www.thedungeons.com
The world's first medieval fully interactive horror attraction. Relive the 'Great Fire of London', unmask 'Jack the Ripper' and take the 'Judgement Day' ride.

London Planetarium
Marylebone Road, London, NW1 5LR
Tel: (0870) 400 3000 www.london-planetarium.com
Visitors can experience a virtual reality trip through space and wander through the interactive Space Zones before the show.

London Transport Museum
Covent Garden Piazza, London, WC2E 7BB
Tel: (020) 7379 6344 www.ltmuseum.co.uk
The history of transport for everyone, from spectacular vehicles, special exhibitions, actors and guided tours to film shows, gallery talks and children's craft workshops.

London Zoo
Regent's Park, London, NW1 4RY
Tel: (020) 7722 3333 www.londonzoo.co.uk
One of the world's most famous zoos and home to over 600 species. Including the new 'Web of Life' exhibition, as well as a full daily events programme.

Madame Tussaud's
Marylebone Road, London, NW1 5LR
Tel: (0870) 400 3000 www.madame-tussauds.com
World-famous collection of wax figures in themed settings which include The Garden Party, 200 Years, Superstars, The Grand Hall, The Chamber of Horrors and The Spirit of London.

National Army Museum
Royal Hospital Road, Chelsea, London, SW3 4HT
Tel: (020) 7730 0717
www.national-armymuseum.ac.uk
The story of the British soldier in peace and war, through five centuries. Exhibits range from paintings to uniforms and from the English Civil War to Kosovo.

National History Museum
Cromwell Road, London, SW7 5BD
Tel: (020) 7942 5000 www.nhm.ac.uk
Home of the wonders of the natural world, one of the most popular museums in the world and one of London's finest landmarks.

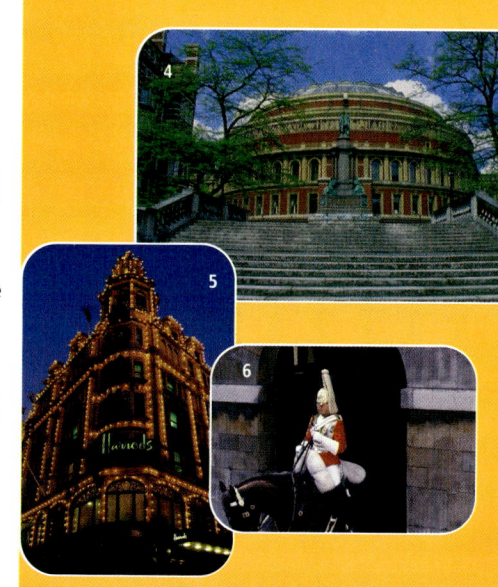

The Pictures:
1 London by night, Piccadilly Circus
2 Big Ben
3 Buckingham Palace
4 Albert Hall
5 Harrods
6 Horseguards Parade

LONDON

National Portrait Gallery

St Martin's Place, London, WC2H 0HE
Tel: (020) 7306 0055 www.npg.org.uk
Permanent collection of portraits of famous men and women from the Middle Ages to the present day. Free, but charge for some exhibitions.

Royal Air Force Museum

Grahame Park Way, Hendon, London, NW9 5LL
Tel: (020) 8205 2266 www.rafmuseum.com
Britain's National Museum of Aviation features over 70 full-sized aircraft, Flight Simulator, 'Touch and Try' Jet Provost Trainer and Eurofighter 2000 Theatre.

Royal Mews

Buckingham Palace, London, SW1A 1AA
Tel: (020) 7839 1377 www.royal.gov.uk
Her Majesty The Queen's carriage horses, carriages and harness used on State occasions (Coronation Coach built 1761).

Royal Observatory Greenwich

Greenwich Park, London, SE10 9NF
Tel: (020) 8858 4422 www.nmm.ac.uk
Museum of time and space and site of the Greenwich Meridian. Working telescopes and planetarium, timeball, Wren's Octagon Room and intricate clocks and computer simulations.

Science Museum

Exhibition Road, London, SW7 2DD
Tel: (0870) 870 4868 www.sciencemuseum.org.uk
See, touch and experience the major scientific advances of the last 300 years. With over 40 galleries, and over 2,000 hands-on exhibits to captivate and inspire all.

Shakespeare's Globe Exhibition and Tour

New Globe Walk, Bankside, London, SE1 9DT
Tel: (020) 7902 1500 www.shakespeares-globe.org
Against the historical background of Elizabethan Bankside, the City of London's playground in Shakespeare's time, the exhibition focuses on actors, architecture and audiences.

St Paul's Cathedral

St Paul's Churchyard, London, EC4M 8AD
Tel: (020) 7236 4128 www.stpauls.co.uk
Wren's famous cathedral church of the diocese of London incorporating the Crypt, Ambulatory and Whispering Gallery.

Tate Britain

Millbank, London, SW1P 4RG
Tel: (020) 7887 8000 www.tate.org.uk
Tate Britain presents the world's greatest collection of British art in a dynamic series of new displays and exhibitions.

Theatre Museum

Russell Street, London, WC2E 7PA
Tel: (020) 7943 4700 www.theatremuseum.org
Five galleries illustrating the history of performance in the United Kingdom. The collection includes displays on theatre, ballet, dance, musical stage, rock and pop music.

Tower of London

Tower Hill, London, EC3N 4AB
Tel: (020) 7709 0765 www.hrp.org.uk
Home of the `Beefeaters' and ravens, the building spans 900 years of British history. On display are the nation's Crown Jewels, regalia and armoury robes.

Victoria and Albert Museum

Cromwell Road, London, SW7 2RL
Tel: (020) 7942 2000 www.vam.ac.uk
The V&A holds one of the world's largest and most diverse collections of the decorative arts, dating from 3000BC to the present day.

Vinopolis, City of Wine

1 Bank End, London, SE1 9BU
Tel: (0870) 241 4040 www.vinopolis.co.uk
Vinopolis offers all the pleasures of wine under one roof. The Wine Odyssey tour includes free tastings from over 200 wines; also 2 restaurants on site.

Westminster Abbey

Parliament Square, London, SW1P 3PA
Tel: (020) 7222 5152 www.westminster-abbey.org
One of Britain's finest Gothic buildings. Scene of the coronation, marriage and burial of British monarchs. Nave and cloisters, Royal Chapels and Undercroft Museum.

LONDON

Find out more about London

Millennium Wheel

LONDON TOURIST BOARD

London Tourist Board and Convention Bureau
6th Floor, Glen House, Stag Place, London SW1E 5LT
www.LondonTouristBoard.com

TOURIST INFORMATION CENTRES

POINT OF ARRIVAL

- **Heathrow Terminals 1, 2, 3** Underground Station Concourse, Heathrow Airport, TW6 2JA.
  Open: Daily 0800-1800; 1 Jun-30 Sep, Mon-Sat 0800-1900, Sun 0800-1800.

- **Liverpool Street Underground Station,** EC2M 7PN.
  Open: Daily 0800-1800; 1 Jun-30 Sep, Mon-Sat 0800-1900, Sun 0800-1800.

- **Victoria Station Forecourt,** SW1V 1JU.
  Open: 1 Jun-30 Sep, Mon-Sat 0800-2100, Sun 0800-1800; 1 Oct-Easter, daily 0800-1800; Easter-31 May, Mon-Sat 0800-2000, Sun 0800-1800.

- **Waterloo International Terminal**
  Arrivals Hall, London SE1 7LT. Open: Daily 0830-2230.

INNER LONDON

- **Britain Visitor Centre,** 1 Regent Street, Piccadilly Circus, SW1Y 4XT.
  Open: Mon 0930-1830, Tue-Fri 0900-1830, Sat & Sun 1000-1600; Jun-Oct, Sat 0900-1700.

- **Greenwich TIC,** Pepys House, 2 Cutty Sark Gardens, Greenwich SE10 9LW.
  Tel: 0870 608 2000; Fax: 020 8853 4607.
  Open: Daily 1000-1700; 1 Jul-31 Aug, daily 1000-2000.

- **Lewisham TIC,** Lewisham Library, 199-201 Lewisham High Street, SE13 6LG.
  Tel: 020 8297 8317; Fax: 020 8297 9241.
  Open: Mon 1000-1700, Tue-Fri 0900-1700, Sat 1000-1600, Sun closed.

- **Liverpool Street Underground Station,** EC2M 7PN.
  Open: Mon-Fri 0800-1800, Sat 0800-1730, Sun 0900-1730.

- **Southwark Information Centre,**
  London Bridge, 6 Tooley Street, SE1 2SY.
  Tel: 020 7403 8299; Fax: 020 7357 6321.
  Open: Easter-31 Oct, Mon-Sat 1000-1800, Sun 1030-1730; 1 Nov-Easter, Mon-Sat 1000-1600, Sun 1100-1600.

- **Tower Hamlets TIC,** 18 Lamb Street, E1 6EA.
  Fax: 020 7375 2539.
  Open: Mon, Tue, Thu & Fri 0930-1330 & 1430-1630, Wed 0930-1300, Sat closed, Sun 1130-1430.

- **Victoria Station Forecourt,** SW1V 1JU.
  Open: Jan-Feb, Mon-Sat 0800-1900; Mar-May, Mon-Sat 0800-2000; Jun-Sep, Mon-Sat 0800-2100; Oct-Dec, Mon-Sat 0800-2000, Sun 0800-1815.

- **London Visitor Centre, Arrivals Hall,**
  Waterloo International Terminal, London SE1 7LT.
  Open: Daily 0830-2230.

OUTER LONDON

- **Bexley Hall Place TIC,** Bourne Road, Bexley, Kent, DA5 1PQ.
  Tel: 01322 558676; Fax 01322 522921.
  Open: Mon-Sat 1000-1630, Sun 1400-1730.

- **Croydon TIC, Katharine Street,** Croydon, CR9 1ET.
  Tel: 020 8253 1009; Fax: 020 8253 1008.
  Open: Mon, Tues, Wed & Fri 0900-1800, Thu 0930-1800, Sat 0900-1700, Sun 1400-1700.

- **Harrow TIC, Civic Centre,** Station Road, Harrow, HA1 2XF.
  Tel: 020 8424 1103; Fax: 020 8424 1134.
  Open: Mon-Fri 0900-1700, Sat & Sun closed.

- **Heathrow Terminals 1,2,3 Underground Station** Concourse, Heathrow Airport, TW6 2JA.
  Open: Daily 0800-1800.

LONDON

- **Hillingdon TIC,** Central Library,
  4-15 High Street, Uxbridge, UB8 1HD.
  Tel: 01895 250706; Fax: 01895 239794.
  Open: Mon, Tue & Thu 0930-2000, Wed 0930-1730,
  Fri 1000-1730, Sat 0930-1600, Sun closed.

- **Hounslow TIC,** The Treaty Centre,
  High Street, Hounslow, TW3 1ES.
  Tel: 020 8583 2929; Fax: 020 8583 4714.
  Open: Mon, Wed, Fri & Sat 0930-1730,
  Tue & Thu 0930-2000, Sun closed.

- **Kingston TIC,** Market House, Market Place,
  Kingston upon Thames, KT1 1JS.
  Tel: 020 8547 5592; Fax: 020 8547 5594.
  Open: Mon-Fri 1000-1700, Sat 0900-1600, Sun closed.

- **Richmond TIC,** Old Town Hall,
  Whittaker Avenue; Richmond, TW9 1TP.
  Tel: 020 8940 9125 Fax: 020 8940 6899.
  Open: Mon-Sat 1000-1700; Easter Sunday-end Sep,
  Sun 1030-1330.

- **Swanley TIC,** London Road, BR8 7AE.
  Tel: 01322 614660; Fax: 01322 666154.
  Open: Mon-Thur 0930-1730, Fri 0930-1800,
  Sat 0900-1600, Sun closed.

- **Twickenham TIC,** The Atrium, Civic Centre, York Street,
  Twickenham, Middlesex, TW1 3BZ.
  Tel: 020 8891 7272; Fax: 020 8891 7738.
  Open: Mon-Thu 0900-1715, Fri 0900-1700,
  Sat & Sun closed.

LONDON LINE

London Tourist Board's recorded telephone information service provides information on museums, galleries, attractions, river trips, sight seeing tours, accommodation, theatre, what's on, changing of the Guard, children's London, shopping, eating out and gay and lesbian London.
Available 24 hours a day. Calls cost 60p per minute as at July 2001. Call 09068 663344.

ARTSLINE

London's information and advice service for disabled people on arts and entertainment. Call (020) 7388 2227.

Getting to London

BY ROAD: Major trunk roads into London include: A1, M1, A5, A10, A11, M11, A13, A2, M2, A23, A3, M3, A4, M4, A40, M40, A41, M25 (London orbital). London Transport is responsible for running London's bus services and the underground rail network. (020) 7222 1234 (24 hour telephone service; calls answered in rotation).

BY RAIL: Main rail termini:
Victoria/Waterloo/Charing Cross - serving the South/South East;
King's Cross - serving the North East; Euston - serving the North West/Midlands;
Liverpool Street - serving the East; Paddington - serving the Thames Valley/West.

The Pictures:
1 China Town
2 Houses of Parliament

LONDON

Where to stay in London

Parks in London are listed in alphabetical order of place name, and then in alphabetical order of park.

Map references refer to the colour location maps at front of this guide. The first number indicates the map to use; the letter and number which follow refer to the grid reference on the map.

At-a-glance symbols can be found inside the back cover flap. Keep this open for easy reference.

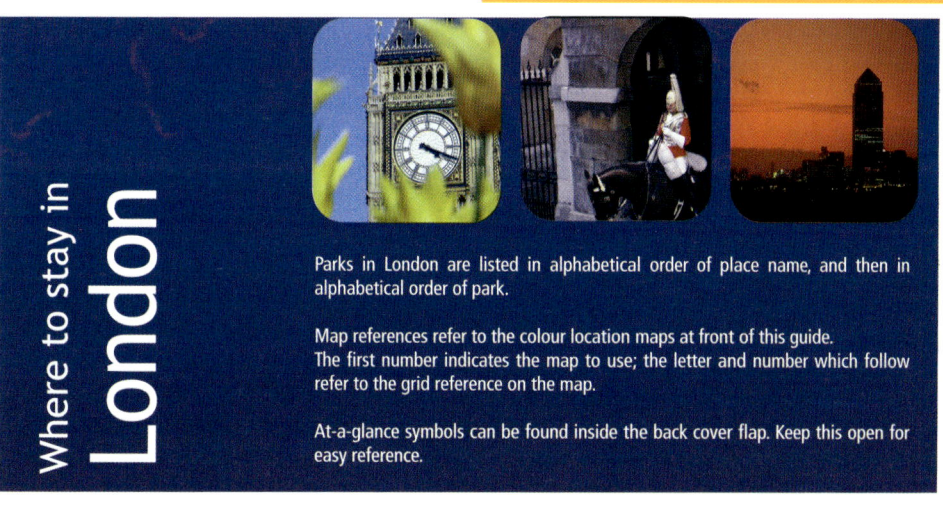

INNER LONDON
CHINGFORD Map ref 2D2

★★★★
TOURING & CAMPING PARK

Ad p58

LEE VALLEY CAMPSITE
Sewardstone Road, Chingford, London E4 7RA
T: (020) 8529 5689
F: (020) 8559 4070
E: scs@leevalleypark.org.uk
I: www.leevalleypark.org.uk

OPEN April–October
CC: Barclaycard, Delta, JCB, Maestro, Mastercard, Solo, Switch, Visa, Visa Electron
5.2 hectares (13 acres) Level, sloping, grassy, hard.

200 — £11.20
— £11.20
— £11.20
200 touring pitches

Take junction 26 off the M25, then follow signs to Chingford. Turn left at the roundabout and the campsite is 2 miles on the right. Signposted.

OUTER LONDON
STANSTED Map ref 4B3

★★★★★
HOLIDAY, TOURING & CAMPING PARK

ROSE AWARD

BH&HPA

THRIFTWOOD CARAVAN & CAMPING PARK
Plaxdale Green Road, Stansted TN15 7PB
T: (01732) 822261
F: (01732) 824636
I: www.ukparks.co.uk/thriftwood

OPEN January, March–December
CC: Barclaycard, Delta, Eurocard, JCB, Mastercard, Solo, Switch, Visa, Visa Electron
8 hectares (20 acres) Level, grassy, hard, sheltered.

150 — £8.00–£11.00
150 — £8.00–£11.00
150 — £8.00–£11.00
4 — £200.00–£340.00
150 touring pitches
13 units privately owned

Situated 3.75 miles south of Brands Hatch motor racing circuit on A20. Signposted.

QUALITY ASSURANCE SCHEME

For an explanation of the quality and facilities represented by the Stars please refer to the front of this guide.

LONDON

Perfectly Placed for the
City of London
and the countryside of Hertfordshire and Essex

Lee Valley Regional Park is a perfect place to stay. All sites have modern facilities, offer value for money and are located in pleasant surroundings with their own leisure attractions.

Lee Valley Caravan Park, Dobbs Weir, Hoddesdon, Herts
Enjoy the peace and tranquillity of this riverside site with good fishing, walking and boating nearby. Get to the West End by train and tube in under an hour.
Tel/Fax: 01992 462090

Lee Valley Campsite, Chingford, London
Situated on the edge of Epping Forest and close to the historic town of Waltham Abbey, this site is easily accessible from the M25 and just 42 minutes from the West End by public transport.
Tel: 020 8529 5689 Fax: 020 8559 4070

For more information, call the Lee Valley Park Information Centre on 01992 702200 or find us on the web at: www.leevalleypark.com

Lee Valley Park

WEB

ON-LINE INFORMATION

In-depth information about travelling in Britain is now available on BTA's VisitBritain website.

Covering everything from castles to leisure parks and from festivals to road and rail links, the site complements Where to Stay perfectly, giving you up-to-the-minute detials to help you with your travel plans.

BRITAIN on the internet
www.visitbritain.com

CUMBRIA

Cumbria's dramatic and breathtaking landscapes, from the famous Lakes to the rugged mountains and fells, have inspired poets and artists for hundreds of years.

classic sights
Hadrian's Wall – a reminder of Roman occupation
Lake Windermere – largest lake in England

coast & country
Scafell Pike – England's highest mountain
Whitehaven – historic port

literary links
William Wordsworth – The poet's homes: Wordsworth House, Dove Cottage and Rydal Mount
Beatrix Potter – Her home, Hill Top; her watercolours at the Beatrix Potter Gallery and the tales at The World of Beatrix Potter

distinctively different
The Gondola – sail Coniston Water aboard the opulent 1859 steam yacht Gondola
Cars of the Stars Museum – cars from TV and film, including Chitty Chitty Bang Bang and the Batmobile

The county of Cumbria

FOR MORE INFORMATION CONTACT:
Cumbria Tourist Board
Ashleigh, Holly Road, Windermere,
Cumbria LA23 2AQ
Tel: (015394) 44444 Fax: (015394) 44041
Email: mail@cumbria-tourist-board.co.uk
Internet: www.golakes.co.uk

The Pictures:
1 Lake Windermere
2 Muncaster Castle
3 Walking at Wasdale

Places to Visit - see pages 60-63
Where to Stay - see pages 64-68

PLACES to visit

You will find hundreds of interesting places to visit during your stay, just some of which are listed in these pages. Contact any Tourist Information Centre in the region for more ideas on days out.

The Dock Museum
North Road, Barrow-in-Furness, Cumbria LA14 2PW
Tel: (01229) 894444 www.barrowtourism.co.uk
The museum presents the story of steel shipbuilding, for which Barrow is famous, and straddles a Victorian graving dock. Interactive displays, nautical adventure playground.

The Beacon
West Strand, Whitehaven, Cumbria CA28 7LY
Tel: (01946) 592302 www.copelandbc.gov.uk
Discover the industrial, maritime and social history of Whitehaven and surrounding area. Includes Meteorology Office weather gallery with satellite-linked equipment.

Dove Cottage and Wandsworth Museum
Town End, Grasmere, Ambleside, Cumbria LA22 9SH
Tel: (015394) 35544 www.wordsworth.org.uk
Wordsworth's home 1799-1808. Poet's possessions. Museum with manuscripts, farmhouse reconstruction, paintings and drawings. Special events throughout the year.

Birdoswald Roman Fort
Gilsland, Carlisle, Cumbria CA8 7DD
Tel: (016977) 47602
Remains of Roman fort on one of the best parts of Hadrian's Wall with excellent views of the Irthing Gorge. Exhibition, shop, tearooms and excavations.

Eden Ostrich World
Langwathby Hall Farm, Langwathby Hall, Langwathby, Penrith, Cumbria CA10 1LW
Tel: (01768) 881771 www.ostrich-world.com
Working farm with ostriches and other rare breed animals. Play areas, riverside walk, tearooms and gift shop. An enjoyable day out for the whole family.

Brantwood, Home of John Ruskin
Coniston, Cumbria LA21 8AD
Tel: (015394) 41396 www.brantwood.org.uk
Superb lake and mountain views. Works by Ruskin and contemporaries, memorabilia, Ruskin watercolours, craft and picture gallery, gardens.

Furness Abbey
Barrow-in-Furness, Cumbria LA13 0TJ
Tel: (01229) 823420
Ruins of 12thC Cistercian abbey, the 2nd wealthiest in England. Extensive remains include transepts, choir and west tower of church, canopied seats, arches, church.

Cars of the Stars Motor Museum
Standish Street, Keswick, Cumbria CA12 5LS
Tel: (017687) 73757 www.carsofthestars.com
Features TV and film vehicles including the Batmobile, Chitty Chitty Bang Bang, the James Bond collection, Herbie, FAB 1, plus many other famous cars and motorcycles.

CUMBRIA

Gleaston Water Mill
Gleaston, Ulverston, Cumbria LA12 0QH
Tel: (01229) 869244 www.watermill.co.uk
Water-driven corn mill in working order. Impressive wooden machinery and water-wheel. Farm equipment and tools display. Craft workshop, craft videos and rare breeds.

Heron Glass
The Lakes Glass Centre, Oubas Hill, Ulverston, Cumbria LA12 7LY
Tel: (01229) 581121
Heron Glass is a combined visitor centre and workshop where you will find traditional glass-making demonstrations daily with a chance of purchasing glassware at the factory shop.

Hill Top
Near Sawrey, Ambleside, Cumbria LA22 0LF
Tel: (015394) 36269 www.nationaltrust.org.uk
Beatrix Potter wrote many of her popular Peter Rabbit stories and other books in this charming little house which still contains her own china and furniture.

Jennings Brothers, The Castle Brewery
Cockermouth, Cumbria CA13 9NE
Tel: (01900) 821011 www.jenningsbrewery.co.uk
Guided tours of Jennings traditional brewery. The brewery uses the finest well water, malt, hops, sugar and yeast to brew distinctive local beers.

K Village Outlet Centre
Lound Road, Netherfield, Kendal, Cumbria LA9 7DA
Tel: (01539) 732363 www.kvillage.co.uk
Famous named brands such as K-shoes, Van Heusen, Denby, National Trust Shop, Tog24 and Ponden Mill, all at discounts. Open 7 days per week with full disabled access.

The Lake District Coast Aquarium
Maryport South Quay, Maryport, Cumbria CA15 8AB
Tel: (01900) 817760
www.lakedistrict-coastaquarium.co.uk
Purpose-built independent aquarium with over 35 displays. Largest collection of native marine species in Cumbria. Cafe and gift shop.

The Lake District Visitor Centre
Brockhole, Windermere, Cumbria LA23 1LJ
Tel: (015394) 46601 www.lake-district.gov.uk
Interactive exhibitions, audio-visual show, shop, gardens, grounds, adventure playground, dry-stone walling area, trails, events and croquet. Cafe with home-cooked food.

Lakeland Motor Museum
Holker Hall, Cark in Cartmel, Grange-over-Sands, Cumbria LA11 7PL
Tel: (015395) 58509 www.holker-hall.co.uk
Over 10,000 exhibits including rare motoring automobilia. A 1930s garage re-creation and the Campbell Legend Bluebird Exhibition.

Lakeland Sheep and Wool Centre
Egremont Road, Cockermouth, Cumbria CA13 0QX
Tel: (01900) 822673 www.shepherdshotel.co.uk
An all-weather attraction with live sheep shows including working-dog demonstrations. Also large screen and other tourism exhibitions on the area, a gift shop and cafe.

Lakeland Wildlife Oasis
Hale Milnthorpe, Cumbria LA7 7BW
Tel: (015395) 63027 www.wildlifeoasis.co.uk
A wildlife exhibition where both living animals and inanimate hands-on displays are used to illustrate evolution in the animal kingdom. Includes gift shop and cafe.

The Pictures:
1 Kirkstile Inn
2 Watendlath Bridge
3 Loughrigg
4 Shoreline, Derwentwater

CUMBRIA

Lowther Parklands
Hackthorpe, Penrith, Cumbria CA10 2HG
Tel: (01931) 712523
Attractions include exotic birds and animals, rides, miniature railway, boating lake, play areas, adventure fort, Tarzan trail, international circus and a puppet theatre.

Muncaster Castle, Gardens, Owl Centre and Meadow Vole Maze
Ravenglass, Cumbria CA18 1RQ
Tel: (01229) 717614 www.muncastercastle.co.uk
Muncaster Castle has the most beautifully situated Owl Centre in the world. See the birds fly, picnic in the gardens, and visit the Pennington family home.

Ravenglass and Eskdale Railway
Ravenglass, Cumbria CA18 1SW
Tel: (01229) 717171 www.ravenglass-railway.co.uk
England's oldest narrow-gauge railway runs for 7 miles through glorious scenery to the foot of England's highest hills. Most trains are steam hauled.

Rheged - The Village in the Hill
Redhills, Penrith, Cumbria CA11 0DQ
Tel: (01768) 868000 www.rheged.com
Cumbria's new visitor attraction with Europe's largest grass-covered building. Discover speciality shops, restaurants, artist exhibitions, pottery demonstrations, children's play area and The National Mountaineering Exhibition.

The Rum Story
27 Lowther Street, Whitehaven, Cumbria CA28 7DN
Tel: (01946) 592933 www.rumstory.co.uk
'The Rum Story' - an authentic, heritage-based experience, depicting the unique story of the UK rum trade in the original Jefferson's wine merchant premises.

Sizergh Castle
Kendal, Cumbria LA8 8AE
Tel: (015395) 60070 www.nationaltrust.org.uk
Strickland family home for 750 years, now National Trust owned. With 14thC pele tower, 15thC great hall, 16thC wings. Stuart connections. Rock garden, rose garden, daffodils.

South Lakes Wild Animal Park Ltd
Crossgates, Dalton-in-Furness, Cumbria LA15 8JR
Tel: (01229) 466086 www.wildanimalpark.co.uk
Wild zoo park in over 17 acres (7 ha) of grounds. Large waterfowl ponds, cafe, toilets, car/coach park, miniature railway. Over 120 species of animals from all around the world.

South Tynedale Railway
Railway Station, Alston, Cumbria CA9 3JB
Tel: (01434) 381696 www.strps.org.uk
Narrow-gauge railway operating along 2.25 mile line from Alston to Kirkhaugh through the scenic South Tyne Valley. Steam- and diesel-hauled passenger trains.

Steam Yacht Gondola
Pier Cottage, Coniston, Cumbria LA21 8AJ
Tel: (015394) 41962
Victorian steam-powered vessel now National Trust owned and completely renovated with an opulently upholstered saloon. Superb way to appreciate the beauty of Coniston Water.

Theatre by the Lake
Lakeside, Keswick, Cumbria CA12 5DJ
Tel: (017687) 74411 www.theatrebythelake.com
Main auditorium of 400 seats, studio of 80. Exhibitions all year round. Cafe and bar.

Tullie House Museum and Art Gallery
Castle Street, Carlisle, Cumbria CA3 8TP
Tel: (01228) 534781 www.historic-carlisle.org.uk
Major tourist complex housing museum, art gallery, education facility, lecture theatre, shops, herb garden, restaurant and terrace bars.

Windermere Lake Cruises
Lakeside Pier, Newby Bridge, Ulverston, Cumbria LA12 8AS
Tel: (015395) 31188
www.windermere-lakecruises.co.uk
Steamers and launches sail between Ambleside, Bowness and Lakeside with connections for the Steam Railway, Brockhole, Ferry House, Fell Foot and the Aquarium of the Lakes.

Windermere Steamboat Museum
Rayrigg Road, Bowness-on-Windermere, Windermere, Cumbria LA23 1BN
Tel: (015394) 45565 www.steamboat.co.uk
A wealth of interest and information about life on bygone Windermere. Regular steam launch trips, vintage vessels and classic motorboats. Model boat pond, lakeside picnic area.

The World Famous Old Blacksmith's Shop Centre
Gretna Green, Gretna DG16 5EA
Tel: (01461) 338441 www.gretnagreen.com
The original Blacksmith's Shop museum and a shopping centre selling cashmere and woollen knitwear, crystal and china. Taste local produce in the Old Smithy Restaurant.

Find out more about Cumbria

Further information about holidays and attractions in Cumbria is available from:

CUMBRIA TOURIST BOARD
Ashleigh, Holly Road, Windermere, Cumbria LA23 2AQ.
Tel: (015394) 44444 Fax: (015394) 44041
Email: mail@cumbria-tourist-board.co.uk
Internet: www.golakes.co.uk

The following publications are available from Cumbria Tourist Board:

Cumbria Tourist Board Holiday Guide (free) Tel: 08705 133059

Events Listings (free)

Cumbria The Lake District Touring Map
including tourist information and touring caravan and camping parks - £3.95

Laminated Poster - £4.50

Getting to Cumbria

BY ROAD: The M1/M6/M25/M40 provide a link with London and the South East and the M5/M6 provide access from the South West. The M62/M6 link Hull and Manchester with the region. Approximate journey time from London is 5 hours, from Manchester 2 hours.

BY RAIL: From London (Euston) to Oxenholme (Kendal) takes approximately 3 hours 30 minutes. From Oxenholme (connecting station for all main line trains) to Windermere takes approximately 20 minutes. From Carlisle to Barrow-in-Furness via the coastal route, with stops at many of the towns in between, takes approximately 2 hours. Trains from Edinburgh to Carlisle take 1 hour 45 minutes. The historic Settle-Carlisle line also runs through the county bringing passengers from Yorkshire via the Eden Valley.

www.travelcumbria.co.uk

The Pictures:
1 Ullswater
2 Buttermere
3 Lake Windermere

CUMBRIA

Where to stay in Cumbria

Parks in this region are listed in alphabetical order of place name, and then in alphabetical order of park.

Map references refer to the colour location maps at the front of this guide. The first number indicates the map to use; the letter and number which follow refer to the grid reference on the map.

At-a-glance symbols can be found inside the bak cover flap. Keep this open for easy reference.

AMBLESIDE, Cumbria Map ref 6A3 *Tourist Information Centre Tel: (015394) 32582*

★★★
HOLIDAY PARK
BH&HPA

GREENHOWE CARAVAN PARK
Great Langdale, Ambleside LA22 9JU
T: (015394) 37231
F: (015394) 37464

OPEN March–November
1.6 hectares (4 acres)
Sloping, stony, sheltered.

46 £150.00–£410.00

From Ambleside take the A593 then the B5343. The site is on the right-hand side. Signposted.

CARLISLE, Cumbria Map ref 6A2 *Tourist Information Centre Tel: (01228) 625600*

★★★★
TOURING &
CAMPING PARK
BH&HPA

DANDY DINMONT CARAVAN AND CAMPING SITE
Blackford, Carlisle CA6 4EA
T: (01228) 674611

OPEN March–October
1.6 hectares (4 acres) Level, grassy, hard.

27 £8.00–£8.25
27 £8.00–£8.25
20 £6.75–£7.25
47 touring pitches
15 units privately owned

Exit the M6 at jct 44. Take A7 north, 1.5 miles. After Blackford sign follow the road directional signs to site. Site is on the right-hand side of the A7. Signposted.

★★★★
HOLIDAY, TOURING
& CAMPING PARK
BH&HPA

ORTON GRANGE CARAVAN PARK
Wigton Road, Carlisle CA5 6LA
T: (01228) 710252
F: (01228) 710252
E: chris@ortongrange.flyer.co.uk

OPEN All year round
CC: Amex, Barclaycard, Delta, Mastercard, Solo, Switch, Visa
2 hectares (5 acres) Level, grassy, sheltered.

30 £8.00–£10.00
30 £8.00–£10.00
20 £8.00–£10.00
4   £99.00–£210.00
50 touring pitches
18 units privately owned

Four miles west of Carlisle on the A595 (south side of the road). Signposted.

CROOK, Cumbria Map ref 6A3

★★★★
HOLIDAY, TOURING
& CAMPING PARK
BH&HPA

RATHERHEATH LANE CAMPING AND CARAVAN PARK
Chain House, Bonningate, Kendal LA8 8JU
T: (01539) 821154 & 0797 163 0226
E: ratherheath@lakedistrictcaravans.co.uk
I: www.lakedistrictcaravans.co.uk

OPEN March–October
.8 hectare (2 acres) Level, sloping, grassy, hard.

10 £7.50–£9.50
10 £5.00–£8.00
12 £6.00–£9.00
4   £145.00–£355.00
20 touring pitches

Leave the M6 at jct 36, 9 miles towards Windermere. From B5274, 1.5 miles, park on right. Signposted.

RATING All accommodation in this guide has been rated, or is awaiting a rating, by a trained Tourist Board assessor.

CUMBRIA

FLOOKBURGH, Cumbria Map ref 6A3

★★★★
HOLIDAY & TOURING PARK

BH&HPA
NCC

Ad p12

LAKELAND LEISURE PARK
Moor Lane, Flookburgh, Grange-over-Sands LA11 7LT
T: (01539) 558556
F: (01539) 558559
E: enquiries@british-holidays.co.uk
I: www.british-holidays.co.uk

OPEN April–October
CC: Delta, Mastercard, Solo, Switch, Visa
42 hectares (105 acres) Level, grassy.

100	£11.00–£32.00
100	£11.00–£32.00
25	£10.00–£20.00
250	£174.00–£668.00

125 touring pitches
531 units privately owned

Leave the M6 at jct 36 and go onto the A590. Turn left onto the A6/A590 for Barrow-in-Furness. Take the B5277 through Grange-over-Sands to Flookburgh. Turn left at the village square. The park is 1 mile down this road.

GRANGE-OVER-SANDS, Cumbria Map ref 6A3 *Tourist Information Centre Tel: (015395) 34026*

★★★★
HOLIDAY & TOURING PARK

BH&HPA

GREAVES FARM CARAVAN PARK
Field Broughton, Grange-over-Sands LA11 6HR
T: (015395) 36329 & 36587

OPEN March–October
1.2 hectares (3 acres) Level, grassy, hard.

3	£9.00–£11.00
3	£9.00–£11.00
5	£8.00–£10.00
2	£190.00–£240.00

8 touring pitches
18 units privately owned

Leave the A590 1 mile south of Newby Bridge, signed Cartmel 4. Proceed 2 miles to 3 bungalows on the left. Approximately 200yds before Field Broughton church. Signposted.

HAWKSHEAD, Cumbria Map ref 6A3

★★★
TOURING & CAMPING PARK

THE CROFT CARAVAN AND CAMP SITE
North Lonsdale Road, Hawkshead, Ambleside LA22 0NX
T: (015394) 36374
F: (015394) 36544
E: enquiries@hawkshead-croft.com
I: www.hawkshead-croft.com

OPEN March–October
CC: Barclaycard, Delta, Eurocard, Mastercard, Solo, Switch, Visa, Visa Electron
2 hectares (5 acres) Level, grassy, sheltered.

15	£11.50–£11.50
	£10.50–£10.50
85	£11.00–£11.00
18	£185.00–£300.00

100 touring pitches

From Ambleside follow B5286, 5 miles to Hawkshead. Signposted.

KENDAL, Cumbria Map ref 6B3 *Tourist Information Centre Tel: (01539) 725758*

★★★★
TOURING & CAMPING PARK

BH&HPA

WATERS EDGE CARAVAN PARK
Crooklands, Kendal LA7 7NN
T: (015395) 67708 & 67527
F: (015395) 67610
E: cromoco@aol.com

OPEN March–November
CC: Barclaycard, Mastercard, Visa
1.2 hectares (3 acres) Level, grassy, hard, sheltered.

30	£11.00–£15.00
30	£11.00–£15.00
5	£5.00–£14.00

35 touring pitches
13 units privately owned

Leave M6 at jct 36. Take A65 to Crooklands. Site about 0.75 miles on the right. Signposted.

PRICES Please check prices and other details at the time of booking

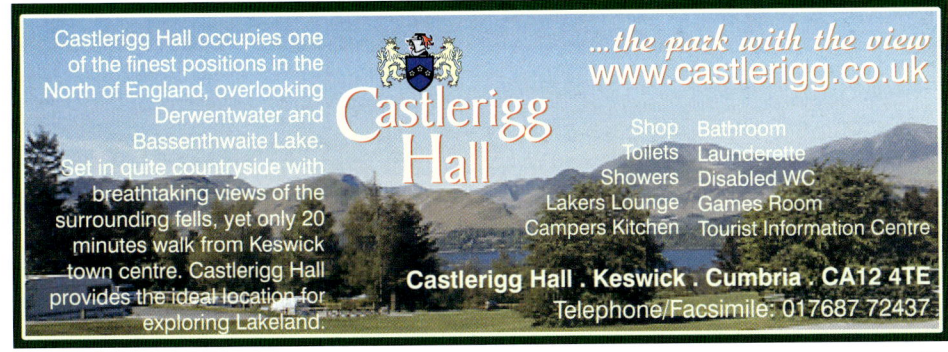

Castlerigg Hall occupies one of the finest positions in the North of England, overlooking Derwentwater and Bassenthwaite Lake. Set in quite countryside with breathtaking views of the surrounding fells, yet only 20 minutes walk from Keswick town centre. Castlerigg Hall provides the ideal location for exploring Lakeland.

...the park with the view
www.castlerigg.co.uk

Shop — Bathroom
Toilets — Launderette
Showers — Disabled WC
Lakers Lounge — Games Room
Campers Kitchen — Tourist Information Centre

Castlerigg Hall . Keswick . Cumbria . CA12 4TE
Telephone/Facsimile: 017687 72437

CUMBRIA

KESWICK, Cumbria Map ref 6A3 *Tourist Information Centre Tel: (017687) 72645*

★★★★
HOLIDAY, TOURING & CAMPING PARK
BH&HPA
Ad p65

CASTLERIGG HALL CARAVAN AND CAMPING PARK
Castlerigg Hall, Keswick CA12 4TE
T: (017687) 72437
F: (017687) 72437
I: www.castlerigg.co.uk

OPEN March–October
CC: JCB, Mastercard, Solo, Switch, Visa
6 hectares (15 acres) Level, sloping, grassy, stony, hard, sheltered.

45	£9.50–£11.50
45	£8.50–£10.00
120	£8.20–£9.60
7	£180.00–£350.00

165 touring pitches
23 units privately owned

About 1.5 miles south east of Keswick off A591, turn right 100yds on the right. Signposted.

★★★★
HOLIDAY & TOURING PARK
BH&HPA

LAKESIDE HOLIDAY PARK
Norman Garner Ltd, Crow Park Road, Keswick CA12 5EW
T: (017687) 72878
F: (017687) 72017
E: welcome@lakesideholidaypark.co.uk
I: www.lakesideholidaypark.co.uk

OPEN March–November
CC: Barclaycard, Delta, JCB, Mastercard, Solo, Switch, Visa, Visa Electron
2.4 hectares (6 acres) Level, grassy, hard, sheltered.

13	£8.00–£16.00
13	£8.00–£16.00
12	£230.00–£460.00

13 touring pitches
20 units privately owned

Leave the M6 at jct 40. Exit A66 at roundabout near Keswick (16 miles). Follow signs for town centre. Follow camping and carvan signs. Signposted.

NEWBY BRIDGE, Cumbria Map ref 6A3

★★★★★
HOLIDAY PARK
BH&HPA

NEWBY BRIDGE CARAVAN PARK
Canny Hill, Newby Bridge, Ulverston LA12 8NF
T: (015395) 31030
F: (015395) 30105
E: newbybridge@hopps.freeserve.co.uk
I: www.cumbriancaravans.co.uk

OPEN March–October
CC: Barclaycard, Eurocard, Mastercard, Visa
10.4 hectares (26 acres) Sloping, hard, sheltered.

7	£14.00–£16.00
7	£14.00–£16.00
7	£140.00–£400.00

7 touring pitches
69 units privately owned

Just before entering Newby Bridge about 2.25 miles beyond High Newton turn left off the A590 signposted Canny Hill. Park entrance 200yds on the right-hand side. Signposted.

PENRITH, Cumbria Map ref 6B2 *Tourist Information Centre Tel: (01768) 867466*

★★★★
TOURING PARK
BH&HPA

FLUSCO WOOD CARAVAN PARK
Flusco, Penrith CA11 0JB
T: (01768) 480020
I: www.fluscowood.co.uk

Large, serviced pitches in beautiful woodland clearings. Centrally heated amenity building. Close to numerous visitor attractions and 1 mile Lake District National Park. Get a friend to stay and get 15% off your 2nd visit. Last year's prices held for 2002.

OPEN March–October & Christmas. Sloping, grassy, hard, sheltered.

Leave M6 at jct 40. Follow A66 west for 3.25 miles. Turn right signed Flusco. Follow road up hill to right, park on the left.

| 47 | £7.50–£9.00 |
| 10 | £7.50–£9.00 |

47 touring pitches

QUALITY ASSURANCE SCHEME

For an explanation of the quality and facilities represented by the Stars please refer to the front of this guide.

CUMBRIA

ST BEES, Cumbria Map ref 6A3

★★★
HOLIDAY, TOURING & CAMPING PARK
BH&HPA

SEACOTE PARK
The Beach, St Bees CA27 0ES
T: (01946) 822777
F: (01946) 824442
E: reception@seacote.com

Beside lovely beach in award-winning historic village on fringe of Lake District. Headland walks, bird sanctuary, golf and indoor pool nearby. Restaurant, bar, entertainment. Tourers, motor caravans and tents-7 nights for the price of 6. Reduction on holiday homes for 2 people or 2 weeks.

OPEN All year round. 9.6 hectares (24 acres) Level, sloping, grassy, hard.
CC: Amex, Barclaycard, Delta, Eurocard, JCB, Maestro, Mastercard, Switch, Visa, Visa Electron

In Whitehaven take B5345 for 4 miles south, follow Beach Road. Signposted.

20		£9.00–£13.00
20		£9.00–£13.00
10		£6.00–£10.00
54		£120.00–£400.00

30 touring pitches
40 units privately owned

SILLOTH, Cumbria Map ref 6A2 Tourist Information Centre Tel: (016973) 31944

★★
HOLIDAY, TOURING & CAMPING PARK
BH&HPA

THE SOLWAY HOLIDAY VILLAGE
Skinburness Drive, Silloth, Carlisle CA7 4QQ
T: (016973) 31236
F: (016973) 32553

OPEN March–October
CC: Barclaycard, Mastercard, Switch, Visa
44 hectares (110 acres) Level, grassy.

60		£7.00–£12.00
60		£7.00–£12.00
60		£7.00–£12.00
76		£120.00–£538.00

60 touring pitches
250 units privately owned

Leave the M6 at jct 41 and make your way to Wigton. Then follow signs to Silloth on the B5302. When you get into Silloth turn right at Raffa Club and follow road for 0.5 miles, holiday park on the right. Signposted.

★★★★★
HOLIDAY, TOURING & CAMPING PARK
BH&HPA
NCC

STANWIX PARK HOLIDAY CENTRE
Greenrow, West Silloth, Silloth, Carlisle CA7 4HH
T: (016973) 32666
F: (016973) 32555
E: stanwix.park@btinternet.com
I: www.stanwix.com

OPEN All year round
CC: Barclaycard, Delta, Eurocard, Mastercard, Solo, Switch, Visa
7.2 hectares (18 acres) Level, grassy, sheltered.

121		£13.60–£16.70
121		£13.60–£16.70
121		£13.60–£16.70
77		£150.00–£485.00

121 touring pitches
135 units privately owned

Leave M6 at jct 44, follow signs to Carlisle, Wigton and Silloth. From south leave M6 at jct 41, follow signs to Wigton and Silloth. Signposted.

ULLSWATER, Cumbria Map ref 6A3

★★★★★
HOLIDAY & TOURING PARK
BH&HPA

WATERFOOT CARAVAN PARK
Pooley Bridge, Penrith CA11 0JF
T: (017684) 86302
F: (01784) 86728
E: lde@netcomuk.co.uk
I: www.ukparks.co.uk/waterfoot

Withing walking distance of Ullswater, a quiet tree-lined site in the grounds of a Georgian mansion, ideal for touring the Lake District. Private boat launching area available. Special discount tickets offered on Ullswater 'Steamers' lake cruises.

OPEN March–October. 8.8 hectares (22 acres) Level, sloping, grassy, hard, sheltered.

Leave the M6 at jct 40, take the A66 west for 1 mile. Follow the A592 for 3.5 miles, site on the right. Signposted.

| 57 | | £9.00–£16.00 |
| 57 | | £9.00–£16.00 |

57 touring pitches
126 units privately owned

CONFIRM YOUR BOOKING
You are advised to confirm your booking in writing.

67

CUMBRIA

WINDERMERE, Cumbria Map ref 6A3 *Tourist Information Centre Tel: (015394) 46499*

★★★★★
**HOLIDAY &
TOURING PARK**

BH&HPA

FALLBARROW PARK
Rayrigg Road, Windermere LA23 3DL
T: (015394) 44422
F: (015394) 88736
I: www.fallbarrow.co.uk

OPEN March–November
CC: Amex, Barclaycard, Delta, Mastercard, Switch, Visa
12.8 hectares (32 acres) Level, grassy, hard.

38		£14.50–£20.50
38		£14.50–£20.50
92		£126.00–£511.00

38 touring pitches
175 units privately owned

From Windermere take the B5284. At Bowness turn right, park on the left. Signposted.

★★★★★
**HOLIDAY, TOURING
& CAMPING PARK**

BH&HPA

LIMEFITT PARK
Windermere LA23 1PA
T: (015394) 32300
I: www.limefitt.co.uk

OPEN March–October
CC: Amex, Barclaycard, Delta, Mastercard, Solo, Switch, Visa
45.2 hectares (113 acres) Level, grassy, hard, sheltered.

110		£9.50–£13.00
110		£9.50–£13.00
55		£9.50–£13.00
9		£169.00–£412.00

165 touring pitches
45 units privately owned

Four miles north of Windermere on the A592 to Ullswater. Signposted.

★★★★★
**HOLIDAY, TOURING
& CAMPING PARK**

BH&HPA

PARK CLIFFE CARAVAN AND CAMPING ESTATE

Birks Road, Windermere LA23 3PG
T: (015395) 31344
F: (015395) 31971
E: info@parkcliffe.co.uk
I: www.parkcliffe.co.uk

A tranquil family park, 600m from Lake Windermere. Mountain-view tourers, lake-view tents. Own pub, heated shower block, with private bathrooms for hire. **Stay 2 nights and get your 3rd night free between 9 Sep–17 Oct.**

OPEN March–November. 10 hectares (25 acres) Level, sloping, grassy, hard, sheltered.
CC: Barclaycard, Delta, Eurocard, Mastercard, Solo, Switch, Visa, Visa Electron

Exit the M6 at jct 36, A590 towards Barrow. At Newby Bridge turn right onto the A592 towards Windermere. After 4 miles turn right into Birks Road, 0.3 miles on the right. Signposted.

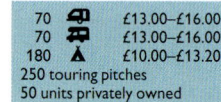

70		£13.00–£16.00
70		£13.00–£16.00
180		£10.00–£13.20

250 touring pitches
50 units privately owned

AT-A-GLANCE SYMBOLS

Symbols at the end of each accommodation entry give useful information about services and facilities. A key to symbols can be found inside the back cover flap. Keep this open for easy reference.

68

CUMBRIA

A brief guide to the main Towns and Villages offering accommodation in Cumbria

A AMBLESIDE, CUMBRIA - Market town situated at the head of Lake Windermere and surrounded by fells. The historic town centre is now a conservation area and the country around Ambleside is rich in historic and literary associations. Good centre for touring, walking and climbing.

C CARLISLE, CUMBRIA - Cumbria's only city is rich in history. Attractions include the small red sandstone cathedral and 900-year-old castle with magnificent view from the keep. Award-winning Tullie House Museum and Art Gallery brings 2,000 years of Border history dramatically to life. Excellent centre for shopping.

- **CROOK, CUMBRIA** - Delightful, unspoilt open farming parish with many attractive and gentle walks giving fine views of the high fells. The village is centred around the local pub and is a good base for touring, having easy access to the motorway link.

F FLOOKBURGH, CUMBRIA - Village, once a market town, renowned for winkle and fluke fishing.

G GRANGE-OVER-SANDS, CUMBRIA - Set on the beautiful Cartmel Peninsula, this tranquil resort, known as Lakeland's Riviera, overlooks Morecambe Bay. Pleasant seafront walks and beautiful gardens. The bay attracts many species of wading birds.

H HAWKSHEAD, CUMBRIA - Lying near Esthwaite Water, this village has great charm and character. Its small squares are linked by flagged or cobbled alleys and the main square is dominated by the market house, or Shambles, where the butchers had their stalls in days gone by.

K KESWICK, CUMBRIA - Beautifully positioned town beside Derwentwater and below the mountains of Skiddaw and Blencathra. Excellent base for walking, climbing, watersports and touring. Motor-launches operate on Derwentwater and motor boats, rowing boats and canoes can be hired.

N NEWBY BRIDGE, CUMBRIA - At the southern end of Windermere on the River Leven, this village has an unusual stone bridge with arches of unequal size. The Lakeside and Haverthwaite Railway has a stop here, and steamer cruises on Lake Windermere leave from nearby Lakeside.

P PENRITH, CUMBRIA - Ancient and historic market town, the northern gateway to the Lake District. Penrith Castle was built as a defence against the Scots. Its ruins, open to the public, stand in the public park. High above the town is the Penrith Beacon, made famous by William Wordsworth.

S SILLOTH, CUMBRIA - Small port and coastal resort on the Solway Firth with wide cobbled roads and an attractive green leading to the promenade and seashore known for its magnificent sunsets.

- **ST BEES, CUMBRIA** - Small seaside village with fine Norman church and a public school founded in the 16th C. Dramatic red sandstone cliffs make up impressive St Bees Head, parts of which are RSPB reserves and home to puffins and black guillemot. Start or finishing point of Wainwright's Coast to Coast Walk.

U ULLSWATER, CUMBRIA - This beautiful lake, which is over 7 miles long, runs from Glenridding to Pooley Bridge. Lofty peaks ranging around the lake make an impressive background. A steamer service operates along the lake between Pooley Bridge, Howtown and Glenridding in the summer.

W WINDERMERE, CUMBRIA - Once a tiny hamlet before the introduction of the railway in 1847, now adjoins Bowness which is on the lakeside. Centre for sailing and boating. A good way to see the lake is a trip on a passenger steamer. Steamboat Museum has a fine collection of old boats.

CHECK THE MAPS

The colour maps at the front of this guide show all the cities, towns and villages for which you will find park entries. Refer to the town index to find the page on which it is listed.

Our Countryside Matters!

Country Code

- Always follow the Country code
- Guard against all risk of fire
- Keep your dogs under close control
- Use gates and stiles to cross fences, hedges and walls
- Take your litter home
- Protect wildlife, plants and trees
- Make no unnecessary noise
- Enjoy the countryside and respect its life and work
- Fasten all gates
- Keep to public paths across farmland
- Leave livestock, crops and machinery alone
- Help to keep all water clean
- Take special care on country roads

We hope the countryside will fully open in 2002. However, given the serious nature of Foot and Mouth Disease please be ready to follow this additional advice and respect any further precautions given in local authority notices:

- Don't go onto farmland if you have handled farm animals in the last 7 days
- Avoid contact with farm animals and keep dogs on a lead where they are present
- If you step in dung, remove it before you leave the field
- Don't go on paths with a local authority 'closed' notice.

For more information contact Tourist information Centres or Countryside Agency web site www.countryside.gov.uk which links to other local authority web sites providing details about rights of way and access opportunities across England.

NORTHUMBRIA

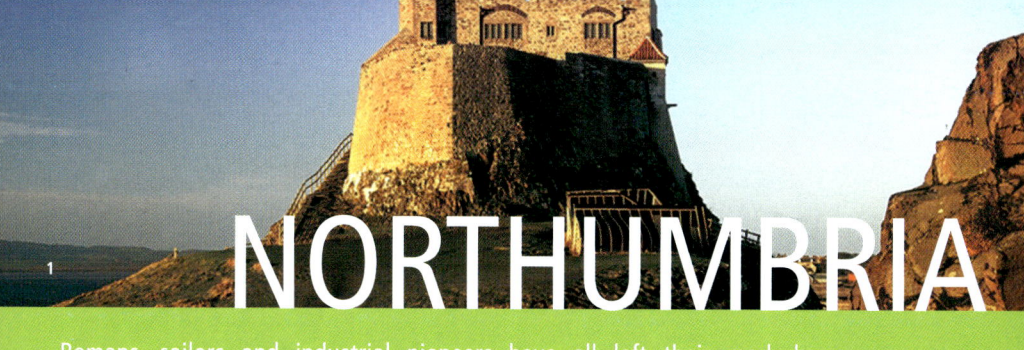

Romans, sailors and industrial pioneers have all left their mark here. Northumbria's exciting cities, castle – studded countryside and white-sanded coastline make it an undiscovered gem.

classic sights
Lindisfarne Castle – on Holy Island
Housesteads Roman Fort – the most impressive Roman fort on Hadrian's Wall

coast & country
Kielder Water and Forest Park – perfect for walking, cycling and watersports
Saltburn – beach of broad sands
Seahouses – picturesque fishing village

maritime history
HMS Trincomalee – magnificent 1817 British warship
Captain Cook – birthplace museum and replica of his ship, Endeavour
Grace Darling – museum commemorating her rescue of shipwreck survivors in 1838

arts for all
Angel of the North – awe-inspiring sculpture by Antony Gormley

distinctively different
St Mary's lighthouse – great views from the top

The counties of County Durham, Northumberland, Tees Valley and Tyne & Wear

FOR MORE INFORMATION CONTACT:
Northumbria Tourist Board
Aykley Heads, Durham DH1 5UX
Tel: (0191) 375 3009 Fax: (0191) 386 0899
Internet: www.visitnorthumbria.com

The Pictures:
1 Lindisfarne Castle, Holy Island
2 Bamburgh, Northumberland
3 Washington Old Hall, Tyne & Wear

Places to Visit - see pages 72-75
Where to Stay - see pages 76-78

PLACES to visit

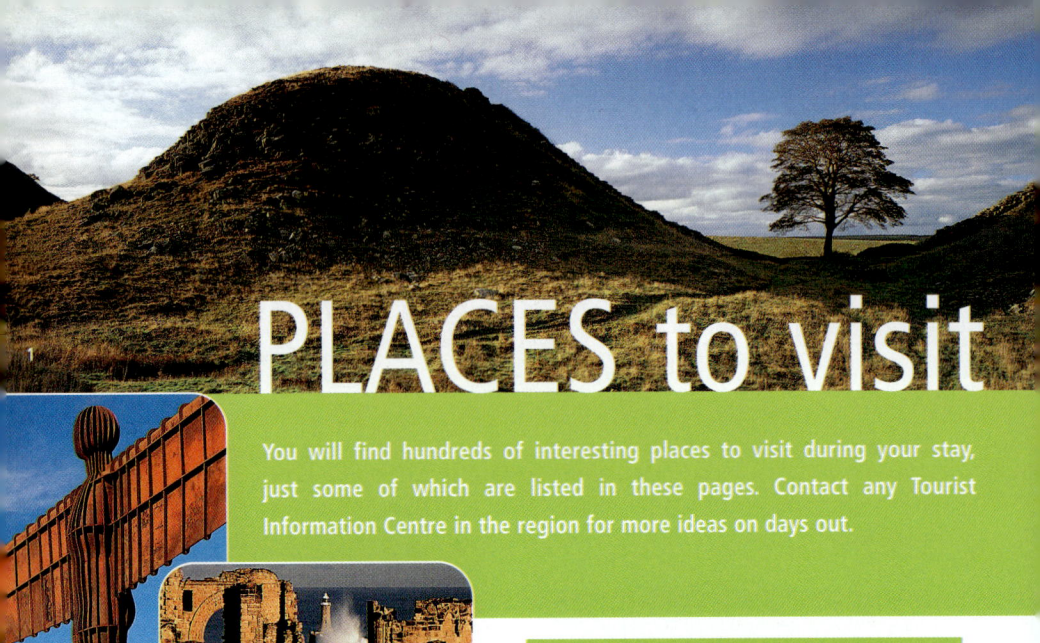

You will find hundreds of interesting places to visit during your stay, just some of which are listed in these pages. Contact any Tourist Information Centre in the region for more ideas on days out.

Alnwick Castle
The Estate Office, Alnwick, Northumberland NE66 1NQ
Tel: (01665) 510777 www.alnwickcastle.com
Largest inhabited castle in England, after Windsor Castle, and home of the Percys, Dukes of Northumberland since 1309.

ARC
Dovecot Street, Stockton-on-Tees, Stockton TS18 1LL
Tel: (01642) 666600 www.arconline.co.uk
Arts venue which aims to provide the region with an extensive and innovative programme. Two theatres, a dance studio, recording studio and rehearsal rooms.

Bamburgh Castle
Bamburgh, Northumberland NE69 7DF
Tel: (01668) 214515 www.bamburghcastle.com
Magnificent coastal castle completely restored in 1900. Collections of china, porcelain, furniture, paintings, arms and armour.

Bede's World
Church Bank, Jarrow, Tyne & Wear NE32 3DY
Tel: (0191) 489 2106 www.bedesworld.co.uk
Discover the exciting world of the Venerable Bede, early medieval Europe's greatest scholar. Church, monastic site, museum with exhibitions and recreated Anglo-Saxon farm.

Bowes Museum
Barnard Castle, Durham DL12 8NP
Tel: (01833) 690606 www.bowesmuseum.org.uk
French-style chateau housing art collections of national importance and archaeology of south west Durham.

Captain Cook Birthplace Museum
Stewart Park, Marton, Middlesbrough, Cleveland TS7 6AS
Tel: (01642) 311211
Early life and voyages of Captain Cook and the countries he visited. Temporary exhibitions. One person free with every group of 10 visiting.

Chesters Roman Fort (Cilurnum)
Chollerford, Hadrian's Wall, Humshaugh, Hexham, Northumberland NE46 4EP
Tel: (01434) 681379
Fort built for 500 cavalrymen. Remains include 5 gateways, barrack blocks, commandant's house and headquarters. Finest military bath house in Britain.

Cragside House, Gardens and Estate
Cragside, Rothbury, Morpeth, Northumberland NE65 7PX
Tel: (01669) 620333 www.nationaltrust.org.uk
House built 1864-84 for the first Lord Armstrong, a Tyneside industrialist. Cragside was the first house to be lit by electricity generated by water power.

Discovery Museum
Blandford House, Blandford Square, Newcastle upon Tyne, Tyne & Wear NE1 4JA
Tel: (0191) 232 6789
The Museum is currently undergoing a £10.7 million redevelopment. Visit the Science Maze, Fashion Works, Live Wires, Maritime Gallery, A Soldier's Life Gallery and The Newcastle Story (the new John George Jolcey Museum).

NORTHUMBRIA

Durham Castle
Palace Green, Durham DH1 3RW
Tel: (0191) 374 3863 www.durhamcastle.com
Castle founded in 1072, Norman chapel dating from 1080, kitchens and great hall dated 1499 and 1284 respectively. Fine example of motte-and-bailey castle.

Durham Cathedral
The Chapter Office, The College, Durham DH1 3EH
Tel: (0191) 386 4266 www.durhamcathedral.co.uk
Durham Cathedral is thought by many to be the finest example of Norman church architecture in England. Visit the tombs of St Cuthbert and The Venerable Bede.

Gisborough Priory
Church Street, Guisborough, Redcar & Cleveland TS14 6HG
Tel: (01287) 633801
Remains of a priory founded by Robert de Brus in AD1119. A priory for Augustinian canons in the grounds of Guisborough Hall. Main arch and window of east wall virtually intact.

Hall Hill Farm
Lanchester, Durham DH7 0TA
Tel: (01388) 730300 www.hallhillfarm.co.uk
Family fun set in attractive countryside with an opportunity to see and touch the animals at close quarters. Farm trailer ride, riverside walk, teashop and play area.

Hartlepool Historic Quay
Maritime Avenue, Hartlepool, Cleveland TS24 0XZ
Tel: (01429) 860006 www.thisishartlepool.com
Hartlepool Historic Quay is an exciting reconstruction of a seaport of the 1800s with buildings and lively quayside, authentically reconstructed.

Housesteads Roman Fort (Vercovicum)
Hadrian's Wall, Haydon Bridge, Hexham, Northumberland NE47 6NN
Tel: (01434) 344363
Best preserved and most impressive of the Roman forts. Vercovicium was a 5-acre fort for an extensive 800 civil settlement. Only example of a Roman hospital.

Killhope, The North of England Lead Mining Museum
Cowshill, Weardale, St John's Chapel, Bishop Auckland, County Durham DL13 1AR
Tel: (01388) 537505 www.durham.gov.uk/killhope
Most complete lead mining site in Great Britain. Mine tours available, 10m (34ft) diameter water-wheel, reconstruction of Victorian machinery, miners lodging and woodland walks.

Kirkleatham Old Hall Museum
Kirkleatham, Redcar, Redcar & Cleveland TS10 5NW
Tel: (01642) 479500
Displays depicting local life, industry, commerce, local history, sea rescue, artists, social and natural history and the story of Kirkleatham.

Laing Art Gallery
New Bridge Street, Newcastle upon Tyne, Tyne & Wear NE1 8AJ
Tel: (0191) 232 7734
Paintings, including watercolours by Northumbrian-born artist John Martin. Award-winning interactive displays 'Art on Tyneside' and 'Children's Gallery'. Cafe and shop.

Life Interactive World
Times Square, Scotswood Road, Newcastle upon Tyne, Tyne & Wear NE1 4EP
Tel: (0191) 243 8210 www.lifeinteractiveworld.co.uk
Life Interactive World is an amazing action-packed journey. Experience the longest motion ride in the world, magical 3D, theatre shows, virtual games and interactives.

The Pictures:
1 Hadrian's Wall
2 The Angel of the North, Gateshead
3 Tynemouth Priory and Castle, Tyne & Wear
4 Dunstanburgh, Northumberland
5 Boulby Cliff, Cleveland
6 Kielder Water, Northumberland

NORTHUMBRIA

National Glass Centre
Liberty Way, Sunderland, Tyne & Wear SR6 0GL
Tel: (0191) 515 5555 www.nationalglasscentre.com
A large gallery presenting the best in contemporary and historical glass. Master craftspeople will demonstrate glass-making techniques. Classes and workshops available.

Nature's World at the Botanic Centre
Nature's World at the Botanic Centre
Ladgate Lane, Acklam, Middlesbrough,
Tees Valley TS5 7YN
Tel: (01642) 594895 www.naturesworld.org.uk
Demonstration gardens, wildlife pond, white garden, environmental exhibition hall, shop, tearooms and River Tees model now open. Hydroponicum and visitor exhibition centre.

Newcastle Cathedral Church of St Nicholas
St Nicholas Street, Newcastle upon Tyne,
Tyne & Wear NE1 1PF
Tel: (0191) 232 1939
www.newcastle-ang-cathedral-stnicholas.org.uk
13thC and 14thC church, added to in 18thC-20thC. Famous lantern tower, pre-reformation font and font cover, 15thC stained glass roundel in the side chapel.

The North of England Open Air Museum
Beamish, County Durham DH9 0RG
Tel: (0191) 370 4000 www.beamish.org.uk
Visit the town, colliery village, working farm, Pockerley Manor and 1825 railway, recreating life in the North East in the early 1800s and 1900s.

Ormesby Hall
Church Lane, Ormesby, Middlesbrough TS7 9AS
Tel: (01642) 324188 www.nationaltrust.org.uk
Georgian, 18thC mansion. Impressive contemporary plasterwork. Magnificent stable block attributed to Carr of York. Model railway exhibition and layout.

Raby Castle
PO Box 50, Staindrop, Darlington, County Durham DL2 3AH
Tel: (01833) 660202 www.rabycastle.com
The medieval castle, home of Lord Barnard's family since 1626, includes a 200-acre deer park, walled gardens, carriage collection, adventure playground, shop and tearooms.

Sea Life Aquarium
Grand Parade, Tynemouth, Tyne & Wear NE30 4JF
Tel: (0191) 257 6100
More than 30 hi-tech displays provide encounters with dozens of sea creatures. Journey beneath the North Sea and discover thousands of amazing creatures.

South Shields Museum and Art Gallery
Ocean Road, South Shields, Tyne & Wear NE33 2JA
Tel: (0191) 456 8740
Discover how the area's development has been influenced by its natural and industrial past through lively hands-on displays. Exciting programme of temporary exhibitions.

Thomas Bewick Birthplace Museum
Cherryburn, Station Bank, Mickley, Stocksfield,
Northumberland NE43 7DB
Tel: (01661) 843276
Birthplace cottage (1700) and farmyard. Printing house using original printing blocks. Introductory exhibition of the life, work and countryside.

Vindolanda (Chesterholm)
Chesterholm Museum, Hadrian's Wall, Bardon Mill,
Hexham, Northumberland NE47 7JN
Tel: (01434) 344277 www.vindolanda.com
Visitors may inspect the remains of the Roman fort and settlement, and see its extraordinary finds in the superb museum. Full-scale replicas of Roman buildings.

Washington Old Hall
The Avenue, District 4, Washington, Tyne & Wear NE38 7LE
Tel: (0191) 416 6879
From 1183 to 1399 the home of George Washington's direct ancestors, remaining in the family until 1613. The manor, from which the family took its name, was restored in 1936.

Wet 'N Wild
Rotary Way, Royal Quays, North Shields,
Tyne & Wear NE29 6DA
Tel: (0191) 296 1333 www.wetnwild.co.uk
Tropical indoor water park. A fun water playground providing the wildest and wettest indoor rapid experience. Whirlpools, slides and meandering lazy river.

Wildfowl and Wetlands Trust
Washington, District 15, Washington, Tyne & Wear NE38 8LE
Tel: (0191) 416 5454 www.wwt.org.uk
Collection of 1,000 wildfowl of 85 varieties. Viewing gallery, picnic areas, hides and winter wild bird-feeding station, flamingos and wild grey heron. Food available.

NORTHUMBRIA

Find out more about Northumbria

Dunstanburgh Castle

Further information about holidays and attractions in Northumbria is available from:

NORTHUMBRIA TOURIST BOARD
Aykley Heads, Durham DH1 5UX.
Tel: (0191) 375 3009 Fax: (0191) 386 0899
Internet: www.visitnorthumbria.com

The following publications are available from Northumbria Tourist Board unless otherwise stated:

Northumbria 2002
information on the region, including hotels, bed and breakfast and self-catering accommodation, caravan and camping parks, attractions, shopping, eating and drinking

Going Places
information on where to go, what to see and what to do. Combined with the award-winning Powerpass promotion which offers 2-for-1 entry into many of the region's top attractions

Group Travel Directory
guide designed specifically for group organisers, detailing group accommodation providers, places to visit, suggested itineraries, coaching information and events

Educational Visits
information to help plan educational visits within the region. Uncover a wide variety of places

to visit with unique learning opportunities

Discover Northumbria on two wheels
information on cycling in the region including an order form allowing the reader to order maps/leaflets from a central ordering point

Freedom
caravan and camping guide to the North of England. Available from Freedom Holidays,
tel: 01202 252179

Getting to Northumbria

BY ROAD: The north/south routes on the A1 and A19 thread the region as does the A68. East/west routes like the A66 and A69 easily link with the western side of the country. Within Northumbria you will find fast, modern interconnecting roads between all the main centres, a vast network of scenic, traffic-free country roads to make motoring a pleasure and frequent local bus services operating to all towns and villages.

BY RAIL: London to Edinburgh InterCity service stops at Darlington, Durham, Newcastle and Berwick upon Tweed. 26 trains daily make the journey between London and Newcastle in just under 3 hours. The London to Middlesbrough journey takes 3 hours. Birmingham to Darlington 3 hours 15 minutes. Bristol to Durham 5 hours and Sheffield to Newcastle just over 2 hours. Direct services operate to Newcastle from Liverpool, Manchester, Glasgow, Stranraer and Carlisle. Regional services to areas of scenic beauty operate frequently, allowing the traveller easy access. The Tyne & Wear Metro makes it possible to travel to many destinations within the Tyneside area, such as Gateshead, South Shields, Whitley Bay and Newcastle International Airport, in minutes.

NORTHUMBRIA

Where to stay in Northumbria

Parks in this region are listed in alphabetical order of place name, and then in alphabetical order of park.

Map references refer to the colour location maps at front of this guide. The first number indicates the map to use; the letter and number which follow refer to the grid reference on the map.

At-a-glance symbols can be found inside the back cover flap. Keep this open for easy reference.

BAMBURGH, Northumberland Map ref 6C1

★★★
HOLIDAY, TOURING & CAMPING PARK

GLORORUM CARAVAN PARK
Glororum, Bamburgh NE69 7AW
T: (01668) 214457 & 214205
F: (01668) 214622
E: info@glororum-caravanpark.co.uk
I: www.glororum-caravanpark.co.uk

OPEN April–October
8 hectares (20 acres) Level, grassy, sheltered.

100		£8.00–£10.00
100		£8.00–£10.00
100		£8.00–£10.00

100 touring pitches
150 units privately owned

From the A1 take the B1341 at Adderstone Garage.

★★★★
HOLIDAY, TOURING & CAMPING PARK

BH&HPA

WAREN CARAVAN PARK
Waren Mill, Bamburgh NE70 7EE
T: (01668) 214366
F: (01668) 214224
E: waren@meadowhead.com
I: www.meadowhead.co.uk/waren

OPEN March–October
CC: Barclaycard, Delta, Maestro, Mastercard, Switch, Visa
40 hectares (100 acres) Level, sloping, grassy, sheltered.

130		£8.50–£14.20
130		£8.50–£14.20
50		£8.50–£14.20
27		£199.00–£445.00

180 touring pitches
250 units privately owned

Follow B1342 from A1 to Waren Mill towards Bamburgh. By Budle Bay turn right, follow Waren Caravan Park signs.

BARDON MILL, Northumberland Map ref 6B2

★★
CAMPING PARK

WINSHIELDS CAMP SITE
Winshields, Bardon Mill, Hexham
NE47 7AN
T: (01434) 344243

OPEN April–October
.4 hectare (1 acre).

| 30 | | £7.50–£8.50 |

30 touring pitches

Take A69 to Bardon Mill. Turn off for Hadrian's Wall at Once Brewed Youth Hostel. Turn left on B6318, 0.5 miles. Signposted.

BEADNELL, Northumberland Map ref 6C1

★★★★
HOLIDAY, TOURING & CAMPING PARK

BH&HPA

BEADNELL LINKS CARAVAN PARK
Beadnell Harbour, Beadnell NE67 5BN
T: (01665) 720526 & 07890 692533
E: b.links@talk21.com
I: www.caravanningnorthumberland

OPEN April–October
4 hectares (10 acres) Level, grassy.

| 17 | | £10.00–£16.50 |
| 17 | | £10.00–£16.50 |

17 touring pitches
138 units privately owned

Follow roads B6347 or B1342 from A1. Signed thereafter.

76

NORTHUMBRIA

BEAL, Northumberland Map ref 6B1

★★★★
HOLIDAY, TOURING & CAMPING PARK

BH&HPA
NCC

Ad p12

HAGGERSTON CASTLE
Beal, Berwick-upon-Tweed TD15 2PA
T: (01289) 381333 & 381481
F: (01289) 381337
E: enquiries@british-holidays.co.uk
I: www.british-holidays.co.uk

OPEN March–November
CC: Delta, Mastercard, Solo, Switch, Visa

156	£16.70–£26.25
156	£16.00–£25.00
280	£174.00–£683.00

156 touring pitches
688 units privately owned

The park is signposted from the A1, 7 miles south of Berwick-upon-Tweed. Situated just off the A1 between Edinburgh and Newcastle.

BELFORD, Northumberland Map ref 6B1

★★★★★
TOURING & CAMPING PARK

BH&HPA
NCC

SOUTH MEADOWS CARAVAN PARK
South Meadows, Belford NE70 7DP
T: (01668) 213326
F: (01668) 213790
E: G.McL@btinternet.com
I: www.southmeadows.co.uk

OPEN March–November
CC: Amex, Barclaycard, Delta, Eurocard, Mastercard, Visa
16 hectares (40 acres) Level, grassy, sheltered.

77	£8.80–£11.00
77	£8.80–£11.00
77	£8.80–£11.00

77 touring pitches

Turn off A1 at jct to B1342 to Belford. Proceed down the straight road until you see the sign to Newlands. Turn left and 1st right to caravan park.

BERWICK-UPON-TWEED, Northumberland Map ref 6B1 Tourist Information Centre Tel: (01289) 330733

★★★
TOURING & CAMPING PARK

BEACHCOMBER CAMPSITE
Goswick, Berwick-upon-Tweed TD15 2RW
T: (01289) 381217 & 07773 726634

OPEN March–September
1.6 hectares (4 acres) Level, grassy.

5	£8.00–£10.00
5	£8.00–£10.00
45	£8.00–£10.00

50 touring pitches

Three miles south of Berwick-upon-Tweed on A1. Take minor road signposted Goswick and Cheswick. Signposted.

★★★★
HOLIDAY PARK

BH&HPA
NCC

Ad p12

BERWICK HOLIDAY CENTRE
Magdalene Fields, Berwick-upon-Tweed TD15 1NE
T: (01289) 307113
F: (01289) 306276
E: enquiries@british-holidays.co.uk
I: www.british-holidays.co.uk

OPEN April–October
CC: Delta, Mastercard, Solo, Switch, Visa
20 hectares (50 acres) Level, grassy, hard.

| 223 | £99.00–£600.00 |

534 units privately owned

From A1 north, exit off the 1st roundabout for Safeway and town centre. Straight forward to town for 0.5 miles. Over railway bridge, turn left, holiday centre at end of road. Same directions from south once at Safeway. Signposted.

★★
TOURING & CAMPING PARK

SALUTATION CARAVAN PARK

Salutation Inn, Shoreswood (A698), Berwick-upon-Tweed TD15 2NL
T: (01289) 382291

Midway between Berwick and Coldstream, 1.5 miles from River Tweed. Peaceful, flat grass park. Traditional pub on site serving food 7 days a week.

OPEN March–November. Level, grassy, hard, sheltered.
CC: Barclaycard, Delta, Eurocard, Maestro, Mastercard, Solo, Switch, Visa

15	£8.00–£12.00
15	£8.00–£12.00
15	£5.00–£8.00

15 touring pitches

From A1 exit westbound onto A698 towards Cornhill. Salutation is about 6 miles on the right.

IDEAS For ideas on places to visit refer to the introduction at the beginning of this section.

77

NORTHUMBRIA

CASTLESIDE, Durham Map ref 6B2

★★★★
HOLIDAY, TOURING & CAMPING PARK
BH&HPA

MANOR PARK CARAVAN PARK (MANOR PARK LTD)
Broadmeadows, Rippon Burn, Castleside, Consett DH8 9HD
T: (01207) 501000
F: (01207) 509271

OPEN April–October
2.8 hectares (7 acres)
Sloping, grassy, sheltered.

30	£5.50–£7.00
7	£5.50–£7.00
5	£5.50–£7.00
30 touring pitches

Just off A68, 2.5 miles south of Castleside and 5 miles north of Tow Law, signposted Broadmeadows. Signposted.

GREENHEAD, Northumberland Map ref 6B2

★★★
TOURING & CAMPING PARK

ROAM-N-REST CARAVAN PARK
Raylton House, Greenhead CA8 7HA
T: (016977) 47213

OPEN March–October
.4 hectare (1 acre) Level, grassy, sheltered.

15	£8.50–£9.00
15	£8.50–£9.00
15	£8.50–£9.00
15 touring pitches

Leave the A69 at Greenhead jct and follow the short link road, turn direct left up the hill. After 250m the park is on the right-hand side. Signposted.

HARTLEPOOL, Tees Valley Map ref 6C2 Tourist Information Centre Tel: (01429) 869706

★★
HOLIDAY & TOURING PARK
BH&HPA

ASH VALE HOMES & HOLIDAY PARK
Easington Road, Hartlepool TS24 9RF
T: (01429) 862111
E: ashvale@compuserve.com
I: www.ashvalepark.demon.co.uk

OPEN March–October
8 hectares (20 acres) Level, sloping, grassy.

20	£10.00–£10.00
20	£10.00–£10.00
20	£10.00–£10.00
21	£100.00–£230.00
20 touring pitches
27 units privately owned

From A19 take A179 at 3rd roundabout. Turn left onto A1086 towards Blackhall. Continue through next roundabout and the park is 300yds on left.

KIELDER FOREST

See under Stonehaugh

SEAHOUSES, Northumberland Map ref 6C1

★★★★
HOLIDAY, TOURING & CAMPING PARK
BH&HPA

SEAFIELD CARAVAN PARK
Seafield Road, Seahouses NE68 7SP
T: (01665) 720628
F: (01665) 720088
E: info@seafieldpark.co.uk
I: www.seafieldpark.co.uk

Luxurious holiday homes for hire on Northumberland's premier park. Fully-appointed caravans offering very best of self-catering accommodation. Superior touring facilities including fully serviced pitches. Seasonal discounts available on 3,4,7 day breaks.
OPEN March–December. 8 hectares (20 acres) Level, grassy.
CC: Barclaycard, Delta, Eurocard, JCB, Mastercard, Solo, Switch, Visa, Visa Electron

26	£10.00–£20.00
26	£10.00–£20.00
10	£165.00–£470.00
26 touring pitches
198 units privately owned

Take the B1340 from Alnwick for 14 miles. East to coast. Signposted.

STONEHAUGH, Northumberland Map ref 6B2

Rating Applied For

STONEHAUGH CAMPSITE
Stonehaugh, Hexham NE48 3DZ
T: (01434) 230798
E: carole@stonehaugh.fsbusiness.co.uk
I: www.stonehaugh.fsbusiness.co.uk

OPEN April–October
2.4 hectares (6 acres) Level, grassy.

15	£8.00–£11.00
15	£5.00–£10.00
15	£5.00–£10.00
15 touring pitches

Take A607A from Hexham and follow road to Chollerford. Go over bridge and straight over roundabout. Follow B6320 for Wark and turn off left following signs for Stonehaugh. Signposted.

78

NORTHUMBRIA

A brief guide to the main Towns and Villages offering accommodation in Northumbria

BAMBURGH, NORTHUMBERLAND - Village with a spectacular red sandstone castle standing 150 ft above the sea. On the village green the magnificent Norman church stands opposite a museum containing mementoes of the heroine Grace Darling.

BARDON MILL, NORTHUMBERLAND - Small hamlet midway between Haydon Bridge and Haltwhistle, within walking distance of Vindolanda, an excavated Roman settlement, and near the best stretches of Hadrian's Wall.

BEADNELL, NORTHUMBERLAND - Charming fishing village on Beadnell Bay. Seashore lime kilns (National Trust), dating from the 18th C, recall busier days as a coal and lime port and a pub is built on to a medieval pele tower which survives from days of the border wars.

BEAL, NORTHUMBERLAND - Tiny hamlet with an inn at the junction of the A1 which leads on to the causeway to Holy Island. Some farmhouses and buildings are dated 1674.

BELFORD, NORTHUMBERLAND - Small market town on the old coaching road, close to the coast, the Scottish border and the north-east flank of the Cheviots. Built mostly in stone and very peaceful now that the A1 has by-passed the town, Belford makes an ideal centre for excursions to the moors and coast.

BERWICK-UPON-TWEED, NORTHUMBERLAND - Guarding the mouth of the Tweed, England's northernmost town with the best 16th C city walls in Europe. The handsome Guildhall and barracks date from the 18th C. Three bridges cross to Tweedmouth, the oldest built in 1634.

CASTLESIDE, DURHAM - Village on the edge of the North Pennines on the A68, one of the main routes from England to Scotland.

GREENHEAD, NORTHUMBERLAND - Small hamlet, overlooked by the ruins of Thirlwall Castle, at the junction of the A69 and the B6318 which runs alongside Hadrian's Wall. Some of the finest sections of the wall and the Carvoran Roman Military Museum are nearby.

HARTLEPOOL, TEES VALLEY - Major industrial port north of Tees Bay. Occupying an ancient site, the town's buildings are predominantly modern. Local history can be followed in the Museum of Hartlepool and adjacent historic quay and there is a marina with restored ships.

SEAHOUSES, NORTHUMBERLAND - Small modern resort developed around a 19th C herring port. Just offshore, and reached by boat from here, are the rocky Farne Islands (National Trust) where there is an important bird reserve.

USE YOUR *i*s

There are more than 550 Tourist Information Centres throughout England offering friendly help with accommodation and holiday ideas as well as suggestions of places to visit and things to do. There may well be a centre in your home town which can help you before you set out. You'll find addresses in the local Phone Book.

Where to Stay 2002

The official and best selling guides, offering the reassurance of quality assured accommodation

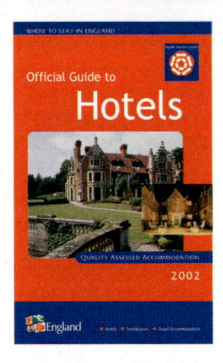

Hotels, Townhouses and Travel Accommodation in England 2002
£10.99

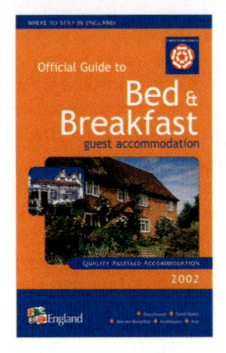

Guesthouses, Bed & Breakfast, Farmhouses and Inns in England 2002
£11.99

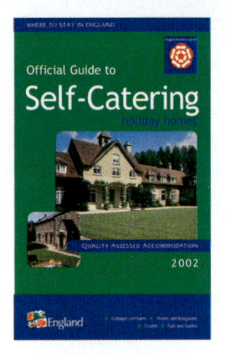

Self Catering Holiday Homes in England 2002
£9.99

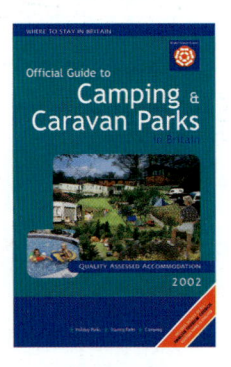

Camping & Caravan Parks in Britain 2002
£5.99

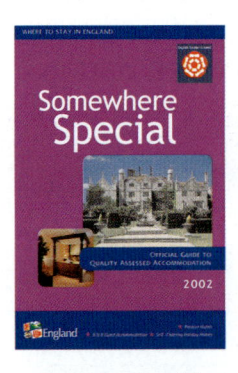

Somewhere Special in England 2002
£7.99

Look out also for: SOMEWHERE SPECIAL IN ENGLAND 2002

Accommodation achieving the highest standards in facilities and quality of service -

the perfect guide for the discerning traveller.

NOW ALSO FEATURING SELF CATERING ACCOMMODATION

The guides include

- Accommodation entries packed with information • Full colour maps
- Places to visit • Tourist Information Centres

INFORMATIVE • EASY TO USE • GREAT VALUE FOR MONEY

From all good bookshops or by mail order from the ETC Fulfilment Centre,
PO Box 22489, London W6 9FR
Tel: 0870 606 7204 Fax: 020 8563 3048
Email: fulfilment@englishtourism.org.uk   Web: www.englishtourism.org.uk

NORTH WEST

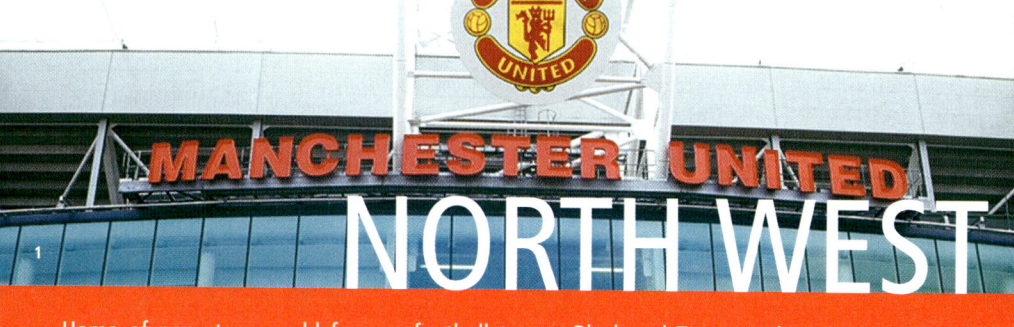

Home of pop stars, world famous football teams, Blackpool Tower and Coronation Street, the great North West has vibrant cities, idyllic countryside and world class art collections too.

classic sights
Blackpool Tower & Pleasure Beach – unashamed razzamatazz
Football – museums and tours at Manchester United and Liverpool football clubs
The Beatles – The Beatles Story, Magical Mystery Tour Bus and Macca's former home

coast & country
The Ribble Valley – unchanged rolling landscapes
Formby – a glorious beach of sand dunes and pine woods
Wildfowl & Wetlands Trust, near Ormskirk – 120 types of birds including flamingoes

arts for all
The Tate Liverpool – modern art
The Lowry – the world's largest collection of LS Lowry paintings

distinctively different
Granada Studios – tour the home of many TV classics

The counties of Cheshire, Greater Manchester, Lancashire, Merseyside and the High Peak District of Derbyshire

FOR MORE INFORMATION CONTACT:

North West Tourist Board
Swan House, Swan Meadow Road,
Wigan Pier, Wigan WN3 5BB
Tel: (01942) 821222 Fax: (01942) 820002
Internet: www.visitnorthwest.com

The Pictures:
1 Manchester United Football Club
2 Healey Dell, Rochdale
3 Blackpool Beach

Places to Visit - see pages 82-85
Where to Stay - see pages 86-87

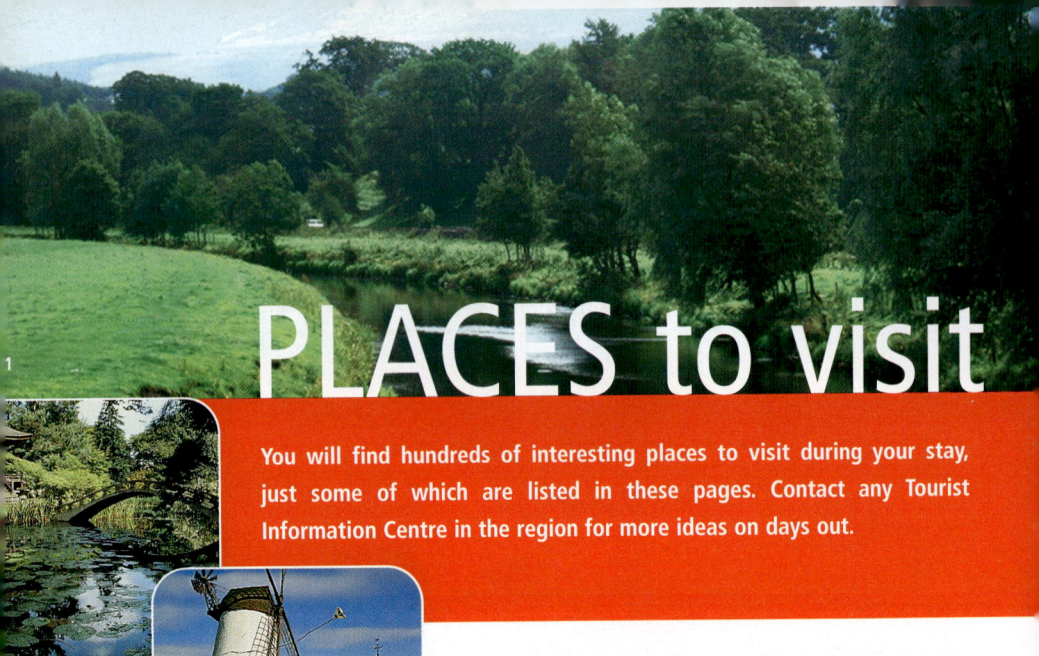

PLACES to visit

You will find hundreds of interesting places to visit during your stay, just some of which are listed in these pages. Contact any Tourist Information Centre in the region for more ideas on days out.

The Albert Dock Company Limited
Suite 22, Edward Pavilion, Albert Dock, Liverpool, Merseyside L3 4AF
Tel: (0151) 708 7334 www.albertdock.com
Britain's largest Grade I Listed historic building. Restored four-sided dock including shops, bars, restaurants, entertainment, marina and the Maritime Museum.

The Beatles Story
Britannia Vaults, Albert Dock, Liverpool, Merseyside L3 4AA
Tel: (0151) 709 1963
Liverpool's award-winning visitor attraction with a replica of the original Cavern Club. Available for private parties.

Beeston Castle
Beeston, Tarporley, Cheshire CW6 9TX
Tel: (01829) 260464
A ruined 13thC castle situated on top of the Peckforton Hills, with views of the surrounding countryside. Exhibitions are also held featuring the castle's history.

Blackpool Pleasure Beach
525 Ocean Boulevard, South Shore, Blackpool, Lancashire FY4 1EZ
(0870) 444 5577
www.blackpoolpleasurebeach.co.uk
Europe's greatest show and amusement park. Blackpool Pleasure Beach offers over 145 rides and attractions, plus spectacular shows.

Blackpool Sea Life Centre
The Promenade, Blackpool, Lancashire FY1 5AA
Tel: (01253) 622445
Tropical sharks up to 8 ft (2.5 m) housed in a 100,000-gallon (454,609-litre) water display with an underwater walkway. The new 'Lost City of Atlantis' is back with the feature exhibition.

Blackpool Tower
The Promenade, Blackpool, Lancashire FY1 4BJ
Tel: (01253) 622242 www.blackpoollive.com
Inside Blackpool Tower you will find the Tower Ballroom, a circus, entertainment for the children, the Tower Top Ride and Undersea World.

Boat Museum
South Pier Road, Ellesmere Port, Cheshire CH5 4FW
Tel: (0151) 355 5017
Over 50 historic crafts, largest floating collection in the world with restored buildings, traditional cottages, workshops, steam engines, boat trips, shop and cafe.

NORTH WEST

Bridgemere Garden World
Bridgemere, Nantwich, Cheshire CW5 7QB
Tel: (01270) 520381
Bridgemere Garden World, 25 fascinating acres (10 ha) of plants, gardens, greenhouses and shop. Coffee shop, restaurant and over 20 different display gardens in the Garden Kingdom.

Camelot Theme Park
Park Hall Road, Charnock Richard, Chorley, Lancashire PR7 5LP
Tel: (01257) 453044 www.camelotthemepark.co.uk
The magical kingdom of Camelot is a world of thrilling rides, fantastic entertainment and family fun, with over 100 rides and attractions to enjoy.

CATALYST: The Museum of Chemical Industry
Gossage Building, Mersey Road, Widnes, Cheshire WA8 0DF
Tel: (0151) 420 1121
Catalyst is the award-winning family day out where science and technology come alive.

Chester Zoo
Upton-by-Chester, Chester, Cheshire CH2 1LH
Tel: (01244) 380280 www.demon.co.uk/chesterzoo
Chester Zoo is one of Europe's leading conservation zoos, with over 5,000 animals in spacious and natural enclosures. Now featuring the new 'Twilight Zone'.

Dunham Massey Hall Park and Garden
Altrincham, Cheshire WA14 4SJ
Tel: (0161) 941 1025 www.thenationaltrust.org.uk
An 18thC mansion in a 250-acre (100ha) wooded deer park with furniture, paintings and silver. A 25-acre (10ha) informal garden with mature trees and waterside plantings.

East Lancashire Railway
Bolton Street Station, Bury, Greater Manchester BL9 0EY
Tel: (0161) 764 7790 www.east-lancs-rly.co.uk
Eight miles of preserved railway, operated principally by steam. Traction Transport Museum close by.

Gawsworth Hall
Gawsworth, Macclesfield, Cheshire SK11 9RN
Tel: (01260) 223456 www.gawsworthhall.com
Gawsworth Hall is a Tudor half-timbered manor-house with tilting ground. Featuring pictures, sculpture and furniture and an open-air theatre.

Jodrell Bank Science Centre, Planetarium and Arboretum
Lower Withington, Macclesfield, Cheshire SK11 9DL
Tel: (01477) 571339 www.jb.man.ac.uk/scicen
Exhibition and interactive exhibits on astronomy, space, energy and the environment. Planetarium and the world-famous Lovell telescope, plus a 35-acre (14-ha) arboretum.

Knowsley Safari Park
Prescot, Merseyside L34 4AN
Tel: (0151) 430 9009 www.knowsley.com
A 5-mile safari through 500 acres (202 ha) of rolling countryside, and the world's wildest animals roaming free – that's the wonderful world of freedom you'll find at the park.

Lady Lever Art Gallery
Port Sunlight Village, Higher Bebington, Wirral, Merseyside CH62 5EQ
Tel: (0151) 478 4136 www.nmgm.org.uk
The 1st Lord Leverhulme's magnificent collection of British paintings dated 1750-1900, British furniture, Wedgwood pottery and oriental porcelain.

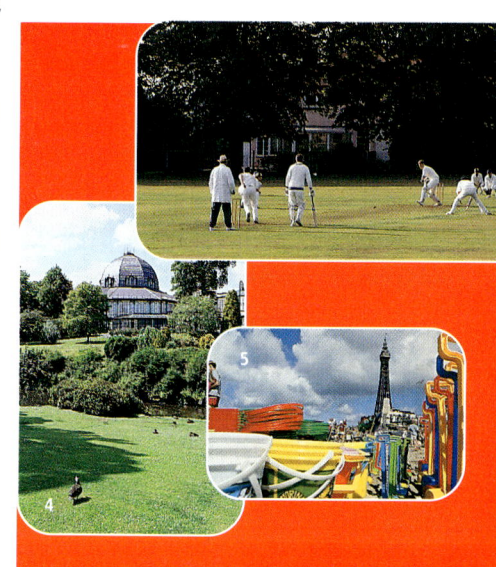

The Pictures:
1 The River Ribble and Pendle Hill, Lancashire
2 Japanese Garden, Tatton Park
3 Lytham, Lancashire
4 Pavilion Gardens, Buxton
5 Blackpool Pleasure Beach

NORTH WEST

Lancaster Castle
Shire Hall, Castle Parade, Lancaster, Lancashire LA1 1YJ
Tel: (01524) 64998
www.lancashire.gov.uk/resources/ps/castle/index.htm
Shire Hall has a collection of coats of arms, a crown court, a grand jury room, a 'drop room' and dungeons. Also external tour of castle.

Lyme Park
Disley, Stockport, Greater Manchester SK12 2NX
Tel: (01663) 762023 www.nationaltrust.org.uk
Lyme Park is a National Trust country estate set in 1,377 acres (541 ha) of moorland, woodland and park. This magnificent house has 17 acres (7 ha) of historic gardens.

The Museum of Science & Industry, in Manchester
Liverpool Road, Castlefield, Manchester M3 4FP
Tel: (0161) 832 1830 www.msim.org.uk
The Museum of Science and Industry in Manchester is based in the world's oldest passenger railway station with galleries that amaze, amuse and entertain.

National Football Museum
Deepdale Stadium, Preston, Lancashire PR1 6RU
Tel: (01772) 908442
www.nationalfootballmuseum.com
The Football Museum exists to explain how and why football has become the people's game.

Norton Priory Museum and Gardens
Tudor Road, Runcorn, Cheshire WA7 1SX
Tel: (01928) 569895 www.nortonpriory.org
Medieval priory remains, purpose-built museum, St Christopher's statue, sculpture trail and award-winning walled garden, all set in 39 acres (16 ha) of beautiful gardens.

Quarry Bank Mill
Styal, Wilmslow, Cheshire SK9 4LA
Tel: (01625) 527468
www.rmplc.co.uk/orgs/quarrybankmill
A Georgian water-powered cotton-spinning mill, with four floors of displays and demonstrations and 300 acres (121 ha) of parkland surroundings.

Rufford Old Hall
Rufford, Ormskirk, Lancashire L40 1SG
Tel: (01704) 821254 www.nationaltrust.org.uk
One of the finest 16thC buildings in Lancashire with a magnificent hall, particularly noted for its immense moveable screen.

Sandcastle
South Promenade, Blackpool, Merseyside FY4 1BB
Tel: (01253) 343602
Wave pool, leisure pools, giant water flumes, white-knuckle water slides, kiddies' safe harbour, play area, catering, bar, shops and amusements.

Smithills Hall & Park Trust
Smithills Hall, Smithills Dean Road, Bolton, Greater Manchester BL1 7NP
Tel: (01204) 332377
Smithills Hall is a fascinating example of the growth of a great house which mirrors the changes in fashion and living conditions from the late 14thC.

Southport Zoo and Conservation Trust
Princes Park, Southport, Merseyside PR8 1RX
Tel: (01704) 538102
Zoological gardens and conservation trust. Southport Zoo has been run by the Petrie family since 1964. Talks on natural history are held in the schoolroom.

Stapley Water Gardens & Palms Tropical Oasis
London Road, Stapeley, Nantwich, Cheshire CW5 7LH
Tel: (01270) 623868
www.stapeleywatergardens.com
Large water garden centre filled with display lakes, pools and fountains. Trees and shrubs, pot plants, gifts, garden sundries and pets. Thousand of items on display.

Tate Liverpool
Albert Dock, Liverpool, Merseyside L3 4BB
Tel: (0151) 702 7445 www.tate.org.uk
The Tate at Liverpool exhibits the National Collection of Modern Art.

Tatton Park
Knutsford, Cheshire WA16 6QN
Tel: (01625) 534400 www.tattonpark.org.uk
Historic mansion with a 50-acre (20-ha) garden, traditional working farm, Tudor manor-house, 2,000-acre (809-ha) deer park and children's adventure playground.

Wigan Pier
Trencherfield Mill, Wigan, Lancashire WN3 4EF
Tel: (01942) 323666 www.wiganmbc.gov.uk
Wigan Pier combines interaction with displays and reconstructions and the Wigan Pier Theatre Company. Facilities include shops and a cafe.

NORTH WEST

Find out more about the North West

Further information about holidays and attractions in the North West is available from:

NORTH WEST TOURIST BOARD
Swan House, Swan Meadow Road, Wigan Pier, Wigan WN3 5BB.
Tel: (01942) 821222 Fax: (01942) 820002
Internet: www.visitnorthwest.com

The following publications are available from North West Tourist Board:

Best of the North West
a guide to information on the region including hotels, self-catering establishments, caravan and camping parks. Also includes attractions, major events, shops and restaurants

Discovery Map
a non-accommodation guide, A1 folded to A4 map including list of visitor attractions, what to see and where to go

Bed and Breakfast Map
forming part of a family of maps for England, this guide provides information on bed and breakfast establishments in the North West region

Freedom
forming part of a family of publications about caravan and camping parks in the north of England

Stay on a Farm
a guide to farm accommodation in the north of England

Group Travel Planner
a guide to choosing the right accommodation, attraction or venue for group organisers

Venues
a 6-monthly newsletter about conference venues in the North West region

Schools Out
a 6-monthly newsletter aimed at schools providing information about where to go and what to see

Getting to the North West

BY ROAD:
Motorways intersect within the region which has the best road network in the country. Travelling north or south use the M6 and east or west the M62.

BY RAIL:
Most North West coastal resorts are connected to InterCity routes with trains from many parts of the country and there are through trains to major cities and towns.

The Pictures:
1 Derbyshire
2 Barca Cafe Bar, Manchester

NORTH WEST

Where to stay in the North West

Parks in this region are listed in alphabetical order of place name, and then in alphabetical order of park.

Map references refer to the colour location maps at front of this guide. The first number indicates the map to use; the letter and number which follow refer to the grid reference on the map.

At-a-glance symbols can be found inside the back cover flap. Keep this open for easy reference.

BLACKPOOL, Lancashire Map ref 5A1 *Tourist Information Centre Tel: (01253) 478 222*

★★★★
HOLIDAY & TOURING PARK
BH&HPA
NCC
Ad p12

MARTON MERE HOLIDAY VILLAGE
Mythop Road, Blackpool FY4 4XN
T: (01253) 767544
F: (01253) 791544
E: enquiries@british-holidays.co.uk
I: www.british-holidays.co.uk

OPEN March–November
CC: Delta, Mastercard, Solo, Switch, Visa
Level, grassy, stony, hard.

310 £11.55–£32.55
310 £11.55–£32.55
118 £192.00–£720.00
310 touring pitches
753 units privately owned

Leave the M55 at jct 4, take the A583 to Blackpool. Turn right at the 2nd set of traffic lights into Mythop Road. The Park is 150yds down on the left-hand side. Signposted.

★★★
HOLIDAY & TOURING PARK

NEWTON HALL CARAVAN PARK
Staining Road, Staining, Blackpool FY3 0AX
T: (01253) 882512 & 885465
F: (01253) 893101
E: sales@partingtons.fsbusiness.co.uk
I: www.partingtons.com

OPEN March–October
CC: Barclaycard, Delta, JCB, Mastercard, Solo, Switch, Visa
11.2 hectares (28 acres) Level, sloping, grassy.

33 £11.50–£16.50
33 £11.50–£16.50
45 £126.00–£420.00
33 touring pitches
380 units privately owned

Leave the M55 at jct 4 onto the A583. Take the 2nd set of lights, turn right onto Mythop Road. Take the 1st left onto Chain Lane. This leads to Staining Road. Newton Hall is on the left-hand side. Signposted.

★★★★
HOLIDAY, TOURING & CAMPING PARK

PIPERS HEIGHT CARAVAN & CAMPING PARK
Peel Road, Peel, Blackpool FY4 5JT
T: (01253) 763767

OPEN March–November
2 hectares (5 acres) Grassy, hard, sheltered.

137 £8.00–£13.00
137 £8.00–£13.00
137 £8.00–£13.00
137 touring pitches
30 units privately owned

Leave the M55 at jct 4. Turn left straight at roundabout to lights turn right. Right and sharp left, park is 30m on right. Signposted.

★★★
HOLIDAY, TOURING & CAMPING PARK

WINDY HARBOUR HOLIDAY CENTRE
Little Singleton, Blackpool FY6 8NB
T: (01253) 883064

OPEN March–October
CC: Barclaycard, Delta, JCB, Mastercard, Switch, Visa
22.8 hectares (57 acres) Level, grassy, hard.

240 £11.50–£18.00
240 £11.50–£18.00
110 £9.50–£13.50
100 £126.00–£420.00
240 touring pitches
580 units privately owned

Leave the M55 at Fleetwood exit and take the A585. The Park is located at T-junction, A586. Signposted.

WHERE TO STAY
Please mention this guide when making your booking.

86

NORTH WEST

CLEVELEYS, Lancashire Map ref 5A1 Tourist Information Centre Tel: (01253) 853378

★★★★
HOLIDAY, TOURING & CAMPING PARK

BH&HPA

KNEPS FARM HOLIDAY PARK
River Road, Stanah, Cleveleys, Blackpool FY5 5LR
T: (01253) 823632
F: (01253) 863967
E: knepsfarm@aol.com
I: www.kneps-farm.co.uk

OPEN March–November
CC: Amex, Barclaycard, Delta, Diners, Eurocard, JCB, Mastercard, Solo, Switch, Visa, Visa Electron
4 hectares (10 acres) Level, grassy, stony, hard, sheltered.

45   £10.00–£12.50
10   £10.00–£12.50
15   £10.00–£12.50
2   £185.00–£370.00
70 touring pitches
78 units privately owned

Leave the A585 at the roundabout, turn right onto the B5412 signposted to Little Thornton. Turn right at mini-roundabout after the school onto Stanah Road leading to River Road. Signposted.

FLEETWOOD, Lancashire Map ref 5A1 Tourist Information Centre Tel: (01253) 773953

★★★★
HOLIDAY PARK

BH&HPA
NCC

Ad p12

CALA GRAN
Fleetwood Road, Fleetwood FY7 8JX
T: (01253) 872555
F: (01253) 771288
E: enquiries@british-holidays.co.uk
I: www.british-holidays.co.uk

OPEN April–November
CC: Delta, Mastercard, Solo, Switch, Visa
17.6 hectares (44 acres) Level, grassy.

231   £99.00–£600.00
496 units privately owned

Exit the M55 at jct 3. Follow the A585 to Fleetwood. At the 4th roundabout with the Nautical College on the left take the 3rd exit. The park is located 800yds on left-hand side. Signposted.

HEYWOOD, Greater Manchester Map ref 5B1

★★★★
TOURING & CAMPING PARK

BH&HPA

GELDER WOOD COUNTRY PARK
Oak Leigh Cottage, Ashworth Road, Heywood, Rochdale OL11 5UP
T: (01706) 364858 & 620300
F: (01706) 364858
E: gelderwood@aol.com
I: www.adultstouring.co.uk

OPEN March–October
19.2 hectares (48 acres)
Level, sloping, grassy, hard.

24   £9.00–£9.00
5   £9.00–£9.00
5   £9.00–£9.00
34 touring pitches

Off the B6222 Bury to Rochdale road, up Ashworth Road. Signposted.

LITTLEBOROUGH, Greater Manchester Map ref 5B1

★★★
HOLIDAY, TOURING & CAMPING PARK

BH&HPA

HOLLINGWORTH LAKE CARAVAN PARK
Rakewood, Littleborough OL15 0AT
T: (01706) 378661

OPEN All year round
52 hectares (130 acres) Level, sloping, grassy, hard, sheltered.

25   £8.00–£12.00
10   £6.00–£12.00
10   £6.00–£12.00
      £150.00–£350.00
45 touring pitches
40 units privately owned

Exit the M62 at jct 21. Follow Hollingworth Lake Country Park signs. Take Rakewood Road. Country Park signs. Signposted.

LYTHAM ST ANNES, Lancashire Map ref 5A1 Tourist Information Centre Tel: (01253) 725610

★★
HOLIDAY & TOURING PARK

BH&HPA

EASTHAM HALL CARAVAN PARK
Saltcotes Road, Lytham St Annes FY8 4LS
T: (01253) 737907

OPEN March–October
CC: Amex, Barclaycard, Eurocard, JCB, Maestro, Mastercard, Solo, Switch, Visa, Visa Electron
10 hectares (25 acres) Level, grassy, hard.

140   £10.00–£13.00
20   £10.00
140 touring pitches
290 units privately owned

On the B5259, 1 mile north of A584 at Lytham. Signposted.

CREDIT CARD BOOKINGS If you book by telephone and are asked for your credit card number it is advisable to check the proprietor's policy should you cancel your reservation.

NORTH WEST

A brief guide to the main Towns and Villages offering accommodation in the North West

B BLACKPOOL, LANCASHIRE - Britain's largest fun resort, with Blackpool Pleasure Beach, 3 piers and the famous Tower. Host to the spectacular autumn illuminations.

C CLEVELEYS, LANCASHIRE - Popular holiday resort on the Fylde coast close to Blackpool, with pleasant promenade, sandy beaches and shopping area. Close by, at Thornton, is a historic Marsh Windmill.

F FLEETWOOD, LANCASHIRE - Major fishing port and resort bounded by the sea on 3 sides. Fine sands, bathing and large model-yacht pond. Good views across Morecambe Bay and peaks of Lake District.

H HEYWOOD, GREATER MANCHESTER - Small industrial town with attractive rural fringe in the Ashworth Valley. Historic buildings and important industrial heritage sites. Access to the East Lancashire Railway (preserved line).

L LITTLEBOROUGH, GREATER MANCHESTER - Attractive small town on the edge of the South Pennine Moors, with many historic buildings and industrial heritage features. Attractions include Hollingworth Lake, the Rochdale Canal and access to the Pennine Way.

• LYTHAM ST ANNES, LANCASHIRE - Pleasant resort famous for its championship golf-courses, notably the Royal Lytham and St Annes. Fine sands and attractive gardens. Some half-timbered buildings and an old restored windmill.

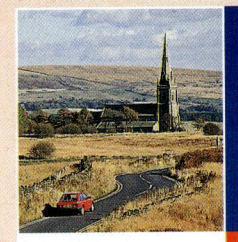

The Safeway Excellence in England AWARDS 2002

The Safeway Excellence in England Awards are all about blowing English tourism's trumpet and telling the world what a fantastic place England is to visit, whether it's for a two week holiday, a weekend break or a day trip.

Formerly called England for Excellence, the Awards are now in their 13th year and are run by the English Tourism Council in association with England's ten regional tourist boards. There are 13 categories including B&B of the Year, Hotel of the Year and Visitor Attraction of the Year. New for 2002 are Short Break Destination of the Year and Most Improved Seaside Resort.

Winners of the 2002 awards will receive their trophies at a fun and festive event to be held on St George's Day (23 April) at the Royal Opera House in London. The day will not only celebrate excellence in tourism but also Englishness in all its diversity.

For a truly exceptional experience, look out for accommodation and attractions displaying a Safeway Excellence in England Award from April 2002 onwards.

Safeway, one of the UK's leading food retailers, is delighted to be sponsoring these awards as a part of a range of initiatives to help farming communities and the tourism industry.

For more information on Safeway Stores please visit: www.safeway.co.uk
For more information about the Excellence in England Awards visit: www.englishtourism.org.uk

YORKSHIRE

Yorkshire combines wild and brooding moors with historic cities, elegant spa towns and a varied coastline of traditional resorts and working fishing ports.

classic sights
Fountains Abbey & Studley Royal – 12th century Cistercian abbey and Georgian water garden
Nostell Prior – 18th century house with outstanding art collection
York Minster – largest medieval Gothic cathedral north of the Alps

coast & country
The Pennines – dramatic moors and rocks
Whitby – unspoilt fishing port, famous for jet (black stone)

literary links
Brontë parsonage, Haworth – home of the Brontë sisters; inspiration for 'Wuthering Heights' and 'Jane Eyre'

arts for all
National Museum of Photography, Film and Television – hi-tech and hands-on

distinctively different
The Original Ghost Walk of York – spooky tours every night

The counties of North, South, East and West Yorkshire, and Northern Lincolnshire

FOR MORE INFORMATION CONTACT:
Yorkshire Tourist Board
312 Tadcaster Road, York YO24 1GS
Tel: (01904) 707070 (24-hr brochure line) Fax: (01904) 701414
Email: info@ytb.org.uk Internet: www.yorkshirevisitor.com

The Pictures:
1 Roseberry Topping
2 Skidby Windmill
3 The Beach at Bridlington

Places to Visit - see pages 90-93
Where to Stay - see pages 94-99

PLACES to visit

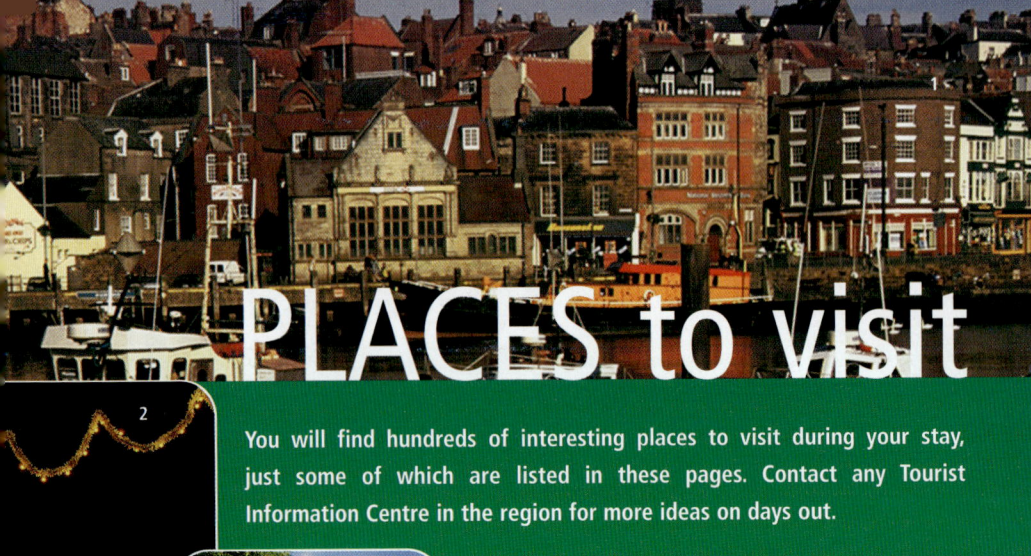

You will find hundreds of interesting places to visit during your stay, just some of which are listed in these pages. Contact any Tourist Information Centre in the region for more ideas on days out.

Beningbrough Hall & Gardens
Beningbrough, York, North Yorkshire YO30 1DD
Tel: (01904) 470666
Handsome Baroque house, built in 1716, with 400 pictures from the National Portrait Gallery, Victorian laundry, potting shed and restored walled garden.

Camp Modern History Theme Museum
Malton, North Yorkshire YO17 6RT
Tel: (01653) 697777 www.edencamp.co.uk
Modern history theme museum depicting civilian way of life during World War II. Millennium features.

Cusworth Hall Museum of South Yorkshire Life
Cusworth Hall, Cusworth Lane, Doncaster,
South Yorkshire DN5 7TU
Tel: (01302) 782342
www.museum@doncaster.gov.uk
Georgian mansion in landscaped park containing Museum of South Yorkshire Life. Special educational facilities.

The Deep
79 Ferensway, Hull, Kingston upon Hull HU2 8LE
Tel: (01482) 615789 www.hull.ac.uk
The Deep consists of 4 elements: a visitor attraction, learning centre, research facility and a business centre.

Eureka! The Museum for Children
Discovery Road, Halifax, West Yorkshire HX1 2NE
Tel: (01422) 330069 www.eureka.org.uk
Eureka! is the first museum of its kind designed especially for children up to the age of 12 with over 400 hands-on exhibits.

Flamingo Land Theme Park, Zoo and Holiday Village
Kirby Misperton, Malton, North Yorkshire YO17 6UX
Tel: (01653) 668287 www.flamingoland.co.uk
One-price family funpark with over 100 attractions, 7 shows and Europe's largest privately owned zoo. Europe's only triple-looping coaster, Magnum Force.

Fountains Abbey and Studley Royal
Studley Park, Ripon, North Yorkshire HG4 3DY
Tel: (01765) 608888 www.fountainsabbey.org.uk
Largest monastic ruin in Britain, founded by Cistercian monks in 1132. Landscaped garden laid between 1720-40 with lake, formal water garden, temples and deer park.

Hornsea Freeport
Rolston Road, Hornsea,
East Riding of Yorkshire HU18 1UT
Tel: (01964) 534211
Set in 25 acres (10 ha) of landscaped gardens with over 40 quality high-street names all selling stock with discounts of up to 50%, licensed restaurant. Leisure attractions.

YORKSHIRE

Last of the Summer Wine Exhibition (Compo's House)
30 Huddersfield Road, Holmfirth, Huddersfield, West Yorkshire HD6 1JS
Tel: (01484) 681408
Collection of photographs and memorabilia connected with the television series 'Last of the Summer Wine'.

Leeds City Art Gallery
The Headrow, Leeds, West Yorkshire LS1 3AA
Tel: (0113) 247 8248
www.leeds.gov.uk/tourinfo/attract/museums/artgall.html
Art gallery containing British paintings, sculptures, prints and drawings of the 19thC and 20thC. Henry Moore gallery with permanent collection of 20thC sculpture.

Lightwater Valley Theme Park
North Stainley, Ripon, North Yorkshire HG4 3HT
Tel: (01765) 635321 www.lightwatervalley.net
Set in 175 acres (71 ha) of parkland, Lightwater Valley features a number of white-knuckle rides and children's rides along with shopping malls, a restaurant and picnic areas.

Magna
Sheffield Road, Templeborough, Rotherham, South Yorkshire S60 1DX
Tel: (01709) 720002 www.magnatrust.org.uk
Magna is the UK's first science adventure centre set in the vast Templeborough steelworks in Rotherham. Fun is unavoidable here with giant interactives.

Midland Railway Centre
Butterley Station, Ripley, North Yorkshire DE5 3QZ
Tel: (01773) 747674
Over 50 locomotives and over 100 items of historic rolling stock of Midland and LMS origin with a steam-hauled passenger service, a museum site, country and farm park.

Mother Shipton's Cave & the Petrifying Well
Prophesy House, High Bridge, Knaresborough, North Yorkshire HG5 8DD
Tel: (01423) 864600 www.mothershipton.co.uk
Mother Shipton's Cave and Petrifying Well are the oldest tourist attractions in Britain, opened in 1630. Cave, well, museum, playground and 12 acres (5 ha) of riverside grounds.

National Museum of Photography, Film & Television
Bradford, West Yorkshire BD1 1NQ
Tel: (01274) 202030 www.nmpft.org.uk
This fascinating and innovative museum houses the three types of media that have transformed the 20thC. Millennium grant awarded.

National Railway Museum
Leeman Road, York, North Yorkshire YO26 4XJ
Tel: (01904) 621261 www.nrm.org.uk
For a fun-packed family day out come along to the National Railway Museum and experience the incredible story of the train.

North Yorkshire Moors Railway
Pickering Station, Park Street, Pickering, North Yorkshire YO18 7AJ
Tel: (01751) 472508 www.nymr.demon.co.uk
Evening and Sunday lunchtime dining service trains offer a unique and nostalgic experience with a wonderful selection of menus to suit all tastes.

The Pictures:
1 Boats in harbour, Whitby, North Yorkshire
2 Hull Fair
3 Countryside near Grimsby
4 The Humber Bridge
5 Flamborough Head
6 Felixkirk, North York Moors

YORKSHIRE

Piece Hall
Halifax, West Yorkshire HX1 1RE
Tel: (01422) 358087 www.calderdale.gov.uk
Built in 1779 and restored in 1976, this Grade I Listed building forms a unique and striking monument to the wealth and importance of the wool trade.

Pleasure Island Family Theme Park
Kings Road, Cleethorpes, North East Lincolnshire DN35 0PL
Tel: (01472) 211511 www.pleasure-island.co.uk
The East Coast's biggest fun day out, with over 50 rides and attractions. Whatever the weather, fun is guaranteed with lots of undercover attractions. Shows from around the world.

Ripley Castle
Ripley, Harrogate, North Yorkshire HG3 3AY
Tel: (01423) 770152 www.ripleycastle.co.uk
Ripley Castle, home to the Ingilby family for over 26 generations, is set in the heart of a delightful estate with Victorian walled gardens, deer park and pleasure grounds.

Royal Armouries Museum
Armouries Drive, Leeds, West Yorkshire LS10 1LT
Tel: (0870) 510 6666 www.armouries.org.uk
Experience more than 3,000 years of history covered by over 8,000 spectacular exhibits and stunning surroundings. Arms and armour.

Sheffield Botanical Gardens
Clarkehouse Road, Sheffield, South Yorkshire S10 2LN
Tel: (0114) 250 0500 www.sbg.org.uk
Extensive gardens with over 5,500 species of plants, Grade II Listed garden pavilion (now closed).

Skipton Castle
Skipton, North Yorkshire BD23 1AQ
Tel: (01756) 792442 www.skiptoncastle.co.uk
Fully-roofed Skipton Castle is in excellent condition. One of the most complete and well-preserved medieval castles in England.

Temple Newsam House
Leeds, West Yorkshire LS15 0AE
Tel: (0113) 264 7321 www.leeds.gov.uk
Tudor/Jacobean house, birthplace of Lord Darnley. Paintings, furniture by Chippendale and others. Gold and silver c1600 onwards. Ceramics, especially Leeds pottery.

Thirsk Museum
14-16 Kirkgate, Thirsk, North Yorkshire YO7 1PQ
Tel: (01845) 527707
Exhibits of local life and industry and cricket memorabilia. The building was the home of Thomas Lord, founder of Lords cricket ground in London.

The Viking City of Jorvick
Coppergate, York, North Yorkshire YO1 9WT
Tel: (01904) 643211 www.jorvik-viking-centre.co.uk
Technology of the 21stC transforms real archaeological evidence into a dynamic vision of the City of York in the10thC.

Wensleydale Cheese Visitor Centre
Wensleydale Creamery, Gayle Lane, Hawes,
North Yorkshire DL8 3RN
Tel: (01969) 667664
Museum, video and interpretation area, viewing gallery. Handmade Wensleydale cheese, licensed restaurant, specialist cheese shop, farm animals in natural environment.

Wigfield Farm
Haverlands Lane, Worsbrough Bridge, Barnsley,
South Yorkshire S70 5NQ
Tel: (01226) 733702
Open working farm with rare and commercial breeds of farm animals including pigs, cattle, sheep, goats, donkeys, ponies, small animals, snakes and other reptiles.

York Castle Museum
The Eye of York, York, North Yorkshire YO1 9RY
Tel: (01904) 653611 www.york.gov.uk
England's most popular museum of everyday life including reconstructed streets and period rooms.

York Dungeon
12 Clifford Street, York, North Yorkshire YO1 9RD
Tel: (01904) 632599 www.thedungeons.com
Set in dark, musty, atmospheric cellars and featuring life-size tableaux of Dark Age deaths, medieval punishments and persecution/torture of heretics.

York Minster
Deangate, York, North Yorkshire YO1 7HH
Tel: (01904) 557200 www.yorkminster.org
York Minster is the largest medieval Gothic cathedral north of the Alps. Museum of Roman/Norman remains. Chapter house.

YORKSHIRE

Find out more about Yorkshire

Further information about holidays and attractions in Yorkshire is available from:

YORKSHIRE TOURIST BOARD
312 Tadcaster Road, York YO24 1GS.
Tel: (01904) 707070 (24-hour brochure line)
Fax: (01904) 701414
Email: info@ytb.org.uk
Internet: www.yorkshirevisitor.com

The following publications are available from Yorkshire Tourist Board:

Yorkshire Visitor Guide 2002
information on the region, including hotels, self-catering, caravan and camping parks.
Also attractions, shops, restaurants and major events

Yorkshire - A Great Day Out
non-accommodation A5 guide listing where to go, what to see and where to eat,
the list goes on! Including map

Bed & Breakfast Touring Map
forming part of a 'family' of maps covering England, this guide provides information on
bed and breakfast establishments in Yorkshire

Group Operators' Guide 2002
a guide to choosing the right venue for travel trade and group organisers including hotels,
attractions and unusual venues

Conference and Venue Guide 2002
a full-colour, comprehensive guide to conference facilities in the region

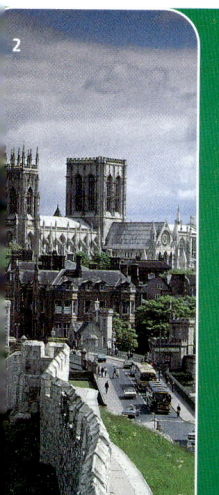

The Pictures:
1 Walker in the Yorkshire Dales
2 York Minster

Getting to Yorkshire

BY ROAD: Motorways: M1, M62, M606, M621, M18, M180, M181, A1(M). Trunk roads: A1, A19, A57, A58, A59, A61, A62, A63, A64, A65, A66.

BY RAIL: InterCity services to Bradford, Doncaster, Harrogate, Kingston upon Hull, Leeds, Sheffield, Wakefield and York. Frequent regional railway services city centre to city centre including Manchester Airport service to Scarborough, York and Leeds.

93

YORKSHIRE

Where to stay in Yorkshire

Parks in this region are listed in alphabetical order of place name, and then in alphabetical order of park.

Map references refer to the colour location maps at front of this guide. The first number indicates the map to use; the letter and number which follow refer to the grid reference on the map.

At-a-glance symbols can be found inside the back cover flap. Keep this open for easy reference.

CLEETHORPES, North East Lincolnshire Map ref 5D1

★★★
HOLIDAY, TOURING & CAMPING PARK
BH&HPA
NCC
Ad p12

THORPE PARK HOLIDAY CENTRE
Cleethorpes DN35 0PW
T: (01472) 813395
F: (01472) 812146
E: enquiries@british-holidays.co.uk
I: www.british-holidays.co.uk

OPEN March–October
CC: Delta, Mastercard, Solo, Switch, Visa
104 hectares (260 acres) Level, grassy, hard.

84	£10.50–£30.50
84	£10.00–£29.00
20	
167	£163.00–£625.00

99 touring pitches
1833 units privately owned

Leave the M180 to A180 towards Grimsby and Cleethorpes. Follow signs for holiday parks and Pleasure Island. Signposted.

FILEY, North Yorkshire Map ref 6D3

★★★★★
TOURING PARK
BH&HPA

LEBBERSTON TOURING PARK
Home Farm, Filey Road, Lebberston, Scarborough
YO11 3PE
T: (01723) 585723

Quiet country location. Well spaced pitches. Extensive south facing views. Ideal park for a peaceful, relaxing break. Fully modernised amenity blocks. Dogs on lead.
OPEN March–October. Sloping, grassy, hard.

| 125 | £7.00–£12.00 |
| 50 | £7.00–£12.00 |

125 touring pitches

From the A64 or the A165 take the B1261 to Lebberston and follow the signs for Lebberston Touring Park.

★★★★★
HOLIDAY, TOURING & CAMPING PARK

ORCHARD FARM HOLIDAY VILLAGE
Stonegate, Hunmanby, Filey YO14 0PU
T: (01723) 891582
F: (01723) 891582

OPEN All year round
5.6 hectares (14 acres) Level, grassy, hard, sheltered.

60	£7.00–£11.00
60	£7.00–£11.00
25	£7.00–£11.00

85 touring pitches
20 units privately owned

Take A165 Scarborough/Bridlington road. Two miles from Filey. Signpost to Hunmanby, site is 1.5 miles down road. Signposted.

REGIONAL TOURIST BOARD The ⋀ symbol after a park name indicates that it is a Regional Tourist Board member.

94

YORKSHIRE

FLAMBOROUGH, East Riding of Yorkshire Map ref 6D3

★★★★
HOLIDAY, TOURING
& CAMPING PARK

BH&HPA

THORNWICK & SEA FARM HOLIDAY CENTRE
Flamborough Holidays Ltd, Flamborough,
Bridlington YO15 1AU
T: (01262) 850369 & 850372
F: (01262) 851550
E: enquiries@thornwickbay.co.uk
I: www.thornwickbay.co.uk

OPEN March–October
CC: Amex, Barclaycard, Delta,
JCB, Mastercard, Switch, Visa
32 hectares (80 acres) Level,
sloping, grassy, hard.

200 — £8.50–£17.50
— £8.50–£12.50
40 — £8.50–£12.50
70 — £125.00–£360.00
240 touring pitches
1000 units privately owned

Follow the B1255 from Bridlington to Flamborough, the park is approximately 1 mile farther towards North Landing. Signposted.

HARROGATE, North Yorkshire Map ref 5B1 Tourist Information Centre Tel: (01423) 537300

★★★★★
HOLIDAY, TOURING
& CAMPING PARK

BH&HPA

RUDDING HOLIDAY PARK
Rudding Park, Follifoot, Harrogate HG3 1JH
T: (01423) 870439
F: (01423) 870859
E: holiday-park@ruddingpark.com
I: www.ruddingpark.com

OPEN March–October
CC: Barclaycard, Delta,
Mastercard, Solo, Switch, Visa
12 hectares (30 acres) Level,
sloping, grassy, hard,
sheltered.

141 — £10.00–£22.50
141 — £10.00–£22.50
141 — £4.00–£14.00
141 touring pitches
90 units privately owned

Three miles south of Harrogate, to the north of the A658 between its jct with the A61 to Leeds and the A661 to Wetherby. Signposted.

★★★
HOLIDAY, TOURING
& CAMPING PARK

BH&HPA

SHAWS TRAILER PARK
Knaresborough Road, Harrogate HG2 7NE
T: (01423) 884432
F: (01423) 883622

OPEN All year round
4.4 hectares (11 acres) Level,
sloping, grassy, hard.

52 — £8.50
52 — £8.50
52 — £6.00–£12.00
52 touring pitches
146 units privately owned

On A59, entrance is adjacent to Johnson's cleaners 50yds south of Ford garage. Signposted.

HELMSLEY, North Yorkshire Map ref 6C3

★★★★★
TOURING &
CAMPING PARK

BH&HPA

GOLDEN SQUARE CARAVAN AND CAMPING PARK
Oswaldkirk, York YO62 5YQ
T: (01439) 788269
F: (01439) 788236
E: barbara@goldensquarecaravanpark.com
I: www.goldensquarecaravanpark.com

OPEN March–October
4 hectares (10 acres) Level,
grassy, hard, sheltered.

129 — £6.50–£10.50
129 — £6.50–£10.50
129 — £6.50–£10.50
— £130.00–£180.00
129 touring pitches

From Helmsley A170 to Thirsk take the 1st left onto the B1257 to York. Take the 1st right to Ampleforth and the turning is after 0.5 miles on the right. Signposted.

HOLMFIRTH, West Yorkshire Map ref 5B1 Tourist Information Centre Tel: (01484) 222444

★★★★
TOURING &
CAMPING PARK

BH&HPA

HOLME VALLEY CAMPING AND CARAVAN PARK

Thongsbridge, Holmfirth HD9 7TD
T: (01484) 665819
F: (01484) 663870
E: pmpeaker@hotmail.com
I: www.holme-valley.co.uk

Picturesque setting in Summer Wine Country, bordering Peak District. Site shop with off-licence, on-site angling, level pitches (grass/gravel), 16-amp hook ups, 5 minutes' walk from village. Book early for angling from own pitch.

OPEN All year round. 1.6 hectares (4 acres) Level, grassy, stony, hard, sheltered.
CC: Amex, Barclaycard, Delta, Maestro, Mastercard, Solo, Switch, Visa, Visa Electron

59 — £7.50–£9.00
59 — £6.50–£8.00
59 — £6.50–£8.00
3 — £95.00–£180.00
59 touring pitches

The entrance to our lane is off the A6024, 5 miles south of Huddersfield. One mile north of Holmfirth, halfway between Honley and Holmfirth. Signposted.

95

YORKSHIRE

HORSFORTH, West Yorkshire Map ref 5B1

★★★★
HOLIDAY, TOURING & CAMPING PARK

BH&HPA

ST HELENA'S CARAVAN SITE
Wardens Bungalow, Otley Old Road,
Horsforth, Leeds LS18 5HZ
T: (0113) 284 1142

OPEN All year round
4.8 hectares (12 acres) Level,
grassy, hard, sheltered.

40		£6.00–£8.00
10		£6.00
10		£5.00
60 touring pitches
40 units privately owned

Follow the A65 to the A658 past the airport to Carlton crossroads, then turn right at sign for Cookridge and Horsforth down Otley Old Road for 0.75 miles. Signposted.

PICKERING, North Yorkshire Map ref 6D3 Tourist Information Centre Tel: (01751) 473791

★★★★
HOLIDAY, TOURING & CAMPING PARK

BH&HPA

WAYSIDE CARAVAN PARK
Wrelton, Pickering YO18 8PG
T: (01751) 472608
F: (01751) 472608
E: wayseparks@talk21.com
I: www.waysideparks.co.uk

OPEN March–September
CC: Barclaycard, Delta, JCB,
Mastercard, Solo, Switch, Visa
4 hectares (10 acres) Level,
grassy, sheltered.

40		£9.00–£13.50
5		£9.00
32		£7.50
72 touring pitches
80 units privately owned

Situated 2.5 miles west of Pickering, 250yds off the A170 by the village of Wrelton. For correct turning watch for signs.

RICHMOND, North Yorkshire Map ref 6C3 Tourist Information Centre Tel: (01748) 850252

★★★★★
HOLIDAY, TOURING & CAMPING PARK

BH&HPA

BROMPTON-ON-SWALE CARAVAN AND CAMPING PARK

Brompton-on-Swale, Richmond DL10 7EZ
T: (01748) 824629
F: (01748) 826383
E: brompton.caravanpark@btinternet.com
I: www.uk.parks.com

Relax and enjoy our family-run park in a lovely natural setting on the banks of the River Swale. Fishing, scenic walks, site shop, heated showers.
OPEN March–October. 4 hectares (10 acres) Level, grassy.
CC: Amex, Barclaycard, Delta, Diners, Eurocard, Mastercard, Solo, Switch, Visa

150		£8.50–£16.00
150		£8.50–£16.00
40		£3.90–£8.50
150 touring pitches
22 units privately owned

On the B6271 halfway between Brompton-on-Swale and Richmond on the left-hand side. Signposted.

RIPON, North Yorkshire Map ref 6C3

★★★★
HOLIDAY, TOURING & CAMPING PARK

BH&HPA

WOODHOUSE FARM CARAVAN & CAMPING PARK
Winksley, Ripon HG4 3PG
T: (01765) 658309
F: (01765) 658882
E: woodhouse.farm@talk21.com
I: www.woodhouse-farm.co.uk

OPEN March–October
CC: Barclaycard, Delta,
Eurocard, Mastercard, Solo,
Switch, Visa, Visa Electron
22.4 hectares (56 acres) Level,
grassy, hard, sheltered.

100		£8.50–£9.50
15		£8.50–£9.50
44		£7.50–£8.50
150 touring pitches
27 units privately owned

From Ripon take the B6265 Pateley Bridge. After Fountains Abbey take 2nd right and follow site signs.

COUNTRY CODE Always follow the Country Code ❧ Enjoy the countryside and respect its life and work ❧ Guard against all risk of fire ❧ Fasten all gates ❧ Keep your dogs under close control ❧ Keep to public paths across farmland ❧ Use gates and stiles to cross fences, hedges and walls ❧ Leave livestock, crops and machinery alone ❧ Take your litter home ❧ Help to keep all water clean ❧ Protect wildlife, plants and trees ❧ Take special care on country roads ❧ Make no unnecessary noise

YORKSHIRE

ROOS, East Riding of Yorkshire Map ref 5D1

★★★
HOLIDAY, TOURING & CAMPING PARK

SAND-LE-MERE CARAVAN & LEISURE PARK

Seaside Lane, Tunstall, Roos, Hull HU12 0JQ
T: (01964) 670403
F: (01964) 671099
E: info@sand-le-mere.co.uk
I: www.sand-le-mere.co.uk

A great place to stay, with its natural park and mere leading to a gentle slope to the beach. No cliffs to climb.

OPEN March–December. Level, grassy.
CC: Delta, Maestro, Mastercard, Solo, Switch, Visa, Visa Electron

From Hull to Hedon take the B1362 at Withernsea, B1242 to Roos. Look for brown signs marked SLM.

18	🚐	£9.00–£12.00
2		£9.00–£12.00
	⛺	£9.00–£12.00
22	🏠	£100.00–£330.00

20 touring pitches
400 units privately owned

SCARBOROUGH, North Yorkshire Map ref 6D3   Tourist Information Centre Tel: (01723) 373333

★★★★
TOURING & CAMPING PARK

BH&HPA

CAYTON VILLAGE CARAVAN PARK LTD

Mill Lane, Cayton Bay, Scarborough YO11 3NN
T: (01723) 583171 & (01904) 624630
E: info@caytontouring.co.uk
I: www.caytontouring.co.uk

Adjoining church, 0.5 miles from beach. Two inns, bus services. Scarborough 3 miles, Filey 4 miles. Free shower, dishwashing facilities, family bathroom. Four-acre dog walk. Low season offers-7 nights for 6, 4 nights for 3 (Sun–Thurs incl). Senior citizens, 10% off full week.

OPEN March–October. 4.4 hectares (11 acres) Level, grassy, hard, sheltered.
CC: Barclaycard, Delta, JCB, Mastercard, Solo, Switch, Visa, Visa Electron

A165, turn inland Cayton Bay traffic lights, 0.5 miles on the right. A64, take B1261 at McDonalds roundabout. In Cayton turn 2nd left after Blacksmiths.

125	🚐	£7.00–£10.00
125		£7.00–£10.00
75	⛺	£7.00–£10.00

200 touring pitches

SLINGSBY, North Yorkshire Map ref 6C3

★★★★
HOLIDAY, TOURING & CAMPING PARK

ROBIN HOOD CARAVAN & CAMPING PARK
Green Dyke Lane, Slingsby, York YO62 4AP
T: (01653) 628391
F: (01653) 628391
E: robinhood.caravan@tesco.net

OPEN March–October
1.6 hectares (4 acres) Level, grassy, hard, sheltered.

32	🚐	£9.00–£16.00
32		£9.00–£16.00
32	⛺	£9.00–£16.00
20	🏠	£160.00–£400.00

32 touring pitches

The caravan park is situated on the edge of the village of Slingsby, with access off the B1257 Malton to Helmsley road. Signposted.

WAKEFIELD, West Yorkshire Map ref 5B1   Tourist Information Centre Tel: (01924) 305000

★★★★
HOLIDAY, TOURING & CAMPING PARK

BH&HPA

NOSTELL PRIORY HOLIDAY HOME PARK
Top Park Wood, Nostell, Wakefield
WF4 1QD
T: (01924) 863938
F: (01924) 862226

OPEN March–October
12.4 hectares (31 acres)
Level, grassy, hard, sheltered.

60	🚐	£8.50–£9.00
7		£8.50–£9.00
60	⛺	£8.00–£9.00
9	🏠	£150.00–£250.00

60 touring pitches
75 units privately owned

Five miles east of Wakefield on A638, Doncaster road. Signposted.

NB **IMPORTANT NOTE** Information on accommodation listed in this guide has been supplied by the proprietors. As changes may occur you are advised to check details at the time of booking.

YORKSHIRE

WHITBY, North Yorkshire Map ref 6D3 *Tourist Information Centre Tel: (01947) 602674*

★★★★
HOLIDAY PARK

ROSE AWARD

BH&HPA

FLASK HOLIDAY HOME PARK
Robin Hoods Bay, Fylingdales, Whitby YO22 4QH
T: (01947) 880592
F: (01947) 880592
E: flaskinn@aol.com
I: www.ukparks.co.uk/flask

Small, family-run site between Whitby and Scarborough, in the North Yorkshire Moors. All super luxury caravans have central heating and double glazing. Rose Award.

OPEN March–October. 2.8 hectares (7 acres) Grassy.
CC: Barclaycard, Mastercard, Switch, Visa, Visa Electron

Situated on the A171, 7 miles to Whitby and 12 miles to Scarborough. Signposted.

10	£150.00–£300.00

42 units privately owned

★★★★★
TOURING & CAMPING PARK

BH&HPA

LADYCROSS PLANTATION CARAVAN PARK
Egton, Whitby YO21 1UA
T: (01947) 895502
E: enquiries@ladycrossplantation.co.uk
I: www.ladycrossplantation.co.uk

OPEN April–October
CC: Barclaycard, Delta, Mastercard, Switch, Visa
11.2 hectares (28 acres) Level, grassy, sheltered.

110	£8.40–£11.00
6	£8.40–£11.00
4	£8.40–£8.40

120 touring pitches

From Whitby to Guisborough (A171) take turning signed Egton/North York Moors Railway/Grosmont/Glaisdale. The caravan site is 200yds on the right.

★★★★★
HOLIDAY, TOURING & CAMPING PARK

BH&HPA

MIDDLEWOOD FARM HOLIDAY PARK
Middlewood Lane, Fylingthorpe, Whitby YO22 4UF
T: (01947) 880414
F: (01947) 880871
E: info@middlewoodfarm.com
I: www.middlewoodfarm.com

OPEN March–December
CC: Barclaycard, Delta, Maestro, Mastercard, Solo, Switch, Visa, Visa Electron
2.8 hectares (7 acres) Level, grassy, hard, sheltered.

20	£6.50–£12.50
50	£6.50–£12.50
50	£6.50–£12.50
30	£119.00–£429.00

50 touring pitches

Follow A171 Scarborough to Whitby road signposted from Fylingthope jct. In Fylingthorpe turn onto Middlewood Lane. Park is 500yds. Signposted.

★★★★★
HOLIDAY, TOURING & CAMPING PARK

BH&HPA

NORTHCLIFFE & SEAVIEW HOLIDAY PARKS
Bottoms Lane, High Hawsker, Whitby YO22 4LL
T: (01947) 880477
F: (01947) 880972
E: enquiries@northcliffe.com
I: www.northcliffe.com

Adjacent family parks. Peaceful heritage coast location. Panoramic seaviews. Fabulous walks/cycling, Yorkshire/England. Winner of Caravan Holiday Park of the Year 1999. Touring/camping-book 7 nights (in advance) for 10% discount, any time of year, any type of pitch!

OPEN All year round except Christmas. 10.4 hectares (26 acres) Level, grassy, hard.
CC: Barclaycard, Delta, Eurocard, JCB, Mastercard, Solo, Switch, Visa, Visa Electron

Three miles south from Whitby. Turn left onto the B1447 to Robin Hood's Bay. Through Hawsker village. Go left at the top of the hill at the Park sign. Follow the private road for 0.5 miles. Signposted.

30	£8.00–£12.00
30	£8.00–£12.00
30	£8.00–£12.00
14	£95.00–£399.00

30 touring pitches
151 units privately owned

STAR RATINGS Were correct at the time of going to press but are subject to change. Please check at the time of booking.

YORKSHIRE

YORK, North Yorkshire Map ref 5C1 *Tourist Information Centre Tel: (01904) 621756*

★★★★★
TOURING PARK

ALDERS CARAVAN PARK
Home Farm, Alne, York YO61 1TB
T: (01347) 838722 & 830109
F: (01347) 838722

OPEN March–October
152 hectares (380 acres)
Level, grassy, hard.

40	🚐	£7.00–£9.50
40	🚙	£7.00–£9.50
	⛺	£6.50

40 touring pitches

Situated 2 miles west of the A19 and 9 miles north of York. In the centre of the village. Signposted.

★★★★★
HOLIDAY, TOURING & CAMPING PARK

BH&HPA

CAWOOD HOLIDAY PARK
Ryther Road, Cawood, Selby YO8 3TT
T: (01757) 268450
F: (01757) 268537
I: www.ukparks.co.uk/cawood

Twixt York and Selby, a quiet rural park for the discerning. Some pitches have views over fishing lake. Bar meals, excellent amenity building.

OPEN January, March–December. 3.6 hectares (9 acres) Level, grassy, hard, sheltered.
CC: Amex, Barclaycard, Delta, Diners, Eurocard, JCB, Maestro, Mastercard, Solo, Switch, Visa, Visa Electron

	🚐	£8.50–£13.00
	🚙	£8.50–£13.00
	⛺	£8.50–£13.00
5	🏠	£195.00–£485.00

57 touring pitches

Take the B1222 from the A1 or York and turn at Cawood traffic lights onto the B1223, signposted Tadcaster. Site is 1 mile farther on. Signposted.

CHECK THE MAPS
The colour maps at the front of this guide show all the cities, towns and villages for which you will find park entries. Refer to the town index to find the page on which it is listed.

99

YORKSHIRE

A brief guide to the main Towns and Villages offering accommodation in Yorkshire

FLAMBOROUGH, EAST RIDING OF YORKSHIRE - Village with strong seafaring tradition, high on chalk headland dominated by cliffs of Flamborough Head, a fortress for over 2000 years. St Oswald's Church is in the oldest part of Flamborough. A nature trail follows the Iron Age earthworks known as Danes Dyke.

HARROGATE, NORTH YORKSHIRE - Major conference, exhibition and shopping centre, renowned for its spa heritage and award-winning floral displays, spacious parks and gardens. Famous for antiques, toffee, fine shopping and excellent tea shops, also its Royal Pump Rooms and Baths. Annual Great Yorkshire Show in July.

- **HELMSLEY, NORTH YORKSHIRE** - Delightful small market town with red roofs, warm stone buildings and cobbled market square, on the River Rye at the entrance to Ryedale and the North York Moors. Remains of 12th C castle, several inns and All Saints' Church.

- **HOLMFIRTH, WEST YORKSHIRE** - Village on the edge of the Peak District National Park, famous as the location for the filming of the TV series 'Last of the Summer Wine'.

PICKERING, NORTH YORKSHIRE - Market town and tourist centre on edge of North York Moors. Parish church has complete set of 15th C wall paintings depicting lives of saints. Part of 12th C castle still stands. Beck Isle Museum. The North York Moors Railway begins here.

RICHMOND, NORTH YORKSHIRE - Market town on edge of Swaledale with 11th C castle, Georgian and Victorian buildings surrounding cobbled market-place. Green Howards' Museum is in the former Holy Trinity Church. Attractions include the Georgian Theatre, restored Theatre Royal, Richmondshire Museum, Easby Abbey.

- **RIPON, NORTH YORKSHIRE** - Ancient city with impressive cathedral containing Saxon crypt which houses church treasures from all over Yorkshire. Charter granted in 886 by Alfred the Great. 'Setting the Watch' tradition kept nightly by horn-blower in Market Square. Fountains Abbey nearby.

SCARBOROUGH, NORTH YORKSHIRE - Large, popular East Coast seaside resort, formerly a spa town. Beautiful gardens and two splendid sandy beaches. Castle ruins date from 1100; fine Georgian and Victorian houses. Scarborough Millennium depicts 1,000 years of town's history. Sea Life Centre.

- **SLINGSBY, NORTH YORKSHIRE** - Large, attractive village with ruined castle and village green, on Castle Howard estate.

WAKEFIELD, WEST YORKSHIRE - Thriving city with cathedral church of All Saints boasting 247-ft spire. Old Bridge, a 9-arched structure, has fine medieval chantry chapels of St Mary's. Georgian architecture and good shopping centre (The Ridings). National Coal Mining Museum for England nearby.

- **WHITBY, NORTH YORKSHIRE** - Holiday town with narrow streets and steep alleys at the mouth of the River Esk. Captain James Cook, the famous navigator, lived in Grape Lane. 199 steps lead to St Mary's Church and St Hilda's Abbey overlooking harbour. Dracula connections. Gothic weekend every April.

YORK, NORTH YORKSHIRE - Ancient walled city nearly 2,000 years old, containing many well-preserved medieval buildings. Its Minster has over 100 stained glass windows and is the largest Gothic cathedral in England. Attractions include Castle Museum, National Railway Museum, Jorvik Viking Centre and York Dungeon.

HEART of England

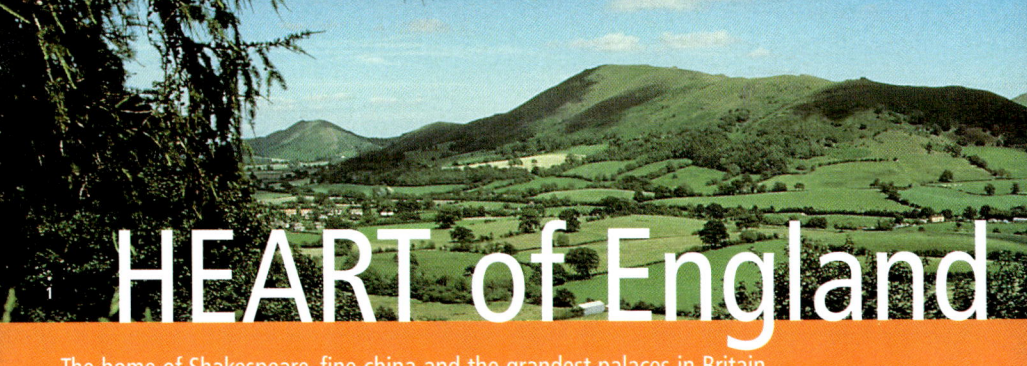

The home of Shakespeare, fine china and the grandest palaces in Britain, the region is full of surprises, from the thriving multicultural cities of Birmingham and Nottingham to countryside both dramatic and picturesque.

classic sights
Hardwick Hall – probably Britain's greatest Elizabethan house
Pottery & porcelain – factory tours of Royal Crown Derby, Wedgewood, Spode and more
Ironbridge Gorge – the world's first cast-iron bridge

country
The Cotswolds – picturebook England
The Peak District – moorland, limestone gorges and ancient woodlands

literary links
Stratford-upon-Avon – Royal Shakespeare Company; the homes of Shakespeare and his family
Nottingham – DH Lawrence Birthplace Museum

arts for all
Walsall – The New Art Gallery
Wightwick Manor – arts & crafts masterpiece
Arts Festivals – Bromsgrove, Malvern and Cheltenham

distinctively different
Cadbury World – Chocaholic heaven

The counties of Derbyshire, Gloucestershire, Herefordshire, Leicestershire, Lincolnshire, Northamptonshire, Nottinghamshire, Rutland, Shropshire, Staffordshire, Warwickshire, Worcestershire and West Midlands

FOR MORE INFORMATION CONTACT:
Heart of England Tourist Board
Larkhill Road, Worcester WR5 2EZ
Tel: (01905) 761100 Fax: (01905) 763450
Internet: www.visitheartofengland.com

The Pictures:
1 South Shropshire Hills
2 Brindley Place, Birmingham
3 Stratford-upon-Avon

Places to Visit - see pages 102-106
Where to Stay - see pages 107-111

101

PLACES to visit

You will find hundreds of interesting places to visit during your stay, just some of which are listed in these pages. Contact any Tourist Information Centre in the region for more ideas on days out.

Acton Scott Historic Working Farm
Wenlock Lodge, Acton Scott, Church Stretton, Shropshire SY6 6QN
Tel: (01694) 781306 www.actonscotmuseum.co.uk
Acton Scott Historic Working Farm demonstrates farming and rural life in south Shropshire at the close of the 19thC.

Alton Towers Theme Park
Alton, Stoke-on-Trent, Staffordshire ST10 4DB
Tel: (0870) 520 4060 www.alton-towers.co.uk
Theme Park with over 125 rides and attractions including Oblivion, Nemesis, Haunted House, Runaway Mine Train, Congo River Rapids, Log Flume and many children's rides.

The American Adventure
Ilkeston, Derbyshire DE7 5SX
Tel: (01773) 531521 www.americanadventure.co.uk
The American Adventure has action and entertainment for all ages including the Missile white-knuckle rollercoaster, Europe's tallest skycoaster and the world's wettest log flume.

Belton House, Park and Gardens
Belton, Grantham, Lincolnshire NG32 2LS
Tel: (01476) 566116
The crowning achievement of restoration country house architecture, built in 1685-88 for Sir John Brownlow with alterations by James Wyatt in 1777.

Belvoir Castle Estate Office
Belvoir, Grantham, Lincolnshire NG32 1PD
Tel: (01476) 870262 www.belvoircastle.com
The present castle is the fourth to be built on this site and dates from 1816. Art treasures include works by Poussin, Rubens, Holbein and Reynolds. Queen's Royal Lancers display.

Birmingham Botanical Gardens and Glasshouses
Westbourne Road, Edgbaston, Birmingham, West Midlands B15 3TR
Tel: (0121) 454 1860
www.bham-bot-gdns.demon.co.uk
15 acres (6 ha) of ornamental gardens and glasshouses. Widest range of plants in the Midlands from tropical rainforest to arid desert. Aviaries with exotic birds, children's play area.

Black Country Living Museum
Tipton Road, Dudley, West Midlands DY1 4SQ
Tel: (0121) 557 9643 www.bclm.co.uk
A warm welcome awaits you at Britain's friendliest open-air museum. Wander around original shops and houses, or ride on fair attractions and take a look down the mine.

HEART OF ENGLAND

Blenheim Palace
Woodstock, Oxford, Oxfordshire OX7 1PX
Tel: (01993) 811325
Home of the 11th Duke of Marlborough, birthplace of Sir Winston Churchill. Designed by Vanbrugh in the English Baroque style. Park landscaped by 'Capability' Brown.

Butlins Family Entertainment Resort
Roman Bank, Skegness, Lincolnshire PE25 1NJ
Tel: (01754) 762311
Butlins Family Entertainment Resort has a skyline pavilion, toyland, sub-tropical waterworld, tenpin bowling and entertainments' centre with live shows.

Cadbury World
Linden Road, Bournville, Birmingham, West Midlands B30 2LD
Tel: (0121) 451 4180 www.cadburyworld.co.uk
Story of Cabdury's chocolate includes chocolate-making demonstration and attractions for all ages.

Chatsworth House and Garden
Bakewell, Derbyshire DE45 1PP
Tel: (01246) 582204 www.chatsworth-house.co.uk
Built in 1687-1707 with a collection of fine pictures, books, drawings and furniture. Garden laid out by 'Capability' Brown with fountains, cascades, a farmyard and playground.

Cotswold Farm Park
Guiting Power, Cheltenham, Gloucestershire GL54 5UG
Tel: (01451) 850307
Collection of rare breeds of British farm animals. Pets' corner, adventure playground, Tractor School, picnic area, gift shop, cafe and seasonal farming displays.

Drayton Manor Family Theme Park
Tamworth, Staffordshire B78 3TW
Tel: (01827) 287979 www.draytonmanor.co.uk
A major theme park with over 100 rides and attractions, plus children's rides, Zoo, farm, museums and the new, live 'Popeye Show'.

The Elgar Birthplace Museum
Crown East Lane, Lower Broadheath, Worcester, Worcestershire WR2 6RH
Tel: (01905) 333224 www.elgar.org
Country cottage birthplace displaying Elgar's desk and family possessions, complemented by new Elgar Centre. Memorabilia, sounds and special events illustrate his life.

The Galleries of Justice
Shire Hall, High Pavement, Lace Market, Nottingham, Nottinghamshire NG1 1HN
Tel: (0115) 952 0555 www.galleriesofjustice.org.uk
A museum of law located in and around a 19thC courthouse and county gaol, brought to life by costumed interpreters.

The Heights of Abraham Cable Cars, Caverns and Country Park
Matlock Bath, Matlock, Derbyshire DE4 3PD
Tel: (01629) 582365 www.heights-of-abraham.co.uk
A spectacular cable car ride takes you to the summit where, within the grounds, there is a wide variety of attractions for young and old alike. Gift shop and coffee shop.

Ikon Gallery
1 Oozells Square, Brindleyplace, Birmingham, West Midlands B1 2HS
Tel: (0121) 248 0708 www.ikongallery.co.uk
Ikon Gallery is one of Europe's foremost galleries for presenting the work of living artists within an innovative educational framework.

The Pictures:
1 Cottage Gardens, River Arrow, Herefordshire
2 Darwin Statue, Shrewsbury
3 Packwood House, Warwickshire
4 Rutland Water
5 Rockingham Castle, Northamptonshire

HEART OF ENGLAND

Ironbridge Gorge Museum
Ironbridge, Telford, Shropshire TF8 7AW
Tel: (01952) 433522 www.ironbridge.org.uk
World's first cast-iron bridge, Museum of the Gorge Visitor Centre, Tar Tunnel, Jackfield Tile Museum, Coalport China Museum, Rosehill House, Blists Hill Museum and Museum of Iron.

Lincoln Castle
Castle Hill, Lincoln, Lincolnshire LN1 3AA
Tel: (01522) 511068
A medieval castle, including towers and ramparts, with a Magna Carta exhibition, a prison chapel experience, reconstructed Westgate and popular events throughout the summer.

Museum of British Road Transport
Hales Street, Coventry, West Midlands CV1 1PN
Tel: (024) 7683 2425 www.mbrt.co.uk
200 cars and commercial vehicles from 1896 to date, 200 cycles from 1818 to date, 90 motorcycles from 1920 to date and the 'Thrust 2' land speed story.

National Sea Life Centre
The Water's Edge, Brindleyplace, Birmingham, West Midlands B1 2HL
Tel: (0121) 633 4700 www.sealife.co.uk
Over 55 fascinating displays. The opportunity to come face-to-face with literally hundreds of fascinating sea creatures, from sharks to shrimps.

The National Tramway Museum
Crich, Matlock, Derbyshire DE4 5DP
Tel: (01773) 852565 www.tramway.co.uk
A collection of over 70 trams from Britain and overseas from 1873-1969 with tram rides on a 1-mile route, a period street scene, depots, a power station, workshops and exhibitions.

Nottingham Industrial Museum
Courtyard Buildings, Wollaton Park, Nottingham, Nottinghamshire NG8 2AE
Tel: (0115) 915 3910 www.nottinghamcity.gov.uk
An 18thC stables presenting the history of Nottingham's industries: printing, pharmacy, hosiery and lace. There is also a Victorian beam engine, a horse gin and transport.

Peak District Mining Museum
The Pavilion, Matlock Bath, Matlock, Derbyshire DE4 3NR
Tel: (01629) 583834 www.peakmines.co.uk
A large exhibition on 3,500 years of lead mining with displays on geology, mines and miners, tools and engines. The climbing shafts make it suitable for children as well.

Rockingham Castle
Rockingham, Market Harborough, Leicestershire LE16 8TH
Tel: (01536) 770240 www.rockinghamcastle.com
An Elizabethan house within the walls of a Norman castle with fine pictures, extensive views, gardens with roses and an ancient yew hedge.

Rugby School Museum
10 Little Church Street, Rugby, Warwickshire CV21 3AW
Tel: (01788) 556109
Rugby School Museum tells the story of the school, scene of 'Tom Brown's Schooldays', and contains the earlier memorabilia of the game invented on the school close.

Severn Valley Railway
The Railway Station, Bewdley, Worcestershire DY12 1BG
Tel: (01299) 403816 www.svr.co.uk
Preserved standard gauge steam railway running 16 miles between Kidderminster, Bewdley and Bridgnorth. Collection of locomotives and passenger coaches.

Shakespeare's Birthplace
Henley Street, Stratford-upon-Avon, Warwickshire CV37 6QW
Tel: (01789) 204016 www.shakespeare.org.uk
The world-famous house where William Shakespeare was born in 1564 and where he grew up. See the highly acclaimed Shakespeare Exhibition.

The Shrewsbury Quest
193 Abbey Foregate, Shrewsbury, Shropshire SY2 6AH
Tel: (01743) 243324 www.shrewsburyquest.com
12thC medieval visitor attraction. Solve mysteries, create illuminated manuscripts, play medieval games and relax in unique herb gardens. Gift shop and cafe.

Shugborough Estate
Shugborough, Milford, Stafford, Staffordshire ST17 0XB
Tel: (01889) 881388 www.staffordshire.gov.uk
18thC mansion house with fine collection of furniture. Gardens and park contain beautiful neo-classical monuments.

HEART OF ENGLAND

Skegness Natureland Seal Sanctuary
North Parade, The Promenade, Skegness, Lincolnshire PE25 1DB
Tel: (01754) 764345 www.skegnessnatureland.co.uk
Collection of performing seals, baby seals, penguins, aquarium, crocodiles, snakes, terrapins, scorpions, tropical birds, butterflies (April-October) and pets.

Snibston Discovery Park
Ashby Road, Coalville, Leicester, Leicestershire LE67 3LN
Tel: (01530) 278444 www.leics.gov.uk/museums
An all-weather and award-winning science and industrial heritage museum.

Spode Visitor Centre
Spode, Church Street, Stoke-on-Trent, Staffordshire ST4 1BX
Tel: (01782) 744011 www.spode.co.uk
Visitors are shown the various processes in the making of bone china. Samples can be bought at the Spode Shop.

The Tales of Robin Hood
30-38 Maid Marian Way, Nottingham, Nottinghamshire NG1 6GF
Tel: (0115) 948 3284
Join the world's greatest medieval adventure. Ride through the magical green wood and play the Silver Arrow game, in the search for Robin Hood.

Twycross Zoo
Twycross, Atherstone, Warwickshire CV9 3PX
Tel: (01827) 880250 www.twycrosszoo.com
A zoo with gorillas, orang-utans, chimpanzees, a modern gibbon complex, elephants, lions, giraffes, a reptile house, pets' corner and rides.

Walsall Arboretum
Lichfield Street, Walsall, West Midlands WS1 1TJ
Tel: (01922) 653148 www.walsallarboretum.co.uk
Picturesque Victorian park with over 79 acres (32 ha) of gardens, lakes and parkland.

Warwick Castle
Warwick, Warwickshire CV34 4QU
Tel: (01926) 406600 www.warwick-castle.co.uk
Set in 60 acres (24 ha) of grounds with state rooms, armoury, dungeon, torture chamber, clock tower, A Royal Weekend Party 1898, Kingmaker – a preparation for battle attractions.

The Wedgwood Story Visitor Centre
Barlaston, Stoke-on-Trent, Staffordshire ST12 9ES
Tel: (01782) 204218 www.thewedgwoodstory.com
New £4.5 million visitor centre. It exhibits centuries of craftsmanship on a plate. Audio guided tour includes exhibition and demonstration areas. Shop and restaurants.

The Wildfowl and Wetlands Trust
The Wildfowl and Wetlands Trust
Slimbridge, Gloucester, Gloucestershire GL2 7BT
Tel: (01453) 890333 www.wwt.org.uk
Tropical house, hides, heated observatory, exhibits, shop, restaurant, children's playground, pond zone.

Worcester Cathedral
10A College Green, Worcester, Worcestershire WR1 2LH
Tel: (01905) 611002
Norman crypt and chapter house, King John's Tomb, Prince Arthur's Chantry, medieval cloisters and buildings. Touch and hearing control visually impaired facilities available.

The Pictures:
1 Alford Craft Market, Lincolnshire
2 Chatsworth House, Derbyshire

HEART OF ENGLAND

Find out more about HEART of England

Further information about holidays and attractions in Heart of England is available from:

HEART OF ENGLAND TOURIST BOARD
Larkhill Road, Worcester WR5 2EZ.
Tel: (01905) 761100 Fax: (01905) 763450
Internet: www.visitheartofengland.com

The following publications are available free from the Heart of England Tourist Board:

Heart of England - The Official Guide 2002
Bed & Breakfast Touring Map including Caravan and Camping

Getting to the HEART of England

BY ROAD: Britain's main motorways (M1/M6/M5) meet in the Heart of England; the M40 links with the M42 south of Birmingham while the M4 provides fast access from London to the south of the region. These road links ensure that the Heart of England is more accessible by road than any other region in the UK.

BY RAIL: The Heart of England lies at the centre of the country's rail network.
There are direct trains from London and other major cities to many towns and cities within the region.

The Pictures:
1 River Avon, Evesham
2 Black Country Museum, Dudley

HEART OF ENGLAND

Where to stay in the Heart of England

Parks in this region are listed in alphabetical order of place name, and then by park. As West Oxfordshire and Cherwell are promoted in both Heart of England and South of England, places in these areas with parks are listed in this section. See South of England for full West Oxfordshire and Cherwell entries if applicable.

Map references refer to the colour location maps at front of this guide. The first number indicates the map to use; the letter and number which follow refer to the grid reference on the map.

At-a-glance symbols can be found inside the back cover flap. Keep this open for easy reference.

ALREWAS, Staffordshire Map ref 5B3

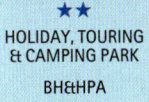

★★
HOLIDAY, TOURING & CAMPING PARK
BH&HPA

WOODSIDE CARAVAN PARK
Fradley Junction, Alrewas, Burton upon Trent DE13 7DN
T: (01283) 790407
F: (01283) 790407
I: www.ukparks.com/woodside

Picturesque old England setting, at busy junction of 2 canals, narrowboats galore, canalside pub, play area, games room, free fishing.

OPEN March–October. 2.8 hectares (7 acres) Level, grassy, hard, sheltered.

From the A38 dual carriageway. Take the A513 signposted for Kings Bromley. After 2 miles turn left for Fradley jct. At canal bridge turn right along canal bank which is tarmac road. We are just past the pub. Signposted.

6	£9.50–£9.50
2	£9.50–£9.50
6	£7.50–£10.00
3	£140.00–£320.00

6 touring pitches
100 units privately owned

ASTON CANTLOW, Warwickshire Map ref 3B1

★★★
HOLIDAY, TOURING & CAMPING PARK
BH&HPA

ISLAND MEADOW CARAVAN PARK
The Mill House, Aston Cantlow B95 6JP
T: (01789) 488273
F: (01789) 488273
E: holiday@islandmeadowcaravanpark.co.uk
I: www.islandmeadowcaravanpark.co.uk

OPEN March–October
2.8 hectares (7 acres) Level, grassy, sheltered.

24	£11.50
24	£11.50
10	£10.00
5	£190.00–£340.00

34 touring pitches
51 units privately owned

From the A3400 between Stratford and Henley-in-Arden or from the A46 between Stratford and Alcester follow the signs for Aston Cantlow. The park is 0.25 miles west of the village. Signposted.

BICESTER, Oxfordshire

See South of England region

BISHOP'S CASTLE, Shropshire Map ref 5A3

★★★
TOURING PARK
BH&HPA

THE OLD SCHOOL CARAVAN PARK
Shelve, Minsterley, Shrewsbury SY5 0JQ
T: (01588) 650410 & 0777 173 1631

OPEN March–November

6	£8.00–£8.00
6	£8.00–£8.00
6	£8.00–£8.00

12 touring pitches

We are on the A488. Signposted.

SYMBOLS The symbols in each entry give information about services and facilities. A key to these symbols appears at the back of this guide.

HEART OF ENGLAND

BOSTON, Lincolnshire Map ref 4A1 *Tourist Information Centre Tel: (01205) 356656*

★★★
HOLIDAY & TOURING PARK
BH&HPA

ORCHARD CARAVAN PARK
Frampton Lane, Hubberts Bridge, Boston
PE20 3QU
T: (01205) 290328
F: (01205) 290247
I: www.orchardpark.co.uk

OPEN January, March–December
14.8 hectares (37 acres)
Level, grassy, sheltered.

60	🚐	£10.00–£12.00
60		£10.00–£12.00
60	▲	£4.00–£10.00
3		£160.00–£180.00

60 touring pitches
125 units privately owned

From A17 take the A1121 towards Boston and at the jct with the B1192 take the Hubberts Bridge turn. Frampton Lane is 1st on the left and the park is 0.25 miles down the lane. Signposted.

BRIDGNORTH, Shropshire Map ref 5A3 *Tourist Information Centre Tel: (01746) 763257*

★★★★
HOLIDAY PARK
BH&HPA

PARK GRANGE HOLIDAYS
Morville, Bridgnorth WV16 4RN
T: (01746) 714285
F: (01746) 714145
E: info@parkgrangeholidays.co.uk
I: www.parkgrangeholidays.co.uk

OPEN All year round
9.6 hectares (24 acres)
Sloping, grassy, hard, sheltered.

	🚐	£4.00–£6.00
		£4.00–£6.00
4		£119.00–£294.00

On the A458 Bridgnorth to Shrewsbury road, 1.5 miles beyond Morville towards Shrewsbury, look for the signs to Park Grange Holiday Luxury Caravans.

BUXTON, Derbyshire Map ref 5B2 *Tourist Information Centre Tel: (01298) 25106*

★★★
TOURING & CAMPING PARK
BH&HPA

COTTAGE FARM CARAVAN PARK
Blackwell in the Peak, Blackwell, Buxton
SK17 9TQ
T: (01298) 85330
E: mail@cottagefarmsite.co.uk
I: www.cottagefarmsite.co.uk

OPEN All year round
1.2 hectares (3 acres) Level, hard, sheltered.

30	🚐	£6.00
30		£6.00
30	▲	£6.00

30 touring pitches

North off A6 signposted with site name.

★★★
HOLIDAY, TOURING & CAMPING PARK
BH&HPA

NEWHAVEN CARAVAN AND CAMPING PARK
Newhaven, Buxton SK17 0DT
T: (01298) 84300
F: (01332) 726027

OPEN March–October
CC: Barclaycard, Delta, Diners, Eurocard, JCB, Mastercard, Switch, Visa
12 hectares (30 acres) Level, sloping, grassy, hard.

95	🚐	£7.25–£8.50
95		£7.25–£8.50
30	▲	£7.25–£8.50

125 touring pitches
73 units privately owned

Halfway between Ashbourne and Buxton on A515 at the jct with the A5012. Signposted.

CHALBURY, Oxfordshire

See South of England region

CIRENCESTER, Gloucestershire Map ref 3B1 *Tourist Information Centre Tel: (01285) 654180*

★★★★
TOURING PARK
BH&HPA

MAYFIELD TOURING PARK
Cheltenham Road, Perrotts Brook,
Cirencester GL7 7BH
T: (01285) 831301
F: (01285) 831301
E: jhutson@btclick.com

OPEN All year round
CC: Amex, Barclaycard, Delta, Eurocard, Mastercard, Solo, Switch, Visa
4.8 hectares (12 acres) Level, sloping, grassy, hard, sheltered.

36	🚐	£7.60–£9.10
25		£7.60–£9.10
36	▲	£6.80–£9.10

72 touring pitches

On the A435 2 miles north of Cirencester, 13 miles south of Cheltenham. Exit A419 at Burford road jct. Signposted.

COTSWOLDS

See under Cirencester

See also Cotswolds in South of England region

COLOUR MAPS Colour maps at the front of this guide pinpoint all places in which you will find parks listed.

108

HEART OF ENGLAND

EVESHAM, Worcestershire Map ref 3B1 Tourist Information Centre Tel: (01386) 446944

★★★★
HOLIDAY &
TOURING PARK

BH&HPA
NCC

THE RANCH CARAVAN PARK
Station Road, Honeybourne, Evesham
WR11 5QG
T: (01386) 830744
F: (01386) 833503
E: enquiries@ranch.co.uk
I: www.ranch.co.uk

OPEN March–November
CC: Barclaycard, Delta,
Eurocard, Mastercard, Switch,
Visa
19.2 hectares (48 acres) Level,
grassy.

120	🚐	£10.50–£15.50
120	🚚	£10.50–£15.50
4	⛺	£215.00–£360.00

120 touring pitches
176 units privately owned

From Evesham take B4035 to Badsey and Bretforton. Left to Honeybourne. Signposted.

LINCOLN, Lincolnshire Map ref 5C2 Tourist Information Centre Tel: (01522) 873213

★★
TOURING &
CAMPING PARK

HARTSHOLME COUNTRY PARK
Skellingthorpe Road, Lincoln LN6 0EY
T: (01522) 873578
F: (01522) 873577

OPEN March–October
.8 hectare (2 acres) Level,
grassy, sheltered.

50	🚐	£7.60–£11.60
50	🚚	£7.60–£11.60
18	⛺	£4.50–£8.00

50 touring pitches

Signposted from A46 Lincoln bypass, brown signs.

MORDIFORD, Herefordshire Map ref 3A1

★★★★
HOLIDAY &
TOURING PARK

BH&HPA

LUCK'S ALL CARAVAN AND CAMPING PARK
Lucksall, Mordiford, Hereford HR1 4LP
T: (01432) 870213

OPEN April–October
CC: Barclaycard, Delta,
Mastercard, Switch, Visa
4 hectares (10 acres) Level,
grassy.

40	🚐	£7.50–£10.25
40	🚚	£7.50–£10.25
40	⛺	£7.00–£9.25
2		£125.00–£285.00

80 touring pitches

On the B4224 between Hereford and Ross-on-Wye. Signposted.

PEAK DISTRICT

See under Buxton, Calver

RUGELEY, Staffordshire Map ref 5B3

★★★★
HOLIDAY &
TOURING PARK

BH&HPA

SILVERTREES CARAVAN PARK
Stafford Brook Road, Penkridge Bank,
Rugeley WS15 2TX
T: (01889) 582185
F: (01889) 582185
I: www.ukparks.co.uk/silvertrees

OPEN March–October
CC: Barclaycard, Mastercard,
Visa
12 hectares (30 acres) Level,
sloping, grassy, hard,
sheltered.

50	🚐	£8.00–£10.00
50	🚚	£8.00–£10.00
8		£199.00–£369.00

50 touring pitches
43 units privately owned

From Rugeley Western Springs Road turn west at traffic lights for Penkridge, after 2 miles turn right into Stafford Brook Road (unclassified). Signposted.

SOUTH CERNEY, Gloucestershire Map ref 3B2

★★★★
HOLIDAY, TOURING
& CAMPING PARK

BH&HPA
NCC

HOBURNE COTSWOLD
Broadway Lane, South Cerney, Cirencester
GL7 5UQ
T: (01285) 860216
F: (01285) 868010
E: enquiries@hoburne.com
I: www.hoburne.com

OPEN March–October
CC: Barclaycard, Delta,
Eurocard, Mastercard, Solo,
Switch, Visa, Visa Electron
28 hectares (70 acres) Level,
grassy, hard.

302	🚐	£11.00–£24.00
302	🚚	£11.00–£24.00
200	⛺	£11.00–£24.00
24		£137.00–£473.00

302 touring pitches
191 units privately owned

From the A419 take the exit towards South Cerney onto Spine Road. After 1 mile turn right into Broadway Lane. The Park is 400 yds on the left. Signposted.

STANDLAKE, Oxfordshire

See South of England region

RATING All accommodation in this guide has been rated, or is awaiting a rating, by a trained Tourist Board assessor.

109

HEART OF ENGLAND

STRATFORD-UPON-AVON, Warwickshire Map ref 3B1 Tourist Information Centre Tel: (01789) 293127

★★★
TOURING & CAMPING PARK
BH&HPA
Ad on this page

DODWELL PARK
Evesham Rd, (B439), Stratford-upon-Avon CV37 9ST
T: (01789) 204957
F: (01926) 620199

OPEN All year round
CC: Barclaycard, Delta, Mastercard, Switch, Visa
.8 hectare (2 acres) Level, sloping, grassy, hard, sheltered.

50	🚐	£9.50–£10.50
20		£9.50–£10.50
50	▲	£6.00–£10.50
50 touring pitches

On the B439 2 miles south west of Stratford-upon-Avon. Signposted.

TELFORD, Shropshire Map ref 5A3 Tourist Information Centre Tel: (01952) 238008

★★★★
TOURING & CAMPING PARK
BH&HPA

SEVERN GORGE PARK
Bridgnorth Road, Tweedale, Telford TF7 4JB
T: (01952) 684789
F: (01952) 684789

OPEN All year round
CC: Barclaycard, Delta, Eurocard, JCB, Mastercard, Solo, Switch, Visa, Visa Electron
3.2 hectares (8 acres) Level, grassy, hard, sheltered.

80	🚐	£10.00–£12.00
80		£10.00–£12.00
40	▲	£10.00–£12.00
80 touring pitches

From M54 jct 4 or 5 take the A442 south signposted Kidderminster (approximately 3 miles). Follow signs for Madeley then Tweedale. Signposted.

TEVERSAL, Nottinghamshire Map ref 5C2

★★★★★
TOURING & CAMPING PARK

SHARDAROBA CARAVAN PARK
Shardaroba, Silverhill Lane, Teversal, Sutton in Ashfield NG17 3JJ
T: (01623) 551838 & 0771 259 0158
F: (01623) 551838
E: stay@shardaroba.co.uk
I: www.shardaroba.co.uk

OPEN All year round
2.4 hectares (6 acres) Level, sloping, grassy, hard.

100	🚐	£8.00–£10.00
40		£8.00–£10.00
100	▲	£8.00–£10.00
100 touring pitches

From the M1 jct 28 take the A38 to Mansfield, take the 1st turning left signed Huthwaite. On the B6027 turn left at the 1st crossroad turn left at the Peacock Hotel. At the T-junction turn left at Carnarvon Arms, site 300 yds right. Signposted.

WEM, Shropshire Map ref 5A3

★★
HOLIDAY, TOURING & CAMPING PARK
BH&HPA

LOWER LACON CARAVAN PARK
Wem, Shrewsbury SY4 5RP
T: (01939) 232376
F: (01939) 233606
E: info@llcp.co.uk
I: www.lowerlaconcaravanpark.co.uk

OPEN All year round
CC: Amex, Barclaycard, Delta, Eurocard, Mastercard, Solo, Switch, Visa, Visa Electron
14.4 hectares (36 acres) Level, grassy, hard, sheltered.

	🚐	£10.90–£15.10
250		£10.90–£15.10
20	▲	£10.90–£15.10
5		£140.00–£310.00
270 touring pitches
50 units privately owned

From Wem over railway crossing, left on the B5065. Site is on the left after 0.5 miles. Signposted.

SB SPECIAL BREAKS
Many establishments offer special promotions and themed breaks. These are highlighted in red. (All such offers are subject to availability.)

DODWELL PARK
Evesham Road (B439), Stratford-upon-Avon, Warwickshire CV37 9ST TEL: 01789 204957

A small, clean, quiet touring park in the countryside on the B439, 2 miles south west of Stratford-Upon-Avon. An ideal location for visiting Shakespeare's birthplace, Warwick Castle and the Cotswolds. We have a well provisioned shop and off licence, electric hook-ups, free hot showers, hard standings, a launderette and country walks to the River Avon.

Free Brochure on request OPEN ALL YEAR

HEART OF ENGLAND

WOODHALL SPA, Lincolnshire Map ref 5D2

★★★★★
**HOLIDAY &
TOURING PARK**

BH&HPA

BAINLAND COUNTRY PARK LTD
Horncastle Road, Woodhall Spa LN10 6UX
T: (01526) 352903 & 353572
F: (01526) 353730
E: bookings@bainland.com
I: www.bainland.com

OPEN All year round
CC: Barclaycard, Delta, Eurocard, Mastercard, Solo, Switch, Visa
16.8 hectares (42 acres) Level, grassy, hard, sheltered.

150	£9.00–£30.00
150	£9.00–£30.00
100	£7.00–£23.00
10	£185.00–£445.00

150 touring pitches

One-and-a-half miles from the centre of Woodhall Spa, going towards Horncastle, on the right just before the petrol station, on the B1191. Signposted.

WYE VALLEY

See under Mordiford

DAVID BELLAMY CONSERVATION AWARDS

If you are looking for a site that's environmentally friendly look for those that have achieved the David Bellamy conservation Award. Recently launched in conjunction with the British Holiday & Home Parks Association, this award is given to sites which are committed to protecting and enhancing the environment – from care of the hedgerows and wildlife to recycling waste – and are members of the Association. More information about this award scheme can be found at the back of the guide.

HEART OF ENGLAND

A brief guide to the main Towns and Villages offering accommodation in the

Heart of England

A ALREWAS, STAFFORDSHIRE - Delightful village of black and white cottages, past which the willow-fringed Trent runs. The Trent and Mersey Canal enhances the scene and Fradley Junction, a mile away, is one of the most charming inland waterway locations in the country.

- **ASTON CANTLOW, WARWICKSHIRE** - Attractive village on the River Alne, with a black and white timbered guild house and a fine old inn.

B BISHOP'S CASTLE, SHROPSHIRE - A 12th C Planned Town with a castle site at the top of the hill and a church at the bottom of the main street. Many interesting buildings with original timber frames hidden behind present day houses. On the Welsh border close to the Clun Forest in quiet, unspoilt countryside.

- **BOSTON, LINCOLNSHIRE** - Historic town famous for its church tower, the Boston Stump, 272 ft high. Still a busy port, the town is full of interest and has links with Boston, Massachusetts, through the Pilgrim Fathers. The cells where they were imprisoned can be seen in the medieval Guildhall.

- **BRIDGNORTH, SHROPSHIRE** - Red sandstone riverside town in 2 parts - High and Low - linked by a cliff railway. Much of interest including a ruined Norman keep, half-timbered 16th C houses, Midland Motor Museum and Severn Valley Railway.

- **BUXTON, DERBYSHIRE** - The highest market town in England and one of the oldest spas, with an elegant Crescent, Poole's Cavern, Opera House and attractive Pavilion Gardens. An excellent centre for exploring the Peak District.

C CIRENCESTER, GLOUCESTERSHIRE - 'Capital of the Cotswolds', Cirencester was Britain's second most important Roman town with many finds housed in the Corinium Museum. It has a very fine Perpendicular church and old houses around the market place.

E EVESHAM, WORCESTERSHIRE - Market town in the centre of a fruit-growing area. There are pleasant walks along the River Avon and many old houses and inns. A fine 16th C bell tower stands between 2 churches near the medieval Almonry Museum.

L LINCOLN, LINCOLNSHIRE - Ancient city dominated by the magnificent 11th C cathedral with its triple towers. A Roman gateway is still used and there are medieval houses lining narrow, cobbled streets. Other attractions include the Norman castle, several museums and the Usher Gallery.

M MORDIFORD, HEREFORDSHIRE - On the River Lugg, which is crossed here by a bridge boasting 9 arches dating from between the 14th C and 16th C. The church retains its Norman south doorway and 13th C tower.

R RUGELEY, STAFFORDSHIRE - Town close to Cannock Chase which has over 2,000 acres of heath and woodlands with forest trails and picnic sites. Nearby is Shugborough Hall (National Trust) with a fine collection of 18th C furniture and interesting monuments in the grounds.

S SOUTH CERNEY, GLOUCESTERSHIRE - The 15,000 acres of lakes and ponds and several Country Parks are being developed at South Cerney as the Cotswold Water Park, for sailing, fishing, bird-watching and other recreational activities.

- **STRATFORD-UPON-AVON, WARWICKSHIRE** - Famous as Shakespeare's home town, Stratford's many attractions include his birthplace, New Place where he died, the Royal Shakespeare Theatre and Gallery and Hall's Croft (his daughter's house).

T TELFORD, SHROPSHIRE - New Town named after Thomas Telford, the famous engineer who designed many of the country's canals, bridges and viaducts. It is close to Ironbridge with its monuments and museums to the Industrial Revolution, including restored 18th C buildings.

- **TEVERSAL, NOTTINGHAMSHIRE** - Village close to Hardwick Hall, the magnificent Elizabethan mansion built for Bess of Hardwick.

W WEM, SHROPSHIRE - Small town connected with Judge Jeffreys who lived in Lowe Hall. Well known for its ales.

- **WOODHALL SPA, LINCOLNSHIRE** - Attractive town which was formerly a spa. It has excellent sporting facilities with a championship golf-course and is surrounded by pine woods.

EAST of England

A region of remote and wild beauty, with vast expanses of open country, unspoilt coastline, sweeping views and big skies. It's renowned for its charming half-timbered towns and villages, ancient sites, historic country houses and nature reserves.

classic sights
Blickling Hall – one of England's great Jacobean houses
Sutton Hoo – important Anglo-Saxon burial site

coast & country
Blakeney Point – good for seal and bird watching
Hatfield Forest – medieval royal hunting forest
Norfolk Broads – miles of waterways through glorious countryside

arts for all
Aldeburgh Festival – classical music in a picturesque setting
Dedham Vale – the landscapes of John Constable; his home and early studio are at East Bergholt. Also the home of Sir Alfred Munnings, famous for his paintings of horses
Sudbury – Gainsborough's house, with fine collection of paintings

delightfully different
Whipsnade Tree Cathedral – unique, 26 acres (10.5ha) cathedral made of trees

The counties of Bedfordshire, Cambridgeshire, Essex, Hertfordshire, Norfolk and Suffolk

FOR MORE INFORMATION CONTACT:
East of England Tourist Board
Toppesfield Hall, Hadleigh, Suffolk IP7 5DN
Tel: (01473) 822922 Fax: (01473) 823063
Email: eastofenglandtouristboard@compuserve.com
Internet: www.eastofenglandtouristboard.com

The Pictures:
1 Horsey Mere, Norfolk
2 King's College, Cambridge
3 Norwich

Places to Visit - see pages 114-118
Where to Stay - see pages 119-123

113

EAST OF ENGLAND

PLACES to visit

You will find hundreds of interesting places to visit during your stay, just some of which are listed in these pages. Contact any Tourist Information Centre in the region for more ideas on days out.

Audley End House and Park
Audley End, Saffron Walden, Essex CB11 4JF
Tel: (01799) 522399
A palatial Jacobean house remodelled in the 18thC-19thC with a magnificent Great Hall with 17thC plaster ceilings. Rooms and furniture by Robert Adam and park by 'Capability' Brown.

Banham Zoo
The Grove, Banham, Norwich, Norfolk NR16 2HE
Tel: (01953) 887771 www.banhamzoo.co.uk
Wildlife spectacular which will take you on a journey to experience tigers, leopards and zebra and some of the world's most exotic, rare and endangered animals.

Barleylands Farm
Barleylands Road, Billericay, Essex CM11 2UD
Tel: (01268) 290209
Visitor centre with a rural museum, animal centre, craft studios, blacksmith's shop, glass-blowing studio with a viewing gallery, miniature steam railway and a restaurant.

Blickling Hall
Blickling, Norwich, Norfolk NR11 6NF
Tel: (01263) 738030 www.nationaltrust.org.uk
A Jacobean redbrick mansion with garden, orangery, parkland and lake. There is also a display of fine tapestries and furniture.

Bressingham Steam Experience and Gardens
Bressingham, Diss, Norfolk IP22 2AB
Tel: (01379) 687386 www.bressingham.co.uk
Steam rides through five miles of woodland. Six acres (2 ha) of the Island Beds plant centre. Mainline locomotives, the Victorian Gallopers and over 50 steam engines.

Bure Valley Railway
Aylsham Station, Norwich Road, Aylsham, Norwich, Norfolk NR11 6BW
Tel: (01263) 733858 www.bvrw.co.uk
A 15-inch narrow-gauge steam railway covering nine miles of track from Wroxham, in the heart of the Norfolk Broads, to Aylsham, a bustling market town.

Colchester Castle
Colchester, Essex CO1 1TJ
Tel: (01206) 282931
www.colchestermuseums.org.uk
A Norman keep on the foundations of a Roman temple. The archaeological material includes much on Roman Colchester (Camulodunum).

EAST OF ENGLAND

Colchester Zoo
Maldon Road, Stanway, Colchester, Essex CO3 5SL
Tel: (01206) 331292 www.colchester-zoo.co.uk
Zoo with 200 species and some of the best cat and primate collections in the UK, 60 acres (27 ha) of gardens and lakes, award-winning animal enclosures and picnic areas.

Ely Cathedral
Chapter House, The College, Ely, Cambridgeshire CB7 4DL
Tel: (01353) 667735
One of England's finest cathedrals with guided tours and tours of the Octagon and West Tower, monastic precincts and also a brass-rubbing centre and Stained Glass Museum.

Fritton Lake Country World
Fritton, Great Yarmouth, Norfolk NR31 9HA
Tel: (01493) 488208
A 250-acre (101-ha) centre with a children's assault course, putting, an adventure playground, golf, fishing, boating, wildfowl, heavy horses, cart rides, falconry and flying displays.

The Gardens of the Rose
The Royal National Rose Society, Chiswell Green, St Albans, Hertfordshire AL2 3NR
Tel: (01727) 850461 www.roses.co.uk
The Royal National Rose Society's Garden with 27 acres (11 ha) of garden and trial grounds for new varieties of rose. Roses of all types displayed with 1,700 different varieties.

Hatfield House, Park and Gardens
Hatfield, Hertfordshire AL9 5NQ
Tel: (01707) 287010 www.hatfield-house.co.uk
Magnificent Jacobean house, home of the Marquess of Salisbury. Exquisite gardens, model soldiers and park trails. Childhood home of Queen Elizabeth I.

Hedingham Castle
Castle Hedingham, Halstead, Essex C09 3DJ
Tel: (01787) 460261
www.hedinghamcastle@aspects.net
The finest Norman keep in England, built in 1140 by the deVeres, Earls of Oxford. Visited by Kings Henry VII and VIII and Queen Elizabeth I and besieged by King John.

Holkham Hall
Wells-next-the-Sea, Norfolk NR23 1AB
Tel: (01328) 710227 www.holkham.co.uk
A classic 18thC Palladian-style mansion. Part of a great agricultural estate and a living treasure house of artistic and architectural history along with a bygones collection.

Ickworth House, Park and Gardens
The Rotunda, Horringer, Bury St Edmunds, Suffolk IP29 5QE
Tel: (01284) 735270 www.nationaltrust.org.uk
An extraordinary oval house with flanking wings, begun in 1795. Fine paintings, a beautiful collection of Georgian silver, an Italian garden and stunning parkland.

Imperial War Museum
Duxford, Cambridge, Cambridgeshire CB2 4QR
Tel: (01223) 835000 www.iwm.org.uk
Over 180 aircraft on display with tanks, vehicles and guns, an adventure playground, shops and a restaurant.

The Pictures:
1 River Wensum, Norfolk
2 Punting on the River Cam, Cambridge
3 Globe Inn, Linslade, Bedfordshire
4 Thorpeness, Suffolk
5 Tulip fields

EAST OF ENGLAND

Kentwell Hall
Long Melford, Sudbury, Suffolk CO10 9BA
Tel: (01787) 310207 www.kentwell.co.uk
A mellow redbrick Tudor manor surrounded by a moat, this family home has been interestingly restored with Tudor costume displays, a 16thC house and mosaic Tudor rose maze.

Knebworth House, Gardens and Park
Knebworth, Stevenage, Hertfordshire SG3 6PY
Tel: (01438) 812661 www.knebworthhouse.com
Tudor manor house, re-fashioned in the 19thC, housing a collection of manuscripts, portraits and Jacobean banquet hall. Formal gardens and adventure playground.

Leighton Buzzard Railway
Page's Park Station, Billington Road, Leighton Buzzard, Bedfordshire LU7 4TN
Tel: (01525) 373888 www.buzzrail.co.uk
An authentic narrow-gauge light railway, built in 1919, offering a 65-minute return journey into the Bedfordshire countryside.

Marsh Farm Country Park
Marsh Farm Road, South Woodham Ferrers, Chelmsford, Essex CM3 5WP
Tel: (01245) 321552
www.marshfarmcountrypark.co.uk
A farm centre with sheep, a pig unit, free-range chickens, milking demonstrations, indoor and outdoor adventure play areas, nature reserve, walks, picnic area and pets' corner.

Melford Hall
Long Melford, Sudbury, Suffolk CO10 9AA
Tel: (01787) 880286
www.nationaltrust.org.uk/eastanglia
Turreted brick Tudor mansion with 18thC and Regency interiors. Collection of Chinese porcelain, gardens and a walk in the grounds. Dogs on leads, where permitted.

Minsmere Nature Reserve
Westleton, Saxmundham, Suffolk IP17 3BY
Tel: (01728) 648281 www.rspb.org.uk
RSPB reserve on the Suffolk coast with bird-watching hides and trails, year-round events, guided walk and visitor centre with large shop and welcoming tearooms.

National Horseracing Museum and Tours
99 High Street, Newmarket, Suffolk CB8 8JL
Tel: (01638) 667333 www.nhrm.co.uk
Award-winning display of the people and horses involved in racing's amazing history. Minibus tours to gallops, stables and equine pool. Hands-on gallery with horse simulator.

National Stud
Newmarket, Suffolk CB8 0XE
Tel: (01638) 663464 www.nationalstud.co.uk
A visit to the National Stud consists of a conducted tour which will include top thoroughbred stallions, mares and foals.

Norfolk Lavender Limited
Caley Mill, Heacham, King's Lynn, Norfolk PE31 7JE
Tel: (01485) 570384 www.norfolk-lavender.co.uk
Lavender is distilled from the flowers and the oil made into a wide range of gifts. There is a slide show when the distillery is not working.

Norwich Cathedral
The Close, Norwich, Norfolk NR1 4EH
Tel: (01603) 218321 www.cathedral.org.uk
A Norman cathedral from 1096 with 14thC roof bosses depicting bible scenes from Adam and Eve to the Day of Judgement. Cloisters, cathedral close, shop and restaurant.

Oliver Cromwell's House
29 St Marys Street, Ely, Cambridgeshire CB7 4HF
Tel: (01353) 662062 www.elyeastcambs.co.uk
The family home of Oliver Cromwell with a 17thC kitchen, parlour, a haunted bedroom, a Tourist Information Centre, souvenirs and craft shop.

Peter Beales Roses
London Road, Attleborough, Norfolk NR17 1AY
Tel: (01953) 454707 www.classicroses.co.uk
Two and a half acres (1 ha) of display rose garden set in rural surroundings.

Pleasure Beach
South Beach Parade, Great Yarmouth, Norfolk NR30 3EH
Tel: (01493) 844585
Rollercoaster, Terminator, log flume, Twister, monorail, galloping horses, caterpillar, ghost train and fun house. Height restrictions are in force on some rides.

EAST OF ENGLAND

Pleasurewood Hills Theme Park
Leisure Way, Corton, Lowestoft, Suffolk NR32 5DZ
Tel: (01502) 586000 pleasurewoodhills.co.uk
Crazy coaster, tidal wave watercoaster, log flume, chairlift, two railways, pirate ship, Aladdin's cave, parrot and sea-lion shows, the cannonball express and rattlesnake rides.

Sainsbury Centre for Visual Arts
University of East Anglia, Norwich, Norfolk NR4 7TJ
Tel: (01603) 456060 www.uea.ac.uk/scva
Housing the Sainsbury collection of works by Picasso, Bacon and Henry Moore alongside many objects of pottery and art. Also a cafe and an art bookshop with activities monthly.

Sandringham
Sandringham, King's Lynn, Norfolk PE35 6EN
Tel: (01553) 772675 www.sandringhamestate.co.uk
The country retreat of HM The Queen. A delightful house and 60 acres (24 ha) of grounds and lakes. There is also a museum of royal vehicles and royal memorabilia.

Shuttleworth Collection
Old Warden Aerodrome, Biggleswade, Bedfordshire SG18 9EP
Tel: (01767) 627288 www.shuttleworth.org
A unique historical collection of aircraft, from a 1909 Bleriot to a 1942 Spitfire (in flying condition), and cars, dating from an 1898 Panhard (in running order).

Somerleyton Hall and Gardens
Somerleyton, Lowestoft, Suffolk NR32 5QQ
Tel: (01502) 730224 www.somerleyton.co.uk
Anglo Italian-style mansion with state rooms, a maze, 12-acre (5-ha) gardens with azaleas and rhododendrons, miniature railway, shop and tearooms.

Stondon Museum
Station Road, Lower Stondon, Henlow Camp, Henlow, Bedfordshire SG16 6JN
Tel: (01462) 850339 www.transportmuseum.co.uk
A museum with transport exhibits from the early 1900s to the 1980s. The largest private collection in England of bygone vehicles from the beginning of the century.

Thursford Collection
Thursford Green, Thursford, Fakenham, Norfolk NR21 0AS
Tel: (01328) 878477
Musical evenings some Tuesdays from mid-July to the end of September. A live musical show with nine mechanical organs and a Wurlitzer show starring Robert Wolfe (daily 29 March-mid October).

Whipsnade Wild Animal Park
Dunstable, Bedfordshire LU6 2LF
Tel: (01582) 872171 www.whipsnade.co.uk
Whipsnade Wild Animal Park has over 2,500 animals and is set in 600 acres (243 ha) of beautiful parkland. The Great Whipsnade Railway and free animal demonstrations.

Wimpole Hall and Home Farm
Arrington, Royston, Hertfordshire SG8 0BW
Tel: (01223) 207257 www.wimpole.org
An 18thC house in a landscaped park with a folly, Chinese bridge. Plunge bath and yellow drawing room in the house, the work of John Soane. Home Farm has a rare breeds centre.

Woburn Abbey
Woburn, Milton Keynes, Bedfordshire MK17 9WA
Tel: (01525) 290666 www.woburnabbey.co.uk
An 18thC Palladian mansion, altered by Henry Holland, the Prince Regent's architect, containing a collection of English silver, French and English furniture and art.

Woburn Safari Park
Woburn, Milton Keynes, Bedfordshire MK17 9QN
Tel: (01525) 290407 www.woburnsafari.co.uk
Drive through the safari park with 30 species of animals in natural groups just a windscreen's width away, plus the action-packed Wild World Leisure Area with shows for all.

The Pictures:
1 St Alban's Cathedral
2 Cromer, Norfolk

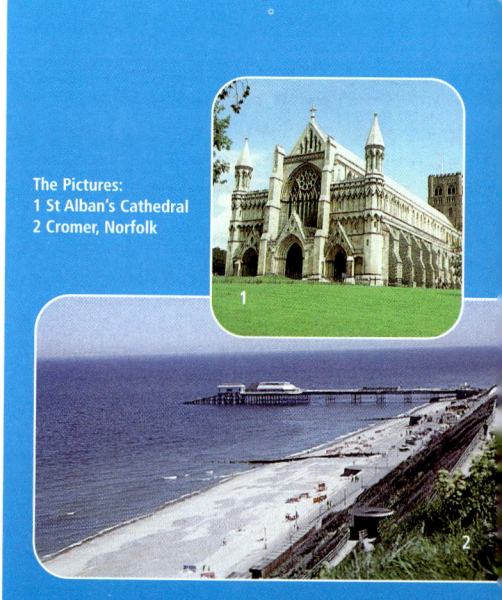

EAST OF ENGLAND

Find out more about the East of England

Further information about holidays and attractions in the East of England is available from:

EAST OF ENGLAND TOURIST BOARD
Toppesfield Hall, Hadleigh, Suffolk IP7 5DN
Tel: (01473) 822922 Fax: (01473) 823063
Email: eastofenglandtouristboard@compuserve.com
Internet: www.eastofenglandtouristboard.com

The following publications are available from The East of England Tourist Board:

East of England - The Official Guide 2002
an information packed A5 guide featuring all you need to know about places to visit and things to see and do in the East of England. From historic houses to garden centres, from animal collections to craft centres - the Guide has it all, including film and TV locations, city, town and village information, events, shopping, car tours plus lots more! Price £3.99 (excl. p&p).

England's Cycling Country
the East of England offers perfect cycling country - from quiet country lanes to ancient trackways. This free publication promotes the many Cycling Discovery Maps that are available to buy (£1.50 excl. p&p), as well as providing useful information for anyone planning a cycling tour of the region

Getting to the East of England

BY ROAD: The region is easily accessible. From London and the south via the A1, M11, M25, A10, M1, A46 and A12. From the north via the A17, A1, A15, A5, M1 and A6. From the west via the A14, A47, A421, A428, A418, A41 and A427.

BY RAIL: Regular fast trains run to all major cities and towns in the region. London stations which serve the region are Liverpool Street, Kings Cross, Fenchurch Street, Moorgate, St Pancras, London Marylebone and London Euston. Bedford, Luton and St Albans are on the Thameslink line which runs to Kings Cross and onto London Gatwick Airport. There is also a direct link between London Stansted Airport and Liverpool Street. Through the Channel Tunnel, there are trains direct from Paris and Brussels to Waterloo Station, London. A short journey on the Underground will bring passengers to those stations operating services into the East of England. Further information on rail journeys in the East of England can be obtained on (0845) 748 4950.

EAST OF ENGLAND

Where to stay in the East of England

Parks in this region are listed in alphabetical order of place name, and then in alphabetical order of park.

Map references refer to the colour location maps at front of this guide. The first number indicates the map to use; the letter and number which follow refer to the grid reference on the map.

At-a-glance symbols can be found inside the back cover flap. Keep this open for easy reference.

BACTON-ON-SEA, Norfolk Map ref 4C1

★★★★★
HOLIDAY PARK
BH&HPA

CABLE GAP CARAVAN PARK
Coast Road, Bacton-on-Sea, Norwich NR12 0EW
T: (01692) 650667 & 0800 0686870
F: (01692) 651388
E: cablegap@freenet.co.uk
I: www.cable-gap.co.uk

25 £120.00–£379.00
43 units privately owned

Family-run park. Situated between the beach and the countryside. 10% discount on selected weeks for 2 persons or 2 persons and a baby under 2 years.

OPEN March–October. 2.4 hectares (6 acres) Level, grassy.
CC: Barclaycard, Delta, JCB, Mastercard, Switch, Visa

From North Walsham take the B1150 to Bacton-on-Sea. At T-junction turn left towards Cromer on the B1159.

BANHAM, Norfolk Map ref 4B1

★★★★
TOURING & CAMPING PARK

APPLEWOOD CARAVAN AND CAMPING PARK
The Grove, Banham, Norwich NR16 2HE
T: (01953) 888370
F: (01953) 887445

OPEN All year round
CC: Barclaycard, Delta, Eurocard, JCB, Maestro, Mastercard, Solo, Switch, Visa, Visa Electron
Level, grassy.

£10.50–£12.50
£10.50–£12.50
100 touring pitches

From the A11 to Attleborough then Banham on the B1077. New Buckenham to the B1113 to Banham. From Diss on the A140 to New Buckenham then to Banham on the B1113. Signposted.

BAWBURGH, Norfolk Map ref 4B1

★★★★
TOURING PARK
Ad on back cover

NORFOLK SHOWGROUND CARAVAN CLUB SITE
Royal Norfolk Showground, Long Lane, Bawburgh, Norwich NR9 3LX
T: (01603) 742708
I: www.caravanclub.co.uk

OPEN May–September
CC: Barclaycard, Mastercard, Visa
2 hectares (5 acres).

60   £6.50–£14.50
60
60 touring pitches

Turn off A47 Norwich Southern Bypass at Longwater intersection (Bawburgh). Follow signpost Bawburgh, site entrance on right 0.25 miles.

PRICES Please check prices and other details at the time of booking

119

EAST OF ENGLAND

BUNGAY, Suffolk Map ref 4C1

★★★
TOURING & CAMPING PARK
BH&HPA

OUTNEY MEADOW CARAVAN PARK
Outney Meadow, Bungay NR35 1HG
T: (01986) 892338
F: (01986) 896627

OPEN March–October
3.2 hectares (8 acres) Level, grassy, hard, sheltered.

45	🚐	£7.50–£12.00
45	🚗	£7.50–£12.00
45	⛺	£7.50–£12.00

45 touring pitches
20 units privately owned

Signposted from roundabout at jct off the A144 and A143.

CAMBRIDGE, Cambridgeshire Map ref 3D1 Tourist Information Centre Tel: (01223) 322640

★★★★★
TOURING & CAMPING PARK
BH&HPA

HIGHFIELD FARM TOURING PARK
Long Road, Comberton, Cambridge CB3 7DG
T: (01223) 262308
F: (01223) 262308

60	🚐	£8.00–£9.25
60	🚗	£8.00–£9.00
60	⛺	£8.00–£9.00

120 touring pitches

A popular family-run park with excellent facilities close to the university city of Cambridge, Imperial War Museum, Duxford. Ideally situated for touring East Anglia.
OPEN April–October. 30.4 hectares (76 acres) Level, grassy, hard, sheltered.

From Cambridge, take A428 to Bedford. After 3 miles, turn left at roundabout and follow sign to Comberton. From M11, take A603 to Sandy at jct 12 for 0.5 miles. Then take B1046 to Comberton. Signposted.

GREAT YARMOUTH, Norfolk Map ref 4C1

★★★★
TOURING PARK
BH&HPA

THE GRANGE TOURING PARK
Ormesby St Margaret, Great Yarmouth NR29 3QG
T: (01493) 730306 & 730023
F: (01493) 730188
E: john.groat@virgin.net

72	🚐	£6.50–£11.50
72	🚗	£6.50–£11.50
72	⛺	£5.00–£11.50

72 touring pitches

Level grass park just 5 minutes from Great Yarmouth, very close to Norfolk Broads. First-class facilities.
OPEN March–September. 1.6 hectares (4 acres) Level, grassy, sheltered.

Three miles north of Great Yarmouth on the B1159 off the A149. Signposted.

★★★
HOLIDAY & TOURING PARK
BH&HPA

GRASMERE CARAVAN PARK (T.B)
Bultitudes Loke, Yarmouth Road, Caister-on-Sea, Great Yarmouth NR30 5DH
T: (01493) 720382

OPEN April–October
CC: Barclaycard, Delta, Mastercard, Switch, Visa
2 hectares (5 acres) Level, grassy, stony, hard.

46	🚐	£6.00–£8.50
46	🚗	£6.00–£8.50
9	⛺	£100.00–£300.00

46 touring pitches
53 units privately owned

Take the A149 from Great Yarmouth and enter Caister at the roundabout by Yarmouth Stadium. After 0.5 miles, turn left 100 yards past the old petrol station site. Signposted.

★★★★
TOURING PARK
Ad on back cover

GREAT YARMOUTH CARAVAN CLUB SITE
Great Yarmouth Racecourse, Jellicoe Road, Great Yarmouth NR30 4AU
T: (01493) 855323
I: www.caravanclub.co.uk

OPEN April–September
CC: Barclaycard, Mastercard, Visa
2 hectares (5 acres) Level, grassy.

| 122 | 🚐 | £6.50–£17.00 |
| 122 | 🚗 | £6.50–£17.00 |

122 touring pitches

Travel north on A149 and turn left at lights. Within 1 mile past 40mph sign on southern outskirts of Caister into Jellicoe Road. Within 0.25 miles, turn left into racecourse entrance and continue across race track.

EAST OF ENGLAND

GREAT YARMOUTH continued

★★★★ HOLIDAY PARK
BH&HPA
NCC
Ad p12

HOPTON HOLIDAY VILLAGE
Warren Lane, Hopton-on-Sea, Great Yarmouth NR31 9BW
T: (01502) 730214
F: (01502) 732305
E: enquiries@british-holidays.co.uk
I: www.british-holidays.co.uk

OPEN April–October
CC: Delta, Mastercard, Solo, Switch, Visa

210 — £99.00–£600.00
700 units privately owned

From the A12, turn off at the sign for Hopton Holiday Village. Signposted.

★★★★ HOLIDAY PARK
BH&HPA
Ad on this page

LIFFENS HOLIDAY PARK
Burgh Castle, Great Yarmouth NR31 9QB
T: (01493) 780357
F: (01493) 782383
I: www.liffens.co.uk

OPEN April–October
CC: Delta, Mastercard, Switch, Visa
12 hectares (30 acres) Level, grassy.

100 — £9.00–£14.00
100 — £9.00–£14.00
50 — £9.00–£14.00
35 — £150.00–£400.00
150 touring pitches
85 units privately owned

From Great Yarmouth, follow signs for Beccles and Lowestoft. Watch for left turn sign for Burgh Castle, follow for 2 miles to T-junction and turn right. Then follow signs to holiday park.

★★★ HOLIDAY PARK
BH&HPA
Ad on this page

LIFFENS WELCOME HOLIDAY CENTRE
Butt Lane, Burgh Castle, Great Yarmouth NR31 9PY
T: (01493) 780481
F: (01493) 781627
I: www.liffens.co.uk

OPEN April–October
CC: Barclaycard, Delta, JCB, Maestro, Mastercard, Solo, Switch, Visa, Visa Electron
Level, grassy, sheltered.

150 — £9.00–£14.00
150 — £9.00–£14.00
150 — £9.00–£14.00
10 — £150.00–£400.00
150 touring pitches
50 units privately owned

On the main A143 from Great Yarmouth to Beccles Road. Proceed through the village of Bradwell to the start of a small dual carriageway. Take 1st right turn, next turning on right and Liffens Holiday Centre is along on right.

★★★★ HOLIDAY PARK
BH&HPA
Ad p122

VAUXHALL HOLIDAY PARK
Acle New Road, Great Yarmouth NR30 1TB
T: (01493) 857231
F: (01493) 331122
E: vauxhall.holidays@virgin.net
I: www.vauxhall-holiday-park.co.uk

OPEN April–October
CC: Barclaycard, Delta, Mastercard, Switch, Visa, Visa Electron
18.8 hectares (47 acres) Level, grassy.

252 — £13.00–£24.00
252 — £13.00–£24.00
— £13.00–£24.00
373 — £172.00–£545.00
252 touring pitches

On the A47 as you approach Great Yarmouth from Norwich. Signposted.

TOWN INDEX

This can be found at the back of the guide. If you know where you want to stay, the index will give you the page number listing all accommodation in your chosen town, city or village.

GREAT YARMOUTH

Liffens – the best choice!

Choose an activity-filled stay at the 4★ Liffens Holiday Park or enjoy the quieter pace of the 3★ Liffens Welcome Holiday Centre – both within 10 mins drive Gt. Yarmouth.

Book on-line or order a brochure from our website:
www.liffens.co.uk

Both parks offer bars, entertainment, restaurants and heated pools with luxury s/c caravans or tenting/touring in landscaped settings. Hook-ups available.

24HR BROCHURE LINE 01493 780357 QUOTE BTA 02
Liffen's Holiday Park, Burgh Castle, Gt. Yarmouth, Norfolk NR31 9QB

EAST OF ENGLAND

KING'S LYNN, Norfolk Map ref 4B1 *Tourist Information Centre Tel: (01553) 763044*

★★★
TOURING PARK

BANK FARM CARAVAN PARK
Bank Farm, Fallow Pipe Road, Saddle Bow,
King's Lynn PE34 3AS
T: (01553) 617305
F: (01553) 617648

OPEN March–October
120 hectares (300 acres)
Level, grassy, sheltered.

15	🚐	£7.00–£7.00
15	🏠	£7.00–£7.00
2	⛺	£5.00–£5.00

15 touring pitches

Off King's Lynn southern bypass (A47) via slip road signposted Saddlebow. Once in the village, cross the river bridge and after 1 mile, fork right into Fallow Pipe Road. The farm is 0.66 miles, by the River Great Ouse. Signposted.

MERSEA ISLAND, Essex Map ref 4B3

★★★
HOLIDAY, TOURING
& CAMPING PARK

BH&HPA

WALDEGRAVES HOLIDAY PARK
Mersea Island, Colchester CO5 8SE
T: (01206) 382898
F: (01206) 385359
E: holidays@waldegraves.co.uk
I: www.waldegraves.co.uk

OPEN March–November
CC: Amex, Barclaycard, Delta,
Eurocard, Mastercard, Switch,
Visa
10 hectares (25 acres) Level,
grassy, sheltered.

40	🚐	£9.00–£15.00
40	🏠	£9.00–£15.00
20	⛺	£9.00–£15.00
21	🏠	£130.00–£350.00

60 touring pitches
205 units privately owned

Take the B1025 from Colchester then left to East Mersea, 2nd right then follow the brown tourist signs.

NORFOLK BROADS

See under Bungay, Great Yarmouth

POLSTEAD, Suffolk Map ref 4B2

★★★★
TOURING &
CAMPING PARK

BH&HPA

POLSTEAD TOURING PARK
Holt Road, Polstead, Colchester CO6 5BZ
T: (01787) 211969
F: (01787) 211969

OPEN March–October
1.6 hectares (4 acres) Level,
grassy, sheltered.

30	🚐	£7.50–£9.00
30	🏠	£7.50–£9.00
30	⛺	£5.00–£8.00

30 touring pitches

Off A1071 between Boxford and Hadleigh opposite the Brewers Arms pub, follow signs.

SAHAM HILLS, Norfolk Map ref 4B1

★★★★
TOURING &
CAMPING PARK

LOWE CARAVAN PARK
Ashdale, Hills Road, Saham Hills, Thetford
IP25 7EZ
T: (01953) 881051
F: (01953) 881051

OPEN All year round

20	🚐	£5.50–£7.50
20	🏠	£5.50–£7.50
20	⛺	£5.50–£7.50
1	🏠	£195.00–£295.00

20 touring pitches

From A11 Thetford, take Watton road and go through Watton High Street. Take 2nd turning on right, Saham Road, past Richmond Golf Club, take 2nd turning on right. At T-junction turn right and then 1st drive on the right.

TOPS FOR TOURING HOLIDAYS IN GREAT YARMOUTH

FREE WITH YOUR HOLIDAY
STAR STUDDED ENTERTAINMENT
INDOOR TROPICAL WATERWORLD
SPORT & FITNESS FUN
KID'S CLUB & NURSERY
SATELLITE T.V.

GREAT YARMOUTH
Vauxhall HOLIDAY PARK 2002
Great Yarmouth No.1 Holiday Park

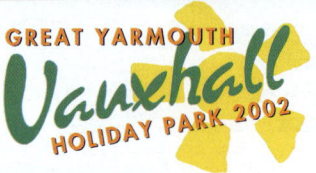

- OVER 250 ALL ELECTRIC SITES • AWNINGS FREE • GRASS & HARD STANDINGS • MODERN HEATED SHOWER & TOILET BLOCKS • FREE CAR PARKING •
- GAS CYLINDER REFILLS ON SITE • NIGHT SECURITY FOR LATE ARRIVALS • HAIRDRYER • BABY CHANGING FACILITIES • NEW SUPER PITCH •

FOR A FREE BROCHURE
TEL: 01493 857231
www.vauxhall-holiday-park.co.uk
5 Acle New Road Great Yarmouth Norfolk NR30 1TB Ref: 5

EAST OF ENGLAND

ST OSYTH, Essex Map ref 4B3

★★★
HOLIDAY, TOURING & CAMPING PARK

BH&HPA
NCC

Ad p12

THE ORCHARDS HOLIDAY VILLAGE
St Osyth, Clacton-on-Sea CO16 8LJ
T: (01255) 820651
F: (01255) 820184
E: enquiries@british-holidays.co.uk
I: www.british-holidays.co.uk

OPEN April–October
CC: Delta, Mastercard, Solo, Switch, Visa

89		£10.50–£25.20
89		£10.50–£25.20
209		£160.00–£602.00

89 touring pitches
963 units privately owned

From Clacton-on-Sea, take B1027 towards Colchester. Approximately 4 miles from Clacton turn left following signs for St Osyth. At crossroads in St Osyth continue across and follow road for 3 miles, park is at the end of the road. Signposted.

SCRATBY, Norfolk Map ref 4C1

★★★★
TOURING & CAMPING PARK

BH&HPA

SCRATBY HALL CARAVAN PARK
Scratby, Great Yarmouth NR29 3PH
T: (01493) 730283

Secluded rural setting, approximately 5 miles north of Great Yarmouth and 0.5 mile from the beach. Free showers, shop, laundrette, children's playground, disabled facilities.

OPEN April–October. 2 hectares (5 acres) Level, grassy, sheltered.

Great Yarmouth A149 to Caister. Onto B1159 Scratby, site signed.

108		£5.25–£11.50
108		£5.25–£11.50
108		£5.25–£11.50

108 touring pitches

STANHOE, Norfolk Map ref 4B1

★★★★
TOURING PARK

THE RICKELS CARAVAN SITE
The Rickels, Bircham Road, Stanhoe, King's Lynn PE31 8PU
T: (01485) 518671
F: (01485) 518969

OPEN March–October
3.2 hectares (8 acres) Level, sloping, grassy, sheltered.

15		£7.00–£8.50
10		£7.00–£8.50
5		£7.00–£8.50

30 touring pitches

From King's Lynn, take the A148 to Hillington and turn left onto the B1153 to Great Bircham. Fork right onto the B1155. Go to the crossroads and straight over. The site is 100yds on the left. Signposted.

WOODBRIDGE, Suffolk Map ref 4C2 *Tourist Information Centre Tel: (01394) 382240*

★★★
TOURING & CAMPING PARK

FOREST CAMPING
Tangham Campsite, Rendlesham Forest, Butley, Woodbridge IP12 3NF
T: (01394) 450707
F: (01394) 450707
E: admin@forestcamping.co.uk
I: www.forestcamping.co.uk

OPEN March–October
CC: Barclaycard, Delta, Maestro, Mastercard, Solo, Switch, Visa, Visa Electron
2.8 hectares (7 acres) Level, sloping, grassy.

90		£9.00–£10.00
90		£9.00–£10.00
90		£9.00–£10.00

90 touring pitches

Six miles east of Woodbridge off B1084 to Orford. Signposted.

AT-A-GLANCE SYMBOLS

Symbols at the end of each accommodation entry give useful information about services and facilities. A key to symbols can be found inside the back cover flap. Keep this open for easy reference.

EAST OF ENGLAND

A brief guide to the main Towns and Villages offering accommodation in the East of England

- **BANHAM, NORFOLK** - Home of an extensive wildlife park and monkey sanctuary.
- **BUNGAY, SUFFOLK** - Market town and yachting centre on the River Waveney with the remains of a great 12th C castle. In the market-place stands the Butter Cross, rebuilt in 1689 after being largely destroyed by fire. Nearby at Earsham the Otter Trust.
- **CAMBRIDGE, CAMBRIDGESHIRE** - A most important and beautiful city on the River Cam with 31 colleges forming one of the oldest universities in the world. Numerous museums, good shopping centre, restaurants, theatres, cinema and fine bookshops.
- **GREAT YARMOUTH, NORFOLK** - One of Britain's major seaside resorts with 5 miles of seafront and every possible amenity including an award winning leisure complex offering a huge variety of all-weather facilities. Busy harbour and fishing centre.
- **KING'S LYNN, NORFOLK** - A busy town with many outstanding buildings. The Guildhall and Town Hall are both built of flint in a striking chequer design. Behind the Guildhall in the Old Gaol House the sounds and smells of prison life 2 centuries ago are recreated.
- **ST OSYTH, ESSEX** - St Osyth was the daughter of the first Christian King of East Anglia. The priory gatehouse and gardens are open to the public during the summer.
- **WOODBRIDGE, SUFFOLK** - Once a busy seaport, the town is now a sailing centre on the River Deben. There are many buildings of architectural merit including the Bell and Angel Inns. The 18th C Tide Mill is now restored and open to the public.

Our Countryside Matters!

Country Code

- Always follow the Country code
- Guard against all risk of fire
- Keep your dogs under close control
- Use gates and stiles to cross fences, hedges and walls
- Take your litter home
- Protect wildlife, plants and trees
- Make no unnecessary noise
- Enjoy the countryside and respect its life and work
- Fasten all gates
- Keep to public paths across farmland
- Leave livestock, crops and machinery alone
- Help to keep all water clean
- Take special care on country roads

We hope the countryside will fully open in 2002. However, given the serious nature of Foot and Mouth Disease please be ready to follow this additional advice and respect any further precautions given in local authority notices:

- Don't go onto farmland if you have handled farm animals in the last 7 days
- Avoid contact with farm animals and keep dogs on a lead where they are present
- If you step in dung, remove it before you leave the field • Don't go on paths with a local authority 'closed' notice.

For more information contact Tourist information Centres or Countryside Agency web site www.countryside.gov.uk which links to other local authority web sites providing details about rights of way and access opportunities across England.

SOUTH WEST

A land of myths and legends – and beautiful beaches. The region has cathedral cities, Georgian Bath and maritime Bristol, mysterious castles, evocative country houses and sub-tropical gardens to discover too.

classic sights
Newquay – surfers' paradise
English Riviera – family-friendly beaches
Dartmoor – wild open moorland and rocky tors

coast & country
Runnymede – riverside meadows and woodland
Pegwell Bay & Goodwin Sands – a haven for birds and seals

glorious gardens
Stourhead – 18th century landscape garden
Lost Gardens of Heligan – 19th century gardens

art for all
Tate Gallery St Ives – modern art and the St Ives School
Arnolfini Gallery, Bristol – contemporary arts

distinctively different
Daphne du Maurier – Cornwall inspired many of her novels
Agatha Christie – follow the trail in Torquay

The counties of Bath, Bristol, Cornwall, Devon, Dorset (Western), Isles of Scilly, Somerset, South Gloucestershire and Wiltshire

FOR MORE INFORMATION CONTACT:
South West Tourism
Admail 3186, Exeter EX2 7WH
Tel: (0870) 442 0880 Fax: (0870) 442 0881
Email: info@westcountryholidays.com
Internet: www.westcountryholidays.com

The Pictures:
1 Weston-super-Mare
2 Bath

Places to Visit - see pages 126-130
Where to Stay - see pages 131-149

PLACES to visit

You will find hundreds of interesting places to visit during your stay, just some of which are listed in these pages. Contact any Tourist Information Centre in the region for more ideas on days out.

At Bristol Harbourside
Bristol, Avon BS1 5DB
Tel: (0117) 915 5000 www.at-bristol.org.uk
A £97 million Millennium Landmark project on Bristol's revitalised harbourside. It consists of 3 world-class visitor attractions.

Atwell-Wilson Motor Museum Trust
Downside, Stockley Lane, Calne, Wiltshire SN11 0NF
Tel: (01249) 813119 www.atwell-wilson.org
Motor museum with vintage, post-vintage and classic cars, including American models. Classic motorbikes. A 17thC water meadow walk. Car clubs welcome for rallies. Play area.

Avebury Manor and Garden
Avebury, Marlborough, Wiltshire SN8 1RF
Tel: (01672) 539250
Manor house, regularly altered and of monastic origins. Present buildings date from the early 16thC with Queen Anne alterations and Edwardian renovations. Gardens.

Babbacombe Model Village
Hampton Avenue, Babbacombe, Torquay, Devon TQ1 3LA
Tel: (01803) 315315
www.babbacombemodelvillage.co.uk
Over 400 models, many with sound and animation, with four acres (1.6 ha) of award-winning gardens. See modern towns, villages and rural areas. Stunning illuminations.

Bristol City Museum & Art Gallery
Queen's Road, Bristol, Avon BS8 1RL
Tel: (0117) 922 3571
www.bristol-city.gov.uk/museums
Collection representing applied, oriental and fine art, archaeology, geology, natural history, ethnography and Egyptology.

Bristol Zoo Gardens
Clifton, Bristol, Avon BS8 3HA
Tel: (0117) 973 8951 www.bristolzoo.org.uk
Enjoy an exciting, real life experience and see over 300 species of wildlife in beautiful gardens.

Buckland Abbey
Yelverton, Devon PL20 6EY
Tel: (01822) 853607
Originally a Cistercian monastery, then home of Sir Francis Drake. Ancient buildings, exhibitions, herb garden, craft workshops and estate walks.

SOUTH WEST

Cheddar Caves and Gorge
Cheddar, Somerset BS27 3QF
Tel: (01934) 742343 www.cheddarcaves.co.uk
Beautiful caves located in Cheddar Gorge. Gough's Cave with its cathedral-like caverns, and Cox's Cave with stalagmites and stalactites. Also 'The Crystal Quest' fantasy adventure.

The Combe Martin Motor Cycle Collection
Cross Street, Combe Martin, Ilfracombe, Devon EX34 0DH
Tel: (01271) 882346
www.motorcycle-collection.co.uk
Collection of motorcycles, scooters and invalid carriages, displayed against a background of old petrol pumps, signs and garage equipment. Motoring nostalgia.

Combe Martin Wildlife and Dinosaur Park
Jurassic Hotel, Combe Martin, Ilfracombe, Devon EX34 0NG
Tel: (01271) 882486
Wildlife park and life-size models of dinosaurs.

Crealy Park
Sidmouth Road, Clyst St Mary, Exeter, Devon EX5 1DR
Tel: (01395) 233200 www.crealy.co.uk
One of Devon's largest animal farms. Milk a cow, feed a lamb and pick up a piglet. Adventure playgrounds. Dragonfly Lake and farm trails.

Dairyland Farm World
Newquay, Cornwall TR8 5AA
Tel: (01872) 510246 www.dairylandfarmworld.com
One hundred and seventy cows milked in rotary parlour. Heritage centre. Farm nature trail. Farm park with animals, pets and wildfowl. Daily events. Also conservation area.

Eden Project
Watering Lane Nursery, Pentewan, St Austell, Cornwall PL26 6EN
Tel: (01726) 222900
A 37-acre (15-ha) china clay pit has been dramatically transformed to accommodate the planthouses, visitor centre and temperate parkland.

Exmoor Falconry & Animal Farm
West Lynch Farm, Allerford, Minehead, Somerset TA24 8HJ
Tel: (01643) 862816 www.exmoorfalconry.co.uk
Farm animals, rare breeds, pets' corner, birds of prey and owls. Flying displays daily. Historic farm buildings.

Flambards Village
Culdrose Manor, Helston, Cornwall TR13 0QA
Tel: (01326) 573404 www.flambards.co.uk
Life-size Victorian village with fully stocked shops, plus carriages and fashions. 'Britain in the Blitz' life-size wartime street, historic aircraft, exploratorium.

Heale Garden & Plant Centre
Middle Woodford, Salisbury, Wiltshire SP4 6NT
Tel: (01722) 782504
Mature, traditional-type garden with shrubs, musk and other roses, and kitchen garden. Authentic Japanese teahouse in water garden. Magnolias. Snowdrops and aconites in winter.

International Animal Rescue Animal Tracks
Ash Mill, South Molton, Devon EX36 4QW
Tel: (01769) 550277 www.iar.org.uk
A 60-acre (24-ha) animal sanctuary with a wide range of rescued animals, from monkeys to chinchillas and shire horses to other horses and ponies. Also rare plant nursery.

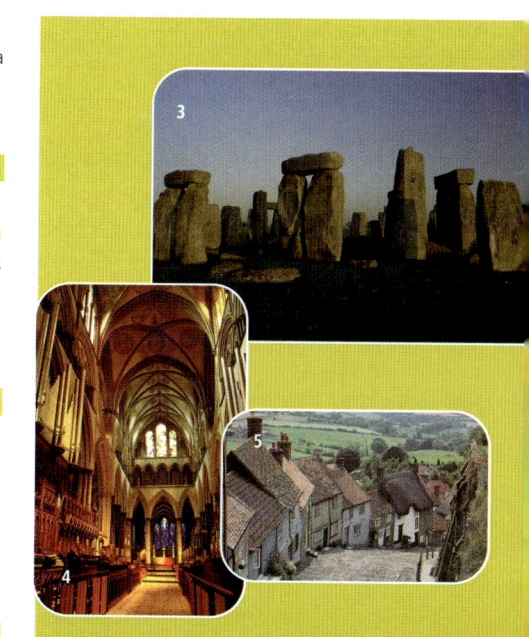

The Pictures:
1 Lands End, Cornwall
2 Clifton Suspension Bridge, Bristol
3 Stonehenge
4 Interior of Salisbury Cathedral
5 Shaftesbury Hill, Dorset

SOUTH WEST

Jamaica Inn Museums (Potters Museum of Curiosity)
Jamaica Inn Courtyard, Bolventor, Launceston, Cornwall PL15 7TS
Tel: (01566) 86838
Museums contain lifetime work of Walter Potter, a Victorian taxidermist. Exhibits include Kittens' Wedding, Death of Cock Robin and The Story of Smuggling.

Longleat
The Estate Office, Warminster, Wiltshire BA12 7NW
Tel: (01985) 844400 www.longleat.co.uk
Elizabethan stately home, safari park, plus a wonderland of family attractions. 'World's Longest Hedge Maze', Safari Boats, Pets' Corner, Longleat railway.

The Lost Gardens of Heligan
Heligan, Pentewan, St Austell, Cornwall PL26 6EN
Tel: (01726) 845100 www.heligan.com
Heligan Gardens is the scene of the largest garden restoration project undertaken since the war. Public access to parts of 'Home Farm'.

Lyme Regis Philpot Museum
Bridge Street, Lyme Regis, Dorset DT7 3QA
Tel: (01297) 443370 www.lymeregismuseum.co.uk
Fossils, geology, local history and lace exhibitions. Museum shop.

National Marine Aquarium
Rope Walk, Coxside, Plymouth, Devon PL4 0LF
Tel: (01752) 600301 www.national-aquarium.co.uk
The United Kingdom's only world-class aquarium, located in the heart of Plymouth. Visitor experiences will include a mountain stream and Caribbean reef complete with sharks.

Newquay Zoo
Trenance Park, Newquay, Cornwall TR7 2LZ
Tel: (01637) 873342 www.newquayzoo.co.uk
A modern, award-winning zoo where you can have fun and learn at the same time. A varied collection of animals, from Acouchi to Zebra.

Paignton Zoo Environmental Park
Totnes Road, Paignton, Devon TQ4 7EU
Tel: (01803) 557479 www.paigntonzoo.org.uk
One of England's largest zoos with over 1,200 animals in the beautiful setting of 75 acres (30 ha) of botanical gardens. The zoo is one of Devon's most popular family days out.

Plant World
St Marychurch Road, Newton Abbot, Devon TQ12 4SE
Tel: (01803) 872939
Four acres (1.6 ha) of gardens including the unique 'map of the world' gardens. Cottage garden. Panoramic views. Comprehensive nursery of rare and more unusual plants.

Powderham Castle
The Estate Office, Kenton, Exeter, Devon EX6 8JQ
Tel: (01626) 890243 www.powderham.co.uk
Built c1390, restored in the 18thC. Georgian interiors, china, furnishings and paintings. Family home of the Courtenays for over 600 years. Fine views across deer park and River Exe.

Plymouth Dome
The Hoe, Plymouth, Devon PL1 2NZ
Tel: (01752) 603300
Purpose-built visitor interpretation centre showing the history of Plymouth and its people from Stone Age beginnings to satellite technology. Situated on Plymouth Hoe.

Railway Village Museum
34 Faringdon Road, Swindon, Wiltshire SN1 5BJ
Tel: (01793) 466553 www.swindon.gov.uk
Foreman's house in original Great Western Railway village. Furnished to re-create a Victorian working-class home.

Roman Baths
Pump Room, Abbey Church Yard, Bath BA1 1LZ
Tel: (01225) 477785 www.romanbaths.co.uk
Roman baths and temple precinct, hot springs and Roman temple. Jewellery, coins, curses and votive offerings from the sacred spring.

St Michael's Mount
Marazion, Cornwall TR17 0HT
Tel: (01736) 710507
Originally the site of a Benedictine chapel, the castle on its rock dates from the 14thC. Fine views towards Land's End and the Lizard. Reached by foot, or ferry at high tide in summer.

Steam – Museum of the Great Western Railway
Kemble Drive, Churchward, Swindon, Wiltshire SN2 2TA
Tel: (01793) 466646 www.steam-museum.org.uk
Historic Great Western Railway locomotives, wide range of nameplates, models, illustrations, posters and tickets.

SOUTH WEST

Stonehenge

Amesbury, Salisbury, Wiltshire SP4 7DE
Tel: (01980) 623108
www.stonehengemasterplan.org
World-famous prehistoric monument built as a ceremonial centre. Started 5,000 years ago and remodelled several times in next 1,500 years.

Stourhead House and Garden

The Estate Office, Stourton, Warminster, Wiltshire BA12 6QD
Tel: (01747) 841152 www.nationaltrust.org.uk
Landscaped garden, laid out c1741-80, with lakes, temples, rare trees and plants. House, begun in c1721 by Colen Campbell, contains fine paintings and Chippendale furniture.

Tate Gallery St Ives

Porthmeor Beach, St Ives, Cornwall TR26 1TG
Tel: (01736) 796226 www.tate.org.uk
Opened in 1993 and offering a unique introduction to modern art. Changing displays focus on the modern movement St Ives is famous for. Also an extensive education programme.

Teignmouth Museum

29 French Street, Teignmouth, Devon TQ14 8ST
Tel: (01626) 777041
Exhibits include a 16thC cannon and artefacts from the Armada wreck, local history, c1920s pier machines and c1877 cannon.

Tintagel Castle

Tintagel, Cornwall PL34 0HE
Tel: (01840) 770328 www.english-heritage.org.uk
Medieval ruined castle on wild, wind-swept coast. Famous for associations with Arthurian legend. Built largely in the 13thC by Richard, Earl of Cornwall. Used as a prison in the 14thC.

Tithe Barn Children's Farm

New Barn Road, Abbotsbury, Weymouth, Dorset DT3 4JF
Tel: (01305) 871817
Extensive children's farm for children under 11 years. Activities include hand-feeding (with bottles) milk to lambs and kids. Replicas of Terracotta Warriors on display in barn.

Totnes Costume Museum – Devonshire Collection of Period Costume

Bogan House, 43 High Street, Totnes, Devon TQ9 5NP
Tel: (01803) 863821
New exhibition of costumes and accessories each season, displayed in one of the historic merchant's houses of Totnes. Bogan House recently restored by Mitchell Trust.

Woodlands Leisure Park

Blackawton, Totnes, Devon TQ9 7DQ
Tel: (01803) 712598
www.woodlands-leisure-park.co.uk
All-weather fun guaranteed with unique combination of indoor and outdoor attractions: 3 watercoasters, toboggan run, massive indoor adventure centre with rides. Falconry and animals.

Wookey Hole Caves and Papermill

Wookey Hole, Wells, Somerset BA5 1BB
Tel: (01749) 672243 www.wookey.co.uk
Spectacular caves and legendary home of the Witch of Wookey. Working Victorian papermill including Old Penny Arcade, Magical Mirror Maze and Cave Diving Museum.

The Pictures:
1 Isles of Scilly
2 Torquay, Devon

SOUTH WEST

Find out more about the
SOUTH WEST

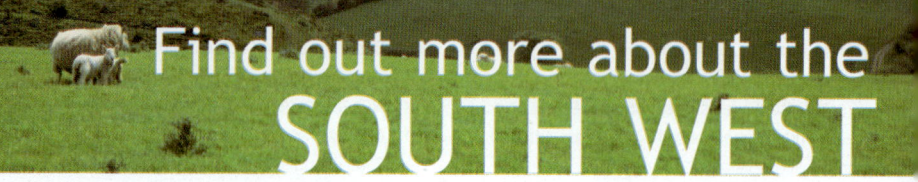

Further information about holidays and attractions in the South West is available from:

SOUTH WEST TOURISM
Admail 3186, Exeter EX2 7WH.
Tel: (0870) 442 0880
Fax: (0870) 442 0881
Email: info@westcountryholidays.com
Internet: www.westcountryholidays.com

The following publications are available free from South West Tourism:
Bed & Breakfast Touring Map
West Country Holiday Homes & Apartments
West Country Hotels and Guesthouses
Glorious Gardens of the West Country
Camping and Caravan Touring Map
Tourist Attractions Touring Map
Trencherman's West Country, Restaurant Guide

Getting to the
SOUTH WEST

BY ROAD: Somerset, Devon and Cornwall are well served from the North and Midlands by the M6/M5 which extends just beyond Exeter, where it links in with the dual carriageways of the A38 to Plymouth, A380 to Torbay and the A30 into Cornwall. The North Devon Link Road A361 joins Junction 27 with the coast of north Devon and A39, which then becomes the Atlantic Highway into Cornwall.

BY RAIL: The main towns in the South West are served throughout the year by fast, direct and frequent rail services from all over the country. InterCity 125 trains operate from London (Paddington) to Chippenham, Swindon, Bath, Bristol, Weston-super-Mare, Taunton, Exeter, Plymouth and Penzance, and also from Scotland, the North East and the Midlands to the South West. A service runs from London (Waterloo) to Exeter, via Salisbury, Yeovil and Crewkerne. Sleeper services operate between Devon and Cornwall and London as well as between Bristol and Glasgow and Edinburgh. Motorail services operate from strategic points to key South West locations.

SOUTH WEST

Where to stay in the South West

Parks in this region are listed in alphabetical order of place name, and then in alphabetical order of park.

Map references refer to the colour location maps at front of this guide. The first number indicates the map to use; the letter and number which follow refer to the grid reference on the map.

At-a-glance symbols can be found inside the back cover flap. Keep this open for easy reference.

ASHBURTON, Devon Map ref 2C2

★★★★
HOLIDAY, TOURING & CAMPING PARK
BH&HPA

ASHBURTON CARAVAN PARK
Waterleat, Ashburton, Newton Abbot TQ13 7HU
T: (01364) 652552
F: (01364) 652552
E: info@ashburtondevon.freeserve.co.uk
I: www.ashburtoncaravanpark.fsnet.co.uk

Select park in sheltered river valley withing Dartmoor National Park. Centrally situated with luxury holiday homes and excellent camping facilities.
OPEN March–October. 1.6 hectares (4 acres) Level, grassy, sheltered.
Off A38 to centre of Ashburton, turn into North Street, bear right before bridge, signed Waterleat with camping logo. One and a half miles north towards moor. Signposted.

35	🚐	£7.50–£10.00
35	🚙	£7.50–£10.00
35	⛺	£7.50–£10.00
8	🏠	£120.00–£260.00

35 touring pitches
28 units privately owned

★★★★
HOLIDAY, TOURING & CAMPING PARK
BH&HPA
Ad p132

PARKERS FARM HOLIDAY PARK
Higher Mead Farm, Alston, Ashburton TQ13 7LJ
T: (01364) 652598
F: (01364) 654004
E: parkersfarm@btconnect.com
I: www.parkersfarm.co.uk

OPEN All year round
CC: Barclaycard, Delta, JCB, Maestro, Mastercard, Solo, Switch, Visa, Visa Electron
148 hectares (370 acres) Level, grassy, hard.

100	🚐	£5.50–£11.00
100	🚙	£5.50–£11.00
100	⛺	£5.50–£11.00
28	🏠	£90.00–£480.00

100 touring pitches

Take A38 from Exeter to Plymouth. When you see sign 26 miles to Plymouth, take 2nd left marked Woodland and Denbury. At Alston Cross. Signposted.

AXMINSTER, Devon Map ref 2D2

★★★
HOLIDAY PARK
BH&HPA

ANDREWSHAYES CARAVAN PARK
Dalwood, Axminster EX13 7DY
T: (01404) 831225
F: (01404) 831893
E: enquiries@andrewhayes.co.uk
I: www.andrewhayes.co.uk

OPEN January, March–December
CC: Barclaycard, Delta, Eurocard, JCB, Mastercard, Solo, Switch, Visa
4 hectares (10 acres) Sloping, grassy, hard.

60	🚐	£7.20–£9.50
10	🚙	£7.20–£9.50
20	⛺	£7.20–£8.00
22	🏠	£120.00–£410.00

90 touring pitches
58 units privately owned

One hundred and fifty yds off A35 signposted Dalwood, Stockland, at Taunton Cross. Three miles Axminster, 6 miles Honiton. Signposted.

CONFIRM YOUR BOOKING
You are advised to confirm your booking in writing.

SOUTH WEST

AXMINSTER continued

★★★★
HOLIDAY PARK
BH&HPA

HUNTERS MOON HOLIDAY PARK
Hawkchurch, Axminster EX13 5UL
T: (01297) 678402
F: (01297) 678402
I: www.ukparks.co.uk/huntersmoon

Set in glorious countryside with views over beautiful Axe Valley, near Lyme Regis. Seasonal pitches and short/long storage. Luxury large caravans for hire. Free hot showers. Over 50s discount.

OPEN March–November. 5.2 hectares (13 acres) Level, sloping, grassy, hard.
CC: Barclaycard, Delta, Mastercard, Switch, Visa, Visa Electron

The park lies approximately 2 miles east of Axminster. Turn off the main A35 onto the B3165 towards Crewkerne then follow the caravan and camping signs. Signposted.

159	🚐	£5.50–£11.00
159	🚙	£5.50–£11.00
159	⛺	£5.50–£11.00
10	🏠	£135.00–£450.00

159 touring pitches
21 units privately owned

BATH, Bath and North East Somerset Map ref 3B2 *Tourist Information Centre Tel: (01225) 477101*

★★★★
TOURING PARK

NEWTON MILL CAMPING
Newton Road, Bath BA2 9JF
T: (01225) 333909
F: (01225) 461556
E: newtonmill@hotmail.com
I: www.campinginbath.co.uk

Beautiful 42-acre setting close to centre of Bath (10 minute bus service). Restaurant, bar beside millstream. Trout fishing, woodland walks. Nearby traffic-free cycle path. Christmas and New Year packages.

OPEN All year round. 17.2 hectares (43 acres) Level, grassy, hard, sheltered.
CC: Amex, Barclaycard, Delta, Eurocard, Maestro, Mastercard, Solo, Switch, Visa, Visa Electron

A4 Bath to Bristol road, take exit road signposted Newton St Loe at roundabout by Globe pub on outskirts of Bath. Site is 1 mile down on left. Signposted.

90	🚐	£10.95–£13.95
90	🚙	£10.95–£14.95
105	⛺	£4.25–£11.95

195 touring pitches

MAP REFERENCES The map references refer to the colour maps at the front of the guide. The first figure is the map number; the letter and figure which follow indicate the grid reference on the map.

Parkers Farm Holiday Park
Higher Mead Farm, Ashburton, Devon, TQ13 7LJ
Tel: 01364 652598 · Fax: 01364 654004
E-mail: parkersfarm@btconnect.com · Web: www.parkersfarm.co.uk

Friendly family run site on edge of Dartmoor National Park. Enjoy a relaxing holiday and visit the animals on a genuine working farm. The touring site has large level terraced pitches, fully tiled shower blocks, laundry room, shop, telephone and family bar and restaurant, all with disabled facilities. Cottages and static caravans are also available for hire. Gold award for quality & service 1999. British Farm Tourist award.

132

SOUTH WEST

BLACKWATER, Cornwall Map ref 2B3

★★★★
HOLIDAY PARK

BH&HPA

TREVARTH HOLIDAY PARK
Blackwater, Truro TR4 8HR
T: (01872) 560266
F: (01872) 560266
E: trevarth@lineone.net

30	⊕	£5.00–£8.75
30	⊕	£5.00–£8.75
30	▲	£5.00–£8.75
20	⊕	£95.00–£440.00

30 touring pitches

Luxury caravan holiday homes, touring and camping. A small, quiet park conveniently situated for north and south coast resorts. Level touring and tent pitches with electric hook up.

OPEN April–October. 1.6 hectares (4 acres) Level, grassy, sheltered.
CC: Barclaycard, Delta, Eurocard, Mastercard, Visa

Three hundred metres from Blackwater exit off Chiverton roundabout on A30. Four and a half miles north east of Redruth. Signposted.

BLUE ANCHOR, Somerset Map ref 2D1

★★★★
HOLIDAY & TOURING PARK

BH&HPA
NCC

BLUE ANCHOR BAY CARAVAN PARK
Blue Anchor (Hoburne), Blue Anchor, Minehead TA24 6JT
T: (01643) 821360
F: (01643) 821572
E: enquiries@hoburne.co.uk
I: www.hoburne.co.uk

OPEN March–October
CC: Barclaycard, Delta, Maestro, Mastercard, Switch, Visa

12 hectares (30 acres) Level, grassy, hard.

103	⊕	£9.00–£17.00
103	⊕	£9.00–£17.00
37	⊕	£95.00–£431.00

103 touring pitches
263 units privately owned

Exit M5 at jct 25 and take A358 for Minehead. After 12 miles turn left onto A39 to Williton. Approximately 4 miles later turn right onto B3191 Carhampton. Follow signs to Blue Anchor Park for 1.5 miles. Park is on the right-hand side. Signposted.

BREAN, Somerset Map ref 2D1

★★★
HOLIDAY PARK

BH&HPA

HOLIDAY RESORT UNITY
Coast Road, Brean Sands, Brean, Burnham-on-Sea TA8 2RB
T: (01278) 751235 & 752100
F: (01278) 751539
E: admin@hru.co.uk
I: www.hru.co.uk

OPEN February–December
CC: Barclaycard, Delta, Eurocard, Mastercard, Solo, Switch, Visa, Visa Electron

32 hectares (80 acres) Level, grassy, hard.

400	⊕	£4.00–£24.00
100	⊕	£4.00–£24.00
300	▲	£4.00–£24.00
120	⊕	

800 touring pitches
400 units privately owned

From M5 jct 22, follow signs for Berrow and Brean. Site on right, 4.5 miles from M5. Signposted.

BRIDPORT, Dorset Map ref 3A3 Tourist Information Centre Tel: (01308) 424901

★★★★
HOLIDAY PARK

BH&HPA

FRESHWATER BEACH HOLIDAY PARK
Burton Bradstock, Bridport DT6 4PT
T: (01308) 897317
F: (01308) 897336
E: enquiries@fbhp.co.uk
I: www.fbhp.co.uk

Own private beach. Surrounded by beautiful countryside on Dorset's 'Sunshine Coast'. Licensed club. Free family entertainment. Heated outdoor pools. Beach, fishing, horse/pony rides. Cliff walks. Pitch prices include up to 6 people and club membership.

OPEN March–November. 12 hectares (30 acres) Level, grassy.
CC: Barclaycard, Delta, Eurocard, JCB, Mastercard, Solo, Switch, Visa, Visa Electron

425	⊕	£9.00–£20.00
425	⊕	£9.00–£20.00
425	▲	£9.00–£20.00
60	⊕	£110.00–£540.00

425 touring pitches
215 units privately owned

From Bridport take B3157, situated 2 miles on the right. Signposted.

IDEAS For ideas on places to visit refer to the introduction at the beginning of this section.

133

SOUTH WEST

BRIDPORT continued

★★★★★
HOLIDAY &
TOURING PARK

BH&HPA

HIGHLANDS END HOLIDAY PARK
Eype, Bridport DT6 6AR
T: (01308) 422139
F: (01308) 425672
E: holidays@wdlh.co.uk
I: www.wdlh.co.uk

OPEN March–October
CC: Mastercard, Switch, Visa
11.2 hectares (28 acres) Level, grassy, hard.

120		£8.00–£12.50
120		£8.00–£12.50
75		£8.00–£12.50
17		£150.00–£460.00

195 touring pitches
144 units privately owned

One mile west of Bridport turn south for Eype, park signposted.

BRIDGWATER, Somerset Map ref 2D1

★★
TOURING PARK

BH&HPA

Ad on this page

SOMERSET VIEW CARAVAN PARK
A38 Taunton Road, North Petherton,
Bridgwater TA6 6NW
T: (01278) 661294
E: someview@somerset-view.co.uk
I: www.somerset-view.co.uk

OPEN February–December

50		£7.50–£9.50
60		£7.50–£9.50
60		£5.00–£8.00

60 touring pitches

Junction 24 off M5. At Bridgwater Services roundabout turn left on to the A38. 500 metres south of North Petherton.

BRIXHAM, Devon Map ref 2D2 Tourist Information Centre Tel: 0906 680 1268 (Premium rate number)

★★★★
TOURING &
CAMPING PARK

BH&HPA

GALMPTON TOURING PARK
Greenway Road, Galmpton, Brixham TQ5 0EP
T: (01803) 842066
F: (01803) 844458
E: galmptontouringpark@hotmail.com
I: www.galmptontouringpark.co.uk

Overlooking the River Dart with superb views from pitches. A quiet base for families and couples to explore Torbay and South Devon. **Off-peak reductions.**

OPEN March–September. 4 hectares (10 acres) Level, sloping, grassy.
CC: Barclaycard, Delta, Eurocard, JCB, Mastercard, Solo, Switch, Visa, Visa Electron

60		£6.80–£11.50
20		£6.80–£11.50
60		£6.80–£11.50

120 touring pitches

Take A380 Torbay ring road then A379 to Brixham, 2nd right to Galmpton Park, through village to park. Signposted.

BUDE, Cornwall Map ref 2C2 Tourist Information Centre Tel: (01288) 354240

★★★
HOLIDAY, TOURING
& CAMPING PARK

PENHALT FARM HOLIDAY PARK
Widemouth Bay, Bude EX23 0DG
T: (01288) 361310
F: (01288) 361310
I: www.holidaybank.co.uk/penhaltfarmholidaypark

OPEN April–October
CC: Barclaycard, Mastercard, Visa
3.2 hectares (8 acres) Level, sloping, grassy.

30		£6.00–£12.00
40		£6.00–£12.00
100		£5.50–£12.00
2		£85.00–£320.00

100 touring pitches

Travelling south 4.5 miles from Bude on A39. Take 2nd right into Widemouth Bay, left at bottom. Our sign is just over 0.5 mile on left. Signposted.

WHERE TO STAY
Please mention this guide when making your booking.

Somerset View
NEW-SITE 5 Mins Off J24 (M5)
Taunton Road, North Petherton, Bridgwater,
Somerset TA6 6NW
50 Pitches (Caravans/Motor Homes/Tents)
Phone/Fax: 01278 661294 E-Mail: someview@somerset-view.co.uk Website: www.somerset-view.co.uk

134

SOUTH WEST

BUDE continued

HOLIDAY PARK ★★★★

PENSTOWE CARAVAN & CAMPING PARK
Penstowe Park, Kilkhampton, Bude
EX23 9QY
T: (01288) 321354 & 321282
F: (01288) 321273
E: info@penstoweleisure.co.uk
I: www.penstoweleisure.co.uk

OPEN March–October
CC: Barclaycard, Mastercard, Switch, Visa
16.8 hectares (42 acres)
Sloping, grassy, hard.

65 £6.50–£12.50
  £6.50–£12.50
15 £6.00–£10.00
80 touring pitches

On the A39 4 miles north of Bude. Signposted.

HOLIDAY & TOURING PARK ★★★★
BH&HPA

UPPER LYNSTONE CARAVAN AND CAMPING SITE
Lynstone, Bude EX23 0LP
T: (01288) 352017
F: (01288) 359034
E: reception@upperlynstone.co.uk
I: www.upperlynstone.co.uk

OPEN April–September
CC: Barclaycard, Delta, Eurocard, Mastercard, Switch, Visa, Visa Electron
2.4 hectares (6 acres) Level, sloping, grassy.

90 £7.00–£11.00
90 £7.00–£11.00
90 £7.00–£11.00
16 £126.00–£345.00
90 touring pitches
25 units privately owned

Half a mile south of Bude on coastal road to Widemouth Bay. Signposted.

HOLIDAY & TOURING PARK ★★★★★
BH&HPA

WOODA FARM PARK
Poughill, Bude EX23 9HJ
T: (01288) 352069
F: (01288) 355258
E: enquiries@wooda.co.uk
I: www.wooda.co.uk

Exceptional views over Bude Bay and countryside. 1.5 miles from safe, sandy beaches. Family owned and run with all facilities, fishing, woodland walks, golf. An ideal base. 10% discount for couples excl Bank Hols and Jul and Aug in our holiday caravans. No groups allowed.

OPEN March–October. 44 hectares (110 acres) Level, sloping, grassy, hard, sheltered.
CC: Barclaycard, Delta, Diners, Eurocard, Mastercard, Switch, Visa

200 £7.50–£11.50
200 £7.50–£11.50
200 £7.50–£11.50
55 £110.00–£480.00
200 touring pitches

From A39 north of Stratton, take coast road to Poughill and Combe Valley. Wooda is 1 mile from A39. Signposted.

BURNHAM-ON-SEA, Somerset Map ref 2D1 Tourist Information Centre Tel: (01278) 787852

HOLIDAY, TOURING & CAMPING PARK ★★★★
BH&HPA
NCC
Ad p12

BURNHAM-ON-SEA HOLIDAY VILLAGE
Marine Drive, Burnham-on-Sea TA8 1LA
T: (01278) 783391
F: (01278) 793776
E: enquiries@british-holidays.co.uk
I: www.british-holidays.co.uk

OPEN April–October
CC: Delta, Mastercard, Solo, Switch, Visa

10 £11.50–£35.00
47 £11.00–£33.00
18 £11.50–£24.50
269 £174.00–£760.00
74 touring pitches
339 units privately owned

Off M5 jct 22, take left on to the A38 to Highbridge, over mini roundabout take right on to railway bridge, B3139 to Burnham-on-Sea, turn left after Elf garage onto Marine Drive. Park situated 400 yds on the left. Signposted.

COUNTRY CODE Always follow the Country Code ❦ Enjoy the countryside and respect its life and work ❦ Guard against all risk of fire ❦ Fasten all gates ❦ Keep your dogs under close control ❦ Keep to public paths across farmland ❦ Use gates and stiles to cross fences, hedges and walls ❦ Leave livestock, crops and machinery alone ❦ Take your litter home ❦ Help to keep all water clean ❦ Protect wildlife, plants and trees ❦ Take special care on country roads ❦ Make no unnecessary noise

SOUTH WEST

CARLYON BAY, Cornwall Map ref 2B3

★★★★★
**HOLIDAY &
CAMPING PARK**

CARLYON BAY CARAVAN & CAMPING PARK

Bethesda, Cypress Avenue, Carlyon Bay, St Austell PL25 3RE
T: (01726) 812735
F: (01726) 815496
E: holidays@carlyonbay.net
I: www.carlyonbay.net

90	🚐	£7.00–£17.00
90	🚚	£6.00–£16.00
180	⛺	£7.00–£17.00

180 touring pitches

Award-winning campsite. Two miles from the Eden Project. Footpath to beach. Exclusively for tourers. Eden: Special offers available excl mid-Jul and Aug, incl camping and Eden tickets.

OPEN March–September. 12.8 hectares (32 acres) Level, grassy, sheltered.
CC: Amex, Barclaycard, Delta, Eurocard, Mastercard, Solo, Switch, Visa, Visa Electron

One mile south west of St Blazey on A390 turn left at Britannia Inn roundabout then 1st right into avenue of cypress trees. Signposted.

CHARD, Somerset Map ref 2D2 Tourist Information Centre Tel: (01460) 67463

★★★
TOURING PARK

ALPINE GROVE TOURING PARK
Alpine Grove, Forton, Chard TA20 4HD
T: (01460) 63479
E: ask@alpinegrovetouringpark.co.uk
I: www.alpinegrovetouringpark.co.uk

OPEN April–September
3.6 hectares (9 acres) Level, sloping, grassy, hard, sheltered.

40	🚐	£4.50–£5.50
40	🚚	£4.50–£5.50
40	⛺	£4.50–£5.50
	🏠	£15.00–£15.00

40 touring pitches

Turn off A303 follow signposts for Chard, turn off before Chard on the left follow signs for Cricket St Thomas, turn off onto B3167. After 1 mile see signpost Alpine Grove, turn right, 0.5 mile on your right. Signposted.

CHARMOUTH, Dorset Map ref 2D2

★★★★
TOURING PARK

BH&HPA

MONKTON WYLD FARM CARAVAN & CAMPING PARK
Charmouth, Bridport DT6 6DB
T: (01297) 34525 & 631131
F: (01297) 33594
E: holidays@monktonwyld.co.uk
I: www.monktonwyld.co.uk

OPEN April–October
CC: Amex, Barclaycard, Delta, Diners, Eurocard, JCB, Maestro, Mastercard, Solo, Switch, Visa, Visa Electron
80 hectares (200 acres) Level, grassy, hard, sheltered.

30	🚐	£7.00–£11.50
	🚚	£7.00–£11.50
30	⛺	£7.00–£11.50

60 touring pitches

A35 from west towards Charmouth, cross Dorset County boundary, site next left (brown tourist sign), 2nd side on left. Signposted.

CHEDDAR, Somerset Map ref 2D1

★★★★
HOLIDAY PARK

BH&HPA

BROADWAY HOUSE HOLIDAY TOURING CARAVAN AND CAMPING PARK
Axbridge Road, Cheddar BS27 3DB
T: (01934) 742610
F: (01934) 744950
E: enquiries@broadwayhouse.uk.com
I: www.broadwayhouse.uk.com

OPEN March–November
CC: Amex, Barclaycard, Delta, Diners, Eurocard, JCB, Mastercard, Solo, Switch, Visa, Visa Electron
12 hectares (30 acres) Level, sloping, grassy, hard, sheltered.

	🚐	£6.00–£14.50
	🚚	£6.00–£10.50
	⛺	£6.00–£14.00
37	🏠	£130.00–£540.00

200 touring pitches

M5 jct 22. Midway betwen Cheddar and Axbridge on A371. Signposted.

DARTMOOR

See under Ashburton, Drewsteignton, Okehampton, Tavistock

REGIONAL TOURIST BOARD The ⋀ symbol after a park name indicates that it is a Regional Tourist Board member.

SOUTH WEST

DAWLISH, Devon Map ref 2D2 *Tourist Information Centre Tel: (01626) 863589*

★★★★
HOLIDAY PARK

BH&HPA

COFTON COUNTRY HOLIDAYS
Starcross, Exeter EX6 8RP
T: (01626) 890111
F: (01626) 891572
E: enquiries@cofton-holidays-devon.co.uk
I: www.cofton-holidays-devon.co.uk

450		£6.50–£11.50
450		£6.50–£11.50
450		£6.50–£11.50
62		£115.00–£485.00

450 touring pitches

Family-owned South Devon park. Close to Exe estuary, short drive to Dawlish Warren beach. Heated swimming pool complex. Pub. Coarse fishing lakes. Woodland walks. Free electric hook-ups low-and mid-season (advance bookings, minimum 3 nights' stay).

OPEN April-October. 6.4 hectares (16 acres) Level, grassy, sheltered.
CC: Barclaycard, Delta, Eurocard, Maestro, Mastercard, Solo, Switch, Visa, Visa Electron

A379 Exeter to Dawlish road, 3 miles Exeter side of Dawlish. Signposted.

DORCHESTER, Dorset Map ref 3B3 *Tourist Information Centre Tel: (01305) 267992*

★★
TOURING PARK

BH&HPA

GIANTS HEAD CARAVAN & CAMPING PARK
Old Sherborne Road, Cerne Abbas,
Dorchester DT2 7TR
T: (01300) 341242

OPEN March-October
1.6 hectares (4 acres) Level,
grassy, sheltered.

50		£7.50–£9.00
50		£7.50–£9.00
50		£7.50–£9.00

50 touring pitches

Into Dorchester, avoiding bypass, at top of town roundabout, take Sherborne road, after 500 yds take right-hand fork at Loder garage. From Cerne Abbas take Buckland Newton road. Signposted.

DREWSTEIGNTON, Devon Map ref 2C2

★★★
TOURING &
CAMPING PARK

BH&HPA

CLIFFORD BRIDGE PARK
Clifford, Drewsteignton, Exeter EX6 6QE
T: (01647) 24226
F: (01647) 24116
E: info@clifford-bridge.co.uk
I: www.clifford-bridge.co.uk

24		£7.95–£11.95
64		£6.95–£11.95
64		£6.95–£11.95

64 touring pitches

Magnificent riverside and forest walks - upstream through Fingle Gorge to Castle Drogo (National Trust) or downstream through Dunsford Nature Reserve. 10% discount to overseas visitors with this guide.

OPEN April-September. 3.2 hectares (8 acres) Level, grassy, sheltered.

M5 jct 31 west along A30 to Woodleigh jct and turn left signed Cheriton Bishop. At Old Thatch Inn follow 'brown tent' signs to Clifford Bridge. Signposted.

DULVERTON, Somerset Map ref 2D1

★★★★
TOURING PARK

Ad on back cover

LAKESIDE CARAVAN CLUB SITE
Higher Grants, Exbridge, Dulverton
TA22 9BE
T: (01398) 324068
I: www.caravanclub.co.uk

OPEN April-October
CC: Barclaycard, Mastercard,
Visa
4.4 hectares (11 acres) Level,
sloping, grassy, hard.

| 50 | | £6.50–£13.50 |
| 50 | | £6.50–£13.50 |

50 touring pitches

Exit M5 jct 27 onto A361 towards Barnstaple. At 1st round-about take A396 signposted for Dulverton. Continue on A396 to Exebridge. Lakeside is on the left-hand side 70 yds past the Exebridge sign.

EXMOOR

See under Dulverton, Porlock, Winsford, Parracombe

STAR RATINGS Were correct at the time of going to press but are subject to change. Please check at the time of booking.

137

SOUTH WEST

FALMOUTH, Cornwall Map ref 2B3 Tourist Information Centre Tel: (01326) 312300

★★ TOURING PARK

PENNANCE MILL FARM
Maenporth, Falmouth TR11 5HJ
T: (01326) 317431 & 312616
F: (01326) 317431

OPEN March–October, December
40 hectares (100 acres) Level, grassy, sheltered.

25 — £7.00–£9.90
20 — £7.00–£9.90
25 — £6.00–£9.90
£110.00–£330.00
70 touring pitches

From Truro to Falmouth on new distributer road straight ahead, past the ASDA superstore roundabout to Maenport. At bottom of hill the site is on the left-hand side. Signposted.

FOWEY, Cornwall Map ref 2B3 Tourist Information Centre Tel: (01726) 833616

★★★ HOLIDAY PARK

BH&HPA

PENHALE CARAVAN AND CAMPING PARK
Fowey PL23 1JU
T: (01726) 833425
F: (01726) 833425
E: penhale@farmersweekly.net

Small, uncrowded park overlooking unspoilt farmland and coast. Close to sandy beaches and many lovely walks. Laundry, free hot showers, small shop for basics.

OPEN April–October. Sloping, grassy.

20 — £5.75–£9.00
6 — £5.75–£9.00
56 — £5.75–£9.00
9 — £100.00–£335.00
56 touring pitches

West from Lostwithiel on A390 turn left after 1 mile onto B3269, after 3 miles turn right on A3082. Penhale 600 yds on left.

GLASTONBURY, Somerset Map ref 3A2 Tourist Information Centre Tel: (01458) 832954

★★★★★ TOURING PARK

BH&HPA

THE OLD OAKS TOURING PARK
Wick Farm, Wick, Glastonbury BA6 8JS
T: (01458) 831337
F: (01458) 833238
E: info@theoldoaks.co.uk
I: www.theoldoaks.co.uk

OPEN March–October
CC: Barclaycard, Delta, JCB, Mastercard, Switch, Visa
40 hectares (100 acres) Level, sloping, grassy, hard, sheltered.

20 — £8.00–£11.00
20 — £8.00–£11.00
20 — £8.00–£11.00
40 touring pitches

From Glastonbury 2 miles towards Shepton Mallet on A361, signed for Wick, site in 1 mile. From Wells left after roundabout entering Glastonbury at sign for Wick. Site 1.5 miles. (Adults only). Signposted.

HAYLE, Cornwall Map ref 2B3

★★★★ HOLIDAY PARK

BH&HPA

BEACHSIDE HOLIDAY PARK
Hayle TR27 5AW
T: (01736) 753080
F: (01736) 757252
E: reception@beachside.demon.co.uk
I: www.beachside.co.uk

OPEN April–October
CC: Barclaycard, Delta, Eurocard, Mastercard, Solo, Switch, Visa, Visa Electron
16 hectares (40 acres) Sloping, grassy.

86 — £6.00–£19.00
86 — £6.00–£19.00
86 — £6.00–£19.00
£85.00–£540.00
86 touring pitches

Leave A30 at the large roundabout at the approach to Hayle, take the Hayle road, turn right beside the putting green and signpost showing 'Beachside'. Situated approximately 0.5 mile on right. Signposted.

CHECK THE MAPS

The colour maps at the front of this guide show all the cities, towns and villages for which you will find park entries. Refer to the town index to find the page on which it is listed.

SOUTH WEST

KENTISBEARE, Devon Map ref 2D2

★★★★
HOLIDAY PARK

BH&HPA

FOREST GLADE HOLIDAY PARK
Kentisbeare, Cullompton EX15 2DT
T: (01404) 841381
F: (01404) 841593
E: forestglade@cwcom.net
I: www.forestglade.mcmail.com

Free indoor heated pool on small, family-managed park surrounded by forest with deer. Large, flat, sheltered pitches. Luxury all-serviced holiday homes for hire. Club members £1 per night discount on pitch fees. Short breaks available in holiday homes during most of season.

OPEN March–October. 6 hectares (15 acres) Level, grassy, hard, sheltered.
CC: Barclaycard, Delta, Mastercard, Solo, Switch, Visa

80	🚐	£6.25–£11.75
80	🚙	£6.25–£11.75
80	⛺	£5.25–£10.75
24	🏠	£98.00–£370.00

80 touring pitches
16 units privately owned

From Honiton take Dunkerswell road and follow Forest Glade signs. From M5 A373, 2.5 miles at Keepers Cottage Inn then 2.5 miles on Sheldon Road. Signposted.

LANDS END, Cornwall Map ref 2A3

★★★
TOURING PARK

CARDINNEY CARAVAN AND CAMPING PARK
Lands End, Main A30, Lands End TR19 6HJ
T: (01736) 810880
F: (01736) 810998
E: cardinney@btinternet.com
I: www.cardinney-camping-park.co.uk

OPEN February–November
CC: Barclaycard, Delta, Eurocard, Mastercard, Solo, Switch, Visa
1.6 hectares (4 acres) Level, grassy, hard.

50	🚐	£5.00–£8.00
25	🚙	£5.00–£8.00
30	⛺	£5.00–£8.00
2	🏠	£84.00–£98.00

105 touring pitches

On the main A30, signposted 5 miles past Penzance. Large name board on right-hand side. Signposted.

MALMESBURY, Wiltshire Map ref 3B2 Tourist Information Centre Tel: (01666) 823748

★★
TOURING PARK

BH&HPA

BURTON HILL CARAVAN AND CAMPING PARK
Burton Hill, Malmesbury SN16 0EH
T: (01666) 826880
F: (01666) 823449
E: burtonhillccp@archesfarm.co.uk

OPEN April–November
.8 hectare (2 acres) Level, grassy, sheltered.

30	🚐	£8.00–£10.00
30	🚙	£8.00–£10.00
30	⛺	£8.00–£10.00

30 touring pitches

Off A429 0.25 mile south, Malmesbury to Chippenham road, opposite hospital, Arches Lane. Signposted.

MARTOCK, Somerset Map ref 3A3

★★★★★
TOURING PARK

BH&HPA
NCC

SOUTHFORK CARAVAN PARK
Parrett Works, Martock TA12 6AE
T: (01935) 825661
F: (01935) 825122
E: southfork.caravans@virgin.net
I: www.ukparks.co.uk/southfork

OPEN All year round
CC: Barclaycard, Delta, Eurocard, JCB, Mastercard, Switch, Visa, Visa Electron
.8 hectare (2 acres) Level, grassy.

23	🚐	£7.00–£9.00
23	🚙	£7.00–£9.00
7	⛺	£7.00–£9.00
3	🏠	£125.00–£240.00

30 touring pitches

From East – A303. Take exit signposted Stoke-sub-Hamdon and Martock. At T-jct turn left and follow camping signs. From West – A303. Six miles east of Ilminster at roundabout take 1st exit, signposted South Petherton, follow signs.

MAWGAN PORTH, Cornwall Map ref 2B2

★★★★★
HOLIDAY &
CAMPING PARK

SUN HAVEN VALLEY CARAVAN PARK & CAMPING PARK
Mawgan Porth, Newquay TR8 4BQ
T: (01637) 860373
F: (01637) 860373
E: sunhaven@freenet.co.uk
I: www.sunhavenvalley.co.uk

OPEN All year round
CC: Barclaycard, Eurocard, Mastercard, Solo, Switch, Visa, Visa Electron
2.8 hectares (7 acres) Level, sloping, grassy, sheltered.

54	🚐	£8.50–£13.50
66	🚙	£8.50–£13.50
58	⛺	£8.50–£13.50
30	🏠	£170.00–£450.00

118 touring pitches

On the B3276 coast road 6 miles north of Newquay turn right at Mawgan Porth beach, 0.75 miles to park entrance. Signposted.

139

SOUTH WEST

MEVAGISSEY, Cornwall Map ref 2B3

★★★★★
HOLIDAY, TOURING & CAMPING PARK

BH&HPA

SEA VIEW INTERNATIONAL
Boswinger, St Austell PL26 6LL
T: (01726) 843425
F: (01726) 843358
E: enquiries@seaviewinternational.com
I: www.seaviewinternational.com

OPEN April–September
CC: Barclaycard, Delta, Eurocard, Mastercard, Solo, Switch, Visa, Visa Electron
11.2 hectares (28 acres) Level, grassy, hard, sheltered.

160		£5.00–£17.00
160		£5.00–£17.00
160		£5.00–£17.00
38		£100.00–£550.00
160 touring pitches		

From St Austell roundabout take B3273 to Mevagissey. Prior to village turn right and follow signs to Gorran and Gorran Haven and brown tourism signs to park.

NEWQUAY, Cornwall Map ref 2B2 Tourist Information Centre Tel: (01637) 854020

★★★★
HOLIDAY PARK

BH&HPA

Ad on this page

HENDRA HOLIDAY PARK
Newquay TR8 4NY
T: (01637) 875778
F: (01637) 879017
E: hendra.cornwall@dial.pipex.com
I: www.hendra-holidays.com

OPEN February–October
CC: Amex, Barclaycard, Delta, Mastercard, Switch, Visa
19.2 hectares (48 acres) Level, sloping, grassy, hard, sheltered.

588		£6.60–£10.30
588		£6.60–£10.30
588		£6.60–£10.30
188		£119.00–£585.00
588 touring pitches		

Take A30 to the Highgate Hill jct, follow the signs for the A392 to Newquay. At Quintrell Downs go straight across the roundabout, Hendra is 0.5 mile on the left. Signposted.

★★★★
TOURING PARK

BH&HPA

Ad p141

NEWPERRAN TOURIST PARK
Rejerrah, Newquay TR8 5QJ
T: (01872) 572407
F: (01872) 571254
E: Trevellapark@cs.com
I: www.newperran.co.uk

OPEN May–September
CC: Amex, Barclaycard, Delta, Eurocard, Mastercard, Solo, Switch, Visa, Visa Electron
10 hectares (25 acres) Level, grassy.

270		£7.20–£12.30
270		£6.50–£11.50
270		£7.20–£12.30
270 touring pitches		

From A30 take B3285 Perranporth road, 2 miles past Mitchell village. Right onto A3075 Newquay road at Goonhavern. Site is 400 yds on left. Signposted.

★★★★
TOURING & CAMPING PARK

BH&HPA

TRELOY TOURIST PARK
Newquay TR8 4JN
T: (01637) 872063 & 876279
F: (01637) 871710
E: holidays@treloy.co.uk
I: www.treloy.co.uk

OPEN April–September
CC: Barclaycard, Delta, Eurocard, Mastercard, Switch, Visa, Visa Electron
4.8 hectares (12 acres) Level, sloping, grassy, hard, sheltered.

140		£6.00–£11.00
140		£6.00–£11.00
140		£6.00–£11.00
140 touring pitches		

Just off the A3059 St Columb Major to Newquay road. Signposted.

CREDIT CARD BOOKINGS If you book by telephone and are asked for your credit card number it is advisable to check the proprietor's policy should you cancel your reservation.

Hendra HOLIDAY PARK

Excellent Camping & Touring Facilities Luxury Static Caravans

Fantastic Family Fun
- Bars · Restaurant
- Live Cabaret Entertainment
- Children's Club
- Fabulous outdoor pool complex
- Indoor fun pool

Newquay
Freephone Brochure Hotline:
0500 242523

ROSE AWARD · AA

Newquay, Cornwall TR8 4NY Tel: 01637 875778 e.mail: hendra.uk@dial.pipex.com www.hendra-holidays.com

SOUTH WEST

NEWQUAY continued

★★★★★
HOLIDAY, TOURING & CAMPING PARK

ROSE AWARD

BH&HPA

Ad on this page

TREVELLA CARAVAN AND CAMPING PARK
Crantock, Newquay TR8 5EW
T: (01637) 830308
F: (01792) 571254
E: Trevellapark@cs.com
I: www.trevella.co.uk

OPEN April–October
CC: Amex, Barclaycard, Delta, Mastercard, Solo, Switch, Visa, Visa Electron
8 hectares (20 acres) Level, sloping, grassy, hard.

230	🚐	£7.20–£12.30
230	🚙	£6.50–£11.50
40	⛺	£7.20–£12.30
57		£155.00–£489.00
270 touring pitches		

Take A3075 Redruth road from Newquay. After 1.5 miles turn right into road signposted Crantock. Signposted.

NEWTON ABBOT, Devon Map ref 2D2 Tourist Information Centre Tel: (01626) 367494

★★★★★
TOURING PARK

BH&HPA

DORNAFIELD
Dornafield Farm, Two Mile Oak, Newton Abbot TQ12 6DD
T: (01803) 812732
F: (01803) 812032
E: enquiries@dornafield.com
I: www.dornafield.com

Beautiful 15thC farmhouse location set amidst glorious South Devon countryside. Ideal for Torquay and Dartmoor. Superb facilities to suit the truly discerning caravanner. *Early and late season bookings. Book for 7 days and only pay for 5. Details on request.*

OPEN March–October. 12 hectares (30 acres) Level, grassy, hard, sheltered.
CC: Barclaycard, Delta, Eurocard, Mastercard, Switch, Visa

135	🚐	£9.00–£13.00
135	🚙	£9.00–£13.00
135	⛺	£9.00–£13.00
135 touring pitches		

Take A381 Newton Abbot to Totnes road. In 2.5 miles at Two Mile Inn turn right. In 0.5 mile 1st turn to left. Site 200 yds on right. Signposted.

QUALITY ASSURANCE SCHEME
For an explanation of the quality and facilities represented by the Stars please refer to the front of this guide.

Trevella Park
34 CRANTOCK, NEWQUAY, CORNWALL TR8 5EW
Award Winning Family Park, set in sheltered parkland, ideal base for touring. Spotless facilities, including shop, cafe, electric pitches. Heated swimming pool. Own 5 acre nature reserve and well stocked coarse fishing lake.
For free colour brochure:
TEL: 01637 830308
www.travella.co.uk

Newperran TOURIST PARK
34 REJERRAH, NEWQUAY, CORNWALL TR8 5QJ
Modern Tourist Park developed from a Cornish farm, in a picturesque, well cared for setting. Spotless facilities with shop, cafe, launderette, games room, TV room, off-licence, & heated swimming pool. *For free colour brochure:*
TEL: 01872 572407
www.newperran.co.uk

SOUTH WEST

OKEHAMPTON, Devon Map ref 2C2

★★★★★
HOLIDAY &
TOURING PARK

BH&HPA

DARTMOOR VIEW HOLIDAY PARK

Whiddon Down, Okehampton EX20 2QL
T: (01647) 231545
F: (01647) 231654
E: jo@dartmoorview.co.uk
I: www.dartmoorview.co.uk

Superb 5 star touring caravan and camping park. Good base for exploring Dartmoor and the West Country. Five star facilities at affordable prices. Super savers available:-£39.95 7 days incl electric, 2 people, caravan/motorhome (excl 14 Jul-31 Aug). Great offers on our luxury holiday homes.

OPEN March–October. 2.4 hectares (6 acres) Level, grassy, hard.
CC: Barclaycard, Delta, Eurocard, JCB, Maestro, Mastercard, Solo, Switch, Visa, Visa Electron

Half a mile off A30 (Merrymeet roundabout). Turn left for Whiddon Down. Three quarters of a mile on the right-hand side. Signposted.

75	🚐	£7.50–£9.75
75	🚗	£7.50–£9.75
75	⛺	£5.00–£9.75
13	🏠	£99.00–£350.00

75 touring pitches
20 units privately owned

OWERMOIGNE, Dorset Map ref 3B3

★★★★
HOLIDAY PARK

BH&HPA

SANDYHOLME HOLIDAY PARK
Moreton Road, Owermoigne, Dorchester DT2 8HZ
T: (01305) 852677
F: (01305) 854677
E: smeatons@sandyholme.co.uk
I: www.sandyholme.co.uk

OPEN March–October
CC: Barclaycard, Delta, Mastercard, Switch, Visa, Visa Electron
2.4 hectares (6 acres) Level, grassy, sheltered.

57	🚐	£7.00–£12.00
57	🚗	£7.00–£12.00
57	⛺	£7.00–£12.00
25	🏠	£125.00–£380.00

57 touring pitches
23 units privately owned

One mile inland off A352. Through village of Owermoigne, 1 mile. Signposted.

PADSTOW, Cornwall Map ref 2B2 Tourist Information Centre Tel: (01841) 533449

★★★★
HOLIDAY, TOURING
& CAMPING PARK

BH&HPA

CARNEVAS FARM HOLIDAY PARK

Carnevas Farm, St Merryn, Padstow PL28 8PN
T: (01841) 520230
F: (01841) 520230

Family-run park for families. Situated on the north Cornish coast. Padstow 4 miles. Nearest beach 0.5 mile. Great surfing. Excellent facilities. Cleanliness assured.

OPEN April–October. 3.2 hectares (8 acres) Level, sloping, grassy.

At end of Bodmin bypass, on A30 carry on under iron bridge turn right onto A3059, St Columb road. Turn onto A39, then left onto B3271, Padstow. At St Merryn turn left onto B3276. Two miles, towards Porthcothan Bay, opposite Tredrea Inn. Signposted.

198	🚐	£6.00–£11.00
198	🚗	£6.00–£11.00
198	⛺	£6.00–£11.00
9	🏠	£140.00–£450.00

198 touring pitches

★★★★
TOURING &
CAMPING PARK

BH&HPA

THE LAURELS TOURING CARAVAN & CAMPING PARK
Padstow Road, Whitecross, Wadebridge PL27 7JQ
T: (01208) 813341
F: (01208) 813341
E: anicholson@thelaurels-park.freeserve.co.uk
I: www.thelaurels-park.freeserve.co.uk

OPEN March–October
.8 hectare (2 acres) Level, grassy, sheltered.

30	🚐	£5.00–£10.00
30	🚗	£5.00–£10.00
30	⛺	£5.00–£10.00

30 touring pitches

Turn onto A389 from Padstow off A39 west of Wadebridge. Entrance 20 yds from jct. Signposted.

SYMBOLS The symbols in each entry give information about services and facilities. A key to these symbols appears at the back of this guide.

SOUTH WEST

PAIGNTON, Devon Map ref 2D2   Tourist Information Centre Tel: 0906 680 1268 (Premium rate number)

★★★★★
**HOLIDAY &
TOURING PARK**

ROSE AWARD

BH&HPA
NCC

Ad on this page

BEVERLEY PARK
Goodrington Road, Paignton TQ4 7JE
T: (01803) 843887
F: (01803) 845427
E: info@beverley-holidays.co.uk
I: www.beverley-holidays.co.uk

OPEN February–December
CC: Barclaycard, Delta,
Eurocard, Mastercard, Solo,
Switch, Visa, Visa Electron
9.2 hectares (23 acres) Level,
sloping, grassy, hard.

189	£9.30–£20.50
50	£9.30–£20.50
120	£7.30–£18.50
197	£108.00–£819.00

189 touring pitches
19 units privately owned

From end of M5 take A380 to Torbay. Then A3022 for 2 miles south of Paignton. Turn left into Goodrington Road.

★★★★
**HOLIDAY, TOURING
& CAMPING PARK**

BH&HPA

HIGHER WELL FARM HOLIDAY PARK
Waddeton Road, Stoke Gabriel, Totnes
TQ9 6RN
T: (01803) 782289

OPEN April–October &
Christmas
3.2 hectares (8 acres) Level,
sloping, grassy, hard,
sheltered.

80	£6.00–£8.50
80	£6.00–£8.50
80	£6.00–£8.50
18	£120.00–£360.00

80 touring pitches

From Paignton, A385 to Totnes turn left at Parkers Arms for Stoke Gabriel, 1.5 miles turn left to Waddeton, situated 200 yds down the road. Signposted.

★★★★
HOLIDAY PARK

BH&HPA
NCC

HOBURNE TORBAY
Grange Road, Goodrington, Paignton
TQ4 7JP
T: (01803) 558010
F: (01803) 696286
E: enquiries@hoburne.com
I: www.hoburne.com

OPEN All year round
CC: Barclaycard, Delta,
Eurocard, Mastercard, Solo,
Switch, Visa
26 hectares (65 acres) Level,
sloping, grassy, hard,
sheltered.

157	£9.00–£24.00
157	£9.00–£24.00
120	£105.00–£536.00

157 touring pitches
430 units privately owned

Turn off Paignton ring road at Nortel into Goodrington Road. After 0.5 mile at bottom of hill turn left into Grange Road. Signposted.

TOURING PARK

BH&HPA

RAMSLADE TOURING PARK
Stoke Road, Stoke Gabriel, Totnes TQ9 6QB
T: (01803) 782575
F: (01803) 782828
E: derek@ramslade.co.uk
I: www.ramslade.co.uk

OPEN March–October
CC: Barclaycard, Delta,
Eurocard, Mastercard, Solo,
Switch, Visa
3.2 hectares (8 acres) Level,
sloping, grassy, hard.

135	£9.00–£14.50
135	£9.00–£14.50
135	£9.00–£14.50

135 touring pitches

From M5 follow A380 towards Torquay. Turn right onto Paignton ring road. At traffic lights turn right (A385). Second left at Parkers Arms, signposted Stoke Gabriel. Signposted.

COLOUR MAPS Colour maps at the front of this guide pinpoint all places in which you will find parks listed.

**LUXURY TOURING PARK
ENGLISH RIVIERA**
EVERY MODERN FACILITY FOR TOURERS
Indoor & Outdoor Heated Swimming Pools • Live Entertainment
Cabaret & Dancing • Sports Facilities • Children's Activities
Call Beverley Holidays on **01803 843887**
for a free colour brochure

Email: info@beverley-holidays.co.uk

www.beverley-holidays.co.uk

SOUTH WEST

PENZANCE, Cornwall Map ref 2A3 *Tourist Information Centre Tel: (01736) 362207*

★★★
TOURING PARK

BH&HPA

TOWER PARK CARAVANS AND CAMPING
St Buryan, Penzance TR19 6BZ
T: (01736) 810286
F: (01736) 810954
E: caravans&camping@towerpark97.freeserve.co.uk
I: www.towerpark97.freeserve.co.uk

OPEN March–December
CC: Barclaycard, Delta, Eurocard, JCB, Mastercard, Solo, Switch, Visa, Visa Electron
2.4 hectares (6 acres) Level, grassy, sheltered.

102		£6.50–£8.50
102		£6.50–£8.50
102		£6.50–£8.50
5		£122.00–£280.00

102 touring pitches

Off A30 3 miles west of Penzance, B3283 to St Buryan, fork right and keep right for 400 yds. Signposted.

POLPERRO, Cornwall Map ref 2C3

★★★★
HOLIDAY, TOURING & CAMPING PARK

BH&HPA

Ad on this page

KILLIGARTH CARAVAN PARK
Polperro, Looe PL13 2JQ
T: (01503) 272216 & 272409
F: (01503) 272065
E: killigarthmanor@breathe.com
I: www.killigarth.co.uk

OPEN April–October
CC: Barclaycard, Delta, Eurocard, Mastercard, Switch, Visa, Visa Electron
12 hectares (30 acres) Level.

202		£8.50–£12.50
202		£8.50–£12.50
202		£8.50–£12.50
146		£105.00–£505.00

202 touring pitches

From Tamar Bridge A38 to roundabout at Trerulefoot, left onto A387 to Looe. Cross bridge to Polperro 3.5 miles turn left at jct just past bus shelter. Signposted.

POLRUAN-BY-FOWEY, Cornwall Map ref 2B3

★★★★
HOLIDAY, TOURING & CAMPING PARK

BH&HPA

POLRUAN HOLIDAYS (CAMPING & CARAVANNING)
Townsend Road, Polruan-by-Fowey, Fowey PL23 1QH
T: (01726) 870263
F: (01726) 870263
E: polholiday@aol.com

OPEN April–September
1.2 hectares (3 acres) Level, sloping, grassy, hard, sheltered.

7		£6.75–£10.50
7		£6.75–£10.50
25		£6.75–£10.50
11		£110.00–£340.00

32 touring pitches

A38 to Dobwalls, left on A390 to East Taphouse. Left on B3359 after 4.5 miles turn right signposted Polruan. Signposted.

AT-A-GLANCE SYMBOLS

Symbols at the end of each accommodation entry give useful information about services and facilities. A key to symbols can be found inside the back cover flap. Keep this open for easy reference.

Killigarth Holiday Centre
POLPERRO near LOOE, CORNWALL

EXCELLENT CAMPING & TOURING CARAVAN FACILITIES
★★ **PLUS LUXURY SELF CATERING HOLIDAY HOMES** ★★

Set in beautiful countryside close to picturesque Polperro and Talland Bay.
Family run holiday park exclusively for families and couples.

★ Bars ★ Top class entertainment ★ Indoor swimming pool
★ Fitness room ★ Sauna ★ Sunbed ★ Amusement arcade ★ Mini cinema
★ Restaurant ★ Takeaway ★ Snooker ★ Pool ★ Darts ★ Mini market
★ Launderette ★ Tennis court

KIDS MEET PUGWASH AND POLLY-PERRO IN THE PIRATE CLUB

FOR BROCHURE & BOOKINGS
TEL: 01503 272216

AA AWARD FOR EXCELLENCE FOR LEISURE FACILITIES

HOLIDAY PARK ★★★★

KILLIGARTH HOLIDAY CENTRE POLPERRO, LOOE, CORNWALL PL13 2JQ

144

SOUTH WEST

PORLOCK, Somerset Map ref 2D1

★★★★
TOURING & CAMPING PARK

BH&HPA

BURROWHAYES FARM CARAVAN AND CAMPING SITE AND RIDING STABLES
West Luccombe, Porlock, Minehead TA24 8HT
T: (01643) 862463
E: info@burrowhayes.co.uk
I: www.burrowhayes.co.uk

Real family site situated in glorious National Trust scenery in Exmoor National Park. Ideal for walking and riding, with stables on site.

OPEN March–October. 3.2 hectares (8 acres) Level, sloping, grassy, sheltered.
CC: Barclaycard, Eurocard, JCB, Maestro, Mastercard, Solo, Switch, Visa, Visa Electron

From Minehead take A39 towards Porlock. Take 1st left after Allerford to Horner and West Luccombe. Burrowhayes is 0.25 along miles on right-hand side before humpback bridge. Signposted.

54		£6.50–£8.50
54		£6.50–£8.50
66		£6.50–£8.50
19		£120.00–£275.00

120 touring pitches

PORTREATH, Cornwall Map ref 2B3

★★★
HOLIDAY PARK

BH&HPA

TEHIDY HOLIDAY PARK
Harris Mill, Illogan, Portreath, Redruth TR16 4JQ
T: (01209) 216489 & 314558
F: (01209) 216489
E: holiday@tehidy.co.uk
I: www.tehidy.co.uk

OPEN April–October
CC: Barclaycard, Delta, JCB, Mastercard, Solo, Switch, Visa, Visa Electron
1.6 hectares (4 acres) Level, sloping, grassy, sheltered.

10		£6.50–£8.00
3		£6.50–£8.00
15		£6.50–£8.00
20		£95.00–£365.00

18 touring pitches

South on A30 take Porthtowan exit. Right 1st roundabout, 1st left to Portreath. Signposted.

ROSUDGEON, Cornwall Map ref 2B3

★★★
HOLIDAY PARK

BH&HPA

KENNEGGY COVE HOLIDAY PARK
Higher Kenneggy, Rosudgeon, Penzance TR20 9AU
T: (01736) 763453
F: (01736) 763453
E: enquiries@kenneggycove.co.uk
I: www.kenneggycove.co.uk

Quiet site in magnificent situation. Sea views. Ten minutes' walk to coastal path and secluded beach. Free hot water. Shop and takeaway service. French and German spoken.

OPEN April–October. 1.6 hectares (4 acres) Level, grassy.

Take the lane to Higher Kenneggy, south off the A394 at the Helston end of Rosudgeon. The park is 0.5 mile down the lane on the left. Signposted.

30		£5.50–£9.00
30		£5.50–£9.00
60		£5.00–£9.00
9		£110.00–£350.00

60 touring pitches

ST AGNES, Cornwall Map ref 2B3

★★★★
TOURING PARK

BH&HPA

BEACON COTTAGE FARM TOURING PARK
Beacon Drive, St Agnes TR5 0NU
T: (01872) 552347 & 553381

OPEN April–September
CC: Diners, JCB, Maestro, Mastercard, Solo, Switch, Visa, Visa Electron
136 hectares (340 acres) Level, grassy, sheltered.

50		£6.00–£14.00
50		£6.00–£14.00
50		£6.00–£14.00

50 touring pitches

From A30 take B3277 to St Agnes, follow signs to park.

RATING All accommodation in this guide has been rated, or is awaiting a rating, by a trained Tourist Board assessor.

SOUTH WEST

ST AUSTELL, Cornwall Map ref 2B3

HOLIDAY PARK
★★★★
BH&HPA

TREWHIDDLE HOLIDAY ESTATE
Pentewan Road, Trewhiddle, St Austell PL26 7AD
T: (01726) 67011
F: (01726) 67010
E: mcclelland@btinternet.com
I: www.trewhiddle.co.uk

Ideally situated for touring Cornwall, 15 minutes from the Eden Project and Heligan Gardens. Three beaches within 4 miles. Touring and camping from £30 per week. Discounts for only 2 people in static caravans during low-and mid-season.

OPEN January, March–December. 6.4 hectares (16 acres) Level, sloping, grassy, sheltered.
CC: Amex, Barclaycard, Delta, Diners, Eurocard, JCB, Mastercard, Switch, Visa, Visa Electron

105	🚐	£6.00–£12.00
105		£6.00–£12.00
105	▲	£6.00–£12.00
22		£110.00–£420.00

105 touring pitches
30 units privately owned

From the A390 turn south on B3273 to Mevagissey, site 0.75 mile from the roundabout on the right. Signposted.

ST IVES, Cornwall Map ref 2B3 Tourist Information Centre Tel: (01736) 796297

TOURING PARK
★★★★★
BH&HPA

POLMANTER TOURIST PARK
St Ives TR26 3LX
T: (01736) 795640
F: (01736) 795640
E: phillip_osborne@hotmail.com
I: www.polmanter.com

OPEN March–October
CC: Barclaycard, Delta, Eurocard, Maestro, Mastercard, Solo, Switch, Visa, Visa Electron
8 hectares (20 acres) Level, sloping, grassy.

75	🚐	£9.00–£15.00
75		£9.00–£15.00
165	▲	£9.00–£15.00

240 touring pitches

A3074 to St Ives from A30, 1st left at mini-roundabout take route to St Ives (Halsetown) turn right at inn, signposted.

TOURING PARK
★★★★
BH&HPA

TREVALGAN HOLIDAY FARM
St Ives TR26 3BJ
T: (01736) 796433
F: (01736) 796433
E: trevalgan@aol.com
I: www.trevalganholidayfarm.co.uk

OPEN April–September
CC: Amex, Barclaycard, Eurocard, Mastercard, Switch, Visa
2 hectares (5 acres) Level, grassy.

40	🚐	£7.00–£12.00
40		£7.00–£12.00
40	▲	£7.00–£12.00

120 touring pitches

From A30 take holiday route to St Ives, jct B3306 turn left, park sign 0.25 mile signposted.

SALCOMBE, Devon Map ref 2C3 Tourist Information Centre Tel: (01548) 843927

TOURING & CAMPING PARK
★★★

BOLBERRY HOUSE FARM
Bolberry, Malborough, Kingsbridge TQ7 3DY
T: (01548) 561251 & 560926
E: bolberry.house@virgin.net
I: www.bolberryparks.co.uk

OPEN March–October
2.4 hectares (6 acres) Level, sloping, grassy.

20	🚐	£7.50–£10.50
20		£7.50–£10.50
50	▲	£6.50–£9.50
5		£95.00–£325.00

70 touring pitches

A381 from Totnes to Kingsbridge. Between Kingsbridge and Salcombe is the village of Malborough. Take sharp right through the village following the signs to Bolberry which is approximately 1 mile. Signposted.

NB **IMPORTANT NOTE** Information on accommodation listed in this guide has been supplied by the proprietors. As changes may occur you are advised to check details at the time of booking.

SOUTH WEST

SIDMOUTH, Devon Map ref 2D2 *Tourist Information Centre Tel: (01395) 516441*

★★★★★
HOLIDAY & TOURING PARK
BH&HPA

SALCOMBE REGIS CAMPING AND CARAVAN PARK
Salcombe Regis, Sidmouth EX10 0JH
T: (01395) 514303
F: (01395) 514303
E: info@salcombe-regis.co.uk
I: www.salcombe-regis.co.uk

OPEN April–October
CC: Barclaycard, Delta, Eurocard, JCB, Mastercard, Solo, Switch, Visa, Visa Electron
6.4 hectares (16 acres) Level, grassy, hard, sheltered.

40		£7.25–£10.50
40		£7.25–£10.50
60		£7.25–£10.50
10		£145.00–£400.00
100 touring pitches		

One and a half miles east of Sidmouth signposted off the A3052 road.

TAUNTON, Somerset Map ref 2D1 *Tourist Information Centre Tel: (01823) 336344*

★★★
TOURING PARK

ASHE FARM CARAVAN AND CAMPSITE
Ashe, Thornfalcon, Taunton TA3 5NW
T: (01823) 442567
F: (01823) 443372
E: camping@ashe-frm.fsnet.co.uk

OPEN April–October
160 hectares (400 acres)
Level, grassy, hard, sheltered.

20		£7.00–£9.00
20		£7.00–£9.00
10		£7.00–£7.00
2		£120.00–£160.00
30 touring pitches		

M5 jct 25. Take A358 south east for 2.5 miles, turn right at Nags Head, site 0.25 mile on right. Signposted.

TAVISTOCK, Devon Map ref 2C2 *Tourist Information Centre Tel: (01822) 612938*

★★★★
HOLIDAY PARK
BH&HPA

HARFORD BRIDGE HOLIDAY PARK
Peter Tavy, Tavistock PL19 9LS
T: (01822) 810349
F: (01822) 810028
E: enquiry@harfordbridge.co.uk
I: www.harfordbridge.co.uk

Beautiful level sheltered park set in Dartmoor with delightful views of Cox Tor. The River Tavy forms a boundary. Ideal for exploring Devon and Cornwall.
Camping: 10% discount for week paid in full on arrival. Holiday let: £15 off 2-week booking. £10 senior citizen discount.

OPEN All year round except Christmas. 6.4 hectares (16 acres) Level, grassy, hard, sheltered.
CC: Barclaycard, Mastercard, Switch, Visa

40		£6.50–£10.50
40		£6.50–£10.50
40		£6.50–£10.50
21		£110.00–£380.00
120 touring pitches		
45 units privately owned		

Two mile north of Tavistock off A386 Okehampton road take the Peter Tavy turning. Signposted.

TINTAGEL, Cornwall Map ref 2B2

★★★★
TOURING PARK
Ad on back cover

TREWETHETT FARM CARAVAN CLUB SITE
Tintagel PL34 0BQ
T: (01840) 770222
I: www.caravanclub.co.uk

OPEN April–October
CC: Barclaycard, Mastercard, Visa
6 hectares (15 acres) Level, grassy, hard.

133		£6.50–£17.00
20		£6.50–£17.00
		£4.00
153 touring pitches		

From A30 onto A359 signposed Camelford. Right onto A39 signposted Bude. Left just before Transmitter. Right onto B3266 signposted Boscastle. Left onto B3263. Site entrance is on the right approximately 2 miles.

TORQUAY, Devon Map ref 2D2 *Tourist Information Centre Tel: 0906 680 1268 (Premium rate number)*

★★★★
TOURING PARK
BH&HPA

WIDDICOMBE FARM TOURING PARK
Ring Road (A380), Compton, Paignton TQ3 1ST
T: (01803) 558325
F: (01803) 559526
E: enquiries@torquaytouring.co.uk
I: www.torquaytouring.co.uk

OPEN March–November
CC: Barclaycard, Delta, Mastercard, Switch, Visa
8 hectares (20 acres) Level, grassy, hard, sheltered.

156		£5.00–£11.50
30		£5.00–£11.50
44		£5.00–£11.50
		£80.00–£295.00
200 touring pitches		

A380 Torquay to Paignton ring road. Signposted.

SOUTH WEST

WELLS, Somerset Map ref 3A2 *Tourist Information Centre Tel: (01749) 672552*

★★★★
TOURING PARK
BH&HPA

MENDIP HEIGHTS CAMPING AND CARAVAN PARK
Townsend, Priddy, Wells BA5 3BP
T: (01749) 870241
F: (01749) 870368
E: bta@mendipheights.co.uk
I: www.mendipheights.co.uk

40		£6.50–£9.90
40		£6.50–£9.90
80		£6.50–£9.90
1		£195.00–£295.00

90 touring pitches

Peaceful quality park situated close to Cheddar and Wells and away from main roads. Spotless heated toilet block. Modern heated luxury caravan for hire.
OPEN March–November. 1.6 hectares (4 acres) Level, sloping, grassy, hard.
CC: Barclaycard, Delta, Mastercard, Solo, Switch, Visa, Visa Electron

Wells north along A39 for 3 miles. Left along B3135 towards Cheddar for 4.5 miles. Park 200 yds on left (signed).

WESTON-SUPER-MARE, North Somerset Map ref 2D1 *Tourist Information Centre Tel: (01934) 888800*

★★
CAMPING PARK
BH&HPA

DULHORN FARM CAMPING SITE
Weston Road, Lympsham, Weston-super-Mare BS24 0JQ
T: (01934) 750298
F: (01934) 750913

OPEN February–December
.8 hectare (2 acres) Level, grassy, sheltered.

42		£8.00–£9.00
42		£8.00–£9.00
42		£5.00–£7.50
3		£100.00–£268.00

42 touring pitches

From M5 jct 22, take the A38 towards Bristol and then A370 to Weston-super-mare, 1.25 miles on left. Signposted.

★★★
TOURING PARK
BH&HPA

WEST END FARM/CARAVAN & CAMPING PARK
Locking, Weston-super-Mare BS24 8RH
T: (01934) 822529
F: (01934) 822529

OPEN All year round
CC: Barclaycard, Delta, Mastercard, Switch, Visa
4 hectares (10 acres) Level, grassy, sheltered.

75		£8.50–£11.00
75		£8.50–£11.00
		£8.50–£11.00

75 touring pitches

M5 to jct 21, onto A370 then onto A371 to Helicopter Museum and follow signs to site.

WHITE CROSS, Cornwall Map ref 2B2

★★★★★
HOLIDAY PARK
ROSE AWARD
BH&HPA

WHITE ACRES HOLIDAY PARK
White Cross, Newquay TR8 4LW
T: (01726) 860220
F: (01726) 860877
E: whiteacres.co.uk

OPEN March–October
CC: Barclaycard, Delta, Eurocard, Mastercard, Solo, Switch, Visa
48 hectares (120 acres) Sloping, grassy, hard.

100		£8.00–£25.00
		£8.00–£25.00
		£8.00–£25.00
209		£220.00–£895.00

100 touring pitches
177 units privately owned

Take the Indian Queens exit from A30. Follow A392 towards Newquay. White Acres Holiday Park is approximately 1 mile on right-hand side. Signposted.

COUNTRY CODE
Always follow the Country Code ❧ Enjoy the countryside and respect its life and work ❧ Guard against all risk of fire ❧ Fasten all gates ❧ Keep your dogs under close control ❧ Keep to public paths across farmland ❧ Use gates and stiles to cross fences, hedges and walls ❧ Leave livestock, crops and machinery alone ❧ Take your litter home ❧ Help to keep all water clean ❧ Protect wildlife, plants and trees ❧ Take special care on country roads ❧ Make no unnecessary noise

SOUTH WEST

WINSFORD, Somerset Map ref 2D1

★★★★
TOURING PARK
BH&HPA

HALSE FARM CARAVAN & TENT PARK
Winsford, Minehead TA24 7JL
T: (01643) 851259
F: (01643) 851592
E: brown@halsefarm.co.uk
I: www.halsefarm.co.uk

22		£6.00–£8.00
22		£6.00–£8.00
22		£6.00–£8.00

44 touring pitches

Exmoor National Park, small, peaceful, adjacent to moor on working farm with spectacular views. Paradise for walkers and country lovers. David Bellamy Gold Conservation Award. 10% discount for one week or more, paid 10 days in advance.

OPEN March–October. 77.2 hectares (193 acres) Level, sloping, grassy, hard, sheltered.

Signposted from A396 Minehead to Tiverton road. Turn off A396 for Winsford. In the village turn left and bear left in front of the Royal Oak Inn. Keep up hill for 1 mile; our entrance is immediately after the cattle grid on the left. Signposted.

WOOLACOMBE, Devon Map ref 2C1 Tourist Information Centre Tel: (01271) 870553

★★★★
HOLIDAY PARK
BH&HPA

GOLDEN COAST HOLIDAY VILLAGE
Station Road, Woolacombe EX34 7HW
T: (01271) 870343
F: (01271) 870089
E: goodtimes@woolacombe.com
I: www.woolacombe.com

OPEN February–December
CC: Barclaycard, Delta, JCB, Mastercard, Solo, Switch, Visa, Visa Electron
4 hectares (10 acres) Level, sloping, grassy, hard.

70		£11.50–£33.00
70		£11.50–£33.00
70		£8.00–£22.00
80		£100.00–£750.00

70 touring pitches

M5 jct 27. A361 to Ilfracombe. At Mullacott Cross take the B3343 towards Woolacombe. Situated on this road on left, approximately 2 miles past 'once upon a time'. Signposted.

★★★
HOLIDAY PARK
BH&HPA

WOOLACOMBE SANDS HOLIDAY PARK
Beach Road, Woolacombe EX34 7AF
T: (01271) 870569
F: (01271) 870606
E: lifesabeach@woolacombe-sands.co.uk
I: www.woolacombe-sands.co.uk

OPEN April–October
CC: Barclaycard, Delta, Eurocard, JCB, Maestro, Mastercard, Solo, Switch, Visa, Visa Electron
Level, sloping, grassy, sheltered.

		£8.00–£25.00
150		£8.00–£25.00
100		£8.00–£25.00
60		£100.00–£650.00

250 touring pitches
14 units privately owned

M5 jct 27 to Barnstaple. A361 to Mullacott Cross then B3343 to Woolacombe. Left just before Woolacombe. Signposted.

CHECK THE MAPS

The colour maps at the front of this guide show all the cities, towns and villages for which you will find park entries. Refer to the town index to find the page on which it is listed.

149

SOUTH WEST

A brief guide to the main Towns and Villages offering accommodation in the

South West

- **A ASHBURTON, DEVON** - Formerly a thriving wool centre and important as one of Dartmoor's four stannary towns. Today's busy market town has many period buildings. Ancient tradition is maintained in the annual ale-tasting and bread-weighing ceremony. Good centre for exploring Dartmoor or the south Devon coast.

- **AXMINSTER, DEVON** - This tree-shaded market town on the banks of the River Axe was one of Devon's earliest West Saxon settlements, but is better known for its carpet making. Based on Turkish methods, the industry began in 1755, declined in the 1830s and was revived in 1937.

- **B BATH, BATH AND NORTH EAST SOMERSET** - Georgian spa city beside the River Avon. Important Roman site with impressive reconstructed baths, uncovered in 19th C. Bath Abbey built on site of monastery where first king of England was crowned (AD 973). Fine architecture in mellow local stone. Pump Room and museums.

- **BLUE ANCHOR, SOMERSET** - Small resort on the Bristol Channel, a station on the West Somerset Railway. Exmoor National Park, Quantocks and Brendon Hills are nearby.

- **BREAN, SOMERSET** - Caravans and holiday bungalows by sand dunes on the flat shoreline south of Brean Down. This rocky promontory has exhilarating cliff walks, bird-watching and an Iron Age fort.

- **BRIDPORT, DORSET** - Market town and chief producer of nets and ropes just inland of dramatic Dorset coast. Old, broad streets built for drying and twisting and long gardens for rope-walks. Grand arcaded Town Hall and Georgian buildings. Local history museum has Roman relics.

- **BRIXHAM, DEVON** - Famous for its trawling fleet in the 19th C, a steeply-built fishing port overlooking the harbour and fish market. A statue of William of Orange recalls his landing here before deposing James II. There is an aquarium and museum. Good cliff views and walks.

- **BUDE, CORNWALL** - Resort on dramatic Atlantic coast. High cliffs give spectacular sea and inland views. Golf-course, cricket pitch, folly, surfing, coarse-fishing and boating. Mother-town Stratton was base of Royalist Sir Bevil Grenville.

- **BURNHAM-ON-SEA, SOMERSET** - Small Victorian resort famous for sunsets and sandy beaches, a few minutes from junction 22 of the M5. Ideal base for touring Somerset, Cheddar and Bath. Good sporting facilities, championship golf-course.

- **C CARLYON BAY, CORNWALL** - Residential and retirement suburb near St Austell, with fine clifftop golf-course.

- **CHARD, SOMERSET** - Market town in hilly countryside. The wide main street has some handsome buildings, among them the Guildhall, court house and almshouses. Modern light industry and dairy produce have replaced 19th C lace making which came at decline of cloth trade.

- **CHARMOUTH, DORSET** - Set back from the fossil-rich cliffs, a small coastal town where Charles II came to the Queen's Armes when seeking escape to France. Just south at low tide, the sandy beach rewards fossil-hunters; at Black Ven an ichthyosaurus (now in London's Natural History Museum) was found.

- **CHEDDAR, SOMERSET** - Large village at foot of Mendips just south of the spectacular Cheddar Gorge. Close by are Roman and Saxon sites and famous show caves. Traditional Cheddar cheese is still made here.

- **D DAWLISH, DEVON** - Small resort, developed in Regency and Victorian periods beside Dawlish Water. Town centre has ornamental riverside gardens with black swans. One of England's most scenic stretches of railway was built by Brunel alongside jagged red cliffs between the sands and the town.

- **DORCHESTER, DORSET** - Busy medieval county town destroyed by fires in 17th and 18th C. Cromwellian stronghold and scene of Judge Jeffreys' Bloody Assize after Monmouth Rebellion of 1685. Tolpuddle Martyrs were tried in Shire Hall. Museum has Roman and earlier exhibits and Hardy relics.

- **DREWSTEIGNTON, DEVON** - Pretty village of thatched cottages overlooking the steep, wooded Teign valley at the northern edge of Dartmoor. The tree-shaded square shelters a fine 15th C church. To the west is Sir Edwin Lutyens' dramatic Castle Drogo in a romantic setting high over the Teign Gorge.

- **DULVERTON, SOMERSET** - Set among woods and hills of south-west Exmoor, a busy riverside town with a 13th C church. The Rivers Barle and Exe are rich in salmon and trout. The information centre at the Exmoor National Park Headquarters at Dulverton is open throughout the year.

- **F FALMOUTH, CORNWALL** - Busy port and fishing harbour, popular resort on the balmy Cornish Riviera. Henry VIII's Pendennis Castle faces St Mawes Castle across the broad natural harbour and yacht basin Carrick Roads, which receives 7 rivers.

- **FOWEY, CORNWALL** - Set on steep slopes at the mouth of the Fowey River, important clayport and fishing town. Ruined forts guarding the shore recall days of 'Fowey Gallants' who ruled local seas. The lofty church rises above the town. Ferries to Polruan and Bodinnick; August Regatta.

- **G GLASTONBURY, SOMERSET** - Market town associated with Joseph of Arimathea and the birth of English Christianity. Built around its 7th C abbey said to be the site of King Arthur's burial. Glastonbury Tor with its ancient tower gives panoramic views over flat country and the Mendip Hills.

- **H HAYLE, CORNWALL** - Former mining town with modern light industry on the Hayle Estuary. Most buildings are Georgian or early Victorian, with some Regency houses along the canal.

- **K KENTISBEARE, DEVON** - Pretty village at the foot of the Blackdown Hills. The church has a magnificent carved 15th C screen, and nearby is a medieval priest's house with a minstrels' gallery and oak screens.

- **L LANDS END, CORNWALL** - The most westerly point of the English mainland, 8 miles south-west of Penzance. Spectacular cliffs with marvellous views. Exhibitions and multi-sensory Last Labyrinth Show.

- **M MALMESBURY, WILTSHIRE** - Overlooking the River Avon, an old town dominated by its great church, once a Benedictine abbey. The surviving Norman nave and porch are noted for fine sculptures, 12th C arches and musicians' gallery.

SOUTH WEST

- **MARTOCK, SOMERSET** - Large village with many handsome buildings of hamstone and a beautiful old church with tie-beam roof. Medieval treasurer's house where a 10' x 6' medieval mural has recently been discovered during National Trust restoration work. Georgian market house, 17th C manor.

- **MAWGAN PORTH, CORNWALL** - Holiday village occupying a steep valley on the popular coastal route to Newquay. Golden sands, rugged cliffs and coves. Nearby Bedruthan Steps offers exhilarating cliff walks and views. The chapel of a Carmelite nunnery, once the home of the Arundells, may be visited.

- **MEVAGISSEY, CORNWALL** - Small fishing town, a favourite with holidaymakers. Earlier prosperity came from pilchard fisheries, boat-building and smuggling. By the harbour are fish cellars, some converted, and a local history museum is housed in an old boat-building shed. Handsome Methodist chapel; shark fishing, sailing.

- **N NEWQUAY, CORNWALL** - Popular resort spread over dramatic cliffs around its old fishing port. Many beaches with abundant sands, caves and rock pools; excellent surf. Pilots' gigs are still raced from the harbour and on the headland stands the stone Huer's House from the pilchard-fishing days.

- **NEWTON ABBOT, DEVON** - Lively market town at the head of the Teign Estuary. A former railway town, well placed for moorland or seaside excursions. Interesting old houses nearby include Bradley Manor, dating from the 15th C, and Forde House, visited by Charles I and William of Orange.

- **O OKEHAMPTON, DEVON** - Busy market town near the high tors of northern Dartmoor. The Victorian church, with William Morris windows and a 15th C tower, stands on the site of a Saxon church. A Norman castle ruin overlooks the river to the west of the town. Museum of Dartmoor Life in a restored mill.

- **OWERMOIGNE, DORSET** - Village 6 miles east of Dorchester, within easy reach of the Dorset coast and the family resort of Weymouth.

- **P PADSTOW, CORNWALL** - Old town encircling its harbour on the Camel Estuary. The 15th C church has notable bench-ends. There are fine houses on North Quay and Raleigh's Court House on South Quay. Tall cliffs and golden sands along the coast and ferry to Rock. Famous 'Obby 'Oss Festival on 1 May.

- **PAIGNTON, DEVON** - Lively seaside resort with a pretty harbour on Torbay. Bronze Age and Saxon sites are occupied by the 15th C church, which has a Norman door and font. The beautiful Chantry Chapel was built by local landowners, the Kirkhams.

- **PENZANCE, CORNWALL** - Resort and fishing port on Mount's Bay with mainly Victorian promenade and some fine Regency terraces. Former prosperity came from tin trade and pilchard fishing. Grand Georgian style church by harbour. Georgian Egyptian building at head of Chapel Street and Morrab Gardens.

- **POLPERRO, CORNWALL** - Picturesque fishing village clinging to steep valley slopes about its harbour. A river splashes past cottages and narrow lanes twist between. The harbour mouth, guarded by jagged rocks, is closed by heavy timbers during storms.

- **POLRUAN-BY-FOWEY, CORNWALL** - Old village linked to Fowey across its estuary by a passenger ferry. Twin medieval forts guard village and town at the river's mouth.

- **PORLOCK, SOMERSET** - Village set between steep Exmoor hills and the sea at the head of beautiful Porlock Vale. The narrow street shows a medley of building styles. South westward is Porlock Weir with its old houses and tiny harbour and further along the shore at Culbone is England's smallest church.

- **PORTREATH, CORNWALL** - Formerly developed as a mining port, small resort with some handsome 19th C buildings. Cliffs, sands and good surf.

- **S SALCOMBE, DEVON** - Sheltered yachting resort of whitewashed houses and narrow streets in a balmy setting on the Salcombe Estuary. Palm, myrtle and other Mediterranean plants flourish. There are sandy bays and creeks for boating.

- **SIDMOUTH, DEVON** - Charming resort set amid lofty red cliffs where the River Sid meets the sea. The wealth of ornate Regency and Victorian villas recalls the time when this was one of the south coast's most exclusive resorts. Museum; August International Festival of Folk Arts.

- **ST AGNES, CORNWALL** - Small town in a once-rich mining area on the north coast. Terraced cottages and granite houses slope to the church. Some old mine workings remain, but the attraction must be the magnificent coastal scenery and superb walks. St Agnes Beacon offers one of Cornwall's most extensive views.

- **ST AUSTELL, CORNWALL** - Leading market town, the meeting point of old and new Cornwall. One mile from St Austell Bay with its sandy beaches, old fishing villages and attractive countryside. Ancient narrow streets, pedestrian shopping precincts. Fine church of Pentewan stone and Italianate Town Hall.

- **ST IVES, CORNWALL** - Old fishing port, artists' colony and holiday town with good surfing beach. Fishermen's cottages, granite fish cellars, a sandy harbour and magnificent headlands typify a charm that has survived since the 19th C pilchard boom. Tate Gallery opened in 1993.

- **T TAUNTON, SOMERSET** - County town, well-known for its public schools, sheltered by gentle hill-ranges on the River Tone. Medieval prosperity from wool has continued in marketing and manufacturing and the town retains many fine period buildings. Museum.

- **TAVISTOCK, DEVON** - Old market town beside the River Tavy on the western edge of Dartmoor. Developed around its 10th C abbey, of which some fragments remain, it became a stannary town in 1305 when tin-streaming thrived on the moors. Tavistock Goose Fair, October.

- **TINTAGEL, CORNWALL** - Coastal village near the legendary home of King Arthur. There is a lofty headland with the ruin of a Norman castle and traces of a Celtic monastery are still visible in the turf.

- **TORQUAY, DEVON** - Devon's grandest resort, developed from a fishing village. Smart apartments and terraces rise from the seafront and Marine Drive along the headland gives views of beaches and colourful cliffs.

- **W WELLS, SOMERSET** - Small city set beneath the southern slopes of the Mendips. Built between 1180 and 1424, the magnificent cathedral is preserved in much of its original glory and with its ancient precincts forms one of our loveliest and most unified groups of medieval buildings.

- **WESTON-SUPER-MARE, NORTH SOMERSET** - Large, friendly resort developed in the 19th C. Traditional seaside attractions include theatres and a dance hall. The museum has a Victorian seaside gallery and Iron Age finds from a hill fort on Worlebury Hill in Weston Woods.

- **WINSFORD, SOMERSET** - Small village in Exmoor National Park, on the River Exe in splendid walking country under Winsford Hill. On the other side of the hill is a Celtic standing stone, the Caratacus Stone, and nearby across the River Barle stretches an ancient packhorse bridge, Tarr Steps.

- **WOOLACOMBE, DEVON** - Between Morte Point and Baggy Point, Woolacombe and Mortehoe offer 3 miles of the finest sand and surf on this outstanding coastline. Much of the area is owned by the National Trust.

Our Countryside Matters!

Country Code

- Always follow the Country code
- Guard against all risk of fire
- Keep your dogs under close control
- Use gates and stiles to cross fences, hedges and walls
- Take your litter home
- Protect wildlife, plants and trees
- Make no unnecessary noise
- Enjoy the countryside and respect its life and work
- Fasten all gates
- Keep to public paths across farmland
- Leave livestock, crops and machinery alone
- Help to keep all water clean
- Take special care on country roads

We hope the countryside will fully open in 2002. However, given the serious nature of Foot and Mouth Disease please be ready to follow this additional advice and respect any further precautions given in local authority notices:

- Don't go onto farmland if you have handled farm animals in the last 7 days
- Avoid contact with farm animals and keep dogs on a lead where they are present
- If you step in dung, remove it before you leave the field • Don't go on paths with a local authority 'closed' notice.

For more information contact Tourist Information Centres or Countryside Agency web site www.countryside.gov.uk which links to other local authority web sites providing details about rights of way and access opportunities across England.

USE YOUR *i*'s

There are more than 550 Tourist Information Centres throughout England offering friendly help with accommodation and holiday ideas as well as suggestions of places to visit and things to do.

You'll find TIC addresses in the local Phone Book.

SOUTH of England

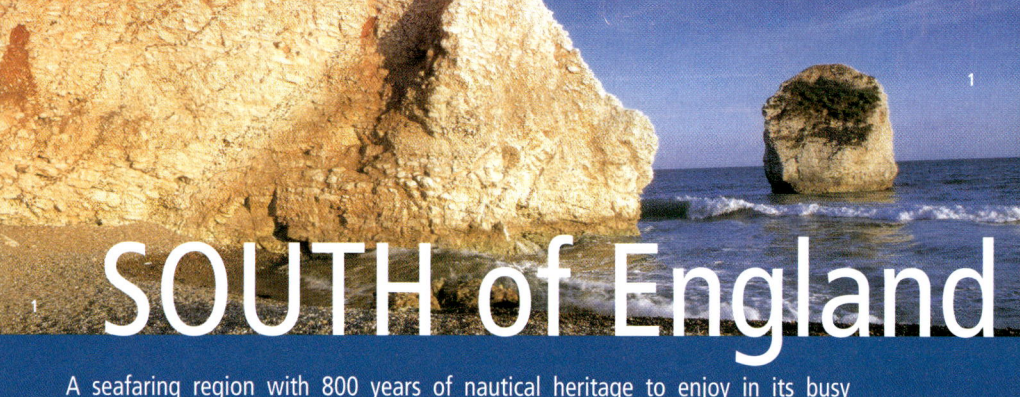

A seafaring region with 800 years of nautical heritage to enjoy in its busy harbours and family resorts. For landlubbers there's gentle countryside, Georgian towns, modern cities and outstanding historic houses too.

classic sights
Blenheim Palace – a gilded Italian palace in an English park
Oxford – University town with ancient colleges
Claydon House – unusual interiors in the Rococo, Gothick and Chinoiserie styles

coast & country
Chiltern Hills – tranquil country walks
New Forest – historic wood and heathland
Studland Bay – glorious sweeping beach

glorious gardens
Cliveden – a series of distinctive and delightful gardens
Mottisfont Abbey – the perfect English rose garden

maritime history
Portsmouth Historic Dockyard – Henry VIII's Mary Rose, HMS Victory and HMS Warrior

distinctively different
Sandham Memorial Chapel – houses Stanley Spencer's WW1 murals

The counties of Berkshire, Buckinghamshire, Dorset (Eastern), Hampshire, Isle of Wight and Oxfordshire

FOR MORE INFORMATION CONTACT:
Southern Tourist Board
40 Chamberlayne Road, Eastleigh,
Hampshire SO50 5JH
Tel: (023) 8062 5505 Fax: (023) 8062 0010
Email: info@southerntb.co.uk
Internet: www.visitbritain.com

The Pictures:
1 Freshwater Bay, Isle of Wight
2 Radcliffe Camera, Oxford
3 Lulworth Cove, Dorset

Places to Visit - see pages 154-157
Where to Stay - see pages 158-168

153

PLACES to visit

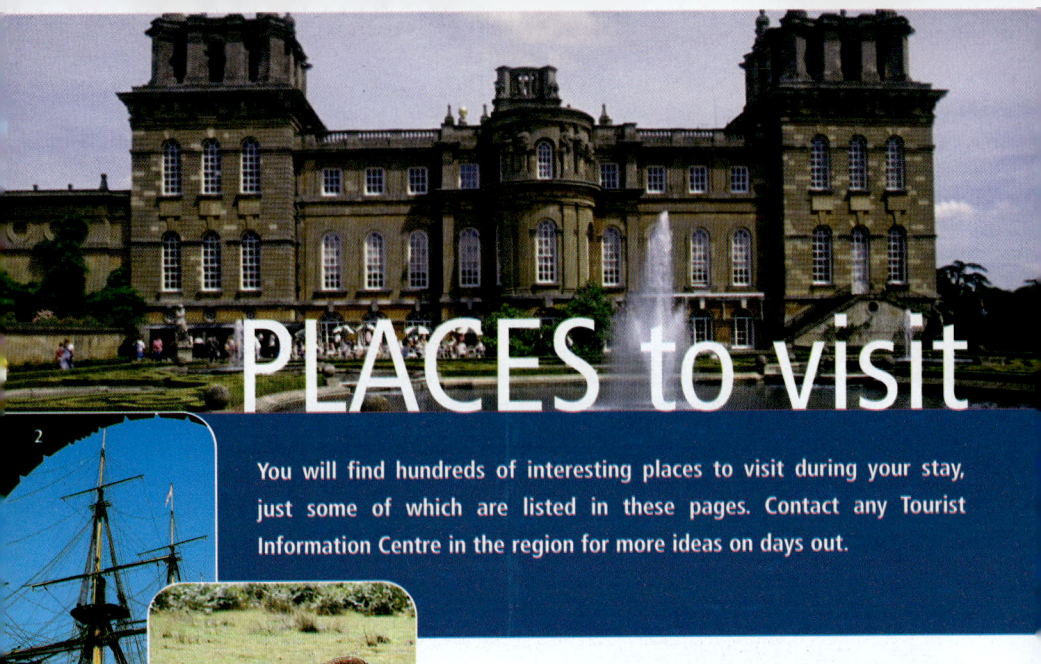

You will find hundreds of interesting places to visit during your stay, just some of which are listed in these pages. Contact any Tourist Information Centre in the region for more ideas on days out.

Beaulieu National Motor Museum
Beaulieu, Brockenhurst, Hampshire SO42 7ZN
Tel: (01590) 612345 www.beaulieu.co.uk
Motor museum with over 250 exhibits showing the history of motoring from 1896. Also Palace House, Wheels Experience, Beaulieu Abbey ruins and a display of monastic life.

Bekonscot Model Village
Warwick Road, Beaconsfield, Buckinghamshire HP9 2PL
Tel: (01494) 672919 www.bekonscot.org.uk
The oldest model village in the world, Bekonscot depicts rural England in the 1930s, where time has stood still for 70 years.

Blenheim Palace
Woodstock, Oxfordshire OX20 1PX
Tel: (01993) 811325 www.blenheimpalace.com
Home of the 11th Duke of Marlborough. Birthplace of Sir Winston Churchill. Designed by Vanbrugh in the English baroque style. Landscaped by `Capability' Brown.

Breamore House
Breamore, Fordingbridge, Hampshire SP6 2DF
Tel: (01725) 512233
Elizabethan manor house of 1583, with fine collection of works of art. Furniture, tapestries, needlework, paintings mainly 17thC and 18thC Dutch School.

Broughton Castle
Banbury, Oxfordshire OX15 5EB
Tel: (01295) 276070
Medieval moated house built in 1300 and enlarged between 1550 and 1600. The home of Lord and Lady Saye and Sele and family home for 600 years. Has Civil War connections.

Buckinghamshire County Museum
Church Street, Aylesbury, Buckinghamshire HP20 2QP
Tel: (01296) 331441
www.buckscc.gov.uk/tourism/museum
Lively hands-on, innovative museum complex consisting of county heritage displays, regional art gallery and Roald Dahl Children's Gallery in lovely garden setting.

Carisbrooke Castle
Newport, Isle of Wight PO30 1XY
Tel: (01983) 522107 www.english-heritage.org.uk
A splendid Norman castle where Charles I was imprisoned. The governor's lodge houses the county museum. Wheelhouse with wheel operated by donkeys.

Compton Acres
Canford Cliffs Road, Canford Cliffs,
Poole, Dorset BH13 7ES
Tel: (01202) 700778 www.comptonacres.co.uk
Ten separate and distinct gardens of the world. The gardens include Italian, Japanese, Indian glen and Spanish water garden. Country crafts and 'Off the Beaten Track Trail'.

SOUTH OF ENGLAND

Cotswold Wildlife Park
Bradwell Grove, Burford, Oxford, Oxfordshire OX18 4JW
Tel: (01993) 823006
Wildlife park in 200 acres (81 ha) of gardens and woodland with a variety of animals from all over the world.

The D Day Museum and Overlord Embroidery
Clarence Esplanade, Portsmouth, Hampshire PO5 3NT
Tel: (023) 9282 7261
www.portsmouthmuseums.co.uk
The magnificent 272 ft- (83 m-) long 'Overlord Embroidery' depicts the allied invasion of Normandy on 6 June 1944. Sound guides available in 4 languages.

Dicot Railway Centre
Great Western Society, Didcot, Oxfordshire OX11 7NJ
Tel: (01235) 817200
www.didcotrailwaycentre.org.uk
Living museum recreating the golden age of the Great Western Railway. Steam locomotives and trains, engine shed and small relics museum.

Exbury Gardens
Exbury Estate Office, Exbury, Southampton, Hampshire SO45 1AZ
Tel: (023) 8089 1203 www.exbury.co.uk.
Over 200 acres (81 ha) of woodland garden, including the Rothschild collection of rhododendrons, azaleas, camellias and magnolias.

Flagship Portsmouth
Porter's Lodge, 1/7 College Road, HM Naval Base, Portsmouth, Hampshire PO1 3LJ
Tel: (023) 9286 1533 www.flagship.org.uk
The world's greatest historic ships: Mary Rose, HMS Victory, HMS Warrior 1860. Royal Naval Museum, 'Warships by Water' tours, Dockyard Apprentice exhibition.

Gilbert White's House and Garden and The Oats Museum
The Wakes, High Street, Selborne, Alton, Hampshire GU34 3JH
Tel: (01420) 511275
Historic house and garden, home of Gilbert White, author of 'The Natural History of Selborne'. Exhibition on Frank Oates, explorer, and Captain Lawrence Oates of Antarctica fame.

The Hawk Conservancy and Country Park
Andover, Hampshire SP11 8DY
Tel: (01264) 772252 www.hawk-conservancy.org
Unique to Great Britain – 'Valley of the Eagles' held here daily at 1400.

Jane Austen's House
Chawton, Alton, Hampshire GU34 1SD
Tel: (01420) 83262
A 17thC house where Jane Austen lived from 1809-1817 and wrote or revised her six great novels. Letters, pictures, memorabilia, garden with old-fashioned flowers.

Kingston Lacy
Wimborne Minster, Dorset BH21 4EA
Tel: (01202) 883402 www.nationaltrust.org.uk
A 17thC house designed for Sir Ralph Bankes by Sir Roger Pratt, altered by Sir Charles Barry in the19thC. Collection of paintings, 250-acre (101-ha) wooded park, herd of Devon cattle.

Legoland Windsor
Winkfield Road, Windsor, Berkshire SL4 4AY
Tel: (0870) 504 0404 www.legoland.co.uk
A family park with hands-on activities, rides, themed playscapes and more Lego bricks than you ever dreamed possible!

The Pictures:
1 Blenheim Palace, Oxfordshire
2 HMS Victory, Portsmouth
3 Deer at Bolderwood, New Forest
4 Poole, Dorset
5 Oxford
6 Swan Green, New Forest

SOUTH OF ENGLAND

The Living Rainforest
Hampstead Norreys, Newbury, Berkshire RG18 0TN
Tel: (01635) 202444 www.livingrainforest.org
Two tropical rainforests, all under cover, approximately 20,000 sq ft (1,858 sq m). Collection of rare and exotic tropical plants together with small representation of wildlife in rainforest.

Manor Farm (Farm and Museum)
Manor Farm Country Park, Pylands Lane, Bursledon, Southampton, Hampshire SO30 2ER
Tel: (01489) 787055
www.hants.gov.uk/countryside/manorfarm
Traditional Hampshire farmstead with range of buildings, farm animals, machinery and equipment, pre-1950s farmhouse and 13thC church set for 1900. Living history site.

Marwell Zoological Park
Colden Common, Winchester, Hampshire SO21 1JH
Tel: (01962) 777407
Set in 100 acres (40.5 ha) of parkland surrounding Marwell Hall. Venue suitable for all age groups including disabled.

Oceanarium
Pier Approach, West Beach, Bournemouth, Dorset BH2 5AA
Tel: (01202) 311993 www.oceanarium.co.uk
Situated in the heart of Bournemouth next to the pier, the Oceanarium will take you on a fascinating voyage of the undersea world with creatures such as elegant seahorses and sinister sharks.

Osborne House
Yorke Avenue, East Cowes, Isle of Wight PO32 6JY
Tel: (01983) 200022 www.english-heritage.com
Queen Victoria and Prince Albert's seaside holiday home. Swiss Cottage where royal children learnt cooking and gardening. Victorian carriage service to Swiss Cottage.

The Oxford Story
6 Broad Street, Oxford, Oxfordshire OX1 3AJ
Tel: (01865) 728822 www.heritageattractions.co.uk
An excellent introduction to Oxford – experience 900 years of University history in one hour. From scientists to poets, astronomers to comedians.

Paultons Park
Ower, Romsey, Hampshire SO51 6AL
Tel: (023) 8081 4442
A full day out for all the family with over 40 attractions. Rides, play areas, entertainments, museums, birds and animals, beautiful gardens and lots more.

River and Rowing Museum
Mill Meadows, Henley-on-Thames, Oxfordshire RG9 1BF
Tel: (01491) 415600 www.rrm.co.uk
A unique, award-winning museum with galleries dedicated to rowing, the River Thames and the town of Henley. Special exhibitions run throughout the year.

Royal Navy Submarine Museum and HMS Alliance
Haslar Jetty Road, Gosport, Hampshire PO12 2AS
Tel: (023) 9252 9217 www.rnsubmus.co.uk
HM Submarine Alliance, HM Submarine No 1 (Holland 1), midget submarines and models of every type of submarine from earliest days to present nuclear age.

Swanage Railway
Station House, Swanage, Dorset BH19 1HB
Tel: (01929) 425800 www.swanrail.demon.co.uk
Enjoy a nostalgic steam train ride on the Purbeck line. Steam trains run every weekend throughout the year with daily running from April to October.

The Vyne
Sherborne St John, Basingstoke, Hampshire RG24 9HL
Tel: (01256) 881337 www.nationaltrust.org.uk
Original house dating back to Henry VIII's time. Extensively altered in the mid 17thC. Tudor chapel, beautiful gardens and lake.

Waterperry Gardens
Waterperry, Oxford, Oxfordshire OX33 1JZ
Tel: (01844) 339254 www.waterperrygardens.co.uk
Ornamental gardens covering six acres (2 ha) of the 83-acre (33.5-ha) 18thC Waterperry House estate. Saxon village church, garden shop, teashop and art and craft gallery.

Whitchurch Silk Mill
28 Winchester Street, Whitchurch, Hampshire RG28 7AL
Tel: (01256) 892065
Unique Georgian silk-weaving watermill, now a working museum producing fine silk fabrics on Victorian machinery. Riverside garden, tearooms for light meals, silk gift shop.

Windsor Castle
Windsor, Berkshire SL4 1NJ
Tel: (01753) 869898 www.royal.gov.uk
Official residence of HM The Queen and royal residence for 9 centuries. State apartments, Queen Mary's Doll's House.

SOUTH OF ENGLAND

Find out more about the SOUTH of England

Further information about holidays and attractions in the South of England is available from:

SOUTHERN TOURIST BOARD
40 Chamberlayne Road, Eastleigh, Hampshire SO50 5JH.
Tel: (023) 8062 5505 Fax: (023) 8062 0010
Email: info@southerntb.co.uk
Internet: www.visitbritain.com

Getting to the SOUTH of England

BY ROAD: A good road network links London and the rest of the UK with major Southern destinations. The M27 provides a near continuous motorway route along the south coast and the M25/M3/A33 provides a direct route from London to Winchester and Southampton. The scenic A31 stretches from London, through Hampshire and to mid Dorset, whilst the M40/A34 have considerably cut travelling times from the West Midlands to the South. The M25 has speeded up access to Berkshire on the M4, Buckinghamshire and Oxfordshire on the M40.

BY RAIL: From London's Waterloo, trains travel to Portsmouth, Southampton and Bournemouth approximately three times an hour. From these stations, frequent trains go to Poole, Salisbury and Winchester. Further information on rail journeys in the South of England can be obtained from 08457 484950.

The Pictures:
1 River Isis, Oxford
2 Alum Bay, Isle of Wight

SOUTH OF ENGLAND

Where to stay in South of England

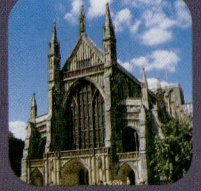

Parks in this region are listed in alphabetical order of place name, and then in alphabetical order of park.

Map references refer to the colour location maps at front of this guide. The first number indicates the map to use; the letter and number which follow refer to the grid reference on the map.

At-a-glance symbols can be found inside the back cover flap. Keep this open for easy reference.

ANDOVER, Hampshire Map ref 3C2 *Tourist Information Centre Tel: (01264) 324320*

★★★
TOURING & CAMPING PARK

WYKE DOWN TOURING CARAVAN & CAMPING PARK
Picket Piece, Andover SP11 6LX
T: (01264) 352048
F: (01264) 324661
E: wykedown@wykedown.co.uk
I: www.wykedown.co.uk

OPEN All year round
CC: Barclaycard, Delta, Diners, Eurocard, Maestro, Mastercard, Solo, Switch, Visa, Visa Electron
12 hectares (30 acres) Level, sloping, grassy, hard, sheltered.

69	🚐	£10.00
69	🚙	£10.00
69	⛺	£10.00

69 touring pitches

Follow international camping signs from A303 trunk road, Andover ring road, then through village. Picket Piece is signposted, approximately 2 miles. Signposted.

BEACONSFIELD, Buckinghamshire Map ref 3C2

★★★★
TOURING & CAMPING PARK

BH&HPA

HIGHCLERE FARM COUNTRY TOURING PARK
Newbarn Lane, Seer Green, Beaconsfield HP9 2QZ
T: (01494) 874505
F: (01494) 875238

Quiet meadowland park, low cost tube prices to London (25 minutes). Eleven miles Legoland. Launderette, showers, play area.

OPEN January, March–December. .8 hectare (2 acres) Level, grassy, hard, sheltered.
CC: Amex, Barclaycard, Delta, Diners, Eurocard, JCB, Mastercard, Solo, Switch, Visa, Visa Electron

45	🚐	£10.00–£13.00
45	🚙	£10.00–£13.00
15	⛺	£8.00–£13.00

60 touring pitches

A40 to Potkiln Lane and follow signs up to site. M40 jct 2 to Beaconsfield, A355 signed Amersham 1 mile, right to Seer Green. Signposted.

BERE REGIS, Dorset Map ref 3B3

★★★
TOURING PARK

BH&HPA

ROWLANDS WAIT TOURING PARK
Rye Hill, Bere Regis, Wareham BH20 7LP
T: (01929) 472727
F: (01929) 472727
E: bta@rowlandswait.co.uk
I: www.rowlandswait.co.uk

OPEN All year round
CC: Barclaycard, Delta, JCB, Mastercard, Switch, Visa
3.2 hectares (8 acres) Level, sloping, grassy, hard, sheltered.

30	🚐	£7.00–£10.00
6	🚙	£7.00–£10.00
35	⛺	£7.00–£10.00

71 touring pitches

From A35 (Poole/Dorchester road) at Bere Regis take Wool/ Bovington Tank Museum road. About 0.5 mile up Rye Hill turn right, site 300 yds. Signposted.

158

SOUTH OF ENGLAND

BICESTER, Oxfordshire Map ref 3C1 *Tourist Information Centre Tel: (01869) 369055*

★
TOURING & CAMPING PARK
BH&HPA

HEYFORD LEYS MOBILE HOME PARK & CAMPING SITE
Camp Road, Upper Heyford, Bicester OX25 5LU
T: (01869) 232048
F: (01869) 233167
E: heyfordleys@aol.com
I: www.ukparks.co.uk/heyfordleys

OPEN All year round
CC: Amex, Barclaycard, Delta, Mastercard, Switch, Visa
2.4 hectares (6 acres) Level, grassy, stony, hard.

22	🚐	£8.00–£11.00
22		£8.00–£11.00
22	▲	£5.00–£6.00
22 touring pitches

Two and a half miles south of M40jct 10, off B430. Signposted.

BOURNEMOUTH, Dorset Map ref 3B3

★★★
TOURING PARK
BH&HPA

ST LEONARDS FARM
Ringwood Road, West Moors, Ferndown BH22 0AQ
T: (01202) 872637
F: (01202) 872637
I: www.st-leonardsfarm.co.uk

A quiet family-run park with well drained and level, widely spaced pitches approximately 8 miles from Bournemouth and close to the beautiful New Forest. £3 per week reduction if you book for 7 nights. Extended stay available to avoid unnecessary towing.

OPEN April–September. 4.8 hectares (12 acres) Level, grassy, sheltered.

On A31, 5.0 miles west of Ringwood, opposite West Moors Garage. Signposted.

110	🚐	£8.00–£12.00
110		£8.00–£12.00
80	▲	£8.00–£12.00
190 touring pitches

BROOK, Isle of Wight Map ref 3C3

★★
HOLIDAY & CAMPING PARK
BH&HPA

COMPTON FARM
Brook, Newport PO30 4HF
T: (01983) 740215
F: (01983) 740215

Working farm with cows, pigs, geese and hens. Families welcome. A small site with acres to fly kites, planes, ride bikes. Sandy beach only quarter mile. SSSI Downland.

OPEN May–September. 160 hectares (400 acres) Grassy.

From Freshwater Bay take A3055 east for 1.5 miles. Signposted.

	🚐	£9.00–£10.00
14	▲	£9.00–£10.00
12		£170.00–£350.00
14 touring pitches

CHARLBURY, Oxfordshire Map ref 3C1

★★★★
TOURING & CAMPING PARK

COTSWOLD VIEW CARAVAN & CAMPING SITE
Enstone Road, Charlbury, Oxford OX7 3JH
T: (01608) 810314
F: (01608) 811891
E: cotswoldview@gfwiddows.f9.co.uk
I: www.cotswoldview.co.uk

OPEN April–October
21.6 hectares (54 acres)
Level, sloping, grassy, hard.

140	🚐	£8.00–£11.00
140		£8.00–£11.00
140	▲	£8.00–£11.00
140 touring pitches

Two miles off A44 on B4022. Signposted.

CHRISTCHURCH, Dorset Map ref 3B3 *Tourist Information Centre Tel: (01202) 471780*

★★★★
TOURING & CAMPING PARK
BH&HPA

HARROW WOOD FARM CARAVAN PARK
Poplar Lane, Bransgore, Christchurch BH23 8JE
T: (01425) 672487
F: (01425) 672487
E: harwood@caravan-sites.co.uk
I: www.caravan-sites.co.uk

OPEN March–December
CC: Barclaycard, Delta, Mastercard, Solo, Switch, Visa
2.4 hectares (6 acres) Level, grassy, hard, sheltered.

60	🚐	£9.75–£14.00
60		£9.75–£14.00
	▲	£9.75–£14.00
60 touring pitches

A35 Lyndhurst to Christchurch road, turn right at Cat and Fiddle pub, 1.5 miles to Bransgore. Signposted.

159

SOUTH OF ENGLAND

CHRISTCHURCH continued

★★★★★
HOLIDAY PARK
BH&HPA

MEADOW BANK HOLIDAYS
Stour Way, Christchurch BH23 2PQ
T: (01202) 483597
F: (01202) 483878
E: enquiries@meadowbank-holidays.co.uk
I: www.meadowbank-holiday.co.uk

44		£6.00–£19.00
44		£6.00–£19.00
75		£135.00–£580.00

44 touring pitches
116 units privately owned

Bournemouth's closest combined holiday and touring park. Ideally located on the pretty river Stour, between Christchurch, Bournemouth and the New Forest.

OPEN March–October. 4 hectares (10 acres) Level, grassy, hard, sheltered.
CC: Barclaycard, Delta, Mastercard, Switch, Visa

A35 from Christchurch, west 1.5 miles, turn right at Crooked Beam Restaurant into the Grove, site 3rd left. Signposted.

COTSWOLDS

See under Charlbury, Standlake

See also Cotswolds in Heart of England region

FORDINGBRIDGE, Hampshire Map ref 3B3

★★★★★
HOLIDAY, TOURING & CAMPING PARK
BH&HPA

Ad on this page

SANDY BALLS HOLIDAY CENTRE
Godshill, Fordingbridge SP6 2JY
T: (01425) 653042
F: (01425) 653067
E: post@sandy-balls.co.uk
I: www.sandy-balls.co.uk

OPEN All year round
CC: Barclaycard, Delta, Mastercard, Switch, Visa
48 hectares (120 acres) Level, grassy, hard, sheltered.

283		£11.25–£24.00
283		£11.25–£24.00
157		£11.25–£24.00
34		£95.00–£885.00

440 touring pitches

From M27 jct 1 join B3078 to Fordingbridge. Signposted.

QUALITY ASSURANCE SCHEME

For an explanation of the quality and facilities represented by the Stars please refer to the front of this guide.

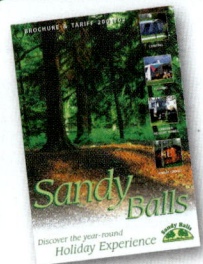

New Forest

For a relaxing award winning break
call for a brochure now on:
01425 653042

Sandy Balls Holiday Centre, Godshill, Fordingbridge, Hants, SP6 2JZ. England.
Fax: +44 (0)1425 653067   e.mail: post@sandy-balls.co.uk   www.sandy-balls.co.uk

Sandy Balls
New Forest Country Holidays
OPEN ALL YEAR ROUND

SOUTH OF ENGLAND

GOSPORT, Hampshire Map ref 3C3 *Tourist Information Centre Tel: (023) 9252 2944*

★★★★
HOLIDAY, TOURING & CAMPING PARK

ROSE AWARD

BH&HPA
NCC

KINGFISHER CARAVAN PARK
Browndown Road, Stokes Bay, Gosport PO13 9BE
T: (023) 9250 2611
F: (023) 9258 3583
E: info@kingfisher-caravan-park.co.uk
I: www.kingfisher-caravan-park.co.uk

Family-run park, 5 minute walk to the beach. On-site clubhouse, restaurant, shop, launderette, children's room. Caravans to hire or buy.

OPEN March–October & Christmas. 5.6 hectares (14 acres) Level, grassy, hard, sheltered.
CC: Amex, Barclaycard, Delta, Diners, Eurocard, Mastercard, Solo, Switch, Visa

M27 jct 11, A32 to Gosport (3 miles approximately) and follow signs to Stokes Bay. Midway between Gosport and Lee on Solent on coast road. Signposted.

90	🚐	£11.00–£16.00
90	🚗	£11.00–£16.00
20	⛺	£6.00–£16.00
20		£120.00–£350.00

110 touring pitches

HAMBLE, Hampshire Map ref 3C3

★★★★
HOLIDAY & TOURING PARK

ROSE AWARD

BH&HPA

RIVERSIDE PARK
Satchell Lane, Hamble, Southampton SO31 4HR
T: (023) 8045 3220
F: (023) 8045 3611
E: enquiries@riversideholidays.co.uk
I: www.riversideholidays.co.uk

Set amongst countryside overlooking the marina and Hamble River below. On the edge of old world village. Touring and camping, 7 nights for price of 6 (Mar–Oct). Shortbreaks for static holiday homes (Mar–Oct) and luxury lodges (all year).

OPEN All year round. 2.4 hectares (6 acres) Level, sloping, grassy, sheltered.
CC: Barclaycard, Delta, Mastercard, Switch, Visa

M27 jct 8, take B3397 south to Hamble. Signposts from Hamble Lane to Riverside Park, via Satchell Lane Signposted.

43	🚐	£8.50–£11.00
43	🚗	£8.50–£11.00
43	⛺	£6.50–£11.00
6		£210.00–£520.00

43 touring pitches
17 units privately owned

HAYLING ISLAND, Hampshire Map ref 3C3

★★★
CAMPING PARK

Ad on this page

FISHERY CREEK CARAVAN & CAMPING PARK
Fishery Lane, Hayling Island PO11 9NR
T: (023) 9246 2164
F: (023) 9246 0741
E: camping@fisherycreek.fsnet.co.uk

OPEN March–October
CC: Barclaycard, Delta, Eurocard, Mastercard, Switch, Visa
3.2 hectares (8 acres) Level, grassy.

Follow brown tourist signs for Fishery Creek. Signposted.

165	🚐	£8.00–£11.00
165	🚗	£8.00–£11.00
165	⛺	£8.00–£11.00

165 touring pitches

FISHERY CREEK CARAVAN & CAMPING PARK

Set in beautiful, quiet location adjoining a tidal creek of **Chichester Harbour**. Two children's play areas, indoor games room, well-stocked shop, constant de luxe hot showers. Facilities for disabled. Rallies welcome. Five minutes to beach, shops, restaurants, pubs and clubs.

Fishery Lane, Hayling Island, PO11 9NR Tel: 023 9246 2164 Fax: 023 9246 0741

161

SOUTH OF ENGLAND

HIGHCLIFFE, Dorset Map ref 3B3

★★★★
HOLIDAY PARK

ROSE AWARD
BH&HPA

COBB'S HOLIDAY PARK
32 Gordon Road, Highcliffe, Christchurch BH23 5HN
T: (01425) 273301
F: (01425) 276090

Pleasant family park, enviable location, near New Forest and beaches. Well provisioned shop, laundrette, children's playground, licensed club with entertainment. Full facility units. Colour TV.

OPEN March–October. 1.6 hectares (4 acres) Level, grassy, sheltered.
CC: Barclaycard, Eurocard, Mastercard, Solo, Switch, Visa

Leave A35 near Christchurch, take A337 to Highcliffe, follow brown tourist signs, turn left at traffic lights in village centre. Park is situated 200yds on the left. Signposted.

45   £160.00–£440.00
17 units privately owned

ISLE OF WIGHT

See under Brook, St Lawrence, Sandown

MILFORD-ON-SEA, Hampshire Map ref 3C3

★★★★
TOURING &
CAMPING PARK

BH&HPA

Ad p10

LYTTON LAWN TOURING PARK
Lymore Lane, Milford-on-Sea, Lymington SO41 0TX
T: (01590) 648331
F: (01590) 645610
E: holidays@shorefield.co.uk
I: www.shorefield.co.uk

OPEN February–August, October–December
CC: Barclaycard, Delta, Mastercard, Switch, Visa
2 hectares (5 acres) Level, sloping, grassy, hard, sheltered.

135   £5.70–£26.00
135   £5.70–£26.00
135   £5.70–£26.00
135 touring pitches

On B3058 coast road midway between Everton and Milford-on-Sea. Signposted.

★★★★★
HOLIDAY PARK

ROSE AWARD
BH&HPA

Ad p10

SHOREFIELD COUNTRY PARK
Shorefield Road, Milford-on-Sea, Lymington SO41 0LH
T: (01590) 648331
F: (01590) 645610
E: holidays@shorefield.co.uk
I: www.shorefield.co.uk

OPEN February–December
CC: Barclaycard, Delta, Mastercard, Switch, Visa
40 hectares (100 acres) Level, grassy, stony.

58   £185.00–£1,080.00
610 units privately owned

From M27 jct 1 take A337 to Downton, turn left at Royal Oak public house. Signposted.

NEW FOREST

See under Fordingbridge, Milford-on-Sea, New Milton, Ringwood

NEW MILTON, Hampshire Map ref 3B3

★★★★
HOLIDAY PARK

BH&HPA

GLEN ORCHARD HOLIDAY PARK
Walkford Lane, New Milton BH25 5NH
T: (01425) 616463
F: (01425) 638655
E: enquiries@glenorchard.co.uk
I: www.glenorchard.co.uk

Small park between forest and beaches, close to swimming/riding/golf facilities. Short breaks April–June/September–October except Easter.

OPEN March–October. .4 hectare (1 acre) Sloping, grassy, sheltered.
CC: Barclaycard, Delta, Mastercard, Solo, Switch, Visa

A35 Lyndhurst to Bournemouth approximately 8 miles, at Hinton turn left into Walkford after 0.75 mile turn left into Walkford Lane. Signposted.

19   £130.00–£460.00

SOUTH OF ENGLAND

NEW MILTON continued

★★★★★
HOLIDAY PARK

ROSE AWARD

BH&HPA
NCC

HOBURNE NAISH ESTATE LTD
Christchurch Road, New Milton BH25 7RE
T: (01425) 273586 & 273786
F: (01425) 282130
E: enquires@hoburne.co.uk
I: www.hoburne.co.uk

OPEN March–October & Christmas
CC: Barclaycard, Mastercard, Switch, Visa
40 hectares (100 acres) Level, grassy, hard.

60 £125.00–£600.00
820 units privately owned

Off A377 between Highcliffe and New Milton Signposted.

OLNEY, Buckinghamshire Map ref 3C1

★★★
TOURING & CAMPING PARK

EMBERTON COUNTRY PARK
Emberton, Olney MK46 5DB
T: (01234) 711575
F: (01234) 711575
E: embertonpark@milton-keynes.gov.uk

OPEN April–October
CC: Barclaycard, Delta, Mastercard, Switch, Visa
70 hectares (175 acres) Level, sloping, grassy, sheltered.

200 £10.00–£14.00
200 £10.00–£14.00
200 £8.00–£12.00
200 touring pitches
115 units privately owned

M1 jct 14, follow A509 north, 10 miles to Emberton, just before Olney. Signposted.

POOLE, Dorset Map ref 3B3 Tourist Information Centre Tel: (01202) 253253

★★★
TOURING PARK

BH&HPA

BEACON HILL TOURING PARK
Blandford Road North, Near Lytchett Minster, Poole BH16 6AB
T: (01202) 631631
F: (01202) 625749
E: bookings@beaconhilltouringpark.co.uk
I: www.beaconhilltouringpark.co.uk

OPEN April–September
12 hectares (30 acres) Level, grassy, hard, sheltered.

120 £9.00–£17.00
120 £8.50–£17.00
50 £8.50–£17.00
170 touring pitches

On A350, 0.25 miles from junction of A35 and A350 towards Blandford. Approximately 3 miles north of Poole. Signposted.

★★★
HOLIDAY, TOURING & CAMPING PARK

BH&HPA

ORGANFORD MANOR CARAVANS & HOLIDAYS
The Lodge, Organford, Poole BH16 6ES
T: (01202) 622202 & 623278
F: (01202) 623278
E: organford@lds.co.uk

OPEN April–October
3.2 hectares (8 acres) Level, grassy, sheltered.

35 £7.50–£9.00
6 £6.00–£7.50
35 £7.50–£9.00
4 £150.00–£200.00
70 touring pitches
41 units privately owned

Take 1st turning left off A35 after roundabout junction of the A35 and A351. Signposted.

★★★★★
HOLIDAY, TOURING & CAMPING PARK

ROSE AWARD

BH&HPA
NCC

Ad p12

ROCKLEY PARK HOLIDAY PARK
Hamworthy, Poole BH15 4LZ
T: (01202) 679393
F: (01202) 683159
E: enquiries@british-holidays.co.uk
I: www.british-holidays.co.uk

OPEN March–October
CC: Delta, Mastercard, Solo, Switch, Visa

71 £11.55–£35.00
71 £11.00–£33.00
27 £10.50–£22.00
95 £202.00–£835.00
71 touring pitches
920 units privately owned

Leave M27 and join A31. Follow signs for Poole town centre, follow signs for Rockley Park. Alternatively take Dorchester bypass into Poole and follow signs for Rockley Park. Signposted.

AT-A-GLANCE SYMBOLS

Symbols at the end of each accommodation entry give useful information about services and facilities. A key to symbols can be found inside the back cover flap. Keep this open for easy reference.

163

SOUTH OF ENGLAND

RINGWOOD, Hampshire Map ref 3B3

★★★
TOURING &
CAMPING PARK

BH&HPA

CAMPING INTERNATIONAL

229 Ringwood Road, St Leonards, Ringwood BH24 2SD
T: (01202) 872817 & 872742
F: (01202) 893986
E: campint.globalnet.co.uk
I: www.users.globalnet.co.uk/~campint

Popular family park with lots of facilities. Ideal for Bournemouth and The New Forest, plus 60 local attractions. Level, marked pitches. Best UK sunshine record.

195	🚐	£8.60–£12.90
195	🚗	£8.60–£12.90
195	⛺	£8.60–£12.90
195 touring pitches		

OPEN March–October. 3.2 hectares (8 acres) Level, grassy, sheltered.
CC: Delta, Mastercard, Switch, Visa

Off A31, 3 miles west of Ringwood. Signposted.

★★★★
CAMPING PARK

Ad on this page

RED SHOOT CAMPING PARK
Linwood, Ringwood BH24 3QT
T: (01425) 473789
F: (01425) 471558
E: enquiries@redshoot_campingpark.com
I: www.redshoot-campingpark.com

OPEN March–October
1.6 hectares (4 acres) Level, grassy.

30	🚐	£9.17–£12.10
70	🚗	£9.17–£12.10
70	⛺	£9.17–£12.10
105 touring pitches		

Two miles north of Ringwood on A338 and follow signs to Linwood or off M27 jct 1, follow signs for Linwood. Signposted.

ROMSEY, Hampshire Map ref 3C3 *Tourist Information Centre Tel: (01794) 512987*

★★★★
HOLIDAY, TOURING
& CAMPING PARK

BH&HPA

HILL FARM CARAVAN PARK

Branches Lane, Sherfield English, Romsey SO51 6FH
T: (01794) 340402
F: (01794) 342358
E: GJB@hillfarmpark.com
I: www.hillfarmpark.com

In 11 acres of beautiful countryside on the edge of the New Forest, our family-run site provides an ideal base to visit the area. **Special rates from £120 per month for seasonal pitches-minimum 3-month stay.**

45	🚐	£9.00–£14.00
45	🚗	£9.00–£14.00
45	⛺	£8.00–£14.00
4	🏠	£150.00–£420.00
45 touring pitches		

OPEN February–December. 4.8 hectares (12 acres) Level, sloping, grassy, sheltered.

A27 from Romsey towards Salisbury, 3rd turn right, called Branches Lane, which is 4 miles from Romsey. Signposted.

SB SPECIAL BREAKS
Many establishments offer special promotions and themed breaks. These are highlighted in red. (All such offers are subject to availability.)

Red Shoot Camping Park

Linwood, Nr Ringwood,
Hants, BH24 3QT
Contact: Mrs. S. Foulds
Tel: 01425 473789 Fax: 01425 471558
Email: enquiries@redshoot-campingpark.com
www.redshoot-campingpark.com

**OPEN MARCH – OCTOBER INCLUSIVE
OFF PEAK TARIFF EARLY & LATE SEASON**
Small Family site in beautiful part of NEW FOREST.
Ideal for walking and touring. Excellent facilities.
Well maintained & personally supervised by owners.
Good Forest Inn adjacent serving meals.
Families welcome. S.A.E. for brochure.

SOUTH OF ENGLAND

ST LAWRENCE, Isle of Wight Map ref 3C3

★★★★★
HOLIDAY PARK

UNDERCLIFF GLEN CARAVAN PARK
The Undercliffe Drive, St Lawrence, Ventnor PO38 1XY
T: (01983) 730261
F: (01983) 730261

9 — £155.00–£405.00

Quiet, beautifully maintained family-run park set in a natural, landscaped valley with superb sea views from every caravan. Shop, laundrette and telephone on site. *Special 3-day breaks available during season (excl mid-Jul to end Aug).*

OPEN March–October. Level, sloping, hard.

A3055 west from Ventnor.

ST LEONARDS, Dorset Map ref 3B3

★★★
HOLIDAY PARK

BH&HPA

Ad p10

OAKDENE FOREST PARK
St Leonards, Ringwood BH24 2RZ
T: (01590) 648331
F: (01590) 645610
E: holidays@shorefield.co.uk
I: www.shorefield.co.uk

OPEN February–December
CC: Barclaycard, Delta, Mastercard, Switch, Visa
22.8 hectares (57 acres) Level, grassy, hard.

246	£5.70–£26.00
246	£5.70–£26.00
246	£5.70–£26.00
115	£160.00–£635.00

246 touring pitches
182 units privately owned

Turn off next to St Leonards hospital westbound on the A31. Signposted.

SANDOWN, Isle of Wight Map ref 3C3 *Tourist Information Centre Tel: (01983) 403886*

★★★
HOLIDAY &
TOURING PARK

BH&HPA

CHEVERTON COPSE HOLIDAY PARK LTD
Scotchells Brook Lane, Sandown PO36 0JP
T: (01983) 403161
F: (01983) 402861

OPEN May–September
CC: Barclaycard, Delta, Mastercard, Visa
2 hectares (5 acres) Sloping, grassy, sheltered.

12	£6.00–£9.50
12	£6.00–£9.50
26	£6.00–£9.50
57	£120.00–£420.00

26 touring pitches

Off A3056 Newport to Sandown road, 0.75 mile out of Lake village. Signposted.

STANDLAKE, Oxfordshire Map ref 3C1

★★★
HOLIDAY, TOURING
& CAMPING PARK

BH&HPA

Ad on this page

HARDWICK PARKS
Downs Road, Standlake, Witney OX29 7PZ
T: (01865) 300501
F: (01865) 300037
E: info@hardwickparks.co.uk
I: www.hardwickparks.co.uk

OPEN April–October
CC: Barclaycard, Eurocard, Mastercard, Solo, Switch, Visa
72 hectares (180 acres) Level, grassy.

100	£8.50–£10.75
100	£8.50–£10.75
50	£8.50–£10.75

250 touring pitches
115 units privately owned

From Witney, take A415. Signposted from A415 outside Standlake.

TOWN INDEX
This can be found at the back of the guide. If you know where you want to stay, the index will give you the page number listing all accommodation in your chosen town, city or village.

HARDWICK Parks

CARAVANNING FOR INDIVIDUALISTS

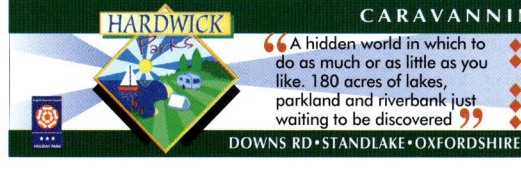

"A hidden world in which to do as much or as little as you like. 180 acres of lakes, parkland and riverbank just waiting to be discovered"

- Air conditioned Showerblock
- Fully equipped Shop & Launderette
- Floating Clubhouse/Bar
- Rally Field
- Long Term Tourers
- Water Skiing & Jet Skiing
- Windsurfing
- Fishing
- Dogs Welcome
- *Holiday Homes for Sale*

DOWNS RD • STANDLAKE • OXFORDSHIRE   01865 300501 (General)   01865 300841 (Watersports)

165

SOUTH OF ENGLAND

Whitecliffe Bay - I.O.W.

SWANAGE, Dorset Map ref 3B3 Tourist Information Centre Tel: (01929) 422885

★★★★
HOLIDAY, TOURING & CAMPING PARK

ROSE AWARD

BH&HPA

Ad on this page

ULWELL COTTAGE CARAVAN PARK
Ulwell, Swanage BH19 3DG
T: (01929) 422823
F: (01929) 421500
E: enq@ulwellcottagepark.co.uk
I: www.ulwellcottagepark.co.uk

OPEN January, March–December
CC: Barclaycard, Delta, Mastercard, Switch, Visa
5.2 hectares (13 acres) Level, sloping, grassy, hard, sheltered.

80 £10.00–£23.00
   £10.00–£23.00
   £10.00–£23.00
   £140.00–£495.00
77 touring pitches
60 units privately owned

Studland Road. On Swanage to Studland road, 1.5 miles on left. Signposted.

THREE LEGGED CROSS, Dorset Map ref 3B3

★★★★
TOURING PARK

BH&HPA

WOOLSBRIDGE MANOR FARM CARAVAN PARK

Ringwood Road, Three Legged Cross, Wimborne Minster BH21 6RA
T: (01202) 826369
F: (01202) 813172

Quiet country setting. Pub/restaurant 5 minutes' walk. Convenient for Bournemouth/New Forest/Moors Valley Country Park. Safe for children. Ideal for cycling, birdwatching, walking. Shop.

OPEN March–October. 40 hectares (100 acres) Level, grassy, hard, sheltered.
CC: Barclaycard, Mastercard, Solo, Switch, Visa, Visa Electron

60 £7.00–£12.00
60 £7.00–£12.00
60 £7.00–£12.00
60 touring pitches

Take A31 west 1 mile past Ringwood turn right at roundabout (A338 junction), signposted to Three Legged Cross, site is 2 miles along on right-hand side. Signposted.

COUNTRY CODE Always follow the Country Code
Enjoy the countryside and respect its life and work ❦ Guard against all risk of fire ❦ Fasten all gates ❦ Keep your dogs under close control ❦ Keep to public paths across farmland ❦ Use gates and stiles to cross fences, hedges and walls ❦ Leave livestock, crops and machinery alone ❦ Take your litter home ❦ Help to keep all water clean ❦ Protect wildlife, plants and trees ❦ Take special care on country roads ❦ Make no unnecessary noise

---

Ulwell Cottage
CARAVAN PARK
Dorset

English Tourism Council
★★★★
HOLIDAY AND CARAVAN PARK

BH&HPA
DAVID BELLAMY CONSERVATION AWARD
SILVER

A family run park in the beautiful Isle of Purbeck nearby sandy beaches, coastal walks and golf.
• 140 holiday homes
• 77 touring pitches
• 2 amenity blocks
• "Village Inn"
• Heated indoor pool
• General shop

www.ulwellcottagepark.co.uk
For Brochure & Information Pack,
Tel: 01929 422823 Fax: 01929 421500

OPEN MARCH 1 TO JANUARY 7

SOUTH OF ENGLAND

WAREHAM, Dorset Map ref 3B3 Tourist Information Centre Tel: (01929) 552740

★★★★
TOURING PARK
BH&HPA

BIRCHWOOD TOURIST PARK
Bere Road, North Trigon, Wareham BH20 7PA
T: (01929) 554763
F: (01929) 556635

Family-run site, in forest location, ideal for Purbecks, Bournemouth and West Dorset. Access into forest for walking and riding.

OPEN March–October. 20 hectares (50 acres) Sloping, grassy, sheltered.
CC: Barclaycard, Delta, Mastercard, Switch, Visa

From Poole (A351) or Dorchester (A352) on north side of railway line at Wareham follow road signposted Bere Regis. Second park on right-hand side after 2.25 miles. Signposted.

175	🚐	£6.50–£11.00
175	🚗	£6.50–£11.00
175	⛺	£6.50–£11.00

175 touring pitches

★★★★
TOURING PARK
BH&HPA
Ad on this page

THE LOOKOUT HOLIDAY PARK
Corfe Road, Stoborough, Wareham
BH20 5AZ
T: (01929) 552546
F: (01929) 556662
E: enquiries@caravan-sites.co.uk
I: www.caravan-sites.co.uk

OPEN All year round
CC: Barclaycard, Delta, Eurocard, Mastercard, Switch, Visa
6 hectares (15 acres) Level, grassy, hard, sheltered.

150	🚐	£9.75–£13.50
150	🚗	£9.75–£13.50
100	⛺	£9.75–£13.50
30		£105.00–£480.00

150 touring pitches
55 units privately owned

From Wareham take the A351 for 1.25 miles towards Corfe Castle. Site on left-hand side. Signposted.

★★★★★
TOURING PARK
BH&HPA
NCC
Ad on this page

WAREHAM FOREST TOURIST PARK
Bere Road, North Trigon, Wareham
BH20 7NZ
T: (01929) 551393
F: (01929) 551393
E: holiday@wareham-forest.co.uk
I: www.wareham-forest.co.uk

OPEN All year round
CC: Barclaycard, Delta, Eurocard, Mastercard, Solo, Switch, Visa
17.6 hectares (44 acres) Level, grassy, stony, hard, sheltered.

200	🚐	£7.00–£12.00
200	🚗	£7.00–£12.00
200	⛺	£7.00–£12.00

200 touring pitches

Located off A35 between Wareham and Bere Regis. Signposted.

"At the gateway to the beautiful Purbeck Hills"

★ Many electric hook-ups ★ Superb amenity blocks ★ Shop & Off-licence ★ Games Room
★ No dogs ★ 150 Touring pitches ★ 86 Hardstandings ★ Modern Launderette
★ Winter storage ★ Large Children's adventure playground

THE Lookout HOLIDAY PARK

AA ▶▶▶
RAC APPOINTED
English Tourism Council ★★★★
ROSE AWARD

Ideally situated: 3 miles from Corfe Castle – 1¼ miles from Wareham and within easy reach of Studland Bay Swanage and Bournemouth.
STATIC HOLIDAY CARAVANS ALSO AVAILABLE.
THE LOOKOUT HOLIDAY PARK STOBOROUGH, WAREHAM, DORSET BH20 5AZ
Or call WAREHAM (01929) 552546 (24 Hours)
E-mail: enquiries@caravan-sites.co.uk

WAREHAM FOREST TOURIST PARK
North Trigon, Wareham, Dorset BH20 7NX Tel/Fax: (01929) 551393
Email: holiday@wareham-forest.co.uk Web: wareham-forest.co.uk
Resident Proprietors: Peter, Pam and Sandra Savage
Direct Forest access. Electric grass/hard standing pitches.
Shop, cafe, launderette, heated swimming pool (high season).
Credit cards accepted. Free colour brochure with pleasure.

OPEN ALL YEAR ROUND

SOUTH OF ENGLAND

WIMBORNE MINSTER, Dorset Map ref 3B3 *Tourist Information Centre Tel: (01202) 886116*

★★★★★
TOURING PARK
BH&HPA

MERLEY COURT TOURING PARK
Merley House Lane, Merley, Wimborne Minster BH21 3AA
T: (01202) 881488
F: (01202) 881484
E: holidays@merley-court.co.uk
I: www.merley-court.co.uk

OPEN March–December
CC: Barclaycard, Delta, Maestro, Mastercard, Solo, Switch, Visa, Visa Electron
8 hectares (20 acres) Level, grassy, hard, sheltered.

160	⊟	£7.50–£12.50
160	🚐	£7.50–£12.50
80	▲	£7.50–£12.50

160 touring pitches

Wimborne 1.5 miles. Off Wimborne bypass A31 junction A349 Poole road, signposted.

★★★★★
TOURING PARK
BH&HPA

SPRINGFIELD TOURING PARK
Candys Lane, Corfe Mullen, Wimborne Minster BH21 3EF
T: (01202) 881719

Family-run park overlooking the Stour Valley. Convenient for coastal resorts, New Forest. Many attractions nearby. Free showers, awnings. Some hard/standing. Tarmac roads. Low season: any 7 days £40 2 adults plus electricity. 10% discount over 60 (excl 7-day offer). 5% discount weekend breaks.

OPEN April–October. 1.6 hectares (4 acres) Level, sloping, grassy, hard, sheltered.

45	⊟	£7.50–£8.50
45	🚐	£7.50–£8.50
45	▲	£6.00–£8.50

45 touring pitches

Close to main A31 trunk road, 1.5 miles west of Wimborne. Signposted.

WOOL, Dorset Map ref 3B3

★★★★
TOURING & CAMPING PARK
BH&HPA

WHITEMEAD CARAVAN PARK
East Burton Road, Wool, Wareham BH20 6HG
T: (01929) 462341
E: nadinechurch@aol.com
I: www.whitmeadcaravanpark.co.uk

OPEN March–October
2 hectares (5 acres) Level, grassy, hard, sheltered.

95	⊟	£6.25–£10.25
95	🚐	£6.25–£10.25
95	▲	£6.25–£10.25

95 touring pitches

On A352 from Wareham turn right before Wool level crossing 350yds. Signposted.

CHECK THE MAPS

The colour maps at the front of this guide show all the cities, towns and villages for which you will find park entries. Refer to the town index to find the page on which it is listed.

SOUTH OF ENGLAND

A brief guide to the main Towns and Villages offering accommodation in the South of England

A ANDOVER, HAMPSHIRE - Town that achieved importance from the wool trade and now has much modern development. A good centre for visiting places of interest.

B BEACONSFIELD, BUCKINGHAMSHIRE - Former coaching town with several inns still surviving. The old town has many fine houses and an interesting church. Beautiful countryside and beech woods nearby.

- **BERE REGIS, DORSET** - This watercress-growing village was in the Middle Ages famed for its fairs and being a resort of kings on their way to the south-west; its former splendour is well commemorated by the medieval church.

- **BICESTER, OXFORDSHIRE** - Market town with a large army depot and well-known hunting centre with hunt established in the late 18th C. The ancient parish church displays work of many periods. Nearby is the Jacobean mansion of Rousham House with gardens landscaped by William Kent.

- **BOURNEMOUTH, DORSET** - Seaside town set among the pines with a mild climate, sandy beaches and fine coastal views. The town has wide streets with excellent shops, a pier, a pavilion, museums and conference centre.

C CHARLBURY, OXFORDSHIRE - Large Cotswold village with beautiful views of the Evenlode Valley just outside the village and close to the ancient Forest of Wychwood.

- **CHRISTCHURCH, DORSET** - Tranquil town lying between the Avon and Stour just before they converge and flow into Christchurch Harbour. A fine 11th C church and the remains of a Norman castle and house can be seen.

G GOSPORT, HAMPSHIRE - From a tiny fishing hamlet, Gosport has grown into an important centre with many naval establishments, including HMS Dolphin, the submarine base, with the Naval Submarine Museum which preserves HMS Alliance and Holland I.

H HAMBLE, HAMPSHIRE - Set almost at the mouth of the River Hamble, this quiet fishing village has become a major yachting centre.

- **HAYLING ISLAND, HAMPSHIRE** - Small island of historic interest, surrounded by natural harbours and with fine sandy beaches, linked to the mainland by an attractive bridge under which boats sail. Birthplace of windsurfing and home to many international sailing events.

- **HIGHCLIFFE, DORSET** - Seaside district of Christchurch some 3 miles to the east. Highcliffe Castle is of interest.

N NEW MILTON, HAMPSHIRE - New Forest residential town on the mainline railway.

P POOLE, DORSET - Tremendous natural harbour makes Poole a superb boating centre. The harbour area is crowded with historic buildings including the 15th C Town Cellars housing a maritime museum.

R RINGWOOD, HAMPSHIRE - Market town by the River Avon comprising old cottages, many of them thatched. Although just outside the New Forest, there is heath and woodland nearby and it is a good centre for horse-riding and walking.

- **ROMSEY, HAMPSHIRE** - Town grew up around the important abbey and lies on the banks of the River Test, famous for trout and salmon. Broadlands House, home of the late Lord Mountbatten, is open to the public.

S SANDOWN, ISLE OF WIGHT - The 6-mile sweep of Sandown Bay is one of the island's finest stretches, with excellent sands. The pier has a pavilion and sun terrace; the esplanade has amusements, bars, eating-places and gardens.

- **STANDLAKE, OXFORDSHIRE** - 13th C church with an octagonal tower and spire standing beside the Windrush. The interior of the church is rich in woodwork.

- **SWANAGE, DORSET** - Began life as an Anglo-Saxon port, then a quarrying centre of Purbeck marble. Now the safe, sandy beach set in a sweeping bay and flanked by downs is good walking country, making it an ideal resort.

W WAREHAM, DORSET - This site has been occupied since pre-Roman times and has a turbulent history. In 1762 fire destroyed much of the town, so the buildings now are mostly Georgian.

- **WIMBORNE MINSTER, DORSET** - Market town centred on the twin-towered Minster Church of St Cuthberga which gave the town the second part of its name. Good touring base for the surrounding countryside, depicted in the writings of Thomas Hardy.

- **WOOL, DORSET** - On the River Frome with a mainline station. Woolbridge Manor is of interest and occupies a prominent position.

169

Where to Stay 2002

The official and best selling guides, offering the reassurance of quality assured accommodation

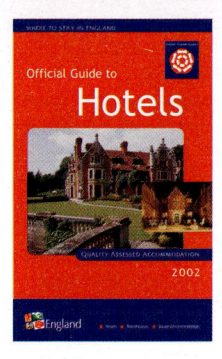

Official Guide to Hotels
Hotels, Townhouses and Travel Accommodation in England 2002
£10.99

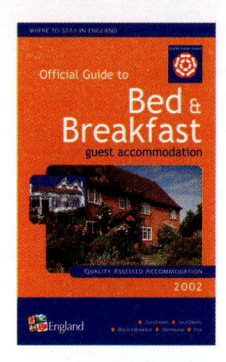

Official Guide to Bed & Breakfast guest accommodation
Guesthouses, Bed & Breakfast, Farmhouses and Inns in England 2002
£11.99

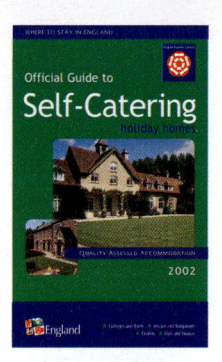

Official Guide to Self-Catering holiday homes
Self Catering Holiday Homes in England 2002
£9.99

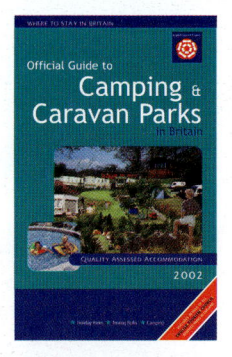

Official Guide to Camping & Caravan Parks in Britain
Camping & Caravan Parks in Britain 2002
£5.99

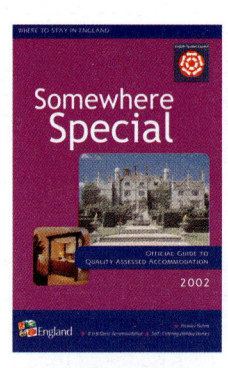

Somewhere Special
Somewhere Special in England 2002
£7.99

Look out also for:
SOMEWHERE SPECIAL IN ENGLAND 2002

Accommodation achieving the highest standards in facilities and quality of service - the perfect guide for the discerning traveller.

NOW ALSO FEATURING SELF CATERING ACCOMMODATION

The guides include

- Accommodation entries packed with information • Full colour maps
- Places to visit • Tourist Information Centres

INFORMATIVE • EASY TO USE • GREAT VALUE FOR MONEY

From all good bookshops or by mail order from the ETC Fulfilment Centre,
PO Box 22489, London W6 9FR
Tel: 0870 606 7204 Fax: 020 8563 3048
Email: fulfilment@englishtourism.org.uk Web: www.englishtourism.org.uk

SOUTH EAST England

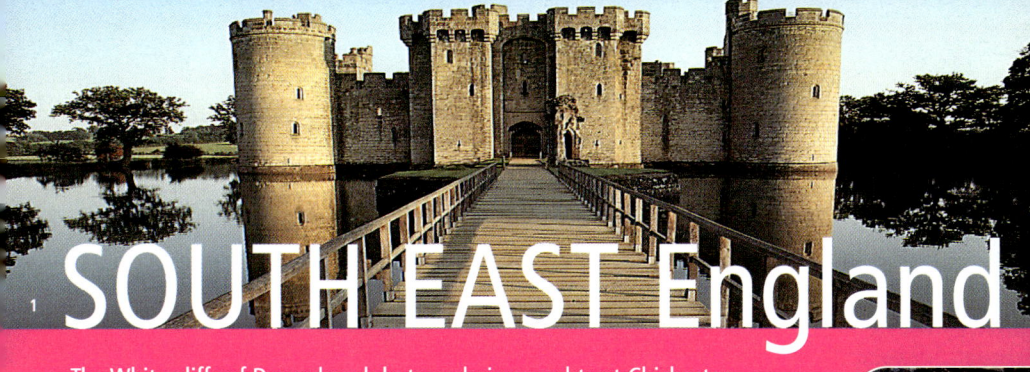

The White cliffs of Dover, beach huts and piers, yachts at Chichester – this distinctive coast combines with famous gardens and the apples and hops of Kent to make a quintessentially English region.

classic sights
Battle of Hastings – audio tour brings the battle to life
Hever Castle – romantic moated castle, home of Anne Boleyn

coast & country
Runnymede – riverside meadows and woodland
Pegwell Bay & Goodwin Sands – a haven for birds and seals

gorgeous gardens
Sissinghurst – celebrated garden of Vita Sackville-West
Leonardslee – rhododendrons and azaleas ablaze with colour in May

literary links
Charles Dickens – Rochester; his home Gad's Hill Place
Rudyard Kipling – Bateman's, his momento filled home
Chaucer – The Canterbury Tales

arts for all
Brighton Festival – international performers, artists and writers every May

distinctively different
Royal Pavilion – exotic palace of King George IV

The counties of East Sussex, Kent, Surrey and West Sussex

FOR MORE INFORMATION CONTACT:
South East England Tourist Board
The Old Brew House, Warwick Park,
Tunbridge Wells, Kent TN2 5TU
Tel: (01892) 540766 Fax: (01892) 511008
Email: enquiries@seetb.org.uk
Internet: www.SouthEastEngland.uk.com

The Pictures:
1 Bodiam Castle, East Sussex
2 Southover Grange Gardens, Lewes, East Sussex

Places to Visit - see pages 172-175
Where to Stay - see pages 176-181

PLACES to visit

You will find hundreds of interesting places to visit during your stay, just some of which are listed in these pages. Contact any Tourist Information Centre in the region for more ideas on days out.

Alfriston Clergy House
The Tye, Alfriston, Polegate, East Sussex BN26 5TL
Tel: (01323) 870001 www.nationaltrust.org.uk
A thatched, half-timbered 14thC building with exhibition on Wealden house-building. It was the first building acquired by The National Trust in 1896. Cottage garden.

Amberley Museum
Houghton Bridge, Amberley, Arundel, West Sussex BN18 9LT
Tel: (01798) 831370 www.amberleymuseum.co.uk
Open-air industrial history centre in chalk quarry. Working craftsmen, narrow-gauge railway, early buses, working machines and other exhibits. Nature trail/visitor centre.

Anne of Cleves House Museum
52 Southover High Street, Lewes, East Sussex BN7 1JA
Tel: (01273) 474610 www.sussexpast.co.uk
A 16thC timber-framed Wealden hall-house which contains collections of Sussex interest. Displays feature Lewes from the 16thC to the present day.

Arundel Castle
Arundel, West Sussex BN18 9AB
Tel: (01903) 883136 www.arundelcastle.org
An impressive Norman stronghold in extensive grounds, much restored in the 18thC and 19thC. 11thC keep, 13thC barbican, barons' hall, armoury, chapel. Van Dyck and Gainsborough paintings.

Basingstoke Canal Visitor Centre
Mytchett Place Road, Mytchett, Camberley, Hampshire GU16 6DD
Tel: (01252) 370073 www.basingstoke-canal.co.uk
A canal interpretation centre with an exhibition displaying the history of canals over the past 200 years. Boat trips and boat hire available. Adventure playground.

Battle Abbey and Battlefield
High Street, Battle, East Sussex TN33 0AD
Tel: (01424) 773792 www.english-heritage.org.uk
An abbey founded by William the Conqueror on the site of the Battle of Hastings. The church altar is on the spot where King Harold was killed. Battlefield views and exhibition.

Beaver Zoological Gardens
Waylands Farm, Approach Road, Tatsfield, Westerham, Kent TN16 2JT
Tel: (01959) 577747 www.beaverwaterworld.com
Visitors to Beaver Zoological Gardens can see reptiles, tropical and cold water fish, Canadian beavers, aviary birds, rabbits and chipmunks. Play area, sandpit and cafe.

Borde Hill Garden
Balcombe Road, Haywards Heath, West Sussex RH16 1XP
Tel: (01444) 450326 www.bordehill.co.uk
Winner of two prestigious awards. A garden of contrasts where botanical interest and garden design play equally important roles. Extended colour throughout the year.

SOUTH EAST ENGLAND

Brooklands Museum
Brooklands Road, Weybridge, Surrey KT13 0QN
Tel: (01932) 857381 www.motor-software.co.uk
Original 1907 motor racing circuit. Features the most historic and steepest section of the old banked track and 1-in-4 test hill. Motoring village and Grand Prix exhibition.

The Canterbury Tales Visitor Attraction
St Margaret's Street, Canterbury, Kent CT1 2TG
Tel: (01227) 479227 www.canterburytales.org.uk
An audiovisual recreation of life in medieval England. Visitors join Chaucer's pilgrims on their journey from London's Tabard Inn to Thomas Becket's shrine at Canterbury.

Charleston
Firle, Lewes, East Sussex BN8 6LL
Tel: (01323) 811265 www.charleston.org.uk
A 17thC-18thC farmhouse, home of Vanessa Bell and Duncan Grant of the Bloomsbury Set. House and contents decorated by the artists. Traditional walled garden.

Chartwell
Westerham, Kent TN16 1PS
Tel: (01732) 866368 www.nationaltrust.org.uk
The home of Sir Winston Churchill with study, studio, museum rooms with gifts, uniforms and photos. Garden, Golden Rose Walk, lakes. 'Years at Chartwell' exhibition.

Chatley Heath Semaphore Tower
Pointers Road, Cobham, Surrey KT11 1PQ
Tel: (01483) 517595
A restored historic semaphore tower, set in woodland, displaying the history of overland naval communications in the early 19thC. Working semaphore mast and models.

Drusillas Park
Alfriston, East Sussex BN26 5QS
Tel: (01323) 874100 www.drusillas.co.uk
South East England Tourist Board Visitor Attraction of the Year. Jungle Adventure Golf, adventure playground, toddlers' play village, zoolympics and small-gauge railway.

Eagle Heights
Hulberry Farm, Lullingstone Lane, Eynsford, Dartford, Kent DA4 0JB
Tel: (01322) 866466 www.eagleheights.co.uk
Bird of prey centre housed undercover where visitors can see eagles, hawks, falcons, owls and vultures from all over the world. Reptile centre, play area and sandpit.

English Wine Centre
Alfriston Roundabout, Alfriston, East Sussex BN26 5QS
Tel: (01323) 870164 www.weddingwine.co.uk
The English Wine Centre was established in 1972 and stocks a large range of English wines, fruit wines and ciders within the attractive wine shop. Tours and tastings available.

Goodwood House
Goodwood, Chichester, West Sussex PO18 0PX
Tel: (01243) 755040 www.goodwood.co.uk
A magnificent Regency house, home to the Earl of March, extensively refurbished in 1997 and set in a large area of open parkland. Fine furnishings, tapestries and porcelain.

Kent & East Sussex Railway
Tenterden Town Station, Tenterden, Kent TN30 6HE
Tel: (01580) 765155 www.kesr.org.uk
Full-size steam railway with restored Edwardian stations at Tenterden and Northiam. 14 steam engines, Victorian coaches and Pullman carriages. Museum and children's play area.

Leeds Castle and Gardens
Maidstone, Kent ME17 1PL
Tel: (01622) 765400 www.leeds-castle.co.uk
A castle built on two islands in a lake, dating from the 9thC. Furniture, tapestries, art treasures, dog collar museum, gardens, duckery, aviaries, maze, grotto, vineyard and greenhouses.

The Pictures:
1 River Wey, Nr. Guildford
2 Chiddingfold Village, Surrey
3 Leeds Castle, Kent
4 Bateman's, East Sussex
5 Chichester Cathedral Gardens, West Sussex
6 Brighton Pier

SOUTH EAST ENGLAND

Port Lympne Wild Animal Park, Mansion and Gardens
Port Lympne, Hythe, Kent CT21 4PD
Tel: (01303) 264647 www.howletts.net
A 300-acre (121-ha) wild animal park specialising in rare breeds including gorillas, deer, rhino, tigers, elephants etc. Mansion with art gallery exhibitions, murals and gardens. Trailer rides.

Rural Life Centre
Old Kiln Museum, Reeds Road, Tilford,
Farnham, Surrey GU10 2DL
Tel: (01252) 792300
www.surreyweb.org.uk/rural-life
A museum with a comprehensive collection of farm machines, implements, wagons, displays on past village life, small arboretum and a woodland walk.

The Savill Garden
Windsor Great Park, Wick Lane, Englefield Green,
Egham, Surrey TW20 0UU
Tel: (01753) 847518 www.savillgarden.co.uk
Woodland garden with formal gardens and herbaceous borders offering much of great interest and beauty in all seasons. Landscaped Queen Elizabeth Temperate House.

Scotney Castle Garden
Lamberhurst, Royal Tunbridge Wells, Kent TN3 8JN
Tel: (01892) 891081 www.nationaltrust.org.uk
Romantic gardens created around the ruins of a 14thC moated castle containing exhibitions. Gardens created by the Hussey family with shrubs, winding paths and good views.

Sculpture at Goodwood
Hat Hill Copse, Goodwood, Chichester, West Sussex PO18 0QP
Tel: (01243) 538449 www.sculpture.org.uk
A changing collection of contemporary British sculpture set in 20 acres (8 ha) of beautiful grounds on the South Downs overlooking Chichester.

St Mary's House and Gardens
Bramber, Steyning, West Sussex BN44 3WE
Tel: (01903) 816205
A medieval, timber-framed Grade I Listed house with rare 16thC wall-leather, fine panelled rooms and a unique painted room. Topiary gardens.

South of England Rare Breeds Centre
Highlands Farm, Woodchurch, Ashford, Kent TN26 3RJ
Tel: (01233) 861493 www.rarebreeds.org.uk
Large collection of rare farm breeds on a working farm with children's play activities. Georgian farmstead under reconstruction. Home to the 'Tamworth Two'. Woodland walks.

Titsey Place and Gardens
Oxted, Surrey RH8 0SD
Tel: (01273) 407056 www.titsey.com
A guided tour of Titsey Place includes the library, old servants' hall, dining room and drawing room. The gardens comprise 10 acres (4 ha) of formal gardens and a walled garden.

Weald and Downland Open Air Museum
Singleton, Chichester, West Sussex PO18 0EU
Tel: (01243) 811348 www.wealddown.co.uk
Over 40 rescued historic buildings from South East England, reconstructed on a downland country park site. Homes and workplaces of the past include a medieval farmstead.

West Dean Gardens
West Dean Estate, West Dean, Chichester,
West Sussex PO18 0QZ
Tel: (01243) 818210 www.westdean.org.uk
Extensive downland garden with specimen trees, 300 ft (91 m) pergola, rustic summerhouses and restored walled kitchen garden. Walk in parkland and 45-acre (18-ha) arboretum.

Wilderness Wood
Hadlow Down, Uckfield, East Sussex TN22 4HJ
Tel: (01825) 830509 www.wildernesswood.co.uk
A family-run working woodland of 60 acres (24 ha), beautiful in all seasons. There are trails, a bluebell walk, a play area, workshop and a timber barn with exhibitions.

The Wildfowl and Wetlands Trust
Mill Road, Arundel, West Sussex BN18 9PB
Tel: (01903) 883355 www.wwt.org.uk
A wildlife paradise and a haven of peace and tranquility for swans, ducks and geese from around the world. Visitor centre and viewing gallery.

Winkworth Arboretum
Hascombe Road, Hascombe, Godalming, Surrey GU8 4AD
Tel: (01483) 208477 www.cornuswwweb.co.uk
One hundred acres (40 ha) of hillside planted with rare trees and shrubs. Good views, lakes, newly restored boathouse, azaleas, bluebells, wild spring flowers and autumn colours.

SOUTH EAST ENGLAND

Find out more about SOUTH EAST England

Further information about holidays and attractions in South East England is available from:

SOUTH EAST ENGLAND TOURIST BOARD
The Old Brew House, Warwick Park, Tunbridge Wells, Kent TN2 5TU.
Tel: (01892) 540766 Fax: (01892) 511008
Email: enquiries@seetb.org.uk
Internet: www.SouthEastEngland.uk.com

The following publications are available from the South East England Tourist Board:

South East Holiday and Short Breaks Guide
a detailed guide to the region including places to visit and inspected accommodation

Bed and Breakfast Touring map 2002 - including Camping and Caravan Parks in the South East
a useful touring map detailing inspected guest accommodation in the South East and London regions. Also contains camping and caravan parks

Eating and Drinking at Traditional Inns
in partnership with Whitbread Pubs, a guide to some of the fine inns to be found in the South and South East of England

Churches and Cathedrals of the South of England
a guide detailing some of the region's finest churches and cathedrals, their fascinating history and architecture

Spoilt for Choice - 100s of Places to Visit in South East England
the definitive guide to over 300 places to visit in South East England. Also contains a Web site directory, map and information on the network of Tourist Information Centres

Leisure Map and Gazetteer - South East England
produced in conjunction with Estate Publications Ltd, a colourful tourist map of the South East showing roads, railways, hundreds of places to visit and the topography of the region

The pictures:
1 Guildford Castle

Getting to SOUTH EAST England

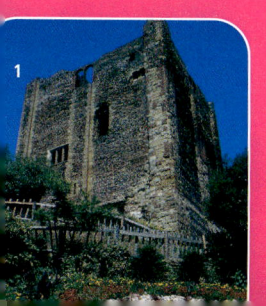

BY ROAD: From the north of England - M1/M25; the west and Wales - M4/M25; the east of England - M25; the south of England M3/M25; London - M20 or M2.

BY RAIL: Regular services from London's Charing Cross, Victoria and Waterloo East stations to all parts of South East England.

SOUTH EAST ENGLAND

Where to stay in South East England

Parks in this region are listed in alphabetical order of place name, and then in alphabetical order of park.

Map references refer to the colour location maps at front of this guide. The first number indicates the map to use; the letter and number which follow refer to the grid reference on the map.

At-a-glance symbols can be found inside the back cover flap. Keep this open for easy reference.

ARUNDEL, West Sussex Map ref 3D3 *Tourist Information Centre Tel: (01903) 882268*

★★★
TOURING & CAMPING PARK

SHIP & ANCHOR MARINA
Heywood & Bryett Ltd, Ford, Arundel
BN18 0BJ
T: (01243) 551262

OPEN March–October
4.8 hectares (12 acres) Level, grassy.

160		£11.00–£13.00
160		
160		
160 touring pitches		

From A27 at Arundel take road south signposted Ford. Site 2 miles on the left, after level crossing. Also signposted from A259 between Littlehampton and Bognor Regis. Signposted.

ASHFORD, Kent Map ref 4B4 *Tourist Information Centre Tel: (01233) 629165*

★★★★★
HOLIDAY, TOURING & CAMPING PARK

BH&HPA

BROADHEMBURY CARAVAN & CAMPING PARK
Steeds Lane, Kingsnorth, Ashford
TN26 1NQ
T: (01233) 620859
F: (01233) 620918
E: holidays@broadhembury.co.uk
I: www.broadhembury.co.uk

OPEN All year round
CC: Barclaycard, Eurocard, Mastercard, Switch, Visa
3.2 hectares (8 acres) Level, grassy, hard, sheltered.

60		£9.00–£15.00
60		£9.00–£15.00
60		£9.00–£15.00
3		£140.00–£320.00
60 touring pitches		
20 units privately owned		

From M20 jct 10 take A2070 for 3 miles, then follow signs for Kingsnorth. Turn left at 2nd crossroads in Kingsnorth. Signposted.

ASHURST, Kent Map ref 3D2

★★★
TOURING & CAMPING PARK

MANOR COURT FARM
Ashurst, Royal Tunbridge Wells TN3 9TB
T: (01892) 740279 & 740210
F: (01892) 740919
E: jsoyke@jsoyke.freeserve.co.uk
I: www.manorcourtfarm.co.uk

Secluded informal camping in garden, orchard, or near ponds on 350-acre mixed farm. Fire sites. New shower facilities. Many pets. Lovely views. Fishing, tennis by arrangement. **Reduced rates for longer stays.**

OPEN All year round. 140 hectares (350 acres) Level, sloping, grassy, hard, sheltered.

On A264 5 miles west of Tunbridge Wells, between Stonecross and Ashurst villages. Signposted.

5		£8.00–£10.00
5		£8.00–£10.00
10		£8.00–£10.00
10 touring pitches		

PRICES Please check prices and other details at the time of booking

176

SOUTH EAST ENGLAND

BATTLE, East Sussex Map ref 4B4 *Tourist Information Centre Tel: (01424) 773721*

★★★★★
HOLIDAY PARK

ROSE AWARD

BH&HPA
NCC

CROWHURST PARK
Crowhurst Park, Telham Lane, Battle TN33 0SL
T: (01424) 773344
F: (01424) 775727
E: enquiries@crowhurstpark.co.uk
I: www.crowhurstpark.co.uk

Quality development of luxury Scandinavian-style pine lodges within the grounds of a 17thC country estate. Facilities include leisure club with indoor swimming pool. Christmas and New Year breaks available.

OPEN March–December. 16 hectares (40 acres) Level, sloping, grassy.
CC: Barclaycard, Mastercard, Visa

£255.00–£870.00
135 units privately owned

Two miles south of Battle on A2100. Signposted.

BEXHILL-ON-SEA, East Sussex Map ref 4B4

★★★★
HOLIDAY, TOURING & CAMPING PARK

BH&HPA

COBBS HILL FARM CARAVAN & CAMPING PARK
Watermill Lane, Sidley, Bexhill-on-Sea,
Bexhill TN39 5JA
T: (01424) 213460 & 221358
F: (01424) 221358

OPEN April–October
2.8 hectares (7 acres) Level, grassy, sheltered.

45   £5.00–£5.80
45   £4.80–£5.50
45   £5.00–£5.80
2   £90.00–£230.00
45 touring pitches

Turning off the A269 into Watermill Lane, 1 mile on left. Signposted.

★★★★★
TOURING & CAMPING PARK

BH&HPA

KLOOFS CARAVAN PARK
Sandhurst Lane, Whydown, Bexhill
TN39 4RG
T: (01424) 842839
F: (01424) 845669
E: camping@kloofs.ndirect.co.uk
I: www.kloofs.ndirect.co.uk

OPEN All year round
8.8 hectares (22 acres) Level, sloping, grassy, hard, sheltered.

25   £10.00
25   £10.00
25   £10.00
50 touring pitches

A259 Bexhill/Little Common roundabout turn into Peartree Lane. At crossroads turn into Whydown Road. Signposted.

BOGNOR REGIS, West Sussex Map ref 3C3 *Tourist Information Centre Tel: (01243) 823140*

★★★
HOLIDAY, TOURING & CAMPING PARK

THE LILLIES NURSERY & CARAVAN PARK
Yapton Road, Barnham, Bognor Regis
PO22 0AY
T: (01243) 552081
F: (01243) 552081
E: thelillies@hotmail.com
I: www.lilliescaravanpark.co.uk

OPEN All year round
CC: Barclaycard, Delta, JCB, Mastercard, Solo, Switch, Visa, Visa Electron
1.2 hectares (3 acres) Level, grassy, sheltered.

19   £8.00–£10.00
19   £8.00–£10.00
16   £8.00–£10.00
6   £160.00–£230.00
35 touring pitches

Three miles north of Bognor Regis. Take the A29 to Westergate bearing right at Labour in Vain public house to Eastergate and onto B2233. From A27 Fontwell roundabout onto A29 then B2233 to park. Signposted.

CANTERBURY, Kent Map ref 4B3 *Tourist Information Centre Tel: (01227) 766567*

★★★★
HOLIDAY, TOURING & CAMPING PARK

BH&HPA

YEW TREE PARK
Stone Street, Petham, Canterbury CT4 5PL
T: (01227) 700306
F: (01227) 700306
E: enquiries@yewtreepark.com
I: www.yewtreepark.com

OPEN March–October
CC: Barclaycard, Delta, Eurocard, JCB, Mastercard, Solo, Switch, Visa
1.6 hectares (4 acres) Level, sloping, grassy, sheltered.

15   £8.50–£12.50
5   £8.00–£12.00
25   £7.50–£11.50
7   £130.00–£305.00
45 touring pitches

On B2068, 4 miles south of Canterbury, 9 miles north of M20, jct 11. Signposted.

CONFIRM YOUR BOOKING
You are advised to confirm your booking in writing.

177

SOUTH EAST ENGLAND

CAPEL LE FERNE, Kent Map ref 4C4

★★★★★
HOLIDAY &
TOURING PARK

ROSE AWARD
BH&HPA

VARNE RIDGE HOLIDAY PARK
145 Old Dover Road, Capel le Ferne,
Folkestone CT18 7HX
T: (01303) 251765
F: (01303) 251765
E: vrcp@varne-ridge.freeserve.co.uk
I: www.varne-ridge.co.uk

OPEN March–October
.4 hectare (1 acre) Level,
grassy.

4		£9.00
4		£9.00
8		£195.00–£350.00

4 touring pitches

Situated on Old Dover Road exit A20 via Capel-Le-Ferne slip road onto B2011 in Folkestone direction for approximately 0.25 mile and follow coast road for approximately 200m and caravan park is on right.

CHICHESTER, West Sussex Map ref 3C3 Tourist Information Centre Tel: (01243) 775888

★★★★★
HOLIDAY, TOURING
& CAMPING PARK

BH&HPA

WICKS FARM CAMPING PARK
Redlands Lane, West Wittering, Chichester
PO20 8QD
T: (01243) 513116
F: (01243) 511296
I: www.wicksfarm.co.uk

OPEN March–October
CC: Barclaycard, Delta,
Mastercard, Switch, Visa
5.6 hectares (14 acres) Level,
grassy, sheltered.

| 42 | | £11.00–£12.50 |
| 42 | | £11.00–£12.50 |

42 touring pitches
72 units privately owned

From A27 at Chichester take A286/B2179 for 6 miles, Wicks Park is 2nd on the right just past Lamb pub. Signposted.

EASTBOURNE, East Sussex Map ref 4B4 Tourist Information Centre Tel: (01323) 411400

★★★
TOURING &
CAMPING PARK

FAIRFIELDS FARM CARAVAN & CAMPING PARK
Eastbourne Road, Westham, Pevensey
BN24 5NG
T: (01323) 763165
F: (01323) 469175
E: enquiries@fairfieldsfarm.com
I: www.fairfieldsfarm.com

OPEN April–October
1.2 hectares (3 acres) Level,
grassy, sheltered.

60		£7.50–£7.50
60		£7.50–£7.50
60		£7.00–£7.50

60 touring pitches

Signposted off A27 Pevensey roundabout. Straight through Pevensey and Westham villages. Then B2191 (left) to Eastbourne east, over level crossing on the left. Signposted.

GATWICK AIRPORT

See under Horsham

HASTINGS, East Sussex Map ref 4B4 Tourist Information Centre Tel: (01424) 781111

★★★
HOLIDAY, TOURING
& CAMPING PARK

BH&HPA
NCC

SHEAR BARN HOLIDAY PARK
Barley Lane, Hastings TN35 5DX
T: (01424) 423583 & 716474
F: (01424) 718740
E: shearbarn@pavilion.co.uk
I: www.shearbarn.co.uk

OPEN March–December
CC: Barclaycard, Delta,
Maestro, Mastercard, Solo,
Switch, Visa, Visa Electron
13.6 hectares (34 acres) Level,
sloping, grassy.

150		£7.50
150		£7.50
300		£6.50
30		£150.00

450 touring pitches
187 units privately owned

From Hastings old town take A259 to Rye/Folkestone. Turn into Harold Road, Gurth Road and Barley Lane signposts on A259.

HENFIELD, West Sussex Map ref 3D3

★★★★
HOLIDAY, TOURING
& CAMPING PARK

BH&HPA

DOWNSVIEW CARAVAN PARK
Bramlands Lane, Woodmancote, Henfield
BN5 9TG
T: (01273) 492801
F: (01273) 495214
E: phr.peter@lineone.net

OPEN February–December
CC: Barclaycard, Delta,
Eurocard, Mastercard, Visa
1.6 hectares (4 acres) Level,
grassy, hard, sheltered.

12		£10.00–£12.00
12		£10.00–£12.00
24		£9.00–£12.00

36 touring pitches
27 units privately owned

Signed from A281 in village of Woodmancote, 9 miles east of Henfield and 6.5 miles north west of Brighton seafront.

IDEAS For ideas on places to visit refer to the introduction at the beginning of this section.

SOUTH EAST ENGLAND

HORSHAM, West Sussex Map ref 3D2 Tourist Information Centre Tel: (01403) 211661

★★★★
TOURING &
CAMPING PARK

BH&HPA

HONEYBRIDGE PARK
Honeybridge Lane, Dial Post, Horsham RH13 8NX
T: (01403) 710923
F: (01403) 710923
E: enquiries@honeybridgepark.free-online.co.uk
I: www.honeybridgepark.co.uk

Delightfully situated, spacious 15-acre park. Adjacent to woodlands. Maintained to highest standards. Relaxed and informal atmosphere. Convenient for ports. Heated amenity block. Ideal touring base. 10% discount on pitch fees for senior citizens and foreign Camping Carnet holders. 3 nights for 2 available mid-week low season.

OPEN All year round. 6 hectares (15 acres) Level, sloping, grassy, hard.
CC: Barclaycard, Delta, Maestro, Mastercard, Solo, Switch, Visa, Visa Electron

On A24 travelling south, turn left 1 mile past Dial Post turning. At Old Barn Nurseries continue for 300yds and site is on the right. Signposted.

100	🚐	£9.00–£13.00
100	🚙	£9.00–£13.00
100	▲	£8.50–£11.00

100 touring pitches

LINGFIELD, Surrey Map ref 3D2

★★★
TOURING PARK

BH&HPA

LONG ACRES CARAVAN & CAMPING PARK
Newchapel Road, Lingfield RH7 6LE
T: (01342) 833205
F: (01622) 735038
E: charlie.pilkington@virgin.net
I: www.ukparks.co.uk/longacres

OPEN All year round
16 hectares (40 acres) Level, sloping, grassy, hard, sheltered.

From M25 jct 6 south on A22 for 6 miles towards East Grinstead. At Newchapel roundabout turn left onto B2028 to Lingfield. Site is 700yds on the right. Signposted.

60	🚐	£10.00–£10.00
60	🚙	£10.00–£10.00
60	▲	£10.00–£10.00

60 touring pitches

MAIDSTONE, Kent Map ref 4B3 Tourist Information Centre Tel: (01622) 602169

★★★★★
TOURING &
CAMPING PARK

BH&HPA

PINE LODGE TOURING PARK
A20 Ashford Road, Hollingbourne, Maidstone ME17 1XH
T: (01622) 730018
F: (01622) 734498

OPEN All year round
CC: Barclaycard, Delta, JCB, Maestro, Mastercard, Solo, Switch, Visa, Visa Electron
2.8 hectares (7 acres) Level, sloping, grassy, hard, sheltered.

From M20 jct 8 onto A20, take turning to Maidstone/Bearsted, site is 0.5 mile on left. Signposted.

60	🚐	£10.00–£12.00
20	🚙	£10.00–£12.00
20	▲	£8.00–£12.00

100 touring pitches

MARDEN, Kent Map ref 4B4

★★★★★
TOURING &
CAMPING PARK

BH&HPA

TANNER FARM TOURING CARAVAN & CAMPING PARK
Goudhurst Road, Marden, Tonbridge TN12 9ND
T: (01622) 832399
F: (01622) 832472
E: tannerfarmpark@cs.com
I: www.tannerfarmpark.co.uk

OPEN All year round
CC: Barclaycard, Delta, Maestro, Mastercard, Solo, Switch, Visa, Visa Electron
60 hectares (150 acres) Level, grassy, hard, sheltered.

From A21 or A229 onto B2079 midway between Marden and Goudhurst. Signposted.

100	🚐	£6.50–£11.50
15	🚙	£6.50–£11.50
20	▲	£6.50–£11.50

100 touring pitches

CREDIT CARD BOOKINGS If you book by telephone and are asked for your credit card number it is advisable to check the proprietor's policy should you cancel your reservation.

179

SOUTH EAST ENGLAND

MINSTER, Kent Map ref 4C3

★★★
HOLIDAY, TOURING & CAMPING PARK

RIVERBANK PARK
The Broadway, Minster, Sheerness ME12 2DB
T: (01795) 870300 & 875211
F: (01795) 871300
E: kirwin.riverbankpark@virgin.net
I: www.ukparks.com/riverbank

60		£9.50–£9.50
30		£9.50–£9.50
10		£9.50–£9.50
2		£250.00–£250.00

100 touring pitches

Quiet, friendly, family-run holiday park. Close to seaside, overlooking countryside, only 50 miles from London. Motel rooms, holiday chalets and caravans also available for hire. **10% discount on motel rooms and holiday chalets for 7 days or more.**

OPEN March–December. 6 hectares (15 acres) Level, sloping, grassy.
CC: Amex, Barclaycard, Diners, JCB, Mastercard, Switch, Visa

Along A249 towards Sheerness. Over Kings Ferry Bridge at roundabout turn right. At traffic lights turn left. At T-junction turn right, at 1st mini-roundabout turn left, travel for 1 mile. Park situated on left behind Abbey Hotel. Signposted.

PAGHAM, West Sussex Map ref 3C3

★★★★
HOLIDAY PARK

BH&HPA
NCC

Ad p12

CHURCH FARM HOLIDAY VILLAGE
Pagham, Chichester PO21 4NR
T: (01243) 262635
F: (01243) 266043
E: enquiries@british-holidays.co.uk
I: www.british-holidays.co.uk

OPEN March–October
CC: Barclaycard, Delta, Mastercard, Switch, Visa
24.8 hectares (62 acres) Level, grassy, sheltered.

| 31 | | £99.00–£600.00 |

880 units privately owned

Where A27 roundabout crosses the A259 on the eastern outskirts of Chichester, take the Pagham exit and follow this road for 1 mile to roundabout. Turn left and follow road to end. Signposted.

ROCHESTER, Kent Map ref 4B3 Tourist Information Centre Tel: (01634) 843666

★★★★
HOLIDAY PARK

BH&HPA
NCC

Ad p12

ALLHALLOWS LEISURE PARK
Allhallows-on-Sea, Allhallows,
Nr Rochester ME3 9QD
T: (01634) 270385
F: (01634) 270081
E: enquiries@british-holidays.co.uk
I: www.british-holidays.co.uk

OPEN April–October
CC: Delta, Mastercard, Solo, Switch, Visa
64 hectares (160 acres) Sloping, grassy.

| 74 | | £99.00–£600.00 |

787 units privately owned

Take M25 jct 2, join A2 to Canterbury. Take A2 to Rochester, turn off at A228 towards Grain. Allhallows is signposted on left hand side of A228. Signposted.

ST NICHOLAS AT WADE, Kent Map ref 4C3

★★
TOURING & CAMPING PARK

ST NICHOLAS CAMPING SITE
Court Road, St Nicholas at Wade,
Birchington CT7 0NH
T: (01843) 847245

OPEN March–September
1.2 hectares (3 acres) Level, grassy, sheltered.

15		£7.50–£10.00
15		£8.20–£10.00
55		£8.20–£10.50

70 touring pitches

Turn left off A299 at St Nicholas at Wade, or turn into the village off A28 at St Nicholas sign. Signposted.

SELSEY, West Sussex Map ref 3C3

★★★★★
TOURING PARK

NCC

Ad p181

WARNER FARM TOURING PARK
Warner Lane, Selsey, Chichester PO20 9EL
T: (01243) 608440 & 604499
F: (01243) 604599
E: warner.farm@btinternet.com
I: www.bunnleisure.co.uk

OPEN March–October
CC: Amex, Barclaycard, Delta, Mastercard, Solo, Switch, Visa
4 hectares (10 acres) Level, grassy, hard, sheltered.

250		£10.00–£25.00
250		£10.00–£25.00
		£10.00–£25.00

250 touring pitches

B2145 into Selsey, turn right into School Lane, 1st right off School Lane, 1st left, proceed until you see sign for all touring caravans. Signposted.

180

SOUTH EAST ENGLAND

UCKFIELD, East Sussex Map ref 3D3

★★★
HOLIDAY & TOURING PARK
BH&HPA

HONEYS GREEN FARM CARAVAN PARK
Easons Green, Framfield, Uckfield TN22 5RE
T: (01825) 840334

OPEN March–October
.8 hectare (2 acres) Level, grassy, sheltered.

18	£9.00–£9.00
4	£9.00–£9.00
6	£155.00–£215.00

22 touring pitches

Turn off A22 at Halland roundabout onto B2192, Heathfield. Site 0.25 mile on left. Signposted.

WASHINGTON, West Sussex Map ref 3D3

★★★★
TOURING & CAMPING PARK

WASHINGTON CARAVAN & CAMPING PARK
London Road, Washington, Pulborough RH20 4AJ
T: (01903) 892869
F: (01903) 893252
E: washcamp@tinyworld.co.uk

OPEN All year round
CC: Barclaycard, Delta, Eurocard, Maestro, Mastercard, Switch, Visa, Visa Electron
1.6 hectares (4 acres), Hard.

21	£9.50–£9.50
21	£9.50–£9.50
40	£9.50–£9.50

60 touring pitches

A24 – A283. Signposted.

WROTHAM HEATH, Kent Map ref 4B3

★★★★★
TOURING & CAMPING PARK
BH&HPA

GATE HOUSE WOOD TOURING PARK
Ford Lane, Wrotham Heath, Sevenoaks TN15 7SD
T: (01732) 843062

OPEN April–October
2.4 hectares (6 acres) Level, grassy, sheltered.

60	£8.00–£10.00
60	£8.00–£10.00
56	£6.00–£10.00

60 touring pitches

From M26/M20 jct 2A, take A20 south towards Maidstone. Through traffic lights at Wrotham Heath. Take 1st left turn signposted Trottiscliffe. Turn left at next junction. Gate House Wood is within 100yds on left. Signposted.

---

the biggest holiday fun for all the family
BUNN leisure

Choose from 4 holiday parks to suit your taste – unbeatable family fun and entertainment

Bunn Leisure really has got something for everyone

4 holiday parks offering a choice of fixed site caravan and touring park holidays for guests of all ages, all promising great value for money. With _free_ access to a selection of daytime activities and a comprehensive evening entertainment programme that is second to none. Beach front location or greener surroundings, whatever your preference Bunn Leisure has got what you're looking for.

Located in Selsey, West Sussex, we're positioned near to the beach with views of the South Downs. Take a look at Bunn Leisure, there's a great holiday waiting for you!

FREE BROCHURE REQUEST YOUR COPY TODAY

Inclusive
✓ Swimming pools
✓ Live entertainment
✓ 3 entertainment venues
✓ Multi-sports play area

For a **FREE** brochure or to make a booking telephone
01243 606080 (Fixed Site Caravans) or **01243 604499** (Touring Park)
Take a look at our web site www.bunnleisure.co.uk

SOUTH EAST ENGLAND

A brief guide to the main Towns and Villages offering accommodation in South East England

A ARUNDEL, WEST SUSSEX - Picturesque, historic town on the River Arun, dominated by Arundel Castle, home of the Dukes of Norfolk. There are many 18th C houses, the Wildfowl and Wetlands Centre and Museum and Heritage Centre.

- **ASHFORD, KENT** - Once a market centre, the town has a number of Tudor and Georgian houses and a museum. Eurostar trains stop at Ashford International station.

- **ASHURST, KENT** - Small hamlet on a hill, at the top of which is the church with its unusual weatherboarded bellcote. The Wealdway long-distance footpath passes nearby at Stone Cross.

B BATTLE, EAST SUSSEX - The Abbey at Battle was built on the site of the Battle of Hastings, when William defeated Harold II and so became the Conqueror in 1066. The museum has a fine collection relating to the Sussex iron industry and there is a social history museum - Buckleys Yesterday's World.

- **BEXHILL-ON-SEA, EAST SUSSEX** - Popular resort with beach of shingle and firm sand at low tide. The impressive 1930s designed De La Warr Pavilion has good entertainment facilities. Costume Museum in Manor Gardens.

- **BOGNOR REGIS, WEST SUSSEX** - Five miles of firm, flat sand has made the town a popular family resort. Well supplied with gardens.

C CANTERBURY, KENT - Place of pilgrimage since the martyrdom of Becket in 1170 and the site of Canterbury Cathedral. Visit St Augustine's Abbey, St Martin's (the oldest church in England), Royal Museum and Art Gallery and the Canterbury Tales. Nearby is Howletts Wild Animal Park. Good shopping centre.

- **CHICHESTER, WEST SUSSEX** - The county town of West Sussex with a beautiful Norman cathedral. Noted for its Georgian architecture but also has modern buildings like the Festival Theatre. Surrounded by places of interest, including Fishbourne Roman Palace, Weald and Downland Open-Air Museum and West Dean Gardens.

E EASTBOURNE, EAST SUSSEX - One of the finest, most elegant resorts on the south-east coast situated beside Beachy Head. Long promenade, well known Carpet Gardens on the seafront, Devonshire Park tennis and indoor leisure complex, theatres, Towner Art Gallery, 'How We Lived Then' Museum of Shops and Social History.

H HASTINGS, EAST SUSSEX - Ancient town which became famous as the base from which William the Conqueror set out to fight the Battle of Hastings. Later became one of the Cinque Ports, now a leading resort. Castle, Hastings Embroidery inspired by the Bayeux Tapestry and Sea Life Centre.

- **HENFIELD, WEST SUSSEX** - Ancient village with many old houses and good shopping facilities, on a ridge of high ground overlooking the Adur Valley. Views to the South Downs.

- **HORSHAM, WEST SUSSEX** - Busy town with much modern development but still retaining its old character. The museum in Causeway House is devoted chiefly to local history and the agricultural life of the county.

L LINGFIELD, SURREY - Wealden village with many buildings dating back to the 15th C. Nearby there is year-round horse racing at Lingfield Park.

M MAIDSTONE, KENT - Busy county town of Kent on the River Medway has many interesting features and is an excellent centre for excursions. Museum of Carriages, Museum and Art Gallery, Mote Park.

- **MARDEN, KENT** - The village is believed to date back to Saxon times, though today more modern homes surrounded the 13th C church.

P PAGHAM, WEST SUSSEX - Around Pagham Harbour is a coastal nature reserve established by the Sussex Naturalists' Trust.

R ROCHESTER, KENT - Ancient cathedral city on the River Medway. Has many places of interest connected with Charles Dickens (who lived nearby) including the fascinating Dickens Centre. Also massive castle overlooking the river and Guildhall Museum.

S SELSEY, WEST SUSSEX - Almost surrounded by water, with the English Channel on two sides and an inland lake, once Pagham Harbour, and the Brook on the other two. Ideal for yachting, swimming, fishing and wildlife.

- **ST NICHOLAS AT WADE, KENT** - Village in the Isle of Thanet with ancient church built of knapped flint.

U UCKFIELD, EAST SUSSEX - Once a medieval market town and centre of the iron industry, Uckfield is now a busy country town on the edge of the Ashdown Forest.

W WASHINGTON, WEST SUSSEX - Near the village is the famous Chanctonbury Ring, an Iron Age camp on a rise nearly 800 ft above sea-level.

SCOTLAND

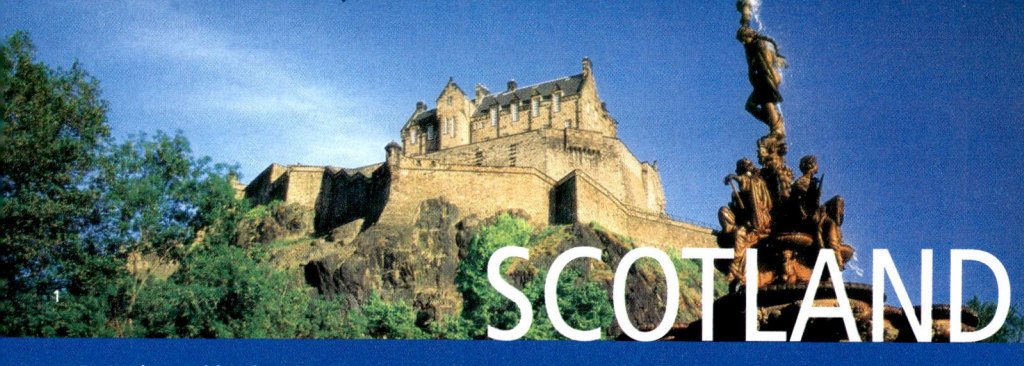

From the Highlands and Islands through the Cairngorms, Lowlands and Big Glens to the Borders, Scotland is a romantic country of snow-capped mountains, sparkling lochs and fairy-tale castles.

classic sights
Loch Lomond – scenic loch in the beautiful Trossachs
Melrose Abbey – burial place of the heart of Robert the Bruce

coast & country
The Highlands – Loch Ness, Ben Nevis and stunning views
Islands – white shell beaches of Iona and Harris, Mull's breathtaking seascapes, scandinavian-style Shetland – many islands, all different

city lights
Edinburgh – elegant and imposing with medieval Old Town and castle, stunning galleries and museums, Festival and Fringe every August.
Glasgow – cosmopolitan and style-conscious, great for shopping, restaurants and nightlife. Home of Scottish Opera and Ballet.

distinctively different
Whisky distilleries – enjoy a wee dram of uisgebeatha – water of life – at one of the beautifully sited distilleries

FOR MORE INFORMATION CONTACT:
VisitScotland
Central Information Department
23 Ravelston Terrace, Edinburgh EH4 3TP
Tel: (0131) 332 2433   Fax: (0131) 315 4545
Email: info@VisitScotland.com
Internet: www.VisitScotland.com

The Pictures:
1 Edinburgh
2 Glencoe

PLACES to visit

You will find hundreds of interesting places to visit during your stay, just some of which are listed in these pages. Contact any Tourist Information Centre in Scotland for more ideas on days out.

Aberdeen Maritime Museum
Shiprow, Aberdeen AB11 2BY
Tel: (01224) 337700 www.aagm.co.uk
Maritime museum with large exhibition area, including hands-on and interactive displays. The North Sea oil and gas industry is featured. Historic ship models.

Achaeolink Prehistory Park
Archaeolink, Oyne, Insch, Aberdeen AB52 6QP
Tel: (01464) 851500 www.archaeolink.co.uk
Ancient history recreated. Triple screen film presentation, Myths and Legends Gallery, interactive displays and outdoor reconstruction park with working Iron Age farm.

Art Gallery and Museum, Kelvingrove
Argyle Street, Glasgow G3 8AG
Tel: (0141) 287 2699 www.GlasgowCityCouncil.com
Enjoy a fabulous range of European paintings and fascinating displays on natural history, archaeology and ethnography in Glasgow's principle art gallery and museum.

Baxters Highland Village
Fochabers, Moray IV32 7LD
Tel: (01343) 820666 www.baxters.com
The Great Hall charts the history of the food company Baxters of Speyside since 1868. Audiovisual demonstration theatre.

The Big Idea
The Harbourside, Irvine, North Ayrshire KA12 8XX
Tel: (08708) 403100 www.bigidea.org.uk
A permanent millennium exhibition celebrating a thousand years of invention, but most importantly the Big Ideas of the visitor.

Brodick Castle, Garden and Country Park
Brodick, North Ayrshire KA27 8HY
Tel: (01770) 302202
The castle was built on the site of a Viking fortress, and parts of it date from the 13thC. It contains superb silver, porcelain, paintings and fine 18thC furniture.

Burrell Collection
2060 Pollockshaws Road, Glasgow G43 1AT
Tel: (0141) 287 2550 www.glasgowcitycouncil.com
The award-winning building welcomes visitors to the riches of Sir William Burrell's unique collection. There are art objects from Iraq, Egypt, Greece and Italy.

Caithness Glass Factory and Visitor Centre
Airport Industrial Estate, Harrowhill, Wick,
Vale of Glamorgan KW1 5BP
Tel: (01955) 602286
Marvel at close quarters the skilled glassmakers transforming fine Scottish sand into exquisite glassware using the heat of the furnace and the skill of hand and eye.

Calanais Standing Stones Visitor Centre
Callanish, Isle of Lewis, Western Isles HS2 9DY
Tel: (01851) 621422
These standing stones are older than Stonehenge and are one of the most remote and ancient monuments in Europe. Visitor centre with multi-lingual interpretation.

SCOTLAND

Chatelherault Country Park
Ferniegair, Hamilton, South Lanarkshire ML3 7UE
Tel: (01698) 426213
Country park with visitor centre exhibits on natural history and history of the restored William Adam lodge (open to the public). River gorge, woodland walks and nature trails.

Cruachan Power Station
Scottish Power, Dalmally, Argyll and Bute PA33 1AN
Tel: (01866) 822618
A unique 30-minute guided tour inside the hollow mountain – a reversible pumped storage scheme hidden 0.6 miles (1 km) inside a granite mountain.

Dawyck Botanic Garden
Stobo, Peebles, Scottish Borders EH45 9JU
Tel: (01721) 760254 www.rbge.org.uk
Spectacular woodland garden with a history of tree planting of over 300 years. Landscaped walks with stunning views of the garden and the countryside of the Scottish Borders.

Deep-Sea World
Battery Quarry, North Queensferry, Inverkeithing, Fife KY11 1JR
Tel: (01383) 411880 www.deepseaworld.com
Discover Scotland's triple award-winning aquarium. Enjoy a spectacular diver's-eye view of our marine environment in the world's longest underwater acrylic tunnel.

Discovery Point and RRS Dicovery
Discovery Quay, Dundee DD1 4XA
Tel: (01382) 201245 www.rrsdiscovery.com
Discovery point centre contains audiovisual displays about Captain Scott's ship 'Discovery' and includes a spectacular film show. Exhibits also depict Antarctic exploration.

Drum Castle
Drumoak, Banchory, Aberdeen AB31 5EY
Tel: (01330) 811204 www.nts.org.uk
The combination over the years of a 13thC square tower, a very fine Jacobean mansion and additions by Victorian lairds makes Drum Castle unique among Scottish castles.

Dynamic Earth
Holyrood Road, Edinburgh EH8 8AS
Tel: (0131) 550 7800 www.dynamicearth.co.uk
See, hear and smell the planet as it was thousands of years ago. Experience everything from boiling volcanoes to freezing ice age, and travel to the future itself.

Edinburgh Castle
Castle Hill, Edinburgh EH1 2NG
Tel: (0131) 225 9846
Dominating Scotland's capital, parts of this famous castle date from the Norman period. Mons Meg, the enormous 500-year-old siege cannon, is located here.

Edinburgh Crystal Visitor Centre
Eastfield Industrial Estate, Penicuik, Mid Lothian EH26 8HB
Tel: (01968) 675128 www.edinburgh-crystal
A stunning exhibition and video presentation reveals the heritage of Edinburgh Crystal. Join a guided tour of the factory and watch the craftsmen at work.

Eilean Donan Castle and Visitor Centre
Dornie, Kyle of Lochalsh, Highlands IV40 8DX
Tel: (01599) 555202 www.eileandonancastle.com
The castle of dreams. Romantic, photogenic, lots to see, not to be missed. Great fun, and great coffee too!

Gallery of Modern Art
Queen Street, Glasgow G1 3AZ
Tel: (0141) 229 1996 www.GlasgowCityCouncil.com
Four floors, each offering a gallery themed on one of the four elements: fire, air, earth, water. Fashionable rooftop cafe with panoramic views across the city.

The Pictures:
1 Rannoch Mor
2 Edinburgh & Castle
3 Edinburgh Festival, Throttke Theatre
4 Dumfries & Galloway
5 Forth Rail Bridge

SCOTLAND

Glamis Castle
Glamis, Forfar, Angus DD8 1RJ
Tel: (01307) 840393
www.great-houses-scotland.co.uk/glamis
Family home of the Earls of Strathmore and Kinghorne and the childhood home of Her Majesty Queen Elizabeth The Queen Mother. Legendary setting of Shakespeare's play 'Macbeth'.

Glenfiddich Distillery
WM Grant & Sons Limited, Dufftown Keith,
Banffshire AB55 4DH
Tel: (01340) 820373
Guided tours around the distillery and bottling hall with a complimentary dram at the end of the tour. Picnic area, shop and car park. Audiovisual display in six languages.

Glenturret Distillery
The Hosh, Crieff, Perthshire PH7 4HA
Tel: (01764) 656565 www.glenturret.com
Scotland's oldest Highland distillery. Guided tours, free tasting, award-winning visitor heritage centre, audiovisual presentation, 3-dimensional exhibition museum. Restaurant.

Highland Mysteryworld
Glencoe, Ballachulish, Highlands PA35 4HL
Tel: (01855) 811660
Prepare to become involved. Learn as you laugh, explore as you touch, and see as you sense the fantastic mysteries around you. Five fabulous indoor attractions.

Highland and Rare Breeds Farm
Scottish Farm Animal Visitor Centre, Elphin,
Lairg, Highlands IV27 4HH
Tel: (01854) 666204
An educational Highland farm with over 30 breeds of animals and poultry to see in a beautiful open setting. Highland cattle, rare breeds of Scottish sheep, goats, pigs and fowl.

Inveraray Jail
Church Square, Inveraray, Argyle and Bute PA32 8TX
Tel: (01499) 302381
Scotland's living 19thC prison featuring an exhibition on torture, death and damnation. Sit and listen to trials.

James Pringle Weavers of Inverness
Holm Woollen Mill, Dores Road, Inverness,
Highlands IV2 4RB
Tel: (01463) 223311 www.clantartan.com
A 200-year-old woollen mill offering a weaving exhibition with interactive displays and a have-a-go area.

Johnstons of Elgin – Cashmere Visitor Centre
Newmill, Elgin, Moray IV30 4AF
Tel: (01343) 554099 www.johnstons-of-elgin.com
Be guided around the only British mill still to transform cashmere from fibre to garment and enjoy an audiovisual presentation. Shop and coffee shop.

Landmark Forest Heritage Park
Carrbridge, Highlands PH23 3AJ
Tel: (01479) 841614
Amazing range of attractions: Microworld exhibition, Wildwater Coaster, Treetop Trail, Steam-powered sawmill, Wild Forest Maze and Clydesdale horse demonstrations.

The Mill on the Fleet
Gatehouse of Fleet, Castle Douglas,
Dumfries and Galloway DG7 2HS
Tel: (01577) 814099
An 18thC cotton mill, rebuilt as a heritage centre, telling the story of the building of Gatehouse. Model of town, craft and art exhibitions and cafe with riverside terrace.

The Pictures:
1 Edinburgh Festival Street Theatre
2 Loch Torridon
3 Loch Lomond

SCOTLAND

Mount Stuart
Mount Stuart, Rothesay, Argyle and Bute PA20 9LR
Tel: (01700) 503877 www.mountstuart.com
A magnificent Victorian Gothic house, the architectural fantasy of the 3rd Marquess of Bute. The profusion of astrological designs and stained glass is breathtaking.

Museum of Scotland
Chambers Street, Edinburgh EH1 1JF
Tel: (0131) 225 7534 www.nms.ac.uk
A new museum which tells the story of Scotland's past – its land, its people and their achievements.

Museum of Transport
1 Bunhouse Road, Kelvin Hall, Glasgow G3 8DP
Tel: (0141) 287 2720 www.glasgow.gov.uk
A unique collection of transport and technology which reflects Glasgow's history as the second city of the British Empire.

National Wallace Monument
Abbey Craig, Hillfoots Road, Causewayhead, Stirling FK9 5LF
Tel: (01786) 472140
Spectacular 220 ft- (67 m-) high 19thC tower built to commemorate Scotland's 'Braveheart', William Wallace. Experience his life through a series of exhibitions.

New Lanark Visitor Centre
New Lanark Mills, New Lanark, Lanark,
South Lanarkshire ML11 9DB
Tel: (01555) 661345 www.newlanark.org
Two hundred-year-old nominated World Heritage Site, birthplace of Robert Owen's radical vision for the future, featuring a new ride called the 'New Millennium Experience'.

Ortak Visitor Centre
Ortak Jewellery, Hatston, Kirkwall, Orkney KW15 1RH
Tel: (01856) 872224 www.ortak.co.uk
The visitor centre, next to the jewellery workshops, houses a permanent exhibition with a video presentation which describes how modern jewellery is made.

Rob Roy & Trossachs Visitor Centre
Ancaster Square, Callander, Stirling FK17 8ED
Tel: (01877) 330342
Exhibition of the life and times of Rob Roy McGregor including a Highland cottage, cinematic tour of the Trossachs, plus play area, gift shop and entertainment.

The Royal Yacht Britannia
100 Ocean Drive, Leith Docks, Edinburgh EH6 6JJ
Tel: (0131) 555 5566 www.royalyachtbritannia.co.uk
The Royal Yacht Britannia is permanently moored in Edinburgh and is open year round as a visitor attraction and hospitality venue. Voted Best New Attraction 1999.

Scone Palace
Scone, Perth, Perth and Kindross PH2 6BD
Tel: (01738) 552300 www.scone-palace.co.uk
This historic house, home of the Earls of Mansfield, is situated at the heart of Scottish history, on the site of the crowning place of the Kings of Scotland.

Scottish Seabird Centre
The Harbour, North Berwick, East Lothian EH39 4SS
Tel: (01620) 890202 www.seabird.org
Located in a spectacular location, attractions include interactive displays, a sound and light show, observation deck, auditorium, cafe and shop.

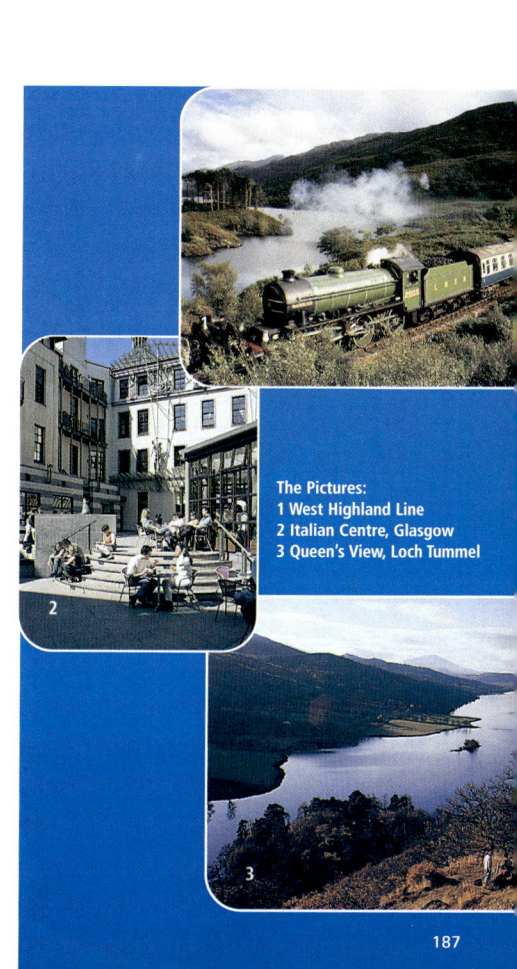

The Pictures:
1 West Highland Line
2 Italian Centre, Glasgow
3 Queen's View, Loch Tummel

SCOTLAND

Shaping a Nation
Fountainpark, Dundee Street, Edinburgh EH11 1AW
Tel: (0131) 229 0300 www.shaping-a-nation.co.uk
Explore the innovative and creative energy of the people of Scotland through the use of interactive technology.

Stirling Castle
Castle Wynd, Stirling FK8 1EJ
Tel: (01786) 450000
A grand castle with outstanding architecture. Many royal connections including strong links with Mary Queen of Scots. Exhibition on life in the royal palace.

The Tall Ship at Glasgow Harbour
Clyde Maritime Centre, 100 Stobcross Road, Glasgow G3 8QQ
Tel: (0141) 339 0631 www.glenlee.co.uk
Visit the tall ship at Glasgow Harbour. The principal attraction is the chance to come aboard the 103-year-old tall ship Glenlee. Exhibitions and children's activities.

Thirlestane Castle
Thirlestane Castle Trust, Lauder, Scottish Borders TD2 6RU
Tel: (01578) 722430 www.thirlestanecastle.co.uk
The castle is famed for its 17thC plasterwork ceilings, fine furniture and newly restored picture collection. Parkland, adventure playground and picnic areas.

Verdant Works
West Henderson's Wynd, Dundee DD1 5BT
Tel: (01382) 225282 www.verdantworks.com
Verdant Works takes you on a tour of the jute trade from its beginnings in the Indian subcontinent to the end product.

Whithorn Priory and Museum
45-47 George Street, Whithorn, Newton Stewart, Dumfries and Galloway
Tel: (01988) 500508 www.whithorn.com
Nowhere in Scotland will you find more periods of history associated with one site. Archaeologists have pieced together evidence to reveal the story of Whithorn.

The Pictures:
1 Highland Cow
2 Walking, Wester Ross

SCOTLAND

Find out more about SCOTLAND

Further information about holidays and attractions in Scotland is available from:

VISITSCOTLAND
Central Information Department, 23 Ravelston Terrace, Edinburgh EH4 3TP
Tel: (0131) 332 2433 Fax: (0131) 315 4545
Email: info@VisitScotland.com
Internet: www.VisitScotland.com

VISITSCOTLAND
19 Cockspur Street (off Trafalgar Square), London SW1Y 5BL

BRITAIN VISITOR CENTRE
Scotland Desk, No. 1 Regent Street, London SW1Y 4XT

Getting to SCOTLAND

BY ROAD: The A1 and M6 bring you quickly over the border and immerse you in beautiful scenery. Scotland's network of excellent roads span out from Edinburgh – Glasgow takes approximately 1hour and 15 minutes by car; Aberdeen 2 hours 30 minutes and Inverness 3 hours.

BY RAIL: The cross-border service from England and Wales to Scotland is fast and efficient, and Scotrail trains offer overnight Caledonian sleepers to make the journey even easier. Telephone (08457) 484950 for further details.

The Pictures:
1 Loch Lomond
2 Blair Atholl

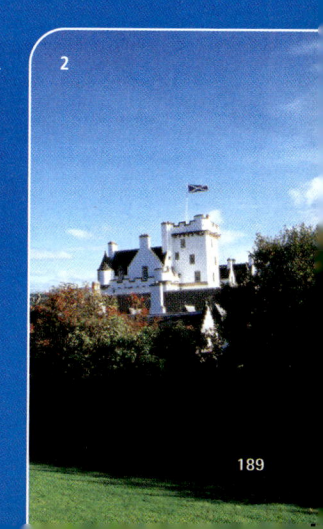

SCOTLAND

Where to stay in Scotland

Parks in Scotland are listed in alphabetical order of place name, and then in alphabetical order of park.

Map references refer to the colour location maps at the front of this guide. The first number indicates the map to use; the letter and number which follow refer to the grid reference on the map.

At-a-glance symbols can be found inside the bak cover flap. Keep this open for easy reference.

ABERDEEN, Aberdeenshire Map ref 8D3 *Tourist Information Centre Tel: (01224) 632727*

★★★
HOLIDAY PARK

SKENE CARAVAN PARK
Mains of Keir, Westhill AB3 6YA
T: (01224) 743282

OPEN April–October
Sloping, grassy, sheltered.

10	£8.00–£10.00
10	£8.00–£10.00
10	£6.00–£8.00
6	£100.00–£220.00

10 touring pitches

From Aberdeen take A944 west for 7 miles, signposted Kirkton of Skene. Turn right up B979, through village, then left. Site half a mile on right. Signposted.

ABERFOYLE, Central Map ref 7B1 *Tourist Information Centre Tel: (01877) 382352*

★★★★★
HOLIDAY PARK

THISTLE AWARD
BH&HPA

TROSSACHS HOLIDAY PARK
Aberfoyle, Stirling FK8 3SA
T: (01877) 382614
F: (01877) 382732

Award-winning 40-acre environmental park, self-catering accommodation, mountain bikes for hire, use of local leisure club.
OPEN March–October. 16.2 hectares (40 acres) Grassy, hard.
CC: Barclaycard, Delta, Eurocard, Mastercard, Switch, Visa
On east side of A81 3 miles south of Aberfoyle. Signposted.

45	£9.00–£12.00
45	£9.00–£12.00
20	£9.00–£12.00
12	£159.00–£449.00

45 touring pitches

AVIEMORE, Highland Map ref 8C3 *Tourist Information Centre Tel: (01479) 810363*

★★★★★
HOLIDAY PARK

THISTLE AWARD
BH&HPA
NCC

ROTHIEMURCHUS CAMPING & CARAVAN PARK
Coylumbridge, Aviemore PH22 1QU
T: (01479) 812800
F: (01479) 812800
E: Rothie@enterprise.net

OPEN All year round
CC: JCB, Mastercard, Solo, Switch, Visa
Level, sloping, grassy, hard, sheltered.

17	£10.00–£13.00
17	£10.00–£13.00
22	£7.00–£8.00
5	£275.00–£400.00

39 touring pitches
40 units privately owned

From A9 take B970. The park is 1.5 miles from Aviemore on the right hand side. Signposted.

NB — IMPORTANT NOTE Information on accommodation listed in this guide has been supplied by the proprietors. As changes may occur you are advised to check details at the time of booking.

190

SCOTLAND

AYR, Ayrshire Map ref 7B2 *Tourist Information Centre Tel: (01292) 290300*

★★★
HOLIDAY PARK

BH&HPA
NCC

HEADS OF AYR CARAVAN PARK
Dunure Road, Ayr KA7 4LD
T: (01292) 442269
F: (01292) 500298

OPEN March–October

3.6 hectares (9 acres) Level,
sloping, grassy.

20		£9.50–£13.00
20		£9.00–£12.00
10		£9.00–£13.00
		£150.00–£370.00

50 touring pitches
100 units privately owned

Five miles (8km) south of Ayr on A719. Site overlooking Arran and the Firth of Clyde. Signposted.

BALLOCH, Strathclyde Map ref 7B2

★★★★★
HOLIDAY PARK

THISTLE AWARD

BH&HPA

LOMOND WOODS HOLIDAY PARK
Old Luss Road, Balloch, Loch Lomond
G83 8QP
T: (01389) 755000
F: (01389) 755563

OPEN All year round

CC: Mastercard, Switch, Visa
6 hectares (15 acres) Level,
grassy, hard, sheltered.

120		£8.50–£13.00
120		£8.50–£13.00
40		£8.50–£13.00
6		£190.00–£495.00

120 touring pitches
23 units privately owned

0.25 mile from junction of A82 and A811, 17 miles north-west of Glasgow. Signposted.

BALMACARA, Highland Map ref 8B3

★★★★
TOURING PARK

RERAIG CARAVAN SITE
Balmacara, Kyle of Lochalsh IV40 8DH
T: (01599) 566215
I: www.reraigcs.co.uk

OPEN May–September

CC: Delta, Eurocard,
Mastercard, Visa
.8 hectare (2 acres) Level,
grassy, hard.

40		£8.30–£8.30
40		£8.30–£8.30
5		£8.30–£8.30

45 touring pitches

1.75 miles (3km) west of junction of A87 and A890 behind Balmacara Hotel. Signposted.

BLAIR ATHOLL, Tayside Map ref 7C1

★★★★★
HOLIDAY PARK

THISTLE AWARD

BH&HPA
NCC

Ad on this page

BLAIR CASTLE CARAVAN PARK
Blair Atholl PH18 5SR
T: (01796) 481263
F: (01796) 481587

OPEN April–October

CC: Barclaycard, Eurocard,
Mastercard, Switch, Visa
12.8 hectares (32 acres) Level,
sloping, grassy, hard,
sheltered.

140		£8.50–£10.50
15		£8.50–£10.50
82		£7.00–£10.50
27		£170.00–£370.00

241 touring pitches
74 units privately owned

Take A9 north from Pitlochry. Turn off for Blair Atholl after 6 miles. Signposted.

BLAIRGOWRIE, Tayside Map ref 7C1 *Tourist Information Centre Tel: (01250) 872960*

★★★★
HOLIDAY PARK

THISTLE AWARD

BH&HPA

FIVE ROADS CARAVAN PARK
by Alyth, Blairgowrie PH11 8NB
T: (01828) 632255
F: (01828) 632255
E: steven.ewart@btopenworld.com
I: www.fiveroads.com

OPEN January–December

1.2 hectares (3 acres) Level,
hard, sheltered.

17		£8.50–£10.25
2		£8.50–£10.25
6		£7.00–£8.00
3		£165.00–£295.00

From Perth take A93 to Blairgowrie then A926 to Alyth. Turn in at Blackbird Inn on left. From Aberdeen take A90 to Forfar junction then A94 to Meigle then B954 to Alyth then A926 to site entrance.

WHERE TO STAY
Please mention this guide when making your booking.

BLAIR CASTLE CARAVAN PARK
BLAIR ATHOLL, PERTHSHIRE PH18 5SR. TEL: (01796) 481263

Stay at our glorious highland park set amidst spectacular mountain scenery. Top quality facilities, tourist board rating "excellent". Thistle Award for our hire caravan holiday homes. Spacious central park and recreation areas, extensive woodland, hill and riverside walks. Water, drainage, electrical hook-ups and flat pitches are available. Blair Castle (open to the public) is a ten minute walk away.
Pony trekking, mountain bikes, fishing and golf, all from Blair Atholl village (100 yds)
Write or telephone today for full colour brochure

AA
Best of British

SCOTLAND

CALLANDER, Central Map ref 7C1 Tourist Information Centre Tel: (01877) 330342

★★★★★
HOLIDAY PARK

BH&HPA

GART CARAVAN PARK
Stirling Road, Callander FK17 8HW
T: (01877) 330002

| 133 🚐 | £12.50 |
| 133 🚙 | £12.50 |

133 touring pitches
77 units privately owned

A peaceful and spacious park maintained to a very high standard with modern heated shower block facilities. The ideal centre for cycling, walking and fishing. *Reduced rates for the over 50's.*

OPEN March–October. 10.4 hectares (26 acres) Level, grassy, sheltered.
CC: Barclaycard, Delta, Mastercard, Switch, Visa

Leave Junction 10 of the M9, west to Callander. Signposted.

DUMFRIES, Dumfries & Galloway Map ref 7C3 Tourist Information Centre Tel: (01387) 253862

★★★
HOLIDAY PARK

BH&HPA

BARNSOUL FARM AND WILD LIFE AREA
Shawhead, Dumfries DG2 9SQ
T: (01387) 730249 & 730453
F: (01387) 730249
E: barnsouldg@aol.com
I: barnsoulfarm.co.uk

20 🚐	£7.00–£10.00
20 🚙	£7.00–£10.00
20 ⛺	£7.00–£10.00
4 🏠	£130.00–£220.00

20 touring pitches

One of Galloway's most scenic farms. 300 acres of meadows, ponds, woodland and historic remains. *Special offers for small groups in bothies, tents or caravans.*

OPEN April–October. 100 hectares (250 acres) Level, sloping, grassy, hard, sheltered.

Off A75 at sign for Shawhead. At Shawhead take right, then within 50m bear left. After 1.5 miles Barnsoul is on left. Signposted.

DUNBAR, Lothian Map ref 7D2 Tourist Information Centre Tel: (01368) 863353

★★★★
HOLIDAY PARK

THISTLE AWARD

BH&HPA

BELHAVEN BAY CARAVAN PARK
Belhaven Bay, Dunbar EH42 1TU
T: (01368) 865956
F: (01368) 865022
E: enquiries@belhavenbay.demon.co.uk

OPEN March–October
CC: Barclaycard, Delta, Mastercard, Switch, Visa
Level, grassy, sheltered.

52 🚐	£6.75–£10.50
52 🚙	£6.75–£10.50
52 ⛺	£3.00–£10.50
5 🏠	£155.00–£375.00

52 touring pitches
25 units privately owned

From the A1 north or south exit at roundabout west of Dunbar. Park is approx .5 mile along the A1087 on left. From south do not take the first exit on the A1087.

DUNDONNELL, Highland Map ref 8B2

★★★★
CAMPING PARK

BADRALLACH BOTHY & CAMPING SITE
Croft No 9, Badrallach, Dundonnell, Garve IV23 2QP
T: (01854) 633281
E: michael.stott2@virgin.net
I: www.badrallach.com

OPEN All year round
16 hectares (40 acres) Level, grassy.

3 🚐	£7.50–£7.50
3 🚙	£7.50–£7.50
12 ⛺	£7.50–£7.50
🏠	£180.00–£250.00

15 touring pitches

Off A832. One mile east of Dundonnell Hotel take single track road 7 miles to lochside site. Signposted.

SB SPECIAL BREAKS

Many establishments offer special promotions and themed breaks. These are highlighted in red. (All such offers are subject to availability.)

SCOTLAND

DUNKELD, Tayside Map ref 7C1 *Tourist Information Centre Tel: (01350) 727688*

★★★★
TOURING PARK

INVERMILL FARM CARAVAN PARK
Inver, Dunkeld PH8 OJR
T: (01350) 727477
F: (01350) 727477

OPEN April–October
4 hectares (10 acres) Level,
grassy, sheltered.

50		£9.00–£10.00
50		£9.00–£10.00
15		£9.00–£10.00

65 touring pitches

Turn off the A9 onto the A822 (signposted Crieff). Immediately turn right following the sign to Inver for 0.5 mile past the static site and cross the bridge. We are the first on the left. Signposted.

EDINBURGH, Lothian Map ref 7C2 *Tourist Information Centre Tel: (0131) 473 3800*

★★★★★
TOURING PARK

BH&HPA
NCC

DRUMMOHR CARAVAN PARK
Levenhall, Musselburgh, Edinburgh EH21 8JS
T: (0131) 665 6867
F: (0131) 653 6859
E: bookings@drummohr.org
I: www.drummohr.org

Premier park close to Princess St, Edinburgh, and the coast of East Lothian. Excellent bus service to city with many retail outlets in the area.

OPEN March–October. 4 hectares (10 acres) Level, grassy, hard, sheltered.
CC: Barclaycard, Delta, Eurocard, Mastercard, Switch, Visa

120		£9.00–£11.00
40		£9.00–£11.00
60		£9.00–£11.00

120 touring pitches

From south on A1, take A199 Musselburgh, then B1361. Follow park signs. From the west on the A1, come off at Wallyford slip road and follow Caravan Park and Mining Museum signs. Signposted.

★★★★★
TOURING PARK

Ad on back cover

EDINBURGH CARAVAN CLUB SITE
Marine Drive, Edinburgh EH4 5EN
T: (0131) 312 6874

OPEN All year round
CC: Barclaycard, Mastercard
Level, grassy, hard.

200		£9.50–£17.50
200		£9.50–£17.50
		£4.00

200 touring pitches

From west, turn left at end of M8 on to A720. At end of bypass turn right on to A8, then left on to A902. After 1.5 miles turn right at Bampton roundabout, then left B9085. Lauriston Farm Rd, Silverknowes Rd, right at roundabout.

★★★★
TOURING PARK

BH&HPA

LINWATER CARAVAN PARK
West Clifton, East Calder, Livingston
EH53 0HT
T: (0131) 333 3326
F: (0131) 333 1952

OPEN April–October
20 hectares (50 acres) Level,
grassy.

50		£8.00–£10.00
50		£8.00–£10.00
10		£8.00–£10.00

60 touring pitches

At junction of M8/A8/M9 at Newbridge, take B7030 signposted Wilkieston for 2 miles. Park signposted on right, 1 mile on.

★★★★
HOLIDAY PARK

THISTLE AWARD

BH&HPA

MORTONHALL CARAVAN PARK
38 Mortonhall Gate, Frogston Road East,
Edinburgh EH16 6TJ
T: (0131) 664 1533 & 664 2104
F: (0131) 664 5387
E: enquiries@mortonhallcp.demon.co.uk

OPEN March–October
CC: Amex, Barclaycard, Delta,
Eurocard, Mastercard, Switch,
Visa
10 hectares (25 acres) Level,
sloping, grassy, hard,
sheltered.

150		£9.50–£13.90
150		£9.50–£13.90
100		£9.50–£13.90
18		£189.00–£470.00

250 touring pitches

From the city bypass at Lothianburn junction, follow signs for Mortonhall. From city centre take the east or west ends of Princes Street. Signposted.

REGIONAL TOURIST BOARD The ⋀ symbol after a park name indicates that it is a Regional Tourist Board member.

SCOTLAND

FORT WILLIAM, Highland Map ref 7B1 Tourist Information Centre Tel: (01397) 703781

★★★★★ **HOLIDAY PARK**
BH&HPA
Ad on this page

LINNHE LOCHSIDE HOLIDAYS
Corpach, Fort William PH33 7NL
T: (01397) 772376
F: (01397) 772007
E: holidays@linnhe.demon.co.uk
I: www.linnhe-lochside-holidays.co.uk

OPEN February–October, Christmas, New Year & January
CC: Barclaycard, Delta, Eurocard, Mastercard, Switch, Visa
8 hectares (20 acres) Level, hard, sheltered.

65	🚐	£12.00–£15.00
65	🚗	£12.00–£15.00
10	⛺	£9.00–£11.00
68	🏠	£175.00–£460.00

75 touring pitches
21 units privately owned

On A830 1.5 miles (3km) west of Corpach village, 5 miles from Fort William. Signposted.

GLASGOW, Strathclyde Map ref 7B2 Tourist Information Centre Tel: (0141) 2044400

★★★ **HOLIDAY PARK**
BH&HPA

CRAIGENDMUIR PARK
Campsie View, Stepps, Glasgow G33 6AF
T: (0141) 779 2973 & 779 4159
F: (0141) 779 4357
E: info@craigendmuir.co.uk
I: www.craigendmuir.co.uk

OPEN All year round
CC: Mastercard, Visa
Level, grassy, hard.

18	🚐	£9.50
6	⛺	£9.50
6		£9.50
6	🏠	£180.00

20 touring pitches

From south or west exit at junction 11 on M8 and take A80 (Cumbernauld and Sterling). From north continue on A80 to Stepps. Signposted.

GLENCOE, Highland Map ref 7B1

★★★★★ **HOLIDAY PARK**
THISTLE AWARD
BH&HPA

INVERCOE CARAVAN & CAMPING PARK
Invercoe, Glencoe PH49 4HP
T: (01855) 811210
F: (01855) 811210
E: invercoe@sol.co.uk

OPEN March–October
2 hectares (5 acres) Level, hard.

55	🚐	£10.00–£14.00
55	🚗	£10.00–£14.00
55	⛺	£8.00–£14.00
5	🏠	£220.00–£370.00

55 touring pitches

Site is 0.25 mile from Glencoe crossroads (A82) on the Kinlochleven road B863. Signposted.

★★ **CAMPING PARK**

RED SQUIRREL CAMP SITE
Glencoe PA49 4HX
T: (01855) 811256

Natural, clean, happy, easy going site by River Coe and mountains. Showers 50p meters. Walking, climbing, touring and historic area. Pubs and shops approximately 1 mile.
OPEN All year round. 8 hectares (20 acres) Level, sloping, grassy, stony, sheltered.

| | 🚐 | £9.00–£9.00 |
| 75 | ⛺ | £9.00–£9.00 |

75 touring pitches

Old Glencoe road between Clachaig Inn and Glencoe village, parallel to A82. Brown and white main road signs.

TOWN INDEX

This can be found at the back of the guide. If you know where you want to stay, the index will give you the page number listing all accommodation in your chosen town, city or village.

Linnhe Lochside Holidays "Best Park in Scotland 1999"
Almost a botanical garden and stunningly beautiful. Luxury chalets and holiday caravans for hire. Touring pitches, licensed shop, private beach & free fishing.
Pets welcome. Colour brochure.
Corpach, Fort William, PH33 7NL Tel: (01397) 772376
www.linnhe-lochside-holidays.co.uk email: holidays@linnhe.demon.co.uk

SCOTLAND

GLENLUCE, Dumfries & Galloway Map ref 7B3

★★★★
HOLIDAY PARK

THISTLE AWARD
NCC

WHITECAIRN FARM CARAVAN PARK
Glenluce, Newton Stewart DG8 0NZ
T: (01581) 300267
F: (01581) 300434
I: www.whitecairncaravans.co.uk

OPEN March–October
2.4 hectares (6 acres) Level, grassy.

10 — £7.50–£9.50
10 — £7.50–£9.50
10 — £7.50–£9.50
15 — £150.00–£290.00
10 touring pitches
25 units privately owned

1.5 miles (2km) north of Glenluce village off A75. Signposted.

INVERUGLAS, Strathclyde Map ref 7B1

★★★★★
HOLIDAY PARK

THISTLE AWARD
NCC

LOCH LOMOND HOLIDAY PARK
Inveruglas, Tarbet G83 7DW
T: (01301) 704224
F: (01301) 704206
E: enquiries@lochlomond-lodges.co.uk
I: www.lochlomond-caravans.co.uk

OPEN January, March–October, December
CC: Barclaycard, Mastercard, Switch
5.2 hectares (13 acres) Sloping, grassy, stony, sheltered.

15 — £10.00–£15.00
18 — £10.00–£15.00
8 — £140.00–£365.00
18 touring pitches
46 units privately owned

From Glasgow A82 north 30 miles (48km) to Tarbet Hotel. Turn right on A82 Oban road for 3 miles (5km) and site on right. Signposted.

ISLE OF ARRAN Map ref 7B2 Tourist Information Centre Tel: (01770) 302140

★★★
TOURING PARK

BH&HPA

LOCHRANZA GOLF CARAVAN AND CAMPING SITE
Lochranza, Brodick KA27 8HL
T: (01770) 830273

OPEN April–October
Level, grassy.

60 — £11.00–£13.00
60 — £10.00–£12.00
60 — £9.00–£13.00
60 touring pitches

At the golf course.

KIPPFORD, Dumfries & Galloway Map ref 7C3

★★★★★
HOLIDAY PARK

THISTLE AWARD
BH&HPA
NCC

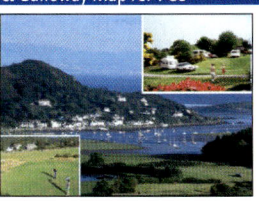

KIPPFORD HOLIDAY PARK
Kippford, Dalbeattie DG5 4LF
T: (01556) 620636
F: (01556) 620607
I: www.kippfordholidaypark.co.uk

Coastal south-west Scotland by beautiful seaside village. Terraced pitches on Bellamy Gold Park, with woodland and coastal walks. Play areas, cycles, fishing , 9-hole golf. Discounts for large families and senior citizens, also 7th night free. Marquee (free) for small rallies.

OPEN All year (Nov–Feb booking only). 7.2 hectares (18 acres) Level, sloping, grassy, hard, sheltered.

30 — £9.00–£11.00
5 — £9.00–£11.00
10 — £7.00–£11.00
10 — £115.00–£350.00
45 touring pitches
105 units privately owned

From A711 Dalbeattie take Solway coast road A710. After 3.5 miles continue straight ahead at junction with Kippford Road. Entrance to park is 200 yards on right. Signposted.

LAUDER, Borders Map ref 7C2

★★★★
TOURING PARK

BH&HPA

THIRLESTANE CASTLE CARAVAN AND CAMPING SITE
Thirlestane Castle, Lauder TD2 6RU
T: (01578) 722254 & 07976 231032
F: (01578) 718749

OPEN April–September
1.6 hectares (4 acres) Level, sloping, grassy.

50 — £8.00–£8.00
50 — £8.00–£8.00
50 — £7.00–£7.00
50 touring pitches

0.25 miles (0.5km) south of Lauder, just off A68 and A697. Edinburgh 28 miles (45km), Newcastle 68 miles (109km). Signposted.

SCOTLAND

LAURENCEKIRK, Grampian Map ref 7D1

★★★★
HOLIDAY PARK

BH&HPA

DOVECOT CARAVAN PARK
North Water Bridge, Laurencekirk
AB30 1QL
T: (01674) 840630
F: (01674) 840630

OPEN April–October
2.4 hectares (6 acres) Grassy, sheltered.

25 £7.50–£8.50
25 £7.50–£8.50
25
2 £200.00–£220.00
25 touring pitches
40 units privately owned

From Laurencekirk (A90) 5 miles south at Northwater Bridge, turn right to Edzell. Site is 300m on left. Signposted.

LINLITHGOW, Lothian Map ref 7C2

★★★★
TOURING PARK

BEECRAIGS CARAVAN AND CAMPING SITE
Beecraigs Country Park, The Park Centre, Linlithgow
EH49 6PL
T: (01506) 844516
F: (01506) 846256
E: mail@beecraigs.com
I: www.beecraigs.com

39 £9.50–£10.50
39 £9.50–£10.50
20 £8.50–£9.50
59 touring pitches

Open all year. Situated near historic Linlithgow town. On-site facilities include electric hook ups, barbecues, play area, modern toilet facilities and laundry. Pets welcome. Leaflets available.

OPEN All year round. 400 hectares (1000 acres) Level, grassy, hard, sheltered.
CC: Delta, Mastercard, Switch, Visa

From Linlithgow, follow Beecraigs Country Park or international caravan park signposts. Park is 2 miles south of Linlithgow. From M8, follow B792.

LOCH LOMOND

See under Balloch

LOCHGILPHEAD, Strathclyde Map ref 7B2

★★★★
HOLIDAY PARK

THISTLE AWARD

BH&HPA

LOCHGILPHEAD CARAVAN PARK
Bank Park, Lochgilphead PA31 8NE
T: (01546) 602003
F: (01546) 603699

OPEN April–October
2.8 hectares (7 acres) Level, grassy, hard, sheltered.

30 £8.00
30 £8.00
10 £8.00
15 £125.00
40 touring pitches
15 units privately owned

Adjacent to junction of A83/A816 within town of Lochgilphead. Signposted.

LOCKERBIE, Dumfries & Galloway Map ref 7C3

★★★★★
HOLIDAY PARK

HODDOM CASTLE CARAVAN PARK
Hoddom, Lockerbie DG11 1AS
T: (01576) 300251

OPEN March–October
CC: Barclaycard, Mastercard, Switch, Visa
11.2 hectares (28 acres) Level, sloping, grassy, hard, sheltered.

170 £6.00–£11.00
170 £6.00–£11.00
170 £5.00–£11.00
170 touring pitches
29 units privately owned

From A74 turn off at Junction 19. Follow signs to Hoddom Castle from A75. Take B723 west of Annan to Lockerbie. Follow signs to Hoddom Castle.

MAP REFERENCES The map references refer to the colour maps at the front of the guide. The first figure is the map number; the letter and figure which follow indicate the grid reference on the map.

SCOTLAND

LONGNIDDRY, Lothian Map ref 7C2

★★★★
HOLIDAY, TOURING & CAMPING PARK

THISTLE AWARD

BH&HPA
NCC

Ad p12

SETON SANDS HOLIDAY VILLAGE
Longniddry, East Lothian EH32 0QF
T: (01875) 813333 & 0845 7697761
F: (01875) 813531
E: enquiries@british-holidays.co.uk
I: www.british-holidays.co.uk

OPEN March–October
CC: Delta, Mastercard, Solo, Switch, Visa
Level, grassy.

64	£9.45–£23.00
64	£9.00–£22.00
30	£8.40–£16.80
124	£99.00–£600.00

60 touring pitches
489 units privately owned

Take A1 until approximately 10 miles south of Edinburgh. Take exit signposted Seton Sands on to B6371 towards Port Seton and Cockenzie. Follow signs through Port Seton. Park is 1 mile along on right hand side. Signposted.

MOTHERWELL, Strathclyde Map ref 7C2 *Tourist Information Centre Tel: (01698) 285590*

★★★★
TOURING PARK

NCC

STRATHCLYDE PARK CARAVAN CAMPING SITE
366 Hamilton Road, Motherwell ML1 3ED
T: (01698) 266155
F: (01698) 252925

OPEN April–October

100	£8.45–£8.45
100	£8.45–£8.45
150	£3.80–£7.30

250 touring pitches

From south follow M74 north, exit at A725 junc 5 signposted with a thistle emblem. From Edinburgh follow M8 south Carlisle road and M74, come down A725. Signposted.

NORTH BERWICK, Lothian Map ref 7D2 *Tourist Information Centre Tel: (01620) 892197*

★★★★★
HOLIDAY PARK

THISTLE AWARD

BH&HPA

TANTALLON CARAVAN PARK
Dunbar Road, North Berwick EH39 5NJ
T: (01620) 893348
F: (01620) 895623
E: enquiries@tantalloncp.demon.co.uk

OPEN March–October
CC: Barclaycard, Delta, Eurocard, Mastercard, Switch, Visa
Level, sloping, grassy.

147	£7.60–£15.00
147	£7.60–£15.00
147	£7.60–£15.00
10	£165.00–£475.00

147 touring pitches
45 units privately owned

From North Berwick take A198 towards Dunbar. Situated on east side of town overlooking golf course and Firth of Forth. From A1 turn onto A198 3 miles west of Dunbar. Signposted.

PITLOCHRY, Tayside Map ref 7C1 *Tourist Information Centre Tel: (01796) 472215*

★★★★
HOLIDAY PARK

THISTLE AWARD

BH&HPA

MILTON OF FONAB CARAVAN PARK
Pitlochry PH16 5NA
T: (01796) 472882
F: (01796) 474363

OPEN March–October
6 hectares (15 acres) Level, grassy, sheltered.

154	£10.50–£11.00
154	£10.50–£11.00
154	£10.50–£11.00
36	£220.00–£350.00

154 touring pitches

From south take Pitlochry filter road. Site is half a mile south of Pitlochry. Signposted.

SANDHEAD, Dumfries & Galloway Map ref 7B3 *Tourist Information Centre Tel: (01776) 702595*

★★★★
HOLIDAY PARK

BH&HPA

SANDS OF LUCE CARAVAN PARK
Sandhead, Stranraer DG9 9JR
T: (01776) 830456
F: (01776) 830456

OPEN March–October
4.8 hectares (12 acres) Level, grassy.

50	£7.50–£9.50
20	£7.00–£9.00
10	£7.50–£9.50
6	£150.00–£310.00

60 touring pitches
37 units privately owned

From Stranraer take A77 to the A716 signposted to Drummore. Park is 7 miles south of Stranraer, 1 mile past the village of Stoneykirk. Signposted.

SKELMORLIE, Ayrshire Map ref 7B2

★★★
HOLIDAY PARK

BH&HPA

MAINS CARAVAN PARK
Skelmorlie Mains, Skelmorlie PA17 5EU
T: (01475) 520794
F: (01475) 520794

OPEN March–October
96 hectares (240 acres) Level, sloping, grassy, stony, hard, sheltered.

26	£10.00–£14.00
26	£9.00–£13.00
70	£8.00–£12.00
10	£175.00–£460.00

96 touring pitches
72 units privately owned

Off A78, 4 miles north of Largs. Signposted.

SCOTLAND

STIRLING, Central Map ref 7C2 *Tourist Information Centre Tel: (01786) 475019*

★★★★★
TOURING PARK
BH&HPA

WITCHES CRAIG CARAVAN PARK
Blairlogie, Stirling FK9 5PX
T: (01786) 474947
E: witchescraig@aol.com

OPEN April–October
2 hectares (5 acres) Level, grassy, hard, sheltered.

60	£10.00–£11.00
60	£10.00–£11.00
60	£10.00–£11.00
60 touring pitches

Leave Stirling on St Andrews road, A91. Site 3 miles (5km) east of Stirling. Signposted.

WEMYSS BAY, Strathclyde Map ref 7B2

★★★★
HOLIDAY PARK
THISTLE AWARD
BH&HPA
NCC
Ad p12

WEMYSS BAY HOLIDAY PARK
Wemyss Bay, Renfrewshire PA18 6BA
T: (01475) 520812
F: (01475) 521137
E: enquiries@british-holidays.co.uk
I: www.british-holidays.co.uk

OPEN March–October
CC: Delta, Mastercard, Switch, Solo, Visa

115 £99.00–£600.00
385 units privately owned

From Glasgow follow the M8 to Greenock and take the A78 to Wemyss Bay. Entrance opposite railway station and Wemyss Bay Ferry terminal. Signposted.

DAVID BELLAMY CONSERVATION AWARDS

If you are looking for a site that's environmentally friendly look for those that have achieved the David Bellamy conservation Award. Recently launched in conjunction with the British Holiday & Home Parks Association, this award is given to sites which are committed to protecting and enhancing the environment – from care of the hedgerows and wildlife to recycling waste – and are members of the Association. More information about this award scheme can be found at the back of the guide.

SCOTLAND

A brief guide to the main Towns and Villages offering accommodation in Scotland

A ABERDEEN, ABERDEENSHIRE - Gleaming granite-built city with a busy fish market and a harbour for deep-sea trawlers. Bordered by fine sandy beaches and backed by hills, castles and the salmon rivers of Royal Deeside and Donside.

• **ABERFOYLE, CENTRAL** - Village on the River Forth. Nearby are the Loch Ard forests and Menteith Hills.

• **AVIEMORE, HIGHLAND** - Popular centre for exploring Speyside and the Cairngorms. Winter sports, fishing, walking and climbing.

• **AYR, AYRSHIRE** - One of Scotland's brightest seaside resorts. Also a Royal Burgh and noted centre for the manufacture of carpets and fabrics. Many associations with the poet Robert Burns. Faces the Isle of Arran across the Firth of Clyde.

B BALLOCH, STRATHCLYDE - Situated at the southern end of Loch Lomond, an ideal starting place for touring the loch.

• **BALMACARA, HIGHLAND** - Small village on the north shore of Loch Alsh with views towards the Sound of Sleat and Skye.

• **BLAIR ATHOLL, TAYSIDE** - Highland village at the foot of the Grampian mountains.

• **BLAIRGOWRIE, TAYSIDE** - Bracing inland resort overlooking the fertile valley of Strathmore.

C CALLANDER, CENTRAL - A favourite centre for exploring the Trossachs and the Highlands, beautifully situated at the entrance to the Pass of Leny.

D DUMFRIES, DUMFRIES & GALLOWAY - Fascinating town with old five-arched bridge spanning the River Nith. County capital and Royal Burgh with associations with Robert Burns, James Barrie and Robert Bruce. Burns died here and the house he occupied contains interesting personal relics. His tomb is in St Michaels.

• **DUNBAR, LOTHIAN** - Popular seaside resort at the foot of the Lammermuir Hills. Good bathing from extensive sands. On the rock above the harbour are the remains of Dunbar Castle. Mary Queen of Scots fled here with Darnley in 1566, immediately after the murder of Rizzio, her secretary.

• **DUNDONNELL, HIGHLAND** - Locality of scattered crofting hamlets round the shores of Little Loch Broom, dominated by the magnificent ridge of An Teallach. Glorious scenery, mountaineering and sea angling.

• **DUNKELD, TAYSIDE** - Picturesque cathedral town beautifully situated in the richly wooded valley of the River Tay on the edge of the Perthshire Highlands. Salmon and trout fishing.

E EDINBURGH, LOTHIAN - Scotland's capital and international festival city. Dominated by its ancient fortress, the city is surrounded by hills, woodlands and rivers. Good shopping on Princes Street.

F FORT WILLIAM, HIGHLAND - One of the finest touring centres in the Western Highlands. A busy holiday town set on the shores of Loch Linnhe at the western end of the Great Glen almost in the shadow of Ben Nevis, the highest mountain in the British Isles. Nearby are fishing, climbing, walking and steamer trips to the islands.

G GLASGOW, STRATHCLYDE - Scotland's largest city, whose shipyards have built many of the world's most famous vessels. Although a commercial city it has also become a famous centre for the arts and was the European City of Culture for 1990. Excellent shopping facilities and nightlife.

• **GLENCOE, HIGHLAND** - Village at the foot of Glen Coe, a deep and rugged defile enclosed by towering mountains. Scene of massacre of MacDonalds of Glencoe by the Campbells of Glen Lyon in 1692. A valley of haunting beauty offering winter sports.

K KIPPFORD, DUMFRIES & GALLOWAY - Beautiful seaside village, part of the Colvend Coast Heritage Trail, with sailing centre, spectacular beach views and pubs. National Trust and Forestry Commission walks and cycle tracks, game and coarse fishing trips and cycle hire.

L LAUDER, BORDERS - Royal Burgh with quaint old tolbooth, 16th C church and medieval Thirlstane Castle.

• **LINLITHGOW, LOTHIAN** - Historic town west of Edinburgh whose industries include electronics, distilling and manufacturing. Close by stand the ruins of Linlithgow Palace, birthplace of Mary Queen of Scots.

• **LOCHGILPHEAD, STRATHCLYDE** - Town at the head of Loch Gilphead.

• **LOCKERBIE, DUMFRIES & GALLOWAY** - Market town in the beautiful Valley of Annandale.

• **LONGNIDDRY, LOTHIAN** - Small village on the Firth of Forth.

N NORTH BERWICK, LOTHIAN - Holiday resort on the Firth of Forth with sandy beaches, golf and a picturesque harbour.

P PITLOCHRY, TAYSIDE - A favourite holiday resort and touring centre in the valley of the Tummel. Points of interest are Pitlochry Dam and Salmon Ladder.

S SKELMORLIE, AYRSHIRE - Firth of Clyde resort opposite Bute.

• **STIRLING, CENTRAL** - Ancient town with a long and turbulent history. The famous castle perched on its towering rock was a vital stronghold which became the scene of several battles, notably the Battle of Bannockburn in 1314.

199

Where to Stay 2002

The official and best selling guides, offering the reassurance of quality assured accommodation

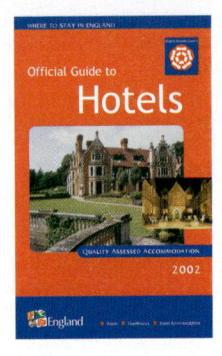

Hotels, Townhouses and Travel Accommodation in England 2002
£10.99

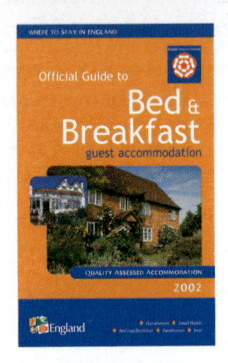

Guesthouses, Bed & Breakfast, Farmhouses and Inns in England 2002
£11.99

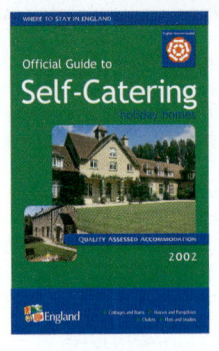

Self Catering Holiday Homes in England 2002
£9.99

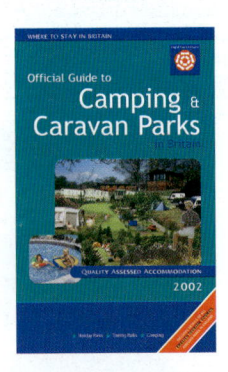

Camping & Caravan Parks in Britain 2002
£5.99

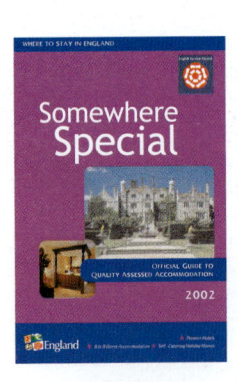

Somewhere Special in England 2002
£7.99

Look out also for:
SOMEWHERE SPECIAL IN ENGLAND 2002

Accommodation achieving the highest standards in facilities and quality of service - the perfect guide for the discerning traveller.

NOW ALSO FEATURING SELF CATERING ACCOMMODATION

The guides include

- Accommodation entries packed with information • Full colour maps
- Places to visit • Tourist Information Centres

INFORMATIVE • EASY TO USE • GREAT VALUE FOR MONEY

From all good bookshops or by mail order from the ETC Fulfilment Centre,
PO Box 22489, London W6 9FR
Tel: 0870 606 7204 Fax: 020 8563 3048
Email: fulfilment@englishtourism.org.uk Web: www.englishtourism.org.uk

WALES

A timeless country of epic mountains, lush green valleys and spectacular coastline, all rich in wildlife. Explore pretty pastel harbours, forbidding stone castles, charming Victorian resorts and the city pleasures of Cardiff.

classic sights
Powis Castle – medieval castle with Italian and French style gardens
Portmeirion – romantic Italian style seaside village set in sub-tropical woodlands
Tintern Abbey – decorative medieval abbey in a riverbank setting

coast & country
Gower peninsula – sweeping golden beaches
Snowdonia National Park – mountains, hill farms and upland lakes
Lake Vyrnwy – dramatic and mountain-ringed

literary links
Dylan Thomas – Carmarthenshire inspired his work. Dylan Thomas Centre at Swansea
Hay Festival of Literature – attracts leading international writers

distinctively different
Dolaucothi Gold Mines – try panning for gold yourself!

FOR MORE INFORMATION CONTACT:
Wales Tourist Board
Brunel House, 2 Fitzalan Road,
Cardiff CF24 0UY
Tel: (029) 2049 9909 Fax: (029) 2048 5031
Email: info@tourism.wales.gov.uk

The Pictures:
1 Gwent, South Wales
2 Brecon Beacons

Places to Visit - see pages 202-207
Where to Stay - see pages 208-214

PLACES to visit

You will find hundreds of interesting places to visit during your stay, just some of which are listed in these pages. Contact any Tourist Information Centre in Wales for more ideas on days out.

The Pictures: 1 Rhossili Bay, North Wales, 2 East Wales, 3 Aberaeron

Aberaeron Sea Aquarium

2 Quay Parade, Aberaeron, Ceredigion SA46 0BT
Tel: (01545) 570142
Sea aquarium reflecting fish, fishing interests and conservation in Cardigan Bay. Voyages on a jet boat to discover the marine ecology of Cardigan Bay.

Aberystwyth Arts Centre

University of Wales, Aberystwyth, Ceredigion SY23 3DE
Tel: (01970) 622882 www.aber.ac.uk/artscentre
Main venue for the arts in mid and west Wales, the centre has undergone a recently completed £3.6 million redevelopment.

Afan Argoed Country Centre

Afan Forest Park, Cynonville, Port Talbot SA13 3HG
Tel: (01639) 850564
The centre has 10,000 acres (4,047 ha) to enjoy and explore including forest trails, picnic sites, barbecue, mountain bike trails, cycle hire and camping. Disabled access.

Alice in Wonderland Centre

The Rabbit Hole, 3-4 Trinity Square, Llandudno, Conwy LL30 2PY
Tel: (01492) 860082 www.wonderland.co.uk
Experience the timeless world of Lewis Carroll's Alice down a walk-through rabbit hole with life-size scenes and recorded narration.

Anglesey Sea Zoo

The Oyster Hatchery, Brynsiencyn, Isle of Anglesey LL61 6TQ
Tel: (01248) 430411 www.angleseyseazoo.co.uk
Anglesey Sea Zoo – with beautiful marine inhabitants of Wales and beyond.

Bala Lake Railway

Llanuwchllyn Station, Llanuwchllyn, Bala, Gwynedd LL23 7DD
Tel: (01678) 540666 www.bala-lake-railway.co.uk
Narrow-gauge steam train trips in the Snowdonia National Park along the shore of the largest natural lake in Wales.

Big Pit Mining Museum

Blaenavon, Torfaen NP4 9XP
Tel: (01495) 790311
Unique, underground tour of a real coal mine given by experienced miner guides.

Bodnant Garden

Tal-y-cafn, Colwyn Bay, Conwy LL28 5RE
Tel: (01492) 650460 www.oxalis.co.uk/bodnant
Interest and colour all year with rhododendrons in spring and laburnum arch late May. Terraces, ponds and giant trees.

Brecknock Museum

Captain's Walk, Brecon, Powys LD3 7DW
Tel: (01874) 624121
Regional museum and art gallery. Displays include prehistory to dark ages, country life, major town life gallery. Natural History including Edwardian Naturalists Study.

WALES

Brecon Cathedral
Cathedral Close, Brecon, Powys LD3 9DP
Tel: (01874) 623344
Cathedral, heritage centre, shop, restaurant.

Borth Animalarium
Ynys Fergi, Borth, Ceredigion SY24 5NA
Tel: (01970) 871224
A unique close encounter with the animal kingdom. Of interest to all age groups.

Castell Coch
Tongwynlais, Cardiff CF15 7JS
Tel: (029) 2081 0101
Rarely used and still perfectly preserved, this Victorian extravaganza must be seen to be believed. A beautiful fairytale castle in the woods.

Castell Henllys Iron Age Fort
Meline, Crymych, Pembrokeshire SA41 3UT
Tel: (01239) 891319
castellhenllys.pembrokeshirecoast.org.uk
A reconstructed Iron Age hill fort with four roundhouses, granary, animal pen, visitor centre, gift shop, picnic areas and pleasant walks.

Carew Castle & Tidal Mill
Carew, Tenby, Pembrokeshire SA70 8SL
Tel: (01646) 651782
www.pembrokeshirecoast.org.uk
A magnificent Norman castle which later became an Elizabethan residence. Links with Henry Tudor and the setting for the Great Tournament of 1507.

Caws Cenarth Welsh Cheese
Fferm Glyneithinog, Pontseli,
Boncath, Pembrokeshire SA37 0LH
Tel: (01239) 710432 www.cawscenarth.co.uk
The making of traditional handmade Caerphilly and other award-winning varieties of cheese.

Celtica
Y Plas, Aberystwyth Road, Machynlleth, Powys SY20 8ER
Tel: (01654) 702702 www.celtica.wales.com
Celtica is a unique heritage centre that interprets the history and culture of the Celts.

Centre for Alternative Technology
Pantperthog, Machynlleth, Powys SY20 9AZ
Tel: (01654) 702400 www.cat.org.uk
This attraction offers a stimulating day out for everyone. Interactive displays on solar and wind power, organic gardens, children's activities, tours, bookshop, restaurant.

Chirk Castle
Chirk, Wrexham LL41 5AF
Tel: (01691) 777701
A magnificent Marcher Fortress, completed in 1310, now owned by the National Trust.

Cilgwyn Candles
Trefelin, Cilgwyn, Newport, Pembrokeshire SA42 0QN
Tel: (01239) 820470
A candle-making workshop with a wide selection of candle-related goods and a mini museum of candle-making traditions and history.

Colby Woodland Garden
Narberth, Stepaside, Narberth, Pembrokeshire SA67 8PP
Tel: (01834) 811885
Tranquil and secluded valley, walled garden, tearooms, arts and crafts, gift shop, events.

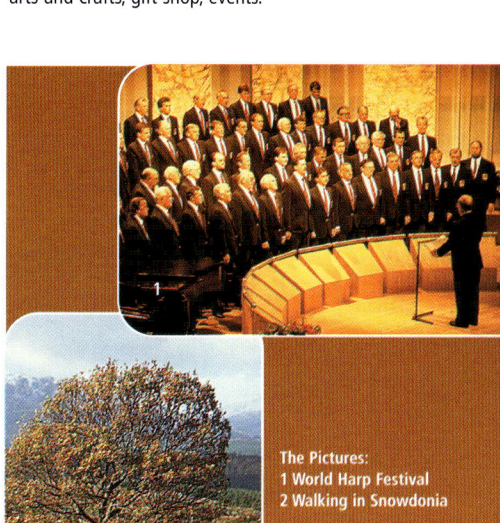

The Pictures:
1 World Harp Festival
2 Walking in Snowdonia

WALES

Conwy Butterfly Jungle
Bodlondeb Park, Bangor Road, Conwy LL32 8DU
Tel: (01492) 593149
Tropical butterflies in free flight around the visitor in exotic jungle surroundings, with birds and other insects to view and real rainforest surround-sound to hear.

Corris Craft Centre
Corris, Machynlleth, Powys SY20 9RF
Tel: (01654) 761584
Six individual craft workshops, where skilled craft workers may be viewed.

Craig-y-nos Country Park
Pen-y-cae, Swansea SA9 1GL
Tel: (01639) 730395 www.breconbeacons.org
Tall trees and rushing rivers fill this delightful country park.

Dan-yr-Ogof The National Showcaves Centre
Glyntawe, Abercraf, Swansea SA9 1GJ
Tel: (01639) 730284 www.showcaves.co.uk
Experience our three award-winning showcaves and dinosaur park. Shire Horse Centre and Barney Owl's covered play area.

Doctor Who Exhibition and Model Railway World
Lower Dee Exhibition Centre, Llangollen, Denbighshire LL20 8RX
Tel: (01978) 860584 www.dapol.co.uk
The BBC Doctor Who exhibition, as seen on telelvision, tells the story of the famous television programme. This is an award-winning site.

Egypt Centre
University of Wales, Singleton Park, Swansea SA2 8PP
Tel: (01792) 295960 www.swan.ac.uk/egypt
The largest collection of Egyptian antiquities in Wales.

Erdigg Hall
Wrexham LL13 0YT
Tel: (01978) 355314 www.nationaltrust.org.uk
A unique family home capturing the life of a bustling household during the early 1900s. The walled garden is one of the most important-surviving 18thC gardens in Britain.

Ffestiniog Railway
Harbour Station, Porthmadog, Gwynedd LL49 9NF
Tel: (01766) 512340 www.festrail.co.uk
The Ffestiniog Railway operates a narrow-gauge steam and diesel service from Porthmadog to Blaenau Ffestiniog, and also between Caernarfon and Waunfawr.

Folly Farm
Begelly, Kilgetty, Pembrokeshire SA68 0XA
Tel: (01834) 812731 www.folly-farm.co.uk
Vintage fun-fair, go-karts, bottle-feeding, hand-milking, birds of prey, adventure play, pet centre, restaurants, shops and more.

Glynn Vivian Art Gallery
Alexandra Road, Swansea SA1 5DZ
Tel: (01792) 655006 www.swansea.gov.uk
Large collection of 20thC paintings and Swansea pottery, plus full programme of temporary exhibitions.

Great Orme Copper Mines
Great Orme, Pyllau Road, Llandudno, Conwy LL30 2XG
Tel: (01492) 870447
Visitor centre, film and displays, underground trip and surface walkway.

Gwili Railway
Bronwydd Arms Station, Bronwydd Arms, Carmarthenshire SA33 6HT
Tel: (01267) 230666 www.gwili-railway.co.uk
Full-size steam railway winding up the beautiful Gwili Valley.

King Arthur's Labyrinth
Corris Craft Centre, Corris, Gwynedd SY20 9RF
Tel: (01654) 761584 www.corris-w.dircon.co.uk
An underground boat takes visitors into spectacular caverns where Welsh tales of King Arthur are told with tableaux and stunning sound and light effects.

Llanerch Vineyard
Hensol, Pontyclun, Rhondda Cyon Taff CF72 8JU
Tel: (01443) 225877
Largest vineyard in Wales producing the internationally acclaimed Cariad wines, set in the Vale of Glamorgan.

Llangloffan Cheese Centre
Llangloffan Farm, Castle Morris, Haverfordwest, Pembrokeshire SA62 5ET
Tel: (01348) 891241 www.welshcheese.co.uk
Visitors to the farm are able to watch cheese being made and are talked through the entire process.

WALES

Llechwedd Slate Caverns
Blaenau Ffestiniog, Gwynedd LL41 3NB
Tel: (01766) 830306 llechwedd.co.uk
Two underground rides, Victorian Village using reminted coins, shops and pub.

The Magical Grounds
Talhenbont Hall, Chwilog, Pwllheli, Gwynedd LL53 6SZ
Tel: (01766) 810247
16thC hall set in 70 acres (28 ha) of woodland and rivers with gardens, an adventure playground and craft shop. Other facilities are also available.

Museum of Childhood Memories
1 Castle Street, Beaumaris, Isle of Anglesey LL58 8AP
Tel: (01248) 712498
www.nwi.co.uk/museumofchildhood
Unlimited viewing of items that have brought pleasure to families over the past 200 years.

Museum of Welsh Life
St Fagans, Cardiff CF5 6XB
Tel: (029) 2057 3500 www.nmgw.ac.uk/mwl
See Wales in a day from Celtic times to the present at Europe's leading open-air museum.

Museum of the Welsh Woollen Industry
Drefach Felindre, Carmarthen, Carmarthenshire SA44 5UP
Tel: (01559) 370929 www.nmgw.ac.uk
One of the seven sites of the 'National Museums and Galleries of Wales'. It tells the story of wool from the middle ages to the present day.

New Quay Honey Farm
Cross Inn, Llandysul, Ceredigion SA44 6NN
Tel: (01545) 560822
Discover the fascinating world of bees in a live exhibition. Relax in the tearoomss, visit the meadery and explore the honey shop.

Oakwood Leisure
Canaston Bridge, Narberth, Pembrokeshire SA67 8DE
Tel: (01834) 891373
Wales' largest theme park set in 80 acres (32 ha) of beautiful countryside with over 40 rides and attractions.

Powis Castle and Garden
The Property Office, Welshpool, Powys SY21 8RF
Tel: (01938) 554338
World-famous terraced garden. Medieval castle with fine collection of paintings and furniture and collection of treasures from India.

Rheidol Hydro Electric Station
Rheidol Power Station, Cwm Rheidol, Aberystwyth, Ceredigion SY23 3NF
Tel: (01970) 880667
Visitor centre with light refreshments, interactive models and videos. Tours of the power station. Fish farm.

Rhiannon Jewellery
Canolfan Aur Cymru, Main Square,
Tregaron, Ceredigion SY25 6JL
Tel: (01974) 298415
Craft design centre and jewellery workshop specialising in the Welsh and Celtic heritage. Established since 1971.

Rhondda Heritage Park
Lewis Merthyr Colliery, Coed Cae Road, Trehafod, Pontypridd, Rhondda Cyon Taff CF37 7NP
Tel: (01443) 682036
An underground mining attraction based at the former Lewis Merthyr Colliery.

St David's Cathedral
The Close, St David's, Haverfordwest,
Pembrokeshire SA62 6RH
Tel: (01437) 720202
Built on the site where St David founded a monastic settlement in the 6thC, the outstanding features of this cathedral are the magnificent ceilings and sloping floor.

Segontium Roman Museum
Beddgelert Road, Caernarfon, Gwynedd LL55 2LN
Tel: (01286) 675625 www.nmgw.ac.uk
The Segontium Roman Museum exhibits many exciting finds from the important fort.

The Pictures:
1 Love Spoons
2 Pony Trekking, Cader Idris

WALES

Skomer Island Nature Reserve
c/o Dyfed Wildlife Trust, 7 Market Street, Haverfordwest, Pembrokeshire SA61 1NF
Tel: (01437) 765462
The most important seabird colony in Southern Britain.

Snowdon Mountain Railway
Llanberis, Caernarfon, Gwynedd LL55 4TY
Tel: (01286) 870223
www.snowdonrailway.force9.co.uk
Britain's only rack and pinion mountain railway, running from the lakeside village of Llanberis to the summit of Snowdon. Spectacular views of Snowdon when weather is clear.

Sygun Copper Mine
Beddgelert, Gwynedd LL55 4NE
www.ourworld.compuserve.com/homepages/SnowdoniaMine
Underground audiovisual tours of 18thC and 19thC copper mines in the heart of Snowdonia.

Techniquest
Stuart Street, Cardiff CF10 5BW
Tel: (029) 2047 5475 www.tquest.org.uk
Launch a hot-air ballon, create your own shadow in colour, or film your own animation! All this and more in the UK's leading hands-on science discovery centre.

Vale of Rheidol Railway
Park Avenue, Aberystwyth, Ceredigion SY23 1PG
Tel: (01970) 625819
Narrow-gauge steam railway running from Aberystwyth to Devil's Bridge, a distance of 11.5 miles (18km).

Welsh Royal Crystal
Unit 5, Brynberth Industrial Estate, Rhayader, Powys LD6 5EN
Tel: (01597) 811005
Handcrafted crystal cut by master craftsmen. Visit the on-site factory shop and pick up a bargain. Coffee shop selling home-made cakes.

The Pictures:
1 Carreg Samson
2 Royal National Eisteddfod

Find out more about WALES

Snowdonia

Further information about holidays and attractions in Wales is available from:

WALES TOURIST BOARD
Brunel House, 2 Fitzalan Road, Cardiff CF24 1UY
Tel: (029) 2049 9909
Fax: (029) 2048 5031
Email: info@tourism.wales.gov.uk

The following publications are available from the Wales Tourist Board:

The Complete Guides to South, Mid and North Wales - £5.60 each

Wales Tourist Map - £2.90

Travelmaster Guide to South Wales - £8.75

A Journey Through Wales - £4.99

Exploring Snowdonia, Anglesey and the Llyn Peninsula - £5.85

Ghosts and Legends of Wales - £5.95

'By Car' Guides - £2.40 each

Ordnance Survey Pathfinder Guides - £9.75 each

Castles Guide - £7.25

All prices include post and packing.

Free publications:

Activity Wales

Discovering Accessible Wales (holidays for disabled people, covering everything from accommodation to activities)

Wales Touring Camping and Caravanning

Beaches Guide

Wales Bus, Rail and Tourist Map and Guide

Wales Countryside Holidays

Cycling, Walking, Fishing and Golfing Wales (4 separate guides)

Freedom Holiday Parks Wales

Wales Farm Holidays

Riding and Trekking Wales

Getting to WALES

BY ROAD: Travelling to South and West Wales is easy on the M4 and the dual carriageway network. The new Second Severn Crossing gives two ways to enter Wales, but those wishing to visit Chepstow and the Wye Valley should use the original Severn Bridge and the M48 (originally part of the M4).

In North Wales the A55 'Expressway' has made travelling speedier, whilst mid Wales is accessible via the M54 which links with the M6, M5 and M1.

BY RAIL: Fast and frequent Great Western Intercity trains travel between London Paddington and Cardiff, departing hourly and half-hourly at peak times, and taking
only two hours. Newport, Bridgend, Port Talbot, Neath and Swansea are also accessible through this service, which encompasses most of West Wales. London Euston links to the North Wales coast via Virgin trains, who also run a service between the North East of England and South Wales. In addition, Wales and West Passenger Trains run Alphaline services from London Waterloo, Manchester and the North East, Brighton and the South, and Nottingham and the Heart of England.

For further rail enquiries, please telephone (08457) 484950.

WALES

Where to stay in Wales

Parks in Wales are listed in alphabetical order of place name, and then in alphabetical order of park.

Map references refer to the colour location maps at the front of this guide. The first number indicates the map to use; the letter and number which follow refer to the grid reference on the map.

At-a-glance symbols can be found inside the bak cover flap. Keep this open for easy reference.

BALA, Gwynedd Map ref 1B1 Tourist Information Centre Tel: (01678) 521102

★★★★
HOLIDAY, TOURING & CAMPING PARK

DRAGON AWARD

BH&HPA

PEN Y GARTH CARAVAN AND CAMPING PARK
Bala LL23 7ES
T: (01678) 520485
F: (01678) 520401
E: stay@penygarth.co.uk
I: www.penygarth.co.uk

30		£8.50–£10.50
5		£8.50–£10.50
28		£8.00–£10.00
5		£150.00–£350.00

63 touring pitches
49 units privately owned

Picturesque, peaceful setting in Snowdonia National Park, close to Bala lake and town - perfect for country lovers. Level pitches, clean, modern facilities, superb hire caravans. Special discounts for tourers and tents for long stays (5 nights or more) on production of this guide book.
OPEN March–October. Level, grassy, sheltered.
CC: Delta, Mastercard, Switch, Visa

By road, take B4391 Bala to Llangynog road. One mile from Bala fork right at sign to Rhosygwaliau. Site is 600 yds on the right. Signposted.

BANGOR, Gwynedd Map ref 1A1 Tourist Information Centre Tel: (01248) 352786

★
TOURING & CAMPING PARK

TREBORTH HALL FARM CARAVAN SITE
Treborth Hall Farm, Bangor LL57 2RX
T: (01248) 364104 & 364399
F: (01248) 364333
E: enquiries@treborthleisure.co.uk
I: www.treborthleisure.co.uk

OPEN Easter–September

	£8.50–£10.20
	£8.50–£10.20
	£4.00–£7.00
	£180.00–£250.00

Take the Bangor A487 with hospital sign turning off A55 Expressway. Bear left at roundabout then straight on at next roundabout. Approx 800 yds on left.

BARMOUTH, Gwynedd Map ref 1A2 Tourist Information Centre Tel: (01341) 280787

★★★★★
TOURING & CAMPING PARK

BARMOUTH TOURING CARAVAN & CAMPING PARK
Llanaber Road, Barmouth LL42 1YR
T: (01341) 280262
F: (01341) 280586
E: mynach@lineone.net

OPEN March–January
CC: Delta, Mastercard, Switch, Visa
Level, grassy, hard, sheltered.

60		£6.00–£14.00
60		£6.00–£13.00
180		£5.00–£13.00

180 touring pitches

Half a mile North of Barmouth, on the A496 Barmouth Harlech Coastal Road, seaward side. Signposted.

WALES

BARMOUTH continued

★★★★ HOLIDAY PARK
DRAGON AWARD
BH&HPA

PARC CAERELWAN
Talybont, Barmouth LL43 2AX
T: (01341) 247236
F: (01341) 247711
E: parc@porthmadog.co.uk
I: www.porthmadog.co.uk/parc/

OPEN All year round
CC: Delta, JCB, Mastercard, Switch, Visa
Level, grassy, hard, sheltered.

53 — £164.00–£360.00
80 units privately owned

On the A496 coast road 5 miles north of Barmouth. Signposted.

BENLLECH, Isle of Anglesey Map ref 1A1 Tourist Information Centre Tel: (01248) 713177

★★★★ HOLIDAY PARK

NANT NEWYDD CARAVAN PARK
Brynteg, Nr Benllech Bay LL78 7JJ
T: (01248) 852842 & 852266
F: (01248) 852281
I: www.nantnewydd.co.uk

Small, select, family-run country park, with beautiful gardens and waterfalls, 2.5 miles from Benllech Bay. Luxury fully-equipped caravans for hire. Dogs on leads welcomed.

OPEN March–October

£8.00–£15.00
£8.00–£15.00
£8.00–£15.00
£155.00–£330.00

From Britannia Bridge take A5025 Amloch Road to Benllech. Turn left at square, take B5108 to Llangefni for approx 2 miles. At crossroads, California Inn on left, turn left onto B5110. 1 mile on right

BRECON, Powys Map ref 1B3 Tourist Information Centre Tel: (01874) 622485

★★★★ HOLIDAY, TOURING & CAMPING PARK
BH&HPA

ANCHORAGE CARAVAN PARK
Bronllys, Brecon LD3 0LD
T: (01874) 711246
F: (01874) 711711

OPEN All year round
Level, sloping, grassy, sheltered.

60 — £9.00
10 — £9.00
40 — £9.00
110 touring pitches

Situated 8 miles North East of Brecon on A438 in the village of Bronllys. Signposted.

★★★★★ TOURING & CAMPING PARK
DAFFODIL AWARD
BH&HPA

BRYNICH CARAVAN PARK
Brecon LD3 7SH
T: (01874) 623325
F: (01874) 623325
E: Brynich@aol.com
I: www.brynich.co.uk

OPEN March–October
CC: Delta, JCB, Mastercard, Switch, Visa
Level, grassy, hard.

50 — £8.50–£10.00
20 — £8.50–£10.00
60 — £8.50–£10.00
130 touring pitches

The caravan park is situated on the A470, 200 yards from the junction with the A40, 2 km east of Brecon. Signposted.

CAERNARFON, Gwynedd Map ref 1A1 Tourist Information Centre Tel: (01286) 672232

★★★★ HOLIDAY PARK
Ad p210

BRYN GLOCH CARAVAN & CAMPING PARK
Betws Garmon, Caernarfon LL54 7YY
T: (01286) 650216
F: (01286) 650591
E: eurig@easynet.co.uk
I: www.bryngloch.co.uk

OPEN All year round
CC: Mastercard, Switch, Visa
Level, grassy.

80 — £10.00–£11.00
80 — £10.00–£10.00
80 — £10.00–£10.00
8 — £130.00–£315.00
160 touring pitches

Located on A4085 Caernarfon to Beddgelert road 5 miles from Caernarfon and 7 miles from Beddgelert. Signposted.

CREDIT CARD BOOKINGS If you book by telephone and are asked for your credit card number it is advisable to check the proprietor's policy should you cancel your reservation.

WALES

CAERNARFON continued

PLAS-Y-BRYN CARAVAN PARK
★★★ HOLIDAY PARK

Bontnewydd, Caernarfon LL54 7YE
T: (01286) 672811
F: (01286) 673336
E: philplasybryn@aol.com
I: www.plasybrynholidayscaernarfon.co.uk

This small park is situated 2 miles from the historic town of Caernarfon. Central for Snowdonia, Anglesey and the Llyn Peninsula. Beaches within 4 miles. Short breaks available throughout the year, with prices to suit all.

OPEN March–December. Sloping, grassy, sheltered.
CC: Delta, Mastercard, Visa

Two and a half miles south of Caernarfon.

10 — £95.00–£285.00

TYN YR ONNEN C/C PARK
★★★ TOURING & CAMPING PARK

Waunfawr, Caernarfon LL55 4AX
T: (01286) 650281
F: (01286) 650043
E: tyn.yr.onnen@gwynedd.net
E: www.gwynedd.net/caernafon/tyn-yr-onnen

Tyn-yr-Onnen is a paradise for walkers, on the edge of the Snowdonia range. High-quality facilities. Central, convenient to find from motorway. Camp fires. Donkeys, nature trail.

OPEN April–October. Level, sheltered.
CC: Barclaycard, Delta, Switch, Visa

London M6, M54, A5/A55 Expressway. Chester – Bangor – A487 Caernafon/ A4085. Farm off A4085 at Waunfawr, village chippy left. Signposted.

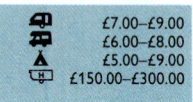

£7.00–£9.00
£6.00–£8.00
£5.00–£9.00
£150.00–£300.00

CARDIGAN, Ceredigion Map ref 1A2 Tourist Information Centre Tel: (01239) 711333

CENARTH FALLS HOLIDAY PARK
★★★★★ TOURING & HOLIDAY PARK

DRAGON AWARD
BH&HPA

Cenarth, Newcastle Emlyn SA38 9JS
T: (01239) 710345
F: (01239) 710344
E: enquiries@cenarth-holipark.co.uk
I: www.cenarth-holipark.co.uk

OPEN March–January
CC: Delta, JCB, Mastercard, Switch, Visa
Level, grassy, sheltered.

30 — £8.00–£15.00
30 — £8.00–£15.00
30 — £8.00–£15.00
6 — £150.00–£485.00
30 touring pitches
83 units privately owned

After 0.25 mile from Cenarth bridge turn right at park signs. Situated off A484 Cardigan-Carmarthen Road. Signposted.

STAR RATINGS Were correct at the time of going to press but are subject to change. Please check at the time of booking.

Bryn Gloch Camping & Caravan Park

Award Winning Family-run Park within Snowdonia National Park

Nestled between Snowdonia mountain ranges and on the banks of the river Gwyrfai with breathtaking views.

- Clean, peaceful site, electric hook-ups, luxury toilet/showers, shop & off-licence, games room, spacious play area, fishing, mini golf.
- Modern Caravans
- Self-Catering Accommodation
- Tent Pitches
- Touring Pitches
- OPEN ALL YEAR

For Brochure call 01286 650216
Email: eurig@easynet.co.uk
Website: www.bryngloch.co.uk

WALES

CONWY, Conwy Map ref 1B1 Tourist Information Centre Tel: (01492) 592248

★★★ TOURING PARK

CONWY TOURING PARK
Trefriw Road, Conwy LL32 8UX
T: (01492) 592856
F: (01492) 580024
I: www.conwytouringpark.com

OPEN Easter–September

£4.85–£11.08
£4.85–£11.08
£4.85–£11.08

Turn left at mini roundabout in front of Conwy Castle. Follow B5106 for 1.5 miles. Look for sign on left.

FISHGUARD, Pembrokeshire Map ref 1A2 Tourist Information Centre Tel: (01348) 873484

★★★★ HOLIDAY, TOURING & CAMPING PARK

DRAGON AWARD

BH&HPA

FISHGUARD BAY CARAVAN & CAMPING PARK
Garn Gelli, Fishguard SA65 9ET
T: (01348) 811415
F: (01348) 811425
E: inquiries@fishguardbay.com
I: www.fishguardbay.com

OPEN January, March–December
CC: Delta, Diners, Mastercard, Switch, Visa
Sloping, grassy.

20 £9.50–£11.50
£9.50–£11.50
30 £8.50–£10.50
11 £150.00–£378.00
50 touring pitches
39 units privately owned

Take A487 Cardigan Road from Fishguard, 3 miles outside Fishguard, turning on left. Signposted.

★★★★ TOURING PARK

BH&HPA

GWAUN VALE TOURING PARK
Llanychaer, Fishguard SA65 9TA
T: (01348) 874698
E: margaret.harries@softhome.net

OPEN March–October
Level, grassy, hard, sheltered.

£7.00–£8.00
£7.00–£8.00
£7.00–£8.00
30 touring pitches

From Fishguard, take B4313 for 1.5 miles. The site is on the right. Signposted.

KEESTON, Pembrokeshire Map ref 1A3 Tourist Information Centre Tel: (01437) 763110

★★★★ HOLIDAY PARK

DRAGON AWARD

BH&HPA

Ad on this page

SCAMFORD CARAVAN PARK
Keeston, Haverfordwest SA62 6HN
T: (01437) 710304
F: (01437) 710304
E: scamford-caravan-holidays@talk21.com
I: www.scamford-caravan-holidays.co.uk

OPEN March–October
CC: Delta, Mastercard, Switch, Visa
Level, grassy.

5 £5.50–£7.50
£5.50–£7.50
25 £112.00–£358.00
5 touring pitches

A487 Haverfordwest to St. Davids, after 4 miles Haverfordwest, turn right for Keeston, and also for Scamford Caravan Park. Signposted.

LLANELLI, Carmarthenshire Map ref 1A3 Tourist Information Centre Tel: (01554) 772020

★★★★★ TOURING PARK

Ad on back cover

PEMBREY COUNTRY PARK CARAVAN CLUB SITE
Llanelli SA16 0EJ
T: (01554) 834369

OPEN April–September
CC: Mastercard, Visa
Level, grassy, hard, sheltered.

115 £8.00–£17.00
£8.00–£17.00
£4.00
115 touring pitches

From M4, leave at Junction 48 onto A4138. After 4 miles turn right onto A484 and continue towards Carmarthen. Within 7 miles in Pembrey Village turn right before park gates. Signposted.

SYMBOLS The symbols in each entry give information about services and facilities. A key to these symbols appears at the back of this guide.

SCAMFORD Caravan Park

The peaceful country park

Colour brochure from resident owners:
Richard and Christine White,
Scamford Caravan Park, Keeston, Haverfordwest, Pembrokeshire SA62 6HN
Tel/Fax: Camrose (01437) 710304
e-mail: scamfordcaravanpark@talk21.com
www.scamford-caravan-holidays.co.uk

WALES

LLANGADOG, Carmarthenshire Map ref 1B3 Tourist Information Centre Tel: (01550) 720693

★★★★
TOURING &
CAMPING PARK

BH&HPA

ABERMARLAIS CARAVAN PARK
Llangadog SA19 9NG
T: (01550) 777868 & 777797

60		£7.50–£7.50
60		£7.50–£7.50
28		£7.00–£7.50

88 touring pitches

A tranquil site in a beautiful woodland valley at the western end of the Brecon National Park, ideal for nature lovers and bird-watchers.
OPEN March–October. Level, sloping, grassy, hard, sheltered.
CC: Amex, Delta, Mastercard, Switch, Visa

Situated on A40, 6 miles west of Llandovery or 6 miles east of Llandeilo. Signposted.

LLANGORSE, Powys Map ref 1B3 Tourist Information Centre Tel: (01874) 622485

★★★★
HOLIDAY PARK

BH&HPA

LAKESIDE CARAVAN PARK
Llangorse Lake, Llangorse, Brecon LD3 7TR
T: (01874) 658226
F: (01874) 658330
E: holidays@lakeside.zx3.net
I: www.lakeside-holidays.net

OPEN March–November
CC: Amex, Delta, Mastercard, Switch, Visa
Level, grassy, sheltered.

50		£7.00–£9.00
50		£7.00–£9.00
50		£7.00–£9.00
10		£140.00–£315.00

50 touring pitches
72 units privately owned

From Abergavenny A40 to Bwlch, turn right onto B4560 to Llangorse. Head for the Lake.

MONMOUTH, Monmouthshire Map ref 1B3 Tourist Information Centre Tel: (01600) 713899

★★★★
TOURING &
CAMPING PARK

MONMOUTH CARAVAN PARK
Rockfield Road, Monmouth NP25 5BA
T: (01600) 714745
F: (01600) 716690
E: mail@monmouthcaravanpark.co.uk
I: www.monmouthcaravanpark.co.uk

OPEN March–October
CC: Delta, Mastercard, Switch, Visa
Level, grassy, hard, sheltered.

40		£8.50–£10.00
5		£8.50–£10.00
5		£5.00–£10.00

40 touring pitches

B4233 Rockfield road out of Monmouth opposite fire station. Signposted.

MORFA BYCHAN, Gwynedd Map ref 1A1 Tourist Information Centre Tel: (01766) 512981

★★★★
HOLIDAY PARK

DRAGON AWARD

Ad p12

GREENACRES HOLIDAY PARK
Blackrock Sands, Morfa Bychan, Black Rock, Porthmadog LL49 9YB
T: (01766) 512781
F: (01766) 512084
E: enquiries@british-holidays.co.uk
I: www.british-holidays.co.uk

OPEN March–October
CC: Delta, Mastercard, Solo, Switch, Visa
Level, grassy.

71		£14.75–£33.00
		£14.00–£31.00
		£14.00–£31.00
201		£99.00–£600.00

50 touring pitches
873 units privately owned

Into Porthmadog High Street, take road to Black Rock sands, follow into village and Greenacres is situated on left at end of village. Signposted.

OXWICH, Swansea Map ref 1A3 Tourist Information Centre Tel: (01792) 361302

★★★
CAMPING PARK

OXWICH CAMPING PARK
Oxwich, Swansea SA3 1LS
T: (01792) 390777

OPEN April–September
Level, sloping, grassy, hard, sheltered.

| 90 | | £10.00–£10.00 |
| 90 | | £10.00–£10.00 |

180 touring pitches

Take A4118 from Swansea. Turn left at Oxwich sighposted. First right, campsite on right.

NB **IMPORTANT NOTE** Information on accommodation listed in this guide has been supplied by the proprietors. As changes may occur you are advised to check details at the time of booking.

212

WALES

PANDY, Monmouthshire Map ref 1B3 Tourist Information Centre Tel: (01873) 857588

★★★★
TOURING PARK

Ad on back cover

PANDY CARAVAN CLUB SITE
Pandy, Abergavenny NP7 8DR
T: (01873) 890370

OPEN March–October
CC: Mastercard, Visa
Level, grassy, hard.

60 — £6.50–£17.00
£6.50–£17.00

From South do not go into Abergavenny, continue onto A465 Hereford in 6.25 metres turn left by Pandy Inn, into Minor Road, site on left after passing under railway bridge. Signposted.

PEMBROKE, Pembrokeshire Map ref 1A3 Tourist Information Centre Tel: (01646) 622388

★★★★★
**TOURING &
CAMPING PARK**

DAFFODIL AWARD

Ad on back cover

FRESHWATER EAST CARAVAN CLUB SITE
Freshwater East, Pembroke SA71 5LN
T: (01646) 672341

OPEN April–October
CC: Mastercard, Visa
Level, grassy, hard.

130 — £6.50–£17.00
£6.50–£17.00
130 touring pitches

Take M4 to Carmarthen, then follow signs to Pembroke. Go under railway bridge, take left onto A4139, in Lamphey continue onto B4584, after 1.75 miles turn right, sign after 0.25 mile at foot of hill. Signposted.

PENDINE, Carmarthenshire Map ref 1A3 Tourist Information Centre Tel: (01267) 231557

★★★★
HOLIDAY PARK

BH&HPA

Ad p12

PENDINE SANDS HOLIDAY PARK
Pendine, Nr Carmarthen SA33 4NZ
T: (01994) 453398
F: (01994) 453654
E: enquiries@british-holidays.co.uk
E: www.british-holidays.co.uk

OPEN March–October
CC: Delta, Mastercard, Solo, Switch, Visa

73 — £99.00–£600.00
425 units privately owned

Take the A40 trunk road from Carmarthen to St. Clears. Pendine/Pentywyn is signposted along the A4066, 8 miles from the A40 junction. Pass through Laugharne and the park reception is 5 miles further on the right hand side.

PENMAENMAWR, Conwy Map ref 1B1 Tourist Information Centre Tel: (01492) 592248

★
**HOLIDAY, TOURING
& CAMPING PARK**

WOODLANDS CAMPING PARK
Pendyffren Hall, Penmaenmawr LL34 6UF
T: (01492) 623219

OPEN March–October
Level, grassy, stony, sheltered.

25 — £12.00–£15.00
£12.00–£15.00
100 — £8.00–£14.00
100 touring pitches

Off A55 between Conwy and Penmaemawr, signposted Dwygyfylchi.

ST DAVIDS, Pembrokeshire Map ref 1A3 Tourist Information Centre Tel: (01437) 720392

★★★★
**HOLIDAY, TOURING
& CAMPING PARK**

BH&HPA

CAERFAI BAY CARAVAN PARK
St Davids, Haverfordwest SA62 6QT
T: (01437) 720274
F: (01437) 721577
E: info@caerfaibay.co.uk
I: www.caerfaibay.co.uk

OPEN April–November

£7.50–£12.00
£5.50–£7.00
£5.50–£7.00
£140.00–£330.00

Turn off A487 (Haverfordwest to St Davids) in St Davids at Visitor Centre. Caerfai Park is at road end, 1 mile, on the right. Signposted.

★★★★
TOURING PARK

Ad on back cover

LLEITHYR MEADOW CARAVAN CLUB SITE
Whitesands, St Davids, Haverfordwest
SA62 6PR
T: (01437) 720401

OPEN April–September
CC: Mastercard, Visa
Level, grassy, sheltered.

120 — £6.50–£17.00
£6.50–£17.00
120 touring pitches

Take M4 to Carmarthen, then A40 to Haverfordwest, then A487 towards St Davids. Before entering St Davids turn right onto B4583, crossroads. Turn sharp right opposite entrance to St Davids golf club. Signposted.

213

WALES

SWANSEA, Swansea Map ref 1B3 Tourist Information Centre Tel: (01792) 468321

★★★★
**TOURING &
CAMPING PARK**

Ad on back cover

GOWERTON CARAVAN CLUB SITE
Pont-Y-Cob Road, Swansea SA4 3QP
T: (01792) 873050

OPEN April–October
CC: Mastercard, Visa
Level, grassy.

150
150 touring pitches

£6.50–£14.50
£6.50–£9.50

Take B4296 towards Gower and then Gowerton. In 0.5 mile, 100 yds after passing under railway bridge (height restriction of 11ft), turn right onto B4295. Turn after 0.5 mile. Signposted Pont-y-Cob Road.

TENBY, Pembrokeshire Map ref 1A3 Tourist Information Centre Tel: (01834) 842402

★★★
HOLIDAY PARK

BH&HPA

Ad p12

KILN PARK HOLIDAY CENTRE
Marsh Road, Tenby SA70 7RB
T: (01834) 844121
F: (01834) 845387
E: enquiries@british-holidays.co.uk
E: www.british-holidays.co.uk

OPEN March–October
CC: Delta, Mastercard, Switch, Visa
Level, grassy.

198
198
104
119
302 touring pitches
587 units privately owned

£14.70–£35.70
£14.00–£34.00
£14.00–£34.00
£135.00–£700.00

On the A477/78 follow signs to Tenby. At mini roundabout follow signs for Penally. 1 mile on left hand side. Signposted.

TREARDDUR BAY, Isle of Anglesey Map ref 1A1 Tourist Information Centre Tel: (01248) 7130177

★
**TOURING &
CAMPING PARK**

TYN RHOS CAMPING SITE
Ravenspoint Road, Trearddur Bay,
Holyhead LL65 2BQ
T: (01407) 860369

OPEN March–October
Level, sloping, grassy, sheltered.

20
14
180
180 touring pitches

£6.50–£8.50
£5.50–£7.50
£5.00–£7.00

A55 across Anglesey joining A5 at Caegeliog, left at Valley onto B4545, for Trearddur Bay. Left onto Ravenspoint Road (after Beach Hotel). 0.75 mile to shared entrance, take left hand branch. Signposted.

WREXHAM Map ref 1B1 Tourist Information Centre Tel: (01978) 292015

★★★★
**TOURING &
CAMPING PARK**

BH&HPA

THE PLASSEY LEISURE PARK
Eyton, Wrexham LL13 0SP
T: (01978) 780277
F: (01978) 780019
E: enquiries@theplassey.co.uk
I: www.theplassey.co.uk

OPEN January–November
CC: Delta, Diners, Switch, Visa
Level, grassy, hard, sheltered.

100
10
10
120 touring pitches

£12.00–£14.50
£12.00–£14.50
£12.00–£14.50

Take Bangor-on-Dee exit off the A483, and 2.5 miles along B5426 to the Plassey. Signposted.

COUNTRY CODE Always follow the Country Code ❀ Enjoy the countryside and respect its life and work ❀ Guard against all risk of fire ❀ Fasten all gates ❀ Keep your dogs under close control ❀ Keep to public paths across farmland ❀ Use gates and stiles to cross fences, hedges and walls ❀ Leave livestock, crops and machinery alone ❀ Take your litter home ❀ Help to keep all water clean ❀ Protect wildlife, plants and trees ❀ Take special care on country roads ❀ Make no unnecessary noise

WALES

A brief guide to the main Towns and Villages offering accommodation in Wales

B BALA, GWYNEDD - Small market town on Bala Lake, the largest natural sheet of water in Wales. Mountain scenery, fishing, walking and boating.

• **BANGOR, GWYNEDD** - Cathedral and university town at the mouth of the Menai Strait, ideal centre for touring North Wales. To the south west the Menai Bridge links the Isle of Anglesey to the mainland.

• **BARMOUTH, GWYNEDD** - Popular seaside resort at the mouth of the beautiful Mawddach estuary, on the edge of the Snowdonia National Park.

• **BENLLECH, ISLE OF ANGLESEY** - Small resort on the north east coast of Anglesey.

• **BRECON, POWYS** - Market town situated at the junction of the rivers Usk and Honddu. Excellent base for exploring the Brecon Beacons National Park.

C CAERNARFON, GWYNEDD - Ancient county town famous for its magnificent and well preserved medieval castle, the birthplace of Edward I and scene of the investiture of the Prince of Wales in 1969.

• **CONWY** - Fascinating medieval fortress town at the mouth of the River Conwy, enclosed by massive walls and dominated by striking 13C castle. Sheltered harbour and small fishing fleet.

F FISHGUARD, PEMBROKESHIRE - Picturesque little town perched high above its harbour. Fine cliff scenery.

L LLANELLI, CARMARTHENSHIRE - Industrial centre on the Burry inlet, with beautiful surrounding countryside. Kidwelly Castle and Wildlife and Wetlands Centre nearby.

M MONMOUTH, MONMOUTHSHIRE - Historic market town, birthplace of Henry V, with unique 13th C gateway built across the Monnow.

P PEMBROKE, PEMBROKESHIRE - Historic county town, dominated by its fine old castle, birthplace of Henry VII. Remains of Monkton Priory.

• **PENMAENMAWR, CONWY** - Holiday resort at the foot of Penmaenmawr Mountain, with excellent sands and bathing, sailing and golf.

S ST DAVIDS, PEMBROKESHIRE - A place of pilgrimage for over eight centuries, situated on the rugged western peninsula within easy reach of some of Britain's finest cliffs and bays. Interesting cathedral.

• **SWANSEA** - Large seaport and modern industrial city with a university and extensive parks and gardens. Swansea is also a seaside resort and a good centre for exploring the Gower Peninsula.

T TENBY, PEMBROKESHIRE - Town with colourful harbour, superb sands, cliff-top hotels and ancient walls and gateways. It stands on a rocky promontory on Carmarthen Bay and is an ideal centre for exploring the coast.

• **TREARDDUR BAY, ISLE OF ANGLESEY** - Charming little resort south of Holyhead with rocky sand-fringed bay, bathing, fishing and golf.

W WREXHAM - Busy market town with medieval church.

CREDIT CARD BOOKINGS If you book by telephone and are asked for your credit card number it is advisable to check the proprietor's policy should you cancel your reservation.

215

Ratings you can trust

When you're looking for a place to stay, you need a rating system you can trust. The British Graded Holiday Parks Scheme, operated jointly by the national tourist boards for England, Scotland and Wales, gives you a clear guide of what to expect.

Based on the internationally recognised rating of One to Five Stars, the system puts great emphasis on quality and reflects customer expectations.

Parks are visited annually by trained, impartial assessors who award a rating based on cleanliness, environment and the quality of services and facilities provided.

STAR QUALITY

★★★★★   Exceptional Quality
★★★★   Excellent Quality
★★★   Very Good Quality
★★   Good Quality
★   Acceptable Quality

Information

Useful Addresses	218
Standards for Caravan and Camping Parks	219
Events for 2002 in England, Scotland and Wales	222
Tourist Information in Britain	232
National Accessible Scheme	233
BTA Overseas Offices	234
David Bellamy Conservation Awards	236
Travel Information - by Car and Train	238
Excellence in England Awards	240
Competition Rules	240
Index to Parks	241
Index to Towns	245
Index to Advertisers	247
Calendar 2002 and 2003	248

INFORMATION

Useful Addresses
ADRESSES UTILES
NÜTZLICHE ANSCHRIFTEN
NUTTIGE ADRESSEN
INDIRIZZI UTILI

AUTOMOBILE ASSOCIATION

Routes can be prepared, avoiding unsuitable routes for caravans and steep gradients if specified. Please write to: AA Routes, Lambert House, Stockport Road, Cheadle, Staffordshire SK8 2DY.
Tel: 08705 500 600 (members only);
Internet: www.theaa.co.uk

BRITISH HOLIDAY & HOME PARKS ASSOCIATION LTD

Chichester House, 6 Pullman Court,
Great Western Road, Gloucester GL1 3ND
Enquiries and brochure requests (01452) 526911
Fax: (01452) 508508

The BH&HPA is recognised as the official representative body of the Parks Industry in the UK.

Member parks are located all over Britain. The parks are situated within some of the most spectacular locations that Britain can offer, from the breathtaking scenery of the Scottish Highlands, the beautiful coastal landscape of Cornwall, to the splendid mountains and lakes of North Wales and Northern Ireland. Parks can also be found nearby historic cities such as Oxford and Cambridge, and Shakespeare's city of Stratford-upon-Avon. Castles and historic sites are within reach of many BH&HPA parks.

Member parks offer pitches for touring caravans, tent and motor homes, caravan holiday homes and chalets to let, and holiday home ownership. The type of park ranges from the large multi-facility park to the smaller park run by a farm. So there is something to suit all needs.

BH&HPA jointly produces a set of full colour guides to holiday parks covering Scotland, Wales, Western England, Southern England, Northern England and Eastern England. These are available free-of-charge by calling (01452) 526911.

THE CAMPING AND CARAVANNING CLUB

Greenfields House, Westwood Way,
Coventry, West Midlands CV4 8JH
Tel: (02476) 856798
Internet: www.campingandcaravanningclub.co.uk

Operates a national network of over 90 camping and caravanning parks throughout Britain, most of which are open to non-members.

The club publishes a detailed guide to the above sites, a Big Sites book listing over 4000 parks in Britain and Ireland including a map with all these sites plotted on, useful for route planning. These are all available free to members.

Foreign visitors can obtain the above guides and map for £10.00 plus postage and by quoting their Camping Card International (CCI) number. Foreign visitors without a CCI may obtain the guide to the Club parks open to them through temporary membership at £10.00 plus postage for three months membership.

THE CARAVAN CLUB

East Grinstead House, East Grinstead,
West Sussex RH19 1UA
Tel: (01342) 326944 Fax: (01342) 410258
Internet: www.caravanclub.co.uk

The Caravan Club offers over 200 sites in the United Kingdom and Ireland. These include city locations such as London, Edinburgh, York and Chester, plus sites near leading heritage attractions such as Longleat, Sandringham, Chatsworth and Blenheim Palace. A further 20 are in National Parks. Over 90% of pitches have an electric hook-up point and most sites offer emptying points for motor caravanners. Foreign visitors are welcomed and holders of International Camping Cards (CCI's) qualify for pitch discounts on selected sites. Non member caravanners pay a supplement of £5 per pitch per night, refunded against the membership fee (£32.50 in 2001) which adds access to a further 3000 small 5-van sites. A 700-page Sites Directory and UK Location Map gives clear directions whilst towing. Tent campers are welcome on 70 sites.

FORESTRY COMMISSION

231 Corstorphine Road, Edinburgh EH12 7AT.
Tel: (0131) 334 0303 Fax: (0131) 334 3047
Internet: www.forestry.gsi.gov.uk

Forest Holidays, run by Forest Enterprise, an executive agency of the Forestry Commission, have almost 30 camping and caravan sites in the scenic forest locations throughout the UK. Choose from the Scottish Highlands, the New Forest, Snowdonia National Park, the Forest of Dean, or the banks of Loch Lomond. Some sites are open all year.

Advance bookings accepted for many sites. Dogs welcome on most sites. For a unique forest experience, call the Forestry Commission for a brochure on Tel: (0131) 334 0066.

THE MOTOR CARAVANNERS' CLUB LTD

22 Evelyn Close, Twickenham TW2 7BN
Tel: (020) 8893 3883 Fax: (020) 8893 8324
Email: info@motorcaravanners.org.uk
Internet: www.motorcaravanners.org.uk

The Motor Caravanners' Club is authorised to issue the Camping Card International (CCI). It also produces a monthly magazine, 'Motor Caravanner' for all members.

INFORMATION

Standards for Caravan and Camping Parks

NORMES REQUISES POUR LES TERRAINS DE CAMPING ET POUR CARAVANES
REGELN FÜR CAMPING- UND CARAVANPLÄTZE
AAN CARAVAN EN CAMPINGPARKEN GESTELDE EISEN
NORME IMPOSTE AI CAMPEGGI PER TENDE E ROULOTTES

These standards should be read in conjunction, where applicable, with the Caravan Sites and Control of Development Act 1960, and, where applicable, the Public Health Act 1936.

A THE PARK

1. The park must have planning permission and site licence readily available, if applicable.
2. Facilities must be clean and in wholesome condition.
3. The park must be well managed and maintained and kept in a clean and presentable manner and attention paid to the road-side sign and entrance.
4. The park must have reception arrangements at appropriate times where advice and assistance can be obtained if necessary.
5. The park operator must be capable of arranging or carrying out repairs to caravans and equipment.
6. Supplies of gas and replacement bottles together with essential (where applicable) spares must be available at all reasonable times.
7. Where provided, all toilet blocks and washing facilities must be lit internally and externally during the hours of darkness, whilst the park is open.
8. All shower blocks must have internal lighting.
9. Where washing and/or shower facilities are provided, an adequate supply of hot and cold water must be available at all reasonable times.
10. A proprietary first-aid kit must be readily available. Emergency notices must be prominently displayed giving details and location of park, contact, telephone, doctor, fire service, local hospital and other essential services.
11. Parks open in the shoulder season (Oct-Mar) must provide adequate heating in at least one toilet, washing and shower facility (both male and female).
12. The park owner must have fire fighting equipment and notices which conform with the conditions of the site licence.
13. All electricity installations on the park both internally and externally must have the appropriate safety certification.
14. Parks providing pitches for touring units must provide facilities for chemical disposal unless specifically prohibited by local authorities.
15. Lighting should be appropriate to the size and type of park.
16. Adequate provision to be made for refuse disposal.
17. The intended use of facilities must be indicated by signage.

NB: Parks providing NO toilet facilities make this clear in all promotional literature and advertising.

B VISITOR INFORMATION

The booking form must be accompanied by details of the park, stating clearly:

1. A description of the park and its amenities, e.g:
   a) Whether cars park by caravans or in a car park.
   b) Whether or not pets are allowed.
   c) Details of shower and bath facilities.
   d) Whether a grocery shop is on site or the distance to nearest shop.
   e) Licensed bar.
   f) Laundry facilities.
   g) Dancing, entertainments.
   h) Television room.
   i) Sports facilities.
   j) Public transport to and from park.
   k) Distance from sea and accessibility to beach (coastal parks only).
2. The prices for the pitch for the period booked and details of any further charges, e.g. electricity, gas, showers, awnings as well as any optional charges, e.g. holiday insurance.
   Note: If Value Added Tax (VAT) is not included in the total charge, this must be clearly stated.
3. Any special conditions for payment of deposits or balance.
4. Wherever possible, a map showing the location of the park and its proximity to main centres and attractions.
5. If bookings in advance are necessary during the summer months.

INFORMATION

C CARAVAN HOLIDAY HOMES AND CHALETS

1. All caravans must be of proprietary make.
2. All caravans/chalets must be in good state of internal and external repair and decoration with no internal dampness.
3. The caravans/chalets must not be occupied by more than the number of persons for which they are designed by the manufacturer ie four persons in a four-berth.
4. It is the park operator's responsibility to ensure that all caravans offered for hire on the park have insurance cover for public liability as letting caravans and comply with the Consumer Protection Act.
5. Equipment must be provided as listed opposite. An inventory of this equipment must be available for each caravan/chalet.
6. All caravans/chalets must have adequate storage space for luggage and food for the maximum number of occupants.
7. All doors, windows, skylights and all ventilation in the caravan/chalet must function correctly. All windows must be properly fitted with opaque curtains or blinds.
8. All caravans/chalets must have adequate internal lighting.
9. All caravans/chalets must be thoroughly cleaned and checked before every letting and equipment maintained and replaced as necessary.
10. Where linen is provided it must be changed on each change of occupier and as appropriate during lets of two weeks or more. All mattresses must be in sound condition.
11. The sink and its waste pipe must be in sound condition with a draining board. A fixed impervious work top for food preparation must be provided.
12. All caravans/chalets must have a fridge and a cooker with at least two boiling rings. The cooker must be in a sound and clean condition and functioning properly.
13. All caravans/chalets must have adequate heating.
14. All caravans must have safe steps or equivalent, to each external door.
15. All caravans must have a supply of hot and cold water.
16. All caravan holiday homes must be fully serviced with water, drainage, mains WC, shower and/or bath.

D INVENTORY OF EQUIPMENT FOR CARAVAN HOLIDAY-HOMES AND CHALETS

The accommodation should contain the following:

- One per caravan/chalet

  Kettle
  Teapot
  Saucepan & lid (large, medium & small)
  Frying pan
  Colander
  Oven roasting tray
  Casserole dish
  Carving knife and fork
  Bread knife
  Bread/cake container
  Bread/chopping board
  Fish slice
  Small vegetable knife
  Tin opener
  Corkscrew/bottle opener
  Potato peeler
  Large fruit dish
  Butter dish
  Sugar bowl
  Tray
  Milk jug
  Mixing bowl or basin
  Bread/cake plate
  Condiment set (two-piece)
  Washing-up bowl
  Dustpan and brush
  Broom
  Floor cloth
  Pot scourer/dish mop
  Bucket
  Mirror
  Doormat
  Covered kitchen refuse container
  Fire extinguisher/blanket
  Smoke detector

- Two per caravan/chalet

  Table spoons
  Dusters
  Ash trays

- Per bed

  Three blankets or one continental quilt and cover (for winter lettings, or letting very early or late in the season the scale of bedding to be increased and adequate heating provided)
  one pillow per person

- One per person

  Knife (table & dessert)
  Fork (table & dessert)
  Spoon (dessert & tea)
  Plate (large & small)
  Tea cup and saucer
  Cereal/soup plate
  Tumbler
  Egg cup

- Four per person

  Coat-hangers

INFORMATION

E INFORMATION FOR HIRERS

The booking form should be accompanied by details of the park and caravan(s)/chalet(s) stating clearly:

1. The accommodation size (length and width) of the caravan and the number of berths. This shall not exceed the maximum number of berths as defined by the manufacturer.
2. Whether caravans are connected to:
   Mains water
   Mains drainage
   Mains sewerage
   Electricity (stating voltage)
   Piped gas (stating LPG or Natural)
3. Type of lighting: Electricity or Gas
4. Type of cooking: Electricity or Gas
5. A full description of park and its amenities.
6. Wherever possible a map showing the location of the park and its proximity to main centres and attractions.
7. The charges for the accommodation/pitch for the period booked and details of any further additional charges, for example, electricity, gas, showers etc, as well as any optional charges, eg holiday insurance.
   Note: If VAT is payable it must be included in the quoted price.

F THE CARAVAN PARKS STANDARD FOR GUESTS WITH DISABILITIES

The National Accessible Scheme is operated by the English Tourism Council and the national and regional tourist boards throughout Britain. They assess places to stay that provide accommodation for wheelchair users or others who may have difficulty walking.

The tourist organisations recognise three categories of accessibility:

CATEGORY 1 Accessible to a wheelchair user travelling independently.

CATEGORY 2 Accessible to a wheelchair user travelling with assistance.

CATEGORY 3 Accessible to a wheelchair user able to walk a few paces and up a maximum of 3 steps.

For holiday home parks, the rating will depend upon access to reception, route to the caravan, food shop and telephone (where provided), and the holiday home itself.

For touring/camping parks, it will depend upon access to reception, routes to pitches, food shop and telephone (where provided), toilet and washing facilities.

Please contact individual park operators for more detailed information you may require.

A list of parks offering accessible accommodation featured in this guide can be found on page 232.

The National Accessible Scheme is currently in the process of being updated. Consultation has been conducted throughout 2001 with introduction during 2002.

G CODE OF CONDUCT

In addition to fulfilling its statutory obligations, the park management undertakes to observe the following Code of Conduct:

1. To ensure high standards of courtesy, cleanliness, catering and service appropriate to the type of site.
2. To describe fairly to all visitors and prospective visitors, the amenities, facilities and service provided by the park, whether by advertisement, brochure, word of mouth, or any other means, and to allow visitors to see pitches, if requested, before booking.
3. To make clear to visitors exactly what is included in all prices quoted for pitches, meals and refreshments, including service charges, taxes and other surcharges. Details of cancellation procedures and charges for additional services or facilities available should also be made clear.
4. To adhere to, and not to exceed, prices current at the time of occupation for accommodation or other services.
5. To advise visitors at the time of booking of the charges that might be incurred if the booking is subsequently cancelled.
6. To advise visitors at the time of booking and subsequent to any change, if the pitch offered is on another park and the location of the park and any difference in the comfort and amenities from the pitch previously booked.
7. To give each visitor, on request, details of payment due and receipt, if required.
8. To deal promptly and courteously with all enquiries, requests, reservations, correspondence and complaints from visitors.
9. To present grading awards and/or accessible awards and/or any other national tourist board awards un-ambiguously.
10. To allow an English Tourism Council or national tourist board representative reasonable access to the establishment, on request, to confirm that the Code of Conduct is being observed.
11. The operator must also comply with the provisions of the caravan industry Codes of Practice.

A selection of events for 2002 in England

MANIFESTATIONS EN ANGLETERRE EN 2002
VERANSTALTUNGEN IN ENGLAND 2002
EVENEMENTEN IN ENGELAND IN 2002
CALENDARIO DEGLI AVVENIMENTI IN INGHILTERRA NEL 2002

This is a selection of the many cultural, sporting and other events that will be taking place throughout England during 2002. Please note, as changes often occur after press date, it is advisable to confirm the date and location before travelling.

- Vous trouverez ci-dessous un choix de manifestations devant se dérouler en Angleterre dans le courant de l'année. Etant donné que des modifications sont susceptibles de survenir après la date de mise sous presse, nous vous conseillons de vous faire confirmer, une fois arrivé en Angleterre, les reseignements donnés dans ce guide auprès du Centre d'Information Touristique de la région où vous séjournez.

- Nachstehend finden Sie eine Auswahl der 2002 in England stattfindenden Veranstaltungen. Da nach Redaktionsschluß oft Änderungen vorkommen, ist es ratsam, sich die Angaben bei Ihrer Ankunft in England vom jeweiligen Tourist Information Centre bestätigen zu lassen.

- Hieronder vindt u een keuze uit de evenementen die er het komende jaar in Engeland zullen plaatsvinden. Eventuele veranderingen vinden vaak pas na de persdatum plaats. Het is daarom raadzaam de gegeven informatie na aankomst in Engeland bij het plaatselijke Toeristen Informatie Bureau te controleren.

- Riportiamo una selezione degli avvenimenti che si svolgeranno in Inghilterra nel corso dell'anno prossimo. Dal momento che dopo la data di stampa si verificano spesso dei cambiamenti, si consiglia di verificare l'esattezza delle informazioni riportate in questa guida rivolgendosi, dopo l'arrivo in Inghilterra, al Tourist Information Centre del luogo.

* Provisional at time of going to press.

January 2002

1 January
The New Year's Day Parade - London
Parliament Square,
SW1 to Berkeley Square, London W1
Tel: (020) 8566 8586
Email: markp@londonparade.co.uk
www.londonparade.co.uk

3-13 January
London International Boat Show
Earls Court Exhibition Centre, Warwick Road,
London SW5 9TA
Tel: (01784) 472222 (Boatline)
www.bigblue.org.uk

13 January
Antique and Collectors' Fair
Alexandra Palace,
Alexandra Palace Way, London N22 7AY
Tel: (020) 8883 7061
Email: info@pigandwhistlepromotions.com
www.allypally-uk.com

27 January
Charles I Commemoration
Banqueting House,
Whitehall, London SW1A 2ER
Tel: (01430) 430695

31 January-3 February
Wakefield Rhubarb Trail and Festival of Rhubarb
Various venues, Wakefield
Tel: (01924) 305841
Email: pventom@wakefield.gov.uk
www.wakefield.gov.uk

February 2002

1 February*
Cheltenham Folk Festival
Town Hall, Imperial Square, Cheltenham
Tel: (01242) 226033
Email: Antoniac@cheltenham.gov.uk
www.visitcheltenham.gov.uk

9-16 February
Jorvik Viking Festival - Jolablot 2002
Various venues - Jorvik, Coppergate, York
Tel: (01904) 643211
Email: marketing.jorvik@lineone.net
www.jorvik-viking.centre.co.uk

17 February
Chinese New Year Celebrations
Centered on Gerrard Street and Leicester Square,
London WC2
Tel: (020) 7287 1118

17 February-24 March
Lambing Sunday and Spring Bulb Days
Kentwell Hall, Long Melford, Sudbury

26 February-3 March
Fine Art and Antiques Fair
Olympia, Hammersmith Road, London W14
Tel: (020) 7370 8212
Email: olympia.antiques@eco.co.uk
www.olympia-antiques.co.uk

March 2002

6 March-1 April
Ideal Home Show
Earls Court Exhibition Centre,
Warwick Road, London SW5 9TA
Tel: (0870) 606 6080

7 March-10 March*
Crufts 2002
National Exhibition Centre, Birmingham

EVENTS

12 March-14 March
Cheltenham Gold Cup National Hunt Racing Festival
Cheltenham Racecourse, Prestbury Park, Cheltenham
Tel: (01242) 513014
www.cheltenham.co.uk

16 March-17 March
Ambleside Daffodil and Spring Flower Show
The Kelsick Centre, St Mary's Lane, Ambleside
Tel: (015394) 32252
www.ambleside-show.org.uk

17 March
Antique and Collectors' Fair
Alexandra Palace, Alexandra Palace Way,
London N22 7AY
Tel: (020) 8883 7061
Email: info@pigandwhistlepromotions.com
www.allypally-uk.com

23 March
Head of the River Race
River Thames, London
Tel: (01932) 220401
Email: secretary@horr.co.uk
www.horr.co.uk

23 March-24 March*
Thriplow Daffodil Weekend
Various Venues, Thriplow, Royston
Tel: (01763) 208132
Email: jmurray@thriplow.fsnet.co.uk
www.thriplow.org.uk

29 March
British and World Marbles Championship
Greyhound Public House,
Radford Road, Tinsley Green, Crawley
Tel: (01403) 730602

29 March-5 April*
Harrogate International Youth Music Festival
Various venues, Harrogate
Tel: (01306) 744360
Email: peurope@kuoni.co.uk
www.performeurope.co.uk

29 March-6 April
Ulverston Walking Festival
Various Venues, Ulverston
Tel: (01229) 585588

30 March
Oxford and Cambridge Boat Race
River Thames, London
Tel: (020) 7611 3500

April 2002

1 April
Old Custom: World Coal Carrying Championship
Start: Royal Oak Public House,
Owl Lane, Ossett
Tel: (01924) 218990
Email: bwilding@gawthorpe.ndo.co.uk
www.gawthorpe.ndo.co.uk

1 April
London Harness Horse Parade
Battersea Park, London SW11
Tel: (01733) 371156
Email: t-g@ic24.net
www.eastofengland.org.uk

1 April-30 April*
Old Custom: Pace Egg Plays
Upper Calder Valley, Various venues, Todmorden, Heptonstall, Hebden Bridge
Tel: (01422) 843831
Email: calderdale_tourism@lineone.net

1 April-30 April*
Trigg Morris Men's Easter Monday Tour
Various Venues Starting in the
Market Square, Launceston
Tel: (01637) 880394
www.triggmorris.freeserve.co.uk

4 April-6 April*
Horse-racing: Martell Grand National Festival
Aintree Racecourse,
Ormskirk Road, Aintree, Liverpool
Tel: (0151) 523 2600
Email: aintree@rht.net
www.aintree.co.uk

14 April
London Marathon
Greenwich Park, London SE10
Tel: (020) 8948 7935

18 April-20 April
Maltings Beer Festival
Tuckers Maltings, Teign Road, Newton Abbot
Tel: (01626) 334734

20 April-6 May
World Snooker Championships
Crucible Theatre, Norfolk Street, Sheffield
Tel: (0114) 249 6006
www.embassysnooker.com

24 April-27 April
Bury St Edmunds Beer Festival
Corn Exchange, Cornhill, Bury St Edmunds
Tel: (01842) 860063

25 April-28 April
Harrogate Spring Flower Show
Great Yorkshire Showground, Harrogate
Tel: (01423) 561049
Email: info@flowershow.org.uk
www.flowershow.org.uk

May 2002

1 May-6 May*
Cheltenham International Jazz Festival
Various venues throughout Cheltenham

1 May-31 May*
Bexhill 100 Festival of Motoring
Seafront, De La Warr Parade, Bexhill
Tel: (01424) 730564
Email: brian@bexhill100.co.uk
www.bexhill100.co.uk

1 May-31 May*
Hay on Wye Literature Festival
Various Venues in Hay-on-Wye,
Hay-on-Wye, Hereford
Tel: (01497) 821299

1 May-31 May*
Jennings Keswick Jazz Festival
Keswick
Tel: (01900) 602122
Email: carnegie@allerdale.gov.uk

EVENTS

1 May-31 Aug
Glyndebourne Festival Opera
Glyndebourne Opera House,
Glyndebourne, Glynde, Lewes

3 May-6 May
Hastings Traditional Jack in the Green Morris Dance and Folk Festival
Various venues, Hastings
Tel: (01424) 781122
Email: greenman@britishlibrary.net
www.jack-in-the-park.co.uk

4 May*
Downton Cuckoo Fair
Village Centre, Downton, Salisbury
Tel: (01725) 510646

4 May-27 May*
Rhododendron and Azalea Time
Leonardslee Gardens,
Lower Beeding, Horsham
Tel: (01403) 891212
Email: leonardslee.gardens@virgin.net
www.leonardslee.com

5 May-6 May*
2002 Dover Pageant
Dover College Grounds, Dover
Tel: (01304) 242990
Email: pageant@port-of-dover.com
www.port-of-dover.com/pageant

6-May
Dunstable Carnival
Bennett Memorial Recreation Ground,
Bull Pond Lane, Dunstable
Tel: (01582) 607895
Email: promotions.dunstable@towns.bedfordshie.gov.uk

11 May-19 May*
Tiverton Spring Festival
Various venues, Tiverton
Tel: (01884) 258952

12-May
Antique and Collectors' Fair
Alexandra Palace, Alexandra Palace Way,
London N22 7AY
Tel: (020) 8883 7061
Email: info@pigandwhistlepromotions.com
www.allypally-uk.com

12-May
South Suffolk Show
Point-to-Point Course, Ampton Park,
Ingham, Bury St Edmunds
Tel: (01638) 750879
Email: geoff@southsuffolkshow.co.uk
www.southsuffolkshow.co.uk

15 May-19 May
Royal Windsor Horse Show
Home Park, Windsor Castle, Windsor
Tel: (01753) 860633
Email: olympia-show-jumping@eco.uk
www.olympia-show-jumping.co.uk

18 May-19 May
London Tattoo
Wembley Arena, Empire Way, Wembley
Tel: (01189) 303239
Email: normanrogerson@telinco.co.uk
www.telinco.co.uk/maestromusic

21 May-24 May
Chelsea Flower Show
Royal Hospital Chelsea,
Royal Hospital Road,
Chelsea, London SW3 4SR

24 May-27 May*
Old Custom: The Hunting of the Earl of Rone
Various venues, Combe Martin, Ilfracombe
Tel: (01271) 882 366
Email: tom.brown1@virgin.net

25 May-26 May*
Air Fete
RAF Mildenhall,
100ARW/CV USAF, Mildenhall,
Bury St Edmunds
Tel: (01638) 543341
www.mildenhall.af.mil/airfete

25 May-26 May
Hertfordshire County Show
Hertfordshire Agricultural Society, Dunstable Road,
Redbourn, St Albans
Tel: (01582) 792626

26 May-27 May
Battle Medieval Fair
Abbey Green, High Street, Battle
Tel: (01424) 774447
Email: chpsmith@lineone.net

27 May-7 Jun
Isle of Man T.T. Motorcycle Festival
Various venues Isle of Man
Tel: (01624) 686801

29 May-30 May
Corpus Christi Carpet of Flowers and Floral Festival
Cathedral of Our Lady and St Philip Howard,
Cathedral House, Arundel
Tel: (01903) 882297
Email: aruncathl@aol.com

31 May-2 Jun
Holker Garden Festival
Holker Hall and Gardens, Cark in Cartmel,
Grange-over-Sands
Tel: (015395) 58328
Email: publicopening@holker.co.uk
www.holker-hall.co.uk

EVENTS

June 2002

1 June-3 June*
Orange WOW
North Shields Fishquay and Town Centre, North Shields
Tel: (0191) 200 5164
Email: carol.alevroyianni@northtyneside.gov.uk
www.orangewow.co.uk

1 June-4 June*
Chatham Navy Days
The Historic Dockyard, Chatham
Tel: (01634) 823800
www.worldnavalbase.org.uk

1 June-31 July*
Exeter Festival
Various Venues, Exeter
Tel: (01392) 265118
www.exeter.gov.uk

6 June-12 June
Appleby Horse Fair
Fair Hill, Roman Road,
Appleby-in-Westmorland
Tel: (017683) 51177
Email: tic@applebytowncouncil.fsnet.co.uk
www.applebytowncouncil.fsnet.co.uk

6 June-16 June
Fine Art and Antiques Fair
Olympia, Hammersmith Road, London W14
Tel: (020) 7370 8212
Email: olympia.antiques@eco.co.uk
www.olympia-antiques.com

7 June*
Robert Dover's Cotswold Olimpick Games
Dovers Hill, Weston Subedge, Chipping Campden
Tel: (01384) 274041
Email: a.greenwood@cix.co.uk

7 June-8 June
Derby Day
Epsom Down, Epsom
Tel: (01372) 470047
19 June-23 June

24 June-7 July
Wimbledon Lawn Tennis Championships
All England Lawn Tennis and Croquet Club,
Church Road, London SW19 5AE
Tel: (020) 8946 2244

28 June-30 June*
The Ordnance Survey Balloon and Flower Festival
Southampton Common, The Avenue, Southampton
Tel: (023) 8083 2525
Email: southampton.gov.uk

29 June-17 July*
Chester Mystery Plays
Cathedral Green, Chester
Tel: (01244) 682617

July 2002

5 July-14 July
Lichfield International Arts Festival
Throughout City of Lichfield
Tel: (01543) 306270
Email: Lichfield.fest@Lichfield-arts.org.uk
www.lichfieldfestival.org

5 July-14 July
York Early Music Festival
Various venues, York
Tel: (01904) 645738
Email: enquiry@yorkearlymusic.org
www.yorkearlymusic.org

6 July-7 July
Sunderland International Kite Festival
Northern Area Playing Fields, District 12, Washington
Tel: (0191) 514 1235
Email: jackie.smithr@edcom.sunderland.gov.uk
www.sunderland.gov.uk/kitefestival

6 July-18 August
Cookson Country Festival
Various Venues in South Shields
Tel: (0191) 424 7985
Email: andy.buyers@s-tyneside-mbc.gov.uk
www.s-tyneside-mbc.gov.uk

10 July-14 July*
Henley Festival
Royal Regatta, Henley-on-Thames
Tel: (01491) 843400
Email: info@henley-festival.co.uk
www.henley-festival.co.uk

13 July
Tendring Hundred Show
Lawford House Park, Lawford, Manningtree
Tel: (01206) 571517
Email: anne@tendringshow.demon.co.uk
www.tendringshow.demon.com

13 July-14 July
Tewkesbury Medieval Festival
The Gastons, Gloucester Road, Tewkesbury
Tel: (01386) 871908

19 July-21 July*
Netley Marsh Steam and Craft Show
Meadow Farm, Ringwood Road, Netley Marsh, Southampton
Tel: (023) 8086 7882

19 July-14 September
BBC Henry Wood Promenade Concerts
Royal Albert Hall, Kensington Gore, London SW7 2AP
Tel: (020) 7765 5575
Email: proms@bbc.co.uk
www.bbc.co.uk/proms

EVENTS

23 July-28 July*
Chulmleigh Old Fair
Various Venues, Chulmleigh
Tel: (01769) 580276

25 July-4 August*
**Manchester 2002
- The 17th Commonwealth Games**
Various venues, Manchester
Tel: (0161) 228 2002

26 July-28 July
Gateshead Summer Flower Show
Gateshead Central Nurseries, Whickam Highway, Lobley Hill, Gateshead
Tel: (0191) 433 3838
Email: g.scott@leisure.gatesheadmbc.gov

27 July-28 July*
Sunderland International Air Show
Promenade, Sea Front, Seaburn, Sunderland
Tel: (0191) 553 2000

31 July
Nantwich and South Cheshire Show
Dorfold Hall, Nantwich
Tel: (01270) 780306

August 2002

1 August-30 August
Last Night of the Proms Outdoor Concert
Castle Howard, York
Tel: (01653) 648444
Email: mec@castlehoward.co.uk
www.castlehoward.co.uk

1 August-31 August*
Lowther Horse Driving Trials and Country Fair
Lowther Castle, Lowther Estate, Lowther, Penrith
Tel: (01931) 712378

1 August-31 August*
Maryport Songs of the Sea Festival
The Harbour, Maryport
Tel: (01900) 813738

3 August*
Stoke Gabriel Grand Carnival Procession
Village Centre, Stoke Gabriel, Totnes
Tel: (01803) 782483

3 August-4 August
Woodvale International Rally
R A F Woodvale, 43 Kenilworth Road, Southport
Tel: (01704) 578816

4 August-11 August
Alnwick International Music Festival
Market-place, Alnwick
Tel: (01665) 510417
Email: jim@alnwick0.demon.co.uk

10 August-17 August
Billingham International Folklore Festival
Town Centre, Queensway, Billingham
Tel: (01642) 651060
www.billinghamfestival.co.uk

16 August-26 August*
Ross on Wye International Festival
Various venues around Ross on Wye, mainly by the riverside, Rope Walk, Ross-on-Wye
Tel: (01594) 544446
Email: info@festival.org.uk
www.festival.org.uk

22 August-27 August
International Beatles Festival
Various venues, Liverpool
Tel: (0151) 236 9091
Email: cavern@fsb.dial.co.uk
www.cavern-liverpool.co.uk

25 August-26 August
Western Union Notting Hill Carnival
Streets around Ladbroke Grove, London W11
Tel: (020) 8964 0544

28 August-1 September
Great Dorset Steam Fair
South Down Farm, Tarrant Hinton, Blandford Forum
Tel: (01258) 860361
Email: enquiries@steam-fair.co.uk
www.steam-fair.co.uk

30 August-3 November
Blackpool Illuminations
Promenade, Blackpool
Tel: (01253) 478222
Email: tourism@blackpool.gov.uk
www.blackpooltourism.gov.uk

31 August-1 September*
Lancashire Vintage and Country Show
Hamilton House Farm, St Michael's on Wyre, Preston
Tel: (01772) 687259

September 2002

1 September*
Egremont Crab Fair and Sports
Baybarrow, Orgill, Egremont
Tel: (01946) 821554
Email: crabfair.homestead.com/mainpage.html

1 September*
Kendal Torchlight Procession
Kendal
Tel: (015395) 63018
Email: ronc@torchlight.net1.co.uk
www.lakesnet.co.uk/kendaltorchlight

1 September-30 September*
Southampton International Boat Show
Western Esplanade, Southampton
Tel: (01784) 223600
Email: boatshow@boatshows.co.uk
www.bigblue.org.uk

EVENTS

5 September-8 September
The Blenheim Petplan International Three Day Event
Blenheim Palace, Woodstock
Tel: (01993) 813335
Email: blenheimht@btconnect.com

7 September-8 September
Berwick Military Tattoo
Berwick Barracks, Berwick-upon-Tweed
Tel: (01289) 307426

7 September-8 September*
Kirkby Lonsdale Victorian Fair
Kirkby Lonsdale
Tel: (015242) 71570

13 September-15 September
Thames Festival
River Thames, London
Tel: (020) 7928 0960
Email: festival@coin-street.org
www.ThamesFestival.org

18 September-21 September*
Barnstaple Ancient Chartered Fair
Seven Brethren Bank, Barnstaple
Tel: (01271) 373311
Email: barnstaple_com_council@northdevon.gov.uk

21 September-22 September*
Newbury and Royal County of Berkshire Show
Newbury Showground, Priors Court, Hermitage, Thatcham

22 September
Antique and Collectors' Fair
Alexandra Palace, Alexandra Palace Way,
London N22 7AY
Tel: (020) 8883 7061
Email: info@pigandwhistlepromotions.com
www.allypally-uk.com

October 2002

1 October-6 October
Horse of the Year Show
Wembley Arena, Empire Way, Wembley
Tel: (020) 8900 9282
Email: info@hoys.co.uk
www.hoys.co.uk

11 October-19 October
Hull Fair
Walton Street Fairground, Walton Street, Hull
Tel: (01482) 615625
Email: city.entertainments@hull.gov.uk

20 October
Trafalgar Day Parade - The Sea Cadet Corps
Trafalgar Square, London WC2
Tel: (020) 7928 8978
Email: rbusby@sea-cadets.org

November 2002

1 November-30 November*
International Guitar Festival of Great Britain
Various venues, Wirral
Tel: (0151) 666 5060
Email: rob@bestguitarfest.com
www.bestguitarfest.com

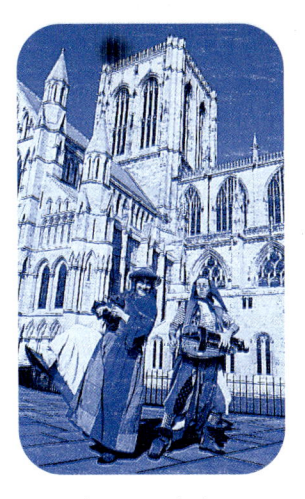

1 November-31 December*
Marwell's Winter Wonderland
Marwell Zoological Park, Colden Common, Winchester
Tel: (01962) 777407
Email: events@marwell.org.uk

3 November
London to Brighton Veteran Car Run
Hyde Park, London W2
Tel: (01753) 765035

9 November
Lord Mayor's Show
City of London, London
Tel: (020) 7606 3030

10 November
Remembrance Day Service and Parade
Cenotaph, Whitehall, London SW1
Tel: (020) 7273 3498
Email: frances.bright@homeoffice.gsi.gov.uk

11 November*
Highbridge and Burnham-on-Sea Guy Fawkes Carnival
Town Centre, Burnham-on-Sea
Tel: (01278) 794557

16 November-23 December
Thursford Christmas Spectacular
Thursford Collection, Thursford Green,
Thursford, Fakenham
Tel: (01328) 878477

17 November
Antique and Collectors' Fair
Alexandra Palace, Alexandra Palace Way,
London N22 7AY
Tel: (020) 8883 7061
Email: info@pigandwhistlepromotions.com
www.allypally-uk.com

December 2002

18 December-22 December
Showjumping: Olympia International Championships
Olympia, Hammersmith Road, London W14
Tel: (020) 7370 8206
Email: olympia-show-jumping@eco.co.uk
www.olympia-show-jumping.co.uk

EVENTS

A selection of events for 2002 in Scotland

January 2002

1 January*
Men's & Boy's "Ba" Games
Kirkwall Town Centre, Kirkwall
Contact: (01856) 872 961

1-31 January*
The Burning of the Clavie
Various venues around village, Burghead, Elgin
Contact:(01343) 542666

25 January
Burn's Night
Various venues across Scotland, Edinburgh
Contact: (0131) 332 2433
www.visitscotland.com

29 January
Festival: Up Helly Aa
Lerwick Town Centre, Lerwick
Contact: (01595) 693 434
Email: shetland.tourism@zetnet.co.uk
www.shetland-tourism.co.uk

February 2002

2 February*
Rugby Football: Six Nations - Scotland v England
Murrayfield Stadium, Edinburgh
Contact: (0131) 346 500
Email: feedback@srn.org.uk
www.sru.org.uk

April 2002

6 April-16 April
Edinburgh International Science Festival
Various venues, Edinburgh
Contact: (0131) 530 2001
www.edinburghfestivals.co.uk

19 April-20 April*
Horse Racing: Ladbroke Casinos Scottish Grand National
Ayr Racecourse
Contact: (01292) 264 179

May 2002

1 May-31 May*
Orkney Folk Festival
Various venues, Orkney
Contact: (01856) 851 331

June 2002

20 June-23 June
Royal Highland Show
Royal Highland Centre, Ingliston, Edinburgh
Contact: (0131) 335 6200
www.rhass.org.uk

July 2002

18 July-21 July
Golf: The Open Championship 2002
Muirfield Golf Club, Duncur Road, Muirfield, Gullane
Contact: (01334) 472 112
www.randa.org

EVENTS

August 2002

2 August-4 August*
Edinburgh Military Tattoo
Edinburgh Castle, Castle Hill, Edinburgh
Contact: (0131) 225 118

11 August-31 August
Edinburgh International Festival
Various venues, Edinburgh
Contact: (0131) 473 2001

September 2002

8 September*
Braemar Gathering
Princess Royal and Duke of York Memorial Park, Braemar, Ballater
Contact: (01339) 755 377
Email: info@braemargathering.org
www.braemargathering.org

October 2002

11 October-18 October
Royal National Mod
Various venues, Stornoway
Contact: (01463) 709 705
www.the-mod.org.uk

December 2002

29 December-2 Jan*
Edinburgh's Hogmanay
Various venues, Edinburgh
Contact: (0131) 473 3800

31 December-1 January*
Stonehaven Fireballing Festival
Various venues, Auld Toon Cross to Cannon, Stonehaven
Contact: (01224) 582272

Since changes often occur after press date, it is advisable to confirm the date and locations of events before travelling.

* provisional at time of going to press.

Britain On-Line

In-depth information about travelling in Britain is now available on BTA's VisitBritain website.

Covering everything from castles to leisure parks and from festivals to road and rail links, the site complements Where to Stay perfectly, giving you up-to-the-minute details to help with your travel plans.

BRITAIN on the internet
www.visitbritain.com

EVENTS

A selection of events for
2002 in Wales

April 2002

7 April
Rugby Football: Six Nations Wales v France
Millennium Stadium,
Westgate Street, Cardiff
Contact: (0870) 5582 582
www.millenniumstadium-plc.co.uk

May 2002

1 May-31 May*
Football: FA Cup Final
Millennium Stadium, Westgate Street, Cardiff
Contact: (020) 7402 7151
www.the-fa.org.uk

June 2002

8 July-14 July
Llangollen International Musical Eisteddfod
Royal International Pavilion,
Abbey Road, Llangollen
Contact: (01978) 860 236
Email: marketing@lime.uk.com
www.lime.uk.com

22 July-25 July*
Royal Welsh Show
Royal Welsh Showground,
Llanelwedd, Builth Wells
Contact: (01982) 553 683
Email: info@rwas.co.uk
www.rwas.co.uk

August 2002

1 August-31 August*
World Bog Snorkelling Championships
Various venues, Llanwrtyd Wells
Contact: (01591) 610 666
Email: tic@celt.ruralwales.org
www.llanwrtyd-wells.powys.uk

9 August-11 August
Brecon Jazz festival
Various venues, Brecon
Contact: (01874) 625 557
Email: breconjazz@brecon.co.uk
www.breconjazz.co.uk

17 August-25 August
Llandrindod Wells Victorian Festival
Old Town Hall,
Temple Street, Llandrindod Wells
Contact: (01597) 823 441
Email: gordon@celt.ruralwales.org

22 August-27 August
Presteigne Festival of Music and Arts
Various venues, Presteigne
Contact: (01544) 267 800

October 2002

5 October-20 October*
Swansea Festival of Music and the Arts
Various venues, Swansea
Contact: (01792) 411570

EVENTS

November 2002

1 November-3 November
Portmeirion Antiques Fair
Various venues, Portmeirion, Porthmadog
Contact: (01202) 604 306

1 November-30 November*
Network Q Rally
Various venues,
City centre/Cardiff Bay, Cardiff
Contact: (029) 2066 7773
Email: ray@cardiffmarketing.co.uk
www.cardiffmarketing.co.uk

Since changes often occur after press date, it is advisable to confirm the date and locations of events before travelling.

* provisional at time of going to press.

Tourist information Centres

When it comes to your next break in Britain, the first stage of your journey could be closer than you think. You've probably got a Tourist Information centre nearby which is there to serve the local community – as well as visitors. Knowledgeable staff will be happy to help you, wherever you're heading.

Many Tourist information Centres can provide you with maps and guides, and sometimes it's even possible to book your accommodation, too.

Across the Britain, there are more than 800 Tourist Information Centres. You'll find the address of your nearest Tourist Information Centre in your local Phone Book.

INFORMATION

Tourist Information in Britain

INFORMATION POUR LES TOURISTES EN GRANDE-BRETAGNE
TOURISTEN-INFORMATION IN GROSSBRITANNIEN
TOERISTISCHE INFORMATIE IN GROOT-BRITTANNIE
INFORMAZIONI PER TURISTI IN GRAN BRETAGNA

To help you explore Britain, to see both the major sites and the fascinating attractions off the beaten track, there is a country-wide service of Tourist Information Centres (TICs), each ready and able to give advice and directions on how best to enjoy your holiday in Britain. A comprehensive list can be obtained from BTA offices overseas.

Call in at these centres while travelling - you'll find them in most towns and many villages - and make use of the help that awaits you. Much development of Tourist Information Centre services has taken place in recent years and you should have no difficulty in locating them as most are well signposted and the use of the following international symbol is becoming more common:

[i] Tourist information

You can rest assured that the Tourist Information Centres in the places you visit will be ready to give you all the help you need when you get to Britain, particularly on matters of detailed local information.

ACCOMMODATION RESERVATION SERVICES

Wherever you go in Britain, you will find TICs which can help and advise you about all types of accommodation. Details of Park Finding Services are outlined on page 32.

THE BRITAIN VISITOR CENTRE

The Britain Visitor Centre offers the most comprehensive information and booking service in London - and it's all under one roof, just two minutes walk from Piccadilly Circus.

The Britain Visitor Centre will book rail, air and car travel, reserve sightseeing tours, theatre tickets and accommodation, change currency and, of course, provide information in many languages on the whole of Britain and Ireland. There is also a bookshop within the Centre.

Open seven days a week, 0900 to 1830 Monday to Friday, 1000 to 1600 Saturday and Sunday (0900 to 1700 Saturdays June to September) at 1 Regent Street, London SW1Y 4XT.

TOURIST ORGANISATIONS

Here is an address list of official tourist organisations in all parts of Britain. All these offices welcome personal callers, except where indicated.

LONDON

London Tourist Board and Convention Bureau
6th floor, Glen House, Stag Place, London SW1E 5LT
(no personal callers please).
Web site: www.londontouristboard.com

For further information on London Tourist Information Centres please refer to pages 55.

Scottish Tourist Board
19 Cockspur Street, London SW1Y 5BL
(personal callers only)
Telephone enquiries: (0131) 332 2433

Wales Tourist Board
1 Regent Street, London SW1Y 4XT
Tel: (020) 7808 3838

British Tourist Authority
Thames Tower, Black's Road,
Hammersmith, London W6 9EL
(written enquiries only)

ENGLAND

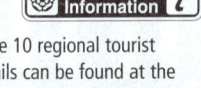

[Tourist Information i]

Information is available from the 10 regional tourist boards in England (contact details can be found at the beginning of each regional section), and a network of around 550 Tourist Information Centres. Look out for the sign shown above.

SCOTLAND

[Tourist Information i]

The Scottish Tourist Board has a substantial network of local tourist boards, backed up by more than 140 information centres.

Scottish Tourist Board
23 Ravelston Terrace, Edinburgh EH4 3TP
Tel: (0131) 332 2433

WALES

[Tourist Information Centre / Canolfan Croeso Cymru]

There are three Regional Tourism Companies and over 84 information centres to help you.

Wales Tourist Board
Brunel House, 2 Fitzalan Road, Cardiff CF24 0UY
Tel: (029) 20499909
(telephone and written enquiries only)

INFORMATION ON THE INTERNET

Visit the BTA's website for a wealth of information including travel information, places to visit and events.
WWW.VISITBRITAIN.COM

INFORMATION

National Accessible Scheme

The English Tourism Council and the National and Regional Tourist Boards throughout Britain assess all types of places to stay, on holiday or business, that provide accessible accommodation for wheelchair users and others who may have difficulty walking.

Accommodation establishments taking part in the National Accessible Scheme, and which appear in this guide are listed below. Use the Town Index at the back to find the page numbers for their full entries.

The Tourist Boards recognise three categories of accessibility:

CATEGORY 1 — Accessible to all wheelchair users including those travelling independently.

CATEGORY 2 — Accessible to a wheelchair user with assistance.

CATEGORY 3 — Accessible to a wheelchair user able to walk short distances and up at least three steps.

If you have additional needs or special requirements of any kind, we strongly recommend that you make sure these can be met by your chosen establishment before you confirm your booking.

The criteria the English Tourism Council and the National and Regional Tourist Boards have adopted do not necessarily conform to British Standards or to Building Regulations. They reflect what the Boards understand to be acceptable to meet the practical needs of wheelchair users.

The National Accessible Scheme is currently in the process of being updated. Consultation has been conducted throughout 2001 with introduction during 2002.

CATEGORY 1
- **Brecon, Powys** - Brynich Caravan Park

CATEGORY 2
- **Brecon, Powys** - Anchorage Caravan Park
- **Canterbury, Kent** - Yew Tree Park
- **Marden, Kent** - Tanner Farm Touring Caravan and Camping Park
- **Pandy, Monmouthshire** - Pandy Caravan Club Site
- **Poole, Dorset** - Beacon Hill Touring Park
- **Portreath, Cornwall** - Tehidy Holiday Park
- **Telford, Shropshire** - Severn Gorge Park
- **Winsford, Somerset** - Halse Farm Caravan & Tent Park

CATEGORY 3
- **Cardigan, Ceredigion** - Cenarth Falls Holiday Park
- **Glasgow, Strathclyde** - Craigendmuir Park
- **Monmouth, Monmouthshire** - Monmouth Caravan Park
- **Morfa Bychan, Gwynedd** - Greenacres Holiday Park
- **Swansea, Swansea** - Gowerton Caravan Club Site
- **Tenby, Pembrokeshire** - Kiln Park Holiday Centre

The National Accessible Scheme forms part of the Tourism for All Campaign that is being promoted by National and Regional Tourist Boards. Additional help and guidance on finding suitable holiday accommodation for those with special needs can be obtained from:

HOLIDAY CARE

Holiday Care, 2nd Floor, Imperial Buildings, Victoria Road, Horley, Surrey RH6 7PZ

Tel: (01293) 774535
Fax: (01293) 784647
Email: holiday.care@virgin.net
Internet: www.holidaycare.org.uk
Minicom: (01293) 776943

INFORMATION

BTA Overseas Offices

ARGENTINA - Buenos Aires
British Tourist Authority
Avenida Córdoba 645, 2 piso
1054 Buenos Aires
Tel: 011 4314 6735/8955
Fax: 011 4315 3161
E-mail: rmartelli@bta.org.uk
Website: www.visitbritain.com/ar
(open to public Mon-Thu 1000-1700; Fri 1000-1300)

AUSTRALIA - Sydney
British Tourist Authority
Level 16, Gateway
1 Macquarie Place
Sydney, NSW 2000
Tel: 02 9377 4400
Fax: 02 9377 4499
E-mail: visitbritainaus@bta.org.uk
Website: www.visitbritain.com/au

AUSTRIA - Vienna
Britain Visitor Centre
Schenkenstr. 4
A-1010 Wien
Tel: 01-533 26 16 81
Fax: 01 533 26 16 85
E-mail: tourist.information@britishcouncil.at
Website: www.visitbritain.com

BELGIUM - Brussels
Visit Britain Centre
Avenue Louise 140, 2nd Floor
1050 Brussels
Tel: 02 646 35 10
Fax: 02 646 39 86
E-mail: british.be@bta.org.uk
Website: www.visitbritain.com/be

BRAZIL - Rio de Janeiro
British Tourist Authority
Rua da Assembleia 10, sala 3707
Rio de Janeiro-RJ 20119-900
Tel: (21) 531 1717/0382
Fax: (21) 531 0383
E-mail: btabras@vetor.com.br
Website: www.visitbritain.com/br

CANADA - Toronto
British Tourist Authority
5915 Airport Road, Suite 120
Mississauga, Ontario L4V 1T1
Toll free: 1 888 VISIT UK
Fax: 905 405 1835
E-mail: travelinfo@bta.org.uk
Website: www.visitbritain.com/ca

DENMARK - Copenhagen
British Tourist Authority
Møntergade 3
1116 Copenhagen K
Tel: 70 21 50 11
Fax: 33 75 50 08
E-mail: dkweb@bta.org.uk
Website: www.visitbritain.com/dk

FINLAND - Helsinki
British Travel Centre
Tammasaarenkatu 7 Vega
00180 Helsinki
Tel: 09 2515 2422
Fax: 09 2512 2410
E-mail: finlandbtc@bta.org.uk

FRANCE - Paris
Office de Tourisme de Grande-Bretagne
19 rue des Mathurins
75009 Paris
Tel: 01 44 51 56 20
Fax: 01 44 51 56 21
MiniTel: 3615 BRITISH
Website: www.grandebretagne.net/fr

GERMANY
(For telephone and written enquiries -
no walk-in visitors please)
British Tourist Authority
Westendstr 16-22
60325 Frankfurt
Tel: 01801-468 642 (local tariff from all over Germany)
Fax: 069-9711 2444
E-mail: gb-info@bta.org.uk
Website: www.visitbritain.com/de

(For walk-in visitors only, from 01.12.2001)
Britain Visitor Centre
Hackescher Markt 1
10178 Berlin

HONG KONG
British Tourist Authority
Room 1504, Eton Tower
8 Hysan Avenue
Causeway Bay
Hong Kong
Tel: 2882 9967
Fax: 2577 1443
E-mail: hko@bta.org.uk
Website: www.visitbritain.com/hk

IRELAND - Dublin
British Tourist Authority
18/19 College Green
Dublin 2
Tel: 01 670 8000
Fax: 01 670 8244
E-mail: Contactus@bta.org.uk
Website: www.visitbritain.com/ie

INFORMATION

ITALY - Milan
British Tourist Authority
Corso Magenta 32
20123 Milano
Tel: 02 88 08 151
Fax: 02 7201 0086
Website: www.visitbritain.com/ciao

JAPAN - Tokyo
British Tourist Authority
Akasaka Twin Tower 1F
2-17-22 Akasaka
Minato-ku
Tokyo 107-0052
Tel: 03 5562 2550
Website: www.uknow.or.jp (Japanese/English);
or www.visitbritain.com/jp (Japanese)

NETHERLANDS - Amsterdam
British Tourist Authority
Aurora Gebouw (5e)
Stadhouderskade 2
1054 ES Amsterdam
Tel: 020 689 0002
Fax: 020 689 0003
E-mail: BritInfo.NL@bta.org.uk
Website: www.visitbritain.com/nl

NEW ZEALAND - Auckland
British Tourist Authority
17th Floor, NZI House
151 Queen Street
Auckland 1
Tel: 09 303 1446
Fax: 09 377 6965
E-mail: bta.nz@bta.org.uk
Website: www.visitbritain.com/nz

NORWAY - Oslo
British Tourist Authority
Dronning Mauds gt 1
POBox 1554 Vika
N-0117 Oslo
Tel: 22 01 20 80
Fax: 22 01 20 84
E-mail: britisketuristkontor@bta.org.uk
Website: www.visitbritain.com/no

SINGAPORE
British Tourist Authority
108 Robinson Road
#01-00 GMG Building
Singapore 068900
Tel: 227 5400
Fax: 227 5411
E-mail: singapore@bta.org.uk
Website: www.visitbritain.com/sg

SOUTH AFRICA - Johannesburg
British Tourist Authority
Lancaster Gate
Hyde Park Lane
Hyde Park 2196 (public address)
PO Box 41896, Craighall 2024 (postal address)
Tel: 011 325 0343
Fax: 011 325 0344
E-mail: johannesburg@bta.org.uk
Website: www.visitbritain.com/za

SPAIN - Madrid
British Tourist Authority
Apartado de Correos 42078
28080 Madrid (public address)
Tel: 902 171 181
Fax: 91 386 10 88
E-mail: turismo.britanico@bta.org.uk
Website: www.visitbritain.com/es
(Call centre service open 1000-1900 daily)

SWEDEN - Stockholm
British Tourist Authority
Box 3102, 103 62 Stockholm (postal address);
Klara Norra Kyrkogata 29, S 111 22 Stockholm
(public address)
Tel: 08 4401 700
Fax: 08 21 31 29
E-mail: stockholm.internet@bta.org.uk
Website: www.visitbritain.com/sverige

SWITZERLAND - Zurich
British Tourist Authority
Limmatquai 78
CH-8001 Zurich
Tel: 0844 007 007 (local rate for Switzerland)
Fax: 01 266 21 61
E-mail: ch-info@bta.org.uk

UNITED ARAB EMIRATES - Dubai
British Tourist Authority
Tariq Bin Zaid Street
Near Rashid Hospital
Al Maktoum Roundabout
PO Box 33342
Dubai
Tel: 04 3350088
Fax: 04 3355335

USA - Chicago
British Tourist Authority
625 North Michigan Avenue
Suite 1001, Chicago
IL 60611
(Open to personal callers only, Mon-Fri 9am-5pm)

For written and telephone enquiries
7th Floor, 551 Fifth Avenue
New York, NY 10176-0799
Toll free: 1 800 GO 2 BRITAIN
E-mail: travelinfo@bta.org.uk
Website: www.travelbritain.org

USA - New York
British Tourist Authority
7th Floor, 551 Fifth Avenue
New York, NY 10176-0799
Tel: 00 1 (212) 986 2266
Toll free: 1 800 GO 2 BRITAIN
E-mail: travelinfo@bta.org.uk
Website: www.travelbritain.org

The David Bellamy
CONSERVATION AWARD

"These well-deserved awards are a signpost to parks which are making real achievements in protecting our environment. Go there and experience wrap-around nature….you could be amazed at what you find!" says Professor David Bellamy.

Many of Britain's holiday parks have become "green champions" of conservation in the countryside, according to leading conservationist David Bellamy. More than 360 gold, silver and bronze parks were this year named in the David Bellamy Conservation Awards, organised in conjunction with the British Holiday and Home Parks Association.

These parks are recognised for their commitment to conservation and the environment through their management of landscaping, recycling policies, waste management, the cultivation of flora and fauna and the creation of habitats designed to encourage a variety of wildlife onto the park. Links with the local community and the use of local materials is also an important consideration.

Parks participating in the scheme are assessed for the awards by holidaymakers who complete postcards to be returned to David Bellamy, an independent inspection by a representative from the local Wildlife Trust and David Bellamy's own study of the parks environmental audit completed when joining the scheme.

Parks with Bellamy Awards offer a variety of accommodation from pitches for touring caravans, motorhomes and tents to caravan holiday homes, holiday lodges and cottages for rent. Holiday parks with these awards are not just those in quiet corners of the countryside. Amongst the winners are much larger centres in popular holiday areas that offer a wide range of entertainments and attractions.

FOR A FREE BROCHURE FEATURING A FULL LIST OF AWARD WINNING PARKS PLEASE CONTACT:

BH&HPA
6 Pullman Court, Great Western Road, Gloucester, GL1 3ND
Tel: 01452 526911 Fax: 01452 508508
Email: enquiries@bhhpa.org.uk   Website: www.ukparks.com/bellamy.htm

The David Bellamy
Conservation Awards

The following parks, which are all featured in this guide, have received a Gold, Silver or Bronze David Bellamy Conservation Award.

LONDON
Thriftwood Caravan Park, Stansted	GOLD

CUMBRIA
Castlerigg Hall Caravan and Camping Park, Keswick	GOLD
Fallbarrow Park, Windermere	GOLD
Greenhowe Caravan Park, Ambleside	SILVER
Lakeland Leisure Park, Flookburgh	SILVER
Waterfoot Caravan Park, Ullswater	GOLD

NORTHUMBRIA
Beadnell Links Caravan Park, Beadnell	GOLD
Haggerston Castle, Beal	GOLD
Seafield Caravan Park, Seahouses	SILVER
Waren Caravan Park, Bamburgh	SILVER

NORTH WEST
Cala Gran, Fleetwood	SILVER
Kneps Farm Holiday Park, Cleveleys	GOLD
Marton Mere Holiday Village, Blackpool	SILVER

YORKSHIRE
Brompton-on-Swale Caravan and Camping Park, Richmond	GOLD
Cawood Holiday Park, York	GOLD
Cayton Village Caravan Park, Scarborough	SILVER
Golden Square Caravan and Camping Park, Helmsley	GOLD
Holme Valley Camping and Caravan Park, Holmfirth	GOLD
Ladycross Plantation Caravan Park, Whitby	SILVER
Lebberston Touring Park, Filey	BRONZE
Northcliffe & Seaview Holiday Parks, Whitby	GOLD
Rudding Holiday Park, Harrogate	SILVER
St Helena's Caravan Site, Horsforth	SILVER
Thornwick & Sea Farm Holiday Centre, Flamborough	SILVER
Thorpe Park Holiday Centre, Cleethorpes	SILVER

HEART OF ENGLAND
Island Meadow Caravan Park, Aston Cantlow	GOLD
Orchard Caravan Park, Boston	GOLD
The Ranch Caravan Park, Evesham	SILVER

EAST OF ENGLAND
Grasmere Caravan Park, Great Yarmouth	BRONZE
Hopton Holiday Village, Great Yarmouth	SILVER
Scratby Hall Caravan Park, Scratby	BRONZE
Vauxhall Holiday Park, Great Yarmouth	BRONZE
Waldegraves Holiday Park, Mersea Island	SILVER

SOUTH WEST
Beverley Park, Paignton	GOLD
Broadway House Holiday Touring Caravan and Camping Park, Cheddar	GOLD
Burnham-on-Sea Holiday Village, Burnham-on-Sea	GOLD
Clifford Bridge Park, Drewsteignton	SILVER
Cofton Country Holiday Park, Dawlish	GOLD
Dornafield, Newton Abbot	GOLD
Forest Glade Holiday Park, Kentisbeare	SILVER
Freshwater Beach Holiday Park, Bridport	BRONZE
Golden Coast Holiday Village, Woolacombe	GOLD
Halse Farm Caravan & Tent Park, Winsford	GOLD
Harford Bridge Holiday Park, Tavistock	GOLD
Highlands End Holiday Park, Bridport	SILVER
Holiday Resort Unity, Brean	SILVER
Mendip Heights Camping and Caravan Park, Wells	GOLD
The Old Oaks Touring Park, Glastonbury	GOLD
Parkers Farm Holiday Park, Ashburton	SILVER
Polruan Holidays (Camping & Caravanning), Polruan-by-Fowey	SILVER
Ramslade Touring Park, Paignton	GOLD
Sandyholme Holiday Park, Owermoigne	SILVER
Sea View International, Megavissy	GOLD
Treloy Tourist Park, Newquay	BRONZE
Trevalgan Holiday Farm, St Ives	SILVER
Trevella Caravan and Camping Park, Newquay	GOLD

SOUTHERN
Beacon Hill Touring Park, Poole	SILVER
Hill Farm Caravan Park, Romsey	SILVER
Merley Court Touring Park, Wimborne Minster	SILVER
Riverside Park, Hamble	BRONZE
Rockley Park Holiday Park, Poole	SILVER
Rowlands Wait Touring Park, Bere Regis	GOLD
Sandy Balls Holiday Centre, Godshill	GOLD
Shorefield Country Park, Milford-on-Sea	GOLD
Ulwell Cottage Caravan Park, Swanage	SILVER

SOUTH EAST ENGLAND
Church Farm Holiday Village, Pagham	GOLD
Crowhurst Park, Battle	GOLD
Honeybridge Park, Horsham	SILVER
Wicks Farm Camping Park, Chichester	GOLD

SCOTLAND
Belhaven Bay Caravan Park, Dunbar	SILVER
Kippford Holiday Park, Kippford	GOLD
Linnhe Lochside Holidays, Fort William	SILVER
Linwater Caravan Park, Edinburgh	SILVER
Lochranza Golf Caravan and Camping Site, Isle of Arran	SILVER
Rothiemurchus Camping & Caravan Park, Aviemore	GOLD
Sands of Luce Caravan Park, Sandhead	SILVER
Seton Sands Holiday Village, Longniddry	SILVER
Trossachs Holiday Park, Aberfoyle	GOLD
Wemyss Bay Holiday Park, Wemyss Bay	SILVER

WALES
Cenarth Falls Holiday Park, Cardigan	GOLD
Greenacres Holiday Park, Morfa Bychan	SILVER
Kiln Park Holiday Centre, Tenby	SILVER
Pendine Sands, Pendine	SILVER

TRAVEL

Distance Chart

The distances between towns on the chart below are given to the nearest mile, and are measured along routes based on the quickest travelling time, making maximum use of motorways or dual-carriageway roads. The chart is based upon information supplied by the Automobile Association.

To calculate the distance in kilometres multiply the mileage by 1.6

For example: Brighton to Dover
82 miles x 1.6
=131.2 kilometres

	Aberdeen	Aberystwyth	Barnstaple	Birmingham	Brighton	Bristol	Cambridge	Cardiff	Carlisle	Carmarthen	Colchester	Dorchester	Dover	Edinburgh	Exeter	Fort William	Glasgow	Gloucester	Guildford	Holyhead	Hull	Inverness	Kendal	Leeds	Lincoln	Liverpool	Maidstone	Manchester	Middlesbrough	Newcastle	Norwich	Nottingham	Oxford	Penzance	Perth	Plymouth	Sheffield	Southampton	Stranraer	Taunton	York	London
468																																										
603	214																																									
431	124	180																																								
605	288	208	171																																							
513	128	99	90	169																																						
462	215	267	97	120	170																																					
531	110	127	109	201	44	203																																				
231	236	372	199	375	282	257	300																																			
513	48	190	171	264	106	266	67	282																																		
516	289	292	171	112	195	48	227	310	290																																	
595	206	94	172	119	62	179	119	363	182	206																																
587	325	273	207	82	206	124	238	400	301	116	200																															
125	335	470	298	473	380	333	398	98	381	385	462	458																														
585	196	53	162	175	82	249	109	353	172	274	55	245	453																													
156	446	581	409	584	491	466	509	209	491	518	573	590	133	563																												
147	333	468	296	472	379	353	397	96	379	405	461	478	49	451	102																										
479	111	125	56	155	35	150	61	247	124	171	117	192	347	107	456	343																										
563	224	175	128	44	106	91	138	332	201	103	97	97	432	147	541	428	99																								
459	101	339	167	343	250	259	201	227	149	333	332	369	327	322	436	323	215	300																								
375	228	321	140	258	231	138	249	170	312	191	313	262	247	303	379	266	196	239	219																							
106	494	630	457	633	540	514	558	257	540	566	622	635	158	612	66	174	505	591	485	428																						
279	190	325	153	329	236	245	254	47	236	319	318	355	147	308	256	143	201	286	181	164	305																					
331	174	302	121	263	212	146	230	126	220	200	294	271	202	284	335	222	177	220	165	60	383	71																				
387	199	276	89	216	186	95	204	182	267	147	245	220	258	258	391	278	151	173	204	46	439	176	72																			
357	110	274	102	277	184	193	202	126	163	268	266	304	225	256	335	222	150	235	101	128	383	79	74	140																		
548	286	234	168	50	167	85	199	361	262	77	161	41	419	206	570	458	153	58	329	223	619	315	233	181	263																	
356	134	261	89	264	171	160	189	123	180	212	253	291	223	243	332	219	137	222	125	97	381	77	44	85	35	251															
276	245	357	177	318	268	198	286	95	291	251	350	322	147	340	280	191	233	276	236	89	308	84	63	123	145	283	115														
234	276	388	208	349	299	229	317	60	322	282	381	353	106	371	239	154	264	307	267	142	266	102	94	154	176	314	146	38													
488	277	329	159	171	233	63	264	282	327	61	241	175	359	311	491	379	212	162	320	150	540	276	173	104	241	135	186	223	254												
393	162	234	54	195	144	86	163	188	226	129	226	218	265	216	397	284	110	153	178	92	446	164	74	38	112	179	71	129	160	119											
503	159	170	68	109	73	81	105	271	168	124	116	371	152	480	367	48	67	239	189	529	225	171	130	173	106	161	226	257	144	103											
697	308	108	274	287	194	361	221	465	284	386	167	357	565	111	674	562	219	259	433	414	723	419	396	369	367	317	355	451	482	423	328	264									
87	382	518	345	521	428	402	446	145	428	454	510	527	42	500	102	62	393	478	373	315	114	193	268	327	271	487	266	192	151	428	334	418	611								
628	239	67	205	218	125	292	152	396	215	316	98	288	496	45	605	492	150	190	364	345	654	350	326	300	298	248	286	382	413	354	259	195	77	542							
365	167	272	76	233	182	122	201	159	264	176	264	247	236	254	368	255	148	191	158	66	417	125	36	47	79	207	39	100	131	147	44	141	366	281	297						
570	225	142	135	66	106	131	138	339	201	159	53	152	439	109	548	435	100	49	307	257	596	292	238	197	241	112	228	293	324	193	171	67	221	484	152	208					
232	342	478	305	481	388	305	406	106	388	415	470	487	133	460	188	89	354	439	333	276	258	153	228	288	231	226	201	163	389	294	378	572	146	503	265	446					
554	165	50	132	160	51	218	79	323	142	243	45	224	423	32	532	419	77	126	291	272	581	276	253	227	225	184	212	308	339	280	186	121	144	469	75	223	94	429			
322	202	315	134	276	225	155	243	117	248	209	307	280	193	297	326	213	191	233	193	38	374	91	24	80	103	240	72	50	89	180	86	184	409	238	340	58	251	223	266		
388	216	120	59	120	60	152	31	215	61	128	79	413	198	522	409	102	30	281	186	571	266	198	143	215	39	202	253	284	115	131	65	310	458	241	168	80	419	167	211		
544	238	216																																								

238

TRAVEL

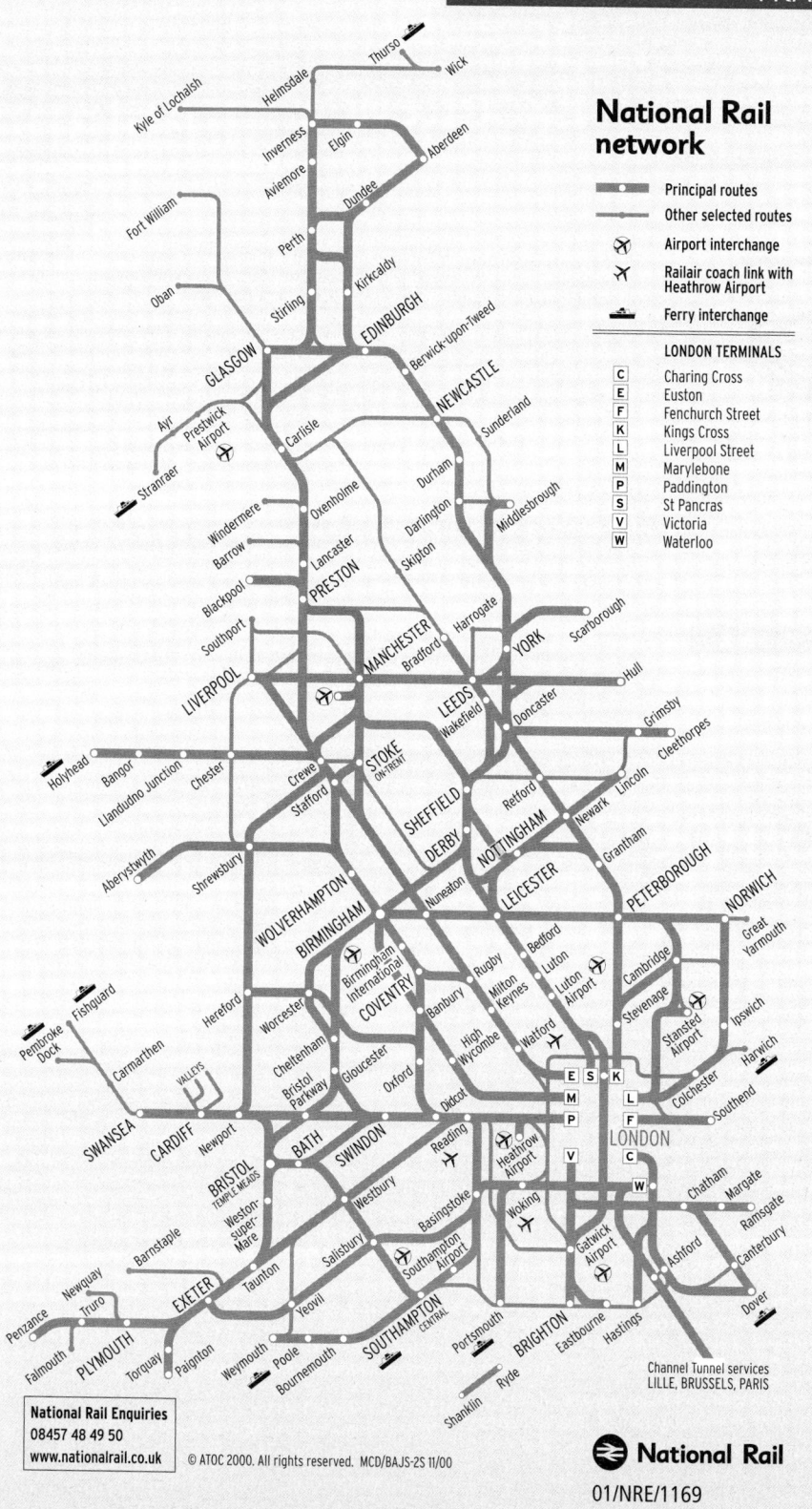

National Rail network

- Principal routes
- Other selected routes
- ✈ Airport interchange
- ✈ Railair coach link with Heathrow Airport
- ⛴ Ferry interchange

LONDON TERMINALS

C	Charing Cross
E	Euston
F	Fenchurch Street
K	Kings Cross
L	Liverpool Street
M	Marylebone
P	Paddington
S	St Pancras
V	Victoria
W	Waterloo

Channel Tunnel services
LILLE, BRUSSELS, PARIS

National Rail Enquiries
08457 48 49 50
www.nationalrail.co.uk

© ATOC 2000. All rights reserved. MCD/BAJS-2S 11/00

National Rail
01/NRE/1169

239

The Safeway Excellence in England

AWARDS 2002

The Safeway Excellence in England Awards are all about blowing English tourism's trumpet and telling the world what a fantastic place England is to visit, whether it's for a two week holiday, a weekend break or a day trip.

Formerly called England for Excellence, the Awards are now in their 13th year and are run by the English Tourism Council in association with England's ten regional tourist boards. There are 13 categories including B&B of the Year, Hotel of the Year and Visitor Attraction of the Year. New for 2002 are Short Break Destination of the Year and Most Improved Seaside Resort.

Winners of the 2002 awards will receive their trophies at a fun and festive event to be held on St George's Day (23 April) at the Royal Opera House in London. The day will not only celebrate excellence in tourism but also Englishness in all its diversity.

For a truly exceptional experience, look out for accommodation and attractions displaying a Safeway Excellence in England Award from April 2002 onwards.

Safeway, one of the UK's leading food retailers, is delighted to be sponsoring these awards as a part of a range of initiatives to help farming communities and the tourism industry.

For more information on Safeway Stores please visit: www.safeway.co.uk
For more information about the Excellence in England Awards visit: www.englishtourism.org.uk

Safeway

EXCELLENCE IN ENGLAND
Awards for Tourism

ENGLISH TOURISM COUNCIL

GNER

Competition Rules

See competition on page 14

1. One entry per household.

2. All entries must be received by 30 November 2002. Entries received after this date will not be accepted. The British Tourist Authority and British Holidays cannot accept responsibility for entries that are damaged, illegible or lost in the mail.

3. All correct entries received by 30 November 2002 will be entered into the draw.

4. The judges' decision is final and no correspondence will be entered into.

5. There will be one winner of the 7-night touring break and three runners up winning either a 3-night weekend break or a 4-night mid-week touring break. Winners can choose from any Haven or British Holidays Park excluding Rockley Park, and Marton Mere. All breaks are subject to availability and must be booked in either Spring 2002 (March-June) or Autumn 2002 (September-October) excluding Bank Holidays in England and Scotland. Towels, insurance, food and transport are not supplied. Parties must be over 21 years of age. Subject to Haven Holidays and British Holidays Terms and Conditions. Call for a copy of the Haven and British Holidays brochures.

6. No cash alternative will be offered and prizes are non-transferable.

7. The winners will be notified within 28 days of the draw taking place.

8. Details of the winners may be obtained by sending an SAE to Julie Freedman, BTA Camping and Caravan Parks Competition, British Holidays, 1 Park Lane, Hemel Hempstead, Herts HP2 4YL

9. Any employee of the British Tourist Authority or Bourne Leisure Group (including Haven and British Holidays), their agents or immediate family are not eligible to enter.

10. All information is correct at time of printing. The British Tourist Authority and British Holidays cannot be held responsible for any changes made thereafter.

INDEX TO PARKS
REPERTOIRE DES TERRAINS/PLATZVERZEICHNIS/ REGISTER VAN CAMPINGS/INDICE DEI CAMPEGGI

A — PAGE

Abermarlais Caravan Park *Llangadog* — 212
Alders Caravan Park *York* — 99
Allhallows Leisure Park *Rochester* — 180
Alpine Grove Touring Park *Chard* — 136
Anchorage Caravan Park *Brecon* — 209
Andrewshayes Caravan Park *Axminster* — 131
Applewood Caravan And Camping Park *Banham* — 119
Ash Vale Homes & Holiday Park *Hartlepool* — 78
Ashburton Caravan Park *Ashburton* — 131
Ashe Farm Caravan And Campsite *Taunton* — 147

B — PAGE

Badrallach Bothy & Camping Site *Dundonnell* — 192
Bainland Country Park Ltd *Woodhall Spa* — 111
Bank Farm Caravan Park *King's Lynn* — 122
Barmouth Touring Caravan & Camping Park *Barmouth* — 208
Barnsoul Farm And Wild Life Area *Dumfries* — 192
Beachcomber Campsite *Berwick-upon-Tweed* — 77
Beachside Holiday Park *Hayle* — 138
Beacon Cottage Farm Touring Park *St Agnes* — 145
Beacon Hill Touring Park *Poole* — 163
Beadnell Links Caravan Park *Beadnell* — 76
Beecraigs Caravan And Camping Site *Linlithgow* — 196
Belhaven Bay Caravan Park *Dunbar* — 192
Berwick Holiday Centre *Berwick-upon-Tweed* — 77
Beverley Park *Paignton* — 143
Birchwood Tourist Park *Wareham* — 167
Blair Castle Caravan Park *Blair Atholl* — 191
Blue Anchor Bay Caravan Park *Blue Anchor* — 133
Bolberry House Farm *Salcombe* — 146
Broadhembury Caravan & Camping Park *Ashford* — 176
Broadway House Holiday Touring Caravan And *Cheddar* — 136
Brompton-on-swale Caravan And Camping Park *Richmond* — 96
Bryn Gloch Caravan & Camping Park *Caernarfon* — 209
Brynich Caravan Park *Brecon* — 209
Burnham-on-sea Holiday Village *Burnham-on-Sea* — 135
Burrowhayes Farm Caravan And Camping Site And Riding Stables *Porlock* — 145
Burton Hill Caravan And Camping Park *Malmesbury* — 139

C — PAGE

Cable Gap Caravan Park *Bacton-on-Sea* — 119
Caerfai Bay Caravan Park *St Davids* — 213
Cala Gran *Fleetwood* — 87
Camping International *Ringwood* — 164
Cardinney Caravan And Camping Park *Lands End* — 139
Carlyon Bay Caravan & Camping Park *Carlyon Bay* — 136
Carnevas Farm Holiday Park *Padstow* — 142
Castlerigg Hall Caravan And Camping Park *Keswick* — 66
Cawood Holiday Park *York* — 99
Cayton Village Caravan Park Ltd *Scarborough* — 97
Cenarth Falls Holiday Park *Cardigan* — 210
Cheverton Copse Holiday Park Ltd *Sandown* — 165
Church Farm Holiday Village *Pagham* — 180
Clifford Bridge Park *Drewsteignton* — 137
Cobbs Hill Farm Caravan & Camping Park *Bexhill-on-Sea* — 177
Cobb's Holiday Park *Highcliffe* — 162
Cofton Country Holidays *Dawlish* — 137
Compton Farm *Brook* — 159
Conwy Touring Park *Conwy* — 211
Cotswold View Caravan & Camping Site *Charlbury* — 159
Cottage Farm Caravan Park *Buxton* — 108
Craigendmuir Park *Glasgow* — 194
The Croft Caravan And Camp Site *Hawkshead* — 65
Crowhurst Park *Battle* — 177

D — PAGE

Dandy Dinmont Caravan And Camping Site *Carlisle* — 64
Dartmoor View Holiday Park *Okehampton* — 142
Dodwell Park *Stratford-upon-Avon* — 110
Dornafield *Newton Abbot* — 141
Dovecot Caravan Park *Laurencekirk* — 196
Downsview Caravan Park *Henfield* — 178
Drummohr Caravan Park *Edinburgh* — 193
Dulhorn Farm Camping Site *Weston-Super-Mare* — 148

E — PAGE

Eastham Hall Caravan Park *Lytham St Annes* — 87
Edinburgh Caravan Club Site *Edinburgh* — 193
Emberton Country Park *Olney* — 163

F — PAGE

Fairfields Farm Caravan & Camping Park *Eastbourne* — 178
Fallbarrow Park *Windermere* — 68
Fishery Creek Caravan & Camping Park *Hayling Island* — 161
Fishguard Bay Caravan & Camping Park *Fishguard* — 211
Five Roads Caravan Park *Blairgowrie* — 191
Flask Holiday Home Park *Whitby* — 98
Flusco Wood Caravan Park *Penrith* — 66
Forest Camping *Woodbridge* — 123
Forest Glade Holiday Park *Kentisbeare* — 139
Freshwater Beach Holiday Park *Bridport* — 133
Freshwater East Caravan Club Site *Pembroke* — 213

G — PAGE

Galmpton Touring Park *Brixham* — 134
Gart Caravan Park *Callander* — 192
Gate House Wood Touring Park *Wrotham Heath* — 181
Gelder Wood Country Park *Heywood* — 87
Giants Head Caravan & Camping Park *Dorchester* — 137
Glen Orchard Holiday Park *New Milton* — 162
Glororum Caravan Park *Bamburgh* — 76
Golden Coast Holiday Village *Woolacombe* — 149
Golden Square Caravan And Camping Park *Helmsley* — 95
Gowerton Caravan Club Site *Swansea* — 214
The Grange Touring Park *Great Yarmouth* — 120
Grasmere Caravan Park (T.b) *Great Yarmouth* — 120
Great Yarmouth Caravan Club Site *Great Yarmouth* — 120
Greaves Farm Caravan Park *Grange-over-Sands* — 65
Greenacres Holiday Park *Morfa Bychan* — 212
Greenhowe Caravan Park *Ambleside* — 64
Gwaun Vale Touring Park *Fishguard* — 211

H — PAGE

Haggerston Castle *Beal* — 77
Halse Farm Caravan & Tent Park *Winsford* — 149
Hardwick Parks *Standlake* — 165
Harford Bridge Holiday Park *Tavistock* — 147
Harrow Wood Farm Caravan Park *Christchurch* — 159

241

Name	Page
Hartsholme Country Park *Lincoln*	109
Heads of Ayr Caravan Park *Ayr*	191
Hendra Holiday Park *Newquay*	140
Heyford Leys Mobile Home Park & Camping Site *Bicester*	159
Highclere Farm Country Touring Park *Beaconsfield*	158
Higher Well Farm Holiday Park *Paignton*	143
Highfield Farm Touring Park *Cambridge*	120
Highlands End Holiday Park *Bridport*	134
Hill Farm Caravan Park *Romsey*	164
Hoburne Cotswold *South Cerney*	109
Hoburne Naish Estate Ltd *New Milton*	163
Hoburne Torbay *Paignton*	143
Hoddom Castle Caravan Park *Lockerbie*	196
Holiday Resort Unity *Brean*	133
Hollingworth Lake Caravan Park *Littleborough*	87
Holme Valley Camping And Caravan Park *Holmfirth*	95
Honeybridge Park *Horsham*	179
Honeys Green Farm Caravan Park *Uckfield*	181
Hopton Holiday Village *Great Yarmouth*	121
Hunters Moon Holiday Park *Axminster*	132

I	PAGE
Invercoe Caravan & Camping Park *Glencoe*	194
Invermill Farm Caravan Park *Dunkeld*	193
Island Meadow Caravan Park *Aston Cantlow*	107

K	PAGE
Kenneggy Cove Holiday Park *Rosudgeon*	145
Killigarth Caravan Park *Polperro*	144
Kiln Park Holiday Centre *Tenby*	214
Kingfisher Caravan Park *Gosport*	161
Kippford Holiday Park *Kippford*	195
Kloofs Caravan Park *Bexhill-on-Sea*	177
Kneps Farm Holiday Park *Cleveleys*	87

L	PAGE
Ladycross Plantation Caravan Park *Whitby*	98
Lakeland Leisure Park *Flookburgh*	65
Lakeside Caravan Club Site *Dulverton*	137
Lakeside Caravan Park *Llangorse*	212
Lakeside Holiday Park *Keswick*	66
The Laurels Touring Caravan & Camping Park *Padstow*	142
Lebberston Touring Park *Filey*	94
Lee Valley Campsite *Chingford*	57
Liffens Holiday Park *Great Yarmouth*	121
Liffens Welcome Holiday Centre *Great Yarmouth*	121
The Lillies Nursery & Caravan Park *Bognor Regis*	177
Limefitt Park *Windermere*	68
Linnhe Lochside Holidays *Fort William*	194
Linwater Caravan Park *Edinburgh*	193
Lleithyr Meadow Caravan Club Site *St Davids*	213
Loch Lomond Holiday Park *Inveruglas*	195
Lochgilphead Caravan Park *Lochgilphead*	196
Lochranza Golf Caravan And Camping Site *Isle of Arran*	195
Lomond Woods Holiday Park *Balloch*	191
Long Acres Caravan & Camping Park *Lingfield*	179
The Lookout Holiday Park *Wareham*	167
Lowe Caravan Park *Saham Hills*	122
Lower Lacon Caravan Park *Wem*	110
Luck's All Caravan And Camping Park *Mordiford*	109
Lytton Lawn Touring Park *Milford-on-Sea*	162

M	PAGE
Mains Caravan Park *Skelmorlie*	197
Manor Court Farm *Ashurst*	176
Manor Park Caravan Park (Manor Park Ltd) *Castleside*	78
Marton Mere Holiday Village *Blackpool*	86
Mayfield Touring Park *Cirencester*	108
Meadow Bank Holidays *Christchurch*	160
Mendip Heights Camping And Caravan Park *Wells*	148
Merley Court Touring Park *Wimborne Minster*	168
Middlewood Farm Holiday Park *Whitby*	98
Milton of Fonab Caravan Park *Pitlochry*	197
Monkton Wyld Farm Caravan & Camping Park *Charmouth*	136
Monmouth Caravan Park *Monmouth*	212
Mortonhall Caravan Park *Edinburgh*	193

N	PAGE
Nant Newydd Caravan Park *Benllech*	209
Newby Bridge Caravan Park *Newby Bridge*	66
Newhaven Caravan And Camping Park *Buxton*	108
Newperran Tourist Park *Newquay*	140
Newton Hall Caravan Park *Blackpool*	86
Newton Mill Camping *Bath*	132
Norfolk Showground Caravan Club Site *Bawburgh*	119
Northcliffe & Seaview Holiday Parks *Whitby*	98
Nostell Priory Holiday Home Park *Wakefield*	97

O	PAGE
Oakdene Forest Park *St Leonards*	165
The Old Oaks Touring Park *Glastonbury*	138
The Old School Caravan Park *Bishop's Castle*	107
Orchard Caravan Park *Boston*	108
Orchard Farm Holiday Village *Filey*	94
The Orchards Holiday Village *St Osyth*	123
Organford Manor Caravans & Holidays *Poole*	163
Orton Grange Caravan Park *Carlisle*	64
Outney Meadow Caravan Park *Bungay*	120
Oxwich Camping Park *Oxwich*	212

P	PAGE
Pandy Caravan Club Site *Pandy*	213
Parc Caerelwan *Barmouth*	209
Park Cliffe Caravan And Camping Estate *Windermere*	68
Park Grange Holidays *Bridgnorth*	108
Parkers Farm Holiday Park *Ashburton*	131
Pembrey Country Park Caravan Club Site *Llanelli*	211
Pen Y Garth Caravan And Camping Park *Bala*	208
Pendine Sands Holiday Park *Pendine*	213
Penhale Caravan And Camping Park *Fowey*	138
Penhalt Farm Holiday Park *Bude*	134
Pennance Mill Farm *Falmouth*	138
Penstowe Caravan & Camping Park *Bude*	135
Pine Lodge Touring Park *Maidstone*	179
Pipers Height Caravan & Camping Park *Blackpool*	86
Plas-y-bryn Caravan Park *Caernarfon*	210
The Plassey Leisure Park *Wrexham*	214
Polmanter Tourist Park *St Ives*	146
Polruan Holidays (Camping & Caravanning) *Polruan-By-Fowey*	144
Polstead Touring Park *Polstead*	122

R	PAGE
Ramslade Touring Park *Paignton*	143
The Ranch Caravan Park *Evesham*	109
Ratherheath Lane Camping And Caravan Park *Crook*	64
Red Shoot Camping Park *Ringwood*	164
Red Squirrel Camp Site *Glencoe*	194
Reraig Caravan Site *Balmacara*	191
The Rickels Caravan Site *Stanhoe*	123
Riverbank Park *Minster*	180
Riverside Park *Hamble*	161
Roam-n-rest Caravan Park *Greenhead*	78
Robin Hood Caravan & Camping Park *Slingsby*	97
Rockley Park Holiday Park *Poole*	163
Rothiemurchus Camping & Caravan Park *Aviemore*	190
Rowlands Wait Touring Park *Bere Regis*	158
Rudding Holiday Park *Harrogate*	95

S	PAGE
St Helena's Caravan Site *Horsforth*	96
St Leonards Farm *Bournemouth*	159
St Nicholas Camping Site *St Nicholas At Wade*	180
Salcombe Regis Camping And Caravan Park *Sidmouth*	147

Salutation Caravan Park *Berwick-upon-Tweed*	77
Sand-le-mere Caravan & Leisure Park *Roos*	97
Sands of Luce Caravan Park *Sandhead*	197
Sandy Balls Holiday Centre *Fordingbridge*	160
Sandyholme Holiday Park *Owermoigne*	142
Scamford Caravan Park *Keeston*	211
Scratby Hall Caravan Park *Scratby*	123
Sea View International *Mevagissey*	140
Seacote Park *St Bees*	67
Seafield Caravan Park *Seahouses*	78
Seton Sands Holiday Village *Longniddry*	197
Severn Gorge Park *Telford*	110
Shardaroba Caravan Park *Teversal*	110
Shaws Trailer Park *Harrogate*	95
Shear Barn Holiday Park *Hastings*	178
Ship & Anchor Marina *Arundel*	176
Shorefield Country Park *Milford-on-Sea*	162
Silvertrees Caravan Park *Rugeley*	109
Skene Caravan Park *Aberdeen*	190
The Solway Holiday Village *Silloth*	67
Somerset View Caravan Park *Bridgwater*	134
South Meadows Caravan Park *Belford*	77
Southfork Caravan Park *Martock*	139
Springfield Touring Park *Wimborne Minster*	168
Stanwix Park Holiday Centre *Silloth*	67
Stonehaugh Campsite *Stonehaugh*	78
Strathclyde Park Caravan Camping Site *Motherwell*	197
Sun Haven Valley Caravan Park & Camping Park *Mawgan Porth*	139

T	PAGE
Tanner Farm Touring Caravan & Camping Park *Marden*	179
Tantallon Caravan Park *North Berwick*	197
Tehidy Holiday Park *Portreath*	145
Thirlestane Castle Caravan And Camping Site *Lauder*	195
Thornwick & Sea Farm Holiday Centre *Flamborough*	95
Thorpe Park Holiday Centre *Cleethorpes*	94
Thriftwood Caravan & Camping Park *Stansted*	57
Tower Park Caravans And Camping *Penzance*	144
Treborth Hall Farm Caravan Site *Bangor*	208
Treloy Tourist Park *Newquay*	140
Trevalgan Holiday Farm *St Ives*	146
Trevarth Holiday Park *Blackwater*	133
Trevella Caravan And Camping Park *Newquay*	141
Trewethett Farm Caravan Club Site *Tintagel*	147
Trewhiddle Holiday Estate *St Austell*	146
Trossachs Holiday Park *Aberfoyle*	190
Tyn Rhos Camping Site *Trearddur Bay*	214
Tyn Yr Onnen C/c Park *Caernarfon*	210

U	PAGE
Ulwell Cottage Caravan Park *Swanage*	166
Undercliff Glen Caravan Park *St Lawrence*	165
Upper Lynstone Caravan And Camping Site *Bude*	135

V	PAGE
Varne Ridge Holiday Park *Capel Le Ferne*	178
Vauxhall Holiday Park *Great Yarmouth*	121

W	PAGE
Waldegraves Holiday Park *Mersea Island*	122
Wareham Forest Tourist Park *Wareham*	167
Waren Caravan Park *Bamburgh*	76
Warner Farm Touring Park *Selsey*	180
Washington Caravan & Camping Park *Washington*	181
Waterfoot Caravan Park *Ullswater*	67
Waters Edge Caravan Park *Kendal*	65
Wayside Caravan Park *Pickering*	96
Wemyss Bay Holiday Park *Wemyss Bay*	198
West End Farm/caravan & Camping Park *Weston-Super-Mare*	148
White Acres Holiday Park *White Cross*	148
Whitecairn Farm Caravan Park *Glenluce*	195
Whitemead Caravan Park *Wool*	168
Wicks Farm Camping Park *Chichester*	178
Widdicombe Farm Touring Park *Torquay*	147
Windy Harbour Holiday Centre *Blackpool*	86
Winshields Camp Site *Bardon Mill*	76
Witches Craig Caravan Park *Stirling*	198
Wooda Farm Park *Bude*	135
Woodhouse Farm Caravan & Camping Park *Ripon*	96
Woodlands Camping Park *Penmaenmawr*	213
Woodside Caravan Park *Alrewas*	107
Woolacombe Sands Holiday Park *Woolacombe*	149
Woolsbridge Manor Farm Caravan Park *Three Legged Cross*	166
Wyke Down Touring Caravan & Camping Park *Andover*	158

Y	PAGE
Yew Tree Park *Canterbury*	177

Our Countryside Matters!

Country Code

- Always follow the Country code
- Guard against all risk of fire
- Keep your dogs under close control
- Use gates and stiles to cross fences, hedges and walls
- Take your litter home
- Protect wildlife, plants and trees
- Make no unnecessary noise
- Enjoy the countryside and respect its life and work
- Fasten all gates
- Keep to public paths across farmland
- Leave livestock, crops and machinery alone
- Help to keep all water clean
- Take special care on country roads

We hope the countryside will fully open in 2002.
However, given the serious nature of Foot and Mouth Disease please be ready to follow this additional advice and respect any further precautions given in local authority notices:

- Don't go onto farmland if you have handled farm animals in the last 7 days
- Avoid contact with farm animals and keep dogs on a lead where they are present
- If you step in dung, remove it before you leave the field
- Don't go on paths with a local authority 'closed' notice.

For more information contact Tourist information Centres or Countryside Agency web site www.countryside.gov.uk which links to other local authority web sites providing details about rights of way and access opportunities across England.

INDEX TO TOWNS
ANNUAIRE PAR VILLES/STÄDTEVERZEICHNIS/ INDEX VAN STEDEN/INDICE DELLE CITTA

A	PAGE
Aberdeen *Aberdeenshire*	190
Aberfoyle *Central*	190
Alrewas *Staffordshire*	107
Ambleside *Cumbria*	64
Andover *Hampshire*	158
Arundel *West Sussex*	176
Ashburton *Devon*	131
Ashford *Kent*	176
Ashurst *Kent*	176
Aston Cantlow *Warwickshire*	107
Aviemore *Highland*	190
Axminster *Devon*	131
Ayr *Ayrshire*	191

B	PAGE
Bacton-on-Sea *Norfolk*	119
Bala *Gwynedd*	208
Balloch *Strathclyde*	191
Balmacara *Highland*	191
Bamburgh *Northumberland*	76
Bangor *Gwynedd*	208
Banham *Norfolk*	119
Bardon Mill *Northumberland*	76
Barmouth *Gwynedd*	208
Bath *Bath and North East Somerset*	132
Battle *East Sussex*	177
Bawburgh *Norfolk*	119
Beaconsfield *Buckinghamshire*	158
Beadnell *Northumberland*	76
Beal *Northumberland*	77
Belford *Northumberland*	77
Benllech *Isle of Anglesey*	209
Bere Regis *Dorset*	158
Berwick-upon-Tweed *Northumberland*	77
Bexhill-on-Sea *East Sussex*	177
Bicester *Oxfordshire*	159
Bishop's Castle *Shropshire*	107
Blackpool *Lancashire*	86
Blackwater *Cornwall*	133
Blair Atholl *Tayside*	191
Blairgowrie *Tayside*	191
Blue Anchor *Somerset*	133
Bognor Regis *West Sussex*	177
Boston *Lincolnshire*	108
Bournemouth *Dorset*	159
Brean *Somerset*	133
Brecon *Powys*	209
Bridgnorth *Shropshire*	108
Bridgwater *Somerset*	134
Bridport *Dorset*	133
Brixham *Devon*	134
Brook *Isle of Wight*	159
Bude *Cornwall*	134
Bungay *Suffolk*	120
Burnham-on-Sea *Somerset*	135
Buxton *Derbyshire*	108

C	PAGE
Caernarfon *Gwynedd*	209
Callander *Central*	192
Cambridge *Cambridgeshire*	120
Canterbury *Kent*	177
Capel Le Ferne *Kent*	178
Cardigan *Ceredigion*	210
Carlisle *Cumbria*	64
Carlyon Bay *Cornwall*	136
Castleside *Durham*	78
Chard *Somerset*	136
Charlbury *Oxfordshire*	159
Charmouth *Dorset*	136
Cheddar *Somerset*	136
Chichester *West Sussex*	178
Christchurch *Dorset*	159
Cirencester *Gloucestershire*	108
Cleethorpes *North East Lincolnshire*	94
Cleveleys *Lancashire*	87
Conwy *Conwy*	211
Cotswolds *Heart of England* (See under Cirencester See also Cotswolds in South of England region)	
Cotswolds *South of England* (See under Charlbury, Standlake See also Cotswolds in Heart of England region)	
Crook *Cumbria*	64

D	PAGE
Dartmoor (See under Ashburton, Drewsteignton, Okehampton, Tavistock)	
Dawlish *Devon*	137
Dorchester *Dorset*	137
Drewsteignton *Devon*	137
Dulverton *Somerset*	137
Dumfries *Dumfries & Galloway*	192
Dunbar *Lothian*	192
Dundonnell *Highland*	192
Dunkeld *Tayside*	193

E	PAGE
Eastbourne *East Sussex*	178
Edinburgh *Lothian*	193
Evesham *Worcestershire*	109
Exmoor (See under Dulverton, Porlock, Winsford, Parracombe)	

F	PAGE
Falmouth *Cornwall*	138
Filey *North Yorkshire*	94
Fishguard *Pembrokeshire*	211
Flamborough *East Riding of Yorkshire*	95
Fleetwood *Lancashire*	87
Flookburgh *Cumbria*	65
Fordingbridge *Hampshire*	160
Fort William *Highland*	194
Fowey *Cornwall*	138

G	PAGE
Gatwick Airport (See under Horsham)	
Glasgow *Strathclyde*	194
Glastonbury *Somerset*	138
Glencoe *Highland*	194
Glenluce *Dumfries & Galloway*	195
Gosport *Hampshire*	161
Grange-over-Sands *Cumbria*	65
Great Yarmouth *Norfolk*	120
Greenhead *Northumberland*	78

H	PAGE
Hamble *Hampshire*	161
Harrogate *North Yorkshire*	95
Hartlepool *Tees Valley*	78
Hastings *East Sussex*	178
Hawkshead *Cumbria*	65
Hayle *Cornwall*	138
Hayling Island *Hampshire*	161
Helmsley *North Yorkshire*	95
Henfield *West Sussex*	178
Heywood *Greater Manchester*	87
Highcliffe *Dorset*	162
Holmfirth *West Yorkshire*	95
Horsforth *West Yorkshire*	96
Horsham *West Sussex*	179

I	PAGE
Inveruglas *Strathclyde*	195
Isle of Arran	195
Isle of Wight (See under Brook, St Lawrence, Sandown)	

K	PAGE
Keeston *Pembrokeshire*	211
Kendal *Cumbria*	65
Kentisbeare *Devon*	139
Keswick *Cumbria*	66
Kielder Forest (See under Stonehaugh)	
King's Lynn *Norfolk*	122
Kippford *Dumfries & Galloway*	195

L	PAGE
Lands End *Cornwall*	139
Lauder *Borders*	195
Laurencekirk *Grampian*	196
Lincoln *Lincolnshire*	109
Lingfield *Surrey*	179
Linlithgow *Lothian*	196
Littleborough *Greater Manchester*	87
Llanelli *Carmarthenshire*	211

245

Llangadog *Carmarthenshire*	212
Llangorse *Powys*	212
Loch Lomond (See under Balloch)	
Lochgilphead *Strathclyde*	196
Lockerbie *Dumfries & Galloway*	196
London	57
Longniddry *Lothian*	197
Lytham St Annes *Lancashire*	87

M — PAGE

Maidstone *Kent*	179
Malmesbury *Wiltshire*	139
Marden *Kent*	179
Martock *Somerset*	139
Mawgan Porth *Cornwall*	139
Mersea Island *Essex*	122
Mevagissey *Cornwall*	140
Milford-on-Sea *Hampshire*	162
Minster *Kent*	180
Monmouth *Monmouthshire*	212
Mordiford *Herefordshire*	109
Morfa Bychan *Gwynedd*	212
Motherwell *Strathclyde*	197

N — PAGE

New Forest (See under Fordingbridge, Milford-on-Sea, New Milton, Ringwood)	
New Milton *Hampshire*	162
Newby Bridge *Cumbria*	66
Newquay *Cornwall*	140
Newton Abbot *Devon*	141
Norfolk Broads (See under Bungay, Great Yarmouth)	
North Berwick *Lothian*	197

O — PAGE

Okehampton *Devon*	142
Olney *Buckinghamshire*	163
Owermoigne *Dorset*	142
Oxwich *Swansea*	212

P — PAGE

Padstow *Cornwall*	142
Pagham *West Sussex*	180
Paignton *Devon*	143
Pandy *Monmouthshire*	213

Peak District (See under Buxton, Calver)	
Pembroke *Pembrokeshire*	213
Pendine *Carmarthenshire*	213
Penmaenmawr *Conwy*	213
Penrith *Cumbria*	66
Penzance *Cornwall*	144
Pickering *North Yorkshire*	96
Pitlochry *Tayside*	197
Polperro *Cornwall*	144
Polruan-By-Fowey *Cornwall*	144
Polstead *Suffolk*	122
Poole *Dorset*	163
Porlock *Somerset*	145
Portreath *Cornwall*	145

R — PAGE

Richmond *North Yorkshire*	96
Ringwood *Hampshire*	164
Ripon *North Yorkshire*	96
Rochester *Kent*	180
Romsey *Hampshire*	164
Roos *East Riding of Yorkshire*	97
Rosudgeon *Cornwall*	145
Rugeley *Staffordshire*	109

S — PAGE

Saham Hills *Norfolk*	122
St Agnes *Cornwall*	145
St Austell *Cornwall*	146
St Bees *Cumbria*	67
St Davids *Pembrokeshire*	213
St Ives *Cornwall*	146
St Lawrence *Isle of Wight*	165
St Leonards *Dorset*	165
St Nicholas At Wade *Kent*	180
St Osyth *Essex*	123
Salcombe *Devon*	146
Sandhead *Dumfries & Galloway*	197
Sandown *Isle of Wight*	165
Scarborough *North Yorkshire*	97
Scratby *Norfolk*	123
Seahouses *Northumberland*	78
Selsey *West Sussex*	180
Sidmouth *Devon*	147
Silloth *Cumbria*	67
Skelmorlie *Ayrshire*	197
Slingsby *North Yorkshire*	97
South Cerney *Gloucestershire*	109
Standlake *Oxfordshire*	165

Stanhoe *Norfolk*	123
Stansted *Greater London*	57
Stirling *Central*	198
Stonehaugh *Northumberland*	78
Stratford-upon-Avon *Warwickshire*	110
Swanage *Dorset*	166
Swansea *Swansea*	214

T — PAGE

Taunton *Somerset*	147
Tavistock *Devon*	147
Telford *Shropshire*	110
Tenby *Pembrokeshire*	214
Teversal *Nottinghamshire*	110
Three Legged Cross *Dorset*	166
Tintagel *Cornwall*	147
Torquay *Devon*	147
Trearddur Bay *Isle of Anglesey*	214

U — PAGE

Uckfield *East Sussex*	181
Ullswater *Cumbria*	67

W — PAGE

Wakefield *West Yorkshire*	97
Wareham *Dorset*	167
Washington *West Sussex*	181
Wells *Somerset*	148
Wem *Shropshire*	110
Wemyss Bay *Strathclyde*	198
Weston-Super-Mare *North Somerset*	148
Whitby *North Yorkshire*	98
White Cross *Cornwall*	148
Wimborne Minster *Dorset*	168
Windermere *Cumbria*	68
Winsford *Somerset*	149
Woodbridge *Suffolk*	123
Woodhall Spa *Lincolnshire*	111
Wool *Dorset*	168
Woolacombe *Devon*	149
Wrexham	214
Wrotham Heath *Kent*	181
Wye Valley (See under Mordiford)	

Y — PAGE

York *North Yorkshire*	99

246

Index to Advertisers

Beverley Holidays, Paignton	143
Blair Castle Caravan Park, Blair Atholl	191
Bryn Gloch Camping & Caravan Park, Caernarfon	210
Bunn Leisure, Selsey	181
The Camping and Caravnning Club	Inside Front Cover
The Caravan Club	Back Cover
Castlerigg Hall, Keswick	65
Dodwell Park, Stratford-upon-Avon	110
Fishery Creek Caravan & Camping Park, Hayling Island	161
Hardwick Parks, Standlake	165
Haven Leisure	12
Hendra Holiday Park, Newquay	140
Killigarth Holiday Centre, Polperro	144
Lee Valley Park, London	58
Liffens, Great Yarmouth	121
Linnhe Lochside Holidays, Fort William	194
The Lookout Holiday Park, Wareham	167
Newperran Tourist Park, Newquay	141
Parkers Farm Holiday Park, Ashburton	132
Red Shoot Camping Park, Ringwood	164
Sandy Balls Holiday Centre, Fordingbridge	160
Scamford Caravan Park, Keeston	211
Shorefield Holidays, Milford on Sea	10
Somerset View, Bridgwater	134
Trevella Park, Newquay	141
Ulwell Cottage Caravan Park, Swanage	166
Vauxhall Holiday Park, Great Yarmouth	122
Wareham Forest Touring Park, Wareham	167

Britain On-Line

In-depth information about travelling in Britain is now available on BTA's VisitBritain website.

Covering everything from castles to leisure parks and from festivals to road and rail links, the site complements Where to Stay perfectly, giving you up-to-the-minute details to help with your travel plans.

BRITAIN on the internet
www.visitbritain.com

CALENDARS

Calendar 2002

JANUARY	FEBRUARY	MARCH	APRIL
M T W T F S S	M T W T F S S	M T W T F S S	M T W T F S S
1 2 3 4 5 6	1 2 3	1 2 3	1 2 3 4 5 6 7
7 8 9 10 11 12 13	4 5 6 7 8 9 10	4 5 6 7 8 9 10	8 9 10 11 12 13 14
14 15 16 17 18 19 20	11 12 13 14 15 16 17	11 12 13 14 15 16 17	15 16 17 18 19 20 21
21 22 23 24 25 26 27	18 19 20 21 22 23 24	18 19 20 21 22 23 24	22 23 24 25 26 27 28
28 29 30 31	25 26 27 28	25 26 27 28 29 30 31	29 30

MAY	JUNE	JULY	AUGUST
M T W T F S S	M T W T F S S	M T W T F S S	M T W T F S S
1 2 3 4 5	1 2	1 2 3 4 5 6 7	1 2 3 4
6 7 8 9 10 11 12	3 4 5 6 7 8 9	8 9 10 11 12 13 14	5 6 7 8 9 10 11
13 14 15 16 17 18 19	10 11 12 13 14 15 16	15 16 17 18 19 20 21	12 13 14 15 16 17 18
20 21 22 23 24 25 26	17 18 19 20 21 22 23	22 23 24 25 26 27 28	19 20 21 22 23 24 25
27 28 29 30 31	24 25 26 27 28 29 30	29 30 31	26 27 28 29 30 31

SEPTEMBER	OCTOBER	NOVEMBER	DECEMBER
M T W T F S S	M T W T F S S	M T W T F S S	M T W T F S S
30 1	1 2 3 4 5 6	1 2 3	30 31 1
2 3 4 5 6 7 8	7 8 9 10 11 12 13	4 5 6 7 8 9 10	2 3 4 5 6 7 8
9 10 11 12 13 14 15	14 15 16 17 18 19 20	11 12 13 14 15 16 17	9 10 11 12 13 14 15
16 17 18 19 20 21 22	21 22 23 24 25 26 27	18 19 20 21 22 23 24	16 17 18 19 20 21 22
23 24 25 26 27 28 29	28 29 30 31	25 26 27 28 29 30	23 24 25 26 27 28 29

Calendar 2003

JANUARY	FEBRUARY	MARCH	APRIL
M T W T F S S	M T W T F S S	M T W T F S S	M T W T F S S
1 2 3 4 5	1 2	1 2	1 2 3 4 5 6
6 7 8 9 10 11 12	3 4 5 6 7 8 9	3 4 5 6 7 8 9	7 8 9 10 11 12 13
13 14 15 16 17 18 19	10 11 12 13 14 15 16	10 11 12 13 14 15 16	14 15 16 17 18 19 20
20 21 22 23 24 25 26	17 18 19 20 21 22 23	17 18 19 20 21 22 23	21 22 23 24 25 26 27
27 28 29 30 31	24 25 26 27 28	24 25 26 27 28 29 30 31	28 29 30

MAY	JUNE	JULY	AUGUST
M T W T F S S	M T W T F S S	M T W T F S S	M T W T F S S
1 2 3 4	1	1 2 3 4 5 6	1 2 3
5 6 7 8 9 10 11	2 3 4 5 6 7 8	7 8 9 10 11 12 13	4 5 6 7 8 9 10
12 13 14 15 16 17 18	9 10 11 12 13 14 15	14 15 16 17 18 19 20	11 12 13 14 15 16 17
19 20 21 22 23 24 25	16 17 18 19 20 21 22	21 22 23 24 25 26 27	18 19 20 21 22 23 24
26 27 28 29 30 31	23 24 25 26 27 28 29 30	28 29 30 31	25 26 27 28 29 30 31

SEPTEMBER	OCTOBER	NOVEMBER	DECEMBER
M T W T F S S	M T W T F S S	M T W T F S S	M T W T F S S
1 2 3 4 5 6 7	1 2 3 4 5	1 2	1 2 3 4 5 6 7
8 9 10 11 12 13 14	6 7 8 9 10 11 12	3 4 5 6 7 8 9	8 9 10 11 12 13 14
15 16 17 18 19 20 21	13 14 15 16 17 18 19	10 11 12 13 14 15 16	15 16 17 18 19 20 21
22 23 24 25 26 27 28	20 21 22 23 24 25 26	17 18 19 20 21 22 23	22 23 24 25 26 27 28
29 30	27 28 29 30 31	24 25 26 27 28 29 30	29 30 31

Notes

Ratings you can trust

When you're looking for a place to stay, you need a rating system you can trust. The British Graded Holiday Parks Scheme, operated jointly by the national tourist boards for England, Scotland and Wales, gives you a clear guide of what to expect.

Based on the internationally recognised rating of One to Five Stars, the system puts great emphasis on quality and reflects customer expectations.

Parks are visited annually by trained, impartial assessors who award a rating based on cleanliness, environment and the quality of services and facilities provided.

STAR QUALITY

★★★★★	Exceptional Quality
★★★★	Excellent Quality
★★★	Very Good Quality
★★	Good Quality
★	Acceptable Quality

British Graded Holiday Parks Scheme

Quality ★

Assessed Parks

On the following pages you will find brief contact details for each park, together with its Star rating and type of site. The listing also shows if an establishment has a National Accessible rating (see the front of the guide for further information).

More detailed information on all the places shown in blue can be found in the regional sections (where establishments have paid to have their details included). To find these entries please refer to the appropriate regional section, or look in the town index at the back of this guide.

The list which follows was compiled slightly later than the regional sections. For this reason you may find that, in a few instances, a Star rating may differ between the two sections. This list contains the most up-to-date information and was correct at the time of going to press. Please note that it does not include parks in Scotland and Wales.

LONDON

LONDON

INNER LONDON
E4
Lee Valley Campsite ★★★★
Touring and Camping Park
Sewardstone Road, Chingford,
London E4 7RA
T: (020) 8529 5689
F: (020) 8559 4070
E: scs@leevalleypark.org.uk
I: www.leevalleypark.org.uk

N9
Lee Valley Leisure Centre ★★★★
Touring and Camping Park
Meridian Way, London N9 OAS
T: (020) 8345 6666 & 8803 6900
F: (020) 8884 4975
E: leisurecentre@leevalleypark.org.uk
I: www.leevalleypark.org.uk

SE19
Crystal Palace C C Site ★★★★★
Touring and Camping Park
Crystal Palace Parade, London SE19 1UF
T: (020) 8778 7155
F: (020) 8676 0980

OUTER LONDON
Loughton
Debden House Camp Site ★★
Touring and Camping Park
Debden Green, Loughton, Essex IG10 2PA
T: (020) 8508 3008 & 85083008
F: (020) 8508 0284

The Elms Caravan and Camping Park ★★★
Touring and Camping Park
Lippitts Hill, High Beech, Loughton, Essex IG10 4AW
T: (020) 8508 3749 & 8508 1000
F: (020) 8502 0016
E: elmscar@aol.com
I: members.aol.com/elmscar

STANSTED
Thriftwood Caravan & Camping Park ★★★★★
Holiday, Touring and Camping Park
Rose Award
Plaxdale Green Road, Stansted, Kent TN15 7PB
T: (01732) 822261
F: (01732) 824636
I: www.ukparks.co.uk/thriftwood

CUMBRIA

ALLONBY
Cumbria
Manor House Caravan Park ★★
Holiday, Touring and Camping Park
Edderside Road, Allonby, Maryport, Cumbria CA15 6RA
T: (01900) 881236
F: (01900) 881199
E: holidays@manorhousepark.co.uk
I: www.manorhousepark.co.uk

Spring Lea Caravan Park ★★★
Holiday, Touring and Camping Park
Allonby, Maryport, Cumbria CA15 6QF
T: (01900) 881331
F: (01900) 881209
E: mail@springlea.co.uk
I: www.springlea.co.uk

AMBLESIDE
Cumbria
Greenhowe Caravan Park ★★★
Holiday Park
Great Langdale, Ambleside, Cumbria LA22 9JU
T: (015394) 37231
F: (015394) 37464

Skelwith Fold Caravan Park ★★★★★
Holiday and Touring Park
Skelwith Fold, Ambleside, Cumbria LA22 0HX
T: (015394) 32277
F: (015394) 34144
E: info@skelwith.com
I: www.skelwith.com

APPLEBY-IN-WESTMORLAND
Cumbria
Wild Rose Park ★★★★★
Holiday, Touring and Camping Park
Ormside, Appleby-in-Westmorland, Cumbria CA16 6EJ
T: (017683) 51077
F: (017683) 52551
E: hs@wildrose.co.uk
I: www.wildrose.co.uk

BASSENTHWAITE
Cumbria
Bassenthwaite Lakeside Lodges ★★★★★
Holiday Park
Scarness, Bassenthwaite, Keswick, Cumbria CA12 4QZ
T: (017687) 76641
F: (017687) 76919
E: enquiries@bll.ac
I: www.bll.ac

BEETHAM
Cumbria
Beetham Caravan Park ★★★★★
Holiday Park
Beetham, Milnthorpe, Cumbria LA7 7AL
T: (015395) 62552

BOUTH
Cumbria
Black Beck Caravan Park ★★★★★
Holiday, Touring and Camping Park
Bouth, Ulverston, Cumbria LA12 8JN
T: (01229) 861274
F: (01229) 861041
E: ribble@netcomuk.co.uk

BRAMPTON
Cumbria
Cairndale Caravan Park ★★★
Holiday and Touring Park
Cumwhitton, Headsnook, Brampton, Carlisle, Cumbria CA8 9BZ
T: (01768) 896280

BRAYSTONES
Cumbria
Tarnside Caravan Park ★★★
Holiday and Touring Park
Braystones, Beckermet, Cumbria CA21 2YL
T: (01946) 841308
E: ann@hotmail.com
I: www.ukparks.co.uk/tarnside

CARLISLE
Cumbria
Dalston Hall Caravan Park ★★★★
Holiday, Touring and Camping Park
Dalston Hall, Dalston, Carlisle CA5 7JX
T: (01228) 710165

Dandy Dinmont Caravan and Camping Site ★★★★
Touring and Camping Park
Blackford, Carlisle CA6 4EA
T: (01228) 674611

Orton Grange Caravan Park ★★★★
Holiday, Touring and Camping Park
Wigton Road, Carlisle, CA5 6LA
T: (01228) 710252
F: (01228) 710252
E: chris@ortongrange.flyer.co.uk

COCKERMOUTH
Cumbria
Violet Bank Holiday Home Park Ltd ★★★
Holiday, Touring and Camping Park
Simoncales Lane, Cockermouth, Cumbria CA13 9TG
T: (01900) 822169

CONISTON
Cumbria
Crake Valley Holiday Park ★★★★★
Holiday Park
Rose Award
Water Yeat, Blawith, Ulverston, Cumbria LA12 8DL
T: (01229) 885203
F: (01229) 885203
I: www.ukparks.co.uk/crake

Park Coppice Caravan Club Site ★★★★★
Touring Park
Coniston, Cumbria LA21 8AU
T: (01539) 441555
I: www.caravanclub.co.uk

CROOK
Cumbria
Ratherheath Lane Camping and Caravan Park ★★★★
Holiday, Touring and Camping Park
Chain House, Bonningate, Kendal, Cumbria LA8 8JU
T: (01539) 821154 & 0797 163 0226
E: ratherheath@lakedistrictcaravans.co.uk
I: www.lakedistrictcaravans.co.uk

CROOKLANDS
Cumbria
Millness Hill Park ★★★★
Holiday, Touring and Camping Park
Crooklands, Milnthorpe, Cumbria LA7 7NU
T: (015395) 67306
F: (015395) 67306
E: holidays@millness.demon.co.uk

ENDMOOR
Cumbria
Gatebeck Park ★★★★★
Holiday and Touring Park
Endmoor, Kendal, Cumbria LA8 0HL
T: (015395) 67875
F: (015395) 67875

ESKDALE
Cumbria
Fisherground Farm Campsite ★★
Camping Park
Fisherground, Eskdale, Holmrook, Cumbria CA19 1TF
T: (019467) 23319
E: holidays@fisherground.co.uk
I: www.fishergroundcamping.co.uk

CUMBRIA

FLOOKBURGH
Cumbria

Lakeland Leisure Park ★★★★
Holiday and Touring Park
Moor Lane, Flookburgh, Grange-over-Sands, Cumbria LA11 7LT
T: (01539) 558556
F: (01539) 558559
E: enquiries@british-holidays.co.uk
I: www.british-holidays.co.uk

GRANGE-OVER-SANDS
Cumbria

Greaves Farm Caravan Park ★★★★
Holiday and Touring Park
Field Broughton, Grange-over-Sands, Cumbria LA11 6HR
T: (015395) 36329 & 36587

Meathop Fell Caravan Club Site ★★★★★★
Touring Park
Grange-over-Sands, Cumbria LA11 6RB
T: (01539) 532912
I: www.caravanclub.co.uk

Old Park Wood Caravan Park ★★★★
Holiday and Touring Park
Holker, Grange-over-Sands, Cumbria LA11 7PP
T: (015395) 58101
F: (015395) 58039
E: pobatopw@aol.com
I: www.holker-estate-parks.co.uk

HAWKSHEAD
Cumbria

The Croft Caravan and Camp Site ★★★
Touring and Camping Park
North Lonsdale Road, Hawkshead, Ambleside, Cumbria LA22 0NX
T: (015394) 36374
F: (015394) 36544
E: enquiries@hawkshead-croft.com
I: www.hawkshead-croft.com

Grizedale Hall Caravan Site ★★★
Camping Park
Grizedale Hall, Hawkshead, Ambleside, Cumbria LA22 0GL
T: (01229) 860257

KENDAL
Cumbria

Camping and Caravanning Club Site Kendal ★★★★
Touring Park
Millcrest, Shap Road, Kendal, Cumbria LA9 6NY
T: (01539) 741363
I: www.campingandcaravanning.co.uk

Waters Edge Caravan Park ★★★★
Touring and Camping Park
Crooklands, Kendal, Cumbria LA7 7NN
T: (015395) 67708 & 67725
F: (015395) 67610
E: cromoco@aol.com

KESWICK
Cumbria

The Camping and Caravanning Club Site, Derwentwater ★★★★
Holiday and Touring Park
Crowe Park Road, Keswick, Cumbria CA12 5EN
T: (017687) 72579
I: www.campingandcaravanningclub.co.uk

Castlerigg Farm Camp Site ★★★
Touring and Camping Park
Keswick, Cumbria CA12 4TE
T: (017687) 72479 & 74718
F: (017687) 74718
E: info@castleriggfarm.freeserve.co.uk
I: www.kesnet.co.uk/castlerigg.htm

Castlerigg Hall Caravan and Camping Park ★★★★
Holiday, Touring and Camping Park
Castlerigg Hall, Keswick, Cumbria CA12 4TE
T: (017687) 72437
F: (017687) 72437
I: www.castlerigg.co.uk

Keswick Camping and Caravanning Club Site ★★★★
Touring Park
Derwentwater, Keswick, Cumbria CA12 5EP
T: (01768) 772392
I: www.campingandcaravanningclub.co.uk

Lakeside Holiday Park ★★★★
Holiday and Touring Park
Norman Garner Ltd, Crow Park Road, Keswick, Cumbria CA12 5EW
T: (017687) 72878
F: (017687) 72017
E: welcome@lakesideholidaypark.co.uk
I: www.lakesideholidaypark.co.uk

Low Briery Holiday Village ★★★★
Holiday Park
Penrith Road, Keswick, Cumbria CA12 4RN
T: (017687) 72044
I: www.keswick.uk.com

Scotgate Holiday Park ★★★★
Holiday, Touring and Camping Park
Braithwaite, Keswick, Cumbria CA12 5TF
T: (017687) 78343
F: (017687) 78099
I: www.scotgateholidaypark.co.uk

KIRKBY LONSDALE
Cumbria

Woodclose Caravan Park
Rating Applied For
Kirkby Lonsdale, Carnforth, Lancashire LA6 2SE
T: (015242) 71597
F: (015242) 72301
E: michaelhodgkins@woodclosecaravanpark.fsnet.co.uk
I: www.woodclosepark.com

KIRKBY STEPHEN
Cumbria

Pennine View Caravan Park ★★★★★
Touring and Camping Park
Station Road, Kirkby Stephen, Cumbria CA17 4SZ
T: (017683) 71717

LAMPLUGH
Cumbria

Inglenook Caravan Park ★★★★
Holiday, Touring and Camping Park
Lamplugh, Workington, Cumbria CA14 4SH
T: (01946) 861240
F: (01946) 861240
E: mesicp@fsbdial.co.uk
I: www.inglenookcaravanpark.co.uk

LOUGHRIGG
Cumbria

Neaum Crag ★★★★★
Holiday Park
Loughrigg, Ambleside, Cumbria LA22 9HG
T: (015394) 33221
F: (015394) 33735
I: www.neaumcrag.co.uk

MILNTHORPE
Cumbria

Fell End Caravan Park ★★★★★
Holiday, Touring and Camping Park
Slack Head Road, Hale, Milnthorpe, Cumbria LA7 7BS
T: (015395) 62122
F: (015395) 63810

NEW HUTTON
Cumbria

The Ashes Exclusively Adult Caravan Park ★★★★
Touring Park
New Hutton, Kendal, Cumbria LA8 0AS
T: (01539) 731833 & 07974 058296
F: (01539) 731833
E: ashes-new-hutton@cwcom.net
I: www.ashes-new-hutton.cwc.net

NEWBY BRIDGE
Cumbria

Newby Bridge Caravan Park ★★★★★
Holiday Park
Canny Hill, Newby Bridge, Ulverston, Cumbria LA12 8NF
T: (015395) 31030
F: (015395) 30105
E: newbybridge@hopps.freeserve.co.uk
I: www.cumbriancaravans.co.uk

ORTON
Cumbria

Tebay Caravan Site ★★★★
Holiday and Touring Park
Orton, Penrith, Cumbria CA10 3SB
T: (015396) 24511 & (015397) 11224
F: (015396) 24511
E: julie@rheged.com

PENRITH
Cumbria

Flusco Wood Caravan Park ★★★★
Touring Park
Flusco, Penrith, Cumbria CA11 0JB
T: (01768) 480020
I: www.fluscowood.co.uk

Lowther Holiday Park ★★★★
Holiday, Touring and Camping Park
Eamont Bridge, Penrith, Cumbria CA10 2JB
T: (01768) 863631
F: (01768) 868126
E: holiday.park@lowther.co.uk
I: www.lowther.co.uk

Melmerby Caravan Park ★★★★
Holiday and Touring Park
Melmerby, Penrith, Cumbria CA10 1HE
T: (01768) 881311
F: (01768) 881311

POOLEY BRIDGE
Cumbria

Waterside House Campsite ★★★★
Camping Park
Waterside House, Howtown Road, Pooley Bridge, Penrith, Cumbria CA10 2NA
T: (017684) 86332
F: (017684) 86332
E: emquire@watersidefarm-campsite.co.uk
I: www.watersidefarm-campsite.co.uk

ST BEES
Cumbria

Seacote Park ★★★
Holiday, Touring and Camping Park
The Beach, St Bees, Cumbria CA27 0ES
T: (01946) 822777
F: (01946) 824442
E: reception@seacote.com

SEDGWICK
Cumbria

Low Park Wood Caravan Club Site ★★★★
Touring Park
Sedgwick, Kendal, Cumbria LA8 0JZ
T: (01539) 560186
I: www.caravanclub.co.uk

SILECROFT
Cumbria

Silecroft Caravan and Camping Park ★★★
Holiday, Touring and Camping Park
Silecroft, Millom, Cumbria LA18 4NX
T: (01229) 772659
F: (01229) 772659
E: silecroftpark@aol.com
I: www.caravanholidayhomes.com

SILLOTH
Cumbria

Seacote Caravan Park ★★★★
Holiday and Touring Park
Skinburness Road, Silloth, Carlisle, Cumbria CA1 4QJ
T: (016973) 31031
F: (016973) 31121

Establishments printed in blue have a detailed entry in this guide

253

CUMBRIA

The Solway Holiday Village ★★
Holiday, Touring and Camping Park
Skinburness Drive, Silloth,
Carlisle CA7 4QQ
T: (016973) 31236
F: (016973) 32553

Stanwix Park Holiday Centre ★★★★★
Holiday, Touring and Camping Park
Greenrow, West Silloth, Silloth,
Carlisle, Cumbria CA7 4HH
T: (016973) 32666
F: (016973) 32555
E: stanwix.park@btinternet.com
I: www.stanwix.com

Tanglewood Caravan Park ★★★
Holiday, Touring and Camping Park
Causewayhead, Silloth, Carlisle
CA7 4PE
T: (016973) 31253

STAVELEY
Cumbria

Ashes Lane Caravan and Camping Park ★★★★
Touring and Camping Park
Ashes Lane, Staveley, Kendal,
Cumbria LA8 9JS
T: (01539) 821119
F: (01539) 821282
I: www.asheslane.com

TROUTBECK
Cumbria

Troutbeck Head Caravan Club Site ★★★★★
Touring Park
Troutbeck Head, Troutbeck,
Penrith, Cumbria CA11 0SS
T: (01768) 483521
F: (01768) 483839
I: www.caravanclub.co.uk

ULLSWATER
Cumbria

The Quiet Camping Site ★★★★★
Holiday, Touring and Camping Park
Ullswater, Penrith, Cumbria
CA11 0LS
T: (017684) 86337
F: (017684) 86610

Waterfoot Caravan Park ★★★★★
Holiday and Touring Park
Pooley Bridge, Penrith, Cumbria
CA11 0JF
T: (017684) 86302
F: (01784) 86728
E: lde@netcomuk.co.uk
I: www.ukparks.co.uk/waterfoot

ULVERSTON
Cumbria

Brook Hollow Caravan Park ★★★★★
Holiday Park
Alpine Road, Newland Bottom,
Ulverston, Cumbria LA12 7QD
T: (01229) 582582

WATERMILLOCK
Cumbria

Cove Caravan and Camping Park ★★★★★
Holiday, Touring and Camping Park
Ullswater, Penrith, Cumbria
CA11 0LS
T: (017684) 86549

WINDERMERE
Cumbria

Fallbarrow Park ★★★★★
Holiday and Touring Park
Rayrigg Road, Windermere,
Cumbria LA23 3DL
T: (015394) 44422
F: (015394) 88736
I: www.fallbarrow.co.uk

Hill of Oaks and Blakeholme Caravan Estate ★★★★★
Holiday and Touring Park
Tower Wood, Windermere,
Cumbria LA23 3PJ
T: (015395) 31578
F: (015395) 30431
E: lde@netcomuk.co.uk
I: www.ukparks.co.uk/hillofoaks

Limefitt Park ★★★★★
Holiday, Touring and Camping Park
Windermere, Cumbria LA23 1PA
T: (015394) 32300
I: www.limefitt.co.uk

Park Cliffe Caravan and Camping Estate ★★★★★
Holiday, Touring and Camping Park
Birks Road, Windermere,
Cumbria LA23 3PG
T: (015395) 31344
F: (015395) 31971
E: info@parkcliffe.co.uk
I: www.parkcliffe.co.uk

White Cross Bay Holiday Park and Marina ★★★★★
Holiday and Touring Park
Ambleside Road, Troutbeck
Bridge, Windermere, Cumbria
LA23 1LF
T: (015394) 43937
F: (015394) 88704
E: wxb@windermere.uk.com
I: www.windermere.uk.com

NORTHUMBRIA

ASHINGTON
Northumberland

Wansbeck Riverside Park ★★★
Holiday, Touring and Camping Park
Green Lane, Ashington,
Northumberland NE63 8TX
T: (01670) 812323
F: (01670) 812323

BAMBURGH
Northumberland

Bradford Kaims Caravan Park ★★
Holiday, Touring and Camping Park
Bamburgh, Northumberland
NE70 7JT
T: (01668) 213432 & 213595
F: (01668) 213891

Glororum Caravan Park ★★★
Holiday, Touring and Camping Park
Glororum, Bamburgh,
Northumberland NE69 7AW
T: (01668) 214457 & 214205
F: (01668) 214622
E: info@glororum-caravanpark.co.uk
I: www.glororum-caravanpark.co.uk

Waren Caravan Park ★★★★
Holiday, Touring and Camping Park
Waren Mill, Bamburgh,
Northumberland NE70 7EE
T: (01668) 214366
F: (01668) 214224
E: waren@meadowhead.com
I: www.meadowhead.co.uk/waren

BARDON MILL
Northumberland

Winshields Camp Site ★★
Camping Park
Winshields, Bardon Mill,
Hexham, Northumberland
NE47 7AN
T: (01434) 344243

BARRASFORD PARK
Northumberland

Barrasford Park Caravan and Camping Site ★★★
Holiday, Touring and Camping Park
1 Front Drive, Barrasford Park,
Hexham, Northumberland
NE48 4BE
T: (01434) 681210

BEADNELL
Northumberland

Beadnell Links Caravan Park ★★★★
Holiday, Touring and Camping Park
Beadnell Harbour, Beadnell,
Northumberland NE67 5BN
T: (01665) 720526 &
07890 692533
E: b.links@talk21.com
I: www.caravanningnorthumberland.com

The Camping And Carravanning Site Beadnell ★★★
Touring and Camping Park
Beadnell, Chathill,
Northumberland NE67 5BX
T: (01665) 720586
I: www.campingandcaravanningclub.co.uk

BEAL
Northumberland

Haggerston Castle ★★★★
Holiday, Touring and Camping Park
Beal, Berwick-upon-Tweed,
Northumberland TD15 2PA
T: (01289) 381333 & 381481
F: (01289) 381337
E: enquiries@british-holidays.co.uk
I: www.british-holidays.co.uk

BEAMISH
Durham

Bobby Shafto Caravan Park ★★★
Holiday, Touring and Camping Park
Beamish, Stanley, County
Durham DH9 0RY
T: (0191) 370 1776
F: (0191) 370 1776

BELFORD
Northumberland

South Meadows Caravan Park ★★★★★
Touring and Camping Park
South Meadows, Belford,
Northumberland NE70 7DP
T: (01668) 213326
F: (01668) 213790
E: G.McL@btinternet.com
I: www.southmeadows.co.uk

BELLINGHAM
Northumberland

Brown Rigg Caravan & Camping Park ★★★★
Touring and Camping Park
Bellingham, Hexham,
Northumberland NE48 2JY
T: (01434) 220175
F: (01434) 220175
I: www.nothumberlandcaravanpark.com

BERWICK-UPON-TWEED
Northumberland

Beachcomber Campsite ★★★
Touring and Camping Park
Goswick, Berwick-upon-Tweed,
Northumberland TD15 2RW
T: (01289) 381217 &
07773 726634

NORTHUMBRIA

Berwick Holiday Centre ★★★★
Holiday Park
Magdalene Fields, Berwick-upon-Tweed, Northumberland TD15 1NE
T: (01289) 307113
F: (01289) 306276
E: enquiries@british-holidays.co.uk
I: www.british-holidays.co.uk

Marshall Meadows Farm ★★★
Holiday, Touring and Camping Park
Berwick-upon-Tweed, Northumberland TD15 1UT
T: (01289) 307375

Ord House Country Park ★★★★★
Holiday, Touring and Camping Park
Rose Award
East Ord, Berwick-upon-Tweed, Northumberland TD15 2NS
T: (01289) 305288
F: (01289) 330832
E: enquiries@ordhouse.co.uk
I: www.ordhouse.co.uk

Salutation Caravan Park ★★
Touring and Camping Park
Salutation Inn, Shoreswood (A698), Berwick-upon-Tweed, Northumberland TD15 2NL
T: (01289) 382291

BIRLING
Northumberland

Rose Cottage Camp Site ★★★
Touring and Camping Park
Rose Cottage, Birling, Morpeth, Northumberland NE65 0XS
T: (01665) 711459

CASTLESIDE
Durham

Manor Park Caravan Park (Manor Park Ltd) ★★★★
Holiday, Touring and Camping Park
Broadmeadows, Rippon Burn, Castleside, Consett, County Durham DH8 9HD
T: (01207) 501000
F: (01207) 509271

COTHERSTONE
Durham

Doe Park Caravan Site ★★★★
Touring and Camping Park
Doe Park, Cotherstone, Barnard Castle, County Durham DL12 9UQ
T: (01833) 650302 &
07710 069682
F: (01833) 650302

CRASTER
Northumberland

Proctors Stead Caravan Site ★★★
Holiday, Touring and Camping Park
Proctors Stead, Craster, Alnwick, Northumberland NE66 3TF
T: (01665) 576613
F: (01665) 576311

CRESSWELL
Northumberland

Cresswell Towers Holiday Park ★★★
Holiday, Touring and Camping Park
Cresswell, Morpeth, Northumberland NE61 5JT
T: (01670) 860411
F: (01670) 860226
I: www.leisuregb.co.uk

Golden Sands Holiday Park ★★★★
Holiday Park
Beach Road, Cresswell, Morpeth, Northumberland NE61 5LF
T: (01670) 860256
F: (01670) 860256

DUNSTAN
Northumberland

Club Dunstan Hill ★★★★
Touring and Camping Park
Camping & Caravanning Club Site, Dunstan, Alnwick, Northumberland NE66 3TQ
T: (01665) 576310
I: www.campingandcaravanningclub.co.uk

DURHAM
Durham

Finchale Abbey Caravan Park ★★★
Holiday, Touring and Camping Park
Finchale Abbey Farm, Finchale Abbey, Durham, County Durham DH1 5SH
T: (0191) 386 6528 &
(01388) 720271
F: (0191) 386 8593
E: godricwatson@hotmail.com
I: www.finchaleabbey.co.uk

Grange Caravan Club Site ★★★★
Touring and Camping Park
Meadow Lane, Durham, DH1 1TL
T: (0191) 384 4778
F: (0191) 383 9161

EBCHESTER
Durham

Byreside Caravan Site ★★★★
Touring and Camping Park
Hamsterley, Ebchester, Newcastle upon Tyne NE17 7RT
T: (01207) 560280

FALSTONE
Northumberland

Kielder Water Caravan Club Site ★★★★
Touring and Camping Park
Leaplish Waterside Park, Falstone, Hexham, Northumberland NE48 1AX
T: (01434) 250278
I: www.caravanclub.co.uk

GREENHEAD
Northumberland

Roam-n-Rest Caravan Park ★★★
Touring and Camping Park
Raylton House, Greenhead, Northumberland CA8 7HA
T: (016977) 47213

HALTWHISTLE
Northumberland

Camping & Caravanning Club Site Haltwhistle ★★★★
Touring and Camping Park
Burnfoot Park Village, Haltwhistle, Northumberland NE49 0JP
T: (01434) 320106
I: www.campingandcaravanningclub.co.uk

HARTLEPOOL
Tees Valley

Ash Vale Homes & Holiday Park ★★
Holiday and Touring Park
Easington Road, Hartlepool, Cleveland TS24 9RF
T: (01429) 862111
E: ashvale@compuserve.com
I: www.ashvalepark.demon.co.uk

HAYDON BRIDGE
Northumberland

Poplars Riverside Caravan Park ★★★★
Holiday, Touring and Camping Park
East Lands Ends, Haydon Bridge, Hexham, Northumberland NE47 6BY
T: (01434) 684427

HEXHAM
Northumberland

Causey Hill Caravan Park ★★★
Holiday, Touring and Camping Park
Causey Hill, Hexham, Northumberland NE46 2JN
T: (01434) 604647

Fallowfield Dene Caravan and Camping Park ★★★★
Touring and Camping Park
Acomb, Hexham, Northumberland NE46 4RP
T: (01434) 603553

Hexham Racecourse Caravan Site ★★★
Touring and Camping Park
High Yarridge, Hexham, Northumberland NE46 2JP
T: (01434) 606847
F: (01434) 605814
E: hexrace@aol.com
I: www.hexham-racecourse.co.uk

Riverside Leisure ★★★★★
Holiday, Touring and Camping Park
Tyne Green, Hexham, Northumberland NE46 3RY
T: (01434) 604705
F: (01434) 606217
E: riverleis@aol.com

KIELDER
Northumberland

Forestry Commission - Kielder Caravan and Camping Site ★★★
Touring and Camping Park
Kielder, Hexham, Northumberland NE48 1EP
T: (01434) 250291 & (0131) 314 6505
E: fe.holidays@forestry.gov.uk
I: www.forestholidays.co.uk

LARTINGTON
Durham

Barnard Castle Camping and Caravanning Club ★★★★
Touring and Camping Park
Dockenflatts Lane, Lartington, Barnard Castle, County Durham DL12 9DG
T: (01833) 630228
I: www.campingandcaravanningclub.co.uk

Pecknell Farm ★★★★
Touring and Camping Park
Lartington, Barnard Castle, County Durham DL12 9DF
T: (01833) 638357

LONGHORSLEY
Northumberland

Forget-me-not Caravan Park ★★★
Holiday, Touring and Camping Park
Longhorsley, Morpeth, Northumberland NE65 8QY
T: (01670) 788364
F: (01670) 788715
E: info@forget-me-notcaravanpark.co.uk
I: www.forget-me-notcaravanpark.co.uk

LOWICK
Northumberland

Barmoor South Moor ★★★★
Holiday Park
Lowick, Berwick-upon-Tweed, Northumberland TD15 2QF
T: (01289) 388205
E: barrgold@farming.co.uk

MELKRIDGE
Northumberland

Hadrian's Wall Caravan and Camping Site ★★
Touring and Camping Park
Melkridge, Haltwhistle, Northumberland NE49 9PG
T: (01434) 320495 & 0777 593 3881

NEWTON
Northumberland

Well House Farm ★★★
Touring and Camping Park
Newton, Stocksfield, Northumberland NE43 7UY
T: (01661) 842193

NEWTON-BY-THE-SEA
Northumberland

Newton Hall Caravan Park ★★★★
Holiday, Touring and Camping Park
Newton Hall, Newton-by-the-Sea, Alnwick, Northumberland NE66 3DZ
T: (01665) 576239 & (01655) 576900
F: (01665) 576900
E: ianpatterson@newtonhall.prestel.co.uk
I: www.commercepark.co.uk/newtonhall

NORTHUMBRIA

NORTH SEATON
Northumberland
Sandy Bay Holiday Park ★★★
Holiday and Touring Park
North Seaton, Ashington, Northumberland NE63 9YD
T: (01670) 815055
F: (01670) 812705
E: Sandybay@gbholidayparks.co.uk
I: www.gbholidayparks.co.uk

OTTERBURN
Northumberland
Border Forest Caravan Park ★★★★
Holiday, Touring and Camping Park
Cottonshopeburnfoot, Otterburn, Newcastle upon Tyne, Northumberland NE19 1TF
T: (01830) 520259

OVINGHAM
Northumberland
The High Hermitage Caravan Park ★★★
Holiday and Touring Park
The Hermitage, Ovingham, Prudhoe, Northumberland NE42 6HH
T: (01661) 832250
F: (01661) 834848

ROTHBURY
Northumberland
Coquetdale Caravan Park ★★★
Holiday, Touring and Camping Park
Whitton, Rothbury, Morpeth, Northumberland NE65 7RU
T: (01669) 620549
F: (01669) 620088
E: enquiry@coquetdalecaravanpark.co.uk
I: www.coquetdalecaravanpark.co.uk

SEAHOUSES
Northumberland
Seafield Caravan Park ★★★★
Holiday, Touring and Camping Park
Seafield Road, Seahouses, Northumberland NE68 7SP
T: (01665) 720628
F: (01665) 720088
E: info@seafieldpark.co.uk
I: www.seafieldpark.co.uk

SOUTH SHIELDS
Tyne and Wear
Lizard Lane Camping & Caravan Site ★★★
Holiday, Touring and Camping Park
Lizard Lane, South Shields, Tyne and Wear NE34 7AB
T: (0191) 424 7988

Sandhaven Caravan and Camping Park ★★★
Holiday, Touring and Camping Park
Bents Park Road, South Shields, Tyne and Wear NE33 2NL
T: (0191) 424 7988

SPITTAL
Northumberland
Seaview Caravan Club Site ★★★★
Touring Park
Billendean Road, Spittal, Berwick-upon-Tweed, Northumberland TD15 1QU
T: (01289) 305198
I: www.caravanclub.co.uk

STOCKTON-ON-TEES
Tees Valley
White Water Caravan Club Park ★★★★★
Touring and Camping Park
Tees Barrage, Stockton-on-Tees, Cleveland TS18 2QW
T: (01642) 634880
I: www.caravanclub.co.uk

STONEHAUGH
Northumberland
Stonehaugh Campsite Rating Applied For
Stonehaugh, Hexham, Northumberland NE48 3DZ
T: (01434) 230798
E: carole@stonehaugh.fsbusiness.co.uk
I: www.stonehaugh.fsbusiness.co.uk

SWARLAND
Northumberland
Percy Wood Caravan Park ★★★★
Holiday and Touring Park
Swarland, Morpeth, Northumberland NE65 9JW
T: (01670) 787649
F: (01670) 787034
E: enquiries@percywood.freeserve.co.uk
I: www.ukparks.co.uk/percywood

WHITLEY BAY
Tyne and Wear
Whitley Bay Holiday Park Great British Holiday Parks Ltd ★★★
Holiday and Touring Park
The Links, Whitley Bay, Tyne and Wear NE26 4RR
T: (0191) 253 1216
F: (0191) 297 1033
E: whitleybay@gbholidayparks.co.uk
I: www.gbholidayparks.co.uk

WINSTON
Durham
Winston Caravan Park ★★★★
Holiday, Touring and Camping Park
The Old Forge, Winston, Darlington, County Durham DL2 3RH
T: (01325) 730228
F: (01325) 730228
E: m.willetts@ic24.net
I: www.touristnetuk.com/ne/winston

WOOLER
Northumberland
Riverside Holiday Village ★★★★
Holiday, Touring and Camping Park
Brewery Road, Wooler, Northumberland NE71 6QG
T: (01668) 281447
F: (01668) 282142

NORTH WEST

AINSDALE
Merseyside
Willowbank Holiday Home and Touring Park ★★★★
Holiday, Touring and Camping Park
Coastal Road, Ainsdale, Southport, Merseyside PR8 3ST
T: (01704) 571566
F: (01704) 571566
E: mail@willowbankcp.co.uk
I: www.willowbankcp.co.uk

ALVANLEY
Cheshire
The Ridgeway Country Holiday Park ★★★
Holiday Park
The Ridgeway, Alvanley, Frodsham WA6 6XQ
T: (01928) 734981 & 07946 033457
F: (01928) 734981
E: enquiries@ridgewaypark.com
I: www.ridgewaypark.com

BAY HORSE
Lancashire
Wyreside Lakes Fishery ★★★
Touring and Camping Park
Sunnyside Farmhouse, Gleaves Hill Road, Bay Horse, Lancaster, Lancashire LA2 9DQ
T: (01524) 792093
F: (01524) 792093
I: www.wyresidelakes.co.uk

BLACKPOOL
Lancashire
Gillett Farm Caravan Park Ltd ★★★
Holiday, Touring and Camping Park
Peel Road, Peel, Blackpool, Lancashire FY4 5JU
T: (01253) 761676

Marton Mere Holiday Village ★★★★
Holiday and Touring Park
Mythop Road, Blackpool, FY4 4XN
T: (01253) 767544
F: (01253) 791544
E: enquiries@british-holidays.co.uk
I: www.british-holidays.co.uk

Newton Hall Caravan Park ★★★
Holiday and Touring Park
Staining Road, Staining, Blackpool FY3 0AX
T: (01253) 882512 & 885465
F: (01253) 893101
E: sales@partingtons.fsbusiness.co.uk
I: www.partingtons.com

Pipers Height Caravan & Camping Park ★★★★
Holiday, Touring and Camping Park
Peel Road, Peel, Blackpool, Lancashire FY4 5JT
T: (01253) 763767

Richmond Hill Caravan Park Rating Applied For
352 St Annes Road, South Shore, Blackpool, Lancashire FY4 2QN
T: (01253) 344266 & 07971 632577
E: marji@richmndhill.free-online.co.uk
I: www.richmndhill.free-online.co.uk

Sunset Park ★★★★
Holiday and Touring Park
Hambleton, Poulton-le-Fylde, FY6 9EQ
T: (01253) 700222
F: (01253) 701756
E: sunset@caravans.com
I: www.caravans.com/parks/sunset

Windy Harbour Holiday Centre ★★★
Holiday, Touring and Camping Park
Little Singleton, Blackpool, FY6 8NB
T: (01253) 883064

CABUS
Lancashire
Claylands Caravan Park ★★★★
Holiday and Touring Park
Claylands Farm, Cabus, Preston PR3 1AJ
T: (01524) 791242
F: (01524) 792406
E: alan@claylands-caravan-park.co.uk
I: www.claylands-caravan-park.co.uk

NORTH WEST

CAPERNWRAY
Lancashire
Old Hall Caravan Park ★★★★★
Holiday and Touring Park
Capernwray, Carnforth, Lancashire LA6 1AD
T: (01524) 733276
F: (01524) 734488
E: oldhall@charis.co.uk
I: www.oldhall.uk.com

CARNFORTH
Lancashire
Netherbeck Holiday Home Park ★★★★★
Holiday Park
North Road, Carnforth, Lancashire LA5 9NG
T: (01524) 735133 & 07967 112961
F: (01524) 735133
E: info@netherbeck.co.uk
I: www.netherbeck.co.uk

CLEVELEYS
Lancashire
Kneps Farm Holiday Park ★★★★
Holiday, Touring and Camping Park
River Road, Stanah, Cleveleys, Blackpool FY5 5LR
T: (01253) 823632
F: (01253) 863967
E: knepsfarm@aol.com
I: www.kneps-farm.co.uk

CLITHEROE
Lancashire
The Camping and Caravanning Club Site Clitheroe ★★★
Touring and Camping Park
Edisford Road, Clitheroe, Lancashire BB7 3LA
T: (01200) 425294
I: www.campingandcaravanningclub.co.uk

COCKERHAM
Lancashire
Cockerham Sands Country Park ★★★★
Holiday and Touring Park
Cockerham, Lancaster LA2 0DB
T: (01524) 751387
F: (01524) 752175

Moss Wood Caravan Park ★★★★★
Holiday and Touring Park
Crimbles Lane, Cockerham, Lancaster, Lancashire LA2 0ES
T: (01524) 791041
F: (01524) 792444
E: info@mosswood.co.uk
I: www.mosswood.co.uk

FLEETWOOD
Lancashire
Cala Gran ★★★★
Holiday Park
Fleetwood Road, Fleetwood, Lancashire FY7 8JX
T: (01253) 872155
F: (01253) 771288
E: enquiries@british-holidays.co.uk
I: www.british-holidays.co.uk

GLASSON DOCK
Lancashire
Marina Caravan Park ★★★★
Holiday Park
Conder Green, Glasson Dock, Lancaster LA2 0BP
T: (01524) 751787 & 751436
F: (01524) 751436

HEYSHAM
Lancashire
Ocean Edge Leisure Park ★★
Holiday and Touring Park
Moneyclose Lane, Heysham, Morecambe, Lancashire LA3 2XA
T: (01524) 855657 & 858828
F: (01524) 855884

HEYWOOD
Greater Manchester
Gelder Wood Country Park ★★★★
Touring and Camping Park
Oak Leigh Cottage, Ashworth Road, Heywood, Rochdale, Lancashire OL11 5UP
T: (01706) 364858 & 620300
F: (01706) 364858
E: gelderwood@aol.com
I: www.adultstouring.co.uk

KIRKHAM
Lancashire
Mowbreck Holiday and Residential Park ★★★★
Holiday Park
Mowbreck Lane, Wesham, Preston PR4 3HA
T: (01772) 682494
F: (01772) 672986

LANCASTER
Lancashire
New Parkside Farm Caravan Park ★★★
Touring Park
Denny Beck, Caton Road, Lancaster, LA2 9HH
T: (01524) 770723 & 770337
I: www.ukparks.co.uk/newparkside

LEYLAND
Lancashire
Royal Umpire Caravan Park ★★★★
Touring and Camping Park
Southport Road, Croston, Leyland, Preston PR5 7JB
T: (01772) 600257
F: (01772) 600662

LITTLE STANNEY
Cheshire
Chester Fairoaks Caravan Club Site ★★★★★
Touring Park
Rake Lane, Little Stanney, Chester CH2 4HS
T: (0151) 355 1600
I: www.caravanclub.co.uk

LITTLEBOROUGH
Greater Manchester
Hollingworth Lake Caravan Park ★★★
Holiday, Touring and Camping Park
Rakewood, Littleborough, Lancashire OL15 0AT
T: (01706) 378661

LONGRIDGE
Lancashire
Beacon Fell View Holiday Park ★★★
Holiday, Touring and Camping Park
110 Higher Road, Longridge, Preston PR3 2TF
T: (01772) 785434 & 783233
F: (01772) 784204

LYTHAM ST ANNES
Lancashire
Eastham Hall Caravan Park ★★
Holiday and Touring Park
Saltcotes Road, Lytham St Annes, Lancashire FY8 4LS
T: (01253) 737907

MEOLS
Merseyside
Burbo Holiday Park
Rating Applied For
Park Lane, Meols, Wirral, Merseyside CH47 8XX
T: (0151) 632 3331
F: (0151) 632 3354

MIDDLETON
Lancashire
Melbreak Caravan Park ★★★
Touring and Camping Park
Carr Lane, Middleton, Morecambe, Lancashire LA3 3LH
T: (01524) 852430

MORECAMBE
Lancashire
Regent Leisure Park ★★★★★
Holiday Park
Westgate, Morecambe, Lancashire LA3 3DF
T: (01524) 413940
F: (01524) 832247

Venture Caravan Park ★★★
Holiday and Touring Park
Langridge Way, Westgate, Morecambe, Lancashire LA4 4TQ
T: (01524) 412986
F: (01524) 422029
E: mark@venturecaravanpark.co.uk
I: www.venturecaravanpark.co.uk

Westgate Caravan Park ★★★
Holiday and Touring Park
Westgate, Morecambe, Lancashire LA3 3DE
T: (01524) 411448 & 414226
F: (01524) 414226
I: www.ukparks.co.uk/westgate

NATEBY
Lancashire
Bridge House Marina and Caravan Park ★★★
Holiday and Touring Park
Nateby Crossing Lane, Nateby, Preston PR3 0JJ
T: (01995) 603207
F: (01995) 601612

NETHER KELLET
Lancashire
The Hawthorns Caravan Park ★★★★★
Holiday Park
Nether Kellet, Carnforth, Lancashire LA6 1EA
T: (01524) 732079
F: (01524) 732079

ORMSKIRK
Lancashire
Abbey Farm Caravan Park ★★★★★
Holiday, Touring and Camping Park
Dark Lane, Ormskirk, Lancashire L40 5TX
T: (01695) 572686
F: (01695) 572686
E: abbeyfarm@yahoo.com
I: www.abbeyfarmcaravanpark.co.uk

PILLING
Lancashire
Fold House Caravan Park Ltd
Rating Applied For
Head Dyke Lane, Pilling, Preston PR3 6SJ
T: (01253) 790267
F: (01253) 790157
E: fhcp@foldhouse.co.uk
I: www.foldhouse.co.uk

PREESALL
Lancashire
Willowgrove Caravan Park ★★★
Holiday and Touring Park
Sandy Lane, Preesall, FY6 0EJ
T: (01253) 811306

PRESTON
Lancashire
Ribby Hall Holiday Village ★★★★★
Holiday Park
Ribby Road, Wrea Green, Preston PR4 2PA
T: (01772) 671111
F: (01772) 673113
E: enquiries@ribbyhall.co.uk
I: www.ribbyhall.co.uk

RIMINGTON
Lancashire
Rimington Caravan Park ★★★★★
Holiday, Touring and Camping Park
Hardcacre Lane, Rimington, Clitheroe, Lancashire BB7 4EE
T: (01200) 445355
F: (01200) 447235

SCARISBRICK
Lancashire
Hurlston Hall Country Caravan Park ★★★★
Holiday and Touring Park
Southport Road, Scarisbrick, Ormskirk, Lancashire L40 8HB
T: (01704) 841064
F: (01704) 841700

SCORTON
Lancashire
Six Arches Caravan Park ★★★
Holiday and Touring Park
Scorton, Preston PR3 1AL
T: (01524) 791683
F: (01524) 792926

SILVERDALE
Lancashire
Far Arnside Caravan Park ★★★★★
Holiday Park
Holgates Caravan Parks Ltd, Middlebarrow Plain, Silverdale, Carnforth, Lancashire LA5 0SH
T: (01524) 701508
F: (01524) 701580
E: caravan@holgates.co.uk
I: www.holgates.co.uk

NORTH WEST

Holgates Caravan Park Ltd ★★★★★
Holiday and Touring Park
Rose Award
Cove Road, Silverdale, Carnforth, Lancashire LA5 0SH
T: (01524) 701508
F: (01524) 701580
E: caravan@holgates.co.uk
I: www.holgates.co.uk

TARLETON
Lancashire
Leisure Lakes Ltd ★★
Touring and Camping Park
Mere Brow, Tarleton, Preston, Lancashire PR9 7TW
T: (01772) 813446 & 814502
F: (01772) 816150
E: gab@leisurelakes.co.uk

THURSTASTON
Merseyside
Wirral Country Park Caravan Club Site ★★★★
Touring Park
Station Road, Thurstaston, Wirral, Merseyside CH61 0HN
T: (0151) 648 5228
I: www.caravanclub.co.uk

TOSSIDE
Lancashire
Crowtrees Park ★★★★
Holiday Park
Tosside, Skipton, North Yorkshire BD23 4SD
T: (01729) 840278
F: (01729) 840278
I: www.holidaysyorkshiredales.com

WARRINGTON
Cheshire
Holly Bank Caravan Park ★★★
Touring and Camping Park
Warburton Bridge Road, Rixton, Warrington, Cheshire WA3 6HU
T: (0161) 775 2842

WEST BRADFORD
Lancashire
Three Rivers Woodland Park ★★★★
Holiday, Touring and Camping Park
Eaves Hall Lane, West Bradford, Clitheroe, Lancashire BB7 3JG
T: (01200) 423523
F: (01200) 442383

WINSFORD
Cheshire
Lakeside Caravan Park ★★★★
Holiday Park
Stockhill, Winsford, Cheshire CW7 4EF
T: (01606) 861043
F: (01606) 861043
E: enquiries@thornleyleisure.co.uk
I: www.thornleyleisure.co.uk

YORKSHIRE

ACASTER MALBIS
North Yorkshire
Chestnut Farm Caravan Park ★★★★★
Holiday, Touring and Camping Park
Acaster Malbis, York YO23 2UQ
T: (01904) 704676
F: (01904) 704676
E: enquiries@chestnutfarmholidaypark.co.uk

Moor End Farm ★★★★
Holiday, Touring and Camping Park
Acaster Malbis, York YO23 2UQ
T: (01904) 706727
F: (01904) 706727
E: moorendfarm@acaster99.fsnet.co.uk
I: www.ukparks.co.uk/moorend

ALLERSTON
North Yorkshire
Vale of Pickering Caravan Park ★★★★★
Touring and Camping Park
Carr House Farm, Allerston, Pickering, North Yorkshire YO18 7PQ
T: (01723) 859280
F: (01723) 850060
E: tony@valeofpickering.co.uk
I: www.valeofpickering.co.uk

BARDSEY
West Yorkshire
Moor Lodge Caravan Park ★★★★
Holiday and Touring Park
Blackmoor Lane, Bardsey, Leeds LS17 9DZ
T: (01937) 572424

BARMBY MOOR
East Riding of Yorkshire
The Sycamores Touring Caravan Park ★★★★
Touring and Camping Park
Feoffe Common Lane, Barmby Moor, York YO42 4HS
T: (01759) 388578
E: sycamores@york-camping.freeserve.co.uk

BARMSTON
East Riding of Yorkshire
Barmston Beach Holiday Park ★★★
Holiday and Touring Park
Sands Lane, Barmston, Driffield, East Riding of Yorkshire YO25 8PJ
T: (01262) 468202
F: (01262) 468670

BEDALE
North Yorkshire
Pembroke Caravan Park ★★★★
Touring and Camping Park
19 Low Street, Leeming Bar, Northallerton, North Yorkshire DL7 9BW
T: (01677) 422608 & 422652

BOLTON ABBEY
North Yorkshire
Howgill Lodge ★★★★★
Holiday, Touring and Camping Park
Barden, Bolton Abbey, Skipton, North Yorkshire BD23 6DJ
T: (01756) 720655
I: www.yorkshirenet.co.uk/stayat/howgill

BRANDESBURTON
East Riding of Yorkshire
Dacre Lakeside Park ★★★★
Touring and Camping Park
New Road, Brandesburton, Driffield, North Humberside YO25 8RT
T: (01964) 543704 & 07785 922478
F: (01964) 544040
E: dacresurf@aol.com
I: www.dacrepark.co.uk

BRIDLINGTON
East Riding of Yorkshire
Park Estate Caravan Park ★★★★
Holiday and Touring Park
Lime Kiln Lane, Bridlington, East Riding of Yorkshire YO16 6TG
T: (01262) 673733
F: (01262) 401851
E: admin@park-estates.co.uk
I: www.park-estates.co.uk

BURTON-IN-LONSDALE
North Yorkshire
Gallaber ★★★★
Holiday, Touring and Camping Park
Gallaber Farm, Burton-in-Lonsdale, Carnforth, Yorkshire LA6 3LU
T: (015242) 61361

CAYTON BAY
North Yorkshire
Browns Caravan Site
Rating Applied For
Mill Lane, Cayton Bay, Scarborough, North Yorkshire YO11 3NN
T: (01723) 582303
F: (01723) 584083
E: info@brownscaravan.co.uk
I: www.brownscaravan.co.uk

Cayton Bay Holiday Park ★★★★
Holiday Park
Cayton Bay, Scarborough, North Yorkshire YO11 3NJ
T: (01723) 583111
F: (01723) 584863

Cliff Farm Caravan Park ★★★★★
Holiday Park
Mill Lane, Cayton Bay, Scarborough, North Yorkshire YO11 3NN
T: (01723) 582239 & 583073
F: (01723) 582239
E: sandrabrown5@btinternet.com

CLEETHORPES
North East Lincolnshire
Thorpe Park Holiday Centre ★★★
Holiday, Touring and Camping Park
South Humberside DN35 0PW
T: (01472) 813395
F: (01472) 812146
E: enquiries@british-holidays.co.uk
I: www.british-holidays.co.uk

CONSTABLE BURTON
North Yorkshire
Constable Burton Hall Caravan Park ★★★★★
Touring and Camping Park
Constable Burton, Leyburn, North Yorkshire DL8 5LJ
T: (01677) 450428
F: (01677) 450622

CROPTON
North Yorkshire
Spiers House Caravan and Camping Site ★★★★
Touring and Camping Park
Forestry Commission, Cropton, Pickering, North Yorkshire YO18 8ES
T: (01751) 417591 & (0131) 314 6505
E: fe.holidays@forestry.gov.uk
I: www.forestholidays.co.uk

FARNHAM
North Yorkshire
Kingfisher Caravan and Camping Park ★★★
Holiday, Touring and Camping Park
Low Moor Lane, Farnham, Knaresborough, North Yorkshire HG5 9DQ
T: (01423) 869411
F: (01423) 869411

FILEY
North Yorkshire
Crows Nest Caravan Park ★★★★★
Holiday, Touring and Camping Park
Gristhorpe, Filey, North Yorkshire YO14 9PS
T: (01723) 582206
F: (01723) 582206
E: crows.nest@tesco.net

Filey Brigg Caravan & Country Park ★★★
Touring and Camping Park
Church Cliff Drive, North Cliff, Arndale, Filey, North Yorkshire YO14 0XX
T: (01723) 513852
E: filey@ytbic.co.uk
I: www.ycc.org.uk

258

Establishments printed in blue have a detailed entry in this guide

YORKSHIRE

Lebberston Touring Park ★★★★★
Touring Park
Home Farm, Filey Road, Lebberston, Scarborough, North Yorkshire YO11 3PE
T: (01723) 585723

Orchard Farm Holiday Village ★★★★★
Holiday, Touring and Camping Park
Stonegate, Hunmanby, Filey, North Yorkshire YO14 0PU
T: (01723) 891582
F: (01723) 891582

Primrose Valley Holiday Park ★★★★
Holiday and Touring Park
Primrose Valley, Filey, North Yorkshire YO14 9RF
T: (01723) 513771
F: (01723) 513777

FLAMBOROUGH
East Riding of Yorkshire

Thornwick & Sea Farm Holiday Centre ★★★★
Holiday, Touring and Camping Park
Flamborough Holidays Ltd, Flamborough, Bridlington, East Riding of Yorkshire YO15 1AU
T: (01262) 850369 & 850372
F: (01262) 851550
E: enquiries@thornwickbay.co.uk
I: www.thornwickbay.co.uk

GARGRAVE
North Yorkshire

Dalesway Caravan Park ★★★★★
Holiday Park
Dale View Bungalow, Marton Road, Gargrave, Skipton, North Yorkshire BD23 3NS
T: (01756) 749592
F: (01756) 749592
E: brenda.bdcaravans@btinternet.com
I: www.ukparks.co.uk/dalesway

GILLING WEST
North Yorkshire

Hargill House Caravan Club Site ★★★★
Touring and Camping Park
Gilling West, Richmond, North Yorkshire DL10 5LJ
T: (01748) 822734
I: www.caravanclub.co.uk

GLAISDALE
North Yorkshire

Hollins Farm ★★
Camping Park
Glaisdale, Whitby, North Yorkshire YO21 2PZ
T: (01947) 897516

GRISTHORPE BAY
North Yorkshire

Blue Dolphin Holiday Park ★★★
Holiday, Touring and Camping Park
Gristhorpe Bay, Filey, North Yorkshire YO14 9PU
T: (01723) 515155
F: (01723) 512059
I: www.havenholidays.co.uk

HARDEN
West Yorkshire

Harden & Bingley Caravan Park ★★★★
Holiday and Touring Park
Goit Stock Private Estate, Goit Stock Lane, Harden, Bingley, West Yorkshire BD16 1DF
T: (01535) 273810
I: www.ukparks.co.uk/harden

HARROGATE
North Yorkshire

Bilton Park ★★★
Touring and Camping Park
Village Farm, Bilton Lane, Harrogate, North Yorkshire HG1 4DH
T: (01423) 863121 & 565070
E: tony@bilton-park.swinternet.co.uk

High Moor Farm Park ★★★★
Holiday, Touring and Camping Park
Skipton Road, Harrogate, North Yorkshire HG3 2LT
T: (01423) 563637 & 564955
F: (01423) 529449

Ripley Caravan Park ★★★★★
Touring and Camping Park
Ripley, Harrogate, North Yorkshire HG3 3AU
T: (01423) 770050
F: (01423) 770050

Rudding Holiday Park ★★★★★
Holiday, Touring and Camping Park
Rudding Park, Follifoot, Harrogate, North Yorkshire HG3 1JH
T: (01423) 870439
F: (01423) 870859
E: holiday-park@ruddingpark.com
I: www.ruddingpark.com

Shaws Trailer Park ★★★
Holiday, Touring and Camping Park
Knaresborough Road, Harrogate, North Yorkshire HG2 7NE
T: (01423) 884432
F: (01423) 883622

Warren Forest Caravan Park ★★★★★
Holiday Park
Warsill, Ripley, Harrogate, North Yorkshire HG3 3LH
T: (01765) 620683
F: (01765) 620683
E: warrenforestpark@barclays.net
I: www.ukparks.co.uk/warrenforrest

HATFIELD
South Yorkshire

Hatfield Water Park ★★★★
Touring Park
Hatfield, Doncaster, South Yorkshire DN7 6EQ
T: (01302) 841572
F: (01302) 846368

HAWES
North Yorkshire

Bainbridge Ings Caravan and Camping Site ★★
Holiday and Camping Park
Hawes, North Yorkshire DL8 3NU
T: (01969) 667354
I: www.bainbridge-ings.co.uk

Honeycott Caravan Park ★★★
Holiday, Touring and Camping Park
Ingleton Road, Hawes, North Yorkshire DL8 3LH
T: (01969) 667310

HELMSLEY
North Yorkshire

Foxholme Touring Caravan Park ★★★★★
Touring and Camping Park
Harome, York YO62 5JG
T: (01439) 770416 & 771696
F: (01439) 771744

Golden Square Caravan and Camping Park ★★★★★
Touring and Camping Park
Oswaldkirk, York YO62 5YQ
T: (01439) 788269
F: (01439) 788236
E: barbara@goldensquarecaravanpark.com
I: www.goldensquarecaravanpark.com

HIGH BENTHAM
North Yorkshire

Riverside Caravan Park ★★★★
Holiday, Touring and Camping Park
High Bentham, Lancaster LA2 7HS
T: (015242) 61272 & 07711 587428
F: (015242) 62163
E: RiversideBentham@cs.com
I: www.riversidecaravanpark.co.uk

HIGH HAWSKER
North Yorkshire

Seaview Holiday Park ★★★★★
Holiday Park
Bottoms Lane, High Hawsker, Whitby, North Yorkshire YO22 4LL
T: (01947) 880477
F: (01947) 880972
I: www.northcliffe-seaview.com

HOLMFIRTH
West Yorkshire

Holme Valley Camping and Caravan Park ★★★★
Touring and Camping Park
Thongsbridge, Holmfirth, HD9 7TD
T: (01484) 665819
F: (01484) 663870
E: pmpeaker@hotmail.com
I: www.holme-valley.co.uk

HORNSEA
East Riding of Yorkshire

Longbeach Leisure Park ★★★★
Holiday, Touring and Camping Park
South Cliff, Hornsea, East Riding of Yorkshire HU18 1TL
T: (01964) 532506 & 533899
F: (01964) 536846
I: www.longbeach-leisure.co.uk

HORSFORTH
West Yorkshire

St Helena's Caravan Site ★★★★
Holiday, Touring and Camping Park
Wardens Bungalow, Otley Old Road, Horsforth, Leeds LS18 5HZ
T: (0113) 284 1142

INGLETON
North Yorkshire

Parkfoot Holiday Homes ★★★★★
Holiday Park
Bentham Road, Ingleton, Carnforth, Lancashire LA6 3HR
T: (015242) 61833 & (01253) 890854
F: (015242) 61961
E: sales@parkfoot.co.uk

KEARBY WITH NETHERBY
North Yorkshire

Maustin Park Ltd ★★★★★
Holiday, Touring and Camping Park
Kearby With Netherby, Wetherby, West Yorkshire LS22 4DA
T: (0113) 288 6234
F: (0113) 288 6234
E: info@maustin.co.uk
I: www.maustin.co.uk

KILLINGHALL
North Yorkshire

Pinemoor Caravan Park ★★★★
Holiday Park
Burley Bank Road, Killinghall, Harrogate, North Yorkshire HG3 2RZ
T: (01423) 503980
F: (01423) 503910

LANGTHORPE
North Yorkshire

Old Hall Caravan Park ★★★★
Holiday, Touring and Camping Park
Skelton Road, Langthorpe, Boroughbridge, York YO51 9BZ
T: (01423) 322130
F: (01423) 322130

LOFTHOUSE
North Yorkshire

Studfold Farm Caravan and Camping Park ★★★
Holiday, Touring and Camping Park
Studfold Farm, Lofthouse, Harrogate, North Yorkshire HG3 5SG
T: (01423) 755210
F: (01423) 755311

MASHAM
North Yorkshire

Black Swan Caravan & Campsite ★★★
Touring Park
Rear Black Swan Hotel, Fearby, Ripon, North Yorkshire HG4 4NF
T: (01765) 689477
F: (01765) 689477
E: blackswanholidaypark@fsmail.net
I: www.geocities.com/theblackswan_uk/

NAWTON
North Yorkshire

Wrens of Ryedale Caravan and Camp Site ★★★★
Touring and Camping Park
Gale Lane, Nawton, York YO62 7SD
T: (01439) 771260
F: (01439) 771260
E: dave@wrensofryedale.fsnet.co.uk
I: www.wrensofryedale.fsnet.co.uk

Establishments printed in blue have a detailed entry in this guide

259

YORKSHIRE

PATRINGTON
East Riding of Yorkshire
Patrington Haven Leisure Park Ltd ★★★★★
Holiday Park
Patrington, Hull, East Yorkshire HU12 0PT
T: (01964) 630071
F: (01964) 631060
E: info@patringtonhavenleisurepark.co.uk
I: www.phlp.co.uk

PICKERING
North Yorkshire
Upper Carr Chalet and Touring Park ★★★★★
Holiday, Touring and Camping Park
Upper Carr Lane, Malton Road, Black Bull, Pickering, North Yorkshire YO18 7JP
T: (01751) 473115
F: (01751) 475325
E: harker@uppercarr.demon.co.uk
I: www.upercarr.demon.co.uk

Wayside Caravan Park ★★★★
Holiday, Touring and Camping Park
Wrelton, Pickering, North Yorkshire YO18 8PG
T: (01751) 472608
F: (01751) 472608
E: waysideparks@talk21.com
I: www.waysideparks.co.uk

POCKLINGTON
East Riding of Yorkshire
South Lea Caravan Park ★★★★
Touring Park
South Lea, The Balk, Pocklington, York YO42 2NX
T: (01759) 303467

REIGHTON GAP
North Yorkshire
Reighton Sands Holiday Park ★★★
Holiday, Touring and Camping Park
Reighton Gap, Filey, North Yorkshire YO14 9SJ
T: (01723) 890476
F: (01723) 891043

RICHMOND
North Yorkshire
Brompton-on-Swale Caravan and Camping Park ★★★★★
Holiday, Touring and Camping Park
Brompton-on-Swale, Richmond, North Yorkshire DL10 7EZ
T: (01748) 824629
F: (01748) 826383
E: brompton.caravanpark@btinternet.com
I: www.uk.parks.com

RIPON
North Yorkshire
River Laver Holiday Park ★★★★★
Holiday and Touring Park
Studley Road, Ripon, North Yorkshire HG4 2QR
T: (01765) 690508
F: (01765) 690708

Sleningford Watermill Caravan and Camping Park ★★★★
Touring and Camping Park
North Stainley, Ripon, North Yorkshire HG4 3HQ
T: (01765) 635201

Woodhouse Farm Caravan & Camping Park ★★★★
Holiday, Touring and Camping Park
Winksley, Ripon, North Yorkshire HG4 3PG
T: (01765) 658309
F: (01765) 658882
E: woodhouse.farm@talk21.com
I: www.woodhouse-farm.co.uk

ROECLIFFE
North Yorkshire
Camping & Caravanning Club Site Boroughbridge ★★★★★★
Touring Park
Bar Lane, Roecliffe, York YO51 9LS
T: (01423) 322683
I: www.campingandcaravanningclub.co.uk

ROOS
East Riding of Yorkshire
Sand-le-Mere Caravan & Leisure Park ★★★
Holiday, Touring and Camping Park
Seaside Lane, Tunstall, Roos, Hull, East Yorkshire HU12 0JQ
T: (01964) 670403
F: (01964) 671099
E: info@sand-le-mere.co.uk
I: www.sand-le-mere.co.uk

ROUNDHAY
West Yorkshire
Roundhay Park Caravan & Campsite ★★★
Touring and Camping Park
Elmete Lane, Roundhay, Leeds, West Yorkshire LS8 2LG
T: (0113) 265 2354
F: (0113) 237 0077
I: www.leeds.gov.uk

RUDSTON
East Riding of Yorkshire
Thorpe Hall Caravan and Camping Site ★★★★
Touring and Camping Park
Thorpe Hall, Rudston, Driffield, East Riding of Yorkshire YO25 4JE
T: (01262) 420393 & 420574
F: (01262) 420588
E: caravansite@thorpehall.co.uk
I: www.thorpehall.co.uk

SALTWICK BAY
North Yorkshire
Whitby Holiday Park ★★★
Holiday, Touring and Camping Park
Saltwick Bay, Whitby, North Yorkshire YO22 4JX
T: (01947) 602664
F: (01947) 820356

SCARBOROUGH
North Yorkshire
Cayton Village Caravan Park Ltd ★★★★
Touring and Camping Park
Mill Lane, Cayton Bay, Scarborough, North Yorkshire YO11 3NN
T: (01723) 583171 & (01904) 624630
E: info@caytontouring.co.uk
I: www.caytontouring.co.uk

Flower of May Holiday Park ★★★★★
Holiday, Touring and Camping Park
Lebberston Cliff, Scarborough, North Yorkshire YO11 3NU
T: (01723) 584311
F: (01723) 581361
E: info@flowerofmay.com
I: www.flowerofmay.com

Jacob's Mount Caravan & Camping Park ★★★★★
Holiday, Touring and Camping Park
Bell Elliott Construction Ltd, Stepney Road, Scarborough, North Yorkshire YO12 5NL
T: (01723) 361178
F: (01723) 361178
I: www.jacobsmount.co.uk

Scalby Close Park ★★★★
Touring and Camping Park
Burniston Road, Scarborough, North Yorkshire YO13 0DA
T: (01723) 365908
E: admin@scalbyclose.co.uk
I: www.scalbyclose.co.uk

Scalby Manor Touring Caravan & Camp Park ★★★
Touring and Camping Park
Burniston Road, Scarborough, North Yorkshire YO13 0DA
T: (01723) 366212
E: scarboroughtic@scarborough.gov.uk
I: www.ycc.org.uk

Scalby Mills Caravan Park ★★★
Holiday Park
12/14 Scalby Mills Road, Scarborough, North Yorkshire YO12 6RW
T: (01723) 374509 & 07770 596033
F: (01723) 374509

SCOTTON
North Yorkshire
Knaresborough Caravan Club Site ★★★★
Touring and Camping Park
New Road, Scotton, Knaresborough, North Yorkshire HG5 9HH
T: (01423) 860196
I: www.caravanclub.co.uk

SEAMER
North Yorkshire
Arosa Caravan & Camping Park ★★★
Touring and Camping Park
Ratten Row, Seamer, Scarborough, North Yorkshire YO12 4QB
T: (01723) 862166
E: neilcherry@arosacaravanpark.co.uk
I: www.mywebpage.net/arosa

SHERIFF HUTTON
North Yorkshire
Sheriff Hutton Camping & Caravanning Club Site ★★★★
Touring and Camping Park
Bracken Hill, Sheriff Hutton, York YO60 6QG
T: (01347) 878660
I: www.campingandcaravanningclub.co.uk

SILSDEN
West Yorkshire
Dales Bank Holiday Park ★★
Touring Park
Low Lane, Silsden, Keighley, West Yorkshire BD20 9JH
T: (01535) 653321 & 656523
E: m.preston@btclick.com
I: home.btclick.com/rm.preston

SKIPSEA
East Riding of Yorkshire
Far Grange Park Ltd ★★★★★
Holiday, Touring and Camping Park
Skipsea, Driffield, East Riding of Yorkshire YO25 8SY
T: (01262) 468293 & 468248
F: (01262) 468648
E: enquiries@fargrangepark.co.uk
I: www.fargrangepark.co.uk

Skipsea Sands Holiday Village ★★★★
Holiday, Touring and Camping Park
Mill Lane, Skipsea, Driffield, East Riding of Yorkshire YO25 8TZ
T: (01262) 468210
F: (01262) 468454

Skirlington Caravan Park ★★★★★
Holiday, Touring and Camping Park
Low Skirlington, Skipsea, Driffield, East Riding of Yorkshire YO25 8SY
T: (01262) 468213 & 468466
F: (01262) 468105
E: info@skirlington.com
I: www.skirlington.com

SKIPWITH
North Yorkshire
Oakmere Caravan Park and Fishery ★★★
Holiday, Touring and Camping Park
Hill Farm, Skipwith, Selby, North Yorkshire YO8 5SN
T: (01757) 288910 & 288430
F: (01757) 288910

SKIRLAUGH
East Riding of Yorkshire
Burton Constable Country Park ★★★★
Holiday, Touring and Camping Park
Old Lodges, Skirlaugh, Hull HU11 4LN
T: (01964) 562508
F: (01964) 563420

YORKSHIRE

SLINGSBY
North Yorkshire
Camping & Caravanning Club Site Slingsby ★★★★★
Touring and Camping Park
Railway Street, Slingsby, York
YO62 4AA
T: (01653) 628335
I: www.
campingandcaravanningclub.
co.uk

Robin Hood Caravan & Camping Park ★★★★
Holiday, Touring and Camping Park
Green Dyke Lane, Slingsby, York, North Yorkshire YO62 4AP
T: (01653) 628391
F: (01653) 628391
E: robinhood.caravan@tesco.net

SNAINTON
North Yorkshire
Jasmine Caravan Park ★★★★★
Touring and Camping Park
Cross Lane, Snainton, Scarborough, North Yorkshire YO13 9BE
T: (01723) 859240
F: (01723) 859240
E: info@jasminepark.co.uk
I: www.jasminepark.co.uk

STAINFORTH
North Yorkshire
Knight Stainforth Hall Caravan and Camping Park ★★★
Touring and Camping Park
Stainforth, Settle, North Yorkshire BD24 0DP
T: (01729) 822200 & 823387
E: info@knightstainforth.co.uk
I: www.knightstainforth.co.uk

STAXTON
North Yorkshire
Spring Willows Touring Caravan Park ★★★★★
Touring and Camping Park
Main Road, Staxton, Scarborough, North Yorkshire YO12 4SB
T: (01723) 891505
E: fun4all@springwillows.fsnet.co.uk
I: www.springwillows.co.uk

STRENSALL
North Yorkshire
Moorside Caravan Park ★★★★★
Touring Park
Moorside Park, Lords Moor Lane, Strensall, York YO32 5XF
T: (01904) 491208 & 491865

THIRSK
North Yorkshire
Nursery Garden Caravan Park ★★★★
Holiday and Touring Park
Baldersby Park, Rainton, Thirsk, North Yorkshire YO7 3PG
T: (01845) 577277 & 07979 543337
F: (01845) 577277
E: nurserygardencp@talk21.com

Quernhow Caravan & Campsite ★★★
Holiday, Touring and Camping Park
Great North Road, Sinderby, Thirsk, North Yorkshire YO7 4LG
T: (01845) 567990

York House Caravan Park ★★★
Holiday, Touring and Camping Park
Balk, Thirsk, North Yorkshire YO7 2AQ
T: (01845) 597495
F: (01845) 597495

THORNE
South Yorkshire
Elder House Touring Park ★★★★
Touring Park
Elder House Farm, Sandtoft Road, Thorne, Doncaster, South Yorkshire DN8 5TD
T: (01405) 813173

THRESHFIELD
North Yorkshire
Long Ashes Park ★★★★
Holiday Park
Threshfield, Skipton, North Yorkshire BD23 5PN
T: (01756) 752261
F: (01756) 752876
E: info@longashespark.co.uk
I: www.longashespark.co.uk

Wood Nook Caravan Park ★★★★
Holiday, Touring and Camping Park
Skirethorns, Threshfield, Skipton, North Yorkshire BD23 5NU
T: (01756) 752412
F: (01756) 752412
E: bookings@wood-nook.demon.co.uk
I: www.woodnook.net

WAKEFIELD
West Yorkshire
Nostell Priory Holiday Home Park ★★★★
Holiday, Touring and Camping Park
Top Park Wood, Nostell, Wakefield, West Yorkshire WF4 1QD
T: (01924) 863938
F: (01924) 862226

WHITBY
North Yorkshire
Flask Holiday Home Park ★★★★
Holiday Park
Rose Award
Robin Hoods Bay, Fylingdales, Whitby, North Yorkshire YO22 4QH
T: (01947) 880592
F: (01947) 880592
E: flaskinn@aol.com
I: www.ukparks.com.co.uk/flask

Ladycross Plantation Caravan Park ★★★★★
Touring and Camping Park
Egton, Whitby, North Yorkshire YO21 1UA
T: (01947) 895502
E: enquiries@ladycrossplantation.co.uk
I: www.ladycrossplantation.co.uk

Middlewood Farm Holiday Park ★★★★★
Holiday, Touring and Camping Park
Middlewood Lane, Fylingthorpe, Whitby, North Yorkshire YO22 4UF
T: (01947) 880414
F: (01947) 880871
E: info@middlewoodfarm.com
I: www.middlewoodfarm.com

Northcliffe & Seaview Holiday Parks ★★★★★
Holiday, Touring and Camping Park
Bottoms Lane, High Hawsker, Whitby, North Yorkshire YO22 4LL
T: (01947) 880477
F: (01947) 880972
E: enquiries@northcliffe.com
I: www.northcliffe.com

Partridge Nest Farm Holiday Caravans ★★★
Holiday Park
Eskdaleside, Sleights, Whitby, North Yorkshire YO22 5ES
T: (01947) 810450 & 811412
F: (01947) 811413
E: pnfarm@aol.com
I: www.tmis.com/partridge-nest/

Sandfield House Farm Caravan Park ★★★★★
Touring and Camping Park
Sandsend Road, Whitby, North Yorkshire YO21 3SR
T: (01947) 602660
F: (01947) 606274
E: sandfieldw@aol.com

WILBERFOSS
East Riding of Yorkshire
The Steer Inn Caravan Park ★★
Touring and Camping Park
The Steer Inn, Hull Road, Wilberfoss, York YO41 5PF
T: (01759) 380211 & 380600
F: (01759) 388904
E: kevin@steerinn.co.uk
I: www.steerinn.co.uk

WILSTHORPE
East Riding of Yorkshire
South Cliff Caravan Park ★★★★
Holiday, Touring and Camping Park
Wilsthorpe, Bridlington, East Riding of Yorkshire YO15 3QN
T: (01262) 671051
F: (01262) 605639

The White House Caravan Park ★★★★★
Holiday Park
The White House, Wilsthorpe, Bridlington, East Yorkshire YO15 3QN
T: (01262) 673894
F: (01262) 401350

WITHERNSEA
East Riding of Yorkshire
Willows Holiday Park
Rating Applied For
Hollym Road, Withernsea, North Humberside HU19 2PN
T: (01964) 612233

WOMBLETON
North Yorkshire
Wombleton Caravan Park ★★★★★
Touring and Camping Park
Moorfield Lane, Wombleton, York YO62 7RY
T: (01751) 431684
I: www.europage.co.uk/wombletonpark

YORK
North Yorkshire
Alders Caravan Park ★★★★★
Touring Park
Home Farm, Alne, York YO61 1TB
T: (01347) 838722 & 830109
F: (01347) 838722

Allerton Park Caravan Park ★★★★★
Holiday, Touring and Camping Park
Allerton Park, Knaresborough, North Yorkshire HG5 0SE
T: (01423) 330569
T: (01759) 371377
E: enquiries@yorkshireholidayparks.co.uk
I: www.yorkshireholidayparks.co.uk

Beechwood Grange Caravan Club Site ★★★★★
Touring Park
Malton Road, York, YO3 9TH
T: (01904) 424637
I: www.caravanclub.co.uk

Castle Howard Caravan and Camping Site ★★★
Holiday, Touring and Camping Park
Coneysthorpe, York YO60 7DD
T: (01653) 648366 & 648316
E: wjmonks1@aol.com
I: www.castlehoward.co.uk

Cawood Holiday Park ★★★★★
Holiday, Touring and Camping Park
Ryther Road, Cawood, Selby, North Yorkshire YO8 3TT
T: (01757) 268450
F: (01757) 268537
I: www.ukparks.co.uk/cawood

Goosewood Caravan Park ★★★★★
Holiday, Touring and Camping Park
Sutton-on-the-Forest, York YO61 1ET
T: (01347) 810829
F: (01347) 811498
E: prince@libertysurf.uk

Mount Pleasant Holiday Park and Park Home Estate ★★★
Holiday, Touring and Camping Park
Acaster Malbis, York YO23 2UA
T: (01904) 707078 & 700088
F: (01904) 700888
E: mountpleasant@holgates.com
I: www.holgates.com

Establishments printed in blue have a detailed entry in this guide

261

YORKSHIRE

Rawcliffe Manor Caravan Park ★★★★★
Touring Park
Manor Lane, Shipton Road, York, YO30 5TZ
T: (01904) 624422
F: (01904) 640845
E: billherbert@rawcliffecaravans.sagehost.co.uk
I: www.ukparks.co.uk/rawcliffemanor

Rowntree Park Caravan Club Site ★★★★★
Touring Park
Terry Avenue, York, YO2 1JQ
T: (01904) 658997
I: www.caravanclub.co.uk

Weir Caravan Park ★★★★★
Holiday, Touring and Camping Park
Stamford Bridge, York YO41 1AN
T: (01759) 371377
F: (01759) 371377
E: enquiries@yorkshireholidayparks.co.uk
I: www.yorkshireholidayparks.co.uk

HEART OF ENGLAND

ALDERTON
Gloucestershire

Winchcombe Camping and Caravanning Site ★★★★
Touring and Camping Park
Brooklands Farm, Alderton, Tewkesbury, Gloucestershire GL20 8NX
T: (01242) 620259
I: www.campingandcaravanningclub.co.uk

ALREWAS
Staffordshire

Woodside Caravan Park ★★
Holiday, Touring and Camping Park
Fradley Junction, Alrewas, Burton upon Trent, Staffordshire DE13 7DN
T: (01283) 790407
F: (01283) 790407
I: www.ukparks.com/woodside

ALSOP-EN-LE-DALE
Derbyshire

Rivendale Caravan and Leisure Park ★★★
Holiday, Touring and Camping Park
Buxton Road, Alsop-en-le-dale, Ashbourne, Derbyshire DE6 1QU
T: (01335) 310311 & 310441
F: (01335) 842311
E: alsopdale@aol.com
I: www.ukparks.co.uk/rivendale

AMBERGATE
Derbyshire

The Firs Farm Caravan and Camping Park ★★★★
Touring and Camping Park
Crich Lane, Nether Heage, Ambergate, Belper, Derbyshire DE56 2JH
T: (01773) 852913

ANDERBY CREEK
Lincolnshire

Anderby Springs Caravan Estate ★★★
Holiday Park
Anderby Creek, Skegness, Lincolnshire PE24 5XW
T: (01754) 872265 & (01507) 441333
F: (01507) 441333

ASHBOURNE
Derbyshire

Callow Top Holiday Park ★★★★
Holiday, Touring and Camping Park
Callow Top Farm, Buxton Road, Ashbourne, Derbyshire DE6 2AQ
T: (01335) 344020
F: (01335) 343726
E: callotop@talk21.com
I: www.callowtop.co.uk

ASTON CANTLOW
Warwickshire

Island Meadow Caravan Park ★★★
Holiday, Touring and Camping Park
The Mill House, Aston Cantlow, Warwickshire B95 6JP
T: (01789) 488273
F: (01789) 488273
E: holiday@islandmeadowcaravanpark.co.uk
I: www.islandmeadowcaravanpark.co.uk

BAKEWELL
Derbyshire

Chatsworth Park Caravan Club Site ★★★★★
Touring Park
Chatsworth, Bakewell, Derbyshire DE45 1PN
T: (01246) 582226
I: www.caravanclub.co.uk

Greenhills Caravan Park ★★
Holiday, Touring and Camping Park
Crow Hill Lane, Bakewell, Derbyshire DE45 1PX
T: (01629) 813052 & 813467
F: (01629) 815131
E: greenhills@talk21.com
I: www.greenhillsleisure.com

BEWDLEY
Worcestershire

Severn Bank Park ★★★★★
Holiday Park
Blackstone, Bewdley, Worcestershire DY12 1QD
T: (01299) 823611
I: www.severnbank.co.uk

BISHOP'S CASTLE
Shropshire

The Old School Caravan Park ★★★
Touring Park
Shelve, Minsterley, Shrewsbury SY5 0JQ
T: (01588) 650410 & 0777 173 1631

BODYMOOR HEATH
West Midlands

Kingsbury Water Park Camping & Caravanning Club Site ★★★
Touring Park
Bodymoor Heath, Sutton Coldfield, West Midlands B76 0DY
T: (01827) 874101
I: www.campingandcaravanningclub.co.uk

BOSTON
Lincolnshire

Orchard Caravan Park ★★★
Holiday and Touring Park
Frampton Lane, Hubberts Bridge, Boston, Lincolnshire PE20 3QU
T: (01205) 290328
F: (01205) 290247
I: www.orchardpark.co.uk

BREWOOD
Staffordshire

Homestead Caravan Park ★★★★
Holiday Park
Shutt Green Lane, Shutt Green, Brewood, Stafford ST19 9LX
T: (01902) 851302
F: (01902) 850099
E: david@caravanpark.fsbusiness.co.uk
I: www.ukparks.co.uk/homesteadcp

BRIDGNORTH
Shropshire

Park Grange Holidays ★★★★
Holiday Park
Morville, Bridgnorth, Shropshire WV16 4RN
T: (01746) 714285
F: (01746) 714145
E: info@parkgrangeholidays.co.uk
I: www.parkgrangeholidays.co.uk

Stanmore Hall Touring Park ★★★★★
Holiday and Touring Park
Stourbridge Road, Bridgnorth, Shropshire WV15 6DT
T: (01746) 761761
F: (01746) 768069
E: stanmore@morris-leisure.co.uk
I: www.morris-leisure.co.uk

BUXTON
Derbyshire

Cottage Farm Caravan Park ★★★
Touring and Camping Park
Blackwell in the Peak, Blackwell, Buxton, Derbyshire SK17 9TQ
T: (01298) 85330
E: mail@cottagefarmsite.co.uk
I: www.cottagefarmsite.co.uk

Lime Tree Park ★★★★
Holiday Park
Dukes Drive, Buxton, Derbyshire SK17 9RP
T: (01298) 22988
I: www.ukparks.co.uk/limetree

Newhaven Caravan and Camping Park ★★★
Holiday, Touring and Camping Park
Newhaven, Buxton, Derbyshire SK17 0DT
T: (01298) 84300
F: (01332) 726027

CASTLE DONINGTON
Leicestershire

Donington Park Farmhouse Hotel ★★★
Touring Park
Melbourne Road, Isley Walton, Castle Donington, Derby DE74 2RN
T: (01332) 862409
F: (01332) 862364
E: info@parkfarmhouse.co.uk
I: www.parkfarmhouse.co.uk

CASTLETON
Derbyshire

Losehill Caravan Club Site ★★★★★
Touring and Camping Park
Castleton, Hope Valley, Derbyshire S33 8WB
T: (01433) 620636
I: www.caravanclub.co.uk

CHAPEL HILL
Lincolnshire

Orchard Caravans ★★
Holiday, Touring and Camping Park
Witham Bank, Chapel Hill, Lincoln LN4 4PZ
T: (01526) 342414
F: (01526) 342414

CHAPEL ST LEONARDS
Lincolnshire

Robin Hood Leisure Park ★★★★
Holiday and Touring Park
South Road, Chapel St Leonards, Skegness, Lincolnshire PE24 5TR
T: (01754) 874444
F: (01754) 874648

Establishments printed in blue have a detailed entry in this guide

HEART OF ENGLAND

CHARLESWORTH
Derbyshire

Woodseats Holiday Home Park
Rating Applied For
Woodseats Lane, Charlesworth, Glossop, Derbyshire SK13 5DR
T: (01457) 863415
F: (01457) 863415
E: woodseatspark@btinternet.com
I: www.btinternet.com/~woodseatspark

CHEDDLETON
Staffordshire

Glencote Caravan Park ★★★★
Holiday, Touring and Camping Park
Station Road, Cheddleton, Leek, Staffordshire ST13 7EE
T: (01538) 360745
F: (01538) 361788
I: www.glencote.co.uk

CHELTENHAM
Gloucestershire

Briarfields Caravan and Camping ★★★★
Touring and Camping Park
Gloucester Road, Cheltenham, Gloucestershire GL51 0SX
T: (01242) 235324 & 07836 274440
F: (01242) 235324

CIRENCESTER
Gloucestershire

Mayfield Touring Park ★★★★
Touring Park
Cheltenham Road, Perrotts Brook, Cirencester, Gloucestershire GL7 7BH
T: (01285) 831301
F: (01285) 831301
E: jhutson@btclick.com

COLEFORD
Gloucestershire

Forest Holidays ★★
Touring and Camping Park
Reception Site Office, Bracelands Drive, Christchurch, Coleford, Gloucestershire GL16 7NN
T: (01594) 833376

EARDISLAND
Herefordshire

Arrow Bank Caravan Park ★★★★
Holiday, Touring and Camping Park
Nun House Farm, Eardisland, Leominster, Herefordshire HR6 9BG
T: (01544) 388312
F: (01544) 388312

EAST FIRSBY
Lincolnshire

Manor Farm Caravan and Camping Site ★★
Touring and Camping Park
Manor Farm, East Firsby, Market Rasen, Lincolnshire LN8 2DB
T: (01673) 878258 & 07850 679189
F: (01673) 878258
E: bookings@lincolnshire-lanes.com
I: www.lincolnshire-lanes.com

ELLESMERE
Shropshire

Fernwood Caravan Park ★★★★★
Holiday and Touring Park
Lyneal, Ellesmere, Shropshire SY12 0QF
T: (01948) 710221
F: (01948) 710324
E: fernwood@caravanpark37.fsnet.co.uk
I: www.ranch.co.uk

EVESHAM
Worcestershire

The Ranch Caravan Park ★★★★
Holiday and Touring Park
Station Road, Honeybourne, Evesham, Worcestershire WR11 5QG
T: (01386) 830744
F: (01386) 833503
E: enquiries@ranch.co.uk
I: www.ranch.co.uk

FISHTOFT
Lincolnshire

Pilgrims Way ★★★
Touring Park
Church Green Road, Fishtoft, Boston, Lincolnshire PE21 0QY
T: (01205) 366646 & 07951 309853
F: (01205) 366646
E: pilgrimswaylincs@yahoo.com
I: www.pilgrims-way.co.uk

FLAGG
Derbyshire

Pomeroy Caravan Park ★★
Touring and Camping Park
Street House Farm, Pomeroy, Flagg, Buxton, Derbyshire SK17 9QG
T: (01298) 83259

FLEET HARGATE
Lincolnshire

Delph Bank Touring Caravan & Camping Park – Just for Adults. ★★★★
Touring and Camping Park
Old Main Road, Fleet Hargate, Holbeach, Spalding, Lincolnshire PE12 8LL
T: (01406) 422910
F: (01406) 422910

FOLKINGHAM
Lincolnshire

Low Farm Touring Park ★★★
Touring Park
Spring Lane, Folkingham, Sleaford, Lincolnshire NG34 0SJ
T: (01529) 497322

HADFIELD
Derbyshire

Camping & Caravanning Club Site ★★★
Touring and Camping Park
Crowden, Hadfield, Hyde, Cheshire SK13 1HZ
T: (01457) 866057
I: www.campingandcaravanningclub.co.uk

HANLEY SWAN
Worcestershire

Camping & Caravanning Club Site ★★★★
Touring and Camping Park
Blackmore Camp No. 2, Hanley Swan, Worcester, Worcestershire WR8 0EE
T: (01684) 310280
I: www.campingandcaravanningclub.co.uk

HAUGHTON
Shropshire

Camping and Caravanning Site Ebury Hill ★★★★
Touring and Camping Park
Ring Bank, Haughton, Telford, Shropshire TF6 6BU
T: (01743) 709334
I: www.campingandcaravanningclub.co.uk

HAYFIELD
Derbyshire

Camping & Caravanning Club Site ★★★
Camping Park
Kinder Road, Hayfield, High Peak, Derbyshire SK22 2LE
T: (01663) 745394
I: www.campingandcaravanningclub.co.uk

HOPTON HEATH
Shropshire

Ashlea Pools Country Park Holiday Homes ★★★★★
Holiday Park
Ashlea, Hopton Heath, Craven Arms, Shropshire SY7 0QD
T: (01547) 530430

HORNCASTLE
Lincolnshire

Elmhirst Lakes Caravan Park ★★★★
Holiday Park
Elmhirst Road, Horncastle, Lincolnshire LN9 5LU
T: (01507) 527533

INGOLDMELLS
Lincolnshire

Coastfield Caravan Park ★★★
Holiday Park
Vickers Point, Roman Bank, Ingoldmells, Skegness, Lincolnshire PE25 1JU
T: (01754) 872592 & 872356
F: (01754) 874450

Country Meadows Touring Park ★★★
Holiday and Touring Park
Anchor Lane, Ingoldmells, Skegness, Lincolnshire PE25 1LZ
T: (01754) 874455 & 873351
F: (01754) 874125
E: bookings@countrymeadows.co.uk
I: www.countrymeadows.co.uk

KIRK IRETON
Derbyshire

Blackwall Plantation Caravan Club Site ★★★
Touring Park
Kirk Ireton, Ashbourne, Derbyshire DE6 3JL
T: (01335) 370903
I: www.caravanclub.co.uk

KIRKBY-ON-BAIN
Lincolnshire

Camping & Caravanning Club Site ★★★★
Touring and Camping Park
Woodhall Spa Club Site, Wellsyke Lane, Kirkby-on-Bain, Woodhall Spa, Lincolnshire LN10 6YU
T: (01526) 352911
I: www.campingandcaravanningclub.co.uk

LADMANLOW
Derbyshire

Grin Low Caravan Club Site ★★★★★
Touring and Camping Park
Grin Low Road, Ladmanlow, Buxton, Derbyshire SK17 6UJ
T: (01298) 77735
I: www.caravanclub.co.uk

LEEK
Staffordshire

The Camping and Caravanning Club Leek ★★★★
Touring and Camping Park
Blackshaw Grange, Blackshaw Moor, Leek, Staffordshire ST13 8TL
T: (01538) 300285
I: www.campingandcaravanningclub.co.uk

LINCOLN
Lincolnshire

Hartsholme Country Park ★★
Touring and Camping Park
Skellingthorpe Road, Lincoln, LN6 0EY
T: (01522) 873578
F: (01522) 873577

Hazelwood Tourer Caravan Park ★
Touring and Camping Park
Moor Lane, Thorpe-on-the-Hill, Lincoln, LN6 9DA
T: (01522) 688245 & 688887
F: (01522) 688891
E: hazelwood@dial.pipex.com

LITTLE TARRINGTON
Herefordshire

The Millpond ★★★★
Touring and Camping Park
Little Tarrington, Hereford, Herefordshire HR1 4JA
T: (01432) 890243
F: (01432) 890243
E: enquiries@millpond.co.uk
I: www.millpond.co.uk

LUDLOW
Shropshire

Orleton Rise Holiday Home Park ★★★★★
Holiday and Touring Park
Green Lane, Orleton, Ludlow, Shropshire SY8 4JE
T: (01584) 831617
F: (01584) 831617

Establishments printed in blue have a detailed entry in this guide

HEART OF ENGLAND

MABLETHORPE
Lincolnshire

Camping & Caravanning Club Site ★★★★
Touring and Camping Park
Highfield, 120 Church Lane, Mablethorpe, Lincolnshire LN12 2NU
T: (01507) 472374
I: www.campingandcaravanningclub.co.uk

Golden Sands Holiday Park ★★★
Holiday Park
Quebec Road, Mablethorpe, Lincolnshire LN12 1QJ
T: (01507) 477871
F: (01507) 472066
E: GeneralGoldenSands/Haven/HOL/Rank@Rank

Trusthorpe Springs Leisure Park ★★
Holiday and Touring Park
Trusthorpe Hall, Mile Lane, Mablethorpe, Lincolnshire LN12 2QQ
T: (01507) 441384 & 07711 829908
F: (01507) 443334
E: d.brailsford@ukonline.co.uk

MATLOCK
Derbyshire

Darwin Forest Country Park ★★★★
Holiday and Touring Park
Darley Moor, Two Dales, Matlock, Derbyshire DE4 5LN
T: (01629) 732428
F: (01629) 735015
E: admin@darwinforest.co.uk
I: www.darwinforest.co.uk

MERIDEN
West Midlands

Somers Wood Caravan and Camping Park ★★★★
Touring and Camping Park
Somers Road, Meriden, Coventry CV7 7PL
T: (01676) 522978
F: (01676) 522978
E: enquiries@somerswood.co.uk
I: www.somerswood.co.uk

MORDIFORD
Herefordshire

Luck's All Caravan and Camping Park ★★★★
Holiday and Touring Park
Lucksall, Mordiford, Hereford HR1 4LP
T: (01432) 870213

MORETON-IN-MARSH
Gloucestershire

Moreton-in-Marsh Caravan Club Site ★★★★★
Touring and Camping Park
Bourton Road, Moreton-in-Marsh, Gloucestershire GL56 0BT
T: (01608) 650519 & 652515
I: www.caravanclub.co.uk

NEWARK
Nottinghamshire

Milestone Caravan Park ★★★★★
Touring Park
Milestone House, North Road, Cromwell, Newark, Nottinghamshire NG23 6JE
T: (01636) 821244 & 822256
E: milestone.cp@pgen.net

NORTON
Gloucestershire

Red Lion Camping and Caravan Park ★★
Touring and Camping Park
Wainlode Hill, Norton, Gloucester GL2 9LW
T: (01452) 730251

OLLERTON
Nottinghamshire

The Shannon Caravan & Camping Park ★★★★
Touring and Camping Park
Wellow Road, Ollerton, Newark, Nottinghamshire NG22 9AP
T: (01636) 869002
I: www.caravansitefinder.co.uk

PETERCHURCH
Herefordshire

Poston Mill Park ★★★★★
Holiday and Touring Park
Poston Mill Park, Golden Valley, Peterchurch, Hereford HR2 0SF
T: (01981) 550225
F: (01981) 550885
E: Enquiries@poston-mill.co.uk
I: www.ukparks.co.uk/postonmill

ROMSLEY
Worcestershire

Camping & Caravanning Club Site, Clent Hills ★★★★
Touring Park
Fieldhouse Lane, Romsley, Halesowen, West Midlands B62 0NH
T: (01562) 710015
I: www.campingandcaravanningclub.co.uk

ROSS-ON-WYE
Herefordshire

Broadmeadow Caravan Park ★★★★★
Holiday, Touring and Camping Park
Broadmeadows, Ross-on-Wye, Herefordshire HR9 7BH
T: (01989) 768076
F: (01989) 566030
E: broadm4811@aol.com

RUGELEY
Staffordshire

Camping and Caravanning Club Site, Cannock Chase ★★★★
Touring and Camping Park
Old Youth Hostel, Wandon, Rugeley, Staffordshire WS15 1QW
T: (01889) 582166
I: www.campingandcaravanningclub.co.uk

Silvertrees Caravan Park ★★★★
Holiday and Touring Park
Stafford Brook Road, Penkridge Bank, Rugeley, Staffordshire WS15 2TX
T: (01889) 582185
F: (01889) 582185
I: www.ukparks.co.uk/silvertrees

SHOBDON
Herefordshire

Pearl Lake Leisure Park Ltd ★★★★
Holiday and Touring Park
Shobdon, Leominster, Herefordshire HR6 9NQ
T: (01568) 708326
F: (01568) 708408
E: enquiries@pearl-lake.freeserve.co.uk

SHREWSBURY
Shropshire

Beaconsfield Farm Caravan Park ★★★★★
Holiday and Touring Park
Battlefield, Shrewsbury, SY4 4AA
T: (01939) 210370 & 210399
F: (01939) 210349
E: mail@beaconsfield-farm.co.uk
I: www.beaconsfield-farm.co.uk

Oxon Hall Touring Park ★★★★★
Holiday and Touring Park
Welshpool Road, Bicton Heath, Shrewsbury, Shropshire SY3 5FB
T: (01743) 340868
F: (01743) 340869
E: oxon@morris-leisure.co.uk
I: www.morris-leisure.co.uk

SKEGNESS
Lincolnshire

Manor Farm Caravan Park ★★
Touring and Camping Park
Sea Road, Anderby, Skegness, Lincolnshire PE24 5YB
T: (01507) 490372

SOUTH CERNEY
Gloucestershire

Hoburne Cotswold ★★★★
Holiday, Touring and Camping Park
Broadway Lane, South Cerney, Cirencester, Gloucestershire GL7 5UQ
T: (01285) 860216
F: (01285) 868010
E: enquiries@hoburne.com
I: www.hoburne.com

STOKE-ON-TRENT
Staffordshire

The Star Caravan and Camping Park ★★★
Holiday and Touring Park
Star Road, Cotton, Oakamoor, Stoke-on-Trent, ST10 3BN
T: (01538) 702256 & 702564

STONEY MIDDLETON
Derbyshire

Peakland Caravans ★★★
Holiday Park
High Street, Stoney Middleton, Hope Valley S32 4TL
T: (01433) 631414
E: peakland2000@aol.com

STOURPORT-ON-SEVERN
Worcestershire

Lickhill Manor Caravan Park ★★★★★
Holiday, Touring and Camping Park
Lickhill Road, Stourport-on-Severn, Worcestershire DY13 8RL
T: (01299) 877820 & 871041
F: (01299) 824998
E: excellent@lickhillmanor.co.uk
I: www.lickhillmanor.co.uk

STRATFORD-UPON-AVON
Warwickshire

Dodwell Park ★★★
Touring and Camping Park
Evesham Rd, (B439), Stratford-upon-Avon, Warwickshire CV37 9ST
T: (01789) 204957
F: (01926) 620199

SUTTON ST EDMUND
Lincolnshire

Orchard View Caravan & Camping Park ★★★
Holiday, Touring and Camping Park
102 Broadgate, Sutton St Edmund, Spalding, Lincolnshire PE12 0LT
T: (01945) 700482

SUTTON ST JAMES
Lincolnshire

Foreman's Bridge Caravan Park ★★★★
Holiday, Touring and Camping Park
Sutton Road, Sutton St James, Spalding, Lincolnshire PE12 0HU
T: (01945) 440346 & 07885 788857
F: (01945) 440346
E: foremansbridge@btinternet.com
I: www.foremans.bridge.co.uk

SYMONDS YAT WEST
Herefordshire

Doward Park Camp Site ★★★
Camping Park
Great Doward, Symonds Yat West, Ross-on-Wye, Herefordshire HR9 6BP
T: (01600) 890438
E: dowardpark@ntlworld.com

Sterretts Caravan Park ★★★
Holiday and Touring Park
Symonds Yat West, Ross-on-Wye, Herefordshire HR9 6BY
T: (01594) 832888 & 833162

Symonds Yat Camping and Caravan Park Ltd. ★★
Touring Park
Premier Leisure Park, Symonds Yat West, Ross-on-Wye, Herefordshire HR9 6BY
T: (01600) 890883 & 891069
F: (01600) 890883

TANSLEY
Derbyshire

Packhorse Farm Bungalow ★★★
Touring and Camping Park
Tansley, Matlock, Derbyshire DE4 5LF
T: (01629) 582781

Establishments printed in blue have a detailed entry in this guide

HEART OF ENGLAND

TELFORD
Shropshire
Severn Gorge Park ★★★★
Touring and Camping Park
Bridgnorth Road, Tweedale, Telford, Shropshire TF7 4JB
T: (01952) 684789
F: (01952) 684789

TEVERSAL
Nottinghamshire
Shardaroba Caravan Park ★★★★★
Touring and Camping Park
Shardaroba, Silverhill Lane, Teversal, Sutton in Ashfield, Nottinghamshire NG17 3JJ
T: (01623) 551838 & 0771 259 0158
F: (01623) 551838
E: stay@shardaroba.co.uk
I: www.shardaroba.co.uk

TEWKESBURY
Gloucestershire
Croft Farm Leisure and Water Park ★★
Touring and Camping Park
Croft Farm, Bredons Hardwick, Tewkesbury, Gloucestershire GL20 7EE
T: (01684) 772321 & 07778 675744
F: (01684) 773379
E: alan@croftfarmleisure.co.uk
I: www.croftfarmleisure.co.uk

Tewkesbury Abbey Caravan Club Site ★★★★
Touring and Camping Park
Gander Lane, Tewkesbury, Gloucestershire GL20 5PG
T: (01684) 294035
I: www.caravanclub.co.uk

TRENTHAM
Staffordshire
Trentham Gardens Caravan Park ★
Touring and Camping Park
Stone Road, Trentham, Stoke-on-Trent, Staffordshire ST4 8AX
T: (01782) 657341 & 07966 247393
F: (01782) 644536
E: Enquiry@trenthamgardens.co.uk
I: Trenthamgardens.co.uk

TRUSTHORPE
Lincolnshire
Sutton Springs Holiday Estate ★★★★
Holiday Park
Sutton Road, Trusthorpe, Mablethorpe, Lincolnshire LN12 2PZ
T: (01507) 441333 & 07774 829908
F: 07711 443334
E: d.brailsford@ukonline.co.uk

TUXFORD
Nottinghamshire
Greenacres Touring Park ★★★
Holiday and Touring Park
Lincoln Road, Tuxford, Newark, Nottinghamshire NG22 0JN
T: (01777) 870264
F: (01777) 872512
E: bailey-security@freezone.co.uk
I: www.freezone.co.uk/bailey-security/

UTTOXETER
Staffordshire
Uttoxeter Racecourse Caravan Club Site
Rating Applied For
Uttoxeter Racecourse, Wood Lane, Uttoxeter, Staffordshire ST14 8BD
T: (01889) 564172
I: www.caravanclub.co.uk

WATERHOUSES
Staffordshire
The Cross Inn Caravan Park ★★
Holiday, Touring and Camping Park
Cauldon Low, Waterhouses, Stoke-on-Trent ST10 3EX
T: (01538) 308338 & 308767
F: (01538) 308767
E: adrian_weaver@hotmail.com
I: www.crossinn.co.uk

WELTON
Lincolnshire
Welton Manor Golf Centre
Rating Applied For
Hackthorn Road, Welton, Lincoln, Lincolnshire LN2 3PD
T: (01673) 860917

WEM
Shropshire
Lower Lacon Caravan Park ★★
Holiday, Touring and Camping Park
Wem, Shrewsbury SY4 5RP
T: (01939) 232376
F: (01939) 233606
E: info@llcp.co.uk
I: www.lowerlaconcaravanpark.co.uk

WHATSTANDWELL
Derbyshire
Birchwood Farm Caravan Park ★★
Holiday, Touring and Camping Park
Wirksworth Road, Whatstandwell, Matlock, Derbyshire DE4 5HS
T: (01629) 822280
F: (01629) 822280
E: enquiries@birchwoodfarm.co.uk
I: www.birchwoodfacp.co.uk

Merebrook Caravan Park ★★★
Holiday, Touring and Camping Park
Derby Road, Whatstandwell, Derbyshire DE4 5HH
T: (01773) 852154 & 857010

WHITNEY-ON-WYE
Herefordshire
Penlan Caravan Park ★★★★
Touring Park
Penlan, Brilley, Whitney-on-Wye, Hereford HR3 6JW
T: (01497) 831485 & 831693
F: (01497) 831485
E: p.joyce@btinternet.com

WOLVERLEY
Worcestershire
Camping and Caravanning Club Site - Wolverley ★★★★
Touring and Camping Park
Brown Westhead Park, Wolverley, Kidderminster, Worcestershire DY10 3PX
T: (01562) 850909
I: www.campingandcaravanningclub.co.uk

WOODHALL SPA
Lincolnshire
Bainland Country Park Ltd ★★★★★
Holiday and Touring Park
Horncastle Road, Woodhall Spa, Lincolnshire LN10 6UX
T: (01526) 352903 & 353572
F: (01526) 353730
E: bookings@bainland.com
I: www.bainland.com

Jubilee Park Camping & Caravan Park ★★★
Touring and Camping Park
Stixwould Road, Woodhall Spa, Lincolnshire LN10 6SP
T: (01526) 352448
I: www.skegness-resort.co.uk

WORKSOP
Nottinghamshire
Camping & Caravanning Club Site ★★★
Touring Park
The Walled Garden, Clumber Park, Worksop, Nottinghamshire S80 3BD
T: (01909) 482303
I: www.campingandcaravanningclub.co.uk

Clumber Park Caravan Club Site ★★★★
Touring Park
Lime Tree Avenue, Clumber Park, Worksop, Nottinghamshire S80 3AE
T: (01909) 484758
I: www.caravanclub.co.uk

Riverside Caravan Park ★★★★
Touring Park
Worksop Cricket Club, Central Avenue, Worksop, Nottinghamshire S80 1ER
T: (01909) 474118

WYRE PIDDLE
Worcestershire
Rivermead Holiday Home Park ★★★★★
Holiday Park
Church Street, Wyre Piddle, Pershore, Worcestershire WR10 2JF
T: (01386) 555566 & 561250

WYTHALL
Worcestershire
Chapel Lane Caravan Club Site ★★★★★
Touring Park
Wythall, Birmingham B47 6JX
T: (01564) 826483
I: www.caravanclub.co.uk

YARWELL
Northamptonshire
Yarwell Mill Caravan Park ★★
Holiday Park
Yarwell, Peterborough PE8 6PS
T: (01780) 782344 & 782247
F: (01708) 221860

YOULGREAVE
Derbyshire
Camping & Caravanning Club Site ★★★
Touring and Camping Park
c/o Hopping Farm, Youlgreave, Bakewell, Derbyshire DE45 1NA
T: (01629) 636555
I: www.campingandcaravanningclub.co.uk

EAST OF ENGLAND

ALDEBY
Norfolk
Waveney Lodge Caravan Site ★★★
Touring Park
Elms Road, Aldeby, Beccles, Suffolk NR34 0EJ
T: (01502) 677445
F: (01502) 677445
E: waveneylodge25@hotmail.com

ASHILL
Norfolk
Brick Kiln Farm ★★★★
Touring and Camping Park
Swaffham Road, Ashill, Thetford, Norfolk IP25 7BT
T: (01760) 441300
E: brick.kiln@btclick.com
I: www.home.btclick.com/brick.kiln

ASHWELL
Hertfordshire
Ashridge Farm Cravan Club Site ★★★★★
Touring Park
Ashwell Street, Ashwell, Baldock, Hertfordshire SG7 5QF
T: (01462) 742527 & 743725

ATTLEBOROUGH
Norfolk
Oak Tree Caravan Park ★★★★
Touring Park
Norwich Road, Attleborough, Norfolk NR17 2JX
T: (01953) 455565
F: (01953) 452690
E: oaktree.cp@virgin.net
I: www.oaktree-caravan-park.co.uk

Establishments printed in blue have a detailed entry in this guide

265

EAST OF ENGLAND

BACTON-ON-SEA
Norfolk
Cable Gap Caravan Park
★★★★★
Holiday Park
Coast Road, Bacton-on-Sea,
Norwich, Norfolk NR12 0EW
T: (01692) 650667 &
0800 0686870
F: (01692) 651388
E: cablegap@freenet.co.uk
I: www.cable-gap.co.uk

BANHAM
Norfolk
Applewood Caravan and Camping Park ★★★★
Touring and Camping Park
The Grove, Banham, Norwich
NR16 2HE
T: (01953) 888370
F: (01953) 887445

BAWBURGH
Norfolk
Norfolk Showground Caravan Club Site ★★★★
Touring Park
Royal Norfolk Showground,
Long Lane, Bawburgh, Norwich
NR9 3LX
T: (01603) 742708
I: www.caravanclub.co.uk

BELTON
Norfolk
Wild Duck Holiday Park ★★★
Holiday Park
Howards Common, Belton,
Great Yarmouth, Norfolk
NR31 9NE
T: (01493) 780268
F: (01493) 782308

BENHALL
Suffolk
Whitearch (Touring Caravan) Park ★★★
Touring Park
Main Road, Benhall,
Saxmundham, Suffolk IP17 1NA
T: (01728) 604646 & 603773

BLAKENEY
Norfolk
Friary Farm Caravan Park
★★★★
Holiday Park
Cley Road, Blakeney, Holt,
Norfolk NR25 7NW
T: (01263) 740393

BRENTWOOD
Essex
Camping and Caravanning Club Site Kelvedon Hatch Site
★★★
Touring and Camping Park
Warren Lane, Doddinghurst,
Brentwood, Essex CM15 0JG
T: (01277) 372773
I: www.campingandcaravanningclub.co.uk

BUNGAY
Suffolk
Outney Meadow Caravan Park
★★★
Touring and Camping Park
Outney Meadow, Bungay,
Suffolk NR35 1HG
T: (01986) 892338
F: (01986) 896627

BURGH CASTLE
Norfolk
Burgh Castle Marina and Caravan Park ★★★
Holiday, Touring and Camping Park
Butt Lane, Burgh Castle, Great
Yarmouth, Norfolk NR31 9PZ
T: (01493) 780331
F: (01493) 780163
E: BurghCastleMarina@cs.com

Cherry Tree Holiday Park
★★★★
Holiday Park
Mill Road, Burgh Castle, Great
Yarmouth, Norfolk NR31 9QR
T: (01493) 780229 & 780024
F: (01493) 780457
E: admin.cherrytree@bourneleisure.co.uk

Kingfisher Holiday Park
★★★★★
Holiday Park
Butt Lane, Burgh Castle, Great
Yarmouth, Norfolk NR31 9PY
T: (01493) 781412 & 728990
F: (01493) 780039
E: kingfisher@freezone.co.uk
I: www.ukparks.uk/kingfisherholidaypark

BURWELL
Cambridgeshire
Stanford Park ★★★
Touring and Camping Park
Weirs Drove, Burwell, Cambridge
CB5 0BP
T: (01638) 741547 &
07802 439997

CAISTER-ON-SEA
Norfolk
Caister Beach Holiday Park
★★★★★
Holiday Park
Rose Award
Branford Road, Caister-on-Sea,
Great Yarmouth, Norfolk
NR30 5NE
T: (01493) 720278
F: (01493) 728947

Caister Holiday Park ★★★
Holiday Park
Ormesby Road, Caister-on-Sea,
Great Yarmouth, Norfolk
NR30 5NQ
T: (01493) 728931
F: (01493) 722016

Elm Beach Caravan Park
★★★★
Holiday Park
Manor Road, Caister-on-Sea,
Great Yarmouth, Norfolk
NR30 5HG
T: (01493) 721630 &
0500 400462
F: (01493) 721630
E: elmbch@bohemian.freeserve.co.uk

CALIFORNIA
Norfolk
Wakefield Court Holidays
★★★★
Holiday Park
Beachside, Rottenstone Lane,
California, Great Yarmouth,
Norfolk NR29 3QT
T: (01493) 730279
E: holidays@theseaside.org
I: www.beachside-holidays.co.uk

CAMBRIDGE
Cambridgeshire
Highfield Farm Touring Park
★★★★★
Touring and Camping Park
Long Road, Comberton,
Cambridge CB3 7DG
T: (01223) 262308
F: (01223) 262308

CAWSTON
Norfolk
Haveringland Hall Park
Rating Applied For
Haveringland, Cawston, Norwich
NR10 4PN
T: (01603) 871302
F: (01603) 879223
E: haveringland@claranet.com
I: www.haveringlandhall.co.uk

CHERRY HINTON
Cambridgeshire
Cherry Hinton Caravan Club Site ★★★★★
Touring and Camping Park
Lime Kiln Road, Cherry Hinton,
Cambridge CB1 8NQ
T: (01223) 244088
I: www.caravanclub.co.uk

CLACTON-ON-SEA
Essex
Valley Farm Caravan Park
★★★
Holiday and Touring Park
Valley Farm Camping Ground
Ltd, Valley Road, Clacton-on-Sea, Essex CO15 6LY
T: (01255) 422484
F: (01255) 422484
E: valley.farm@virgin.net
I: www.valleyfarm.co.uk

CLIPPESBY
Norfolk
Clippesby Holidays ★★★★
Holiday Park
Hall Lane, Clippesby, Great
Yarmouth, Norfolk NR29 3BL
T: (01493) 367800
F: (01493) 367809
E: holidays@clippesby.com
I: www.clippesby.com

COLCHESTER
Essex
Colchester Camping and Caravanning Park ★★★★
Touring and Camping Park
Cymbeline Way, Lexden,
Colchester, CO3 4AG
T: (01206) 545551
F: (01206) 710443
E: enquiries@colchestercamping.co.uk
I: www.colchestercamping.co.uk

CORTON
Suffolk
Broadland Sands Holiday Park
★★★★
Holiday Park
Coast Road, Corton, Lowestoft,
Suffolk NR32 5LG
T: (01502) 730939
F: (01502) 730071
E: admin@broadlandsands.co.uk
I: www.broadlandsands.co.uk/holidaypark.htm

Corton Adult Holiday Village
★★★★
Holiday Park
Corton, Lowestoft, Suffolk
NR32 5HR
T: (01502) 730226
F: (01502) 732334

CROMER
Norfolk
Forest Park Caravan Site ★★★
Holiday Park
Northrepps Road, Northrepps,
Cromer, Norfolk NR27 0JR
T: (01263) 513290
F: (01263) 511992
E: forestpark@netcom.co.uk
I: www.forest-park.co.uk

Seacroft Caravan Park ★★★★
Touring and Camping Park
Runton Road, Cromer, Norfolk
NR27 9NJ
T: (01263) 511722
F: (01263) 511512
E: seacroft@lc24net
I: www.seacroftcamping.co.uk

DUNWICH
Suffolk
Cliff House (Dunwich) ★★★★
Holiday Park
Minsmere Road, Dunwich,
Saxmundham, Suffolk IP17 3DQ
T: (01728) 648282
F: (01728) 648282
E: enquiries@cliffhouseholidays.co.uk
I: www.cliffhouseholidays.co.uk

EAST BERGHOLT
Suffolk
The Grange Country Park
★★★★
Holiday, Touring and Camping Park
East End, East Bergholt,
Colchester, Suffolk CO7 6UX
T: (01206) 298567 & 298912
F: (01206) 298770

EAST HARLING
Norfolk
The Dower House Touring Park
★★★★
Touring and Camping Park
East Harling, Norwich NR16 2SE
T: (01953) 717314
F: (01953) 717843
E: info@dowerhouse.co.uk
I: www.dowerhouse.co.uk/

EAST MERSEA
Essex
Cosway Holiday Home Park
★★★★★
Holiday Park
Fen Lane, East Mersea,
Colchester CO5 8UA
T: (01206) 383252
F: (01206) 385524
E: comersea@aol.com
I: www.cosways.co.uk

Fen Farm Caravan and Camping Site ★★★
Holiday, Touring and Camping Park
East Mersea, Colchester
CO5 8UA
T: (01206) 383275
F: (01206) 386316
E: fenfarm@talk21.com
I: www.fenfarm.co.uk

Establishments printed in blue have a detailed entry in this guide

EAST OF ENGLAND

EAST RUNTON
Norfolk
Woodhill Park ★★★★
Holiday, Touring and Camping Park
Rose Award
Cromer Road, East Runton, Cromer, Norfolk NR27 9PX
T: (01263) 512242
F: (01263) 515326
E: info@woodhill-park.com
I: www.woodhill-park.com

FAKENHAM
Norfolk
Fakenham Racecourse ★★★
Touring Park
The Racecourse, Fakenham, Norfolk NR21 7NY
T: (01328) 862388
F: (01328) 855908

The Old Brick Kilns Caravan and Camping Park ★★★★★
Touring and Camping Park
Little Barney Lane, Barney, Fakenham, Norfolk NR21 0NL
T: 0870 901 8877
F: (01328) 878305
E: enquire@old-brick-kilns.co.uk
I: www.old-brick-kilns.co.uk

The Paddocks ★★★★★
Touring Park
Little Barney, Fakenham, Norfolk NR21 0NL
T: (01328) 878803
F: (01328) 878802
E: gent.paddocks@btinternet.com
I: www.paddocks-cottages.co.uk

FELIXSTOWE
Suffolk
Peewit Caravan Park ★★★★
Touring and Camping Park
Walton Avenue, Felixstowe, Suffolk IP11 2HB
T: (01394) 284511
F: (01473) 659824

FENSTANTON
Cambridgeshire
Crystal Lakes Touring Caravan Park
Rating Applied For
Low Road, Fenstanton, Huntingdon, Cambridgeshire PE28 9HU
T: (01480) 497728 & 07976 840765

FOXHALL
Suffolk
Low House Touring Caravan Centre ★★★
Holiday and Camping Park
Low House, Bucklesham Road, Foxhall, Ipswich IP10 0AU
T: (01473) 659437 & 07710 378029
F: (01473) 659880
E: john.e.booth@talk21.com

GOLDHANGER
Essex
Osea Leisure Park ★★★
Holiday Park
Goldhanger, Maldon, Essex CM9 4SA
T: (01621) 854695
F: (01621) 854695
I: jamie@osea.freeserve.co.uk

GRAFHAM
Cambridgeshire
Old Manor Caravan Park ★★★★
Touring and Camping Park
Church Road, Grafham, Huntingdon, Cambridgeshire PE28 0BB
T: (01480) 810264
F: (01480) 819099
E: camping@old-manor.co.uk
I: www.old-manor.co.uk

GREAT SHELFORD
Cambridgeshire
Camping and Caravanning Club Site Cambridge ★★★★
Touring Park
19 Cabbage Moor, Great Shelford, Cambridge CB2 5NB
T: (01223) 841185
I: www.campingandcaravanningclub.co.uk

GREAT YARMOUTH
Norfolk
The Grange Touring Park ★★★★
Touring Park
Ormesby St Margaret, Great Yarmouth, Norfolk NR29 3QG
T: (01493) 730306 & 730023
F: (01493) 730188
E: john.groat@virgin.net

Grasmere Caravan Park (T.B.) ★★★
Holiday and Touring Park
Bultitudes Loke, Yarmouth Road, Caister-on-Sea, Great Yarmouth, Norfolk NR30 5DH
T: (01493) 720382

Great Yarmouth Caravan Club Site ★★★★
Touring Park
Great Yarmouth Racecourse, Jellicoe Road, Great Yarmouth, Norfolk NR30 4AU
T: (01493) 855223
I: www.caravanclub.co.uk

Hopton Holiday Village ★★★★
Holiday Park
Warren Lane, Hopton-on-Sea, Great Yarmouth, Norfolk NR31 9BW
T: (01502) 730214
F: (01502) 732305
E: enquiries@british-holidays.co.uk
I: www.british-holidays.co.uk

Liffens Holiday Park ★★★★
Holiday Park
Burgh Castle, Great Yarmouth, Norfolk NR31 9QB
T: (01493) 780357
F: (01493) 782383
I: www.liffens.co.uk

Liffens Welcome Holiday Centre ★★★
Holiday Park
Butt Lane, Burgh Castle, Great Yarmouth, Norfolk NR31 9PY
T: (01493) 780481
F: (01493) 781627
I: www.liffens.co.uk

Seashore Holiday Park ★★★
Holiday Park
North Denes, Great Yarmouth, Norfolk NR30 4HG
T: (01493) 851131
F: (01493) 332267

Summerfields Holiday Village ★★★★
Holiday Park
Beach Road, Scratby, Great Yarmouth, Norfolk NR29 3NW
T: (01493) 731419 & 733733
F: (01493) 730292

Vauxhall Holiday Park ★★★★
Holiday Park
Acle New Road, Great Yarmouth, Norfolk NR30 1TB
T: (01493) 857231
F: (01493) 331122
E: vauxhall.holidays@virgin.net
I: www.vauxhall-holiday-park.co.uk

HEACHAM
Norfolk
Heacham Beach Holiday Park ★★★
Holiday Park
South Beach Road, Heacham, King's Lynn, Norfolk PE31 7BD
T: (01485) 570270
F: (01485) 572055

HEMINGFORD ABBOTS
Cambridgeshire
Quiet Waters Caravan Park ★★★★
Holiday, Touring and Camping Park
Hemingford Abbots, Huntingdon, Cambridgeshire PE28 9AJ
T: (01480) 463405
F: (01480) 463405

HEMSBY
Norfolk
Newport Caravan Park (Norfolk) Ltd ★★★
Holiday, Touring and Camping Park
Newport Road, Hemsby, Great Yarmouth, Norfolk NR29 4NW
T: (01493) 730405
F: (01493) 733122
E: enquiries@newportcaravanpark.co.uk
I: www.newportcaravanpark.co.uk

HERTFORD
Hertfordshire
Camping and Caravanning Club Site Hertford ★★★★
Touring and Camping Park
Mangrove Road, Hertford, SG13 8QF
T: (01992) 586696
I: www.campingandcaravanningclub.co.uk

HEYBRIDGE
Essex
Barrow Marsh Caravan and Chalet Park ★
Holiday, Touring and Camping Park
Goldhanger Road, Heybridge, Maldon, Essex CM9 4RA
T: (01621) 852859

HODDESDON
Hertfordshire
Lee Valley Caravan Park ★★★★
Touring and Camping Park
Essex Road, Hoddesdon, Hertfordshire EN11 0AS
T: (01992) 462090
F: (01992) 462090
I: caravanpark@leevalleypark.org.uk

HOLME NEXT THE SEA
Norfolk
Sunnymead Holiday Park ★★★★
Holiday Park
Sunnymead Corner, 2 Kirkgate Street, Holme next the Sea, Hunstanton, Norfolk PE36 6LH
T: (01485) 525381 & 571838
F: (01485) 525381
E: sunnymedholpark@aol.com
I: www.sunnymead-holidays.co.uk

HUNSTANTON
Norfolk
Manor Park Holiday Village ★★★
Holiday and Touring Park
Manor Road, Hunstanton, Norfolk PE36 5AZ
T: (01485) 532300
F: (01485) 533881
E: info@manor-park.co.uk
I: www.manor-park.co.uk

Searles Holiday Centre ★★★★
Holiday, Touring and Camping Park
Rose Award
South Beach, Hunstanton, Norfolk PE36 5BB
T: (01485) 534211
F: (01485) 533815
E: bookings@searles.co.uk
I: www.searles.co.uk

IPSWICH
Suffolk
Orwell Meadows Leisure Park ★★★★
Holiday, Touring and Camping Park
Priory Lane, Nacton Road, Ipswich, IP10 0JS
T: (01473) 726666
F: (01473) 721441
E: recept@orwellmeadows.co.uk

JAYWICK
Essex
Tower Holiday Park ★★★
Holiday, Touring and Camping Park
Jaywick, Clacton-on-Sea, Essex CO15 2LF
T: (01255) 820372
F: (01255) 820060

KESSINGLAND
Suffolk
Alandale Holiday Estate ★★
Holiday Park
Bethel Drive, Kessingland, Lowestoft, Suffolk NR33 7SD
T: (01502) 740610
F: (01502) 740610
E: mikevlyne@aol.com

Establishments printed in blue have a detailed entry in this guide

EAST OF ENGLAND

Camping and Caravanning Club ★★★★
Touring and Camping Park
Suffolk Wildlife Park, Whites Lane, Kessingland, Lowestoft, Suffolk NR33 7SL
T: (01502) 742040
I: www.campingandcaravanningclub.co.uk

Heathland Beach Caravan Park ★★★★
Holiday, Touring and Camping Park
London Road, Kessingland, Lowestoft, Suffolk NR33 7PJ
T: (01502) 740337
F: (01502) 742355
E: heathlandbeach@btinternet.com
I: www.heathlandbeach.co.uk

Kessingland Beach Holiday Village ★★★
Holiday, Touring and Camping Park
Kessingland Beach, Beach Road, Kessingland, Lowestoft, Suffolk NR33 7RN
T: (01502) 740636
F: (01502) 740907

KING'S LYNN
Norfolk

Bank Farm Caravan Park ★★★
Touring Park
Bank Farm, Fallow Pipe Road, Saddle Bow, King's Lynn, Norfolk PE34 3AS
T: (01553) 617305
F: (01553) 617648

LITTLE CORNARD
Suffolk

Willowmere Caravan Park ★★★
Touring and Camping Park
Bures Road, Little Cornard, Sudbury, Suffolk CO10 0NN
T: (01787) 375559
F: (01787) 375559

LOWESTOFT
Suffolk

Beach Farm Residential and Holiday Park Limited ★★★
Holiday, Touring and Camping Park
1 Arbor Lane, Pakefield, Lowestoft, Suffolk NR33 7BD
T: (01502) 572794 & 519398
F: (01502) 537460
E: beachfarmpark@aol.com
I: www.beachfarmpark.co.uk

Gunton Hall Classic Resort ★★★★
Holiday Park
Gunton Avenue, Lowestoft, Suffolk NR32 5DF
T: (01502) 730288
F: (01502) 732139

MARCH
Cambridgeshire

Floods Ferry Touring Park ★★
Touring and Camping Park
Staffurths Bridge, Floods Ferry Road, March, Cambridgeshire PE15 0YP
T: (01354) 677302
F: (01354) 677302
I: www.floodsferrytouringpark.co.uk

MERSEA ISLAND
Essex

Waldegraves Holiday Park ★★★
Holiday, Touring and Camping Park
Mersea Island, Colchester, Essex CO5 8SE
T: (01206) 382898
F: (01206) 385359
E: holidays@waldegraves.co.uk
I: www.waldegraves.co.uk

MUNDESLEY
Norfolk

Sandy Gulls Caravan Park ★★
Holiday and Touring Park
Cromer Road, Mundesley, Norwich NR11 8DF
T: (01263) 720513

MUTFORD
Suffolk

Beulah Hall Caravan Park ★★★
Touring and Camping Park
Beulah Hall, Dairy Lane, Mutford, Beccles, Suffolk NR34 7QJ
T: (01502) 476609
F: (01502) 476453
E: carol.stuckey@fsmail.net

NEWMARKET
Suffolk

Camping and Caravanning Club Site
Rating Applied For
Rowley Mile Racecourse, Newmarket, Suffolk CB8 8JL
T: (01638) 663235
I: www.campingandcaravanningclub.co.uk

NORTH WALSHAM
Norfolk

North Walsham Caravan and Chalet Park ★★★
Holiday Park
Bacton Road, North Walsham, Norfolk NR28 0RA
T: (01692) 500526

Two Mills Touring Park ★★★★★
Touring Park
Old Yarmouth Road, Scarborough Hill, North Walsham, Norwich, Norfolk NR28 9NA
T: (01692) 405829
F: (01692) 405829
E: enquiries@twomills.co.uk
I: www.twomills.co.uk

NORWICH
Norfolk

Camping and Caravanning Club Site ★★★
Touring Park
Martineau Lane, Norwich, Norfolk NR1 2HX
T: (01603) 620060
I: www.campingandcaravanningclub.co.uk

Reedham Ferry Touring and Camping Park ★★★
Touring and Camping Park
Reedham, Norwich NR13 3HA
T: (01493) 700429 & 07909 780747
F: (01493) 700999

OULTON BROAD
Suffolk

Broadland Holiday Village ★★★★★
Holiday Park
Rose Award
Marsh Road, Oulton Broad, Lowestoft, Suffolk NR33 9JY
T: (01502) 573033
F: (01502) 512681
E: broadlandhv@hotmail.com
I: www.broadlandvillage.co.uk

OVERSTRAND
Norfolk

Ivy Farm Caravan Park ★★★
Holiday, Touring and Camping Park
No 1 High Street, Overstrand, Cromer, Norfolk NR27 0PS
T: (01263) 579239
I: www.ivy-farm.co.uk

PAKEFIELD
Suffolk

Pakefield Caravan Park ★★★
Holiday, Touring and Camping Park
Arbor Lane, Pakefield, NR33 7BQ
T: (01502) 561136 & 511884
F: (01502) 539264

PENTNEY
Norfolk

Pentney Park Caravan Site ★★★
Touring and Camping Park
Pentney, King's Lynn, Norfolk PE32 1HU
T: (01760) 337479
F: (01760) 338118
E: holidays@pentney.demon.co.uk
I: www.pentney-park.co.uk

PETERBOROUGH
Cambridgeshire

Ferry Meadows Caravan Club Site ★★★★★
Touring Park
Ferry Meadows, Ham Lane, Peterborough, PE2 5UU
T: (01733) 233526
I: www.caravanclub.co.uk

POLSTEAD
Suffolk

Polstead Touring Park ★★★★
Touring and Camping Park
Holt Road, Polstead, Colchester CO6 5BZ
T: (01787) 211969
F: (01787) 211969

POTTER HEIGHAM
Norfolk

Norfolk Broads Caravan Park ★★★★
Holiday Park
Bridge Road, Potter Heigham, Great Yarmouth, Norfolk NR29 5JB
T: (01692) 670461
F: (01692) 670461
E: info@norfolkcaravans.co.uk
I: www.norfolkcaravans.co.uk

ROYDON
Essex

Roydon Mill Leisure Park ★★★
Holiday, Touring and Camping Park
Roydon, Harlow, Essex CM19 5EJ
T: (01279) 792777
F: (01279) 792695
E: info@roydonpark.com
I: www.roydonpark.com

SAHAM HILLS
Norfolk

Lowe Caravan Park ★★★★
Touring and Camping Park
Ashdale, Hills Road, Saham Hills, Thetford, Norfolk IP25 7EZ
T: (01953) 881051
F: (01953) 881051

ST NEOTS
Cambridgeshire

Camping and Caravanning Club Site St Neots ★★★★
Touring Park
Hardwick Road, Eynesbury, St Neots, Cambridgeshire PE19 2UD
T: (01480) 474404
I: www.campingandcaravanningclub.co.uk

ST OSYTH
Essex

The Orchards Holiday Village ★★★
Holiday, Touring and Camping Park
St Osyth, Clacton-on-Sea, Essex CO16 8LJ
T: (01255) 820651
F: (01255) 820184
E: enquiries@british-holidays.co.uk
I: www.british-holidays.co.uk

SANDRINGHAM
Norfolk

Camping and Caravanning Club Site ★★★★★
Touring Park
Sandringham Estate, Double Lodges, Sandringham, Norfolk PE36 6EA
T: (01485) 542555
I: www.campingandcaravanningclub.co.uk

The Sandringham Estate Caravan Club Site ★★★★★
Touring Park
Glucksburg Woods, Sandringham, Norfolk PE35 6EZ
T: (01553) 631614
I: www.caravanclub.co.uk

SAXMUNDHAM
Suffolk

Lakeside Leisure Park Rendham Road ★★★★
Touring and Camping Park
Saxmundham, Suffolk IP17 2QP
T: (01728) 603344
F: (01728) 603344

SCRATBY
Norfolk

California Cliffs Holiday Resort Park ★★★
Holiday Park
Rottenstone Lane, Scratby, Great Yarmouth, Norfolk NR29 3QU
T: (01493) 730584
F: (01493) 733146

Establishments printed in blue have a detailed entry in this guide

EAST OF ENGLAND

Green Farm Caravan Park
★★★★
Holiday and Touring Park
Beach Road, Scratby, Great Yarmouth, Norfolk NR29 3NW
T: (01493) 730440
F: (01493) 733500
I: www.greenfarm-caravan-park.co.uk

Scratby Hall Caravan Park
★★★★
Touring and Camping Park
Scratby, Great Yarmouth, Norfolk NR29 3PH
T: (01493) 730283

SEA PALLING
Norfolk

Golden Beach Holiday Centre
★★★
Holiday and Touring Park
Beach Road, Sea Palling, Norwich NR12 0AL
T: (01692) 598269
F: (01692) 598693

SHOEBURYNESS
Essex

East Beach Caravan Park ★★
Holiday, Touring and Camping Park
East Beach, Shoeburyness, Southend-on-Sea SS3 9SG
T: (01702) 292466
F: (01702) 290634
E: east.beach@care4free.net

SNETTISHAM
Norfolk

Diglea Caravan and Camping Park ★★★
Holiday, Touring and Camping Park
Beach Road, Snettisham, King's Lynn, Norfolk PE31 7RA
T: (01485) 541367

STANHOE
Norfolk

The Rickels Caravan Site
★★★★
Touring Park
The Rickels, Bircham Road, Stanhoe, King's Lynn, Norfolk PE31 8PU
T: (01485) 518671
F: (01485) 518969

TATTERSETT
Norfolk

Manor Park Touring Caravans
★★★
Touring Park
Manor Farm, Tattersett, King's Lynn, Norfolk PE31 8RS
T: (01485) 528310

TRIMINGHAM
Norfolk

Woodland Caravan Park ★★★
Holiday and Touring Park
Trimingham, Norwich NR11 8AL
T: (01263) 579208 &
07768 720109
F: (01263) 576477
E: info@woodland-park.co.uk
I: www.woodland-park.co.uk

UPPER SHERINGHAM
Norfolk

Woodlands Caravan Park
★★★★
Holiday and Touring Park
Holt Road, Upper Sheringham, Sheringham, Norfolk NR26 8TU
T: (01263) 823802

WALTHAM CROSS
Hertfordshire

Camping and Caravanning Club Site ★★
Touring and Camping Park
Theobalds Park, Bulls Cross Ride, Waltham Cross, Hertfordshire EN7 5HS
T: (01992) 620604
I: www.campingandcaravanningclub.co.uk

WALTON-ON-THE-NAZE
Essex

Naze Marine Holiday Park
Rating Applied For
Hall Lane, Walton-on-the-Naze, Essex CO14 8HL
T: 0870 442 9292 &
(01255) 682415
F: (01255) 682427
E: nazemarine@gbholidayparks.co.uk
I: www.gbholidayparks.co.uk

WEELEY
Essex

Weeley Bridge Holiday Park
★★★
Holiday Park
Weeley, Clacton-on-Sea CO16 9DH
T: (01255) 830403
F: (01255) 831544
E: info@weeleybridge.fsnet.co.uk
I: www.leisuregb.co.uk

WELLS-NEXT-THE-SEA
Norfolk

Pinewood Holiday Park ★★★
Holiday Park
Beach Road, Wells-next-the-Sea, Norfolk NR23 1DR
T: (01328) 710439
F: (01328) 711060
E: holiday@pinewoods.co.uk
I: www.pinewoods.co.uk

WEST RUNTON
Norfolk

Beeston Regis Caravan Park Ltd
Rating Applied For
Cromer Road, West Runton, Cromer, Norfolk NR27 9NG
T: (01263) 823614 & 823820
F: (01263) 823944
E: beestonregis@btinternet.com
I: www.beestonregis.co.uk

Camping and Caravanning Club Site ★★★★
Touring and Camping Park
Holgate Lane, West Runton, Cromer, Norfolk NR27 9NW
T: (01263) 837544
I: www.campingandcaravanningclub.co.uk

Laburnum Caravan Park ★★★
Holiday Park
Water Lane, West Runton, Cromer, Norfolk NR27 9QP
T: (01263) 837473
E: laburnum@primex.co.uk
I: www.ukparks.co.uk/laburnum

WEYBOURNE
Norfolk

Kelling Heath Holiday Park
★★★★★
Holiday, Touring and Camping Park
Rose Award
Sandy Hill Lane, Weybourne, Holt, Norfolk NR25 7HW
T: (01263) 588181
F: (01263) 588599
E: info@kellingheath.co.uk
I: www.kellingheath.co.uk

WISBECH
Cambridgeshire

Virginia Lake Caravan Park
★★★
Holiday and Touring Park
Virginia House, St John's Fen End, Wisbech, Cambridgeshire PE14 8JF
T: (01945) 430332 & 430858
F: (01945) 430128

WOODBRIDGE
Suffolk

Forest Camping ★★★
Touring and Camping Park
Tangham Campsite, Rendlesham Forest, Butley, Woodbridge, Suffolk IP12 3NF
T: (01394) 450707
F: (01394) 450707
E: admin@forestcamping.co.uk
I: www.forestcamping.co.uk

WORTWELL
Norfolk

Little Lakeland Caravan Park
★★★★
Holiday and Touring Park
Wortwell, Harleston, Norfolk IP20 0EL
T: (01986) 788646
F: (01986) 788646
E: information@littlelakeland.co.uk
I: www.littlelakeland.co.uk

SOUTH WEST

ASHBURTON
Devon

Ashburton Caravan Park
★★★★
Holiday, Touring and Camping Park
Waterleat, Ashburton, Newton Abbot, Devon TQ13 7HU
T: (01364) 652552
F: (01364) 652552
E: info@ashburtondevon.freeserve.co.uk
I: www.ashburtoncaravanpark.fsnet.co.uk

Parkers Farm Holiday Park
★★★★
Holiday, Touring and Camping Park
Higher Mead Farm, Alston, Ashburton, Devon TQ13 7LJ
T: (01364) 652598
F: (01364) 654004
E: parkersfarm@btconnect.com
I: www.parkersfarm.co.uk

River Dart Country Park
★★★★
Touring and Camping Park
Holne Park, Ashburton, Newton Abbot, Devon TQ13 7NP
T: (01364) 652511
F: (01364) 652020

AVONWICK
Devon

Webland Farm Holiday Park
★★
Holiday Park
Avonwick, South Brent, Devon TQ10 9EX
T: (01364) 73273

AXMINSTER
Devon

Andrewshayes Caravan Park
★★★
Holiday Park
Dalwood, Axminster, Devon EX13 7DY
T: (01404) 831225
F: (01404) 831893
E: enquiries@andrewhayes.co.uk
I: www.andrewhayes.co.uk

Hunters Moon Holiday Park
★★★★
Holiday Park
Hawkchurch, Axminster, Devon EX13 5UL
T: (01297) 678402
F: (01297) 678402
I: www.ukparks.co.uk/huntersmoon

BARTON
Devon

Torquay Holiday Park ★★★★
Holiday Park
Kingskerswell Road, Barton, Torquay TQ2 8JU
T: (01803) 323077
F: (01803) 323503

SOUTH WEST

BATH
Bath and North East Somerset

Bath Marina and Caravan Park ★★★★
Touring Park
Brassmill Lane, Bath, BA1 3JT
T: (01225) 428778
F: (01225) 428778
I: www.bathcaravanpark.co.uk

Newton Mill Camping ★★★★
Touring Park
Newton Road, Bath, BA2 9JF
T: (01225) 333909
F: (01225) 461556
E: newtonmill@hotmail.com
I: www.campinginbath.co.uk

BATHPOOL
Somerset

Tanpits Cider Farm Camping and Caravan Park ★★
Touring Park
Bathpool, Taunton, Somerset
TA2 8BZ
T: (01823) 270663
F: (01823) 270663

BAWDRIP
Somerset

Fairways International Touring Caravan and Camping Park ★★★
Touring and Camping Park
Bath Road, Bawdrip, Bridgwater, Somerset TA7 8PP
T: (01278) 685569
F: (01278) 685569
E: FairwaysInt@Btinternet.com

BEETHAM
Somerset

Five Acres Caravan Club Site ★★★★
Touring Park
Beetham, Chard, Somerset
TA20 3QA
T: (01460) 234519
I: www.caravanclub.co.uk

BERROW
Somerset

Sandyglade Caravan Park Ltd ★★★★
Holiday Park
Coast Road, Berrow, Burnham-on-Sea, Somerset TA8 2QX
T: (01278) 751271
F: (01278) 751036
E: info@sandyglade.co.uk
I: www.sandyglade.co.uk

BERRY HEAD
Devon

Landscove Holiday Village ★★★★
Holiday Park
Rose Award
Gillard Road, Berry Head, Brixham, Devon TQ5 9EP
T: (01803) 859759 & 853176
F: (01803) 851139
E: info@landscoveholidayvillage.com
I: www.landscoveholidayvillage.com

BERRYNARBOR
Devon

Sandaway Beach Holiday Park ★★★
Holiday Park
Berrynarbor, Ilfracombe, Devon
EX34 9ST
T: (01271) 883155 & 866766
F: (01271) 866791
E: bookings@johnfowlerholidays.com
I: www.jfhols.co.uk

BICKINGTON
Devon

The Dartmoor Halfway ★★★★
Touring Park
Bickington, Newton Abbot, Devon TQ12 6JR
T: (01626) 821270
F: (01626) 821820

Lemonford Caravan Park ★★★★
Holiday, Touring and Camping Park
Bickington, Newton Abbot, Devon TQ12 6JR
T: (01626) 821242
F: (01626) 821242
E: mark@lemonford.co.uk
I: www.lemonford.co.uk

BIDEFORD
Devon

Bideford Bay Holiday Park ★★★
Holiday Park
Buck's Cross, Bideford, Devon
EX39 5DU
T: (01237) 431331
F: (01237) 431624
E: gm_bideford@rank.com

BISHOP SUTTON
Bath and North East Somerset

Bath Chew Valley Caravan Park ★★★★★
Touring and Camping Park
Ham Lane, Bishop Sutton, Bristol
BS39 5TZ
T: (01275) 332127
F: (01275) 332664

BLACKAWTON
Devon

Woodlands Leisure Park
Rating Applied For
Blackawton, Totnes, Devon
TQ9 7DQ
T: (01803) 712598
F: (01803) 712680
E: fun@woodlands-leisure-park
I: www.woodlandspark.com

BLACKWATER
Cornwall

Trevarth Holiday Park ★★★★
Holiday Park
Blackwater, Truro, Cornwall
TR4 8HR
T: (01872) 560266
F: (01872) 560266
E: trevarth@lineone.net

BLUE ANCHOR
Somerset

Blue Anchor Bay Caravan Park ★★★★
Holiday and Touring Park
Blue Anchor (Hoburne), Blue Anchor, Minehead, Somerset
TA24 6JT
T: (01643) 821360
F: (01643) 821572
E: enquiries@hoburne.co.uk
I: www.hoburne.co.uk

BODMIN
Cornwall

Camping & Caravanning Club Site ★★★★
Touring and Camping Park
Old Callywith Road, Bodmin, Cornwall PL31 2DZ
T: (01208) 73834
I: www.campingandcaravanningclub.co.uk

Ruthern Valley Holidays ★★★
Holiday, Touring and Camping Park
Ruthernbridge, Bodmin, Cornwall PL30 5LU
T: (01208) 831395
F: (01208) 832324
E: ruthernvalley@hotmail.com
I: www.self-catering.ruthern.co.uk

BOSSINEY
Cornwall

Ocean Cove Caravan Park ★★
Holiday Park
Bossiney, Tintagel, Cornwall
PL34 0AZ
T: (01840) 770325
F: (01840) 770031

BOVISAND
Devon

Bovisand Lodge Estate Ltd ★★★★
Holiday Park
Bovisand, Plymouth, Devon
PL9 0AA
T: (01752) 403554
F: (01752) 482646
E: blodge@netcomuk.co.uk
I: www.bovisand.com

BRATTON FLEMING
Devon

Greenacres Farm Touring Caravan Par ★★★★
Touring Park
Bratton Fleming, Barnstaple, Devon EX31 4SG
T: (01598) 763334

BRAUNTON
Devon

Lobb Fields Caravan and Camping Park ★★★
Touring Park
Saunton Road, Braunton, Devon
EX33 1EB
T: (01271) 812090
F: (01271) 812099
E: lobbfields@compuserve.com
I: www.lobbfields.com

BREAN
Somerset

Beachside Holiday Park ★★★★
Holiday Park
Coast Road, Brean Sands, Brean, Burnham-on-Sea, Somerset
TA8 2QZ
T: (01278) 751346 &
0800 190322
F: (01278) 751683
E: beachside@breansands.fsnet.co.uk
I: www.beachsideholidaypark.co.uk

Brean Beach Holiday Parks ★★★★
Holiday Park
Coast Road, Brean, Burnham-on-Sea, Somerset TA8 2RH
T: (01278) 751349
F: (01278) 751666
E: icj@breanbeach.co.uk
I: www.breanbeach.co.uk

Brightholme Holiday Park ★★★
Holiday Park
Coast Road, Brean, Burnham-on-Sea, Somerset TA8 2QY
T: (01278) 751327
F: (01278) 751327
E: brightholme@burnham-on-sea.co.uk
I: www.burnham-on-sea.co.uk/brightholme

Diamond Farm ★★★
Touring Park
Weston Road, Brean, Burnham-on-Sea, Somerset TA8 2RL
T: (01278) 751263 & 751041
E: trevorfeelfreetoemailme@diamondfarm42.freeserve.co.uk
I: www.diamondfarm.co.uk

Dolphin Caravan Park ★★★★
Holiday Park
Coast Road, Brean, Burnham-on-Sea, Somerset TA8 2QY
T: (01278) 751258
F: (01278) 751258

Holiday Resort Unity ★★★
Holiday Park
Coast Road, Brean Sands, Brean, Burnham-on-Sea, Somerset
TA8 2RB
T: (01278) 751235 & 752100
F: (01278) 751539
E: admin@hru.co.uk
I: www.hru.co.uk

Isis and Wyndham Park ★★★★
Holiday Park
Rose Award
Warren Road, Brean, Burnham-on-Sea, Somerset TA8 2RP
T: (01278) 751227

Northam Farm Touring Park ★★★★
Touring Park
Brean Sands, Brean, Burnham-on-Sea, Somerset TA8 2SE
T: (01278) 751244 & 751222
F: (01278) 751150

SOUTH WEST

Warren Farm Holiday Park ★★★
Holiday Park
Warren Road, Brean, Burnham-on-Sea, Somerset TA8 2RP
T: (01278) 751227
F: (01278) 751033
E: enquiries@warren-farm.co.uk
I: www.warren-farm.co.uk

BRIDESTOWE
Devon

Glebe Park ★★★
Holiday and Touring Park
Bridestowe, Okehampton, Devon EX20 4ER
T: (01837) 861261

BRIDGWATER
Somerset

Somerset View Caravan Park ★★
Touring Park
A38 Taunton Road, North Petherton, Bridgwater, Somerset TA6 6NW
T: (01278) 661294
E: someview@somerset-view.co.uk
I: www.somerset-view.co.uk

BRIDPORT
Dorset

Binghams Farm Touring Caravan Park ★★★★
Touring Park
Binghams Farm, Melplash, Bridport, Dorset DT6 3TT
T: (01308) 488234
F: (01308) 488234
E: binghamsfarm@hotmail.com
I: www.binghamsfarm.co.uk

Freshwater Beach Holiday Park ★★★★
Holiday Park
Burton Bradstock, Bridport, Dorset DT6 4PT
T: (01308) 897317
F: (01308) 897336
E: enquiries@fbhp.co.uk
I: www.fbhp.co.uk

Golden Cap Holiday Park ★★★★
Holiday and Touring Park
Seatown, Chideock, Bridport, Dorset DT6 6JX
T: (01308) 422139
F: (01308) 425672
E: holidays@wdlh.co.uk
I: www.wdlh.co.uk

Highlands End Holiday Park ★★★★★
Holiday and Touring Park
Eype, Bridport, Dorset DT6 6AR
T: (01308) 422139
F: (01308) 425672
E: holidays@wdlh.co.uk
I: www.wdlh.co.uk

BRISTOL

Baltic Wharf Caravan Club Site ★★★★
Touring Park
Cumberland Road, Bristol, BS1 6XG
T: (0117) 926 8030
I: www.caravanclub.co.uk

BRIXHAM
Devon

Brixham Holiday Park ★★★★
Holiday Park
Fishcombe Cove, Brixham, Devon TQ5 8RB
T: (01803) 853324
F: (01803) 853569
E: enquiries@brixhamholidaypark.co.uk

Centry Touring Caravans & Tents ★★
Touring Park
Mudberry House, Centry Road, Brixham, Devon TQ5 9EY
T: (01803) 853215
F: (01803) 853261
E: jlacentry.touring@talk21.com
I: www.english-riviera.co.uk

Galmpton Touring Park ★★★★
Touring and Camping Park
Greenway Road, Galmpton, Brixham, Devon TQ5 0EP
T: (01803) 842066
F: (01803) 844458
E: galmptontouringpark@hotmail.com
I: www.galmptontouringpark.co.uk

St Mary's Bay Holiday Village ★★★★
Holiday Park
Mudstone Lane, Brixham, Devon TQ5 9EJ
T: (01803) 856335
F: (01803) 883855
E: admin@weststarholidays.co.uk
I: www.weststarholidays.co.uk

South Bay Holiday Park
Rating Applied For
St Mary's Road, Brixham, Devon TQ5 9QW
T: (01803) 853004
F: (01803) 882738
E: bookings@johnfowlerholidays.com
I: www.johnfowlerholidays.com

BRYHER
Isles of Scilly

Bryher Campsite ★★★
Camping Park
Jenford, Bryher, Isles of Scilly TR23 0PR
T: (01720) 422886
F: (01720) 423092

BUDE
Cornwall

Budemeadows Touring Holiday Park ★★★★★
Touring Park
Bude, Cornwall EX23 0NA
T: (01288) 361646
F: (01288) 361646
E: wendyjo@globalnet.co.uk
I: www.budemeadows.com

Penhalt Farm Holiday Park ★★★
Holiday, Touring and Camping Park
Widemouth Bay, Bude, Cornwall EX23 0DG
T: (01288) 361210
F: (01288) 361210
I: www.holidaybank.co.uk/penhaltfarmholidaypark

Penstowe Caravan & Camping Park ★★★★
Holiday Park
Penstowe Park, Kilkhampton, Bude, Cornwall EX23 9QY
T: (01288) 321354 & 321282
F: (01288) 321273
E: info@penstoweleisure.co.uk
I: www.penstoweleisure.co.uk

Sandymouth Bay Holiday Park ★★★
Holiday Park
Sandymouth Bay, Bude, Cornwall EX23 9HW
T: (01288) 352563 & 07831 213932
F: (01288) 352563
E: sandymouth@aol.com
I: www.sandymouthbay.co.uk

Upper Lynstone Caravan and Camping Site ★★★★
Holiday and Touring Park
Lynstone, Bude, Cornwall EX23 0LP
T: (01288) 352017
F: (01288) 359034
E: reception@upperlynstone.co.uk
I: www.upperlynstone.co.uk

Wooda Farm Park ★★★★★
Holiday and Touring Park
Poughill, Bude, Cornwall EX23 9HJ
T: (01288) 352069
F: (01288) 355258
E: enquiries@wooda.co.uk
I: www.wooda.co.uk

BURNHAM-ON-SEA
Somerset

Burnham-on-Sea Holiday Village ★★★★
Holiday Park
Marine Drive, Burnham-on-Sea, Somerset TA8 1LA
T: (01278) 783391
F: (01278) 793776
E: enquiries@british-holidays.co.uk
I: www.british-holidays.co.uk

Home Farm Holiday Park ★★★★★
Holiday Park
Edithmead, Burnham-on-Sea, Somerset TA9 4HD
T: (01278) 788888
F: (01278) 780113

Lakeside Holiday Park ★★★★
Holiday Park
Westfield Road, Burnham-on-Sea, Somerset TA8 2AE
T: (01278) 792222
F: (01278) 795592

The Retreat Caravan Park ★★★★
Holiday Park
Berrow Road, Burnham-on-Sea, Somerset TA8 2ES
T: (01458) 860504
F: (01458) 860330

BURTON BRADSTOCK
Dorset

Coastal Caravan Park ★★★
Holiday Park
Annings Lane, Burton Bradstock, Bridport, Dorset DT6 4QP
T: (01308) 422139 & 897361
F: (01308) 425672
E: holidays@wdlh.co.uk
I: www.wdlh.co.uk

CAMELFORD
Cornwall

Juliot's Well Holiday Park ★★★
Holiday Park
Camelford, Cornwall PL32 9RF
T: (01840) 213302
F: (01840) 212700
E: juliot.well@bun.com
I: www.holidaysincornwall.net

CARLYON BAY
Cornwall

Carlyon Bay Caravan & Camping Park ★★★★★
Holiday and Camping Park
Bethesda, Cypress Avenue, Carlyon Bay, St Austell, Cornwall PL25 3RE
T: (01726) 812735
F: (01726) 815496
E: holidays@carlyonbay.net
I: www.carlyonbay.net

CARNON DOWNS
Cornwall

Carnon Downs Caravan and Camping Park ★★★★★
Touring Park
Carnon Downs, Truro, Cornwall TR3 6JJ
T: (01872) 862283
E: park@carnon-downs.caravanpark.co.uk
I: www.carnon-downs-caravanpark.co.uk

CHACEWATER
Cornwall

Chacewater Park ★★★★
Touring Park
Cox Hill, Chacewater, Truro, Cornwall TR4 8LY
T: (01209) 820762
F: (01209) 820544
E: ajpeterken@aol.com

CHARD
Somerset

Alpine Grove Touring Park ★★★
Touring Park
Alpine Grove, Forton, Chard, Somerset TA20 4HD
T: (01460) 63479
E: ask@alpinegrovetouringpark.co.uk
I: www.alpinegrovetouringpark.co.uk

CHARMOUTH
Dorset

The Camping and Caravanning Club Site ★★★★
Touring Park
Monkton Wylde Farm, Charmouth, Bridport, Dorset DT6 6DB
T: (01297) 32965
I: www.campingandcaravanningclub.co.uk

Dolphins River Park ★★★★
Holiday Park
Berne Lane, Charmouth, Dorset DT6 6RD
T: 0800 074 6375
F: (01308) 868 180

Establishments printed in blue have a detailed entry in this guide

SOUTH WEST

Manor Farm Holiday Centre ★★★
Holiday Park
Charmouth, Bridport, Dorset
DT6 6QL
T: (01297) 560226
F: (01297) 560429
E: enq@
manorfarmholidaycentre.co.uk
I: www.
manorfarmholidaycentre.co.uk

Monkton Wyld Farm Caravan & Camping Park ★★★★
Touring Park
Charmouth, Bridport, Dorset
DT6 6DB
T: (01297) 34525 & 631131
F: (01297) 33594
E: holidays@monktonwyld.co.uk
I: www.monktonwyld.co.uk

Newlands Holidays ★★★★
Holiday Park
Charmouth, Bridport, Dorset
DT6 6RB
T: (01297) 560259
F: (01297) 560787
E: enq@www.
newlandsholidays.co.uk
I: www.newlandsholidays.co.uk

Seadown Holiday Park ★★★★
Holiday Park
Bridge Road, Charmouth,
Bridport, Dorset DT6 6QS
T: (01297) 560154
E: www.seadowncaravanpark.co.uk

Wood Farm Caravan and Camping Park ★★★★★
Holiday and Touring Park
Axminster Road, Charmouth,
Bridport, Dorset DT6 6BT
T: (01297) 560697
F: (01297) 560697
E: holidays@woodfarm.co.uk
I: www.woodfarm.co.uk

CHEDDAR
Somerset

Broadway House Holiday Touring Caravan and Camping Park ★★★★
Holiday Park
Axbridge Road, Cheddar,
Somerset BS27 3DB
T: (01934) 742610
F: (01934) 744950
E: enquiries@broadwayhouse.uk.com
I: www.broadwayhouse.uk.com

CHIPSTABLE
Somerset

Oxenleaze Farm Caravans ★★★★
Holiday Park
Rose Award
Chipstable, Taunton, Somerset
TA4 2QH
T: (01984) 623427
F: (01984) 623427
E: enquires@oxenleazefarm.co.uk
I: www.oxenleazefarm.co.uk

CHUDLEIGH
Devon

Holmans Wood Touring Park ★★★★
Touring Park
Harcombe Cross, Chudleigh,
Newton Abbot, Devon TQ13 0DZ
T: (01626) 853785

COLYTON
Devon

Leacroft Touring Park ★★★★
Touring Park
Colyton Hill, Colyton, Devon
EX24 6HY
T: (01297) 552823

COMBE MARTIN
Devon

Manleigh Holiday Park ★★★★
Holiday Park
Rectory Road, Combe Martin,
Ilfracombe, Devon EX34 0NS
T: (01271) 883353
E: info@manleighpark.co.uk
I: www.manleighpark.co.uk

Newberry Farm Touring Caravans and Camping ★★★
Touring Park
Woodlands, Combe Martin,
Ilfracombe, Devon EX34 0AT
T: (01271) 882334
T: (01271) 882880
E: enq@newberrycampsite.co.uk
I: www.newberrycampsite.co.uk

Stowford Farm Meadows ★★★★
Touring Park
Berry Down, Combe Martin,
Ilfracombe, Devon EX34 0PW
T: (01271) 882476
F: (01271) 883053
E: enquiries@stowford.co.uk
I: www.stowford.co.uk

CONNOR DOWNS
Cornwall

Higher Trevaskis Caravan & Camping Park ★★★★
Touring and Camping Park
Gwinear Road, Connor Downs,
Hayle, Cornwall TR27 5JQ
T: (01209) 831736

COOMBE BISSETT
Wiltshire

Summerlands Caravan Park ★★★
Touring Park
College Farm, Rockbourne Road,
Coombe Bissett, Salisbury,
Wiltshire SP5 4LP
T: (01722) 718259
E: summerlands-park@compaquet.co.uk
I: www.summerlands-park.com

CROSSWAYS
Dorset

Crossways Caravan Club Site ★★★★
Touring Park
Crossways, Dorchester, Dorset
DT2 8BE
T: (01305) 852032
I: www.caravanclub.co.uk

CROWCOMBE
Somerset

Quantock Orchard Caravan Park ★★★★★
Touring Park
Crowcombe, Taunton, Somerset
TA4 4AW
T: (01984) 618618
F: (01984) 618618
E: qocp@flaxpool.freeserve.co.uk
I: www.flaxpool.freeserve.co.uk

CUBERT
Cornwall

Trewogans Holiday Park ★★★★
Holiday Park
Pennros Cottage, Cubert,
Newquay, Cornwall TR8 5HH
T: (01637) 830200

DARTMOUTH
Devon

Hillfield Holiday Park ★★★★
Holiday Park
Hillfield, Dartmouth, Devon
TQ6 0LX
T: (01803) 712322
F: (01803) 712322

Little Cotton Caravan Park ★★★★★
Touring Park
Little Cotton, Dartmouth, Devon
TQ6 0LB
T: (01803) 832558
F: (01803) 834887
I: www.littlecotton.co.uk

DAWLISH
Devon

Cofton Country Holidays ★★★★
Holiday Park
Starcross, Exeter, Devon EX6 8RP
T: (01626) 890111
F: (01626) 891572
E: enquiries@
cofton-holidays-devon.co.uk
I: www.cofton-holidays-devon.co.uk

Dawlish Sands Holiday Park ★★★★
Holiday Park
Warren Road, Dawlish Warren,
Dawlish, Devon EX7 0PG
T: (01626) 862038
F: (01626) 866298

Golden Sands Holiday Park ★★★★
Holiday Park
Week Lane, Dawlish, Devon
EX7 0LZ
T: (01626) 863099
F: (01626) 867149
E: info@goldensands.co.uk
I: www.goldensands.co.uk

Leadstone Camping ★★★
Camping Park
Warren Road, Dawlish, Devon
EX7 0NG
T: (01626) 872239 & 864411
F: (01626) 873833
E: info@leadstonecamping.co.uk
I: www.leadstonecamping.co.uk

Oakcliff Holiday Park ★★★★
Holiday Park
Mount Pleasant Road, Dawlish
Warren, Dawlish, Devon
EX7 0ND
T: (01626) 863347
F: (01626) 866636
E: info@oakcliff.co.uk
I: www.oakcliff.co.uk

Peppermint Park ★★★★
Holiday, Touring and Camping Park
Warren Road, Dawlish Warren,
Dawlish, Devon EX7 0PQ
T: (01626) 863436
F: (01626) 866482
E: www.peppermintpark.co.uk

Welcome Family Holiday Park ★★★★
Holiday Park
Warren Road, Dawlish Warren,
Dawlish, Devon EX7 0PH
T: (01626) 862070
F: (01626) 868988
E: fun@welcomefamily.co.uk
I: www.welcomefamily.co.uk

DOBWALLS
Cornwall

Hoburne Doublebois ★★★★
Holiday Park
Rose Award
Dobwalls, Liskeard, Cornwall
PL14 6LD
T: (01579) 320049
F: (01579) 321415
E: mail@hoseasons.co.uk
I: www.hoseasons.co.uk

DONIFORD
Somerset

Doniford Bay Holiday Park ★★★★
Holiday Park
Doniford, Watchet, Somerset
TA23 0TJ
T: (01984) 632423
F: (01984) 633649

Sunnybank Caravan Park ★★★★★
Holiday Park
Doniford, Watchet, Somerset
TA23 0UD
T: (01984) 632237
F: (01984) 634834
E: holidays@sunnybank.co.uk
I: sunnybankcp.co.uk

DORCHESTER
Dorset

Giants Head Caravan & Camping Park ★★
Touring Park
Old Sherborne Road, Cerne
Abbas, Dorchester, Dorset
DT2 7TR
T: (01300) 341242

Morn Gate Caravan Park ★★★
Holiday Park
Bridport Road, Dorchester,
Dorset DT2 9DS
T: (01305) 889284 &
(01202) 668060
F: (01202) 669595
E: morngate@ukonline.co.uk

DOUBLEBOIS
Cornwall

Pine Green Caravan Park ★★★★
Holiday, Touring and Camping Park
Doublebois, Liskeard, Cornwall
PL14 6LE
T: (01579) 320183
E: mary.ruhleman@btinternet.com
I: www.jpr1994sagehost.co.uk/pine.htm

DREWSTEIGNTON
Devon

Clifford Bridge Park ★★★
Touring and Camping Park
Clifford, Drewsteignton, Exeter,
Devon EX6 6QE
T: (01647) 24226
F: (01647) 24116
E: info@clifford-bridge.co.uk
I: www.clifford-bridge.co.uk

SOUTH WEST

DULVERTON
Somerset

Exmoor House Caravan Club Site ★★★★
Touring Park
Dulverton, Somerset TA22 9HL
T: (01398) 323268
I: www.caravanclub.co.uk

Lakeside Caravan Club Site ★★★★
Touring Park
Higher Grants, Exbridge, Dulverton, Somerset TA22 9BE
T: (01398) 324068
I: www.caravanclub.co.uk

EAST WORLINGTON
Devon

Yeatheridge Farm Caravan Park ★★★
Holiday Park
East Worlington, Crediton, Devon EX17 4TN
T: (01884) 860330
F: (01884) 860330

EXFORD
Somerset

Westermill Farm ★★
Camping Park
Westermill, Exford, Minehead, Somerset TA24 7NJ
T: (01643) 831238 & 831216
F: (01643) 831660
E: www.holidays@westermill-exmoor.co.uk
I: www.exmoorcamping.co.uk

EYPE
Dorset

Eype House Caravan Park ★★★
Holiday Park
Eype, Bridport, Dorset DT6 6AL
T: (01308) 424903
F: (01308) 424903
E: enquires@eypehouse.co.uk
I: www.eypehouse.co.uk

FALMOUTH
Cornwall

Maen Valley Holiday Park ★★★
Holiday Park
Falmouth, Cornwall TR11 5BJ
T: (01326) 312190
F: (01326) 211120
E: maenvalley@aol.com
I: www.chycor.co.uk/maen-valley

Pennance Mill Farm ★★
Touring Park
Maenporth, Falmouth, Cornwall TR11 5HJ
T: (01326) 317431 & 312616
F: (01326) 317431

FIDDINGTON
Somerset

Mill Farm Caravan and Camping Park ★★★★
Touring Park
Fiddington, Bridgwater, Somerset TA5 1JQ
T: (01278) 732286

FOWEY
Cornwall

Penhale Caravan and Camping Park ★★★
Holiday Park
Fowey, Cornwall PL23 1JU
T: (01726) 833425
F: (01726) 833425
E: penhale@farmersweekly.net

GLASTONBURY
Somerset

The Isle of Avalon Touring Caravan Park ★★★★★
Touring Park
Godney Road, Glastonbury, Somerset BA6 9AF
T: (01458) 833618
F: (01458) 833618

The Old Oaks Touring Park ★★★★★
Touring Park
Wick Farm, Wick, Glastonbury, Somerset BA6 8JS
T: (01458) 831437
F: (01458) 833238
E: info@theoldoaks.co.uk
I: www.theoldoaks.co.uk

GOONHAVERN
Cornwall

Penrose Farm Touring Park ★★★★
Touring Park
Goonhavern, Truro, Cornwall TR4 9QF
T: (01872) 573185
E: col@penrose99.freeserve.co.uk
I: members.xoom.com/penrosefarm/

Silverbow Park ★★★★★
Holiday Park
Goonhavern, Truro, Cornwall TR4 9NX
T: (01872) 572347

GORRAN
Cornwall

Tregarton Park ★★★★
Touring Park
Gorran, Mevagissey, St Austell, Cornwall PL26 6NF
T: 0870 744 9971
F: (01726) 844481
E: touristboard@tregartonpark.co.uk
I: www.tregartonpark.co.uk

GWINEAR
Cornwall

Parbola Holiday Park ★★★★
Holiday Park
Wall, Gwinear, Hayle, Cornwall TR27 5LE
T: (01209) 831503
F: (01209) 831503
E: bookings@parbola.co.uk
I: www.parbola.co.uk

HAYLE
Cornwall

Beachside Holiday Park ★★★★
Holiday Park
Hayle, Cornwall TR27 5AW
T: (01736) 753080
F: (01736) 757252
E: reception@beachside.demon.co.uk
I: www.beachside.co.uk

Churchtown Farm Caravan & Camping Site ★★
Touring Park
Gwithian, Hayle, Cornwall TR27 5BX
T: (01736) 753219 & 753188

Riviere Sands Holiday Park ★★★
Holiday Park
Riviere Towans, Hayle, Cornwall TR27 5AX
T: (01736) 752132
F: (01736) 756368

St Ives Bay Holiday Park ★★★★
Holiday Park
73 Loggans Road, Upton Towans, Hayle, Cornwall TR27 5BH
T: (01736) 752274
F: (01736) 754523
E: stivesbay@pipex.com
I: www.stivesbay.co.uk

HELSTON
Cornwall

Poldown Caravan Park ★★★★
Holiday and Touring Park
Poldown, Carleen, Helston, Cornwall TR13 9NN
T: (01326) 574560
F: (01326) 574560
E: poldown@poldown.co.uk
I: www.poldown.co.uk

HIGHBRIDGE
Somerset

Greenacre Place Touring Caravan Park ★★★
Touring Park
Bristol Road, Edithmead, Highbridge, Somerset TA9 4HA
T: (01278) 785227
F: (01278) 785227

HONITON
Devon

Camping and Caravanning Club Site ★★★
Touring Park
Otter Valley Park, Northcote, Honiton, Devon EX14 4PX
T: (01404) 44546
I: www.campingandcaravanningclub.co.uk

ILFRACOMBE
Devon

Beachside Holiday Park ★★★★★
Holiday Park
Hele Bay, Ilfracombe, Devon EX34 9QZ
T: (01271) 863006
F: (01271) 867296
E: enquiries@beachsidepark.co.uk
I: www.beachsidepark.co.uk

Hidden Valley Touring & Camping Park ★★★★
Touring Park
West Down, Ilfracombe, Ilfracombe, Devon EX34 8NU
T: (01271) 813837
E: hvpdevon@aol.com
I: www.hiddenvalleypark.com

Mullacott Cross Caravan Park ★★★
Holiday Park
Mullacott Cross, Ilfracombe, Devon EX34 8NB
T: (01271) 862212
F: (01271) 862979
E: info@mullacottcaravans.co.uk
I: www.mullacottcaravans.co.uk

IPPLEPEN
Devon

Ross Park ★★★★★
Touring Park
Park Hill Farm, Moor Road, Ipplepen, Newton Abbot, Devon TQ12 5TT
T: (01803) 812983
F: (01803) 812983
E: enquiries@rossparkcaravanpark.co.uk

Woodville Touring Park ★★★★
Touring Park
Totnes Road, Ipplepen, Newton Abbot, Devon TQ12 5TN
T: (01803) 812240
F: (01803) 813984
E: woodvillepark@lineone.net
I: www.caravan-sitefinder.co.uk/sthwest/devon/woodville.html

ISLES OF SCILLY

Saint Martins Campsite ★★★★
Camping Park
St Martin's, Isles of Scilly TR25 0QN
T: (01720) 422888
F: (01720) 422888
E: chris@stmartinscampsite.freeserve.co.uk

KENTISBEARE
Devon

Forest Glade Holiday Park ★★★★
Holiday Park
Kentisbeare, Cullompton, Devon EX15 2DT
T: (01404) 841381
F: (01404) 841593
E: forestglade@cwcom.net
I: www.forestglade.mcmail.com

KEWSTOKE
North Somerset

Ardnave Holiday Park ★★★
Holiday Park
Kewstoke, Weston-super-Mare BS22 9XJ
T: (01934) 622319

Kewgardens Chalet and Caravan Park ★★
Holiday Park
Off Crooks Lane, Sand Bay, Kewstoke, Weston-super-Mare BS22 9XL
T: (01934) 622598 & 645733

Kewside Caravans ★★
Holiday Park
Royal Oak Stores, Kewstoke, Weston-super-Mare BS22 9XF
T: (01934) 623187

KINGSBRIDGE
Devon

Challaborough Bay Holiday Park ★★
Holiday Park
Challaborough Beach, Kingsbridge, Devon TQ7 4HU
T: (01548) 810771
F: (01548) 810842
E: reception@challaboroughbay.freeserve.co.uk
I: www.parkdeanholidays.com

Establishments printed in blue have a detailed entry in this guide

SOUTH WEST

KINGTON LANGLEY
Wiltshire
Plough Lane Caravan Site ★★★★★
Touring Park
Plough Lane, Kington Langley, Chippenham, Wiltshire SN15 5PS
T: (01249) 750795
F: (01249) 750795
E: ploughlane@lineone.net
I: www.ploughlane.co.uk

LACOCK
Wiltshire
Piccadilly Caravan Site ★★★★★
Touring Park
Folly Lane (West), Lacock, Chippenham, Wiltshire SN15 2LP
T: (01249) 730260

LANDRAKE
Cornwall
Dolbeare Caravan and Camping Park ★★★★
Touring and Camping Park
St Ive Road, Landrake, Saltash, Cornwall PL12 5AF
T: (01752) 851334
E: dolbeare@compuserve.com
I: www.dolbeare.co.uk

LANDS END
Cornwall
Cardinney Caravan and Camping Park ★★★
Touring Park
Lands End, Main A30, Lands End, Cornwall TR19 6HJ
T: (01736) 810880
F: (01736) 810998
E: cardinney@btinternet.com
I: www.cardinney-camping-park.co.uk

LANGPORT
Somerset
Bowdens Crest Caravan and Camping Park ★★
Holiday Park
Bowdens, Langport, Somerset TA10 0DD
T: (01458) 250553
F: (01458) 253360
E: bowcrest@aol.com
I: www.scoot.co.uk/bowdens

LEEDSTOWN
Cornwall
Calloose Caravan and Camping Park ★★★★★
Holiday Park
Rose Award
Leedstown, Hayle, Cornwall TR27 5ET
T: (01736) 850431
F: (01736) 850431
E: calloose@hotmail.com
I: www.calloose.co.uk

LITTLE TORRINGTON
Devon
Smytham Manor Leisure ★★★
Holiday Park
Little Torrington, Torrington, Devon EX38 8PU
T: (01805) 622110
F: (01805) 625451
E: info@smtham.fsnet.co.uk

LOOE
Cornwall
Dolphin Holidays ★★★★
Holiday Park
Tencreek Caravn Park, Looe, Cornwall PL13 2JR
T: (01503) 262447
F: (01503) 262760
E: tencreek@aol.com
I: www.tencreek.co.uk

Looe Bay Holiday Park ★★★★
Holiday Park
St Martins, Looe, Cornwall PL13 1NX
T: (01503) 263737 & (01392) 447447
F: (01503) 264511
E: admin@weststarholidays.co.uk
I: www.weststarholidays.co.uk

Polborder House Caravan and Camping Park ★★★★
Holiday and Touring Park
Bucklawren Road, St Martins by, Looe, Cornwall PL13 1QR
T: (01503) 240265
F: (01503) 240700
E: rlf.polborder@virgin.net
I: www.cornwallexplore.co.uk/Polborder

Tregoad Farm Camping & Caravanning Park ★★★
Touring and Camping Park
St Martin's, Looe, Cornwall PL13 1PB
T: (01503) 262718
F: (01503) 264777
E: tregoadfarmccp@aol.com
I: www.cornwall-online.co.uk/tregoad

Trelawne Manor Holiday Park ★★★★
Holiday Park
Trelawne Manor, Looe, Cornwall PL13 2NA
T: (01503) 272151
F: (01503) 272176
E: bookings@johnfowlerholidays.com
I: www.johnfowlerholidays.com

Waterfront Holiday & Leisure ★★
Holiday Park
Millendreath, Looe, Cornwall PL13 1NY
T: (01503) 263281
F: (01503) 264467

LOWER METHERELL
Cornwall
Trehorner Farm Holiday Park ★★★★★
Holiday Park
Lower Metherell, Callington, Cornwall PL17 8BJ
T: (01579) 351122
F: (01579) 351239

LUXULYAN
Cornwall
Croft Farm Holiday Park ★★★★
Holiday, Touring and Camping Park
Luxulyan, Bodmin, Cornwall PL30 5EQ
T: (01726) 850228
F: (01726) 850498
E: lynpick@globalnet.co.uk
I: www.croftfarm.co.uk

LYDFORD
Devon
Camping & Caravanning Club Site - Lydford ★★★★
Touring and Camping Park
Lydford, Okehampton, Devon EX20 4BE
T: (01822) 820275
I: www.campingandcaravanningclub.co.uk

LYNTON
Devon
Camping & Caravanning Club Site - Lynton ★★★
Touring Park
Caffyn's Cross, Lynton, Devon EX35 6JS
T: (01598) 752379
I: www.campingandcaravanningclub.co.uk

Channel View Caravan Park ★★★★
Holiday and Touring Park
Manor Farm, Barbrook, Lynton, Devon EX35 6LD
T: (01598) 753349 & 752777
F: (01598) 752777
E: channelview@bushinternet.com
I: www.channel-view.co.uk

MALMESBURY
Wiltshire
Burton Hill Caravan and Camping Park ★★
Touring Park
Burton Hill, Malmesbury, Wiltshire SN16 0EH
T: (01666) 826880
F: (01666) 823449
E: burtonhillccp@archesfarm.co.uk

MARLDON
Devon
Widend Touring Park ★★★★
Touring Park
Berry Pomeroy Road, Marldon, Paignton, Devon TQ3 1RT
T: (01803) 550116
F: (01803) 550116

MARTOCK
Somerset
Southfork Caravan Park ★★★★★
Touring Park
Parrett Works, Martock, Somerset TA12 6AE
T: (01935) 825661
F: (01935) 825122
E: southfork.caravans@virgin.net
I: www.ukparks.co.uk/southfork

MAWGAN PORTH
Cornwall
Mawgan Porth Holiday Park ★★★★
Holiday Park
Mawgan Porth, Newquay, Cornwall TR8 4BD
T: (01637) 860322
E: mawganporthhp@fsbdial.co.uk
I: www.mawganporth.co.uk

Sun Haven Valley Caravan Park & Camping Park ★★★★★
Holiday and Camping Park
Mawgan Porth, Newquay, Cornwall TR8 4BQ
T: (01637) 860373
F: (01637) 860373
E: sunhaven@freenet.co.uk
I: www.sunhavenvalley.co.uk

Trevarrian Holiday Park
Rating Applied For
Trevarrian, Mawgan Porth, Newquay, Cornwall TR8 4AQ
T: (01637) 860381

MEVAGISSEY
Cornwall
Penhaven Touring Park ★★★★
Touring Park
Pentewan Road, St Austell, Cornwall PL26 6DL
T: (01726) 843687
F: (01726) 843870
E: penhaven.cornwall@virgin.net
I: www.penhaventouring.co.uk

Sea View International ★★★★★
Holiday, Touring and Camping Park
Boswinger, St Austell, Cornwall PL26 6LL
T: (01726) 843425
F: (01726) 843358
E: enquiries@seaviewinternational.com
I: www.seaviewinternational.com

MINEHEAD
Somerset
Beeches Holiday Park ★★★★
Holiday Park
Rose Award
Blue Anchor Bay, Minehead, Somerset TA24 6JW
T: (01984) 640391
F: (01984) 640361
E: info@beeches-park.co.uk
I: www.beeches-park.co.uk

Camping and Caravanning Club Site ★★★★
Touring Park
Hill Road, North Hill, Minehead, Somerset TA24 5SF
T: (01643) 704138
I: www.campingandcaravanningclub.co.uk

MODBURY
Devon
Camping & Caravanning Club Site - California Cross ★★★★
Touring and Camping Park
California Cross, Modbury, Ivybridge, Devon PL21 0SG
T: (01548) 821297
I: www.campingandcaravanningclub.co.uk

Moor View Touring Park ★★★
Touring Park
California Cross, Modbury, Ivybridge, Devon PL21 0SG
T: (01548) 821485
F: (01548) 821485
E: moorview@tinyworld.co.uk
I: www.ukparks.co.uk/moorviewtouring

SOUTH WEST

Pennymoor Camping and Caravan Park ★★★★
Holiday, Touring and Camping Park
Modbury, Ivybridge, Devon PL21 0SB
T: (01548) 830269 & 830542
F: (01548) 830542
I: www.pennymoor-camping.co.uk

MOORTOWN
Devon

Langstone Manor Caravan and Camping Park ★★★
Holiday Park
Moortown, Tavistock, Devon PL19 9JZ
T: (01822) 613371
F: (01822) 613371
E: web@langstone-manor.co.uk
I: www.langstone-manor.co.uk

MORTEHOE
Devon

Easewell Holiday Park ★★★★
Holiday Park
Easewell Farm, Mortehoe, Woolacombe, Devon EX34 7EH
T: (01271) 870225

North Morte Farm Caravan and Camping Park ★★★
Holiday Park
North Morte Road, Mortehoe, Woolacombe, Devon EX34 7EG
T: (01271) 870381
F: (01271) 870115
E: info@northmortefarm.co.uk
I: www.northmortefarm.co.uk

Twitchen Parc ★★★★
Holiday Park
Mortehoe, Woolacombe, Devon EX34 7ES
T: (01271) 870343
F: (01271) 870089
E: goodtimes@woolacombe.com
I: www.woolacombe.com

Warcombe Farm Camping Park ★★★
Touring Park
Station Road, Mortehoe, Woolacombe, Devon EX34 7EJ
T: (01271) 870690 & 07774 428770
F: (01271) 871070

MUCHELNEY
Somerset

Thorney Lakes and Caravan Park ★★★
Touring Park
Thorney West Farm, Muchelney, Langport, Somerset TA10 0DW
T: (01458) 250811

MULLION
Cornwall

Criggan Mill ★★★★★
Holiday Park
Mullion Cove, Mullion, Helston, Cornwall TR12 7EU
T: (01326) 240496
F: 0870 1640 549
E: info@crigganmill.co.uk
I: www.crigganmill.co.uk

Mullion Holiday Park ★★★★
Holiday Park
Mullion, Helston, Cornwall TR12 7LJ
T: (01392) 447447 & (01326) 240000
F: (01392) 445202
E: admin@weststarholidays.co.uk
I: www.weststarholidays.co.uk

NEWQUAY
Cornwall

Crantock Beach Holiday Park ★★★★
Holiday Park
Crantock, Newquay, Cornwall TR8 5RH
T: (01637) 871111
F: (01637) 850818
E: bookings@newquay-hol-park.demon.co.uk
I: www.newquay-holiday-parks.co.uk

Hendra Holiday Park ★★★★
Holiday Park
Newquay, Cornwall TR8 4NY
T: (01637) 875778
F: (01637) 879017
E: hendra.cornwall@dial.pipex.com
I: www.hendra-holidays.com

Holywell Bay Holiday Park ★★★★
Holiday Park
Holywell Bay, Newquay, Cornwall TR8 5PR
T: (01637) 871111
F: (01637) 850818
E: bookings@newquay-hol-park.demon.co.uk
I: www.newquay-holiday-parks.co.uk

Nancolleth Farm Caravan Gardens ★★★★
Holiday Park
Rose Award
Newquay, Cornwall TR8 4PN
T: (01872) 510236
F: (01872) 510948
E: nanluckraft@farmersweekly.net
I: www.nancolleth.co.uk

Newperran Tourist Park ★★★★
Touring Park
Rejerrah, Newquay, Cornwall TR8 5QJ
T: (01872) 572407
F: (01872) 571254
E: Trevellapark@cs.com
I: www.newperran.co.uk

Newquay Holiday Park ★★★★
Holiday Park
Newquay, Cornwall TR8 4HS
T: (01637) 871111
F: (01637) 850818
E: bookings@newquay-hol-park.demon.co.uk
I: www.newquay-holiday-parks.co.uk

Porth Beach Tourist Park ★★★★
Touring Park
Alexandra Road, Porth, Newquay, Cornwall TR7 3NH
T: (01637) 876531
F: (01637) 871227
E: info@porthbeach.co.uk
I: www.porthbeach.co.uk

Resparva House Touring Park ★★★★
Touring Park
Chapel Town, Summercourt, Newquay, Cornwall TR8 5AH
T: (01872) 510332
E: touringpark@resparva.co.uk
I: www.resparva.co.uk

Riverside Holiday Park ★★★
Holiday Park
Gwills Lane, Newquay, Cornwall TR8 4PE
T: (01637) 873617
F: (01637) 877051
E: info@riversideholidaypark.co.uk
I: www.riversideholidaypark.co.uk

Trekenning Tourist Park ★★★★
Touring Park
Newquay, Cornwall TR8 4JF
T: (01637) 880462
F: (01637) 880500
E: trekenning@aol.com
I: www.crescom.co.uk/trekenning

Treloy Tourist Park ★★★★
Touring and Camping Park
Newquay, Cornwall TR8 4JN
T: (01637) 872063 & 876279
F: (01637) 871710
E: holidays@treloy.co.uk
I: www.treloy.co.uk

Trenance Holiday Park ★★★
Holiday Park
Edgcumbe Avenue, Newquay, Cornwall TR7 2JY
T: (01637) 873447
F: (01637) 852677
E: tony.hoyte@virgin.net
I: www.mywebpage.net/trenance

Trethiggey Touring Park ★★★★
Touring Park
Quintrell Downs, Newquay, Cornwall TR8 4LG
T: (01637) 877672
E: suttonjw@m.s.n.com
I: www.trethiggey.co.uk

Trevella Caravan and Camping Park ★★★★★
Holiday, Touring and Camping Park
Rose Award
Crantock, Newquay, Cornwall TR8 5EW
T: (01637) 830308
F: (01872) 571254
E: Trevellapark@cs.com
I: www.trevella.co.uk

Trevornick Holiday Park ★★★★★
Holiday Park
Holywell Bay, Newquay, Cornwall TR8 5PW
T: (01637) 830531
F: (01637) 831000
E: info@trevornick.co.uk
I: www.trevornick.co.uk

NEWTON ABBOT
Devon

Dornafield ★★★★★
Touring Park
Dornafield Farm, Two Mile Oak, Newton Abbot, Devon TQ12 6DD
T: (01803) 812732
F: (01803) 812032
E: enquiries@dornafield.com
I: www.dornafield.com

OARE
Wiltshire

Hill-View Park ★★★
Touring Park
Oare, Marlborough, Wiltshire SN8 4JE
T: (01672) 563151 & 562271

OKEHAMPTON
Devon

Dartmoor View Holiday Park ★★★★★
Holiday and Touring Park
Whiddon Down, Okehampton, Devon EX20 2QL
T: (01647) 231545
F: (01647) 231654
E: jo@dartmoorview.co.uk
I: www.dartmoorview.co.uk

Yertiz Caravan and Camping Park ★★★
Holiday and Camping Park
Exeter Road, Okehampton, Devon EX20 1QF
T: (01837) 52281
E: yertiz@dial.pipex.com
I: www.dspace.dial.pipex.com/yertiz

ORCHESTON
Wiltshire

Stonehenge Touring Park ★★★
Touring Park
Orcheston, Salisbury, Wiltshire SP3 4SH
T: (01980) 620304 & 620902
F: (01980) 621121
E: stp@orcheston.freeserve.co.uk
I: www.orcheston.freeserve.co.uk

OSMINGTON
Dorset

White Horse Holiday Park ★★★
Holiday Park
Osmington Hill, Osmington, Weymouth, Dorset DT3 6ED
T: (01305) 832164
F: (01305) 832164
E: enquiries@whitehorsepark.co.uk
I: www.whitehorsepark.co.uk

OWERMOIGNE
Dorset

Sandyholme Holiday Park ★★★★
Holiday Park
Moreton Road, Owermoigne, Dorchester, Dorset DT2 8HZ
T: (01305) 852677
F: (01305) 854677
E: smeatons@sandyholme.co.uk
I: www.sandyholme.co.uk

Establishments printed in blue have a detailed entry in this guide

SOUTH WEST

PADSTOW
Cornwall

Carnevas Farm Holiday Park ★★★★
Holiday, Touring and Camping Park
Carnevas Farm, St Merryn, Padstow, Cornwall PL28 8PN
T: (01841) 520230
F: (01841) 520230

The Laurels Touring Caravan & Camping Park ★★★★
Touring and Camping Park
Padstow Road, Whitecross, Wadebridge, Cornwall PL27 7JQ
T: (01208) 813341
F: (01208) 813341
E: anicholson@thelaurels-park.freeserve.co.uk
I: www.thelaurels-park.freeserve.co.uk

Mother Ivey's Bay Caravan Park ★★★★
Holiday, Touring and Camping Park
Trevose Head, Padstow, Cornwall PL28 8SL
T: (01841) 520990
F: (01841) 520550
E: info@motheriveysbay.com
I: www.motheriveysbay.com

Treretheran Touring Park ★★★★
Touring Park
Padstow, Cornwall PL28 8LE
T: (01841) 532061
F: (01841) 532061
E: camping.treretheran@btinternet.com
I: www.btinternet.com/~camping.treretheran

PAIGNTON
Devon

Ashvale Holiday Park ★★★★
Holiday Park
Goodrington Road, Paignton, Devon TQ4 7JD
T: (01803) 843887
F: (01803) 845427
E: info@beverley-holidays.co.uk
I: www.beverley-holidays.co.uk

Beverley Park ★★★★★
Holiday and Touring Park
Rose Award
Goodrington Road, Paignton, Devon TQ4 7JE
T: (01803) 843887
F: (01803) 845427
E: info@beverley-holidays.co.uk
I: www.beverley-holidays.co.uk

Bona Vista Holiday Park ★★★★
Holiday Park
Totnes Road, Paignton, Devon TQ4 7PY
T: (01803) 551971
E: user@bonavista.softnet.co.uk

Byslades International Touring and Camping Park ★★★★
Touring and Camping Park
Totnes Road, Paignton, Devon TQ4 7PY
T: (01803) 555072
E: byslidesitp@lineone.net
I: www.byslidestouringpark.co.uk

Higher Well Farm Holiday Park ★★★★
Holiday, Touring and Camping Park
Waddeton Road, Stoke Gabriel, Totnes, Devon TQ9 6RN
T: (01803) 782289

Hoburne Torbay ★★★★
Holiday and Touring Park
Grange Road, Goodrington, Paignton, Devon TQ4 7JP
T: (01803) 558010
F: (01803) 696286
E: enquiries@hoburne.com
I: www.hoburne.com

Marine Park Holiday Centre ★★★★
Holiday and Touring Park
Grange Road, Paignton, Devon TQ4 7JR
T: (01803) 843887
F: (01803) 845427
E: info@beverley-holidays.co.uk
I: www.beverley-holidays.co.uk

Ramslade Touring Park
Rating Applied For
Stoke Road, Stoke Gabriel, Totnes, Devon TQ9 6QB
T: (01803) 782575
F: (01803) 782828
E: derek@ramslade.co.uk
I: www.ramslade.co.uk

Waterside Holiday Park ★★★★
Holiday Park
Three Beaches, Dartmouth Road, Paignton, Devon TQ4 6NS
T: (01803) 842400
F: (01803) 844876
I: www.watersidepark.co.uk

PAR
Cornwall

Par Sands Holiday Park ★★★★
Holiday, Touring and Camping Park
Par Beach, Par, St Austell, Cornwall PL24 2AS
T: (01726) 812868 & 07831 461403
F: (01726) 817899
E: holidays@parsands.co.uk
I: www.parsands.co.uk

PELYNT
Cornwall

Trelay Farm Park ★★★★
Holiday and Touring Park
Pelynt, Looe, Cornwall PL13 2JX
T: (01503) 220900
F: (01503) 220900

PENTEWAN
Cornwall

Pentewan Sands Holiday Park ★★★★
Holiday, Touring and Camping Park
Pentewan, St Austell, Cornwall PL26 6BT
T: (01726) 843485
F: (01726) 844142
E: info@pentewan.co.uk
I: www.pentewan.co.uk

PENZANCE
Cornwall

Tower Park Caravans and Camping ★★★
Touring Park
St Buryan, Penzance, Cornwall TR19 6BZ
T: (01736) 810286
F: (01736) 810954
E: caravans&camping@towerpark97.freeserve.co.uk
I: www.towerpark97.freeserve.co.uk

PERRANPORTH
Cornwall

Perran Sands Holiday Centre Haven Holidays ★★★
Holiday Park
Perranporth, Cornwall TR6 0AQ
T: (01872) 573551
F: (01872) 571158
E: admin.perransands@bourne-leisure.co.uk
I: www.Haven-Holidays.co.uk

POLGOOTH
Cornwall

Saint Margaret's Holiday Bungalows ★★★★★
Holiday Park
Tregongeeves Lane, Polgooth, St Austell, Cornwall PL26 7AX
T: (01726) 74283
T: (01726) 71680
E: reception@stmargarets-holidays
I: www.stmargarets-holidays.co.uk

POLPERRO
Cornwall

Killigarth Caravan Park ★★★★
Holiday, Touring and Camping Park
Polperro, Looe, Cornwall PL13 2JQ
T: (01503) 272216 & 272409
F: (01503) 272065
E: killigarthmanor@breathe.com
I: www.killigarth.co.uk

POLRUAN-BY-FOWEY
Cornwall

Polruan Holidays (Camping & Caravanning) ★★★★
Holiday, Touring and Camping Park
Townsend Road, Polruan-by-Fowey, Fowey, Cornwall PL23 1QH
T: (01726) 870263
F: (01726) 870263
E: polholiday@aol.com

PORLOCK
Somerset

Burrowhayes Farm Caravan and Camping Site and Riding Stables ★★★★
Touring and Camping Park
West Luccombe, Porlock, Minehead, Somerset TA24 8HT
T: (01643) 862463
E: burrowhayes.co.uk
I: www.burrowhayes.co.uk

Porlock Caravan Park ★★★
Holiday and Touring Park
Highbanks, Porlock, Minehead, Somerset TA24 8ND
T: (01643) 862269
F: (01643) 862239
E: ADHPCP@aol.com
I: www.exmoortourism.org/porlockcaravanpark.htm

PORTHTOWAN
Cornwall

Rose Hill Touring Park ★★★★
Touring Park
Porthtowan, Truro, Cornwall TR4 8AR
T: (01209) 890802
E: reception@rosehillcamping.co.uk
I: www.rosehillcamping.co.uk

PORTREATH
Cornwall

Cambrose Touring Park ★★★
Touring Park
Portreath Road, Redruth, Cornwall TR16 4HT
T: (01209) 890747
F: (01209) 891665
E: cambrosetouringpark@supanet.com
I: www.cambrosetouringpark.co.uk

Tehidy Holiday Park ★★★
Holiday Park
Harris Mill, Illogan, Portreath, Redruth, Cornwall TR16 4JQ
T: (01209) 216489 & 314558
F: (01209) 216489
E: holiday@tehidy.co.uk
I: www.tehidy.co.uk

PRESTON
Dorset

Seaview Holiday Park ★★★
Holiday Park
Preston, Weymouth, Dorset DT3 6DZ
T: (01305) 833037
F: (01305) 833169

Weymouth Bay Holiday Park ★★★
Holiday Park
Preston Road, Preston, Weymouth, Dorset DT3 6BQ
T: (01305) 832271
F: (01305) 835101

REDHILL
North Somerset

Brook Lodge Farm Touring Caravan & Tent Park ★★★
Touring and Camping Park
Cowslip Green, Bristol, BS40 5RD
T: (01934) 862311
F: (01934) 862311

REDRUTH
Cornwall

Lanyon Holiday Park ★★★★
Holiday Park
Losombe Lane, Four Lanes, Redruth, Cornwall TR
T: (01209) 313474 & 07775 782269
F: (01209) 313422
E: jamierielly@supanet.com
I: www.lanyonholidaypark.co.uk

276

Establishments printed in blue have a detailed entry in this guide

SOUTH WEST

RELUBBUS
Cornwall

River Valley Country Park ★★★★★
Holiday Park
Rose Award
Relubbus, Penzance, Cornwall TR20 9ER
T: (01736) 763398
F: (01736) 763398
E: rivervalley@surfbay.dircon.co.uk
I: www.rivervalley.co.uk

RODNEY STOKE
Somerset

Bucklegrove Caravan & Camping Park ★★★★
Holiday Park
Wells Road, Rodney Stoke, Cheddar, Somerset BS27 3UZ
T: (01749) 870261
F: (01749) 870101
E: info@bucklegrove.co.uk
I: www.bucklegrove.co.uk

ROSUDGEON
Cornwall

Kenneggy Cove Holiday Park ★★★
Holiday Park
Higher Kenneggy, Rosudgeon, Penzance, Cornwall TR20 9AU
T: (01736) 763453
F: (01736) 763453
E: enquiries@kenneggycove.co.uk
I: www.kenneggycove.co.uk

ROUSDON
Devon

Pinewood Homes ★★★★★
Holiday Park
Rousdon, Lyme Regis, Dorset DT7 3RD
T: (01297) 22055
F: (01297) 22055
E: info@pinewood.uk.net
I: www.pinewood.uk.net

Westhayes Caravan Park ★★★★
Holiday Park
Sidmouth Road, Rousdon, Lyme Regis, Dorset DT7 3RD
T: (01297) 23456
F: (01297) 625079
I: welome.to/westhayes

RUAN MINOR
Cornwall

Sea Acres Holiday Park ★★★★
Holiday Park
Kennack Sands, Ruan Minor, Helston, Cornwall TR12 7LT
T: (01326) 290064 & 292000
F: (01326) 290063
E: seaacres1@aol.com
I: www.seaacres.co.uk

Silver Sands Holiday Park ★★★
Holiday and Touring Park
Gwendreath, Kennack Sands, Ruan Minor, Helston, Cornwall TR12 7LZ
T: (01326) 290631
F: (01326) 290631
E: enquiries@silversandsholidaypark.co.uk
I: www.silversandsholidaypark.co.uk

ST AGNES
Cornwall

Beacon Cottage Farm Touring Park ★★★★
Touring Park
Beacon Drive, St Agnes, Cornwall TR5 0NU
T: (01872) 552347 & 553381

Troytown Farm Campsite ★★★
Camping Park
Troytown Farm, St Agnes, Isles of Scilly TR22 0PL
T: (01720) 422360
E: troytown@talk21.com
I: www.isles-of-scilly.co.uk

ST AUSTELL
Cornwall

Duporth Holiday Park ★★★
Holiday Park
St Austell Bay, St Austell, Cornwall PL26 6AJ
T: (01726) 65511
F: (01726) 68497
E: duporth@aol.com

River Valley Holiday Park ★★★★
Holiday, Touring and Camping Park
Rose Award
Pentewan Road, London Apprentice, St Austell, Cornwall PL26 7AP
T: (01726) 73533
F: (01726) 73533
E: JohnClemo@aol.com
I: river-valley.co.uk

Sun Valley Holiday Park ★★★★★
Holiday Park
Rose Award
Pentewan Road, St Austell, Cornwall PL26 6DJ
T: (01726) 843266 & 843842
F: (01726) 843266
E: reception@sunvalley-holidays.co.uk
I: www.sunvalley-holidays.co.uk

Trewhiddle Holiday Estate ★★★★
Holiday Park
Pentewan Road, Trewhiddle, St Austell, Cornwall PL26 7AD
T: (01726) 67011
F: (01726) 67010
E: mcclelland@btinternet.com
I: www.trewhiddle.co.uk

ST BURYAN
Cornwall

Camping and Caravanning Club Site ★★★★
Touring Park
Sennen Cove Club Site, Higher Tregiffian Farm, St Buryan, Penzance, Cornwall TR19 6JB
T: (01736) 871588
I: www.campingandcaravanningclub.co.uk

ST COLUMB MAJOR
Cornwall

Tregatillian Holiday Park ★★★★
Holiday Park
Rose Award
St Columb Major, Cornwall TR9 6JH
T: (01637) 880482
F: (01637) 880482
E: tregatillian@fsbdial.co.uk
I: www.chycor.co.uk/parks/tregatillian

ST EWE
Cornwall

Pengrugla Caravan Park ★★★★
Holiday, Touring and Camping Park
Pengrugla, St Ewe, St Austell, Cornwall PL26 6EL
T: (01726) 843485 & 844414
F: (01726) 844142
E: info@pentewan.co.uk
I: www.pentewan.co.uk

ST GENNYS
Cornwall

Camping and Caravanning Club Site ★★★★
Touring Park
Bude Club Site, Gillards Moor, St Gennys, Bude, Cornwall EX23 0BG
T: (01840) 230650
I: www.campingandcaravanningclub.co.uk

ST IVES
Cornwall

Ayr Holiday Park ★★★★
Holiday Park
Higher Ayr, Ayr, St Ives, Cornwall TR26 1EJ
T: (01736) 795855
F: (01736) 798797
E: andy@ayr-holiday-park.demon.co.uk

Little Trevarrack Touring Park ★★★
Touring Park
Laity Lane, Carbis Bay, St Ives, Cornwall TR26 3HW
T: (01736) 797580 & 795640
F: (01736) 797580
E: littletrevarrack@hotmail.com
I: www.littletrevarrack.com

Polmanter Tourist Park ★★★★★
Touring Park
St Ives, Cornwall TR26 3LX
T: (01736) 795640
F: (01736) 795640
E: phillip_osborne@hotmail.com
I: www.polmanter.com

Trevalgan Holiday Farm ★★★★
Touring Park
St Ives, Cornwall TR26 3BJ
T: (01736) 796433
F: (01736) 796433
E: trevalgan@aol.com
I: www.trevalganholidayfarm.co.uk

ST JUST-IN-PENWITH
Cornwall

Roselands Caravan Park ★★★
Holiday Park
Dowran, St Just-in-Penwith, Penzance, Cornwall TR19 7RS
T: (01736) 788571
F: (01736) 788571
E: camping@roseland84.freeserve.co.uk
I: www.roselands

ST JUST IN ROSELAND
Cornwall

Trethem Mill Touring Park ★★★★★
Touring Park
St Just in Roseland, Truro, Cornwall TR2 5JF
T: (01872) 580504
F: (01872) 580968
E: reception@trethem-mill.co.uk
I: www.trethem-mill.co.uk

ST MARY'S
Isles of Scilly

Garrison Farm Campsite
Rating Applied For
St Mary's, Isles of Scilly TR21 0LS
T: (01720) 422670
F: (01720) 422670
E: tedmoulson@cs.com
I: www.isles-of-scilly.co.uk

ST MERRYN
Cornwall

Higher Harlyn Park ★★★
Holiday Park
St Merryn, Padstow, Cornwall PL28 8SG
T: (01841) 520022 & 520879
F: (01841) 520879

Point Curlew Holiday Estate ★★★
Holiday, Touring and Camping Park
St Merryn, Padstow, Cornwall PL28 8PY
T:
I: www.pointcurlew.co.uk

Trethias Farm Caravan Park ★★
Touring Park
Treyarnon Bay, St Merryn, Padstow, Cornwall PL28 8PL
T: (01841) 520323 & 520055
F: (01841) 520055

Trevean Farm ★★★
Touring and Camping Park
St Merryn, Padstow, Cornwall PL28 8PR
T: (01841) 520772

ST MINVER
Cornwall

Little Dinham Woodland Caravan Park
Rating Applied For
St Minver, Rock, Wadebridge, Cornwall PL27 6RH
T: (01208) 812538
E: littledinham@hotmail.com
I: www.littledinham.co.uk

St Minver Holiday Park ★★★
Holiday Park
St Minver, Wadebridge, Cornwall PL27 6RR
T: (01208) 862305
F: (01208) 862265
E: office_stminver@lineone.co.uk

Establishments printed in blue have a detailed entry in this guide

SOUTH WEST

ST TUDY
Cornwall
Hengar Manor ★★★★★
Holiday Park
St Tudy, Bodmin, Cornwall
PL30 3PL
T: (01208) 850382
F: (01208) 850722
E: holidays@hengarmanor.co.uk
I: www.hengarmanor.co.uk

SALCOMBE
Devon
Bolberry House Farm ★★★
Touring and Camping Park
Bolberry, Malborough,
Kingsbridge, Devon TQ7 3DY
T: (01548) 561251 & 560926
E: bolberry.house@virgin.net
I: www.bolberryparks.co.uk

Higher Rew Touring Caravan & Camping Park ★★★★
Touring and Camping Park
Malborough, Salcombe,
Kingsbridge, Devon TQ7 3DW
T: (01548) 842681 & 843681
F: (01548) 843681
E: enquiries@higherrew.co.uk
I: www.higherrew.co.uk

Karrageen Caravan and Camping Park ★★★★
Touring and Camping Park
Karrageen, Bolberry,
Malborough, Kingsbridge, Devon
TQ7 3EN
T: (01548) 561230
F: (01548) 560192
E: phil@karrageen.co.uk
I: www.karrageen.co.uk

SALCOMBE REGIS
Devon
Kings Down Tail Caravan & Camping Park★★★★
Touring Park
Salcombe Regis, Sidmouth,
Devon EX10 0PD
T: (01297) 680313
F: (01297) 680313
I: www.uk.parks.
co.uk/kingsdowntail

SALISBURY
Wiltshire
Camping And Caravanning Club Site★★★★
Touring and Camping Park
Hudsons Field, Castle Road,
Salisbury, Wiltshire SP1 3RR
T: (01722) 320713
I: www.
campingandcaravanningclub.
co.uk

SANDY BAY
Devon
Devon Cliffs Holiday Park ★★★
Holiday Park
Sandy Bay, Exmouth, Devon
EX8 5BT
T: (01395) 226226
F: (01395) 223111

SEATON
Devon
Axe Vale Caravan Park ★★★
Holiday Park
Colyford Road, Seaton, Devon
EX12 2DF
T: (01297) 21342 &
0800 0688826
F: (01297) 21712
E: info@axevale.co.uk
I: www.axevale.co.uk

SEEND
Wiltshire
Camping and Caravanning Club Site ★★★★★
Touring Park
Spout Lane, Seend, Melksham,
Wiltshire SN12 6RN
T: (01380) 828839
I: www.
campingandcaravanningclub.
co.uk

SHALDON
Devon
Coast View Holiday Park ★★★★
Holiday Park
Torquay Road, Shaldon,
Teignmouth, Devon TQ14 0BG
T: (01626) 872392
F: (01626) 872719

Devon Valley Holiday Village ★★★★
Holiday Park
Rose Award
Coombe Road, Ringmore,
Shaldon, Teignmouth, Devon
TQ14 0EY
T: (01626) 872525 &
(01803) 852600
F: (01626) 873634
E: devalley@aol.com
I: devonvalleyholidayvillage.
co.uk

SIDBURY
Devon
Putts Corner Caravan Club Site ★★★★
Touring Park
Sidbury, Sidmouth, Devon
EX10 0QQ
T: (01404) 42875
I: www.caravanclub.co.uk

SIDMOUTH
Devon
Salcombe Regis Camping and Caravan Park★★★★★
Holiday and Touring Park
Salcombe Regis, Sidmouth,
Devon EX10 0JH
T: (01395) 514303
F: (01395) 514303
E: info@salcombe-regis.co.uk
I: www.salcombe-regis.co.uk

SLAPTON
Devon
Camping & Caravanning Club Site – Slapton Sands★★★★
Touring and Camping Park
Middle Grounds, Slapton,
Kingsbridge, Devon TQ7 1QW
T: (01548) 580538
I: www.
campingandcaravanningclub.
co.uk

STICKLEPATH
Devon
Olditch Farm Caravan and Camping Park★★★
Holiday, Touring and Camping Park
Sticklepath, Okehampton, Devon
EX20 2NT
T: (01837) 840734
F: (01837) 840877
E: info@olditch.co.uk
I: www.olditch.co.uk

STRATTON
Cornwall
Ivyleaf Combe ★★★★
Holiday Park
Ivyleaf Hill, Stratton, Bude,
Cornwall EX23 9LD
T: (01288) 321323
E: tony@ivyleafcombe.com
I: www.ivyleafcombe.com

TAUNTON
Somerset
Ashe Farm Caravan and Campsite ★★★
Touring Park
Ashe, Thornfalcon, Taunton,
Somerset TA3 5NW
T: (01823) 442567
F: (01823) 443372
E: camping@ashe-frm.fsnet.
co.uk

Holly Bush Park ★★★★
Touring Park
Culmhead, Taunton, Somerset
TA3 7EA
T: (01823) 421515
F: (01823) 421885
E: beaumont@hollybushpark.
ndo.co.uk
I: www.hollybushpark.co.uk

TAVISTOCK
Devon
Harford Bridge Holiday Park ★★★★
Holiday Park
Peter Tavy, Tavistock, Devon
PL19 9LS
T: (01822) 810349
F: (01822) 810028
E: enquiry@harfordbridge.co.uk
I: www.harfordbridge.co.uk

Woodovis Park ★★★★
Holiday Park
Gulworthy, Tavistock, Devon
PL19 8NY
T: (01822) 832968
F: (01822) 832948
E: info@woodovis.com
I: www.woodovis.com

TEDBURN ST MARY
Devon
Springfield Holiday Park
Rating Applied For
Tedburn Road, Tedburn St Mary,
Exeter, Devon EX6 6EW
T: (01647) 24242
F: (01647) 24131
E: springhol@aol.com
I: www.springfieldholidaypark.
co.uk

TEIGNGRACE
Devon
Twelve Oaks Farm Caravan Park ★★★★
Touring Park
Twelve Oaks Farm, Teigngrace,
Newton Abbot, Devon TQ12 6QT
T: (01626) 352769 & 335015
F: (01626) 352769

TINTAGEL
Cornwall
Bossiney Farm Caravan and Camping Park★★★★
Holiday Park
Tintagel, Cornwall PL34 0AY
T: (01840) 770481
F: (01840) 770025
I: www.bossineyfarm.co.uk

Trewethett Farm Caravan Club Site ★★★★
Touring Park
Tintagel, Cornwall PL34 0BQ
T: (01840) 770222
I: www.caravanclub.co.uk

TORQUAY
Devon
Widdicombe Farm Touring Park ★★★★
Touring Park
Ring Road (A380), Compton,
Paignton, Devon TQ3 1ST
T: (01803) 558325
F: (01803) 559526
E: enquiries@torquaytouring.
co.uk
I: www.torquaytouring.co.uk

TOWEDNACK
Cornwall
Penderleath Caravan & Camping Park
Rating Applied For
Towednack, St Ives, Cornwall
TR26 3AF
T: (01736) 798403

TREGURRIAN
Cornwall
Camping and Caravanning Club Site★★★★
Touring Park
Tregurrian, Newquay, Cornwall
TR8 4AE
T: (01637) 860448
I: www.
campingandcaravanningclub.
co.uk

TRURO
Cornwall
Leverton Place ★★★★★
Camping Park
Greenbottom, Truro, Cornwall
TR4 8QW
T: (01872) 560462
F: (01872) 560668

Liskey Holiday Park ★★★★★
Holiday Park
Greenbottom, Truro, Cornwall
TR4 8QN
T: (01872) 560274
F: (01872) 561413
I: www.liskeyholidaypark.co.uk

Ringwell Valley Holiday Park ★★★★★
Holiday Park
Bissoe Road, Carnon Downs,
Truro, Cornwall TR3 6LQ
T: (01872) 862194
F: (01872) 864343
E: keith@ringwell.co.uk
I: www.ringwell.co.uk

Summer Valley Touring Park ★★★★
Touring Park
Shortlanesend, Truro, Cornwall
TR4 9DW
T: (01872) 277878
I: summervalley.co.uk

UMBERLEIGH
Devon
Camping & Caravanning Club Site ★★★★
Touring Park
Over Weir, Umberleigh, Devon
EX37 9DU
T: (01769) 560009
I: www.
campingandcaravanningclub.
co.uk

SOUTH WEST

UPHILL
North Somerset
Slimeridge Farm ★★★★
Touring Park
Links Road, Uphill, Weston-super-Mare BS23 4XY
T: (01934) 641641

VERYAN
Cornwall
Camping & Caravanning Club Site ★★★★
Touring Park
Tretheake Manor, Veryan, Truro, Cornwall TR2 5PP
T: (01872) 501658
F: (01872) 501658
I: www.campingandcaravanningclub.co.uk

WADEBRIDGE
Cornwall
Little Bodieve Holiday Park ★★★★
Holiday Park
Bodieve Road, Wadebridge, Cornwall PL27 6EG
T: (01208) 812323
I: www.chycor.co.uk/parks/little-bodieve

Trewince Farm Holiday Park ★★★★
Holiday and Touring Park
Rose Award
St Issey, Wadebridge, Cornwall PL27 7RL
T: (01208) 812830
F: (01208) 812835

WALTON
Somerset
Bramble Hill Caravan & Camping Park ★★
Touring Park
Bramble Hill, Walton, Street, Somerset BA16 9RQ
T: (01458) 442548 & 07711 893670

WARMINSTER
Wiltshire
Longleat Caravan Club Site ★★★★
Touring Park
Warminster, Wiltshire BA12 7NL
T: (01985) 844663
I: www.caravanclub.co.uk

WARMWELL
Dorset
Warmwell Country Touring Park ★★★★
Touring Park
Warmwell, Weymouth, Dorset DT2 8JD
T: (01305) 852313
F: (01305) 851824
I: welcome.to/warmwell

Warmwell Leisure Resort ★★★
Holiday Park
Warmwell, Dorchester, Dorset DT2 8JE
T: (01305) 852911
F: (01305) 854588

WATCHET
Somerset
Lorna Doone Caravan Park ★★★★★
Holiday Park
Watchet, Somerset TA23 0BJ
T: (01984) 631206
F: (01984) 633537
E: mail@lornadoone.co.uk
I: www.lornadoone.co.uk

West Bay Caravan Park ★★★★★
Holiday Park
Cleeve Hill, Watchet, Somerset TA23 0BJ
T: (01984) 631261
F: (01984) 634944
E: alistair@westbay2000.freeserve.co.uk
I: www.westhaycavavanpark.co.uk

WATERROW
Somerset
Waterrow Touring Park ★★★★
Touring Park
Waterrow, Taunton, Somerset TA4 2AZ
T: (01984) 623464 & 624280
F: (01984) 624280
E: taylor@waterrowpark.u-net.com
I: www.waterrowpark.u-net.com

WELLS
Somerset
Mendip Heights Camping and Caravan Park ★★★★
Touring Park
Townsend, Priddy, Wells, Somerset BA5 3BP
T: (01749) 870241
F: (01749) 870368
E: bta@mendipheights.co.uk
I: www.mendipheights.co.uk

WEMBURY
Devon
Churchwood Valley Holiday Cabins ★★★★
Holiday Park
Churchwood Valley, Wembury Bay, Wembury, Plymouth PL9 0DZ
T: (01752) 862382
F: (01752) 863274
E: Churchwoodvalley@btinternet.com
I: www.ukparks.co.uk/churchwoodvalley

WEST BAY
Dorset
West Bay Holiday Park ★★★
Holiday Park
West Bay, Bridport, Dorset DT6 4HB
T: (01308) 422424
F: (01308) 421371
I: www.parkdeanholidays.com

WEST BEXINGTON
Dorset
Gorselands Caravan Park ★★★★
Holiday Park
West Bexington, Dorchester, Dorset DT2 9DJ
T: (01308) 897232
F: (01308) 897239

WEST QUANTOXHEAD
Somerset
Home Farm Holiday Centre
Rating Applied For
St Audries Bay, Williton, Taunton, Somerset TA4 4DP
T: (01984) 632487
F: (01984) 634687

St Audries Bay Holiday Club ★★★
Holiday Park
West Quantoxhead, Taunton, Somerset TA4 4DY
T: (01984) 632515
F: (01984) 632785
E: mrandle@staudriesbay.demon.co.uk
I: www.staudriesbay.co.uk

WESTON
Devon
Oakdown Touring and Holiday Home Park ★★★★★
Holiday and Touring Park
Weston, Sidmouth, Devon EX10 0PH
T: (01297) 680387
F: (01297) 680541
E: oakdown@btinternet.com
I: www.bestcaravanpark.co.uk

Stoneleigh Holiday and Leisure Village ★★★★
Holiday Park
Weston, Sidmouth, Devon EX10 0PJ
T: (01395) 513619
F: (01395) 513629

WESTON-SUPER-MARE
North Somerset
Brean Leisure Park Limited ★★★
Holiday Park
Coast Road, Brean, Burnham-on-Sea, Somerset TA8 2RF
T: (01278) 751595 & 752100
F: (01278) 752102
E: admin@brean.com
I: www.brean.com

Camping and Caravanning Club Site ★★★
Touring Park
West End Farm, Locking, Weston-super-Mare, Somerset BS24 8RH
T: (01934) 822548
I: www.campingandcaravanningclub.co.uk

Carefree Holiday Park ★★★★★
Holiday Park
12 Beach Road, Sand Bay, Weston-super-Mare, BS22 9UZ
T: (01934) 624541
F: (01934) 613636

Country View Caravan Park ★★★
Holiday Park
Sand Road, Sand Bay, Weston-super-Mare, BS22 9UJ
T: (01934) 627595
F: (01934) 627595

WESTON-SUPER-MARE
North Somerset
Dulhorn Farm Camping Site ★★
Camping Park
Weston Road, Lympsham, Weston-super-Mare BS24 0JQ
T: (01934) 750298
F: (01934) 750913

WESTON-SUPER-MARE
North Somerset
Purn International Holiday Park ★★★★
Holiday Park
Bridgwater Road, A370 Bleadon, Weston-super-Mare, BS24 0AN
T: (01934) 812342
F: (01934) 812342
E: gavin@purn-international.freeserve.co.uk

Sand Bay Caravan Park ★★★★
Holiday Park
52 Beach Road, Sand Bay, Weston-super-Mare, BS22 9UW
T: (01934) 633126

West End Farm/Caravan & Camping Park ★★★
Touring Park
Locking, Weston-super-Mare BS24 8RH
T: (01934) 822529
F: (01934) 822529

Weston Gateway Tourist Caravan Park
Rating Applied For
West Wick, Weston-super-Mare, BS24 7TF
T: (01934) 510384

WESTWARD HO!
Devon
Beachside Holiday Park ★★★★
Holiday Park
Merley Road, Westward Ho!, Bideford, Devon EX39 1JX
T: (01237) 421163
F: (01237) 472100
E: beachside@surfbay.dircon.co.uk
I: www.beachsideholidays.co.uk

Surf Bay Holiday Park ★★★★
Holiday Park
Golf Links Road, Westward Ho!, Bideford, Devon EX39 1HD
T: (01237) 471833
F: (01237) 474387
E: surfbayholidaypark@surfbay.dircon.co.uk
I: www.surfbay.co.uk

WEYMOUTH
Dorset
Bagwell Farm Touring Park ★★★★
Touring Park
Chickerell, Weymouth, Dorset DT3 4EA
T: (01305) 782575
F: (01305) 786987
E: enquiries@bagwellfarm.co.uk
I: www.bagwellfarm.co.uk

Chesil Beach Holiday Park ★★★
Holiday Park
Chesil Beach, Weymouth, Dorset DT4 9AG
T: (01305) 773233

East Fleet Farm Touring Park ★★★
Touring Park
Fleet Lane, Chickerell, Weymouth, Dorset DT3 4DW
T: (01305) 785768
E: richard@eastfleet.co.uk
I: www.eastfleet.co.uk

Establishments printed in blue have a detailed entry in this guide

SOUTH WEST

Littlesea Holiday Park ★★★
Holiday Park
Lynch Lane, Weymouth, Dorset
DT4 9DT
T: (01305) 774414
F: (01305) 760038

Pebble Bank Caravan Park ★★★
Holiday, Touring and Camping Park
90 Camp Road, Wyke Regis,
Weymouth, Dorset DT4 9HF
T: (01305) 774844
F: (01305) 774844
E: ian@pebbank.freeserve.co.uk
I: www.westcountry.net/dorset/pebble_bank_caravan_park.htm

Waterside Holiday Park ★★★★★
Holiday Park
Bowleaze Cove, Weymouth,
Dorset DT3 6PP
T: (01305) 833103
F: (01305) 832830
E: info@watersideholidays.co.uk
I: www.watersideholidays.co.uk

WHITE CROSS
Cornwall

Summer Lodge Holiday Park ★★★★
Holiday Park
White Cross, Newquay, Cornwall
TR8 4LW
T: (01726) 860415
F: (01726) 861490
E: reservations@summerlodge.co.uk
I: www.summerlodge.co.uk

White Acres Holiday Park ★★★★★
Holiday Park
Rose Award
White Cross, Newquay, Cornwall
TR8 4LW
T: (01726) 860220
F: (01726) 860877
E: whiteacres.co.uk

WIDEMOUTH BAY
Cornwall

Widemouth Bay Caravan Park ★★★
Holiday Park
Widemouth Bay, Bude, Cornwall
EX23 0DF
T: (01288) 361208 &
(01271) 866766
F: (01271) 866791
E: bookings@johnfowlerholidays.com
I: www.johnfowlerholidays.com

WINSFORD
Somerset

Halse Farm Caravan & Tent Park ★★★★
Touring Park
Winsford, Minehead, Somerset
TA24 7JL
T: (01643) 851259
F: (01643) 851592
E: brown@halsefarm.co.uk
I: www.halsefarm.co.uk

WOODBURY
Devon

Castle Brake Holiday Park ★★★
Holiday Park
Castle Lane, Woodbury, Exeter,
Devon EX5 1HA
T: (01395) 232431
E: reception@castlebrake.co.uk
I: www.castlebrake.co.uk

Webbers Farm Caravan & Camping Park ★★★★★
Touring Park
Castle Lane, Woodbury, Exeter,
Devon EX5 1EA
T: (01395) 232276
F: (01395) 233389
E: reception@webbersfarm.co.uk
I: www.webbersfarm.co.uk

WOOLACOMBE
Devon

Golden Coast Holiday Village ★★★★
Holiday Park
Station Road, Woolacombe,
Devon EX34 7HW
T: (01271) 870343
F: (01271) 870089
E: goodtimes@woolacombe.com
I: www.woolacombe.com

Woolacombe Bay Holiday Village ★★★★
Holiday Park
Seymour, Sandy Lane,
Woolacombe, Devon EX34 7AH
T: (01271) 870343
F: (01271) 870089
E: goodtimes@woolacombe.com
I: www.woolacombe.com

Woolacombe Sands Holiday Park ★★★
Holiday Park
Beach Road, Woolacombe,
Devon EX34 7AF
T: (01271) 870569
F: (01271) 870606
E: lifesabeach@woolacombe-sands.co.uk
I: www.woolacombe-sands.co.uk

YEOVIL
Somerset

Long Hazel International Caravan and Camping Park ★★★★
Touring Park
High Street, Sparkford, Yeovil,
Somerset BA22 7JH
T: (01963) 440002
F: (01963) 440002
E: longhazelpark@hotmail.com
I: www.sparkford.f9.co.uk/lhi.htm

SOUTH OF ENGLAND

ALDERHOLT
Dorset

Hill Cottage Farm Caravan Park ★★★★
Touring Park
Sandleheath Road, Alderholt,
Fordingbridge, Hampshire
SP6 3EG
T: (01425) 650513
F: (01425) 652339

ANDOVER
Hampshire

Wyke Down Touring Caravan & Camping Park ★★★
Touring and Camping Park
Picket Piece, Andover,
Hampshire SP11 6LX
T: (01264) 352048
F: (01264) 324661
E: wykedown@wykedown.co.uk
I: www.wykedown.co.uk

APSE HEATH
Isle of Wight

Old Barn Touring Park ★★★★
Touring and Camping Park
Cheverton Farm, Newport Road,
Apse Heath, Sandown, Isle of
Wight PO36 9PJ
T: (01983) 866414
E: oldbarn@weltinet.com
I: www.oldbarntouring.co.uk

Village Way Camping Site ★★★
Holiday, Touring and Camping Park
Newport Road, Apse Heath,
Sandown, Isle of Wight
PO36 9PJ
T: (01983) 863279

ASHURST
Hampshire

Forestry Commission Ashurst Caravan & Camping Site ★★★★
Camping Park
Lyndhurst Road, Ashurst,
Southampton, Hampshire
SO40 2AA
T: (0131) 3146505
E: fe.holidays@forestry.gov.uk
I: www.forestholidays.co.uk

ATHERFIELD BAY
Isle of Wight

Chine Farm Camping Site
Rating Applied For
Chine Farm, Military Road,
Atherfield Bay, Ventnor, Isle of
Wight PO38 2JH
T: (01983) 740228

BANBURY
Oxfordshire

Bo-Peep Caravan Park ★★★★
Touring Park
Aynho Road, Adderbury,
Banbury, Oxfordshire OX17 3NP
T: (01295) 810605
F: (01295) 810605
E: warden@bo-peep.co.uk
I: www.bo-peep.co.uk

BEACONSFIELD
Buckinghamshire

Highclere Farm Country Touring Park ★★★★
Touring and Camping Park
Newbarn Lane, Seer Green,
Beaconsfield, Buckinghamshire
HP9 2QZ
T: (01494) 874505
F: (01494) 875238

BEMBRIDGE
Isle of Wight

Sandhills Holiday Park ★★★
Holiday Park
Whitecliff Bay, Bembridge, Isle
of Wight PO35 5QB
T: (01983) 872277
F: (01983) 874888

Whitecliff Bay Holiday Park Ltd ★★★★
Holiday Park
Rose Award
Hillway Road, Bembridge, Isle of
Wight PO35 5PL
T: (01983) 872671
F: (01983) 872941
E: holiday@whitecliff-bay.com
I: www.whitecliff-bay.com

BERE REGIS
Dorset

Rowlands Wait Touring Park ★★★
Touring Park
Rye Hill, Bere Regis, Wareham,
Dorset BH20 7LP
T: (01929) 472727
F: (01929) 472727
E: bta@rowlandswait.co.uk
I: www.rowlandswait.co.uk

BICESTER
Oxfordshire

Heyford Leys Mobile Home Park & Camping Site ★
Touring and Camping Park
Camp Road, Upper Heyford,
Bicester, Oxfordshire OX25 5LU
T: (01869) 232048
F: (01869) 233167
E: heyfordleys@aol.com
I: www.ukparks.co.uk/heyfordleys

SOUTH OF ENGLAND

BLANDFORD FORUM
Dorset
The Inside Park ★★★★
Touring and Camping Park
Blandford Forum, Dorset
DT11 9AD
T: (01258) 453719 &
07778 313293
F: (01258) 459921
E: inspark@aol.com
I: members.aol.
com/inspark/inspark

BLETCHINGDON
Oxfordshire
**Diamond Farm Caravan &
Camping Park** ★★★
Touring Park
Islip Road, Bletchingdon, Oxford,
Oxfordshire OX5 3DR
T: (01869) 350909
F: (01869) 350918
E: diamondfarm@supanet.com
I: www.
diamondfarmcaravanpark.co.uk

BOURNEMOUTH
Dorset
St Leonards Farm ★★★
Touring Park
Ringwood Road, West Moors,
Ferndown, Dorset BH22 0AQ
T: (01202) 872637
F: (01202) 872637
I: www.st-leonardsfarm.co.uk

BRIGHSTONE
Isle of Wight
**Grange Farm Camping &
Caravan** ★★★
Holiday and Camping Park
Military Road, Brighstone Bay,
Brighstone, Isle of Wight
PO30 4DA
T: (01983) 740296
F: (01983) 741233
E: grangefarm@brighstonebay.
fsnet.co.uk
I: www.brighstonebay.fsnet.
co.uk/main.htm

Lower Sutton Farm ★★★
Holiday Park
Military Road, Brighstone,
Newport, Isle of Wight
PO30 4PG
T: (01983) 740401
F: (01983) 740844

BROCKENHURST
Hampshire
**Forestry Commission Hollands
Wood Caravan & Camping Site**
★★★★
Camping Park
Lyndhurst Road, Brockenhurst,
Hampshire SO42 7QH
T: (0131) 314 6505
F: (0131) 334 0849
E: fe.holidays@forestry.gov.uk
I: www.forestry.gov.uk

**Forestry Commission Roundhill
Caravan & Camping Site** ★★★
Touring and Camping Park
Beaulieu Road, Brockenhurst,
Hampshire SO42 7QL
T: (0131) 314 6505
F: (0131) 334 0849
E: fe.holidays@forestry.gov.uk
I: www.forestry.gov.uk

BROOK
Isle of Wight
Compton Farm ★★
Holiday and Camping Park
Brook, Newport, Isle of Wight
PO30 4HF
T: (01983) 740215
F: (01983) 740215

BURFORD
Oxfordshire
Burford Caravan Club Site
★★★★★
Touring and Camping Park
Bradwell Grove, Burford,
Oxfordshire OX18 4JJ
T: (01993) 823080
I: www.caravanclub.co.uk

CHADLINGTON
Oxfordshire
**Camping & Caravanning Club
Site** ★★★★
Touring and Camping Park
Chipping Norton Road,
Chadlington, Oxford,
Oxfordshire OX7 3PE
T: (01608) 641993
I: www.
campingandcaravanningclub.
co.uk

CHARLBURY
Oxfordshire
**Cotswold View Caravan &
Camping Site** ★★★★
Touring and Camping Park
Enstone Road, Charlbury,
Oxford, Oxfordshire OX7 3JH
T: (01608) 810314
F: (01608) 811891
E: cotswoldview@gfwiddows.f9.
co.uk
I: www.cotswoldview.co.uk

CHRISTCHURCH
Dorset
Beaulieu Gardens Holiday Park
★★★★★
Holiday Park
Rose Award
Beaulieu Avenue, Christchurch,
Dorset BH23 2EB
T: (01202) 486215
F: (01202) 483878
E: enquiries@
meadowbank-holidays.co.uk
I: www.meadowbank-holidays.
co.uk

**Harrow Wood Farm Caravan
Park** ★★★★
Touring and Camping Park
Poplar Lane, Bransgore,
Christchurch, Dorset BH23 8JE
T: (01425) 672487
F: (01425) 672487
E: harwood@caravan-sites.
co.uk
I: www.caravan-sites.co.uk

Hoburne Park ★★★★★
Holiday and Touring Park
Hoburne Lane, Christchurch,
Dorset BH23 4HU
T: (01425) 273379
F: (01425) 270705
E: enquiries@hoburne.com
I: www.hoburne.com

Meadow Bank Holidays
★★★★★
Holiday Park
Stour Way, Christchurch, Dorset
BH23 2PQ
T: (01202) 483597
F: (01202) 483878
E: enquiries@
meadowbank-holidays.co.uk
I: www.meadowbank-holiday.
co.uk

Mount Pleasant Touring Park
★★★★★
Touring Park
Matchams Lane, Hurn,
Christchurch, Dorset BH23 6AW
T: (01202) 475474
E: enq@mount-pleasant-cc.
co.uk
I: www.mount-pleasant-cc.co.uk

COLWELL BAY
Isle of Wight
Colwell Bay Holiday Club
Rating Applied For
Madeira Lane, Colwell Bay,
Freshwater, Isle of Wight
PO40 9SR
T: (01983) 752403
E: james.bishop1@tinyworld.
co.uk

COWES
Isle of Wight
Sunnycott Caravan Park ★★★
Holiday Park
Rew Street, Cowes, Isle of Wight
PO31 8NN
T: (01983) 292859
F: (01983) 295389

CRANMORE
Isle of Wight
Silver Glades Caravan Park
★★★★
Holiday Park
Solent Road, Cranmore,
Yarmouth, Isle of Wight
PO41 0XZ
T: (01983) 760172
E: michele@silverglades.
worldonline.co.uk

EAST COWES
Isle of Wight
Waverley Park Holiday Centre
★★
*Holiday, Touring and Camping
Park*
Old Road, East Cowes, Isle of
Wight PO32 6AW
T: (01983) 293452
F: (01983) 200494
E: waverleypark@
netscapeonline.co.uk
I: come.to/waverleypark

FAREHAM
Hampshire
**Ellerslie Touring Caravan &
Camping Park** ★★
Touring and Camping Park
Downend Road, Fareham,
Hampshire PO16 8TS
T: (01329) 822248
F: (01329) 822248

FORDINGBRIDGE
Hampshire
Sandy Balls Holiday Centre
★★★★★
*Holiday, Touring and Camping
Park*
Godshill, Fordingbridge,
Hampshire SP6 2JY
T: (01425) 653042
F: (01425) 653067
E: post@sandy-balls.co.uk
I: www.sandy-balls.co.uk

FRESHWATER
Isle of Wight
Heathfield Farm Camping Site
★★★
Camping Park
Heathfield Road, Freshwater, Isle
of Wight PO40 9SH
T: (01983) 756756
F: (01983) 756756
E: heathfield@netguides.co.uk
I: www.netguides.co.uk

FRINGFORD
Oxfordshire
Glebe Lakes Caravan Park
Rating Applied For
Glebe Farm, Stoke Lyne Road,
Fringford, Bicester, Oxfordshire
OX6 9RJ
T: (01869) 271410
F: (01869) 277704
E: ann.herring@btinternet.com

FRITHAM
Hampshire
**Forestry Commission Ocknell/
Longbeech Caravan & Camping
Site** ★★★
Camping Park
Fritham, Lyndhurst, Hampshire
SO43 7HH
T: (0131) 314 6505
F: (0131) 3340849
E: fe.holidays@forestry.gov.uk
I: www.forestholidays.co.uk

GILLINGHAM
Dorset
**Thorngrove Caravan &
Camping Park** ★★
Touring and Camping Park
Common Mead Lane,
Gillingham, Dorset SP8 4RE
T: (01747) 822242
F: (01747) 826386
I: 821221

GOSPORT
Hampshire
Kingfisher Caravan Park
★★★★
*Holiday, Touring and Camping
Park*
Browndown Road, Stokes Bay,
Gosport, Hampshire PO13 9BG
T: (023) 9250 2611
F: (023) 9258 3583
E: info@
kingfisher-caravan-park.co.uk
I: www.kingfisher-caravan-park.
co.uk

SOUTH OF ENGLAND

GURNARD
Isle of Wight
Gurnard Pines Holiday Village ★★★★★
Holiday Park
Rose Award
Cockleton Lane, Gurnard, Cowes, Isle of Wight PO31 8QE
T: (01983) 292395
F: (01983) 299415
E: info@gurnardpines.co.uk
I: www.gurnardpines.co.uk

Solent Lawn Holiday Park ★★★
Holiday Park
Shore Road, Gurnard, Cowes, Isle of Wight PO31 8JX
T: (01983) 293243
E: info@isleofwightselfcatering.co.uk
I: www.isleofwightselfcatering.co.uk

HAMBLE
Hampshire
Riverside Park ★★★★
Holiday and Touring Park
Satchell Lane, Hamble, Southampton, Hampshire SO31 4HR
T: (023) 8045 3220
F: (023) 8045 3611
E: enquiries@riversideholidays.co.uk
I: www.riversideholidays.co.uk

HAYLING ISLAND
Hampshire
Fishers Caravan Park ★★★★
Holiday Park
31 Fishery Lane, Hayling Island, Hampshire PO11 9NU
T: (023) 9246 3501

Fishery Creek Caravan & Camping Park ★★★
Camping Park
Fishery Lane, Hayling Island, Hampshire PO11 9NR
T: (023) 9246 2164
F: (023) 9246 0741
E: camping@fisherycreek.fsnet.co.uk

Mill Rythe Holiday Village ★★★★★
Holiday Park
Havant Road, Hayling Island, Hampshire PO11 0PB
T: (023) 9246 3805
F: (023) 9246 4842

Woodcot Caravan Park ★★★★
Holiday Park
29 Fishery Lane, Hayling Island, Hampshire PO11 9NU
T: (023) 9246 3501
F: (023) 9246 3501

HENLEY-ON-THAMES
Oxfordshire
Swiss Farm International Touring and Camping ★★
Touring and Camping Park
Swiss Farm, Marlow Road, Henley-on-Thames, Oxfordshire RG9 2HY
T: (01491) 573419
F: (01494) 573419
E: borlase@borlase.demon.co.uk

HIGHCLIFFE
Dorset
Cobb's Holiday Park ★★★★
Holiday Park
Rose Award
32 Gordon Road, Highcliffe, Christchurch, Dorset BH23 5HN
T: (01425) 273301
F: (01425) 276090

HOLMSLEY
Hampshire
Forestry Commission Holmsley Caravan & Camping Site ★★★★
Touring and Camping Park
Forest Road, Holmsley, Christchurch, Dorset BH23 7EQ
T: (0131) 314 6505
E: fe.holidays@forestry.gov.uk
I: www.forestryholidays.co.uk

HOLTON HEATH
Dorset
Tanglewood Holiday Park ★★★★
Holiday Park
Organford Road, Holton Heath, Poole, Dorset BH16 6JY
T: (01305) 780209 &
(01202) 632618
F: (01305) 777218

HURLEY
Berkshire
Hurley Farm Caravan & Camping Park ★★★
Holiday, Touring and Camping Park
Shepherds Lane, Hurley, Maidenhead, Berkshire SL6 5NE
T: (01628) 823501 & 824493
F: (01628) 825533
E: enquiries@hurleyfarm.co.uk
I: www.hurleyfarm.co.uk

HURN
Dorset
Tall Trees Holiday Caravan Park ★★★★
Holiday Park
Matchams Lane, Hurn, Christchurch, Dorset BH23 6AW
T: (01202) 477144
F: (01202) 479546
E: talltrees.park@talk21.com
I: www.tall-trees.co.uk

LIPHOOK
Hampshire
The Deer's Hut ★★★
Touring and Camping Park
Griggs Green, Longmoor Road, Liphook, Hampshire GU30 7PD
T: (01428) 724406

MILFORD-ON-SEA
Hampshire
Carrington Park ★★★★★
Holiday Park
New Lane, Milford-on-Sea, Lymington, Hampshire SO41 0UQ
T: (01590) 642654
F: (01590) 642951

Downton Holiday Park ★★★★
Holiday Park
Shorefield Road, Milford-on-Sea, Lymington, Hampshire SO41 0LH
T: (01425) 476131 &
(01590) 642515

Lytton Lawn Touring Park ★★★★
Touring and Camping Park
Lymore Lane, Milford-on-Sea, Lymington, Hampshire SO41 0TX
T: (01590) 648331
F: (01590) 645610
E: holidays@shorefield.co.uk
I: www.shorefield.co.uk

Shorefield Country Park ★★★★★
Holiday Park
Shorefield Road, Milford-on-Sea, Lymington, Hampshire SO41 0LH
T: (01590) 648331
F: (01590) 645610
E: holidays@shorefield.co.uk
I: www.shorefield.co.uk

MOLLINGTON
Oxfordshire
Mollington Touring Caravan Park ★★★
Touring and Camping Park
The Yews, Mollington, Banbury, Oxfordshire OX17 1AZ
T: (01295) 750731 &
07966 171959
F: (01295) 750731
I: www.ukparks.co.uk/mollington

MORETON
Dorset
Camping & Caravanning Club Site ★★★★
Camping Park
Station Road, Moreton, Dorchester, Dorset DT2 8BB
T: (01305) 853801
I: www.campingandcaravanningclub.co.uk

NEW MILTON
Hampshire
Forestry Commission Setthorns Caravan and Camping Site. ★★★★
Touring and Camping Park
Wootton, New Milton, Hampshire BH25 5UA
T: (0131) 314 6505
E: fe.holidays@forestry.gov.uk
I: www.forestholidays.co.uk

Glen Orchard Holiday Park ★★★★
Holiday Park
Walkford Lane, New Milton, Hampshire BH25 5NH
T: (01425) 616463
F: (01425) 638655
E: enquiries@glenorchard.co.uk
I: glenorchard.co.uk

Hoburne Bashley Park Ltd ★★★★
Holiday and Touring Park
Sway Road, New Milton, Hampshire BH25 5QR
T: (01425) 612340 & 616422
F: (01425) 632732
E: enquires@hobourne.co.uk
I: www.hobourne.co.uk

Hoburne Naish Estate Ltd ★★★★★
Holiday Park
Christchurch Road, New Milton, Hampshire BH25 7RE
T: (01425) 273586 & 273786
F: (01425) 282130
E: enquires@hobourne.co.uk
I: www.hobourne.co.uk

NEWCHURCH
Isle of Wight
Southland Camping Park ★★★★★
Touring and Camping Park
Newchurch, Sandown, Isle of Wight PO36 0LZ
T: (01983) 865385
F: (01983) 867663
E: info@southland.co.uk
I: www.southland.co.uk

NITON
Isle of Wight
Meadow View Caravan Site ★
Holiday Park
Hoyes Farm, Newport Lane, Niton, Ventnor, Isle of Wight PO38 2NS
T: (01983) 730015 &
07977 856795

NORTH BOARHUNT
Hampshire
South Hants Country Club ★★★★
Holiday and Touring Park
Stockers, North Boarhunt, Fareham, Hampshire PO17 6JS
T: (01329) 832919
F: (01329) 834506
E: contact@southhants.swinternet.co.uk
I: www.southhants.swinternet.co.uk

OLNEY
Buckinghamshire
Emberton Country Park ★★★
Touring and Camping Park
Emberton, Olney, Buckinghamshire MK46 5DB
T: (01234) 711575
F: (01234) 711575
E: embertonpark@milton-keynes.gov.uk

OWER
Hampshire
Green Pastures Caravan Park ★★★
Touring Park
Green Pastures Farm, Ower, Romsey, Hampshire SO51 6AJ
T: (023) 8081 4444 &
07796 188641
E: enquiries@greenpasturesfarm.com
I: www.greenpasturesfarm.com

OXFORD
Oxfordshire
The Camping & Caravanning Club Site ★★★★
Touring and Camping Park
426 Abingdon Road, Oxford, Oxfordshire OX1 4XN
T: (01865) 244088
I: www.campingandcaravanningclub.co.uk

Cassington Mill Caravan Park ★★
Touring and Camping Park
Eynsham Road, Cassington, Witney, Oxfordshire OX29 4DB
T: (01865) 881081
F: (01865) 884167
E: cassingtonpark@talk21.com

Establishments printed in blue have a detailed entry in this guide

SOUTH OF ENGLAND

PENNINGTON
Hampshire

Hurst View Caravan Park ★★★
Holiday Park
Lower Pennington Lane, Pennington, Lymington, Hampshire SO41 8AL
T: (01590) 671648 & 07798 938911
F: (01590) 689244
E: enquiries@hurstview.freeserve.co.uk
I: www.hurstview.co.uk

POOLE
Dorset

Beacon Hill Touring Park ★★★
Touring Park
Blandford Road North, Near Lytchett Minster, Poole, Dorset BH16 6AB
T: (01202) 631631
F: (01202) 625749
E: bookings@beaconhilltouringpark.co.uk
I: www.beaconhilltouringpark.co.uk

Organford Manor Caravans & Holidays ★★★
Touring Park
The Lodge, Organford, Poole, Dorset BH16 6ES
T: (01202) 622202 & 623278
F: (01202) 623278
E: organford@lds.co.uk

Pear Tree Touring Park ★★★★★
Touring Park
Organford Road, Holton Heath, Poole, Dorset BH16 6LA
T: (01202) 622434
F: (01202) 631985
E: info@visitpeartree.co.uk
I: www.visitpeartree.co.uk

Rockley Park Holiday Park ★★★★★
Holiday Park
Hamworthy, Poole, Dorset BH15 4LZ
T: (01202) 679393
F: (01202) 683199
E: enquiries@british-holidays.co.uk
I: www.british-holidays.co.uk

Sandford Holiday Park ★★★★
Holiday Park
Holton Heath, Poole, Dorset BH16 6JZ
T: (01202) 631600 & (01392) 447447
F: (01202) 625678
E: admin@weststarholidays.co.uk
I: www.weststarholidays.co.uk

PORTSMOUTH & SOUTHSEA
Hampshire

Southsea Leisure Park ★★★
Holiday, Touring and Camping Park
Melville Road, Southsea, Hampshire PO4 9TB
T: (023) 9273 5070
F: (023) 9282 1302

RINGWOOD
Hampshire

Camping International ★★★
Touring and Camping Park
229 Ringwood Road, St Leonards, Ringwood, Hampshire BH24 2SD
T: (01202) 872817 & 872742
F: (01202) 893986
E: enquiries@globalnet.co.uk
I: www.users.globalnet.co.uk/~campint

Red Shoot Camping Park ★★★★
Camping Park
Linwood, Ringwood, Hampshire BH24 3QT
T: (01425) 473789
F: (01425) 471558
E: enquiries@redshoot-campingpark.com
I: www.redshoot-campingpark.com

RISELEY
Berkshire

Wellington Country Park ★★★★
Touring and Camping Park
Riseley, Reading, Berkshire RG7 1SP
T: (0118) 932 6444
F: (0118) 932 3445
I: www.wellington-country-park.co.uk

ROMSEY
Hampshire

Hill Farm Caravan Park ★★★★
Holiday, Touring and Camping Park
Branches Lane, Sherfield English, Romsey, Hampshire SO51 6FH
T: (01794) 340402
F: (01794) 342358
E: GJB@hillfarmpark.com
I: www/hillfarmpark.com

ROOKLEY
Isle of Wight

Rookley Country Park ★★★
Holiday Park
Main Road, Rookley, Ventnor, Isle of Wight PO38 3RU
T: (01983) 721606
F: (01983) 721607
I: www.webwight.co.uk.islandview

RYDE
Isle of Wight

Beaper Farm Camping Site ★★★
Camping Park
Beaper Farm, Ryde, Isle of Wight PO33 1QJ
T: (01983) 615210 & (01993) 875184
E: beaper@btinternet.com

Harcourt Sands Holiday Village ★★★★★
Holiday Park
Ryde, Isle of Wight PO33 1PJ
T: (01983) 567321
F: (01983) 611422

Pondwell Holiday Park ★★★
Holiday and Touring Park
Pondwell Hill, Ryde, Isle of Wight PO33 1QA
T: (01983) 612100
F: (01983) 613511
E: info@isleofwightselfcatering.co.uk
I: www.isleofwightselfcatering.co.uk

ST HELENS
Isle of Wight

Carpenters Farm ★★
Touring and Camping Park
St Helens, Ryde, Isle of Wight PO33 1YL
T: (01983) 872450

Field Lane Holiday Park ★★★★
Holiday Park
Field Lane, St Helens, Ryde, Isle of Wight PO33 1UX
T: (01983) 872779
F: (01983) 873000
E: fieldlane@freeuk.com

Hillgrove Park ★★★★
Holiday Park
Field Lane, St Helens, Ryde, Isle of Wight PO33 1UT
T: (01983) 872802
F: (01983) 872100
E: info@hillgrove.co.uk
I: www.hillgrove.co.uk

Nodes Point Holiday Park ★★★
Holiday, Touring and Camping Park
St Helens, Ryde, Isle of Wight PO33 1YA
T: (01983) 872401 & 07802 466186
F: (01983) 874696

Old Mill Holiday Park ★★★★★
Holiday Park
Mill Road, St Helens, Ryde, Isle of Wight PO33 1UE
T: (01983) 872507
E: oldmill@fsbdial.co.uk
I: www.oldmill.co.uk

ST LAWRENCE
Isle of Wight

Undercliff Glen Caravan Park ★★★★★
Holiday Park
The Undercliffe Drive, St Lawrence, Ventnor, Isle of Wight PO38 1XY
T: (01983) 730261
F: (01983) 730261

ST LEONARDS
Dorset

Oakdene Forest Park ★★★
Holiday Park
St Leonards, Ringwood, Hampshire BH24 2RZ
T: (01590) 648331
F: (01590) 645610
E: holidays@shorefield.co.uk
I: www.shorefield.co.uk

SANDOWN
Isle of Wight

The Camping & Caravanning Club Site Adgestone Club Site ★★★★★
Touring and Camping Park
Lower Adgestone Road, Adgestone, Sandown, Isle of Wight PO36 0HL
T: (01983) 403432
I: www.campingandcaravanningclub.co.uk

Cheverton Copse Holiday Park Ltd ★★★
Holiday and Touring Park
Scotchells Brook Lane, Sandown, Isle of Wight PO36 0JP
T: (01983) 403161
F: (01983) 402861

Fairway Holiday Park Ltd ★★★
Holiday Park
The Fairway, Sandown, Isle of Wight PO36 9PS
T: (01983) 403462
F: (01983) 405713

Fort Holiday Park ★★
Holiday Park
Avenue Road, Sandown, Isle of Wight PO36 8BD
T: (01983) 402858

Fort Spinney Holiday Chalets ★★★★★
Holiday Park
Yaverland Road, Sandown, Isle of Wight PO36 8QB
T: (01983) 402360 & 404025
F: (01983) 404025
E: clem@fortspinney.freeserve.co.uk
I: www.isle-of-wight.uk.com/spinney

Sandown Holiday Chalets ★★★★
Holiday Park
Avenue Road, Sandown, Isle of Wight PO36 9AP
T: (01983) 404025 & 402360
F: (01983) 404025
E: clem@fortspinney.freeserve.co.uk
I: www.isle-of-wight.uk.com/chalets

SEAVIEW
Isle of Wight

Salterns Holidays ★★★
Holiday Park
Isle of Wight Self-Catering Ltd, Seaview, Isle of Wight PO34 5AQ
T: (01983) 612330
F: (01983) 613511
E: info@isleofwightselfcatering.co.uk
I: www.isleofwightselfcatering.co.uk

Tollgate Holiday Park ★★★
Holiday Park
The Duver, Seaview, Isle of Wight PO34 5AJ
T: (01983) 612107
E: info@isleofwightselfcatering.co.uk
I: www.isleofwightselfcatering.co.uk

SOUTH OF ENGLAND

SHANKLIN
Isle of Wight

Landguard Camping Park ★★★★
Touring and Camping Park
Rose Award
Landguard Manor Road,
Shanklin, Isle of Wight
PO37 7PH
T: (01983) 867028
F: (01983) 865988
E: landguard@fsbdial.co.uk
I: www.landguard-camping.
co.uk

Landguard Holidays ★★★★
Holiday Park
Landguard Manor Road,
Shanklin, Isle of Wight PO37 7PJ
T: (01983) 863100
F: (01983) 867896
E: enquiries@
landguardholidays.co.uk
I: www.landguardholidays.co.uk

Lower Hyde Holiday Village ★★★★
Holiday, Touring and Camping Park
Landguard Road, Shanklin, Isle of Wight PO37 7LL
T: (01983) 866131
F: (01983) 862532

Ninham Country Holidays ★★★★
Holiday, Touring and Camping Park
Rose Award
Shanklin, Isle of Wight PO37 7PL
T: (01983) 864243
F: (01983) 868811
E: office@ninham-holidays.
co.uk
I: www.ninham-holidays.co.uk

SIXPENNY HANDLEY
Dorset

Church Farm Caravan & Camping Park ★★
Holiday and Camping Park
The Bungalow, Church Farm,
High Street, Sixpenny Handley,
Salisbury, Wiltshire SP5 5ND
T: (01725) 552563
F: (01725) 552563

STANDLAKE
Oxfordshire

Hardwick Parks ★★★
Holiday, Touring and Camping Park
Downs Road, Standlake, Witney,
Oxfordshire OX29 7PZ
T: (01865) 300501
F: (01865) 300037
E: info@hardwickparks.co.uk
I: www.hardwickparks.co.uk

Lincoln Farm Park Limited ★★★★★
Touring Park
High Street, Standlake, Witney,
Oxfordshire OX8 7RH
T: (01865) 300239
E: info@lincolnfarm.touristnet.
uk.com
I: www.lincolnfarm.touristnet.
uk.com

SWANAGE
Dorset

Cauldron Barn Farm Caravan Park ★★★★★
Holiday Park
Landopen Ltd, Cauldron Barn
Road, Swanage, Dorset
BH19 1QQ
T: (01929) 422080
F: (01929) 427870
I: cauldronbarn@fsbdial.co.uk

Haycraft Caravan Club Site ★★★★★
Touring Park
Haycrafts Lane, Harmans Cross,
Swanage, Dorset BH19 3EB
T: (01929) 480572
I: www.caravanclub.co.uk

Priestway Holiday Park ★★★
Touring Park
Priestway, Swanage, Dorset
BH19 2RS
T: (01929) 422747 & 424154
F: (01929) 421822

Swanage Caravan Park ★★★
Holiday Park
Priests Road, Swanage, Dorset
BH19 2QS
T: (01929) 422130
F: (01929) 427952

Ulwell Cottage Caravan Park ★★★★
Holiday, Touring and Camping Park
Rose Award
Ulwell, Swanage, Dorset
BH19 3DG
T: (01929) 422823
F: (01929) 421500
E: enq@ulwellcottagepark.co.uk
I: www.ulwellcottagepark.co.uk

Ulwell Farm Caravan Park ★★★★
Holiday Park
Ulwell, Swanage, Dorset
BH19 3DG
T: (01929) 422825
I: www.ukparks.co.uk/ulwellfarm

THORNESS BAY
Isle of Wight

Thorness Bay Holiday Park ★★★
Holiday and Touring Park
Thorness Bay, Cowes, Isle of
Wight PO31 8NJ
T: (01983) 523109
F: (01983) 822213

THREE LEGGED CROSS
Dorset

Woolsbridge Manor Farm Caravan Park ★★★★
Touring Park
Ringwood Road, Three Legged
Cross, Wimborne Minster,
Dorset BH21 6RA
T: (01202) 826369
F: (01202) 813172

TOTLAND BAY
Isle of Wight

Ivylands Holiday Park ★★★★
Holiday Park
The Broadway, Totland Bay, Isle
of Wight PO39 0AN
T: (01983) 752480
F: (01983) 752480

WAREHAM
Dorset

Birchwood Tourist Park ★★★★
Touring Park
Bere Road, North Trigon,
Wareham, Dorset BH20 7PA
T: (01929) 554763
F: (01929) 556635

The Lookout Holiday Park ★★★★
Touring Park
Corfe Road, Stoborough,
Wareham, Dorset BH20 5AZ
T: (01929) 552546
F: (01929) 556662
E: enquiries@caravan-sites.
co.uk
I: www.caravan-sites.co.uk

Wareham Forest Tourist Park ★★★★★
Touring Park
Bere Road, North Trigon,
Wareham, Dorset BH20 7NZ
T: (01929) 551393
F: (01929) 551393
E: holiday@wareham-forest.
co.uk
I: www.wareham-forest.co.uk

WARSASH
Hampshire

Dibles Park Company Ltd ★★★★
Touring Park
Dibles Park, Dibles Road,
Warsash, Southampton,
Hampshire SO31 9SA
T: (01489) 575232

WEST LULWORTH
Dorset

Durdle Door Holiday Park ★★★★
Holiday Park
West Lulworth, Wareham,
Dorset BH20 5PU
T: (01929) 400200
F: (01929) 400260
E: durdledoor@lulworth.com
I: www.lulworth.com

WIMBORNE MINSTER
Dorset

Charris Camping & Caravan Park ★★★★
Touring and Camping Park
Candy's Lane, Corfe Mullen,
Wimborne Minster, Dorset
BH21 3EF
T: (01202) 885970
F: (01202) 881281
E: jandjcharris@iclway.co.uk
I: www.charris.co.uk

Merley Court Touring Park ★★★★★
Touring Park
Merley House Lane, Merley,
Wimborne Minster, Dorset
BH21 3AA
T: (01202) 881488
F: (01202) 881484
E: holidays@merley-court.co.uk
I: www.merley-court.co.uk

Springfield Touring Park ★★★★★
Touring Park
Candys Lane, Corfe Mullen,
Wimborne Minster, Dorset
BH21 3EF
T: (01202) 881719

Wilksworth Farm Caravan Park ★★★★★
Holiday Park
Cranborne Road, Wimborne
Minster, Dorset BH21 4HW
T: (01202) 885467
I: www.
wilksworthfarmcaravanpark.
co.uk

WINCHESTER
Hampshire

Morn Hill Caravan Club Site ★★★★
Touring Park
Morn Hill, Winchester,
Hampshire SO21 1HL
T: (01962) 869877
I: www.caravanclub.co.uk

WOKINGHAM
Berkshire

California Chalet & Touring Park ★★★★
Holiday, Touring and Camping Park
Nine Mile Ride, Finchampstead,
Wokingham, Berkshire
RG40 4HU
T: (0118) 973 3928
F: (0118) 932 8720

WOODLANDS
Dorset

Sutton Hill Camping & Caravanning Club Site ★★★★
Camping Park
Sutton Hill, Woodlands,
Wimborne Minster, Dorset
BH21 8NQ
T: (01202) 822763
I: www.
campingandcaravanningclub.
co.uk

WOOL
Dorset

Whitemead Caravan Park ★★★★
Touring and Camping Park
East Burton Road, Wool,
Wareham, Dorset BH20 6HG
T: (01929) 462241
E: nadinechurch@aol.com
I: www.whitemeadcaravanpark.
co.uk

WOOTTON BRIDGE
Isle of Wight

Kite Hill Farm Caravan & Camping Park ★★★★
Touring and Camping Park
Wootton Bridge, Ryde, Isle of
Wight PO33 4LE
E: barry@kitehillfarm.freeserve.
co.uk
I: www.campingparksisleofwight.
com

WROXALL
Isle of Wight

Appuldurcombe Gardens Caravan & Camping Park ★★★★
Holiday, Touring and Camping Park
Appuldurcombe Road, Wroxall,
Ventnor, Isle of Wight PO38 3EP
T: (01983) 852597
F: (01983) 856225
E: appuldurcombe@freeuk.com
I: www.appuldurcombe.freeuk.
com

Establishments printed in blue have a detailed entry in this guide

SOUTH OF ENGLAND

YARMOUTH
Isle of Wight
The Orchards Holiday Caravan Park ★★★★★
Holiday and Touring Park
Main Road, Newbridge, Yarmouth, Isle of Wight
PO41 0TS
T: (01983) 531331 & 531350
F: (01983) 531666
E: info@orchards-holiday-park.co.uk
I: www.orchards-holiday-park.co.uk

Savoy Holiday Village ★★★
Holiday Park
Halletts Shute, Yarmouth, Isle of Wight PO41 0RJ
T: (01983) 760355
F: (01983) 761277

SOUTH EAST ENGLAND

ARUNDEL
West Sussex
Ship & Anchor Marina ★★★
Touring Park
Heywood & Bryett Ltd, Ford, Arundel, West Sussex BN18 0BJ
T: (01243) 551262

ASHFORD
Kent
Broadhembury Caravan & Camping Park ★★★★★
Holiday, Touring and Camping Park
Steeds Lane, Kingsnorth, Ashford, Kent TN26 1NQ
T: (01233) 620859
F: (01233) 620918
E: holidays@broadhembury.co.uk
I: www.broadhembury.co.uk

ASHURST
Kent
Manor Court Farm ★★★
Touring and Camping Park
Ashurst, Royal Tunbridge Wells, Kent TN3 9TB
T: (01892) 740279 & 740210
F: (01892) 740919
E: jsoyke@jsoyke.freeserve.co.uk
I: www.manorcourtfarm.co.uk

BATTLE
East Sussex
Crowhurst Park ★★★★★
Holiday Park
Rose Award
Crowhurst Park, Telham Lane, Battle, East Sussex TN33 0SL
T: (01424) 773344
F: (01424) 775727
E: enquiries@crowhurstpark.co.uk
I: www.crowhurstpark.co.uk

Normanhurst Court Caravan Club Site ★★★★★
Touring Park
Stevens Crouch, Battle, East Sussex TN33 9LR
T: (01424) 773808
I: www.caravanclub.co.uk

BEXHILL-ON-SEA
East Sussex
Cobbs Hill Farm Caravan & Camping Park ★★★★
Holiday, Touring and Camping Park
Watermill Lane, Sidley, Bexhill-on-Sea, Bexhill, East Sussex TN39 5JA
T: (01424) 213460 & 221358
F: (01424) 221358

Kloofs Caravan Park ★★★★★
Touring and Camping Park
Sandhurst Lane, Whydown, Bexhill, East Sussex TN39 4RG
T: (01424) 842839
F: (01424) 845669
E: camping@kloofs.ndirect.co.uk
I: www.kloofs.ndirect.co.uk

BIDDENDEN
Kent
Woodlands Park ★★★★
Touring Park
Tenterden Road, Biddenden, Ashford, Kent TN27 8BT
T: (01580) 291216
F: (01580) 291216
E: woodlandsp@aol.com
I: www.campingsite.co.uk

BIRCHINGTON
Kent
Quex Caravan Park ★★★★★
Holiday and Touring Park
Park Road, Birchington, Kent CT7 0BL
T: (01843) 841273
F: (01227) 740585
E: info@keatfarm.co.uk/
I: www.keatfarm.co.uk/

Two Chimneys Caravan Park ★★★★
Holiday, Touring and Camping Park
Shottendane Road, Birchington, Kent CT7 0HD
T: (01843) 841068 & 843157
F: (01843) 843157
E: info@twochimneys.co.uk
I: www.twochimneys.co.uk

BOGNOR REGIS
West Sussex
Bognor Regis Caravan Club Site ★★★★★
Touring and Camping Park
Rowan Way, Bognor Regis, West Sussex PO22 9RP
T: (01243) 828515
I: www.caravanclub.co.uk

Copthorne Caravans ★★★★
Holiday Park
Rose Green Road, Bognor Regis, West Sussex PO21 3ER
T: (01243) 262408
F: (01243) 262408
E: copthornecaravans@ukgateway.net

The Lillies Nursery & Caravan Park ★★★
Holiday, Touring and Camping Park
Yapton Road, Barnham, Bognor Regis, West Sussex PO22 0AY
T: (01243) 552081
F: (01243) 552081

Riverside Caravan Centre (Bognor) Ltd ★★★★★
Holiday Park
Shripney Road, Bognor Regis, West Sussex PO22 9NE
T: (01243) 865823 & 865824
F: (01243) 841570
E: info@rivcentre.co.uk
I: www.rivcentre.co.uk

BRIGHTON & HOVE
East Sussex
Sheepcote Valley Caravan Club Site ★★★★★
Touring and Camping Park
East Brighton Park, Brighton, East Sussex BN2 5TS
T: (01273) 626546
F: (01273) 682600
I: www.caravanclub.co.uk

CAMBER
East Sussex
Camber Sands Holiday Park ★★★
Holiday and Touring Park
Lydd Road, Camber, Rye, East Sussex TN31 7RT
T: (01797) 225555 & 0870 442 9284
F: (01797) 225756
E: cambersands@gbholidayparks.co.uk
I: www.gbholidayparks.co.uk

CANTERBURY
Kent
Canterbury Camping & Caravanning Club Site ★★★★
Touring and Camping Park
Bekesbourne Lane, Canterbury, Kent CT3 4AB
T: (01227) 463216
I: www.campingandcaravanning.co.uk

Yew Tree Park ★★★★
Holiday, Touring and Camping Park
Stone Street, Petham, Canterbury, Kent CT4 5PL
T: (01227) 700306
F: (01227) 700306
E: enquiries@yewtreepark.com
I: www.yewtreepark.com

CAPEL LE FERNE
Kent
Varne Ridge Holiday Park ★★★★★
Holiday and Touring Park
Rose Award
145 Old Dover Road, Capel le Ferne, Folkestone, Kent CT18 7HX
T: (01303) 251765
F: (01303) 251765
E: vrcp@varne-ridge.freeserve.co.uk
I: www.varne-ridge.co.uk

CHERTSEY
Surrey
Chertsey Camping & Caravanning Club Site ★★★★
Camping Park
Bridge Road, Chertsey, Surrey KT16 8JX
T: (01932) 562405
I: www.campingandcaravanningclub.co.uk

CHICHESTER
West Sussex
Bell Caravan Park ★★
Holiday and Touring Park
Bell Lane, Birdham, Chichester, West Sussex PO20 7HY
T: (01243) 512264

Wicks Farm Camping Park ★★★★★
Holiday and Touring Park
Redlands Lane, West Wittering, Chichester, West Sussex PO20 8QD
T: (01243) 513116
F: (01243) 511296
I: www.wicksfarm.co.uk

CROWBOROUGH
East Sussex
Crowborough Camping and Caravanning Club Site ★★★★
Touring and Camping Park
Goldsmith Recreation Ground, Crowborough, East Sussex TN6 2TN
T: (01892) 664827
I: www.campingandcaravanningclub.co.uk

Establishments printed in blue have a detailed entry in this guide

SOUTH EAST ENGLAND

DOVER
Kent

Hawthorn Farm Caravan & Camping Park ★★★★
Holiday, Touring and Camping Park
Station Road, Martin Mill, Dover, Kent CT15 5LA
T: (01304) 852658 & 852914
F: (01304) 853417
E: info@keatfarm.co.uk
I: www.keatfarm.co.uk

Sutton Vale Country Club & Caravan Park ★★★★
Holiday and Touring Park
Vale Road, Sutton-by-Dover, Dover, Kent CT15 5DH
T: (01304) 374155
F: (01304) 381132
E: office@sutton-vale.co.uk
I: www.ukparks.co.uk/suttonvale

DYMCHURCH
Kent

Dymchurch Caravan Park ★★★★
Holiday Park
St Mary's Road, Dymchurch, Romney Marsh, Kent TN29 0PW
T: (01303) 872303
F: (01303) 875179

New Beach Holiday Village ★★★★
Holiday Park
Hythe Road, Dymchurch, Romney Marsh, Kent TN29 0JX
T: (01303) 872233
F: (01303) 872939
E: newbeachholiday@aol.com

New Beach Holiday Village Touring Park ★★★★
Touring Park
Hythe Road, Dymchurch, Romney Marsh, Kent TN29 0JX
T: (01303) 872234
F: (01303) 872939
E: newbeachholiday@aol.com

EAST HORSLEY
Surrey

Horsley Camping & Caravanning Club ★★★★
Touring and Camping Park
Ockham Road North, East Horsley, Leatherhead, Surrey KT24 6PE
T: (01483) 283273
I: www.campingandcaravanningclub.co.uk

EASTBOURNE
East Sussex

Fairfields Farm Caravan & Camping Park ★★★
Touring and Camping Park
Eastbourne Road, Westham, Pevensey, East Sussex BN24 5NG
T: (01323) 763165
F: (01323) 469175
E: enquiries@fairfieldsfarm.com
I: www.fairfieldsfarm.com

EASTCHURCH
Kent

Ashcroft Holiday Park ★★★
Holiday Park
Plough Road, Minster-on-Sea, Eastchurch, Kent ME12 4JH
T: (01795) 880324
F: (01795) 880090

Bramley Park Ltd ★★★
Holiday Park
Second Avenue, Warden Road, Eastchurch, Sheerness, Kent ME12 4EP
T: (01795) 880338
F: (01795) 880629
E: bramley.park@btinternet.com
I: www.ukparks.co.uk/bramley

Coconut Grove Holiday Park ★★★★
Holiday Park
Warden Road, Eastchurch, Sheerness, Kent ME12 4EN
T: (01795) 880353
F: (01795) 881198
E: coconutgrove@palmtreemanagement.co.uk
I: www.palmtreemanagement.co.uk

Copperfields Holiday Park ★★★★
Holiday Park
Fourth Avenue, Warden Road, Eastchurch, Sheerness, Kent ME12 4EW
T: (01795) 880080
F: (01795) 881198
E: copperfields@palmtreemanagement.co.uk
I: www.palmtreemanagement.co.uk

Palm Trees Holiday Park ★★★
Holiday Park
Second Avenue, Eastchurch, Sheerness, Kent ME12 4ET
T: (01795) 880080

Warden Springs Caravan Park Ltd ★★★★
Holiday, Touring and Camping Park
Warden Point, Eastchurch, Sheerness, Kent ME12 4HF
T: (01795) 880216 & 880217
F: (01795) 880218
E: jackie@wscp.freeserve.co.uk
I: www.wardensprings.co.uk

FOLKESTONE
Kent

Black Horse Farm Caravan Club Site ★★★★★
Touring and Camping Park
385 Canterbury Road, Densole, Folkestone, Kent CT18 7BG
T: (01303) 892665
I: www.caravanclub.co.uk

Folkestone Camping & Caravanning Club Site ★★
Touring and Camping Park
The Warren, Folkestone, Kent CT19 6PT
T: (01303) 255093
I: www.campingandcaravanningclub.co.uk

GRAFFHAM
West Sussex

Camping & Caravanning Club Site ★★★★
Camping Park
Great Bury, Graffham, Petworth, West Sussex GU28 0QJ
T: (01798) 867476
I: www.campingandcaravanningclub.co.uk

HASTINGS
East Sussex

Combe Haven Holiday Park ★★★★
Holiday Park
Harley Shute Road, St Leonards-on-Sea, Hastings, East Sussex TN38 8BZ
T: (01424) 427891
F: (01424) 442991

Rocklands Holiday Park ★★★★
Holiday Park
Rocklands Lane, East Hill, Hastings, East Sussex TN35 5DY
T: (01424) 423097

Shear Barn Holiday Park ★★★
Holiday, Touring and Camping Park
Barley Lane, Hastings, East Sussex TN35 5DX
T: (01424) 423583 & 716474
F: (01424) 718740
E: shearbarn@pavilion.co.uk
I: www.shearbarn.co.uk

Stalkhurst Camping & Caravan Site ★★★
Holiday, Touring and Camping Park
Stalkhurst Cottage, Ivyhouse Lane, Hastings, East Sussex TN35 4NN
T: (01424) 439015
F: (01424) 445206

HENFIELD
West Sussex

Downsview Caravan Park ★★★★
Holiday, Touring and Camping Park
Bramlands Lane, Woodmancote, Henfield, West Sussex BN5 9TG
T: (01273) 492801
F: (01273) 495214
E: phr.peter@lineone.net

HERNE BAY
Kent

Keat Farm Holiday Park ★★★★★
Holiday Park
Reculver Road, Herne Bay, Kent CT6 6SR
T: (01227) 374381
F: (01227) 740585
E: info@keatfarm.co.uk/
I: www.keatfarm.co.uk/

HERSTMONCEUX
East Sussex

Orchard View Park ★★★★★
Holiday Park
Victoria Road, Windmill Hill, Herstmonceux, Hailsham, East Sussex BN27 4SY
T: (01323) 832335
F: (01323) 832335
E: orchardviewpark@yahoo.co.uk

HORAM
East Sussex

Horam Manor Touring Park ★★★★
Touring and Camping Park
Horam, Heathfield, East Sussex TN21 0YD
T: (01435) 813662
E: horam.manor@virgin.net
I: www.handbooks.co.uk/horam-manor

HORSHAM
West Sussex

Honeybridge Park ★★★★
Touring and Camping Park
Honeybridge Lane, Dial Post, Horsham, West Sussex RH13 8NX
T: (01403) 710923
F: (01403) 710923
E: enquiries@honeybridgepark.free-online.co.uk
I: www.honeybridgepark.co.uk

KINGSDOWN
Kent

Kingsdown Park Holiday Village ★★★★★
Holiday Park
Upper Street, Kingsdown, Deal, Kent CT14 8AU
T: (01304) 361205
F: (01304) 380125
E: info@kingsdownpark.co.uk
I: www.kingsdownpark.co.uk

LEYSDOWN ON SEA
Kent

Priory Hill Holiday Park ★★★★
Holiday, Touring and Camping Park
Wing Road, Leysdown on Sea, Sheerness, Kent ME12 4QT
T: (01795) 510267 & 07979 530600/1
F: (01795) 510267
E: info@prioryhill.co.uk
I: www.prioryhill.co.uk

LINGFIELD
Surrey

Long Acres Caravan & Camping Park ★★★
Touring and Camping Park
Newchapel Road, Lingfield, Surrey RH7 6LE
T: (01342) 833205
F: (01622) 735038
E: charlie.pilkington@virgin.net
I: www.ukparks.co.uk/longacres

MAIDSTONE
Kent

Pine Lodge Touring Park ★★★★★
Touring and Camping Park
A20 Ashford Road, Hollingbourne, Maidstone, Kent ME17 1XH
T: (01622) 730018
F: (01622) 734498

MARDEN
Kent

Tanner Farm Touring Caravan & Camping Park ★★★★★
Touring and Camping Park
Goudhurst Road, Marden, Tonbridge, Kent TN12 9ND
T: (01622) 832399
F: (01622) 832472
E: tannerfarmpark@cs.com
I: www.tannerfarmpark.co.uk

MERSTHAM
Surrey

Alderstead Heath Caravan Club Site ★★★★★
Touring Park
Dean Lane, Merstham, Redhill, Surrey RH1 3AH
T: (01737) 644629
I: www.caravanclub.co.uk

Establishments printed in blue have a detailed entry in this guide

SOUTH EAST ENGLAND

MINSTER
Kent
Riverbank Park ★★★
Holiday, Touring and Camping Park
The Broadway, Minster, Sheerness, Kent ME12 2DB
T: (01795) 870300 & 875211
F: (01795) 871300
E: kirwin.riverbankpark@virgin.net
I: www.ukparks.com/riverbank

MINSTER-IN-SHEPPEY
Kent
Golden Leas Holiday Park ★★★★
Holiday Park
Bell Farm Lane, Minster-in-Sheppey, Sheerness, Kent ME12 4JA
T: (01795) 874874
F: (01795) 872086

Seacliff Holiday Estate Ltd ★★
Holiday, Touring and Camping Park
Oak Lane, Minster-in-Sheppey, Sheerness, Kent ME12 3QS
T: (01795) 872262

Willow Trees Holiday Park ★★★
Holiday Park
Oak Lane, Minster-in-Sheppey, Sheerness, Kent ME12 3QR
T: (01795) 875833
F: (01795) 881198
E: willowtrees@palmtreemanagement.co.uk
I: www.palmtreemanagement.co.uk

MINSTER-IN-THANET
Kent
Wayside Caravan Park ★★★★★
Holiday Park
Way Hill, Minster-in-Thanet, Ramsgate, Kent CT12 4HP
T: (01843) 821272
F: (01843) 822668

MONKTON
Kent
The Foxhunter Park ★★★★★
Holiday Park
Monkton, Ramsgate, Kent CT12 4JG
T: (01843) 821311
F: (01843) 821458
E: foxhunterpark@netscapeonline.co.uk
I: www.saundersparkhomes.co.uk

NEW ROMNEY
Kent
Romney Sands Holiday Park ★★★
Holiday Park
The Parade, Greatstone On Sea, New Romney, Kent TN28 8RN
T: (01797) 363877
F: (01797) 367497

PAGHAM
West Sussex
Church Farm Holiday Village ★★★★
Holiday Park
Pagham, Chichester, West Sussex PO21 4NR
T: (01243) 262635
F: (01243) 266043
E: enquiries@british-holidays.co.uk
I: www.british-holidays.co.uk

PEVENSEY
East Sussex
Normans Bay Camping and Caravanning Club Site ★★★★
Touring and Camping Park
Pevensey, East Sussex BN24 6PR
T: (01323) 761190
I: www.campingandcaravanningclub.co.uk

PEVENSEY BAY
East Sussex
Bay View Caravan & Camping Park ★★★★★
Holiday, Touring and Camping Park
Rose Award
Old Martello Road, Pevensey Bay, Eastbourne, East Sussex BN24 6DX
T: (01323) 768688
T: (01323) 769637
E: holidays@bay-view.co.uk
I: www.bay-view.co.uk

Martello Beach Park ★★★★★
Holiday and Touring Park
Pevensey Bay, Pevensey, East Sussex BN24 6DH
T: (01323) 761424
F: (01323) 460433
I: www.m.smart@martellobeachpark.fsbusiness.co.uk

POLEGATE
East Sussex
Peel House Farm Caravan Park ★★★★
Holiday, Touring and Camping Park
Polegate, East Sussex BN26 6QX
T: (01323) 845629
F: (01323) 845629
E: peelhocp@tesco.net

RAMSGATE
Kent
Manston Caravan & Camping Park ★★★★
Holiday, Touring and Camping Park
Manston Court Road, Manston, Ramsgate, Kent CT12 5AU
T: (01843) 823442
E: enquiries@manston-park.co.uk
I: www.manston-park.co.uk

Nethercourt Touring Park ★★★
Touring Park
Nethercourt Hill, Ramsgate, Kent CT11 0RX
T: (01843) 595485
F: (01843) 595485

RECULVER
Kent
Blue Dolphin Park ★★★★
Holiday Park
Reculver, Herne Bay, Kent CT6 6SS
T: (01227) 375406
F: (01227) 375406

RINGMER
East Sussex
Bluebell Holiday Park ★★
Holiday Park
The Broyle, Shortgate, Ringmer, Lewes, East Sussex BN8 6PJ
T: (01825) 840407
I: www.bluebellholidaypark.co.uk

ROCHESTER
Kent
Allhallows Leisure Park ★★★★
Holiday Park
Allhallows-on-Sea, Allhallows, Nr Rochester, Kent ME3 9QD
T: (01634) 270385
F: (01634) 270081
E: enquiries@british-holidays.co.uk
I: www.british-holidays.co.uk

Woolmans Wood Caravan Park ★★★★
Touring and Camping Park
Rochester/Maidstone Road, Bridgewood, Rochester, Kent ME5 9SB
T: (01634) 867685
F: (01634) 867685
E: woolmans.wood@currantbun.com

ST NICHOLAS AT WADE
Kent
Frost Farm Thanet Way Caravan Co ★★★
Holiday and Touring Park
Thanet Way, St Nicholas at Wade, Birchington, Kent CT7 0NA
T: (01843) 847219

St Nicholas Camping Site ★★
Touring and Camping Park
Court Road, St Nicholas at Wade, Birchington, Kent CT7 0NH
T: (01843) 847245

SANDWICH
Kent
Sandwich Leisure Park ★★★★
Holiday, Touring and Camping Park
Woodnesborough Road, Sandwich, Kent CT13 0AA
T: (01304) 612681
F: (01227) 273512
E: info@coastandcountryleisure.com
I: www.coastandcountryleisure.com

SEAFORD
East Sussex
Sunnyside Caravan Park ★★★
Holiday Park
Marine Parade, Seaford, East Sussex BN25 2QW
T: (01323) 892825
F: (01323) 892825

SEAL
Kent
Oldbury Hill Camping & Caravanning Club Site ★★★★
Touring and Camping Park
Styants Bottom Road, Styants Bottom, Seal, Sevenoaks, Kent TN15 0ET
T: (01732) 762728
I: www.campingandcaravanningclub.co.uk

SEASALTER
Kent
Homing Caravan Park ★★★★
Holiday Park
Church Lane, Seasalter, Whitstable, Kent CT5 4BU
T: (01227) 771777
F: (01227) 273512
E: info@coastandcountryleisure.com
I: www.coastandcountryleisure.com

SELSEY
West Sussex
Green Lawns Caravan Park ★★★★
Holiday Park
Paddock Lane, Selsey, Chichester, West Sussex PO20 9EJ
T: (01243) 604121
F: (01243) 602355
E: bunn.leisure@btinternet.com
I: www.bunnleisure.co.uk

Warner Farm Touring Park ★★★★★
Touring Park
Warner Lane, Selsey, Chichester, West Sussex PO20 9EL
T: (01243) 608440 & 604499
F: (01243) 604499
E: warner.farm@btinternet.com
I: www.bunnleisure.co.uk

West Sands Caravan Park ★★★★
Holiday Park
Mill Lane, Selsey, Chichester, West Sussex PO20 9BH
T: (01243) 606080
F: (01243) 606068
E: west.sands@btinternet.com
I: www.westsands.co.uk

White Horse Caravan Park ★★★★
Holiday Park
Paddock Lane, Selsey, Chichester, West Sussex PO20 9EJ
T: (01243) 604121
F: (01243) 602355
E: white.horse@btinternet.com
I: www.bunnleisure.co.uk

SLINDON
West Sussex
Camping & Caravanning Club Site, Slindon ★★★
Touring Park
Slindon Park, Slindon, Arundel, West Sussex BN18 0RG
T: (01243) 814387
I: www.campingandcarvanning.co.uk

Establishments printed in blue have a detailed entry in this guide

SOUTH EAST ENGLAND

SMALL DOLE
West Sussex

Southdown Caravan Park ★★★
Holiday Park
Henfield Road, Small Dole,
Henfield, West Sussex BN5 9XH
T: (01903) 814323
F: (01903) 812572
I: www.southdowncaravanpark.co.uk

SOUTHBOURNE
West Sussex

Camping & Caravanning Club Site Chichester ★★★★
Touring Park
345 Main Road, Southbourne, Emsworth, Hampshire PO10 8JH
T: (01243) 373102
I: www.campingandcaravanningclub.co.uk

SOUTHWATER
West Sussex

Raylands Park ★★★★
Holiday, Touring and Camping Park
Jackrells Lane, Southwater, Horsham, West Sussex RH13 7DH
T: (01403) 730218 & 731822
F: (01403) 732828
E: raylands@roundstonecaravans.com
I: www.roundstonecaravans.com

ST-MARGARETS-AT-CLIFFE
Kent

St Margarets Holiday Park ★★★★
Holiday Park
Reach Road, St-Margarets-at-Cliffe, Dover, Kent CT15 6AE
T: (01304) 853262 & 852255
F: (01304) 853434
I: www.leisuregb.co.uk

UCKFIELD
East Sussex

Honeys Green Farm Caravan Park ★★★
Holiday and Touring Park
Easons Green, Framfield, Uckfield, East Sussex TN22 5RE
T: (01825) 840334

WALTON-ON-THAMES
Surrey

Camping & Caravanning Club Site ★★★
Camping Park
Fieldcommon Lane, Walton-on-Thames, Surrey KT12 3QG
T: (01932) 220392
I: www.campingandcaravanningclub.co.uk

WASHINGTON
West Sussex

Washington Caravan & Camping Park ★★★★
Touring and Camping Park
London Road, Washington, Pulborough, West Sussex RH20 4AJ
T: (01903) 892869
F: (01903) 893252
E: washcamp@tinyworld.net

WOODGATE
West Sussex

Willows Caravan Park ★★★★★
Holiday Park
Lidsey Road, Woodgate, Chichester, West Sussex PO20 6SU
T: (01243) 543124
F: (01243) 543124

WORTHING
West Sussex

Northbrook Farm Caravan Club Site ★★★★
Touring Park
Titnore Way, Worthing, West Sussex BN13 3RT
T: (01903) 502962
I: www.caravanclub.co.uk

Onslow Caravan Park ★★★★
Holiday Park
Onslow Drive, Ferring-by-Sea, Worthing, West Sussex BN12 5RX
T: (01903) 243170 & (01243) 513084
F: (01243) 513053
E: islandmeadow@virgin.net
I: www.islandmeadow.co.uk

WROTHAM HEATH
Kent

Gate House Wood Touring Park ★★★★★
Touring and Camping Park
Ford Lane, Wrotham Heath, Sevenoaks, Kent TN15 7SD
T: (01732) 843062

ON-LINE INFORMATION

In-depth information about travelling in Britain is now available on BTA's VisitBritain website.

Covering everything from castles to leisure parks and from festivals to road and rail links, the site complements Where to Stay perfectly, giving you up-to-the-minute detials to help you with your travel plans.

BRITAIN on the internet
www.visitbritain.com

Establishments printed in blue have a detailed entry in this guide